THE DIARY OF
SAMUEL PEPYS

Elizabeth Pepys, from an engraving by James Thomson after John Hayls's portrait
(*Pepys Library, Magdalene College, Cambridge*)

THE DIARY
OF
SAMUEL PEPYS

A new and complete
transcription edited by

ROBERT LATHAM
AND
WILLIAM MATTHEWS

CONTRIBUTING *EDITORS*
WILLIAM A. ARMSTRONG · MACDONALD EMSLIE
OLIVER MILLAR · the late T. F. REDDAWAY

VOLUME VII · *1666*

UNIVERSITY OF CALIFORNIA PRESS
BERKELEY AND LOS ANGELES
1972

Library of Congress Catalog Card No. 70-96950

ISBN 0 520 02094 4

Printed in Great Britain

CONTENTS

LIST OF ILLUSTRATIONS

READER'S GUIDE

This section is meant for quick reference. More detailed information about the editorial methods used in this edition will be found in the Introduction and in the section 'Methods of the Commentary' in vol. I, and also in the statement preceding the Select Glossary at the end of each text volume.

I. THE TEXT

The fact that the MS. is mostly in shorthand makes exact reproduction (e.g. of spelling, capitalisation and punctuation) impossible.

Spelling is in modern British style, except for those longhand words which Pepys spelt differently, and words for which the shorthand indicates a variant pronunciation which is also shown by Pepys's longhand elsewhere. These latter are given in spellings which reflect Pepys's pronunciations.

Pepys's capitalisation is indicated only in his longhand.

Punctuation is almost all editorial, except for certain full-stops, colons, dashes and parentheses. Punctuation is almost non-existent in the original since the marks could be confused with shorthand.

Italics are all editorial, but (in e.g. headings to entries) often follow indications given in the MS. (by e.g. the use of larger writing).

The **paragraphing** is that of the MS.

Abbreviations of surnames, titles, place names and ordinary words are expanded.

Single **hyphens** are editorial, and represent Pepys's habit of disjoining the elements of compound words (e.g. Wh. hall/White-hall). Double hyphens represent Pepys's hyphens.

Single **angle-brackets** mark additions made by Pepys in the body of the MS.; double angle-brackets those made in the margins.

Light **asterisks** are editorial (see below, Section II); heavy asterisks are Pepys's own.

Pepys's **alterations** are indicated by the word 'replacing' ('repl.') in the textual footnotes.

II. THE COMMENTARY

1. Footnotes deal mainly with events and transactions. They also identify MSS, books, plays, music and quotations, but give only occasional and minimal information about persons and places, words and phrases. The initials which follow certain notes indicate the work of the contributing editors. Light asterisks in the text direct the reader to the Select Glossary for the definition of words whose meanings have changed since the time of the diary. References to the diary are given by volume and page where the text is in page-proof at the time of going to press; in other cases, by entry-dates. In notes to the Introduction, since almost all the references there are to the text, a simpler form of reference (by entry-date only) is used.

2. The **Select List of Persons** is printed unchanged in each text volume. It covers the whole diary and identifies the principal persons, together with those who are described in the MS. by titles or in other ways that make for obscurity.

3. The **Select Glossary** is printed at the end of each text volume. It gives definitions of most recurrent English words and phrases, and identifications of certain recurrent places.

4. The **Companion** (vol. X) is a collection of reference material. It contains maps, genealogical tables, and a Large Glossary, but consists mainly of articles, printed for ease of reference in a single alphabetical series. These give information about matters which are dealt with briefly or not at all in the footnotes and the Select Glossary: i.e. persons, places, words and phrases, food, drink, clothes, the weather etc. They also treat systematically the principal subjects with which the diary is concerned: Pepys's work, interests, health etc. References to the *Companion* are given only rarely in the footnotes. Its principal contents are as follows:

'Bibliography of Works Cited'
'Books' (*General; Catalogues; Book-cases*)
'Christenings'
'Christmas' (*General; Twelfth Night*)
'Clothes'
'Currency' (*Coins etc.*)
'Drink'
'Exchequer'
'Food' (*Meals; Dishes*)
'Funerals'
'Games, Sports and Pastimes'
'Gunpowder Plot Day'
'Health' (*Medical history of Pepys and his wife; Diseases etc.; Medicines*)
'Household' (*General; Servants; Furniture and Furnishings etc.*)
'Language'
'May Day'
'Music' (*General; Dances; Musical Instruments; Songs and Song-Books*)
'Navy' (*Admiralty; Chatham Chest; Dockyards and Dockyard Officers; Navy Board and its Officers; Tickets; Victualling*). See also *Ships*

'Ordnance Office'
Persons (*under names*)
Places (*Buildings, streets, inns etc., under names or titles; mainly London; other places under place names*)
'Postal Services'
'Privy Seal Office'
'Religion' (*General; Sermons; Sunday Observance; Lent, Whitsuntide etc.*)
'Royal Fishery'
'St Valentine's Day'
'Science' (*General; Royal Society; Scientific Instruments*)
Ships (*Types and individual ships under names*)

'Shrove Tuesday'
'Tangier' (*General; the Mole*)
'Theatre' (*General; Theatres: buildings, companies*)
'Toilet' (*Washing, Shaving, Cosmetics etc.*)
'Travel' (*By river; By road*)
'Trinity House'
'Wardrobe, the King's Great'
'Wealth'
'Weather'
'Weddings'
'Large Glossary' (*Words; Phrases; Proverbs*)

III. DATES

In Pepys's time two reckonings of the calendar year were in use in Western Europe. Most countries had adopted the New Style – the revised calendar of Gregory XIII (1582); Britain until 1752 retained the Old Style – the ancient Roman, or Julian, calendar, which meant that its dates were ten days behind those of the rest of Western Europe in the seventeenth century. 1 January in England was therefore 11 January by the New Style abroad. On the single occasion during the period of the diary when Pepys was abroad (in Holland in May 1660) he continued to use the Old Style, thus avoiding a break in the run of his dates. In the editorial material of the present work dates relating to countries which had adopted the new reckoning are given in both styles (e.g. '1/11 January') in order to prevent confusion.

It will be noticed that the shortest and longest days of the year occur in the diary ten days earlier than in the modern calendar. So, too, does Lord Mayor's Day in London – on 29 October instead of 9 November.

For most legal purposes (from medieval times until 1752) the new year in England was held to begin on Lady Day, 25 March. But in accordance with the general custom, Pepys took it to begin on 1 January, as in the Julian calendar. He gives to all dates within the overlapping period between 1 January and 24 March a year-date which comprehends both styles – e.g. 'January 1 16$\frac{59}{60}$.' In the present commentary a single year-date, that of the New Style, has been used: e.g. '1 January 1660'.

THE DIARY
1666

JANUARY. $166\frac{5}{6}$.

1. *New yeare's Day.* Called up by 5 a-clock by my order by Mr. Tooker, who wrote, while I dictated to him, my business of the Pursers, and so without eating or drinking till 3 in the afternoon, and then to my great content finished it.[1] So to dinner, Gibson and he and I – and then to Copying it over, Mr. Gibson reading and I writing, and went a good way in it till interrupted by Sir W Warren's coming, of whom I alway learn something or other, his discourse being very good, and his brains also. He being gone, we to our business again, and wrote more of it fair; and then late to bed.

2. Up by candlelight again, and wrote the greatest part of my business fair; and then to the office, and so home to dinner, and after dinner up and made an end of my fair-writing it. And that being done, set [?my clerks] to entering, while I to my Lord Bruncker's; and there find Sir J. Mennes and all his company, and Mr. Boreman and Mrs. Turner, but above all, my dear Mrs. Knipp, with whom I sang; and in perfect pleasure I was to hear her sing, and especially her little Scotch song of *Barbary Allen*.[2] And to make our mirth the completer, Sir Jo Minnes was in the highest pitch of mirth, and his Mimicall tricks, that ever I saw;

1. Pepys to Coventry, 1 January; BM, Lansdowne 253, ff. 242–54; printed in *Further Corr.*, pp. 93–111 from copy in NMM, LBK/8, pp. 337–53. Other contemporary copies in Rawl. C 302, ff. 46+; BM, Harl. 6003, ff. 137+; ib. 6287, ff. 48+ (in Hayter's hand); BM, Add. 9311, ff. 33+; ib. 11602, ff. 302+ (in Gibson's); Adm. Lib. MSS 9, ff. 33+. Pepys refers to it as his 'New Year's Gift' to Coventry, and it is one of the most powerful and elaborate of his office memoranda. He examines the various methods of holding the pursers to account, and suggests a reversion to the oldest method, whereby the pursers were held fully accountable for wages, but in respect of victuals were allowed the benefit of short allowances and absences. His scheme, after discussion by the Board, was adopted in April by the Council with only one alteration, and that in favour of the pursers: below, p. 106; *Further Corr.*, pp. 126–30; cf. *Priv. Corr.*, i. 125–6. On pursers in general, see above, vi. 306 & n. 1.

2. The well-known ballad. There is no evidence that the modern tune was that used in the 17th century. (E)

and most excellent pleasant company he is, and the best Mimique that ever I saw, and certainly would have made an excellent Actor, and now would be an excellent teacher of Actors. Thence, it being post-night, against my will took leave; but before I came to my office, longing for more of her company, returned and met them coming home in coaches; so I got into the coach where Mrs. Knipp was, and got her upon my knee (the coach being full) and played with her breasts and sung; and at last set her at her house, and so good-night. So home to my lodgings, and there endeavoured to have finished the examining my paper of Pursers business to have sent away tonight; but I was so sleepy with my late early risings and late goings to bed, that I could not do it, but was forced to go to bed and leave it to send away tomorrow by an Expresse.

3. Up, and all the morning till 3 in the afternoon examining and fitting up my pursers' paper, and so sent it away by an express. Then comes my wife, and I set her to get supper ready against I go to the Duke of Albemarle; and back again – and at the Dukes, with great joy, I received the good news of the decrease of the plague this week to 70, and but 253 in all;[1] which is the least Bill hath been known these twenty years in the City – though the want of people in London is it that must make it so low, below the ordinary number for Bills. So home, and find all my good company I had bespoke, as, Coleman and his wife and Laneare, Knipp, and her surly husband. And good music we had, and among other things, Mrs. Coleman sang my words I set of *Beauty retire*,[2] and I think it is a good song and they praise it mightily. Then to dancing and supper, and mighty merry till Mr. Rolt came in, whose pain of the Tooth ake made him no company and spoilt ours; so he away, and then my wife's teeth fell of akeing, and she to bed; so forced to break up all with a good song, and so to bed.

4. Up, and to the office – where my Lord Brouncker and I (against Sir W. Batten and Sir J. Mennes and the whole table) for Sir W Warren in the business of his mast-contract, and overcame them and got them to do what I had a mind to; endeed, my Lord

---

1. GL, A.1.5, no. 96 (26 December–　　2. See above, vi. 320, n. 4.　(E).
2 January).

Sir John Mennes, painted in the studio of Sir Anthony van Dyck
(*The Earl of Clarendon*)

being unconcerned in what I aimed at.[1] So home to dinner, where Mr. Sheldon came by invitation from Woolwich; and as merry as I could be, with all my thoughts about me, and my wife still in pain of her teeth. He anon took leave and took Mrs. Barbary his niece home with him, and seems very thankful to me for the 10*l* I did give him for my wife's rent of his*a* house;[2] and I am sure I am beholding to him, for it was a great convenience to me. And then my wife home to London by water, and I to the office till 8 at night; and so to my Lord Brouncker, thinking to have been merry, having appointed a meeting for Sir*b* J. Mennes and his company and Mrs. Knipp again; but whatever hindered I know not, but no company came, which vexed me, because it disappointed me of the glut of mirth I hoped for. However, good discourse with my Lord, and merry with Mrs. Williams's descants upon Sir J. Mennes and Mrs. Turner's not coming; so home and to bed.

5. I, with my Lord Brouncker and Mrs. Williams, by coach with four horses to London, to my Lord's house in Covent Guarden. But Lord, what staring to see a nobleman's coach come to town – and porters everywhere bow to us, and such begging of beggars. And a delightful thing it is to see the town full of people again, as now it is, and shops begin to open, though in many places, seven or eight together, and more, all shut; but yet the town is full compared with what it used to be – I mean the City-end, for Covent Gu[a]rden and Westminster are yet very empty of people, no Court nor gentry being there.[3] Set Mrs.

a repl. 'is'   *b* repl. 'Mr.'

1. Warren had failed to deliver by the end of 1665 the number of 'great masts' which he had promised under contract in 1664: see above, v. 215–16 & n. His explanation was that there was a shortage in Sweden of the longest mast-timber, and that he had lost four ships at sea. He added that he had already allowed the Navy Board a credit of £22,000: Warren to Navy Board, 2 January 1666 (*CSPD 1665–6*, p. 188). He was exonerated by a decision of the Board on 18 January after an enquiry ordered

by Albemarle: PRO, Adm. 106/3520, f. 27*v*. Pepys had had a 'firm league' with him since February 1665: above, vi. 32 & n. 2.

2. William Sheldon was Clerk of the Cheque at Woolwich dockyard. Mrs Pepys lodged at his house during the worst of the Plague: see above, vi. 315 & n. 4.

3. The court did not return to Whitehall until 1 February. For its movements during the Plague, see above, vi. 142, n. 1.

B

Williams down at my Lord's house, and he and I to Sir G. Carteret at his chamber at Whitehall, he being come to town last night to stay one day. So my Lord and he and I, much talk about the Act,[1] what credit we find upon it; but no private talk between him and I. So I to the Change, and there met Mr. Povey, newly-come to town, and he and I to Sir George Smith's and there dined nobly. He tells me how my Lord Bellases[2] complains for want of money, and of him and me therein; but I value it not, for I know I do all that can be done. We had no time to talk of per-ticulars, but leave it to another day; and I away to Cornhill to expect my Lord Brouncker's coming back again; and I stayed at my Stationer's house,[3] and by and by comes my Lord and did take me up; and so to Greenwich, and after sitting with them a while at their house, home, thinking to get Mrs. Knipp but could not, she being busy with company; but sent me a pleasant letter, writing herself *Barbary Allen*.[4] I went therefore to Mr. Boreman's for pastime, and there stayed an hour or two, talking with him and reading a discourse about the River of Thames the reason of its being choked up in several places with Shelfes;[5] which is plain, is by the encroachments made upon the River, and running-out of Cawse ways into the River at every wood wharfe, which was not heretofore when Westminster-hall and White-hall was built, and Redriffe church, which now are sometimes overflown[a] with water.[6] I had great satisfaction herein; so home, and to my papers for lack of company, but by and by comes little Mrs.

a repl. same symbol badly formed

1. The Additional Aid, 1665; see above, vi. 292 & n. 3.
2. Governor of Tangier.
3. John Cade's, on Cornhill.
4. Cf. above, p. 1. (E).
5. Boreman may have been George Boreman, ballast merchant. The choking up of the river was the subject of many complaints. The 'discourse' has not been traced.
6. For floods at Westminster, see above, i. 92 & n. 2. Proposals for embanking the Thames were made from time to time (see e.g. below, 23

September 1668), but no scheme was put into effect until the early 19th century. In 1684–7 the Navy Board and Trinity House made surveys of the buildings and encroachments on the riverside (copy in PL 297). The Board then calculated that the channel of the river had been narrowed by one-fifth in the vicinity of the 'new encroachments'. Cf. Pepys's notes made on a journey of inspection, April 1686: Rawl. A 171, ff. 98r–101v.

Tooker and sat and supped with me, and I kept her very late, talking and making her comb my head; and did what I will with her et tena grande plaisir con ella, tocando sa cosa con mi cosa, and hazendo la cosa par cette moyen. So late to bed.

6. Up betimes, and by water to the Cockepitt; there met Sir G. Carteret, and after discourse with*a* the Duke all together, and there saw a letter wherein Sir W. Coventry did take notice to the Duke with a commendation of my paper about pursers. I to walk in the park with the vicechamberlain, and received his advice about my deportment about the advancing the credit of the Act, giving me caution to see that we do not misguide the King by making them believe greater matters from it then will be found. But I see that this arises from his great trouble to see the Act succede, and to hear my name so much used, and my letters shown at Court about goods served us in upon the credit of it. But I do make him believe that I do it with all respect to him, and on his behalf too, as endeed I do, as well as my own, that it may not be said that he or I do not assist therein. He tells me that my Lord Sandwich doth proceed on his voyage[1] with the greatest kindness that can be imagined from the King and Chancellor – which was joyful news to me.

Thence with Lord Brouncker to Greenwich by water to a great dinner; and much company, Mr. Cottle and his lady and others, and I went hoping to get Mrs. Knipp to us, having wrote a letter to her in the morning, calling myself *Dapper Dicky*[2] in answer to hers of *Barb. Allen* – but could not; and am told by the boy that carried my letter that he found her crying; and I fear she lives*b* a sad life with that ill-natured fellow her husband. So we had a great, but I a melancholy, dinner, having not her there as I hoped. After dinner to Cards; and then comes notice that my wife is come unexpectedly to me to town, so I to her. It is only to see what I do and why I come not home; and she is in the right, that I would have a little more of Mrs. Knip's company before I go away. My wife to fetch away my things from Woolwich, and I

a repl. 'at table'   *b* repl. 'meets'

---

1. He sailed as ambassador to Spain in late February.
2. See BM, H. 1601 (226), G. 309

(66). A song (Scottish, like *Barbara Allen*) in which a girl laments her lover's absence. (E).

back to Cards; and after cards, to choose King and Queene;[1] and a good cake there was, but no marks found; but I privately found the clove, the mark of the knave, and privately put it into Captain Cockes piece, which made some mirth because of his lately being known by his buying of clove and mace of the East India prizes.[2] At night home to my lodging, where I find my wife returned with my things; and there also Captain Ferrers is come upon business of my Lord's to this town, about getting some goods of his put on board, in order to his going to Spain; and Ferrers presumes upon my finding a bed for him, which I did not like to have done without my invitation, because I had done several times before during the plague, that he could not provide himself safely elsewhere. But it being Twelve-Night, they had got the fiddler, and mighty merry they were; and I above came not to them – but when I had done my business among my papers, went to bed, leaving them dancing and choosing King and Queen.

7. *Lords day.* Up, and being trimmed, I was invited by Captain Cocke; so I left my wife, having a mind to some discourse with him, and dined with him. He tells me of new difficulties about his goods, which troubles me and I fear they will be great. He tells me too, what I hear everywhere, how the town talks of my Lord Craven being to come into Sir[a] G. Carteret's place;[3] but sure it cannot be true. But I do fear those two families, his and my Lord Sandwiches, are quite broken – and I must now stand upon my own legs.

Thence to my lodging; and considering how I am hindered by company there to do anything among[b] my papers, I did resolve to

a repl. 'my'   *b* MS. 'away'

---

1. For the Twelfth Night game: cf. above, i. 10 & n. 3.
2. See above, vi. 231 & n. 1.
3. Craven was a distinguished soldier and close friend of Albemarle. In a letter of the 13th, Pepys reported the rumour to Carteret himself, assuring him that Craven was reckoning on it as a certainty: *Shorthand Letters*, p. 78. On 30 December Craven had headed the list of those lending money on the Additional Aid: PRO, E 401/1938. Carteret's profits had been reduced by this act. He was replaced in June 1667 by Anglesey.

go away today, rather then stay to no purpose till tomorrow; and so got all my things packed up – and spent half an hour with W How[1] about his papers of accounts for contingencies and my Lord's accounts, and so took leave of my landlady and daughters, having paid dear for what time I have spent there;[2] but yet, having been quiet and in[a] health, I am very well contented therewith. So with my wife and Mercer took boat, and away home. But in the evening, before I went, comes Mrs. Knipp just to speak with me privately, to excuse her not coming to me yesterday, complaining how like a devil her husband treats her, but will be with us in town a week hence; and so I kissed her and parted.

Being come home, my wife and I to look over our house, and consider of laying out a little money to hang our bedchamber better then it is; and so resolved to go and buy something[b] tomorrow; and so after supper, with great joy in my heart for my coming once again hither, to bed.

8.   Up, and my wife and I by coach to Bennetts in Paternoster-row (few shops there being yet open), and there bought velvett for a coat and Camelott for a cloak for myself. And thence to a place to look over some fine counterfeit damasks to hang my wife's closet, and pitched upon one. And so by coach home again, I calling at the Change; and so home to dinner, and all the afternoon look after my papers at home and my office against tomorrow; and so after supper, and[c] considering the uselessness of laying out so much money upon my wife's closet, but only the chamber[3] – to bed.

9.   Up, and then to the office, where we met first since the plague, which God preserve us in.[4] At noon home to dinner,

---

a   MS. 'my'   b   repl. 'somewhat'   c   repl. 'to bed'

---

1. Deputy-Treasurer of Sandwich's fleet, 1665.
2. Pepys had paid £5 10s. 0d. monthly for his rooms at Mrs Clerke's, and had been there since 11 October 1665.

3. See below, pp. 10, 14.
4. Since 16 August 1665 the Board had met at the royal palace, Greenwich.

where Uncle Tho. with me, and in comes Pierce, lately come from Oxford, and Ferrers. After dinner Pierce and I up to my chamber, where he tells me how a great difference hath been between the Duke and Duchesse, he suspecting her to be naught with Mr. Sidny – but some way or other the matter is made up; but he was banished the Court, and the Duke for many days did not speak to the Duchesse at all.[1] He tells me that my Lord Sandwich is lost there at Court, though the King is perticularly his friend. But people do speak everywhere slightly of him. Which is a sad story to me, but I hope it may be better again. And that Sir G. Carteret is neglected, and hath great enemies at work against him. That matters must needs go*a* bad while all the town and every boy in the street openly cries*b* the King cannot go away till my Lady Castlemayne be ready to come along with him, she being lately brought to bed.[2] And that he visits her and Mrs. Stewart every morning before he eats his breakfast. All this put together makes me very sad; but yet I hope I shall do pretty well among them for all this, by my not meddling with either of their matters. He and Ferrers gone, I paid Uncle Tho. his last quarters money.[3] And then comes Mr. Gawden, and he and I talked above-stairs together a good while about his business; and to my great joy, got him to declare that of the 500*l* he did give me the other day,[4] none of it was for my Treasurershipp for Tanger – (I first telling him how matters stood between Povy and I, that he was to have half of whatever was coming to me by that office); and that he will gratify me at two per cent for that when he next receives any money – so there is 80*l* due to me more then I

a repl. 'good'   *b* repl. 'says'

---

1. Cf. above, vi. 302 & n. 1. Reresby says that the association was innocent and that Sidney was, 'according to report, banished from the court "for another reason" ': *Memoirs* (ed. Browning), p. 55. James Pearse was surgeon to the Duke.

2. The court was still at Oxford, where, on 28 December, in a fellow's chamber at Merton College, Lady

Castlemaine had given birth to George (Fitzroy), cr. Earl (1674) and Duke (1683) of Northumberland, the fifth child of her union with the King. HMC, *Laing*, i. 445.

3. This was an annuity payable from the estate of Robert Pepys of Brampton: above, iii. 17 & nn.

4. See above, vi. 323.

thought of. He gone, I with a glad heart to the office to write my letters; and so home to supper and bed. My wife mighty full of her work she hath today in furnishing her bedchamber.

10. Up, and by coach to Sir G Downing, where Mr. Gawden met me by agreement to talk upon the Act. I do find Sir G. Downing to be a mighty talker, more then is true; which I now know to be so, and suspected it before; but for all that, I have good grounds to think it will succeed for goods, and in time for money too; but not presently.[1] Having done with him, I to my Lord Brunckers house in Covent Guarden; and among other things, it was to acquaint him with my paper of pursers;[2] and read it to him and had his good liking of it. Showed him Mr. Coventry's sense of it, which he sent me last post, much to my satisfaction.[3] Thence to the Change, and there hear, to our grief, how the plague is encreased this week from 70 to 89.[4] We have also great fear of our Hambrough fleet, of their meeting the Dutch; as also have certain news that by storms Sir Jer. Smith's fleet is scattered, and three of them come without masts back to Plymouth; which is another very exceeding great disappointment, and if the victualling ships are miscarried, will tend to the loss of the garrison of Tanger.[5] Thence home; in my way,[a] had the opportunity I longed for, of seeing and saluting Mrs. Stokes,

a MS. 'wife'

---

1. Cf. Downing's brusque and confident letter to Pepys, 9 January, reporting Albemarle's support for the act (the Additional Aid) and a merchant's promise of masts on its credit – so that 'Holland shall not outdoe us in point of credite . . .': PRO, SP 29/144, no. 84.

2. See above, p. 1 & n. 1.

3. Coventry's notes for this letter are in Berks. Rec. Off., Trumbull Add. MSS 19/26. The letter itself has not been traced.

4. GL, A.1.5, no. 96 (2–9 January).

5. Smith had sailed from Plymouth for Tangier and the Straits on 19 December 1665. The three ships which returned had no news of the rest of the fleet. Hence Pepys's relief at hearing in February of their safe arrival off Spain: below, p. 45 & n.2. CSPD 1665–6, p. 193; Allin, vol. ii, p. xvi.

my little goldsmiths wife in Paternoster-row; and there bespoke something, a silver chafing-dish for warming plates. And so home to dinner. Found my wife busy about making her hangings for her chamber with the Upholster. So I to the office, and anon to the Duke of Albemarle by coach at night (taking, for saving time, Sir W. Warren with me, talking of our businesses all the way going and coming) and there got his reference of my pursers' paper to the Board, to consider of it before he read it, for he will never understand it I am sure.[1] Here I saw Sir W Coventry's kind letter to him[2] concerning my paper. And among other of his letters (which I see all, and that is a strange thing, that whatever is writ to this Duke of Albemarle, all the world may see; for this very night he did give me Mr. Coventry's letter to read as soon as it came to his hand, before he had read it himself, and bid me take out of it what concerned the Navy; and many things there was in it which I should not have thought fit for him to have let anybody so suddenly seen).*a* But among other things, find him profess himself to the Duke a friend into the enquiring further into the business of Prizes, and advises that it may be public, for the righting the King and satisfying the people and getting the blame to be rightly laid where it should be – which strikes very hard upon my Lord Sandwich[3] – and troubles me to read it. Besides, what vexed me more, I heard the damned Duchesse again say, to twenty gentlemen publicly in the room, that she would have Mountagu sent once more to sea, before he goes his Embassy, that we may see whether he will make amends for his cowardize;[4] and repeated the answer she did give the other day in my hearing to Sir G Downing – wishing her Lord had been a coward, for then perhaps he might have been made an Embassador and not been sent now to sea. But one good thing she said – she cried mightily out against the having of gentlemen Captains with feathers and ribbands, and wished the King would send her

a no bracket in MS.

---

1. See Albemarle to Navy Board, 10 January (*CSPD 1665–6*, p. 198), asking to be told of Mr Pepys's proposals, since no part of navy business needed more regulation than the disorderly conduct of pursers.

2. Untraced.

3. The enquiry was held privately, by the Prize Commissioners, and resulted in Sandwich's acquittal: below, p. 52. For Coventry's severe criticism of Sandwich on this matter, see Clarendon, *Life*, ii. 464, 469.

4. Cf. above, vi. 291 & n. 1.

husband to sea with the old plain sea-Captains that he served with formerly, that would make their ships swim with blood, though they could not make legs as captains nowadays can.[1]

It grieved me to see how slightly the Duke doth everything in the world, and how the King and everybody suffers whatever he will to be done in the Navy, though never so much against reason – as in the business of recalling Tickets,[2] which will be done notwithstanding all the arguments against it. So back again to my office and there to business, and so to bed.

11. Up, and to the office. By and by to the Custome-house to the Farmers there, with a letter of Sir G. Carteret's for 3000*l* which they ordered to be paid me.[3] And so away back again to the office; and at noon to dinner, all of us by invitation, to Sir W Pen's; and much other company, among others, the Lieutenant of

---

1. Gentlemen captains had been introduced into the navy in the 1630s to command the fighting force on board, and because some thought that it was improper to have the King's ships commanded by men of mean birth. But gentlemen usually knew nothing of navigation, and friction easily developed between them and the 'plain sea-Captains' (or 'tarpaulins') trained in the merchant ships. Commissioner Middleton and Sir William Coventry took much the same view as the Duchess: below, pp. 333–4; 29 June 1667. Pepys's clerk Richard Gibson later expressed the commonest objection. Gentlemen captains, he wrote, 'have had the honour to bring drinking, gameing, whoring, swearing, and all impiety into the navy . . . They bring seamen to covett to act like gentlemen, where gentlemen should learn to act like seamen': qu. J. Charnock, *Marine Archit.* (1800–2), vol. i, p. lxxxviii. Pepys's own views were substantially the same, although he could be critical of

both types and saw the need for both. See *Cat.*, i. 201; *Further Corr.*, pp. 356–7; *Naval Minutes*, pp. 53–4, 64, 83, 119, 194, 230, 267, 315, 426; *Tangier Papers*, pp. 106, 122, 206–7, 212–13, 229. He insisted above all on 'downright diligence, sobriety, and seamanship' (letter to Capt. Rooth, 24 January 1674, in *Cat.*, ii. 232). The best discussion is in Ehrman, pp. 139–41. Cf. also Macaulay, *Hist. Engl.* (1876 ed.), iii. 21–2; I. G. Powell in *Mar. Mirr.*, 9/358+; D. Ogg, *Engl. in reigns of James II and William III*, pp. 326–7; M. Lewis, *England's Sea-officers*, esp. p. 195.

2. Albemarle had favoured, and Pepys had opposed, the recall of tickets: *Further Corr.*, pp. 112, 113. See Pepys to Coventry, 11 January, reporting this interview: ib., pp. 113–14.

3. The first fruits of the new method of payment of bills: above, vi. 304 & n. 3. For this sum, see above, vi. 322.

the Tower and Broome his Poet[1] – and Dr. Whistler and his son-in-law Lowder, servant to Mrs. Margt. Pen[2] – and Sir Edw. Spragg[3] a merry man that sang a pleasant song pleasantly. Rose from table before half-dined, and with Mr. Mountney of the Custome-house to the East India-house and there delivered to him tallies for 3000*l*, and received a note for the money on Sir R. Viner and so ended the matter; and back to my company, where stayed a little, and thence away with Lord Brouncker for discourse sake; and he and I to Gresham College to have seen Mr. Hooke and a new-invented chariot of Dr. Wilkins, but met with nobody at home.[4] So to Dr. Wilkins's, where I never was before – and very kindly received, and met with Dr Merritt;[5] and fine discourse among them, to my great joy – so sober and so ingenious. He is now upon finishing his discourse of a Universall Character.[6] So away, and I home to my office about my letters, and so home to supper and to bed.

12. By coach to the Duke of Albemarle, where Sir W. Batten and I only met. Troubled at my heart to see how things are ordered there – without consideration or understanding. Thence back by coach, and called at Wottons my shoemaker, lately come to town, and bespoke shoes; as also got him to find me a Taylor

1. Alexander Brome was a friend of Sir John Robinson, Lieutenant of the Tower, and had dedicated to him his *Songs and other poems* (1661), presenting the book to his patron as a 'Volunteer' in his regiment. He craved the same safety and subsistence which the Lieutenant gave to the 'great and serious Emblems and instruments of power' and to 'the Apes and Catamountains and other properties of diversion' in his charge.
2. Anthony Lowther, step-son of Whistler, married Margaret Penn in February 1667.
3. A naval commander.
4. The weekly meetings of the Royal Society were not resumed after the Plague until 14 March: see below

p. 51, n. 2. For the new chariot, see below, p. 20 & n. 2.
5. Christopher Merrett, Librarian of the Royal College of Physicians.
6. John Wilkins, *Essay towards a real character, and a philosophical language*, published in 1668; Pepys bought it on 15 May 1668. For this attempt to produce a universal written language, see above, v. 12, n. 3; O. Funke, *Zum Weltsprachenproblem in Engl. im 17 Jahrhundert*, pp. 107+ ; E. N. da C. Andrade in *Annals of Science*, 1/4+ ; cf. also ib., 4/150+ . The scheme seems to have attracted very little support. Pepys himself later found fault with the chapter on 'Naval Relation': *Naval Minutes*, p. 177.

to make me some clothes, my own[1] being not yet in Towne, nor
Pym, my Lord Sandwiches tailor.   So he helped me to a pretty
man, one Mr. Penny, against St. Dunstan's Church.   Thence to
the Change, and there met Mr. Moore, newly come to town, and
took him home to dinner with me; and after dinner to talk – and
he and I do conclude my Lord's case to be very bad, and may be
worse if he do not get a pardon for his doings about the prizes, and
his business at Bergen and other thing[s] done by him at sea, before
he goes for Spayne.[2]   I do use all the art I can to get him to get
my Lord to pay my cosen Pepys, for it is a great burden to my
mind, my being bound for my Lord in 1000*l* to him.[3]   Having
done discourse with him, and directed him to go with my advice
to my Lord express tomorrow to get his pardon perfected before
his going, because*a* of what I read the other night[4] in Sir W.
Coventry's letters, I to the office and there had an extraordinary
meeting of Sir J. Mennes, Sir W. Batten, Sir W. Penn, and
my Lord Brouncker and I, to hear my paper read about pursers,
which they did all of them, with great good will and great
approbation of my method and pains in all; only Sir W. Penn,
who must except against everything and remedy nothing, did
except against my proposal, for some reasons which I could not
understand, I confess, nor my Lord Brouncker neither.   But he
did detect, endeed, a failure or two of mine in my report about
the ill-condition of the present pursers, which I did magnify in one
or two little things; to which I think he did with reason except.
But at last, with all respect did declare the best thing he ever heard
of this kind; but when Sir W. Batten did say, "Let us that do
know the practical part of the Victualling meet Sir J. Mennes,
Sir W. Penn and I, and see what we can do to mend all," he was
so far from offering*b* or furthering it, that he declined it and said
he must be out of town.   So, as I ever knew him, never did in his
life ever attempt to mend anything, but suffer all things to go on
in the way they are, though never so bad, rather then improve his
experience to the King's advantage.   So we broke up; however,
they promising to meet to offer something in it of their opinions –

a repl. 'but'   b repl. 'furthering'

1. William Langford.
2. For the pardon, see below, p. 260
& n. 2.
3. See below, p. 31 & n. 3.
4. See above, p. 10.

and so we rise; and I and my Lord Brouncker by coach a little way, I with him for discourse sake – till our coach broke and tumbled me over him quite down the side of the coach, falling on the ground about the Stockes.[1] But up again, and thinking it fit to have for my honour something reported in writing to the Duke in favour of my pains in this, lest[a] it should be thought to be rejected as Frivolous, I did move it to my Lord, and he will see it done tomorrow. So we parted; and I to the office, and thence home to my poor wife, who works all day at home like a horse at the making of her hanging for our chamber and the bed. So to supper and to bed.

13. At the office all the morning – where my Lord Brouncker moved to have something wrote in my matter, as I desired him last night; and it was ordered, and will be done next sitting. Home with his Lordship to Mrs. Williams's in Covent-garden to dinner (the first time I ever was there), and there met Captain Cocke; and pretty merry, though not perfectly so, because of the fear that there is of a great encrease again of the plague this week.[2] And again my Lord Brouncker doth tell us that he hath it from Sir John Baber, that relates to my Lord Craven, that my Lord Craven doth look after Sir G. Carteret's place and doth reckon himself sure of it.[3] After dinner, Cocke and I together by coach to the Exchange, in our way talking of our matters, and do conclude that everything must break in pieces while no better counsels govern matters then there seem to do, and that it will become him and I and all men to get their reckonings even as soon as they can, and expects all to break. Besides, if the plague continues among us another year, the Lord knows what will become of us. I set him down at the Change, and I home to my office, where late writing letters and doing business; and thence home to supper and to bed – my head full of cares, but pleased with my wife's minding her work so well and busying herself about her house; and I trust in God, if I can but clear myself of my Lord Sandwiches

a　repl. 'let'

---

1. The Stocks market, just north of the site of the present Mansion House. (R).

2. See below, p. 17 & n. 2.

3. See above, p. 6 & n. 3.

bond, wherein I am bound with him for 1000*l* to T. Pepys, I shall do pretty well, come what will come.

14. *Lords day.* Long in bed – till raised by my new Taylor, Mr. Penny; comes and brings me my new velvet coat, very handsome but plain; and a day hence will bring me my Camelott cloak. He gone, I close to my papers to set all in order, and to perform my vow to finish my Journall and other things before I kiss any woman more, or drink any wine,[1] which I must be forced to do tomorrow if I go to Greenwich, as I am invited by Mr. Boreman to hear Mrs. Knipp sing. And I would be glad to go, so as we may be merry. At noon eat the*ᵃ* second of the two Cygnets Mr. Sheply sent us for a New-Year's gift;[2] and presently to my chamber again, and so to work hard all day about my Tanger accounts, which I am going again to make up – as also upon writing a letter to my father about Pall, whom it is time now, I find, to think of disposing of, while God Almighty hath given me something to give with her; and in my letter to my father I do offer to give her 450*l*, to make her own 50*l*, given her by my uncle, up 500*l*.[3] I do also therein propose Mr. Harman the upholster for a husband for her, to whom I have a great love, and did heretofore love his former wife, and a civil man he is, and careful in his way. Besides, I like*ᵇ* his trade and place he lives in, being Cornehill. Thus late at work; and so to supper and to bed. ⟨This afternoon after sermon comes my dear fair beauty of the Exchange, Mrs. Batelier,[4] brought by her sister, an acquaintance of Mercer's, to see my wife. I saluted her with as much pleasure as I had done any a great while. We sat and talked together an hour, with infinite pleasure to me; and so the fair creature went away, and proves one of the modestest women, and

a repl. ? 'this'   *b* repl. 'l'-

1. See above, vi. 336, where the oath is referred to more briefly. Cf. below, p. 25.
2. Shipley was steward of Sandwich's estate at Hinchingbrooke. Cf. also above, v. 2 & n. 2.
3. Paulina had received £50 as a legacy from Robert Pepys of Brampton.

4. Mary Batelier, linen-draper. She, her sister, and her brother Will soon became close friends of the Pepyses. They lived in Crutched Friars within sight of the Navy Office: below, p. 110.

pretty, that ever I saw in my life; and my [wife] judges her so too.⟩ᵃ

15. Busy all the morning in my chamber in my old ᵇ cloth suit, while my usual one is to my tailor's to mend; which I had at noon again, and an answer to a letter I had sent this morning to Mrs. Pierce to go along with my wife and I down to Greenwich tonight, upon an invitation to Mr. Boreman's to be merry, to dance and sing with Mrs. Knipp. Being dressed and having dined, I took coach and to Mrs. Pierce, to her new house in Covent-garden, a very fine place and fine house. Took her thence home to my house, and so by water to Boremans by night – where the greatest disappointment that ever I saw in my life: much company – a good supper provided, and all come with expectation of excess of mirth; but all blank through the waywardnesse of Mrs. Knipp, who, though she had appointed the night, could not be got to come – not so much as her husband could get her to come; but, which was a pleasant thing in all my anger – I asking him (while we were in expectation what answer one of our many messengers would bring) what he thought, whether she would come or no, he answered that for his part he could not so much as think. By and by we all to supper, which the silly maister of the feast commanded; but what with my being out of humour, and the badness of the meat dressed, I did never eat a worse supper in my life. At last, very late and supper done, she came undressed; but it brought me no mirth at all; only, after all being done, without singing, or very little, and no dancing – Pierce and I to bed together; and he and I very merry to find how little and thin clothes they give us to cover us, so that we were fain to lie in our stockings and drawers and lay all our coats and clothes upon the bed. So to sleep.

16. Up, and I leaving the women in bed together (a pretty black and white), I to London to the office, and there forgot, through business, to bespeak any dinner for my wife and Mrs. Pierce. However, by noon they came and a dinner we had, and Kate Joyce comes to see us – with whom very merry. After dinner she and I up to my chamber, who told me her business was chiefly for my advice about her husband's leaving of his trade –

a addition crowded in between entries   *b* repl. 'gown'

which, though I wish enough, yet I did advise against, for he is a man will not know how to live idle, and imployment he is fit for none.¹ Thence I anon carried her, and so Mrs. Pierce, home; and so to the Duke of Albemarle, and mighty kind he to me still. So home late at my letters, and so to bed – being mightily troubled at the news of the plague's being increased, and was much the saddest news that the plague hath brought me from the beginning of it, because of the lateness of the year, and the fear we may with reason have of its continuing with us the next summer – the total being now 375; and the plague, 158.²

17. Busy all the morning, settling things against my going out of town this night. After dinner late, took horse, having sent for Lashmore³ to go with me; and so he and I rode to Dagenhams⁴ in the dark. There find the whole family well. It was my Lord Crew's desire that I should come, and chiefly*ᵃ* to discourse with me of Lord Sandwich's matters; and therein to persuade, what I had done already, that my Lord should sue out a pardon⁵ for his business of the prizes, as also for Bergen and all he hath done this year past, before he begins his Embassy to Spain. For it is to be feared that the Parliament will fly out against him and perticular men the next session. He is glad also that my Lord is clear of his sea imployment, though sorry, as I am, only in the manner of its bringing about. By and by to supper, my Lady Wright very kind. After supper up to wait on my Lady Crew, who is the same weak silly lady as*ᵇ* ever, asking such saintly questions. Down to my Lord again and sat talking an hour or two; and anon to prayers, the whole family, and then all to bed – I handsomely used, lying in the chamber Mr. Carteret formerly did – but sat up an hour talking sillily with Mrs. Carter and Mr. Marre, and so to bed.

a repl. 'an'   *b* MS. 'that'

---

1. Anthony Joyce was a tallow-chandler; he now became an inn-keeper in Clerkenwell. Cf. above, v. 347 & n. 2.
2. The corresponding figures for the previous week (2–9 January) had been 265 and 89: GL, A.1.5, no. 96.
3. Navy Office messenger.
4. A house near Romford, Essex; home of Lady Wright, the widowed daughter of Lord Crew.
5. See below, p. 260 & n. 2.

18. Up before day, and thence rode to London before office time – where I met a note at the door to invite me to supper to Mrs. Pierce's because of Mrs. Knipp, who is in town and at her house. To*ᵃ* the office, where, among other things, vexed with Major Norwood's coming, who takes it ill my not paying a bill of exchange of his.¹ But I have good reason for it, and so the less troubled; but yet troubled, so as at noon, being carried by my Lord Bruncker to Captain Cockes to dinner, where Mrs. Williams was and Mrs. Knipp, I was not heartily merry, though a glass of wine did a little cheer me. After dinner to the office. Anon comes to me thither my Lord Brouncker, Mrs. Williams, and Knipp; I brought down my wife in her night-gown, she not being indeed very well, to the office to them. There, by and by, they parted all; and my wife and I anon, and Mercer, by coach to Pierce, where mighty merry and sing and dance with great pleasure; and I danced, who never did in company in my life.² And Captain Cocke came for a little while and danced, but went away – but we stayed, and had a pretty supper and spent till 2 in the morning; but got home well by coach, though as dark as pitch. And so to bed.

19. Up and ready, called on by Mr. Moone, my Lord Bellaces³ secretary, who and I good friends, though I have failed him in some payments. Thence with Sir J. Mennes to the Duke of Albemarles, and carried all well. And met Norwood, but prevented him in desiring a meeting of the Commissioners for Tanger. Thence to look out Sir H. [Cholmley]; but he not within, he coming to town last night. It is a remarkable thing how infinitely naked all that end of the town, Covent-garden, is at this day of people; while the City is almost as full again of people as ever it was. To the Change, and so home to dinner and the office, whither anon comes Sir H Cholmly to me; and he and I to my house, there to settle his accounts with me; and so with great pleasure we agreed, and great friends became, I think, and

a repl. 'mighty merry'

---

1. See below, p. 23 & n. 2.   3. Belasyse, Governor of Tangier.
2. But see above, ii. 61.

he presented me upon the foot of our accounts for this year's service for him, 100*l*, whereof Povy must have half.[1]   Thence to the office and wrote a letter to Norwood to satisfy him about my non-payment of his bill, for that doth still stick in my mind.   So at night, home to supper and to bed.

20.   To the office, where upon Mr. Kinaston's coming to me about some business of Collonell Norwood's, I sent my boy[2] home for some papers; where, he staying longer then I would have him and being vexed at the business and to be kept from my fellows in the office longer then was fit, I became angry and boxed my boy when he came, that I do hurt my Thumb so much, that I was not able to stir all*a* the day after and in great pain.   At noon to dinner, and then to the office again late, and so to supper and to bed.

21.   *Lords day.*   Lay almost till noon, merrily and with pleasure talking with my wife in bed.   Then up, looking about my house and the room which my wife is dressing up, having new-hung our bedchamber with blue, very handsome.   After dinner to my Tanger accounts, and there stated them against tomorrow very distinctly for the Lords to see who meet tomorrow; and so to supper and to bed.

22.   Up, and set my people to work in copying Tanger accounts, and I down the River to Greenwich to the office to fetch away some papers; and thence to Deptford, where by*b* agreement my Lord Brouncker was to come; but stayed almost till noon, after I had spent an hour with W. How talking of my Lord Sandwiches matters and his folly in minding his pleasures too much nowadays and submitting himself to be governed by Cuttance, to the displeasing of all the commanders almost of the fleet;[3] and thence we may conceive endeed, the rise of all my

a repl. 'in'   *b* MS. 'my'

---

1. The accounts were for the construction of the mole at Tangier, of which Cholmley was engineer. In 1665 he had promised Pepys £200 p.a.: above, vi. 306.

2. Tom Edwards.

3. Sir Roger Cuttance was not a flag-officer, and his influence in the prize goods scandal had been disastrous.

c

Lord's misfortunes of late.   At noon my Lord Brouncker did come, but left the keys of the chests we should open at Sir G. Carteret's lodgings, of my Lord[a] Sandwiches, wherein Hows's supposed Jewells are;[1]   so we could not, according to my Lord Arlington's order, see them today; but we parted, resolving to meet here at night, my Lord Brouncker being going with Dr. Wilkins, Mr. Hooke, and others to Collonell Blunts to consider again of the business of Charriots, and to try their new invention which I saw here my Lord Brouncker ride in; where the coachman sits astride upon a pole over[b] the horse, but doth not touch the horse; which is a pretty odde thing, but it seems it is most easy for the horse, and as they say, for the man also.[2]   Thence, I with speed by water home and eat a bit, and took my accounts and to the Duke of Albemarle – where, for all I feared of Norwood, he was very civil, and Sir Tho. Ingram beyond expectation, I giving them all content; and I thereby settled mightily in my mind, for I was weary of the imployment and had had thoughts of giving it over.   I did also go a good step in a business of Mr. Hublands, about getting a ship of his to go to Tanger; which during this strict Imbargo is a great matter, and I shall have a good reward for it I hope.[3]   Thence by water in the dark down to Deptford: and

a repl. 'Lords'   *b* repl. 'on'

1. See above, vi. 299–300.
2. Thomas Blount lived at Wricklemarsh, near Blackheath. He was a magistrate, and a Fellow of the Royal Society interested in mechanical inventions. (For his plough and his waywiser, see Evelyn, iii. 170, 196.) The present experiment was one of a series made with chariots by members of the Royal Society: cf. above, vi. 94 & n. 2. A report was made to the Society on 14 March: Birch, ii. 66. The design (which was claimed to be better than the rival French designs) was by Hooke and Wilkins, and Hooke had in September 1664 taken out a patent for its manufacture: PRO, SP 44/14, f. 35r. It held one passenger, and the driver sat in a

sprung saddle. Brouncker rode in it from London to Wricklemarsh on one occasion: Boyle, *Works* (1744), v. 349. For descriptions, see Birch, loc. cit., and PRO, SP 44, loc. cit. See also Gunther, vi. 192, etc. Sir William Petty made similar experiments in the 1670s: *Petty–Southwell Corr.* (ed. Marquess of Lansdowne), i. 13, 40–2, 124.
3. Since the beginning of the war, ships had been forbidden, by a proclamation of 1 March 1665, to go to sea except under licence: Steele, no. 3409. The Houblons sent two ships (below, p. 38) and Pepys received £200 on 5 March for what appears to be this service: below, p. 66.

there find my Lord Brouncker come and gone, having stayed long for me. I back presently to the Crowne tavern behind the Exchange by appointment, and there met the first meeting of Gresham College since the plague.[1] Dr. Goddard did fill us with talk in defence of his and his fellow-physicians' going out of town in the plague-time; saying that their perticular patients were most gone out of town, and they left at liberty – and a great deal more, &c.[2] But what, among other fine discourse, pleased me most, was Sir G. Ent about Respiration; that it is not to this day known or concluded on among physicians, nor to be done either, how that action is managed by nature or for what use it is.[3] Here late, till poor Dr. Merritt was drunk; and so all home, and I to bed.

23. Up, and to the office and then to dinner. After dinner, to the office again all the afternoon, and much business with me. Good news, beyond all expectation, of the decrease of the plague; being now but 79, and the whole but 272.[4] So home with comfort to bed. A most furious storme all night and morning.[5]

1. An informal meeting (not recorded in the society's minutes) of which there were several: C. R. Weld, *Hist. Roy. Soc.* (1848), i. 184. It seems that the first Council meeting after the Plague was on 21 February, and the first meeting of the society on 14 March. See below, p. 51 & n. 2; Birch, ii. 63, 65.
2. Many physicians had left London during the Plague, the President of the College of Physicians (Sir Edward Alston) and the great Sydenham among them. See Bell, *Plague*, pp. 62, 292.
3. The discovery by William Harvey (d. 1657) of the circulation of the blood had led investigators to examine the difficulty of explaining the change from venous to arterial blood, and the part played in the process by the lungs. It was English scientists who in this generation made the greatest contributions to the

subject – Boyle, Hooke, and Ent himself, who published a book on it in 1672. Lower showed that it was the lungs not the heart which effected the change; Mayow that the active agent was not the whole air, but only part of it (what we now know as oxygen). See Sir M. Foster, *Lectures on hist. physiol.*, pp. 172+; D. McKie in *Science medicine and history* (ed. E. A. Underwood), i. 469+; T. S. Patterson in *Isis*, 15/47+, 504+.
4. Plague burials had gone down from 158: GL, A.1.5, no. 96.
5. Dr D. J. Schove writes: 'This gale was termed a hurricane by a contemporary meteorologist, John Goad: *Astro-meteorologica* (1686), p. 186. Cf. *Philos. Trans.*, i (for 1665–6) no. 14, p. 247 (which gives 24 January as the date). Cf. Rugge, ii, ff. 582, 583 (26 January; probably a wrong date).'

24. By agreement, my Lord Brouncker called me up; and though it was a very foul windy and rainy morning, yet down to the waterside we went, but no boat could go, the storm continued so. So my Lord, to stay till fairer weather, carried me into the Tower to Mr. Hores,[1] and there we stayed talking an hour; but at last we found no boat yet could go, so we to the office, where we met upon an occasion extraordinary, of examining abuses of our clerks in taking money for examining of tickets, but nothing done in it.[2] Thence my Lord and I, the weather being a

《*Great Storme.*》 little fairer, by water to Detford*a* to Sir G Carteret's house,[3] where W How met us; and there we opened the chests and saw the poor sorry Rubys which have caused all this ado to the undoing of W How; though I am not much sorry for it, because of his pride and ill-nature. About 200 of these very small stones and a cod of Muske (which it is strange I was not able to smell) is all we could find. So locked them up again, and my Lord and I, the wind being again very furious, so as we durst not go by water, walked to London quite round the Bridge, no boat being able to Stirre; and Lord, what a dirty walk we had, and so strong the wind, that in the fields we many times could not carry our bodies against it, but was driven backward. We went through Horsydowne, where I never was since a little boy, that I went to enquire after my father, whom we did give over for lost, coming from Holland.[4] It was dangerous to walk the streets, the bricks and tiles falling from the houses, that the whole streets were covered with them – and whole chimneys, nay, whole houses in two or three places, blowed down. But above all, the pales on London-bridge on both sides were blown away, so that we were fain to stoop very low, for fear of blowing off of the bridge. We could see no boats in the Thames afloat but what were broke loose and carried through the bridge, it being

a repl. 'Greenwich'

---

1. Probably James Hoare, sen., Comptroller of the Mint.
2. The Board made an order this day inviting complaints to be laid before it on 31 January: PRO, Adm. 106/3520, f. 27*v*.
3. An official residence of the Treasurers of the Navy.
4. There is evidence of a visit to Holland by 'John Pepys and a servant' in 1656 (*CSPD 1656–7*, p. 582) when Pepys was 23, but none apparently of any earlier visit.

ebbing water. And the greatest sight of all was, among other parcels of ships driven here and there in clusters together, one was quite overset, and lay with her masts all along in the water and keel above water. So walked home; my Lord away to his house and I to dinner, Mr. Creede being come to town and to dine with me, though now it was 3 a-clock. After dinner, he and I to our accounts; and very troublesome he is and with tricks, which I found plainly and was vexed at. While we were together, comes Sir G Downing with Collonell Norwood, Rumball and Warcupp to visit me;[1] I made them drink good wine – and discoursed above alone a good while with Sir G. Downing, who is very troublesome. And then with Collonell Norwood, who hath a great mind to have me concerned with him in everything;[2] which I like, but am shy of adventuring too much, but will think of it. They gone, Creed and I to finish the settling his accounts. Thence to the office, where the Houblans and we discoursed upon a rubb which we have for one of the ships I hoped to have got to*a* go out to Tanger for them. They being gone, I to my office-business late, and then home to supper and even sack, for lack of a little wine, which I was therefore forced to drink against my oath,[3] but without pleasure.

25. Up, and to the office. At noon home to dinner. So abroad to the Duke of Albemarle and K. Joyces and her husband, with whom I talked a great deal about Pall's business; and told them what portion I would give her, and they do mightily like of it and will proceed further in speaking with Harman, who hath already been spoke to about it, as from them only; and he is mighty glad of it, but doubts it may be an offence*b* to me if I should know of*c* it; so thinks that it doth come only from Joyce, which I like the better. So I do believe the business will go on, and I desire it were over. I to the office then, where I did much

---

a repl. 'them'   b MS. 'office'   c repl. 'not'

---

1. All Pepys's visitors had subscribed loans under the Additional Aid, of which Downing was the principal author.

2. Henry Norwood (appointed Lieutenant-Governor of Tangier on 21 February) was proposing to enter into some trading ventures: see below, p. 24.

3. See above, p. 15 & n.1.

business and set my people to work against furnishing me to go to
Hampton Court, where the King and Duke will be on Sunday
next.   It is now certain that the King of France hath publicly declared war against us,[1] and God knows how little fit we are for it.
At night comes Sir W. Warren, and he and I into the garden and
talked over all our businesses.   He gives me good advice, not to
imbark into trade (as I have had it in my thoughts about
⟨Collonell⟩ Norwood) so as to be seen to mind it, for it will do
me hurt, and draw my mind off from my business and imbroil
my estate too soon.   So to the office business, and I find him as
cunning a man in all points as ever I met with in my life; and
mighty merry we were in the discourse of our own tricks.   So
about 10 a-clock at night, I home and stayed with him there,
settling my Tanger=Boates business,[2] and talking and laughing at
the folly of some of our neighbours of this office, till 2 in the
morning; and so to bed.

26.   Up, and pleased mightily with what my poor wife hath
been doing these eight or ten days with her own hands, like a
drudge, in fitting the new hangings*a* of our bed-chamber of blue,
and putting the old red ones into my dressing-room.   And so by
coach to White-hall, where I had just now notice that Sir G
Carteret is come to town.   He seems pleased, but I perceive he is
heartily troubled at this act[3] and the report of his losing his place,
and more at my not writing to him to*b* the prejudice of the Act.
But I carry all fair to him, and he to me.   He bemoans the Kingdom as in a sad state, and with too much reason I doubt, having so
many enemies about us, and no friends abroad, nor money nor
love at home.   Thence to the Duke of Albemarle, and there a
meeting with all the officers of the Navy; where, Lord, to see how
the Duke of Albemarle flatters himself with false hopes of money
and victuals, and all without reason.   Then comes the Committee
of Tanger to sit, and I there carry all before me very well.
Thence with Sir J Bankes and Mr. Gawden to the Change, they
both very wise men.   After Change, and agreeing with Houblon

---

a repl. 'and old'   *b* repl. 'against'

1. On 16/26 January.   3. See above, vi. 292 & n. 3.
2. See above, vi. 146 & n. 2.

about our ships,[1] D. Gauden and I to the Pope's-head and there dined, and little Chaplin (who a rich man grown);[2] he gone after dinner, and D. Gauden and I to talk of the victualling business of the Navy in what posture it is, which is very sad, also for want of money. Thence home to my chamber by oath,[3] to finish my Journall. Here W Hewres comes to me with 320*l* from Sir W. Warren, whereof 220*l* is got clearly by a late business of insurance of the Gottenborough ships,[4] and the other 100*l* what was due and he had promised me before[5] to give me, to my very extraordinary joy, for which I ought and do bless God; and so to my office, where late, providing a letter to send to Mr. Gawden in a manner we concluded on today; and so to bed.

27. Up very betimes to finish my letter and write it fair to Mr. Gawden, it being to demand several queries in the present state of the victualling, partly to the King's [advantage], and partly to give him occasion to say something relating to the want of money on his own behalf.[6] This done, I to the office – where all the morning. At noon, after a bit of dinner, back to the office, and there fitting myself in all points to give an account to the Duke and Mr. Covent[r]y in all things[7] and in my Tanger businesses, till 3 a-clock in the morning; and so to bed, and up again about 6. *Lords day.* And being dressed in my velvet coat 《28.》 and plain Cravatt, took a hackney-coach provided ready for me by 8 a-clock; and so to my Lord Brouncker with all my papers. And there took his coach with four horses and away

1. See below, p. 98 & n. 2.
2. Francis Chaplin, provision merchant and navy victualler, whom Pepys had known in his Exchequer days, became Sheriff and Alderman in 1668, Lord Mayor in 1677, and a knight in 1679.
3. Cf. above, p. 15.
4. Cf. above, vi. 328.
5. Cf. above, vi. 146 & n. 2.
6. Copy (in Pepys's hand) in Longleat, Coventry MSS 97, ff. 9+, 26 January, with covering note to Coventry, 27 January. A copy of Gauden's answer (27 January) is ib., 96, ff. 133–4.

7. See Pepys's memorandum (in his own hand); 'Minutes of Matters thought fitt to bee layd before his R. H. by discourse of the Board at their attending him at Hampton Court January 28 1665 as well in answer to his Royall Highness's letter of the 25th instant, as for his generall Information in the present Worke of the Office'. They concerned the refitting and building of ships, and the effects of the Plague: Longleat, Coventry MSS 98, ff. 173–5.

towards Hampton Court, having a great deal of good discourse with him – perticularly about his coming to lie at the office; which I went further in inviting him to then*ª* I intended, having not yet well considered whether it will be convenient for me or no to have him here so near us.   And then of getting Mr. Eveling or Sir Robt. Murry into the Navy in the room of Sir Tho. Harvy.[1] At Branford I light, having need to shit; and went into an Inne doore that stood open, found the house of office, and used it, but saw no people: only after I was in the house, heard a great dog bark and so was afeared how I should get safe back again, and therefore drew my sword and scabbard out of my belt to have ready in my hand – but did not need to use it, but got safe into the coach again.   But lost my belt by that shift, not missing it till I came to Hampton Court.   At the Wicke[2] found Sir J. Mennes and Sir W. Batten at a lodging provided for us by our Messenger, and there a good dinner ready.   After dinner took coach, and to Court, where we find the King and Duke and Lords all in council; so we walked up and down – there being none of the ladies come, and so much the more business I hope will be done.   The Council being up, out comes the King, and I kissed his hand and he grasped me very kindly by the hand.   The Duke also, I kissed his; and he mighty kind, and Sir W Coventry.   I found my Lord Sandwich there, poor man, I saw, with a melancholy face and suffers his beard to grow on his upper lip more then usual.[3] I took him a little aside, to know when I should wait on him, and where; he told me, and that it would be best to meet at his lodgings, without being seen to walk together – which I liked very well; and Lord, to see in what difficulty I stand, that I dare*ᵇ* not

---

a   repl. 'then' (badly-formed)   *b*   repl. 'dare' (smudged)

---

1. Harvey had only just been appointed a Navy Commissioner on 20 January in Berkeley's place. He had been brought in, according to Pepys's later comment, 'for want of other ways of gratification' (*Naval Minutes*, p. 257), and did very little work. He did not resign his place until 1668. Evelyn was a Commissioner for the Sick and Wounded; Moray a distinguished soldier and amateur of science. He was a friend of Brouncker, and with him one of the founders of the Royal Society. Neither Evelyn nor Moray became an officer of the Navy Board.

2. Presumably Hampton Wick, on the Middlesex bank opposite Kingston and about a mile east of the Palace. (R).

3. Cf. the portrait above, iii, front.

walk with Sir W. Coventry for fear my Lord or Sir G. Carteret should see me; nor with any of them, for fear Sir W. Coventry should. After changing a few words with Sir W. Coventry, who assures me of his respect and love to me and his concernment for my health in all this sickness – I went down into one of the Courts and there met the King and Duke; and the Duke called me to him – and the King came to me of himself and told me: "Mr. Pepys," says he, "I do give you thanks for your good service all this year, and I assure you I am very sensible of it." And the Duke of Yorke did tell me with pleasure that he had read over my discourse about Pursers[1] and would have it ordered in my way, and so fell from one discourse to another; I walked with them quite out of the Court into the fields, and then back and to my Lord Sandwich's chamber, where I find him very melancholy and not well satisfied, I perceive, with my carriage to Sir G. Carteret; but I did satisfy him, and made him confess to me that I have a very hard game to play; and told me that he was sorry to see it, and the inconveniences which likely may fall upon me with him. But for all that, I am not much afeared, if I can but keep out of harm's way, in not being found too much concerned in my Lord's or Sir G. Carteret's matters; and that I will not be if I can help it. He hath got over his business of the prizes so far as to have a Privy Seale passed for all that was in his distribucion to the officers, which I am heartily glad of; and for the rest, he must be answerable for what he is proved to have.[2] But for his pardon for anything else, he thinks it not seasonable to ask it, and not useful to him; because that will not stop a Parliaments mouth, and for the King, he is sure enough of him. I did ask him whether he was sure of the interest and friendship of any great Ministers of State, and he told me yes. As we were going further, in comes my Lord Mandeville, so we were forced to break off; and I away and to Sir W Coventry's chamber, where he not come in; but I find Sir W Pen, and he and I to discourse. I find him very much out of humour, so that I do not think matters go very well

1. See above, p. 1 & n. 1.
2. A privy-seal order (24 January) franked the goods granted to Sandwich by the King, on condition that customs dues were paid: *CSPD 1665–6*, p. 218. 'The rest' were certain other prize goods which Sandwich had in December sent by ketch to King's Lynn, and thence to Hinchingbrooke: Harris, ii. 28–31. For the pardon, see below, p. 260 & n. 2.

with him, and I am glad of it.   He and I staying till late, and Sir
W. Coventry not coming in (being shut up close all the afternoon
with the Duke of Albemarle), we took boat and by water to
Kingstone; and so to our Lodgeings, where a good supper and
merry; only, I sleepy, and therefore after supper I slunk away
from the rest to bed, and lay very well and slept soundly – my
mind being in a great delirium, between joy for what the King
and Duke have said to me and Sir W. Coventry – and trouble for
my Lord Sandwiches concernments and how hard it will be for
me to preserve myself from feeling thereof.

    29.   Up, and to Court by coach, where to council before the
Duke of Yorke – the Duke of Albemarle with us.   And after
Sir W. Coventry had gone over his notes that he had provided
with the Duke of Albemarle, I went over all mine, with good
success.   Only, I fear I did once offend the Duke of Albemarle,
but I was much joyed to find the Duke of Yorke so much con-
tending for my discourse about the pursers against Sir W. Penn,
who opposed it like a fool.   My Lord Sandwich came in in the
middle of the business; and, poor man, very melancholy methought, and said little at all or to the business, and sat at the lower
end, just as he comes, no room being made for him;   only, I did
give him my stool, and another was reached me.
    This council done, I walked to and again up and down the
house, discoursing with this and that man.   Among others, took
occasion to thank the Duke of Yorke for his good opinion in
general of my service, and perticularly his favour in conferring on
me the victualling business.[1]   He told me that he knew nobody
so fit as I for it.   And next, he was very glad to find that to give
me for my encouragement – speaking very kindly of me.
    So to Sir W. Coventry's to dinner with him, whom I took
occasion to thank for his favour and good thoughts of what little
service I did, desiring he would do the last act of friendship, in
telling me of my faults also.   He told me he would [be] sure he
would do that also, if there were any occasion for it.   So that, as
much as it is possible under so great a fall of my Lord Sandwich's
and difference between them, I may conclude that I am
thoroughly right with Sir W. Coventry.

               1. See above, vi. 254–5 & n.

I dined with him with a great deal of company and much merry discourse. I was called away before dinner ended, to go to my company who dined at our lodgings – whither I went with Mr. Eveling (whom I met) in his coach going that way – but found my company gone; but my Lord Brouncker left his coach for me, so Mr. Eveling and I into my Lord's coach and rode together, with excellent discourse till we came to Clapham – talking of the vanity and vices of the Court, which makes it a most contemptible thing; and endeed, in all his discourse I find him a most worthy person. Perticularly,[a] he intertained me with discourse of an Infirmery which he hath projected for the sick and wounded seamen against the next year, which I mightily approve of[1] – and will endeavour to promote, it being a worthy thing – and of use and will save money. He set me down at Mr. Gawden's,[2] where nobody yet come home, I having left him and his sons and Creed at Court. So I took a book, and into the gardens and there walked and read till dark – with great pleasure; and then in, and in comes Osborne and he and I to talk, and Mr. Jaggard, who came from London; and great hopes there is of a decrease this week also of the plague. Anon comes in Creed, and after that, Mr. Gauden and his sons – and then they bring in three ladies who were in the house, but I do not know of them;

a repl. 'Perfectly'

---

1. Evelyn, as one of the Commissioners for Sick and Wounded Mariners, wrote to Pepys on 31 January sending him, at his request, a 'draught' of the infirmary (for 400–500 men) projected at Chatham: PRO, SP 29/146, f. 73 (printed in C. Marburg, *Mr. Pepys and Mr. Evelyn*, pp. 98–9; summary in *CSPD 1665–6*, p. 226). Already half the accommodation at three London hospitals (St Bartholomew's, St Thomas's and the Savoy) was reserved for the wounded, but the greater number were boarded out. A hospital would not only, as Pepys said, save money, but also avoid 'intemperance' and 'the clamour of landladies': Pepys to Evelyn, 17 March (*Further Corr.*, pp. 116–18). In March a site at Chatham was chosen and estimates prepared (Rawl. A 195a, ff. 249–54), but because of lack of funds nothing was done until Greenwich Hospital was opened in 1705. The history of the present proposal is summarised in Evelyn, iii. 430, n. 2. See also Evelyn, *Diary and corr.* (ed. Wheatley), iii. 329, 331–40; *CSPD 1665–6*, pp. 230, 233, 272; *Letters*, pp. 26–7, 252–3.

2. At Clapham: for the house, see above, iv. 244, n. 1.

his daughter and two nieces, daughters of Dr. Whistlers – with whom, and Creed, mighty sport at supper, the ladies very pretty – and mirthful. I perceive they know Creeds gut and stomach as well as I, and made as much mirth as I with it at supper. After supper I made the ladies sing, and they have been taught; but Lord, though I was forced to commend them, yet it was the saddest stuff I ever heard. However, we sat up late; and then I, in the best chamber like a prince, to bed – and Creede with me. And being sleepy, talked but little.

30. Lay long, till Mr. Gawden was gone out, being to take a little journy. Up, and Creed and I some good discourse, but with some trouble for the state of my Lord's matters. After walking a turn or two in the garden, and bid good-morrow to Mr. Gauden's sons and sent my service to the ladies, I took coach after Mr. Gawden's; and home, finding the town keeping the day solemly, it being the day of the King's Murther;[1] and they being at church, I presently into the church,[a] thinking to see Mrs. Lethulier or Batelier, but did not – and a dull sermon of our young Lecturer[2] to boot.[b] This is the first time I have been in this church since I left London for the plague; and it frighted me indeed to go through the church, more then I thought it could have done, to see so [many] graves lie so high upon the churchyard, where people have been buried of the plague.[3] I was much troubled at it, and do not think to go through it again a good while. So home to my wife, whom I find not well in bed; and it seems hath not been well these two days. She rose, and we to dinner. After dinner up to my chamber, where she entertained me with what she hath lately

a repl. symbol rendered illegible   *b* MS. 'bed'

---

1. For the service, see above, ii. 24, n. 2.

2. The unidentified Scotsman: see above, iv. 12, n. 1.

3. Detailed figures of the burials in St Olave's are given in *Gent. Mag.*, 24 (1845)/355. Since June 1665, 326 plague victims had been buried and a new churchyard opened for the

purpose, first mentioned in the registers on 21 November 1664: *Harl. Soc. Reg.*, 46/199. In 1891 workmen excavating for a sewer came across a considerable collection of skull-bones, halfway between church door and the gateway: unpub. typescript on St Olave's by the Rev. T. Wellard.

bought of clothes for herself, and Damaske, linen, and other things for the house. I did give her a serious account how matters stand with me, of favour with the King and Duke, and of danger in reference to my Lord's and Sir G. Carteret's falls, and the dissatisfaction*ᵃ* I have heard the Duke of Albemarle hath acknowledged to somebody; among other things, against my Lord Sandwich, that he did bring me into the Navy against his desire and endeavour for another, which was our doting fool Turner.[1] Thence, from one discourse to another, and looking over ⟨my⟩ house and other things, I spent the day at home; and at night betimes to bed. ⟨After dinner this day, I went down by water to Deptford and fetched up what money there was of W. How's contingencies in the chest there, being 516*l*. 13*s*. 03*d*, and brought it home to dispose of.⟩*ᵇ*

31. Lay pretty long in bed, and then up and to the office, where we met on extraordinary occasion about the business of tickets.[2] By and by, I to the Change and there did several businesses. Among others, brought home my Cosen Pepys, whom I appointed to be here today, and Mr. Moore met us up[on] the business of my Lord's bond.[3] Seeing my neighbour Mr. Knightly*ᶜ*[4] walk alone from the Change, his family not being yet come to town, I did invite him home with me, and he dined with me. A very sober pretty man he is. He is mighty solicitous, as I find many about the City that live near*ᵈ* the churchyards, to have the churchyards covered with Lime, and I think it is needful, and ours I hope will be done. Good pleasant discourse at dinner, of the practices of merchants to cheat the customers,* occasioned by Mr. Moore's being with much trouble freed of his prize-goods which he bought, which fell into the customers hands and with

---

a repl. 'mistakes'   *b* addition crowded in between entries
c repl. 'GC'   *d* repl. 'next'

---

1. See above, i. 183–4. For Albemarle's attitude, see below, 21 May 1667.
2. See above, p. 22 & n. 1.
3. See above, ii. 43 & n. 2.
4. Robert Knightley, merchant (knighted, 1676).

much ado hath cleared them.[1]   Mr. Knightly being gone, my cousin Pepys and Moore and I to our business, being the clearing of my Lord Sandwiches bond, wherein I am bound with him to my cousin for 1000*l*; I have at last by my dexterity got my Lord's consent to have it paid out of the money raised by his prizes.   So the bond is Cancelled, and he paid by having a note upon Sir Rob. Viner, in whose hands I had lodged my Lord's money – by which I am, to my extraordinary comfort, eased of a liableness to pay that sum in case of my Lord's death or troubles in estate, or my Lord's greater fall, which God defend.

Having settled this matter at Sir Robt. Viner's, I took up Mr. Moore (my cousin going home), and to my Lord Chancellors new house which he is building, only to view it, hearing so much from Mr. Evelyn of it; and endeed, it is the finest pile I ever did see in my life, and will be a glorious house.[2]   Thence to the Duke of Albemarle, who tells me Mr. Coventry is come to town, and directs me to go to him about some business in hand – whether out of displeasure or desire of ease, I know not; but I asked him not the reason of it but went to White-hall, but could not find him there, though to my great joy people begin to bustle up and down there, the King holding his resolution to be in town to-morrow, and hath good encouragement, blessed be God, to do so, the plague being decreased this week to 56, and the total to 227.[3]

So after going to the Swan in the Palace,[4] and sent for Spicer[5] to

---

1. For the prize-goods, see above, vi. 231, n. 1. Henry Moore had bought about £800-worth from Sandwich: Sandwich MSS, Journal, x. 234.

2. Clarendon House, built 1664–8 to the design of Roger Pratt, on the n. side of Piccadilly opposite the n. end of St James's St, and occupied in 1667. Evelyn (iii. 379) called it a 'palace' and praised its design lavishly. (Cf. ib., p. 470 & n. 4: and his letter of 20 January 1666 describing it as 'the best contrived, the most usefull, gracefull and magnificent house in England'; *Diary and corr.*, ed. Wheat-

ley, ii. 417 n.) It became a model for English country houses over a whole generation: H. M. Colvin, *Biog. dict. Engl. architects*, p. 472. It was demolished some sixteen years after its completion. View in C. L. Kingsford, *Early hist. Piccadilly*, opp. p. 106.

3. GL, A.1.5, no. 96 (23–30 January). In the previous week there had been 79 plague burials.

4. The Swan, New Palace Yard. (R).

5. Jack Spicer, a messenger of the Receipt at the Exchequer.

discourse about my last Tanger tallies, that have some of the words washed out with the rain, to have them new writ – I home, and there did some business at, the*ᵃ* office; and so home to supper and to bed.*ᵇ*

    a   MS. 'and the'   *b*   followed by one blank page

FEBRUARY.

1. Up, and to the office, where all the morning till late ⟨and Mr. Coventry with us, the first time since before the plague⟩. Then hearing*a* my wife was gone abroad to buy things and see her mother and father, whom she hath not seen since before the plague, and no dinner provided for me ready, I walked to Captain Cockes, knowing my Lord Brouncker dined there; and there very merry, and a good dinner. Thence my Lord and his mistress Madam Williams set me down at the Exchange, and I to Alderman Backewell's to set all my reckonings straight there, which I did, and took up all my notes. So evened to this day, and thence to Sir Rob. Viner's, where I did the like, leaving clear in his hands just 2000*l* of my own money, to be called for when I pleased.[1] Having done all this, I home;*b* and there to the office, did my business there by the post, and so home and spent till one in the morning in my chamber to set right all my money matters, and so to bed.

2. Up betimes, and knowing that my Lord Sandwich is come to town with the King and Duke, I to wait upon him; which I did and find him in very good humour, which I am glad to see with all my heart.*c* Having received his commands and discoursed with some of his people about my Lord's going, and with Sir Rog. Cuttance, who was there and finds himself slighted by Sir W Coventry, I advised him however to look after imployment, lest it be said that my Lord's friends do forsake the service after he hath made them rich with the prizes. I to London, and there, among other things, did look over some pictures at Cades[2] for my house, and did carry home a Silver Drudger for my cupboard of plate, and did*d* call for my silver chafing-dishes, but they

a blot over symbol	*b* repl. 'to'
c repl. 'time'	*d* repl. 'would'

1. For Pepys's banking methods, see above, v. 269, n. 1.
2. John Cade was a stationer on Cornhill; the pictures would be prints.

are sent home and the man would not be paid for them, saying that he was paid for them already, and with much ado got him to tell me, by Mr. Wayth;[1] but I would not accept of that, but will send him his money, not knowing any courtesy I have yet done him to deserve it. So home, and with my wife looked over our plate and picked out 40*l* worth I believe, to change for more useful plate, to our great content; and then we shall have a very handsome cupboard of plate. So to dinner, and then to the office, where we had a meeting extraordinary about stating to the*a* Duke the present debts of the Navy for which ready money must be had.[2] And that being done, I to my business, where late; and then home to supper and to bed.

3. Up, and to the office, very busy till 3 a-clock; and then home, all of us, for half an hour to dinner; and to it again till 8*b* at night about stating our wants of money for the Duke, but could not finish it. So broke up, and I to my office;*c* then about letters and other businesses very late, and so home to supper, weary with business, and to bed.

4. *Lords day.* And my wife and I the first time together at church since the plague, and now only because of Mr. Mills his coming home to preach his first sermon, expecting a great excuse for his leaving the parish before anybody went, and now staying till all are come home; but he made but a very poor and short excuse, and a bad sermon.[3] It was a frost, and had snowed last night, which covered the graves in the churchyard, so I was the less afeared for going through. Here I had the content to see my noble Mrs. Lethulier;[4] and so home to dinner, and all the afternoon at my Journall till supper, it being a long while behindhand.

a   symbol blotted   *b*   repl. '9'   *c*   repl. 'clos'-

---

1. Robert Waith, Paymaster to the Navy Treasurer. Contrary to regulations, he supplied canvas to the Navy Office. An order to pay him over £720 was signed on 20 February: Rawl. A 211, p. 344.

2. See below, pp. 36-7 & n.

3. Hewer reported the sermon in his shorthand notebook: Houghton Lib., Harvard, MS. Eng. 991.1. (Cf. below, p. 374, n. 1.) The text was Leviticus, xxvi. 21: 'And if ye walk contrary unto me, and will not hearken unto me, I will bring seven times more plagues unto you, according to your sins.'

4. See below, p. 41, n. 1.

D

At supper my wife tells me that W. Joyce hath been with her this evening, the first time since the plague – and tells her my aunt James is lately dead of the stone, and what she had hath given to his and his brother's wife and my cousin Sarah. So after supper to work again, and late to bed.

5. Up, and with Sir W. Batten (at whose lodgings, calling for him, I saw his Lady the first time since her coming to town since the plague, having absented myself designedly, to show some discontent and that I am not at all the more suppliant because of my Lord Sandwiches fall) to my Lord Bruncker's, to see whether he goes to the Dukes this morning or no. But it is put off, and so we parted. My Lord invited me to dinner today, to dine with Sir W. Batten and his Lady there, who were invited before; but lest he should think so little*a* an invitation would serve my turn, I refused and parted, and to Westminster about business; and so back to the Change and there met Mr. Hill, newly-come to town, and with him the Houbland's, preparing for their ship's and his going to Tanger, and agreed that I must sup with them tonight. So home and eat a bit, and then to White-hall to a Committee for Tanger, but it did not meet but was put off to tomorrow. So I did some little business, and visited my Lord Sandwich; and so, it raining, went directly to the Sun behind the Exchange about 7 a-clock, where I find all the five brothers Houblons,[1] and mighty fine gentlemen they*b* are all, and used me mighty respectfully. We were mighty civilly merry, and their discourses (having been all abroad) very fine. Here late, and at last accompanied*c* home with Mr. James Houblon and Hill, whom I invited to sup with me on Friday; and so parted, and I home to bed.

6. Up, and to the office, where very ⟨busy⟩ all the morning; we met upon a report to the Duke of Yorke of the debts of the

---

a   repl. symbol rendered illegible
b   repl. 'their'   c   repl. 'let'

---

1. All were merchants in the Spanish, Portuguese and N. African trades. They were a by-word for their mutual affection. Pepys was to become an intimate of James Houblon.

Navy,[1] which we finished by 3 [a] a-clock; and having eat one little bit of meat, I by water before the rest to White-hall (and they to come after me) because of a committee for Tanger; where I did my business of stating my accounts perfectly well and to good liking, and do not discern but the Duke of Albemarle is my friend in his intentions, notwithstanding my general fears. After that to our Navy business, where my fellow-officers were called in; and did that also very well. And then broke up, and I home by coach, Tooker with me, and stayed in Lumberdstreete at Viners and sent home for the plate which my wife and I had a mind to change, and there changed it – about 50*l* worth – into things more useful, whereby we shall now have a very handsome cupboard of plate. So home to the office, wrote my letters by the post, and to bed.

7. It being fast-day,[2] I stayed at home all day long to set things to rights in my chamber, by taking out all my books and putting my chamber in the same condition it was before the plague. But in the morning, doing of it and knocking [b] up a nail, I did bruise my left thumb, so as broke a great deal of my flesh off, that it hung by a little. It was a sight frighted my wife – but I put some balsam of Mrs. Turners to it, and though in great pain, yet went on with my business; and did it to my full content, setting everything in order, in hopes now that the worst of our fears are over as to the plague for the next year. Interrupted I was by two or three occasions this day, to my great vexation, having this the only day I have been able to set apart for this work since my coming to town. At night to supper, weary, and to bed – having had [c] the plasterers and joiners also to do some jobbs.

a repl. '2'   *b* repl. 'cl'-   *c* repl. 'had' (different symbol)

1. 'Minutes in proofe of the State of Navy debts presented to D. Yorke. Febr. 6. 1665': BM, Add 9316, ff. 23–5 (title and endorsement in Pepys's hand; remainder in Hayter's); copies ib., 9311, ff. 99*v*–100*v*; Longleat, Coventry MSS 96, f. 100*r*. See below, p. 48 & n. 2. Throughout January the newspapers had carried notices informing creditors of the office that two clerks would be on duty every morning and afternoon to receive information about any outstanding debts incurred since 24 June 1660.

2. For the Plague: see above, vi. 155, n. 4.

8. Up, and all the morning at the office. At noon to the Change, expecting to have received from Mr. Houbland, as he promised me, an assignment upon Viner for my reward for my getting them the going of their two ships to Tanger; but I find myself much disappointed therein, for I spoke with him and he said nothing of it, but looked coldly, through some disturbance he meets with in our business through Collonell Norwoods pressing them to carry more goods then will leave room for some of their own.[1] But I shall ease them. Thence to Captain Cockes, where Mr. Williamson, Wren, Boltele, and Madam Williams;[2] and by and by Lord Brouncker (he having been with the King and Duke upon the water today to see Greenwich-house and the Yacht Castle is building of),[3] and much good discourse. So to ⟨White-hall to see my Lord Sandwich⟩,[a] and then home to my business till night, and then to bed.

9. Up, and betimes to Sir Ph. Warwicke, who was glad to see me and very kind. Thence to Collonell Norwood's lodgings, and there set right Houblons business about their ships. Thence to Westminster to the Exchequer about my Tanger business, to get orders for tallies,[4] and so to the Hall, where the first day of the Tearme and the hall very full of people, and much more then was expected, considering the plague that hath been. Thence to the Change, and to the Sun behind it to dinner with the Lieutenant of the Tower and Collonell Norwood and others – where strange pleasure they seem to take in their wine and meat, and discourse of it with the curiosity and joy that methinks was below men of worth. Thence home, and there very much angry with my people till I had put all things in good forwardness about my supper for the Houblons; but that being done, I was in good

a repl. 'Lumberdstreete'

---

1. Cf. above, pp. 20, 23 & nn.
2. The guests were Joseph Williamson (head of Arlington's secretariat) Matthew Wren (Clarendon's secretary, cousin of the architect and a great friend of Cocke), John Bulteel (another secretary of Clarendon), and Abigail Williams, Brouncker's mistress.
3. The *Monmouth* (103 tons). For the work on Greenwich Palace, see above, v. 75, n. 3.
4. £17,500 for the Tangier garrison: *CTB*, i. 717.

humour again, and all things in good order. Anon the five brothers Houblons came, and Mr. Hill, and a very good supper we had, and good company and discourse, with great pleasure. My new plate sets off my cupboard very nobly. Here they were till about 11 at night, with great pleasure; and a fine sight it is to see these five brothers thus loving one to another, and all industrious merchants. Our subject was principally Mr. Hills going for them to Portugall, which was the occasion of this entertainment. They gone, we to bed.

10. Up, and to the office. At noon, full of business, to dinner. This day came first Sir Tho. Harvy after the plague, having been out of town all this while.[1] He was coldly received by us – and he went away before we rose also, to make himself appear yet a man less necessary. After dinner, being full of care and multitude of business, I took coach, and my wife with me; I set her down at her mother's (having first called at my Lord Treasurer's and there spoke with Sir Ph. Warwicke), and I to the Exchequer about Tanger orders, and so to the Swan and there stayed a little; and so by coach took up my wife and at the old Exchange bought a muff, and so home and late at my letters, and so to supper and to bed – being nowadays, for these four or five months, mightily troubled with my snoring in my sleep, and know not how to remedy it.

11.[a] *Lords day.* Up, and put on a new black cloth suit to an old coat that I make to be in mourning at Court, where they are all, for the King of Spain.[2] To church I, and at noon dined well; and then by water to White-hall, carying a Captain of the Tower (who desired his freight thither); there I to the park, and walk two or three turns of the Pall Mall with the company about the King and Duke – the Duke speaking to me a good deal. There met Lord Brouncker and Mr. Coventry and discoursed about the Navy business, and all of us much at a loss that we yet can hear nothing of Sir Jere. Smith's fleet that went away to the Streights

a repl. '12'

---

1. For Harvey, see above, p. 26, n. 1. He had a house in Bury St Edmund's, Suff.   2. Philip IV had died on 7/17 September 1665.

the middle of December[1] – through all the storms that we have had since, that have driven back three or four of them, with their masts by the board.

Yesterday came out the King's Declaracion of war against the French; but with such mild invitations of both them and [the] Duch to come over hither,[a] with promise of their protection, that everybody wonders at it.[2]

Thence home with my Lord Brouncker for discourse sake; and thence by hackney-coach home; and so my wife and I mighty pleasant discourse, supped, and to bed – the great wound I had Wednesday last in my thumb having, with once dressing by Mrs. Turners balsam, been perfectly cured, whereas I did not hope to save my nail, whatever else trouble it did give me.

My wife and I are much thoughtful nowadays about Pall's coming up, in order to a husband.

12. Up, and very busy to perform an oath in finishing my Journall this morning for seven or eight days past. Then to several people attending upon business; among others, Mr.[b] Grant and the executors of Barlow for the 25*l* due for the quarter before he died; which I scruple to pay, being obliged but to pay every half-year.[3] Then[c] comes Mr. Cæsar, my boy's lute-master, whom I have not seen since the plague before, but he hath been in Westminster all this while very well – and tells me how, in the heighth of it, how bold people there were to go in sport to

a repl. 'here'   *b* repl. 'to'   *c* repl. 'dined'

---

1. See above, p. 9 & n. 5.

2. *His Majesties declaration against the French*; dated 9 February, but published on the 10th: Steele, no. 3455. The passage Pepys remarks on runs (pp. 5–6): 'We do declare, That if any of the French or Low-Country Subjects, either out of affection to Us or our Government, or because of the oppression they meet with at home, shall come into Our Kingdomes, they shall be by Us protected in Their

Persons and Estates, and especially those of the Reformed Religion . . . '. Charles also gave assurances to French and Dutch subjects who already lived in Great Britain, provided that they did not correspond with the enemy.

3. Pepys had allowed £100 p.a. to Thomas Barlow, his predecessor as Clerk of the Acts: see above, i. 202 & n. 1. John Graunt, Barlow's friend and agent, was the pioneer social statistician.

one another's burials. And in spite to well people, would breathe in the faces (out of their windows) of well people going by.

Then to dinner before the Change, and so to the Change and then to the tavern to talk with Sir Wm. Warren; and so by coach to several places, among others, to my Lord Treasurer's, there to meet my Lord Sandwich, but missed; and met him at Lord Chancellors and there talked with him about his accounts, and then about Sir G. Carteret; and I find by him that Sir G. Carteret hath a worse game to play then my Lord Sandwich, for people are heaving *a* at him. And he cries out of the business of Sir W. Coventry, who strikes at all and doth all. Then to my bookseller's, and then received some books I have new bought; and here late, choosing some more to new bind, having resolved to give myself 10*l* in books. And so home to the office, and then home to supper, where Mr. Hill was, and supped with us, and good discourse; a excellent person he still appears to me. After supper, and he gone, we to bed.

13. Up, and all the morning at the office. At noon to the Change, and thence, after business, dined at the Sheriffes (Hooker), being carried by Mr. Lethulier; where to my heart's content I met his wife, a most beautiful fat woman.[1] But all the house melancholy upon the sickness of a daughter of the house in childbed, Mr. Vaughans lady[2] – so all of them undressed; but however, this lady a very fine woman – I had a salute of her; and after dinner some discourse, the Sheriff and I, about a parcel of tallow I am buying for the office of him, I away home, and there at the office all the afternoon till late at night, and then away home to supper and to bed.

Ill news this night, that the plague is encreased this week,*b*3 and

---

a repl. 'heave'   *b* MS. 'well'

---

1. John Lethieulier, merchant, had married Sir William Hooker's daughter, Anne. Pepys had admired her recently (above, vi. 316, 328), but had had 'no opportunity of beginning acquaintance'.

2. Letitia Hooker had married John Vaughan, son of the prominent M.P.

of the same name (cf. above, v. 102–3). She survived and lived to a good age.

3. In 6–13 February there were 59 plague burials as against 52 in the previous week: GL, A.1.5, no. 96.

in many places else about the town, and at Chatham and else-where.[1]

This day, my wife wanting a chambermaid, with much ado got[a] our old little Jane[2] to be found out, who came to ⟨see⟩ her; and hath lived all this[b] while in one place, but is so well, that we will not desire her removal; but are mighty glad to see the poor wench, who is very well, and doth well.

14. *St. Valentine's day.* This morning called up by Mr. Hill, who my wife thought had been come to be her Valentine, she it seems having drawn him last night,[3] but it proved not; however, calling him up to our bedside, my wife challenged him. I up and made myself ready, and so with him by coach to my Lord Sandwiches by appointment – to deliver Mr. How's accounts to my Lord. Which done, my Lord did give me hearty and large studied thanks[c] for all my kindnesses to him and care of him and his business. I, after profession of all duty to his Lordshipp, took occasion to bemoan myself that I should fall into such a difficulty about Sir G. Carteret, as not to be for him but I must be against Sir W. Coventry, and therefore desired to be neutrall – which my Lord approved and confessed reasonable, but desired me to be-friend him privately. Having done in private with my Lord, I brought Mr. Hill to kiss his hands, to whom my Lord professed great respects upon my score. My Lord being gone, I took Mr. Hill to my Lord Chancellors new house that is building,[4] and went with trouble up to the top of it and there is there the noblest prospect that ever I saw in my life, Greenwich being nothing to it. And in everything is a beautiful house – and most strongly built in every respect – and as if, as it hath, it had the Chancellor for its maister. Thence with him to his painter, Mr. Hales, who is drawing his picture – which will be mighty like him, and pleased

a repl. 'f' -   *b* repl. 'of'   *c* repl. 'things'

---

1. For the plague at Chatham and other riverside towns nearby (in which it spread freely), see J. F. D. Shrewsbury, *Hist. bubonic plague in Brit. Isles*, pp. 488+.

2. Jane Birch, the Pepyses' first servant. For her periods of service with them (since 1658), see above, ii. 162, n. 1.

3. See *Comp.*: 'Valentine's Day'.

4. In Piccadilly: see above, p. 32, n. 2.

me, so that I am resolved presently to have my wife's and mine done by him, he having a very maisterly hand.[1] So with mighty satisfaction to*ª* the Change, and thence home; and after dinner abroad, taking Mrs. Mary Batelier with us, who was just come to see my wife; and they set me down at my Lord Treasurer's, and themselfs went with the coach into the fields to take the ayre. I stayed a meeting of the Duke of Yorkes and the officers of the Navy and Ordinance – my Lord Treasurer lying in bed of the gowte. Our business was discourse of the straits of the Navy for want of money; but after long discourse, as much out of order as ordinary people's, we came to no issue, nor any money promised or like to be had, and yet the work must be done. Here I perceive Sir G. Carteret had prepared himself to answer a Choque of Sir W. Coventry, by offering of himself to show all he had paid, and what is unpaid and what moneys*ᵇ* and assignments he hath in his hands – which, if he makes good, was the best thing he ever did say in his life – and the best timed, for else*ᶜ* it must have fallen very foul on him.

The meeting done, I away, my wife and they being come back and staying for me at the gate. But Lord, to see how afeared I was that Sir W. Coventry should have spied me once whispering with Sir G. Carteret; though not intended by me, but only Sir G. Carteret came to me and I could not avoid it. So home; they set me down at the Change, and I to the Crowne, where my Lord Bruncker was come, and several of the Virtuosi;[2] and after a small supper*ᵈ* and but little good discourse, I with Sir W Batten (who was brought thither with my Lord Brouncker) home, where I find my wife gone to Mrs. Mercers to be merry – but presently

a repl. 'home'   *b* repl. 'sums'   *c* repl. 'use'   *d* repl. 's'-

---

1. For the portraits of Pepys's wife and himself, see below, p. 44 & n. 2; p. 75 & n. 1. That of Thomas Hill (of which Pepys acquired a copy: below, p. 125) does not appear to survive. (There is however a portrait of him in the Pepys Library, presented in 1945 by a member of the Hill family, which is close in style to Hayls.) The painter, John Hayls

(Hales), is an obscure figure and his *œuvre* has not been established. He seems to have been well established in the 1640s; he died in January 1680. (OM).

2. Fellows of the Royal Society; an informal meeting. For the resumption of the society's meetings, see above, p. 21, n. 1.

came in with Mrs. Knipp, who it seems is in town and was gone thither with my wife and Mercer to dance; and after eating a little supper, went thither again to spend the whole night, there being W. How there, at whose chamber they are, and Lawd Crisp by chance. I to bed.

15. Up, and my wife not come home all night. To the office, where sat all the morning. At noon to Starkys, a great cook's in Austin Fryers, invited by Collonell Atkins, and a good dinner for Collonell Norwood and his friends;[1] among others, Sir Edw. Spragg and others – but ill attendance. Before dined, called on by my wife in a coach; and so I took leave, and there with her and Knipp and Mercer*a* (Mr. Hunt, newly come out of the country, being there also, come to see us) to Mr. Hales the painter's, having set down Mr. Hunt by the way. Here Mr. Hales begun my wife in the posture we saw one of my Lady Peters, like a St. Katharine.[2] While he painted, Knipp and Mercer*b* and I sang; and by and by comes*c* Mrs. Pierce with my name in her bosom for her Valentine, which will cost me money. But strange, how like his very first dead Colouring is, that it did me good to see it, and pleases me mightily – and I believe will be a noble picture. Thence with them all as far as Fleet-street and there set Pierce and Knipp down; and we home, I to the office, whither the Houb[l]ons come, telling me of a little new trouble

a l.h. repl. s.h. 'Kercer'   *b* symbol smudged
c repl. 'Mrs.'

---

1. Henry Norwood was on 21 February appointed Lieutenant-Governor of Tangier. Samuel Atkins was a London merchant who supplied provisions to the garrison.
2. For Lady 'Peters' (Petre), see above, v. 109, n. 3. Neither portrait is known to have survived. That of Elizabeth Pepys (paid for on 17 March when Pepys began to sit for his own) was finished on 20 March. Its present whereabouts is unknown. In the early 19th century it was in the possession of the Pepys Cockerell family, and an engraving of it by James Thomson was reproduced in the first edition of the diary (Braybrooke, 1825, vol. i, opp. p. 2) and in subsequent editions. See illust. above, front. According to a family tradition the painting was destroyed by an infuriated cook in the late 19th century. The vogue for being painted as St Catherine was stimulated by Huysmans' portrait of the Queen in that guise which Pepys had seen in 1664: above, v. 254 & n. 4. (OM).

from Norwood about their ship, which troubles me, though without reason.[1] So late home to supper and to bed.

We hear this night of Sir Jerem. Smith that he and his fleet have been seen at Malaga – which is good news.[2]

16. Up betimes, and by appointment to the Exchange, where I met Mr. Houblons, and took them up in my coach and carried them to Charing-cross, where they to Collonell Norwood to see how they can settle matters with him, I having informed them by the way with advice to be easy with him, for he may hereafter do us service – and they and I are like to understand one another to very good purpose. I to my Lord Sandwich, and there alone with him to talk of his affairs, and perticularly of his prize-goods, wherein I find he is wearied with being troubled, and gives over the care of it, to let it come to what it will, having the King's[a] release for the Dividend made;[3] and for the rest, he thinks himself safe from being proved to have anything more. Thence to the Exchequer, and so by coach to the Change, Mr. Moore with me, who tells me very odde passages of the indiscretion of my Lord in the management of his family, of his carelessness, &c.; which troubles me, but makes me [b] rejoice with all my heart of my being rid of the bond of 1000*l* for that would have been a cruel blow to me.[4] With Moore to the coffee-house, the first time I have been there,[5] where very full, and company it seems hath been there all the plague time. So to the Change, and then home to dinner. And, after dinner, to settle accounts with him for my Lord, and so evened with him to this day. Then to the office, and out with Sir W Warren for discourse, by coach to White-hall, thinking to

a repl. 'King'   *b* MS. 'be'

---

1. See above, p. 20; below, p. 98.

2. Smith had been sent to the Mediterranean with a strong squadron as soon as war was declared on the French in January. For the importance of his voyage, see J. S. Corbett, *Engl. in Medit.*, ii. 54–6, 58–60.

3. See above, p. 27, n. 2.

4. See above, p. 31 & n. 3.

5. I.e. the first time since the Plague. Pepys had not visited the coffee house near the Royal Exchange since 24 May 1665, when the Plague was beginning. (R).

have spoke with Sir W. Coventry but did not – and to see the Queene; but she comes but to Hampton Court tonight.   Back to my office and there late, and so home to supper and bed.   ⟨I walked a good while tonight with Mr. Hater in the garden, talking about a husband for my sister and reckoning up all our clerks about us, none of which he thinks fit for her and her portion.   At last I thought of young Gawden,¹ and will think of it again.⟩ᵃ

17.   Up, and to the office, where busy all the morning.   Late to dinner, and then to the office again and there busy till past 12 at night, and so home to supper and to bed.

We have news of Sir Jer Smith's being well with his fleet at Cales.

18.   *Lords day.*   Lay long in bed, discoursing with pleasure with my wife; among other things, about Pall's coming up, for she must be here a little to be fashioned.   And my wife hath a mind to go down for her – which I am not much against, and so I rose and to my chamber to settle several things.   At noon comes my Uncle Wight to dinner, and brings with him Mrs. Wight;² sad company to me, nor was I much pleased with it – only, I must show respect to my Uncle.   After dinner, they gone and it being a brave day, I walked to White-hall, where the Queene and ladies are all come; I saw some few of them, but not the Queen nor any of the great beauties.   I endeavoured to have seen my Lord Hinchingbrooke, who came to town yesterday, but I could not. Met with Creed, and walked with him a turn or two in the park, but without much content, having now designs of getting money in my head, which allows me not the leisure I used to have with him.   Besides, an odde story lately told of him for a great truth, of his endeavouring to lie with a woman at Oxford, and her crying out saved her; and this being publicly known, doth a little make me hate him.   Thence took coach, and calling by the way at my bookseller's for a book, writ about twenty years ago in prophecy of this year coming on, 1666, explaining it to be the

---

a addition crowded in between entries

---

1. Benjamin, second son of the Navy victualler: below, pp. 88–9.   2. Possibly the cousin mentioned below, p. 87.

mark of the beast.¹ I home and there fell to reading, and then to supper and to bed.

19. Up, and by coach to my Lord Sandwiches, but he was gone out. So I to White-hall, and there waited on the Duke of Yorke with some of the rest of our brethren; and thence back again to my Lord's to see my Lord Hinchingbrooke, which I did, and I am mightily out of countenance, in my great expectation of him by others' report;² though he is endeed a pretty Gentleman, yet nothing what I took him for methinks, either as to person, or discourse discovered to me – but I must try him more before I go too far in censuring. Thence to the Exchequer from office to office, to set my business of my tallies³ in doing, and there all the morning. So at noon by coach to St. Paul's churchyard to my bookseller's, and there bespoke a few more books, to bring all I have lately bought to 10l. Here I am told for certain, what I have heard once or twice already, of a Jew in town, that in the name of the rest doth offer to give any man 10l, to be paid 100l if a certain person now at Smirna be within these two years owned by all the princes of the East, and perticularly the Grand Segnor, as the King of the world, in the same manner we do the King of England here, and that this man is the true Messiah.⁴ One named a friend of his that had received ten pieces in gold upon this score, and says that the Jew hath disposed of 1100l in this manner – which is very strange; and certainly this year of 1666 will be a year of great action, but what the consequence of it will be, God knows.

Thence to the Change, and from my stationer's⁵ thereabouts

1. Francis Potter, *An interpretation of the number 666* (1642); PL 1769; cf. Selden, *Table Talk* (ed. Pollock), p. 158; Aubrey, ii. 161+. For Pepys's views on it, see below, p. 364. 666 was the number of the Beast in the Book of Revelation (xiii. 17).

2. Hinchingbrooke (Sandwich's eldest son, now 18) had returned from abroad in August 1665. He had been away for four years, studying in Paris, and travelling in France and Italy.

3. See above, p. 38 & n. 4.

4. The fame of Sabbatai Zevi, the false Messiah of Smyrna, was now at its height, and had made some impression in England: *CSPD 1665-6*, pp. 50, 526; ib., *1666-7*, pp. 191-2. He died in obscurity in 1676, a Moslem. Evelyn wrote about him in his *History of the three late famous impostors* (1669). See *Trans. Jewish Hist. Soc. Engl.*, 6/17-18: *Occ. papers Pepys Club*, i. 151+.

5. John Cade, of Cornhill.

carried home by coach two books of Ogilbys, his *Æsop* and *Coronacion*, which fell to my lot at his lottery;[1] cost me 4*l*, besides the binding. So home.

I find my wife gone out to Hales her painter's, and I after a little dinner do fallow her, and there do find him at work, and with great content I do see it will be a very rare picture. Left her there, and I to my Lord Treasurer's, where Sir G. Carteret and Sir J. Mennes met me; and before my Lord Treasurer and Duke of Albemarle, the state of our Navy debts was laid open, being very great, and their want of money to answer them openly professed – there being but 1500000*l* to answer a certain expense and debt of 2300000*l*.[2]

Thence walked with Fenn down to White-hall, and there saw the Queene at Cards with many ladies, but none of our beauties were there. But glad I was to see the Queen so well, who looks prettily – and methinks hath more life then before, since it is confessed of all that she miscarryed[a] lately – Dr. Clerke telling me yesterday at White-hall that he had the membranes and other

a l.h. repl. s.h. 'miscarried' badly written

---

1. The books were two folios: *The fables of Aesop paraphras'd in verse: adorn'd with sculptures and illustrated with annotations* (1665); and *The entertainment of his most excellent majestie Charles II, in his passage through the city of London to his coronation . . .* (1662). The first has plates by David Loggan; the second by Hollar. The PL copies (PL 2832, 2903) are in identical white vellum bindings decorated with the royal arms. John Ogilby, an enterprising man, regularly held these lotteries to finance his publications (cf. E. Arber, *Term Cat.*, i. 131). A catalogue of what appears to be this sale is now at the Huntington Library, Calif.: Wing, (W 181*b*). Tickets cost 40*s*., and there was only one blank. 500 copies of the Aesop (never published before) were offered, and 225 of the *Entertainment*. For his other lotteries, see *The Intelligencer*, 1 and 29 May 1665; *London Gazette*, 18 May 1668; *Gent. Mag.*, 84 (1814)/64–6; J. Ashton, *Hist. Engl. lotteries*, esp. pp. 44–5. See also *Pepysiana*, p. 128.

2. The meeting is reported and the figures set out in detail in a letter from Pepys to Coventry of this date: Longleat, Coventry MSS 97, ff. 15+, printed in *Further Corr.*, pp. 120–2. See also Pepys's memorandum (below, p. 308, n. 3) in PL 2589; summarised in *Cat.*, i. 100+. Credit consisted mostly of a parliamentary grant of £1¼ m. made in October 1665; the debts (running from 24 June 1660) did not include expenses of the ordnance, the charge for the sick and wounded, or wages from 1 August to 31 December 1665: see *Cat.*, i. 101. Current needs were estimated at £25,000 a week: *Further Corr.*, p. 135.

vessels in his hands which she voided, and were perfect as ever woman's was that bore a child.[1]

Thence, hoping to find my Lord Sandwich, away by coach to my Lord Chancellors, but missed him; and so home and to office, and then to supper and my Journall, and to bed.

20. Up, and to the office – where, among other businesses, Mr. Evelyn's proposition about public Infirmarys was read and agreed on, he being there.[2] And at noon I took him home to dinner, being desirous of keeping my acquaintance with him; and a most excellent-humourd man I still find him, and mighty knowing. After dinner I took him by coach to White-hall, and there he and I parted; and I to my Lord Sandwiches, where, coming and bolting into the dining-room, I there found Captain Ferrer[3] going to christen a child of his, born yesterday, and I came just pat to be a godfather, along with my Lord Hinchingbrooke and Madam Pierce my valentine – which for that reason I was pretty well contented with – though a little vexed to see myself so beset with people to spend my money, as, she for a Valentine, and little Mrs. Tooker, who is come to my house this day from Greenwich, and will cost me 20s, my wife going out with her this afternoon, and now this Christening. Well, by and by the child is brought, and christened Katharine. And I this day on this occasion drank a glass of wine, which I have not professedly done these two years I think – but a little in the time of the sickness. After that done, and gone and kissed the mother in bed – I away to Westminster-hall and there hear that Mrs. Lane is come to town. So I stayed loitering up and down, till anon she comes and agreed to meet at Swayns;[4] and there I went anon and she

1. Cf. Dr William Quartermaine to Williamson (5 February; also reporting her miscarriage), *CSPD 1665–6*, p. 232; *Hatton Corr.* (ed. E. M. Thompson), i. 48. Charles however referred to her pregnancy of 1668 as her first: C. H. Hartmann, *The King my brother*, pp. 216–17.
2. See above, p. 29 & n. 1. Cf.

Evelyn, under this date: 'To the *Commissioners* of the *Navy*, who having seene the project of the Infirmary encouragd the worke, & were very earnest it should be set about speedily; but I saw no mony . . .'.
3. Sandwich's Master of the Horse.
4. A victualling-house in New Palace Yard.

came, but stayed but little, the place not being private. I have not seen her since before the plague. So thence parted, and rencontrai à her last logis, and in that place did hazer what I tena a mind para faire con her. At last she desired to borrow money of me, 5*l*, and would pawn gold with me for it; which I accepted, and promised in a day or two to supply her. So away home to the office, and thence home, where little Mrs. Tooker stayed all night with us; and a pretty child she is, and happens to be niece to my beauty that is dead, that lived at the Jackeanapes in Cheapside.[1] So to bed – a little troubled that I have been at two houses this afternoon with Mrs. Lane that were formerly shut up of the plague.

21. Up, and with Sir J. Mennes to White-hall by his coach, by the way talking of my brother John, to get a spiritual promotion for him, which I now am to look after, forasmuch as he is shortly to be Maister*a* in Arts, and writes me this week a Latin letter that he is to go into Orders this Lent.[2] There to the Duke's chamber and find *b* our fellows discoursing there on our business; so I was sorry to come late, but no hurt was done thereby. Here the Duke, among other things, did bring out a book, of great antiquity, of some of the customs of the Navy about 100 years since, which he did lend us to read and deliver him back again.[3] Thence I to the Exchequer, and there did strike my tallies for a quarter for Tanger and carried them home with me. And thence to Trinity-house, being invited to an Elder Brother's feast. And there met and sat by Mr. Prin and had good discourse about the privileges of Parliament, which he says are few to the Commons' house, and those not examinable by them but only by the

a repl. 'Mistress'   *b* repl. 'by and by'

---

1. This last was possibly 'the pretty woman that I always loved at the beginning of Cheapeside that sells children's coates': above, i. 250.
2. After ordination John Pepys took his M.A., but did not obtain any spiritual preferment. In 1670, by Pepys's recommendation, he became Clerk to Trinity House.
3. Probably James Humphrey's MS. collections (1568), from which Pepys later made extracts: see below, 29 March 1669 & n.

House of Lords.¹ Thence with my Lord Bruncker to Gresham College, the first time after the sickness that I was there, and the second time any met.² And hear a good lecture of Mr. Hookes about the trade of Felt-making, very pretty.³ And anon alone with me about art of drawing pictures by Prince Roberts rule and machine, and another of Dr Wren's; but he says nothing doth like Squares, or, which is the best in the world, like a darke roome⁴ – which pleased me mightily.

Thence with Povy home to my house, and there late, settling accounts with him – which was very troublesome to me. And he gone, found Mr. Hill below, who sat with me till late talking; and so away, and we to bed.

1. Most M.P.s claimed, on the contrary, that the Commons were the proper judge of cases concerning the privileges of the House. Prynne's view (which Pepys states rather too baldly) rested on the contention that the House's privileges were not an inherent part of its constitution, but a grant made by the King, and that therefore disputes about them were to be settled in the King's courts. In that case they would go, on appeal, to the Lords. See William Prynne, *Fourth part of a brief register of all parl. writs* (1664), esp. pp. 846+. Prynne's reverence for what he regarded as the ancient constitution of the kingdom led him always to stress the powers of the Lords, which had suffered eclipse during the Interregnum.

2. Cf. above, p. 21 & n. 1. This was another informal meeting of the Royal Society. Its proceedings were not recorded in the council's minutes (although a council was held on this day), and the weekly sessions were not resumed until 14 March.

3. The Society had established a committee for the study of trades in 1664, and from that date Hooke had given the Cutlerian lectures on their history: Birch, i. 392, 473, ii. 141;

Gunther, vi. 182. He made several experiments in new methods of cloth-making in 1669: Gunther, p. 360.

4. Professor A. R. Hall writes: 'Perspective machines are first referred to by Leon Battista Alberti (d. 1475). He describes the use of a network of rectangular threads by means of which the artist plotted points onto squared paper: *On Painting* (trans., 1956), pp. 68–9, 121, n. 28. The method was approved by Leonardo, Dürer and others, and may well be the method referred to above by Brouncker. The 'darke roome' was the *camera obscura* in which the image was projected onto a screen by means of a lens. The machines invented by Prince Rupert and Christopher Wren were mechanical tracing devices. Rupert's was demonstrated at the Royal Society in November 1663, and improved by Hooke: Birch, i. 329; Gunther, vi. 159 etc. Wren's was already being manufactured in June 1663 (Monconys, ii. 74–5); illust. and descriptions in R. and M. Hall (ed.), *Letters of H. Oldenburg*, ii. 285+; *Philos. Trans.*, iv, no. 45 (25 March 1669), pp. 898–9. Cf. also Aubrey, ii. 165.'

22. Up, and to the office, where sat all the morning; at noon home to dinner, and thence by coach with my wife for ayre, principally for her. I alone stopped at Hales's, and there mightily am pleased with my wife's picture that is begun there – and with Mr. Hill's, though I must [own] I am not more pleased with it, now the face is finished, then I was when I saw the second time of sitting. Thence to my Lord Sandwiches, but he not within, but goes tomorrow. My wife to Mrs. Hunts, who is lately come to town, and grown mighty fat. I called her there, and so home – and late at the office, and so home to supper and to bed.

We are much troubled that the sickness in general (the town being so full of people) should be [up] by 3, and yet of the perticular disease of the plague, there should be 10 encrease.[1]

23. Up betimes, and out of doors by 6 of the clock and walked (W How with me) to my Lord Sandwiches, who did lie the last night at his house in Lincolns Inne-fields – it being fine walking in the morning, and the streets full of people again. There I stayed, and the house full of people come to take leave of my Lord, who this day goes out of Towne upon his Embassy towards Spayne. And I was glad to find Sir W. Coventry to come, though I know it is only a piece of Courtshipp. I had much discourse with my Lord, he telling me how fully he leaves the King his friend, and the large discourse he had with him the other day, and how he desired to have the business of the prizes examined before he went, and that he yielded to it and it is done, as far as concerns himself, to the full, and the Lords Commissioners for Prizes did reprehend all the Informers in what related to his Lordshipp – which I am glad of in many respects.[2] But we could not make an end of discourse, so I promised to wait upon [him] on Sunday at Cranborne.[3] And took leave, and away thence to Mr. Hales's (with Mr. Hill and two of the Houblons, who came thither to speak with me) and there*a* saw my wife's picture,

a repl. 'then'

---

1. In 13–20 February, plague burials had increased over the previous week from 59 to 69; burials from other causes, from 249 to 252: GL, A.1.5, no. 96.

2. See above, p. 10 & n. 3.

3. The house near Windsor occupied by Sir George Carteret as Vice-Chamberlain of the King's Household. See above, vi. 197, n. 4.

which pleases me well; but Mr. Hills picture never a whit so well as it did before it was finished, which troubled me – and I begin[a] to doubt the picture of my Lady Peters my wife's takes her posture from, and which is an excellent picture, is not of his making, it is so master-like.

I set them down at the Change, and I home to the office, and at noon dined at home, and to the office again. Anon comes Mrs. Knipp to see my wife, who is gone out; so I fain to entertain her, and took her out by coach to look my wife at Mrs. Pierces and Unthankes,[1] but find her not; so back again, and then my wife comes home, having been buying of things. And at home I spent all the night talking with this baggage[2] and teaching her my song of *Beauty retire*,[3] which she sings and makes go most rarely, and a very fine song it seems to be. She also entertained me with repeating many of her own and others' parts of the play-house, which she doth most excellently; and tells me the whole practices of the play-house and players, and is in every respect most excellent company. So I supped, and was merry at home all the evening, and the rather it being my Birthday, 33 years – for which God be praised that I am in so good a condition of health and state and everything else as I am, beyond expectation in all. So she to Mrs. Turner's to lie, and we to bed – mightily pleased to find myself in condition to have these people come about me, and to be able to entertain them and have the pleasure of their qualities, then which no man can have more in this world.

24. All the morning at the office, till past[b] 3 a-clock. At that hour home and eat a bit alone, my wife being gone out. So abroad by coach with Mr. Hill, who stayed for me to speak about business; and he and I to Hales's, where I find my wife and her woman, and Pierce and Knipp, and there sung and was mighty merry, and I joyed myself in it; but vexed at first, to find my wife's picture not so good[c] as I expected; but it was only his having finished one part, and not another, of the face; but before

---

a repl. same symbol badly formed   *b* repl. 'almost'
c MS. 'little' (a closely similar symbol)

---

1. Mrs Pepys's dressmaker.   3. See above, vi. 320 & n. 4. (E).
2. Mrs Knepp. 'Baggage' was sometimes used in a playful sense.

I went, I was satisfied it will be an excellent picture. Here we had ale and cakes, and mighty merry and sung my song, which she now sings rarely, and makes me proud of myself.

Thence left my wife to go home with Mrs. Pierce, while I home to the office; and there*^a* pretty late, and to bed – after fitting myself for tomorrow's journey.

25. *Lords day.* My wife up between 3 and 4 of the clock in the morning to dress herself, and I about 5, and were all ready to take coach, she and I and Mercer, a little past 5; but to our trouble, the coach did not come till 6. Then, with our coach of four horses I hire on purpose, and Lashmore to ride by, we through the City, it being clear day, to Branford, and so to Windsor (Captain Ferrer overtaking us at Kensington, being to go with us) and here drank; and so through, making no stay, to Cranborne about 11 a-clock, and found my Lord and the ladies at a sermon in the house – which being ended, we to them; and all the company glad to see us, and mighty merry to dinner. Here was my Lord, and Lord Hinchingbrooke and Mr. Sidny – Sir Ch. Herbert and Mr. Carteret – my Lady Carteret, my Lady Jemimah, and Lady Slaning. After dinner to talk to and again, and then to walk in the Parke, my Lord and I alone, talking upon these heads – first, he hath left his business of the prizes as well as is possible for him, having cleared himself before the Commissioners by the King's commands, so that nothing or little is to be feared from that point – he goes fully assured, he tells me, of the King's favour. That upon occasion I may know, I desired to know his friends I may trust to. He tells me, but that he is not yet in England but continues this summer in Ireland, my Lord Orrery is his father almost in affection.[1] He tells me, my Lord of Suffolke – Lord Arlington – Archbishop of Canterbury[2] – Lord Treasurer – Mr. Atturny Mountagu – (Sir Tho. Clifford in the House of Commons), Sir G Carteret, and some others I cannot presently remember, are friends that I may rely on for him.

a   repl. 'late'

---

1. Cf. above, vi. 301 & n. Orrery was one of Ormond's principal lieutenants in the government of Ireland.

2. Gilbert Sheldon.

He tells me my Lord Chancellor seems his very good friend, but doubts that he may not think him as much a servant of the Duke of York's as he would have him; and endeed my Lord tells me he hath lately made it his business to be seen studious of the King's favour, and not of the Duke's, and by the King will stand or fall – for factions there are, as he tells me, and God knows how high they may come.

The Duke of Albemarles post is so great, having had the name of bringing in the King, that he is like to stand; or, if it were not for him, God knows in what troubles we might be from some private factions, if an army could be got into another hand, which God forbid.[1]

It is believed that though Mr. Coventry be in appearance so great against the Chancellor, yet that there is a good understanding between the Duke[2] and him.

He dreads the issue of this year, and fears there will be some very great revolutions* before his coming back again.

He doubts it is needful for him to have a pardon for his last year's action, all which he did without commission, and at most but the King's private single word for that of Bergen;[3] but he dares not ask it at this time, lest it should make them think that there is something more in it then yet they know; and if it should be denied, it would be of very ill consequence.

He says also, if it should in Parliament be enquired into, the selling of Dunkirke (though the Chancellor was the man that would have it sold to France, saying the King of Spain had no money to give for it), yet he will be found to have been the greatest adviser of it[4] – which he is a little apprehensive may be called upon this Parliament.

---

1. Possibly a reference to the rumour that the Duke of York might replace Albemarle; cf. above, vi. 321 & n. 1.
2. The Duke of York.
3. See above, vi. 195–6 & n. For the pardon, see below, p. 260 & n.2.
4. Together with Southampton and Albemarle, Sandwich had conducted the negotiations for the sale of Dunkirk with the French ambassador,

d'Estrades. For his reasons (the weaknesses of the place as a port, the greater tactical advantages of Tangier, etc.), see Harris, i. 218+. He was not, however, as active in the bargaining itself as his colleagues. Pepys's report exactly tallies with Sandwich's statement to Southwell (made in 1667, but reported in 1698): HMC, *Leyborne-Popham*, p. 250.

He told me it would not be necessary for him to tell me his debts, because he thinks I know them so well.

He tells me that for the match propounded of Mrs. Mallet for my Lord Hinchingbrooke, it hath been lately off, and now her friends bring it on again, and an overture hath been made to him by a servant of hers to compass the thing without consent of friends,* she herself having a respect to my Lord's family, but my Lord will not listen to it but in a way of honour.[1]

The Duke hath for this week or two been very kind to him, more then lately, and so others; which he thinks is a good sign of fair weather again.

He says the Archbishop of Canterbury hath been very kind to him, and hath plainly said to him that he and all the world knows the difference between his judgment and brains and the Duke of Albema[r]les – and then calls my Lady Duchess the veriest slut and drudge, and the foulest word that can be spoke of a woman almost.[2]

My Lord having walked an hour with me talking thus, and going in, and my Lady Carteret not suffering me to go back again tonight, my Lord to walk again with me about some of this and other discourse; and then in a-doors and to talk, he alone with my Lady Carteret, and I with*a* the young ladies and gentlemen, who played on the guittarr[3] and mighty merry, and anon to supper; and then my Lord going away to write, the young gentlemen to flinging of cushions[4] and other mad sports. At this late, till towards 12 at night; and then being sleepy,*b* I and my wife in a passage-room to bed, and slept not very well, because of noise.

a repl. 'without'   *b* repl. 'weary with'

---

1. The proposed match did not come off.

2. She had been Monck's laundress when he was a prisoner in the Tower during the Civil War – 'a blacksmith's daughter', wrote Aubrey (ii. 73), who 'was kind to him; in a double capacity', and whom he married only after the birth of their son. Aubrey adds that she was 'not at all handsome, nor cleanly'. Pepys more than once remarks on her sluttishness. Cf. below, p. 354; Magalotti, p. 470.

3. For guitars, see above, i. 172 n. 2. (E).

4. A popular game.

26. Called up about 5 in the morning, and my Lord upp and took coach a little after 6, very kindly, of me and the whole company. Then I in, and my wife up and to visit my Lady Slaning in her bed, and there sat three hours, with Lady Jemimah with us, talking and laughing. And by and by my Lady Carteret comes, and she and I to talk – I glad to please her, in discourse of Sir G. Carteret, that all will do well with him, which*a* she is much pleased with, having had great noises and fears about his well-doing – and I fear hath doubted that I have not been a friend to him. But cries out against my Lady Castlemayne, that makes the King neglect his business; and seems much to fear that all will go to wrack, and I fear with great reason. Exclaims against the Duke of Albemarle, and more the Duchess, for a filthy woman, as endeed she is.

Here stayed till 9 a-clock almost, and then took coach, with so much love and kindness from my Lady Carteret, Lady Jemimah, and Lady Slaning, that it joys my heart (and when I consider the manner of my going hither, with a coach and four horses, and servants and a woman with us, and coming hither, being so much made of, and used with that state, and then going to Windsor and being shown all that we were there, and had wherewith to give everybody something for their pains, and then going home, and all in fine weather, and no fears nor cares upon me, I do think myself obliged to think myself happy, and do look upon myself at this time in the happiest occasion a man can be; and whereas we take pains in expectation of future comfort and ease, I have taught myself to reflect upon myself at present as happy and enjoy myself in that consideration, and not only please myself with thoughts of future wealth, and forget the pleasures we at present enjoy).

So took coach and to Windsor to the guarter,[1] and thither sent for Dr. Childe[2] – who came to us, and carried us to St.*b* Georges

a symbol smudged   *b* repl. 'the'

---

1. The Garter Inn, at the junction of High St and Peascod St, the principal inn of the town; mentioned in *The Merry Wives of Windsor*. See R. R. Tighe and J. E. Davis, *Annals of Windsor*, i. 668–70; ii. 24, 95.

2. Dr William Child; organist and master of the choristers at St George's Chapel, 1632–97; also (after 1660) one of the organists of Whitehall Chapel, and private organist to Sandwich.

Chapel and there placed us among the Knights' Stalls (and pretty the observation, that no man, but a woman, may sit in a Knight's place where any brasse-plates are set).[1] And hither comes cushions to us, and a young singing-boy to bring us a copy of the Anthemne to be sung. And here, for our sakes, had this anthem and the great service[2] sung extraordinary, only to entertain us. It is a noble place endeed,[3] and a good Quire of voices. Great bowing by all the people, the poor Knights[4] perticularly, to the Alter. After prayers, we to see the plate of the Chapel[5] and the Robes of Knights, and a man to show us the banners of the several Knights in being, which hang up over the stalls. And so to other discourse, very pretty, about that Order. Was shown where the late [King] is buried, and King Henry the 8, and my Lady Seymour.[6] This being done, to the King's house and to observe the neatness and contrivance of the house and gates; it is the most

1. Then, as now, canons – and their wives – occupied the knights' stalls in their absence. Nothing is known of the rule which Pepys mentions.

2. I.e. the service set in a rich, contrapuntal style, with repetitions of phrases of the text. (E).

3. Descriptions in Magalotti, pp. 282–3 [1669]: Celia Fiennes, *Journeys* (ed. Morris), pp. 274–5 [c. 1698]. See the engravings by Hollar (c. 1663) in Elias Ashmole, *Institution, laws and ceremonies of the . . . Order of the Garter* (1672), pp. 131+; two are reproduced in W. H. St John Hope, *Windsor Castle*, pl. 53.

4. The Poor Knights (now the Military Knights) were part of the foundation of the chapel. They attended services daily and prayed for the good estate of the sovereign and of the Knights of the Garter.

5. See Edward A. Jones, *Plate of St George's Chapel*; C. Oman, in *Report Soc. Friends St George's* (1954), pp.

16–25. Inventory (1667) in M. F. Bond (ed.), *Inventories of St George's, 1384–1667*, pp. 247–50, and pl. viii.

6. I.e. Jane Seymour, Henry's third wife. For the royal tombs in the chapel, see J. Pote, *Hist. antiq. Windsor Castle* (1749), pp. 360–3; Tighe and Davis, *Annals of Windsor*, ii. 235–6. Clarendon (*Hist.*, iv. 495) has a story that after the Restoration an attempt to locate the tomb and body of Charles I was unsuccessful because so many alterations in the building had been made. He was buried before the altar and Evelyn on 8 June 1654 was shown the place. A plan to transfer the body to Westminster was abandoned for lack of funds: J. G. Muddiman, *Trial of Charles I*, pp. 163+. Cf. also E. Ashmole, *Antiq. Berks.* (1719), iii. 186–8; *Greville Memoirs* (ed. Strachey and Fulford), ii. 169; E. H. Fellowes, *Charles I, his death*.

Romantique*ᵃ* castle that is in the world.¹   But Lord, *ᵇ* the prospect that is in the Balcone in the Queen's lodgings,² and the Tarrace and walk, are strange things to consider, being the best in the world, sure.

Infinitely satisfied, I and my wife with all this; she being in all points mightily pleased too, which added to my pleasure.   And so giving a great deal of money to this and that man and woman, we to our tavern and there dined, the Doctor with us; and so took coach and away to Eaton, the Doctor with me.

Before we went to Chapel this morning, Kate Joyce, in a stage-coach going toward London, called to me.   I went to her and saluted her, but could not get her to stay with us, having company.

At Eaton I left my wife in the coach, and he and I to the college and there find all mighty fine.³   The school⁴ good, and the custom pretty of boys cutting their names in the shuts of the window when they go to Cambrige;⁵ by which many a one hath lived to see himself Provost and Fellow, that had his name in the window standing.   To the hall, and there find the boys' verses, *De peste*; it being their custom to make verses at Shrovetide.⁶   I read

---

a l.h. preceded by s.h. 'a' and symbol rendered illegible
b repl.? 'other'

---

1. Pepys preserved a Hollar engraving (c. 1663) of the castle (PL 2972, pp. 206–7). Description c. 1660 (with reproductions of some of the Hollar engravings) in W. H. St John Hope, *Windsor Castle*, ch. xviii. Cf. Evelyn, 8 June 1654; Fiennes, op. cit., pp. 274–82 [c. 1698]; views in *Drawings of Engl. in 17th cent.* (ed. P. H. Hulton), ii, pl. 24 (by Schellinks); Magalotti, opp. p. 281.

2. Either the gallery built by Elizabeth in the Star building (now the Royal Library), or the 'pergula' built c. 1635 on the present n. terrace (now obscured by the rebuilding of 1675). Magalotti (p. 281) admired the view from the former. Hope, op. cit., pp. 301, 324–5.

3. Views in Ashmole, *Institution . . . of the . . . Order of the Garter* (1672), opp. p. 136 (Hollar, 1672);

R. Willis and J. W. Clark, *Archit. hist. Cambridge*, vol. i, opp. p. 418 (Loggan, c. 1688). The buildings dated mostly from the late 15th and early 16th centuries. Description (1683) in Molyneux's letters, *Dublin Univ. Mag.*, 18 (1841)/320+.

4. I.e. the 15th-century schoolroom known as Lower School.

5. The names of boys proceeding to King's College were carved on the shutters in Lower School. Since 1645 the pillars had been used. H. C. Maxwell Lyte, *Hist. Eton* (1911 ed.), p. 266 n.

6. The 'Bacchus verses': compositions by the upper forms, hung up from the hooks which may still be seen on either side of the hall. The practice disappeared sometime after 1824. Maxwell Lyte, op. cit., pp. 146–7, 152.

several, and very good they *a* were, and better I think then ever I
made when I was a boy – and in rolls as long and longer then the
whole hall by much.[1]   Here is a picture of Venice hung up,
given, and a Monument made of Sir H. Wottons giving it, to the
College.[2]

Thence to the Porters, in the absence of the Butler, and did drink
of the College beer, which is very good,[3] and went into the back
fields to see the scholars play.[4]   And so to the Chapel and there
saw,*b* among other things, Sir H. Wottons stone, with this
Epitaph –

> *Hic Jacet primus hujus Sententiæ Author.*
> *Disputandi pruritus fit ecclesiæ scabies.*

But unfortunately, the word *Author* was wrong writ, and now so
basely altered, that it disgraces the stone.[5]

Thence took leave of the Doctor; and so took coach, and finely, *c*
but sleepy, away home, and got thither about 8 at night; and
after a little at my office, I to bed.

And an hour after was waked with my wife's quarrelling with
Mercer, at which I was angry, and my wife and I fell out – but
with much ado to sleep again, I beginning to practise more
temper,* and to give her her way.

---

a repl. 'for'   *b* repl. 'have'   *c* preceded by blot

---

1. An exaggeration.

2. In 1636 Sir Henry Wotton
(Provost of Eton, 1624–39, and ambassador to Venice under James I) had
presented the large painted map of
Venice by Odoardo Fialetti which until 1970 hung in College hall, with an
inscription on wood recording the
gift.   Cf. L. Pearsall Smith, *Life Sir
H. Wotton*, i. 210. It is now in the
college picture gallery. (OM).

3. Charles II and Rupert regularly
drank the college beer when at
Windsor. The brewhouse was just
outside the hall, and now houses *inter
alia* the picture gallery. Maxwell
Lyte, p. 266, n. 3.

4. The playing fields are first
mentioned in 1507: VCH, *Berks.*, ii.
174.

5. The tombstone, now in the
antechapel, has been restored, and the
inscription rewritten: '*Hic iacet Huius
sententiæ Primus auctor Disputandi
pruritus fit Ecclesiarum scabies/Nomen
alias quaere.*' ('Here lies the author of
the saying: "The itch for disputation
is the plague of churches." Ask
elsewhere for his name.') Molyneux
(op. cit., p. 320) reproduces it more
accurately than Pepys.

27. Up, and after a harsh word or two, my wife and I good friends; and so up and to the office, where all the morning. At noon, late to dinner, my wife gone out to Hales's about her picture. And after dinner I after her, and do mightily like her picture and think it will be as good as my Lady Peters's.[1] So home, mightily pleased, and there late at business; and so home and set down my three last days' Journalls, and so to bed – over-joyed to think of the pleasure of the last Sunday and yesterday, and my ability to bear the charge of those pleasures – and with profit too – by obliging my Lord and reconciling Sir G. Carteret's family.

28. *Ashwendsday.* Up, and after doing a little business at my office, I walked (it being a most curious dry and cold morning) to White-hall; and there I went into the parke, and meeting Sir Ph. Warwicke, took a turn with him in the Pell Mell, talking of the melancholy posture of affairs, where everybody is snarling one at another, and all things put together look ominously. This new Act,[a] too, putting us out of a power of raising money[2] – so that he fears as I do, but is fearful of enlarging in that discourse of a whole confusion in everything, and the State and all. We appointed another time to meet to talk of the business of the Navy alone, seriously, and so parted and I to White-hall; and there we did our business with the Duke of Yorke, and so parted and walked to Westminster-hall, where I stayed talking with Mrs. Michell and Howlett long, and her daughter,[3] which is become a mighty pretty woman; and thence, going out of the hall, was called to by Mrs. Martin. So I went to her, and bought two bands and so parted, and by and by met at her chamber and there did what I would; and so away home, and there find Mrs. Knipp and we dined together, she the pleasantest company in the world. After dinner I did give my wife money to lay out on Knipp, 20s, and I abroad to White-hall to visit ⟨Collonell Norwood and then⟩ Sir G. Carteret, with whom I have brought myself right again,

a l.h. repl. l.h. 'Act' badly written

---

1. See above, p. 44, n. 2.
2. The Additional Aid of 1665: see above, vi. 292 & n. 3. Warwick was secretary to the Lord Treasurer.

3. Betty Howlett, now married to Mrs Mitchell's son.

and he very open to me.   Is very melancholy, and matters, I fear, go down with him; but he seems most afeared of a general catastrophe to the whole Kingdom, and thinks, as I fear, that all things will come to nothing.   Thence to the Palace-yard to the Swan and there stayed till it was dark; and then to Mrs. Lanes and there lent her 5*l*, upon 4*l*. o1*s*. in gold – and then did what I would with her; and I perceive she is come to be very bad and offers anything, that it is dangerous to have to do with her; nor will I see any more a good while.   Thence by coach home and to the office, where a while; and then betimes to bed, by 10 a-clock, sooner then I have done many a day.

And thus ends this month, with my mind full of resolution to apply myself better, from this time forward, to my business then I have done within these six or eight days – visibly to my prejudice, both in quiet of mind and setting backward of my business, that I cannot give a good account of it as I ought to do.*a*

a   followed by one blank page

MARCH.

1. Up, and to the office and there all the morning sitting; and at noon to dinner with my Lord Brouncker, Sir W. Batten, and Sir W. Penn at the White*a* Horse in Lumbard-street – where, God forgive us, good sport with Captain Cockes having his maid sick of the plague a day or two ago, and sent to the pest-house, where she now is – but he will not say anything but that she is well. But, blessed be God, a good Bill this week we have – being but 237 in all, and 42 of the plague, and of them, but 6 in the City – though my Lord Brouncker says that these 6 are most of them in new parishes, where they were not the last week.[1] Here was with us*b* also Mr Williamson,[2] who the more I know, the more I honour.

Thence I slipped after dinner without notice home, and there close to my business at my office till 12 at night, having with great comfort returned to my business by some fresh vows, in addition to my former and more severe; and a great joy it is to me to see myself in a good disposition to business.

So home to supper, and to my journall and to bed.

2. Up, as I have of late resolved, before 7 in the morning, and to the office, where all the morning; among other things, setting my wife and Mercer with much pleasure to work upon the ruling of some paper for the making of books for pursers,[3] which will require a great deal of work, and they will earn*c* a good deal of money by it – the hopes of which makes them work mighty hard.

At noon dined, and to the office again; and about 4 a-clock

---

a repl. symbol rendered illegible   *b* smudges under symbols
c MS. 'enter'

---

1. I.e. in the parishes of St Benet Fink, St Dunstan-in-the-East, St James Garlickhithe, St Mildred Poultry and St Stephen Coleman St: GL, A.1.5, no. 96.

2. Joseph Williamson, head of Secretary Arlington's secretariat; later (1674–8) Secretary of State.

3. Cf. his plans for a reorganisation of the pursers' work: above, p. 1 & n. 1.

took coach and to my Lord Treasurer's, and thence to Sir Ph. Warwicke's new house[1] by appointment, there to spend an hour in talking; and we were together above an hour, and very good discourse about the state of the King as to money, and perticularly, in that point, of the Navy. He endeavours hard to come to a good understanding of Sir G. Carteret's accounts. And by his discourse, I find Sir G. Carteret must be brought to it, and[a] he is a madman that he doth not do it of himself, for the King expects the Parliament will call upon him for his promise of giving an[b] account of the money, and ⟨he⟩ will be ready for it, which cannot be, I am sure, without Sir G. Carteret's accounts be better understood then they are.[2]

He seems to have a great esteem of me, and my opinion and thoughts of things. After we had spent an hour thus discoursing, and vexing that we do but grope so in the dark as we do, because the people that should enlighten us do not help us – we resolved for fitting some things for another meeting, and so broke up. He showed me his house, which is yet all unhung, but will be a very noble house indeed.

Thence[c] by coach, calling at my bookseller's, and carried home 10*l*-worth of books, all I hope I shall buy a great while.

There by appointment find Mr. Hill come to sup and take his last leave of me;[3] and by and by in comes Mr. ⟨James⟩ Houbland to bear us company, a man I love mightily, and will not lose his acquaintance. He told me in my eare this night what he and his brothers have resolved to give me, which is 200*l* ⟨for helping them out with two or three ships⟩[4] – a good sum, and that which I did believe they would give me, and I did expect little less.

Here we talked, and very good company till late, and then took leave of one another; and endeed I am heartily sorry for Mr. Hill's leaving us – for he is a very worthy gentleman, as most I

a MS. 'and which'   *b* repl. 'an any'   *c* repl. 'thus'

1. In the Outer Spring Garden, near St James's Palace.
2. On 14 March Pepys sent to Warwick a detailed summary of the debts of the Navy not included in Carteret's estimate: *Further Corr.*, pp. 124–6; PL 2589, pp. 1–3. Carteret's figure was c. £800,000;

Pepys now reckoned that there were additional debts of just over £462,000. Cf. above, p. 48 & n. 2.
3. He was going to Portugal where he was to act as the Houblons' agent: above, p. 39.
4. See above, p. 20 & n. 3.

know – God give him a good voyage and success in his business. Thus we parted, and my wife and I to bed, heavy for the loss of our friend.

3. All the morning at the office. At noon to the Old James, being sent for, and there dined with Sir Wm. Rider, Cutler and others, to make an end with two Scots Maisters about the freight of two*a* ships of my Lord Rutherfords.[1] After a small dinner and a little discourse, I away to the Crowne behind the Exchange to Sir W Pen, Captain Cocke, and Fenn, about getting a bill of Cocke's paid to Pen, in part for the East India goods he sold us. Here Sir W. Penn did give me the reason in my eare of his importunity for money, for that he is now to marry his daughter.[2] God send her better fortune then her father deserves I should wish him, for a false rogue.

Thence by coach to Hales's; and there saw my wife sit, and I do like her picture mightily, and very like it will be, and a brave piece of work. But he doth complain that her nose hath cost him as much work as another's face, and he hath done it finely indeed. Thence home, and late at the office, and then to bed.

4. *Lords day.* And all day at my Tanger and private accounts, having neglected them since Christmas;[3] which I hope I shall never do again, for I find the inconvenience of it, it being ten times the labour to remember and settle things; but I thank God I did it at last, and brought them all fine and right; and I am, I think, by all appears to me (and I am sure I cannot be 10*l* wrong), worth above 4600*l*; for which the Lord be praised, being the biggest sum I ever was worth yet. I was at it till past 2 a-clock on Monday morn-
《5.》ing, and then read my vows and to bed, with great joy and content that I have brought my things to so good a settlement; and now, having my mind fixed to fallow my business again, and sensible*b* of Sir W Coventry's jealousies,* I doubt,

a repl. 'my'   *b* repl. 'since'-

1. Heir of the Earl of Teviot (d. 1664), late Governor of Tangier. This business has not been traced elsewhere.
2. Penn married off his daughter

Margaret to Anthony Lowther in February 1667.
3. Cf. above, vi. 336 & n. 1; below, p. 113.

concerning me; partly my siding with Sir G. Carteret, and partly that endeed I have been silent in my business of the office a[a] great while and given but little account of myself, and least of all to him, having not made him one visit since he came to town from Oxford, I am resolved to fall hard to it again and fetch up the time and interest I have lost, or am in a fair way of doing it.[1]

Up about 8 a-clock, being called up by several people; among others, by Mr. Moone,[2] with whom I went to Lumbert-street to Colvill; and so back again, and in my chamber he and I did end all our businesses together of accounts for money upon bills of exchange; and am pleased to find myself reputed a man of business and method, as he doth give me out to be. To the Change at noon, and so home to dinner. News for certain of the King of Denmarcke's declaring for the Dutch and resolution to assist them.[3]

To the office, and there all the afternoon. In the evening came Mr. James and brother Houblon to agree upon charter[b]-parties for their ships, and did acquaint me that they had paid my messenger, whom I sent this afternoon for it, 200*l* for my friendship in that business, which pleases me mightily.[4] They being gone, I forth late to Sir R. Viner's to take a receipt of them for that 200*l* lodged for me there with them. And so back home, and after supper, to bed.

6. Up betimes, and did much business before office-time. Then to the office and there till noon, and so home to dinner, and to the office again till night. In the evening, being at Sir W. Batten's, stepped in (for I have not used to go thither a great while); I find my Lord Bruncker and Mrs. Williams, and they would of their own accord, though I had never obliged them (nor my wife neither) with one visit for many of theirs, go see my

---

a repl. 'great' (badly-formed)   *b* MS. 'char'-

---

1. Pepys this day wrote to Coventry about the business of the office: Longleat, Coventry MSS 97, f. 17*r*. Coventry's 'jealousies' soon disappeared (cf. below, p. 67) and Pepys's letters to him resumed their frank and easy tone: e.g. Coventry MSS 97, f. 35*r*.

2. Secretary to Lord Belasyse, Governor of Tangier.

3. A treaty of alliance with the Dutch was ratified by Denmark on 12/22 February.

4. See above, p. 20 & n. 3.

house and my wife; which I showed them, and made them welcome with wine and ⟨China⟩ oranges (now a great rarity since the war; none to be had),[1] there being also Captain Cocke and Mrs. Turner, who had never been in my house since I came to the office before, and Mrs. Carcasse, wife of Mr. Carcasse's. My house happened to be mighty clean and did me great honour, and they mightily pleased with it. They gone, I to the office and did some business; and then home to supper and to bed, my mind troubled through a doubtfulness of my having incurred Sir W Coventry's displeasure by not having waited on him since his coming to town, which is a mighty fault and that I can bear the fears of the bad effects of till I have been with him, which shall be tomorrow, God willing. So to bed.

7. Up betimes and to St. James's, thinking Mr. Coventry had lain there, but he doth not, but at White-hall; so thither I went, and had as good a time as heart could wish; and after an hour in his chamber about public business, he and I walked up; and the Duke being gone abroad, we walked an hour in the Matted Gallery, he of himself beginning to discourse of the unhappy differences between him and my Lord of Sandwich, and from the beginning to the end did run through all passages wherein my Lord hath at any time gathered any dissatisfaction, and cleared himself to me most honourably; and in truth, I do believe he doth as he says. I did afterward purge myself of all partiality in the business of Sir G. Carteret (whose story Sir W. Coventry did also run over), that I do mind the King's interest notwithstanding my relation to him; all which he declares he firmly believes, and assures me he hath the same kindness and opinion of me as[a] ever. And when I said I was jealous of myself, that having now come to such an income as I am by his favour, I should not be found to do as much service as might deserve it, he did assure me he thinks it not too much for me, but thinks I deserve it as much as any man in England. All this discourse did cheer my heart, and sets me right again, after a good deal of melancholy, out of fears of his

a MS. 'that'

1. Many were imported from France: Evelyn, *Kalendarium Hortense* (1679), p. 34. Wood in his *Life and* *Times* mentions the purchase of oranges in 1659, 1661 and 1662 but none during the war period.

disinclination to me upon the differences with my Lord Sandwich and Sir G. Carteret; but I am satisfied thoroughly, and so went away quite another man, and by the grace of God will never lose it again by my folly in not visiting and writing to him*a* as I used heretofore to do. Thence by coach to the Temple;*b* and it being a holiday, a fast-day,[1] I there light and took water, being invited, and down to Greenwich to Captain Cockes, where dined he and Lord Brouncker and Matt Wrenn, Boltele, and Major Cooper, who is also a very pretty companion – but they all drink hard; and after dinner, to gaming at cards – so I provoked my Lord to be gone; and he and I to Mr. Cottles and met Mrs. Williams (without whom he cannot stir out of doors), and there took coach and away home. They carry me to London and set me down at the Temple; where my mind changed, and I home and to writing and hear my boy play on the lute, and a turn with my wife pleasantly in the garden by moonshine, my heart being in great peace. And so home to supper and to bed. ⟨The King and Duke are to go tomorrow to Audly-end in order to the seeing and buying of it of my Lord Suffolke.⟩*c*[2]

8. Up betimes and to the office, where all the morning – sitting; and did discover three or four fresh*d* instances of Sir W Pen's old cheating dissembling tricks – he being as false a fellow as ever was born. Thence with Sir W. Batten and Lord Brouncker to the White-horse in Lumberd-street, to dine with Captain Cocke upon perticular business of Canvas to buy for the King. And here by chance I saw the mistress of the house I have heard much of; and a very pretty woman she is endeed – and her husband the simplest-looked fellow and old that ever I saw.[3]

---

a MS. 'me'   *b* repl. symbol rendered illegible
c addition crowded in between entries   *d* repl. 'of'

---

1. For the Plague; see above, vi. 155, n. 4.
2. They went with Prince Rupert and spent the rest of the week there: *London Gazette*, 12 March. The warrant to execute the conveyances was not issued until 8 May 1669: *CSPD 1668–9*, p. 319. When the house was returned to the Earls of Suffolk in 1701 two-thirds of the purchase price of £50,000 was still unpaid: W. Addison, *Audley End*, p. 52.
3. She was Frances, second wife of Abraham Browne. She committed suicide in the following year: below, 24 February 1667.

After dinner I took coach and away to Hales's, where my wife is sitting; and endeed, her face and neck, which are now finished, do so please me, that I am not myself almost, nor was not all the night after, in writing of my letters, in consideration of the fine picture that I shall be maister of.

Thence home and to the office, where very late, and so home to supper and to bed.

9. Up, and being ready, to the Cockepitt – to make a visit to the Duke of Albemarle; and to my great joy find him the same man to me that heretofore, which I was in great doubt of through my negligence in not visiting of him a great while; and having now set all to rights there, I am in mighty ease in my mind, and I think shall never suffer matters to run so far backward again, as I have done of late with reference to my neglecting him and Sir W. Coventry.

Thence by water down to Deptford, where I met my Lord Brouncker and Sir W. Batten by agreement, and to measuring Mr. Castles new third-rate ship, which is to be called the *Defyance*.[1] And here I had my end, in saving the King some money and getting myself some experience in knowing how they do measure ships.[2] Thence I left them and walked to Redriffe, and there taking water, was overtaken by them in their boat, and so they would have me in with them*a* to Castle's house, where my Lady Batten and Madame Williams were, and there dined and a deal of doings. I had a good dinner, and counterfeit mirth and pleasure with them, but had but little, thinking how I neglected my business. Anon all home to Sir W. Batten's, and there, Mrs. Knipp coming, we did spend the even together very merry, she and I singing; and God forgive me, I do still see that my nature is not to be quite conquered, but will esteem pleasure above all things; though, yet in the middle of it, it hath reluctancy after my business, which is neglected by my fallowing my pleasure. However, music and women I cannot but give way to, whatever

a repl. 'me'

---

1. Cf. above, vi. 7 & n. 2. Disputes arose about payment for the ship, the builder having made it larger than was required by the Board's specifications: Longleat, Coventry MSS 96, ff. 271-2, 274r, 275r.

2. Cf. above, v. 358, n. 1.

my business is. They being gone, I to the office a while, and so home to supper and to bed.

10. Up and to the office, and there busy sitting till noon. I^a find at home Mrs. Pierce and Knipp, come to dine with me. We were mighty merry. And after dinner I carried them and my wife out by coach to the New Exchange, and there I did give my valentine, Mrs. Pierce, a dozen pair of gloves and a pair of silk stockings – and Knipp, for company sake (though my wife had by my consent laid out 20*s* upon her the other day), six pair of gloves. Thence to Hales's to have seen our pictures; but could not get in, he being abroad. And so^b to the cake-house[1] hard by, and there sat in the coach with great pleasure and eat some fine cakes; and^c so carried them to Pierces, and away home. It is a mighty fine witty boy, Mrs. pierce's little boy. Thence home and to the office, where late writing letters; and leaving a great deal to do on Monday – I home to supper and to bed.

The truth is, I do indulge myself a little the more pleasure, knowing that this is the proper age of my life to do it, and out of my observation that most men that do thrive in the world do forget to take pleasure during the time that they are getting their estate but reserve that till they have got one, and then it is too late for them to enjoy it with any pleasure.

11. *Lords day.* Up, and by water to Whitehall. There met Mr. Coventry coming out, going along with the Commissioners of the Ordinance to^d the water-side to take barge, they being going down to the Hope. I returned with them as far as the Tower in their barge, speaking with Sir W Coventry. And so home and to church – and at noon dined; and then to my chamber, where with great pleasure about one business or other till late, and so to supper and to bed.

---

a repl. 'where'	*b* repl. 'then'
c preceded by blot	*d* repl. 'by water'

---

1. This was in the market place of the Earl of Southampton's estate development, now the area round Bloomsbury Sq. (R).

12. Up betimes, and called on by abundance of people about business. And then away by water to Westminster, and there to the Exchequer about some business and thence by coach, calling at several places: to the Old Exchange and there did much business, and so homeward and bought a silver salt for my ordinary table to use, and so home to dinner; and after dinner comes my Uncle and Aunt Wight, the latter I having not seen since the plague – a silly, froward, ugly woman she is. We made mighty much of them, and she talks mightily of her fear of the sickness, and so a deal of tittle-tattle; and I left them and to my office, where late; and so home to supper and to bed. This day I hear my Uncle Talbott Pepys died the last week, and was buried.[1] All the news now is that Sir Jerem. Smith is at Cales with his fleet[2] – and Mings in the Elve.[3]

The King is come this noon to town from Audly End with the Duke of Yorke and a fine train of gentlemen.

13. Up betimes and to the office, where busy sitting all the morning – and I begin to find a little convenience by holding up my head to Sir W Pen, for he is come to be more supple. At noon to dinner and then to the office again, where mighty business, doing a great deal till midnight, and then home to supper and to bed. The plague encreased this week 29 from 28, though the Totall fallen from 238 to 207[4] – which doth never a whit please me.

14. Up, and met by 6 a-clock in my chamber, Mr. Povy (from White-hall) about evening reckonings between him and me on our Tanger business, and at it hard till toward 8 a-clock; and then he carried me in his chariot to White-hall, where by and by my fellow officers met me and we had a meeting before the Duke. Thence with my Lord Brouncker towards London, and in our way called in Covent-garden and took in Sir John (formerly

---

1. He had died in his 83rd year on the 1st, and was buried on the 5th at Impington, near Cambridge. He was Pepys's great-uncle.
2. For Smith's voyage to the Mediterranean, see above, p. 45, n. 2; for his visit to Cadiz (where he was

allowed to water), see HMC, *Heathcote*, p. 237.
3. Elbe. See below, p. 76 & n. 1.
4. The comparison is between the week of 6–13 March and the previous week: GL, A.1.5, no. 96.

Dr) Baber[1] – who hath this humour, that he will not enter into discourse while any stranger is in company, till he [hath] been told who he is that seems a stranger to him. This he did declare openly to me, and asked my Lord who I was – giving this reason, that he hath been inconvenienced by being too free in discourse till he knew who all the company were. Thence to Guildhall (in our way taking in Dr. Wilkins), and there my Lord and I had full and large discourse with Sir Tho. Player, the Chamberlain of the City (a man I have much heard of for his credit and punctuality in the City, and[a] on that score have had a desire to be made known to him), about the credit of our tallies which are lodged there for security to such as should lend money thereon to the use of the Navy[2] – and I had great satisfaction therein. And the truth is, I find all our matters of credit to be in an ill condition. Thence, I being in a little haste, walked before, and to[b] the Change a little, and then home; and presently to Trinity-house to dinner, where Captain Cox made his Elder Brother's dinner – but it seemed to me a very poor sorry dinner. I, having many things in my head, rose when my belly was full, though the dinner not half-done; and home and there to do some business, and by and by out of doors and met Mr. Povy, coming to me by appointment, but it being a little too late, I took a little pride in the street not to go back with him – but prayed him to come another time; and I away – to Kate Joyces, thinking to have spoke to her husband about Pall's business; but a stranger, the Welch Dr. Powell, being there, I forebore and went away, and so to Hales's to see my wife's picture, which I like mighty well; and there had the pleasure to see how suddenly he draws the Heavens, laying a dark ground and then lightening it when and where he will. Thence to walk all alone in the fields behind Grays Inne, making an end of reading over my dear *Faber Fortunæ* of my Lord Bacon's;[3] and thence, it growing dark, took two or three wanton turns about the idle places and lanes about Drury-lane,[c] but to no satisfaction, but a

---

a repl. bracket   *b* repl. 'home'   *c* repl.'Drury-lane St.'

---

1. Physician-in-ordinary to the King.
2. These loans were probably secured on the Hearth Tax of 1662 and/or the Royal Aid of 1664.
3. Cf. above, ii. 102 & n. 1.

great fear of the plague among*a* them; and so anon I walked by invitation to Mrs. Pierce's, where I find much good company; that is to say, Mrs. Pierce, my wife, Mrs. Worship and her daughter, and Harris the player and Knipp, and my wife and Mercer, and Mrs. Barbary Shelden, who is come this day*b* to spend a week with my wife.[1] And here, with music, we danced and sung and supped, and then to sing and dance*c* till past one in the morning. And much mirth with Sir Anthony Apsly*d* and one Collonell Sidny, who lodge in the house – and above all, they are mightily taken with Mrs. Knipp. Hence, weary and sleepy, we broke up, and I and my company home well by coach and to bed.

15. Lay till it was full time to rise, it being 8 a-clock, and so to the office and there sat till almost 3 a-clock, and then to dinner; and after dinner (my wife and Mercer and Mrs. Barbary being gone to Hales's before), I and my Cosen ⟨Anth.⟩ Joyce, who came on purpose to dinner with me. And he and I to discourse of our proposition of marriage between Pall and Harman. And upon discourse, he and I to Harman's house, and took him to a tavern hard by and we to discourse of our business, and I offered 500*l*. And he declares most ingenuously that his trade[2] is not to be trusted on – that he however needs no money, but would have her money bestowed on her – which I like well, he saying that he would adventure 2 or 300*l* with her. I like him as a most good-natured and discreet man, and I believe very cunning.* We came to this conclusion, for us to meet one another the next week, and then we hope to come to some end, for I did declare myself well satisfied with the mach. Thence to Hales, where I met my wife and people, and do find the picture, above all things, a most pretty picture and mighty like*e* my wife – and I asked him his price: he says, 14*l*; and the truth is, I think he doth deserve it. Thence toward London and home, and I to the office, where I did*f*

---

a MS. 'away'   *b* repl. 'to'   *c* repl. 'sup'   *d* repl. 'Apls'-
     e repl. 'I'-   *f* repl. 'I stated my queries to him'

---

1. Her stay was prolonged until 2 April, but (perhaps because she was 'odd looked': below, p. 250) is not much noticed in the diary. She was the niece of William Sheldon of Woolwich, in whose house Mrs Pepys had lodged during the worst months of the Plague.

2. That of upholsterer.

much, and betimes to bed, having had of late so little sleep, and there slept till 7 this morning.

16. Up, and all the morning about the Victuallers business, passing his account.[1] And then[a] at noon to the Change and did several businesses; and thence to the Crowne behind the Change and dined with my Lord Brouncker and Captain Cocke and Fenn, and Madam Williams – who without question must be my Lord's wife, and else she could not fallow him else wherever he goes and kiss and use him publicly as she doth.[2]   Thence to the office, where Sir W. Penn and I made an end of the Victuallers business; and thence abroad about several businesses, and so in the evening back again; and anon called on by Mr. Povy and he and I stayed together in my chamber till 12 at night, ending our reckonings and giving him tallies for all I was to pay him.   And so parted, and I to make good my Journall for two or three days, and begun it,[b] till I came to the other side, where I have scrached so much, for, for want of sleep, I begun to write idle and from the purpose – so forced to break off, and to bed.

17. Up, and to finish my Journall, which I had not sense enough the last night to make an end of – and thence to the office, where very busy all the morning.   At noon home to dinner, and presently with my wife out to Hales's, where I am still infinitely pleased with my wife's picture.   I paid him 14*l* for it, and 25*s* for the frame, and I think it not a whit too dear for so good a picture. It is not yet quite finished and dry, so as to be fit to bring home yet. This day I begun to sit, and he will make me, I think, a very fine picture.   He promises it shall be as good as my wife's, and I sit to have it full of shadows, and do almost break my neck looking

a repl. 'Sir Wm. Bat. and I would you had told me on it further, for'
     b blot above symbol

---

1. See Pepys's notes (16 March) on these accounts: NWB, pp. 114–15.
2. Brouncker died unmarried in 1684. But he left most of his estate to his 'beloved freind Mrs Abigail Williams alias Cromwell', his sole executrix: PCC, Hare, 39.

over my shoulder to make the posture for him to work by.[1] Thence home and to the office; and so home, having a great cold, and so my wife and Mrs. Barbary have very great ones – we are at a loss how we all come by it together. So to bed, drinking butter-ale.[2] This day my W. Hewers comes from Portsmouth – and gives me an instance of another piece of knaveries of Sir W. Penn, who wrote to Comissioner Middleton that[a] it was my negligence the other day he was not acquainted, as the Board directed, with our clerks coming down to the pay. But I need no new arguments to teach me that he is a false rogue to me, and all the world besides.

18. *Lords day.* Up, and my cold better. So to church, and then home to dinner; and so walked out to St. Jones's Church, thinking to have seen fair Mrs. Butler;[3] but could not, she not being there – nor, I believe, lives thereabouts now.

So walked to Westminster; very fine fair dry weather, but all cry out for lack of rain.[4] To Herberts and drank, and thence to Mrs. Martins and did what I would with her, her husband going for some wine for us. The poor man, I do think, would take pains if I can get him a purser's place, which I will endeavour.[5] She tells me as a secret that Betty Howlet of the Hall, my little sweetheart that I use to call my second wife, is married to a younger son of Mr. Michells (his elder brother, who should have had her, being dead this plague), at which I am glad, and that they are to live near me in Thames-street by the Old Swan.

a repl. 'who'

---

1. The portrait is reproduced above, vol. i, front. It was finished towards the end of April, after six sittings for the likeness, and was paid for on 16 May. Pepys was painted on one other occasion in the diary period, by Saville (above, ii. 218 & n. 4). See D. Piper, *Cat. 17th-cent. portraits in Nat. Portrait Gall.*, p. 271; ib., *Book Collector*, 21/65+; R. Barber, *Samuel Pepys Esquire*, nos 2–8, 56–7. (OM).
2. Drunk hot, this was Pepys's favourite remedy for a cold.

3. Frances Butler (*'la belle Boteler'*), a cousin of Pepys's friend Will Bowyer, and a beauty he had not seen since October 1664. The church was St John's, Clerkenwell.
4. Dr D. J. Schove writes: 'The "cold, dry time at London" was remarked on by Josselin (*Diary*, ed. Hockliffe, p. 152). For its connection with the Fire of London, see below, esp. p. 283 & n. 2.'
5. See below, p. 360 & n. 3.

Thence by coach home, and to my chamber about some accounts, and so to bed.

Sir Chr. Mings is come home from Hambrough, without anything done, saving bringing home some pipestaves for us.[1]

19.[a] Up betimes, and upon a meeting extraordinary at the office most[b] of the morning, with Lord Brouncker, Sir W. Coventry, Sir W. Penn – upon the business of the accounts – where, now we have got almost as much as we would have, we begin to lay all on the Controller[2] – and I fear he will be run down with it, for he is every day less and less capable of doing business. Thence with my Lord Brouncker [and] Sir W. Coventry to the ticket-office to see in what little order things are there; and there it is a shame to see how the King is served. Thence to the Chamberlain of London and satisfy ourselfs more perticularly how much credit we have there, which proves very little. Thence to Sir Rob. Long's[3] [in his] absence – about much the same business, but have not the satisfaction we would have there neither. So Sir W. Coventry parted, and my Lord and I to Mrs. Williams's and there I saw her closet, where endeed a great many fine things there are – but the woman I hate. Here we dined, and Sir J. Minnes came to us – and after dinner we walked to the King's play-house, all in dirt, they being altering of the Stage to make it wider[4] – but God knows when they will begin to act again.[5] But my business here was to see the inside of the Stage and all the tiring roomes and Machines; and endeed it was a sight worthy seeing. But to see their clothes and the various sorts, and what a

---

a number smudged   b repl. 'all'

---

1. Myngs's squadron had arrived in the Downs on the 15th escorting six of the Hamburg fleet – fewer than were expected. Earlier in the month, there had been reports on the Exchange that he had taken 14 Dutch ships: CSPD 1665-6, pp. 280, 301.
2. Sir John Mennes.
3. Auditor of the Receipt of the Exchequer.
4. Pepys had earlier complained

(8 May 1663) of inaudibility at this theatre (the TR, Drury Lane) and had ascribed it to the distance between the stage and the boxes. (A).
5. Because of the plague, the King had issued an order on 5 June 1665 that the playhouses should be closed. They did not resume regular activities until the latter part of November 1666. (A).

mixture of things there was, here a wooden leg, there a ruff, here a hobby-horse, there a Crowne, would make a man split himself to see with laughing – and *a* perticularly Lacys wardrobe, and Shotrell's.[1] But then again, to think how fine they show on the stage by candle-light, and how poor things they are to look now too near-hand, is not pleasant at all. The Machines are fine, and the paintings very pretty.[2]

Thence, mightily satisfied in my curiosity, I away with my Lord to see him at her house again; and so take leave, and by coach home and to the office. And thence sent for to Sir G. Carteret by and by to the [Navy Treasury in] Broadstreete, where he and I walked two or three hours, till it was quite dark, in his gallery, talking of his affairs – wherein I assure him all will do well, and did give him (with great liberty, which he accepted kindly) my advice to deny the Board nothing they would ask about his accounts, but rather call upon them to know whether there was anything more they desired or was wanting. But our great discourse and serious reflections was upon the bad state of the Kingdom in general, through want of money and good conduct, which we fear will undo all. Thence, mightily satisfied with this good fortune of this discourse with him, I home; and there walked in the dark till 10 a-clock at night in the garden with Sir W Warren – talking of many things belonging to us perticularly; and I hope to get something considerably by him before the year be over. He gives me good advice of circumspection in my place, which I am now in great mind to improve; for I think our office stand on very

a repl. badly-formed symbol – ? 'all'

---

1. John Lacy was a popular comedian. Shoterell was either Robert or William. Both were members of the King's Company: Downes, p. 2. (A).

2. The chief 'machines' of the Restoration stage were the large central trapdoor, which could be mechanically lowered and raised, and the systems of ropes, windlasses, and pulleys, whereby characters or properties could seem to fly, or be lowered to the stage and raised from it. But Pepys may here be using the term to describe the grooves attached to the stage and the underside of the flies by means of which the painted wings and rear flats could be shunted into position and withdrawn: cf. above, ii. 131, n. 2. By 'paintings' he means the scenes represented on the wings and rear flats, or on back drops. For scenery, see the engravings in Elkanah Settle's *The Empress of Morocco* (1673). (A).

ticklish terms, the Parliament likely to sit shortly and likely to be asked more money, and we able to give a very bad account of the expense of what we have done with what they did give before. Besides, the turning out the prize-officers may be an example for the King's[a] giving us up to the Parliament's pleasure as easily, for we deserve it as much.[1]

Besides, Sir G. Carteret did tell me tonight how my Lord Brouncker himself, whose good-will I could have depended as much on as any, did himself to him take notice of the many places I have; and though I was a painful man, yet the Navy was enough for any man to go through with in his own single place there – which much troubles me, and shall yet provoke me to more and more care and diligence then ever.

Thence home to supper, where I find my wife and Mrs. Barbary with great colds, as I also at this time have.

This day, by letter from my father, he propounds a match in the country for Pall, which pleased me well; of one that hath seven score and odd pounds land per annum in possession, and expects 1000*l* in money by the death of an old aunt. He hath neither father, mother, sister, nor brother. But demands 600*l* down, and 100*l* on birth of first child – which I had some inclinations to stretch to. He is kinsman and lives with Mr. Phillips.[2] But my wife tells me he is a drunken, ill-favoured, ill-bred country fellow – which sets me off of it again, and I will go on with Harman. So after supper, to bed.

20. Up, and to the office, where busy all the morning. At noon dined in haste, and so my wife, Mrs. Barbary, Mercer, and I by coach to Hales, where I find my wife's picture now perfectly finished in all respects, and a beautiful picture it is, as almost I ever saw. I sat again, and had a great deal done; but whatever the matter is, I do not fancy that it hath the ayre of my face, though it

a repl. symbol rendered illegible

---

1. In January the number of sub-commissioners for the ports had been reduced: *CSPD Add. 1660–85*, pp. 153–4.

2. He was Robert Ensum, of Elling-ton, Hunts.; nephew of Lewis Philipps, a lawyer whom Pepys had several times consulted. The proposal did not prosper, and Ensum died later in the year.

will be a very fine picture. Thence home and to my business, being post-night; and so home to supper and to bed.

21. Up betimes, and first by coach to my Lord Generall to visit him, and then to the Duke of Yorke, where we all met and did our usual business with him. But Lord, how anything is yielded to presently, even by Sir W. Coventry, that is propounded by the Duke; as now, to have Troutbacke, his old surgeon, and entended to go Surgeon-General of the fleet, to go Physician-General of the fleet, of which there never was any precedent in the world, and he for that to have 20*l* per month.[1] Thence with Lord Brouncker to Sir Robt. Long, whom we found in his closet; and after some discourse of business, he fell to discourse at large, and pleasant; and among other things, told us of the plenty of partridges in France, where he says the King of France and his company killed with their guns in the Plain de Versaille, 300 and odd partridges at one bout.

Thence I to the Excise Office behind the Change, and there find our business of our tallies in great disorder as to payment, and thereupon do take a resolution of thinking how to remedy it*ᵃ* as soon as I can. Thence home and there met Sir W Warren, and after I had eat a bit of victuals (he staying in the office), he and I to White-hall – he to look after the business of the prize-ships, which we are endeavouring to buy, and hope to get money by them. So*ᵇ* I to London by coach and to Gressham College, where I stayed half an hour; and so away home to my office, and there walking late, alone in the dark in the garden with Sir W. Warren,

a repl. 'as'   *b* repl. 'and'

<hr>

1. This arrangement was perhaps made in order to avoid displacing Pepys's friend, James Pearse, from his post as Surgeon-General. Pearse continued to serve in this capacity, while John Troutbeck (surgeon to the King and to Albemarle's troop of Life Guards) was in fact given no position in the fleet beyond that of personal physician to Rupert and Albemarle: PRO, Adm. 20/7, pt i. 253; NMM, MS. 9588, ff. 120*v*-121*r*. Physicians were normally paid much more than surgeons, and in this case Troutbeck's pay was almost twice that of Pearse. Pearse's pay was in 1673 raised to that now paid to Troutbeck: NMM, MS. 9588, loc. cit. Physicians were not normally employed in the navy except during epidemics. J. J. Keevil, *Medicine and the navy*, i. 69; ii. 113. Their first appointment to a fleet dates from 1691: *Sergison Papers* (ed. R. D. Merriman), p. 207.

who tells me that at the Committee of the Lords for the Prizes today there passed very high words between my Lord Ashly[1] and Sir W. Coventry about our business of the prize-ships. And that my Lord Ashly did snuff and talk as high to him as he used to do to any ordinary seaman. And that Sir W. Coventry did take it very quietly; but yet for all, did speak his mind soberly and with reason, and went away saying he had done his duty therein, and so left it to them whether they would let so many ships go for masts or not.[2] Here he and I talked of a thousand businesses, all profitable discourse; and late parted, and I home to supper and to bed – troubled a little at a letter from my father, telling me how [he] is like to be sued for a debt of Tom's by Smith the Mercer.[3]

22. Up, and to the office all the morning. At noon, my wife being gone to her father's, I dined with Sir W. Batten, he inviting me. After dinner, to my office close and did very much business; and so late home to supper, and to bed.

The plague encreased 4 this week, which troubles me – though but one in the whole City.[4]

23. Up, and going out[a] of my dressing-room when[b] ready to go downstairs,[c] I spied little Mrs. Tooker, my pretty little girl, which it seems did come yesterday to our house to stay a little while with us, but I did not know of it till now.[5]   I was glad of

a MS.'out out'   *b* repl. same symbol badly formed
          c repl. same symbol badly formed

---

1. Treasurer of the Prize Commission.
    2. The Prize Commissioners on the 23rd agreed to the Navy Board's request for the sale of fireships to Warren, who would use them for the transport of masts from Gothenburg. BM, Harl, 1510, f. 38r.
    3. In a letter to 'Mr Smith' (8 April 1666: probably composed and written by the diarist), John Pepys did not deny the fact of the debt, but simply regretted that there was no money to pay it with: Rawl. A 182, f. 334r; printed *Family Letters*, pp. 15-16.

The mercer may have been Theophilus Smith, woollen draper at the Sign of the White Lion, Paul's Churchyard.
    4. Plague burials had increased from 29 (6-13 March) to 33 (13-20 March); deaths in general from 207 to 233. The city parish affected was that of St Mary Mounthaw. GL, A.1.5, no. 96.
    5. Frances Tooker was the daughter of Pepys's neighbour when he was in lodgings with Mrs Clerke at Greenwich during the Plague.

her coming, she being a very pretty child and now grown almost a woman. I out by 6 a-clock by appointment to Hales's, where we fell to my picture presently very hard, and it comes on a very fine picture – and very merry; pleasant discourse we had all the morning while he was painting. Anon comes my wife, and Mercer and little Tooker. And having done with me, we all to a picture drawer's hard by, Hales carrying me to see some lanskip of a man's doing – but I do not [like] any of them, save only a piece of fruit, which endeed was very fine. Thence I to Westminster to the Chequer about a little business, and then to the Swan and there sent for a bit of meat and dined, and after dinner had opportunity of being pleased with Sarah; and so away to Westminster-hall, and there Mrs. Michell tells me with great joy how little Betty Howlet is married to her young son Michell; which is a pretty odd thing, that he should so soon succeed in that match to his elder brother, that died of the plague – and to the house and trade entended for him.[1] And more, they say that the girle hath*a* heretofore said that she did love this little one more then the other brother that was entended her all along. I am glad of this match, and more that they are likely to live near me in Thames-street – where I may see Betty now and then, whom I from a girl did use to call my second wife, and mighty pretty she is.

Thence by coach to Anthony Joyce to receive Harman's answer; which did trouble me to receive, for he now demands 800*l*, whereas he never made exception at the portion, but accepted of 500*l* – this I do not like; but however, I cannot much blame the man, if he thinks he can get more of another then of me. So home, and hard to my business at the office, where much business; and so home to supper and to bed.

24. Up, and to the office, where all the morning. At noon home to dinner, where Ant. Joyce; and I did give my final answer, I would give but 500*l* with my sister, and did show him the good offer made us in the country,[2] to which I did now more

a repl. 'says'

---

1. They seem to have kept a strong-water house.

2. See above, p. 78 & n. 2.

and more incline, and entend to pursue that. After dinner I to White-hall to a committee for Tanger, where the Duke of York was – and I acquitted myself well in what I had to do. After the committee up, I had occasion to fallow the Duke into his lodgings into a chamber where the Duchesse was sitting to have her picture drawn by Lilly,[1] who was there at work. But I was well pleased to see that there was nothing near so much resemblance of her face in his work, which is now the second, if not the third time, as there was of my wife's at the very first time. Nor do I think at last it can be like, the lines not being in proportion to those of her face.

So home and to the office, where late; and so to bed.

25. *Lady day and Sunday.* Up, and to my chamber, in my gown all the morning, about settling my papers there. At noon to dinner, where my wife's brother, whom I sent for to offer making him a muster-master and send to sea;[2] which the poor man likes well of and will go, and it will be a good preferment to him – only hazardous. I hope he will prove a good discreet man.

After dinner, to my papers and Tanger accounts again till supper, and after supper, again to them; but by my mixing them, I know not how, my private and public accounts, it makes me mad to see how hard it is to bring them to be understood; and my head is confounded, that though I did swear to sit up till one a-clock upon them, yet I fear it will be to no purpose, for I cannot understand what I do or have been doing of them today.

26. Up, and a meeting extraordinary there was, of Sir W. Coventry, Lord Brouncker, and myself, about the business of settling the ticket office, where infinite room is left for abusing the King in the wages of seamen. Our being done, my Lord Brouncker and I to the Tower to see the famous ingraver,[3] to get

---

1. This portrait may be the seated three-quarter length, of which there are many versions but of which the original, probably the portrait recorded later in James II's collection, is still in the royal collection; or the full-length derivation, now at Hampton Court, from the same design:

O. Millar, *Tudor, Stuart and early Georgian pictures in coll. H.M. Queen* (1963), nos 242, 243. (OM).

2. Balty St Michel served this summer in Harman's fleet in this capacity.

3. John Roettiers, engraver to the Mint.

him to grave a seal for the office. And did see some of the finest pieces of work in embossed work that ever I did see in my life, for fineness and smallness of the images thereon – and I will carry my wife thither to show them her. Here I also did see bars of gold melting, which was a fine sight. So with my Lord to the Pope's-head tavern in Lumberd-street to dine, by appointment with Captain Taylor – whither Sir W. Coventry came to us, and were mighty merry. And I find reason to honour him every day more and more.

Thence alone to Broad-street to Sir G. Carteret, by his desire to confer with him; who is, I find, in great pain about the business of the office, and not a little, I believe, in fear of falling there, Sir W. Coventry having so great a pique against him. And herein I first learn an iminent instance how great a man this day, that nobody could think could be shaken, is the next overthrow[n], dashed out of countenance, and every small thing of irregularity in his business taken notice of, where nobody the other day darst cast an eye upon them. And next, I see that he that the other day nobody durst come near, is now as supple as a spaniel, and sent and speaks to me with great submission, and readily*[a]* hears to advice. Thence home to the office, where busy late; and so home a little to my account[s] public and private, but*[b]* could not get myself rightly to know how to dispose of them in order to passing.

27.*[c]* All the morning at the office busy. At noon dined at home; Mr. Cooke, our old acquaintance at my Lord Sandwiches, came to see and dine with me, but I quite out of humour, having many other and better things to think of.[1] Thence to the office to settle my people's work, and then home to my public account of Tanger; which it is strange, by meddling with evening reckonings with Mr. Povy lately, how I myself am become intangled therein so that after all I could do, ready to break my head and brains, I thought of another way, though not so perfect,*[d]* yet the

a repl. 'doth'   *b* repl. 'that'   *c* repl. '26'   *d* MS. 'perfectly'

---

1. Cooke was a servant of Sand-wich. Pepys could rarely bring him-self to be polite to him. In 1662 Cooke had misled him about a proposed match for Pall (above, iii. 231–2), and in 1663 had begged to be appointed to a post in the navy before it had been established: above, iv. 66.

G

only one which this account is capable of. Upon this latter I sat up till past 2 in the morning, and then to bed.

28.[a] Up, and with Creed, who came hither betimes to speak with me about his accounts, to White-hall by water – mighty merry in discourse, though I had been very little troubled with him or did countenance it, having now, blessed be God, a great deal of good business to mind, to better purpose then chatting with him.

Waited[b] on the Duke. After that walked with Sir W Clerke[1] into St. James's Park, and by and by met with Mr. Hays, Prince Robert's Secretary; who are mighty, both, brisk blades, but I fear they promise themselfs more then they expect. Thence to the Cockpit and dined with a great deal of company at the Duke of Albemarles, and a bad and dirty nasty dinner.

So by coach to Hales and there sat again; and it is become mighty like. Hither came my wife and Mercer, brought by Mrs. Pierce and Knipp; we were mighty merry, and the picture goes on[c] the better for it.

Thence set them down at Pierces, and we home, where busy, and at my chamber till 12 at night, and so to bed.

This night I am told the Queen of Portugall, the mother to our Queen, is lately dead, and news brought of it hither this day.[2]

29. All the morning hard at the office. At noon dined, and then out to Lumbard-street to look after the getting in of some money that is lodged there of mine in Viner's hands, I having no mind to have it lie there longer. So back again and to the office, where, and at home, about public and private business and accounts till past 12 at night, and so to bed. This day poor Jane, my old little Jane,[3] came to us again, to my wife's and my great content; and we hope to take mighty pleasure in her, she having

a repl. '27'   *b* repl. same symbol blotted   *c* repl. 'out'

---

1. Secretary at War.
2. Luisa Maria de Gusmão, widow of John IV, and mother of the reigning King Afonso VI and of Catherine

of Braganza, had died in Lisbon on 17/27 February.
3. Jane Birch: see above, p. 42 & n. 2.

all the marks and qualities of a good and loving and honest servant – she coming by force away from the other place where she hath lived ever since she went from us, and at our desire – her late mistress having used all the stratagems she could to keep her.

30. My wife and I mightily pleased with Janes coming to us again. Up, and away goes Alce our cook-maid, a good servant, whom we loved and did well by her; and she an excellent servant, but would not bear being told of any fault in the fewest and kindest words, and would go away of her own accord, after having given her mistress warning fickly for quarter of a year together. So we shall take another girl, and make little Jane our Cooke; at least, make a trial of it.

Up, and after much business, I out to Lumbard-street[1] and there received 2200*l* and brought it home; and contrary to expectation, received 35*l* for the use of 2000*l* of it a quarter of a year, where it hath produced me this profit – and hath been a convenience to me as to care and security of my house, and demandable at two days' warning, as this hath been.

This morning Sir W Warren came to me a second time about having 2000*l* of me upon his bills on the Act, to enable him to pay for the ships he is buying – wherein I shall have considerable profit.[2] I am loath to do it, but yet, speaking with Colvill, I do not see but I shall be able to do it, and get money by it too.

Thence home and eat one mouthful, and so to Hales's and there sat till almost quite dark upon working my gowne, which I hired to be drawn [in] it – an Indian gown, and I do see all the reason to expect a most excellent picture of it.

Thus[a] home, and to my private accounts in my chamber till past one in the morning; and so to bed – with my head full of thoughts for my evening of all my accounts tomorrow, the latter end of the month; in which God give me good issue, for I never was in such a confusion in my[b] life, and that in great sums.

a MS. 'Those'   *b* repl. same symbol

---

1. To Vyner's, the goldsmith-banker's: see above, p. 34.
2. For the ships, see above, p. 80
& n. 2. The act was the Additional Aid of 1665.

31.   All the morning at the office busy. At noon to dinner, and thence to the office and did my business there as soon as I could, and then home and to my accounts, where very late at them. But Lord, what a deal of do I have to understand any part of them. And in short, do what I could, I could not come to an understanding of them; but after I had thoroughly wearied myself, I was forced to go to bed and leave them, much against my will, and vow too; but I hope God will forgive me in it, for I have sat up these four nights till past 12 at night*a* to master them, but cannot.

Thus ends this month – with my head and mind mightily full and disquiet because of my accounts, which I have let go too long and confounded my public with my private, that I cannot come to any liquidating of them.   However, I do see that I must be grown richer then I was by a good deal the last month.

Busy also I am in thoughts for a husband for my sister; and to that end, my wife and I have determined that she shall presently go into the country to my father and mother, and consider of a proffer made them for her in the country;[1] which, if she likes, shall go forward.

a   MS. 'noon'

---

1. See above, p. 78 & n. 2.

APRILL.

1. *Lords day.* Up and abroad, and by coach to Charing-cross*a* to wait on Sir Ph. Howard[1] – whom I found in bed, and he doth receive me very civilly. My request was about suffering my wife's brother to go to sea, and to save his pay in the Duke's guards – which, after a little difficulty, he did with great respect agree to. I find him a very fine-spoken gentleman, and one*b* of great parts – and very courteous. Much pleased with this visit, I to White-hall, where I met Sir G Downing; and to discourse with him an hour about the Exchequer payments upon the late act, and informed myself of him thoroughly in my safety in lending 2000*l* to Sir W Warren upon an order of his upon the Exchequer for 2602*l* – and I do purpose to do it.[2]

Thence, meeting Dr. Allen the physician, he and I and another walked in the park, a most pleasant warm day, and to the Queen's chapel – where I do not so dislike the music.[3] Here I saw on a post an invitation to all good Catholics to pray for the soul of such a one, departed this life.

The Queen, I hear, doth not yet hear of the death of her mother, she being in a course of physic, that they dare not tell it her.[4]

At noon by coach home, and there by invitation met my uncle and aunt Wight and their cousin Mary – and dined with me and very merry. After dinner, my uncle and I abroad by coach to White-hall, up and down the House, and I did some business; and thence with him and a gentleman he met with to my Lord Chancellors*c* new house;[5] and there viewed it again and again, and up to the top, and I like it as well as ever and think it a most noble house. So all up and down my Lord St. Albans his new building and market-house, and the tavern under the market-house, looking

---

a repl. 'White-hall'   b MS. 'whom'   c repl. 'Tr'-

---

1. Captain of Albemarle's troop of Life Guards.
2. See below, pp. 89–90 & n.
3. Cf. above, iii. 202; below, p. 99. (E).
4. Cf. Lamplugh to Williamson,

8 April: 'The . . . death is yet kept from our Queen, and the Gazetteer had a cheque for his forwardness in publishing it' (*CSPD 1665–6*, p. 342).
5. See above, p. 32, n. 2.

to and again into every place of building;[1] and so away, and took coach and home – where to my accounts, and was at them till I could not hold open my eyes; and so to bed.

I this afternoon made a visit to my Lady Carteret, whom I understood newly come to town. And she took it mighty kindly, but I see her face and heart are dejected from the condition her husband's matters stand in. But I hope they will do all well enough – and I do comfort her as much as I can, for she is a noble lady.

2. Up, and to the office; and thence with Mr. Gawden to guild hall to see the books and tallies there in the chamber[2] – (and by the way in the street his new coach broke, and we fain to take an old hackney); thence to the Exchequer again to inform myself of some other points in the new act, in order to my lending Sir W. Warren 2000*l* upon an order of his upon the act,[3] which they all encourage me to.

There, walking with Mr. Gawden in Westminster-hall, he and I to talk from one business to another, and at last to the marriage of his daughter: he told me the story of Creeds pretences to his daughter, and how he would not believe but she loved him, while his daughter was in great passion on the other hand against him.[4] Thence to talk of his son Benj; and I proposed a match for him, and at last named my sister, which he imbraces heartily; and speaking of the lowness of her portion, that it would be less then

---

1. St Albans had been engaged since 1662 in developing the area north of Pall Mall and west of the modern Lower Regent Street. It included several streets, a 'Piazza' (the modern St James's Square) and, after 1665, a large house for St Albans himself in the south-east corner. There was by 1664 a covered market to the east of the square. This development was one of the principal building projects of the time, similar to that carried out by the Earl of Southampton in Bloomsbury. St Albans was one of the main creators of the modern West End. Cf. above, iv. 295–6. See C. L. Kingsford, *Early hist.*

Piccadilly, pp. 94+; LCC, *Survey of London*, vols xxix and xxx (esp. xxix. 1–5). (R).

2. The city chamber made loans to the government, on behalf of the city corporation and of individuals, which were secured on taxes, such as the Royal Aid of 1664. The tallies represented credits on these revenues.

3. See below, p. 90 & n. 1. The accounts of the Additional Aid were open to inspection at the Exchequer in order to encourage lending.

4. Sarah Gauden was 'a buxom lass' (above, vi. 172), but to Creed all heiresses were beautiful. This match did not come off.

1000*l*, he tells me, if everything else agrees, he will, out of what he means to give me yearly, make a portion for her shall cost me nothing more than I entend freely. This did mightily rejoice me; and, full of it, did go with him to London to the Change and there did much business, and at the Coffee-house with Sir W Warren – who very wisely did show me that my matching my sister with Mr. Gawden would undo me in all my places, everybody suspecting me in all I do, and I shall neither be able to serve him nor free myself from imputation of being of his faction, while I am placed for his severest check. I was convinced that it would be for neither of our interests to make this alliance, and so am quite off of it again; but with great satisfaction in the motion.

Thence to the Crown tavern behind the Exchange to meet with Cocke and Fenn; and did so, and dined with them; and after dinner had the intent of our meeting, which was some private discourse with Fenn,[1] telling him what I hear and think of his business; which he takes very kindly, and says he will look about him – it was about his giving of ill language and answers to people that come to him about money – and some other perticulars. This morning Mrs. Barbary and little Mrs. Tooker[2] went away home hence. Thence, my wife by coach calling me, we to White-hall, to visit my Lady Carteret; she was not within. So to Westminster-hall, where I purposely took my wife well-dressed into the hall, to see and be seen; and among others, Howlet's daughter, who is newly married, and is she I call wife and one I love mightily. So to Broad-street, and there met my Lady and Sir G. Carteret and sat and talked with them a good while; and so home and to my accounts, which I cannot get through with. But at it till I grow drowzy; and so to bed, mightily vexed that I can come to no better issue in my accounts.

3. Up, and Sir W Warren with me betimes, and signed a bond and assigned his order on the Exchequer to a blank for me to fill – and I did deliver him 1900*l*; the truth is, it is a great venture to venture so much on the act; but thereby I hedge in 300*l* gift for my service about some ships that he hath bought, prizes, and

good interest besides, and his bond to repay me the money at six weeks' warning.¹ So to the office, where busy all the morning. At noon home to dinner, and there my brother Balty dined with me and my wife; who is become a good serious man and I hope to do him good, being sending him a muster-maister of one of the squadrons of the fleet. After dinner and he gone, I to my accounts hard all the afternoon till it was quite dark; and I thank God I do come to bring them very fairly to make me worth 5000*l* stock*ᵃ* in the world, which is a great mercy to me; though I am a little troubled to find 50*l* difference between the perticular account I make to myself of my profits and loss in each month – and the account which I raise from my acquittance[s] and money which I have at the end of every month in my chest and other men's hands. However, I do well believe that I am effectually 5000*l* – the greatest sum I ever was in my life yet; and this day I have, as I have said before, agree[d] with Sir W. Warren and got of him 300*l* gift.

At night a while to the office, and then home and supped and to my accounts again till I was ready to [have] slept, there being no pleasure to handle them if they are not kept in*ᵇ* good order. So to bed.

4. Up, and with Sir W. Penn in his coach to White-hall – in his way talking simply and fondly as he used to do; but I find myself to slight him and his simple talk, I thank God, and that my condition will enable me to do it. Thence ⟨after doing our business with the Duke of Yorke⟩, with Captain Cocke home to the Change in his coach. He promises me presently a dozen of silver salts, and proposes a business for which he hath promised Mrs. Williams, for my Lord Bruncker, a set of plate shall cost him 500*l*, and me the like – which will be a good business indeed. After done several businesses at the Change, I home, and being

a repl. 'strock'   *b* repl. 'better'

---

1. Pepys's memorandum on this transaction, dated this day, is in Rawl. A 174, f. 436. He had consulted Downing about the security provided by the act (the Additional Aid of 1665). On 13 August he cashed the order at Colvill's for £2,432, and on the whole transaction (excluding the gift) made a profit of £230 in four months. For details, see D. C. Coleman's summary in *Essays . . . in honour of R. H. Tawney* (ed. F. J. Fisher), p. 223.

washing-day, dined upon cold meat; and so abroad by coach to Hales's, and there sat till night, mightily pleased with my picture, which is now almost finished. So by coach home, it being the fast-day,[1] and to my chamber; and so after supper to bed – consulting how to send my wife into the country to advise about Pall's marriage, which I much desire, and my father too – and two or three offers are*a* now in hand.

5. Up, and before office time to Lumbard-street; and there at Viner's was shown the silver plates made for Captain Cocke to present my Lord Brouncker; and I chose a dozen of the same weight to be bespoke for myself, which he told me yesterday he would give me on the same occasion. To the office, where the falseness and impertinencies of Sir W Pen would make a man mad to think of. At noon would have avoided, but could not, dining with my Lord Brouncker and his mistress with Captain Cocke at the Sun tavern in Fish-street; where a good dinner, but the woman doth tire me. And endeed, to see how simply my Lord Brouncker (who is otherwise a wise man) doth proceed at the table[2] in serving of Cocke, without any means of understanding in his proposal or defence when opposed,*b* would make a man think him a fool.

After dinner home, where I find my wife hath on a sudden, upon notice of a coach going away tomorrow, taken a resolution of going in it to Brampton – we having lately thought it fit for her to go, to satisfy herself and me in the nature of the fellow that is there proposed to my sister.[3] So she to fit herself for her journy, and I to the office all the afternoon till late; and so home, and late putting notes to *It is decreed, nor shall thy fate*, &c.,[4] and then to bed.

The plague this week is to our great grief increased 9 this week, though decreased a few in the total.[5] And this increase runs

a MS. 'or'   *b* MS. 'proposed'

1. For the Plague.
2. The office-table, not the dining-table.
3. See above p. 78 & n. 2.
4. The words are Catiline's first soliloquy in Jonson's play of that name (I, i. 73–97). Pepys now composed a voice-line; his organist friend John Hingston later provided

a bass: below, p. 414. The setting (in the hand of Morelli, Pepys's domestic musician in the 1670s) is in PL 2803, ff. 108*v*–111*r*. (E).
5. Plague deaths in the week 27 March–3 April were 26 (as against 17 in the previous week); deaths from all causes 211 (as against 224): GL, A.1.5, no. 96.

through many parishes, which makes us much fear the next year.

6. Up mighty betimes, upon my wife's going this day toward Brampton. I could not go to the coach with her, but W Hewers did, and hath leave from me to go the whole day's journey with her. All the morning upon business at the office, and at noon dined; and Mrs. Hunt coming, lent her 5*l* on her occasions, and so carried her to axe-yard-end at Westminster and there left her – a good and understanding woman, and her husband, I perceive, thrives mightily in his business of the Excise.[1]

Thence to Mr. Hales, and there sat and my picture almost finished; which, by the word of Mr. and Mrs. Pierce (who came in accidentally), is mighty like, and I am sure I am mightily pleased, both in the thing and the posture. Thence with them home a little, and so to White-hall and there met by agreement with Sir St. Fox and Mr. Ashburnham, and discoursed the business of our Excize tallies – the former being Treasurer of the guards, and the other Cofferer of the King's household[2] – I benefited much by their discourse. We came to no great conclusion upon our discourse; but parted, and I home, where all things methinks melancholy in the absence of my wife.

This day great news of the Swedes declaring for us against the Dutch; and so far as that, I believe it.[3] After a little supper,[a] to bed.

7. Lay pretty long today, lying alone and thinking on several businesses. So up to the office, and there till noon; thence with my Lord Brouncker home by coach to Mrs. Williams's, where Bab Allen[4] and Dr Charleton dined. Bab and I sang, and were

a repl. 'discourse'

---

1. The Hunts (once neighbours of the Pepyses in Axe Yard) were old friends.

2. Payments for the Guards, the Household and for Tangier had all been secured on the revenue from the excise: *CTB*, i. 683.

3. It was, however, untrue. Since January, the English envoy Henry Coventry had been trying to tempt Sweden into supporting England against the Dutch and the Danes, but without success. Pepys's story perhaps derived from the news in the *London Gazette* of 5 April that the Swedes were angry with the Danes and concerned about the freedom of the Baltic. See below, p. 107 & n. 1.

4. Mrs Knepp's nickname: above, p. 4.

mighty merry as we could be there, where the rest of the company did not overplease. Thence took her by coach to Hales's, and there find Mrs. Pierce and her boy and Mary. She had done sitting the first time, and endeed her face is mighty like, at first dash.[1] Thence took them to the cake-house,[2] and there called in the coach for cakes, and drank; and thence I carried them to my Lord Chancellors new house to show them that, and all mightily pleased; thence set each down at home, and so I home to the office – where about 10 of the clock W Hewers comes to[a] me, to tell me that he left my wife well this morning at Bugden (which was great riding),[3] and brings me a letter from her. She is very well got thither, of which I am heartily glad. After writing several letters, I home to supper and to bed.

The Parliament, of which I was afeared of their calling us of the Navy to an account of the expense of money and stores, and wherein we were so little ready to give them a good answer.[4]

The Bishop of Munster, everybody says, is coming to peace with the Dutch, we having not supplied him with the monies promised him.[5]

8. Up, and was in great trouble how to get a passage to White-hall, it raining – and no coach to be had. So I walked to the Old Swan and there got a scull. To the Duke of Yorke, where we all met to hear the debate between Sir Tho. Allen and Mr. Wayth – the former complaining of the latter's ill-usage of him at the late pay of his ship – but a very sorry poor occasion he had for it. The Duke did determine it with great judgment, chiding both, but encouraging Wayth to continue to be a check to all Captains in anything to the King's right. And endeed I

---

a repl. 'home'

---

1. Hayls's portrait of Mrs Pierce is not known to survive. Pepys records the progress of the portrait; it was apparently finished by 9 May, but was not considered a very satisfactory effort: below, p. 131. (OM).

2. See above, p. 70, n. 1.

3. To Buckden, Hunts., was a distance of some 60 miles.

4. Sentence incomplete. Parlia-

ment now stood prorogued until 23 April, and on meeting then was again prorogued until 18 September. For the navy accounts, see below, p. 294, n. 1.

5. See below, p. 107, n. 1. For the unpaid subsidies, see Sir W. Temple, *Works* (1814), i. 214+; Feiling, p. 154.

never did see the Duke do anything more in order, nor with more judgment, then he did pass the verdict in this business.[1]

The Court*[a]* full this morning of the news of Tom Cheffins's death, the King's closet-keeper.[2] He was well last night as ever, playing at tables in the house – and not very ill this morning, 6 a-clock; yet dead before 7 – they think of an impostume in his breast. But it looks fearfully among people nowadays, the plague, as we hear, increasing everywhere again.[3]

To the Chapel, but could not get in to hear well. But I had the pleasure once in my life to see an Ar[ch]bishop (this was of Yorke)[4] in a pulpit.

Then at a loss how to get home to dinner, having promised to carry Mrs. Hunt thither. At last got my Lord Hinchingbrooke's coach, he staying at Court; and so took her up in axe yard, and home and dined – and good discourse of the old matters of the Protector and his family, she having a relation to them.[5] The Protector lives in France; spends about 500*l* per annum.[6]

Thence carried her home again; and then to Court, and walked over to St. James's chapel, thinking to have heard a Jesuite preach but came too late. So got a hackney, and home and there to

---

a repl. 'news'

---

1. According to a letter of Pepys, Allin had complained that Waith had refused to allow him pay for some of his seamen 'absent by sickness or his particular leave'. 'They were doubtless some boys wherein he was interested': Pepys to Mennes, 5 April (NMM, LBK/8, p. 376). The Duke had reserved the matter to his own decision, and Pepys added, 'I doubt not this little storme will be smothred with a gentle interpretation on all hands.' Cf. below, pp. 96–7 & n.

2. Chiffinch had died on 6 April.

3. The week ending on 3 April had seen an increase of 9 deaths, whereas in the week before there had been a decrease of 16: GL, A.1.5, no. 96. Cf. below, p. 108 & n. 2.

4. Richard Sterne, Archbishop of York, 1664–83.

5. Both she and her husband John were by origin East Anglian.

6. Richard Cromwell (son and successor of Oliver) was living in Paris under the name of John Clarke, and passed his time reading and sketching. Cf. above, v. 296 & n. 2. William Mumford, a servant of his wife, who lived at Hursley, Herts., had recently (15 March) been examined 'about Cromwell's movements': *CSPD 1665–6*, p. 299. Richard returned to England c. 1680 and spent the remainder of his life at Cheshunt, Herts.

business. At night had Mercer comb my head; and so to supper, sing a psalm, and to bed.

9. Up betimes, and with my Joyner begun the making of the window in my boy's chamber bigger, purposing it shall be a room to eat and for hav[ing] Musique in.

To the office, where a meeting upon extraordinary business. At noon to the Change about more, and then home with Creed and dined, and then with him to the Committee of Tanger, where I got two or three things done I had a mind to – of convenience to me. Thence by coach to Mrs. Pierces, and with her and Knipp and Mrs. Pierce's boy and girl abroad, thinking to have been merry at Chelsey; but being come almost to the house by coach near the waterside, a house alone, I think the Swan – a gentleman walking by called to us to tell us that the house was shut up of the sickness. So we with great affright turned back, being holden to the gentleman, and went away (I for my part in great disorder) for Kensington; and there I spent about 30s upon the jades with great pleasure – and we sang finely, and stayed till about 8 at night, the night coming on apace; and so set them down at*a* Pierce's, and so away home – where a while with Sir W. Warren about business, and then to bed.

10. Up betimes, and many people to me about business. To the office and there sat till noon, and then home and dined; and to the office again all the afternoon, where we sat all, the first time of our resolution to sit both forenoons and afternoons. Much business at night, and then home, and though late, did see some work done by the plasterer to my new window in the boy's chamber plastered. Then to supper, and after having my head combed by the little girl,[1] to bed. Bad news, that the plague is decreased in the general again and two encreased in the sickness.[2]

11. To White-hall, having first set my people to work about setting my rails upon the leads of my wife's closet, a thing I have

a repl. 'in'

---

1. Susan.
2. Burials from all causes were down by 16 from the previous week (27 March–3 April), but plague burials up from 26 to 28: GL, A.1.5, no. 96.

long designed, but never had a fit opportunity till now. After having done with the Duke of Yorke, I to Hales's, where there was nothing found to be done more to my picture but the Musique; which now pleases me mightily, it being painted true.[1] Thence home; and after dinner to Gresham College, where a great deal of do and formality in choosing of the Council and Officers. I had three votes to be of the Council – who am but a stranger, nor expected any.[2] So my Lord Brouncker being continued President, I home, where I find to my great content my rails up upon my leads. To the office and did a little business, and then home and did a great Jobb at my Tanger accounts – which I find are mighty apt to run into confusion – my head also being too full of other businesses and pleasures. This noon Bagwell's wife came to me to the office, after her being long at Portsmouth. After supper, and past 12 at night, to bed.[a]

12. Up, and to the office, where all the morning. At noon dined at home, and so to my office again; and taking a turn in the garden, my Lady Pen comes to me and takes me into her house, where I find her daughter and a pretty lady of her acquaintance, one[b] Mrs. Lowder (sister, I suppose, of her servant* Lowder's), with whom I, notwithstanding all my resolution to fallow business close this afternoon, did stay talking and playing the fool almost all the afternoon. And there saw two or three foolish sorry pictures of her[3] doing, but very ridiculous compared to what my wife doth. She grows mighty homely, and looks old.[4] Thence, shamed at myself for this loss of time, yet not able to leave it, I to the office; where my Lord Brouncker came, and he and I had a little fray, he being, I find, a very peevish man if he be

a entry crowded into bottom of page   b repl. 'once'

---

1. For the picture, see above, p. 75, n. 1. For the music, see below, p. 98, n. 1.
    2. At this election meeting (postponed from St Andrew's Day 1665 because of the plague), 46 fellows were present. Evelyn (with 27 votes) and John Creed were among the ten new councillors, but Evelyn was excused service. Birch, ii. 74, 80; Evelyn, 11

April. Pepys's silence about Creed's election perhaps betrays his dislike of him. Pepys himself was first elected to the Council in 1672. He was to serve five terms (of one year each) as Councillor and two terms (1684–6) as President of the society.
    3. Lady Penn's.
    4. She was about 44.

denied what he expects, and very simple in his argument in this business – (about signing a warrant for paying Sir Tho. Allen 1000*l* out of the groats);[1] but we were pretty good friends before we parted; and so we broke up, and I to the writing my letters by the post; and so home to supper and to bed.

13.[a] Up, being called up by my wife's brother, for whom I have got a commission from the Duke of Yorke for muster-master of one of the Divisions of which Harman is Reread-mirall, of which I am glad as well as he. After I had acquainted him with it and discoursed a little of it, I went forth and took him with me by coach to the Duke of Albemarle; who being not up, I took a walk with Balty into the park, and to the Queen's chapel, it being Goodfriday; where people were all upon their knees, very silent – but it seems no Masse this day. So back, and waited on the Duke and received some commands of his; and so by[b] coach to Mr. Hales's – where it is pretty strange to see[c] that his second doing, I mean the second time of her sitting, is less like Mrs. Pierce then the first – and yet I am confident will be most like her, for he is so curious* that I do not see how it is possible for him to mistake.

Here, he and I presently resolved of going to White-hall, to spend an hour in the galleries there among the pictures; and we did so to my extraordinary satisfaction, he showing me the difference in the painting; and when I come more and more to distinguish and observe the workmanship, I do not find so many good things as I thought there was – but yet great difference be-tween the works of some and others – and while my head and judgment was full of these, I would go back again to his house to see his pictures. And endeed, though I think at first sight some difference doth open, yet very inconsiderably; but that I may judge his to be very good pictures. Here we fell into discourse of

a repl. '15'   *b* repl. 'to'   *c* repl. 'say

---

1. These were the payments made at the rate of a groat (fourpence) a month out of seamen's wages, for the provision of chaplains. By an order of 2 February 1665 any surplus from this fund was to go to the command-ing admiral: cf. *CSPD Add. 1660–85*, p. 133. The present dispute seems to have been about the *Royal James*: above, pp. 93–4 & n.; PRO, SP 29/153, no. 25. Allin had received £1000 out of the groats in the pre-vious July by the Duke of York's order: PRO, Adm. 2/1725, f. 144.

my picture, and I am for his putting out the Lanskipp, though he says it is very well done; yet I do judge it will be best without it, and so it shall be put out – and be made a plain sky, like my wife[s] picture, which will be very noble.[1]

Thence called upon an old woman in pannier ally to agree for ruling of some paper for me, and she will do it pretty cheap. Here I find her have a very comely black* maid to her servant, which I liked very well.

So home to dinner and to see my Joyner do the bench upon my leads, to my great content. After dinner, I abroad to carry paper to my old[a] woman; and so to Westminster-hall, and there, beyond my intention or design, did see and speak with Betty Howlett at her father's still. And it seems they carry her to her own house to begin the world with her young husband on Monday next, Easter Monday. I please myself with the thoughts of her neighbourhood,[b] for I love the girl mightily.

Thence home; and thither comes Mr. Houblon and a brother, with whom I evened for the charter-parties of their ships for Tanger, and paid them the third advanced on their freight – to full satisfaction;[2] and so they being gone, comes Creed, and with him till past one in the morning, evening his accounts till 《14.》 my head aked and I was fit for nothing. However, coming at last luckily to see through and settle all to my mind, it did please me mightily; and so with my mind at rest, to bed, and he with me – and hard to sleep.

Up about 7 and finished our papers, he and I; and I delivered him tallies and some money – and so away – I to the office, where we sat all the morning. At noon dined at home, and Creed with me. Then parted, and I to the office, and anon called thence by Sir H. Cholmly; and he and I to my chamber, and there settled our matters of accounts and did give him tallies and money to

a repl. 'work'   *b* repl. 'hol'-

---

1. X-ray photographs taken in 1954 did not reveal the original landscape here referred to. They showed alterations to the sitter's left hand, and to the sheet of music with the song *Beauty Retire*. (Perhaps the notes were not legible enough for Pepys's taste.) Less certainly, they suggested that the sheet of music was an afterthought. They also showed that Pepys's right arm and hand were originally included. See illust., opp.; also D. Piper in *Cat. 17th-cent. portraits in NPG* (1963), pp. 269-70; *Book Collector*, 21/65+. (OM).

2. See above p. 20, n. 3.

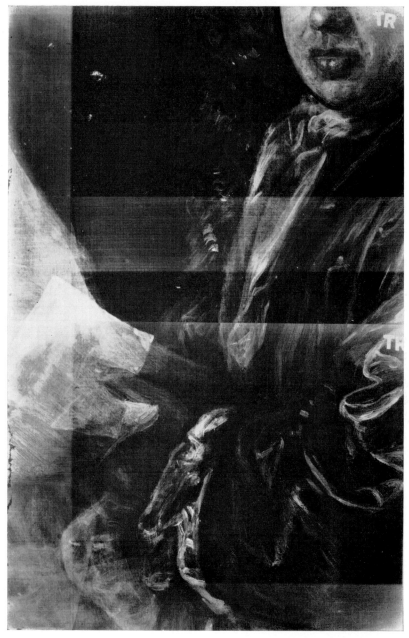

Samuel Pepys. X-ray detail of section of portrait by John Hayls.
Cf. Vol. I, front
(*National Portrait Gallery, photograph The Book Collector*)

clear him; and so he being gone and all these accounts cleared, I shall be even with the King, so as to make a very clear and short account in a very few days, which pleases me very well.

Here he and I discoursed a great while about Tanger, and he doth convince me, as things are now ordered by my Lord Bellases, and will be by Norwood (men that do only mind themselfs),[a] the garrison will never come to anything. And he proposes his own being governor; which in truth I do think will do very well, and that he will bring it to something.

He gone, I to my office, where to write letters late; and then home and looked over a little more my papers of accounts lately passed; and so to bed.

15. *Easter day.* Up, and by water to Westminster[b] to the Swan to lay down my cloak, and there found Sarah alone; with[c] whom after I had stayed awhile, I to White-hall chapel; and there coming late, could hear nothing of the Bishop of London's sermon;[1] so walked into the park to the Queen's chapel and there heard a good deal of their mass and some of their Musique, which is not so contemptible, I think, as our people would make it, it pleasing me very well[2] – and indeed, better then the Anthemne I heard afterward at White-hall at my coming back.

I stayed till the King went down to receive the Sacrament; and stood in his Closett with a great many others and there saw him receive[d] it – which I did never see the manner of before. But do see very little difference between the degree of the ceremonies used by our people in the administration thereof and that in the Roman church, saving that methought our chapel was not so fine, nor the manner of doing it so glorious, as it was in the Queenes chapel.

Thence walked to Mr. Pierce's and there dined, I alone with him and her and their children. Very good company, and good discourse,[e] they being able to tell me all the businesses of the

---

a closing bracket at end of sentence   b repl. 'White-hall'
c repl. 'all' 'when'   d repl. 'which'   e symbol smudged

---

1. Cf. Magalotti, p. 366. Humphrey Henchman was Bishop of London, 1663–75. As Lord Almoner he had the duty of preaching on Easter Day.

2. For Pepys's opinion of the music at St James's Chapel, see above, p. 87 & n. 3. (E).

H

Court[1] – the Amours and the mad doings that are there – how for certain, Mrs. Steward doth do everything now with the King that a mistress should do – and that the King hath many bastard children that are known and owned, besides the Duke of Monmouth.[2] After a great deal of this discourse – I walked thence into the park, with her little boy James with me, who is the wittiest boy, and the best company in the world. And so back again through White-hall both coming and going. And people did generally take him to be my boy – and some would ask me.

Thence home to Mr. Pierce again; and he being gone forth, she and I and the children out by coach to Kensington, to where we were the other day, and with great pleasure stayed till night; and were mighty late getting home, the horses tiring and stopping at every twenty steps. By the way we discoursed of Mrs. Clerke,[3] who she says is grown mighty high, fine, and proud. But tells me an odd story, how Captain Rolt did see her the other day accost a gentleman in Westminster-hall and went with him; and he dogged them to Moore fields to a little blind bawdy house, and there stayed watching three hours and they came not out; so could stay no longer, but left them there. And he is sure it was she, he knowing her well and describing her very clothes to Mrs. Pierce, which she knows are what she wears.

Seeing them well at home – I homeward; but the horses at Ludgate-hill made a final stop, so there I lighted and with a link, it being about 10 a-clock, walked home. And after singing a psalm or two, and supped, to bed.

16. Up, and set my people, Mercer, W Hewers, Tom, and the girl, at work at ruling and stitching my ruled books for the Muster maisters.[4] And I hard toward the settling of my Tanger accounts. At noon dined alone; the girl Mercer taking physic, can eat nothing, and W. Hewer went forth to dinner. So up to

---

1. James Pearse was a surgeon to the Duke of York, and a Groom of the Bedchamber to the Queen.

2. By now, there were nine (in the end, fourteen) acknowledged bastards. List in GEC, *Comp. Peerage*, vi, App. F.

3. The wife of Dr Timothy Clarke, physician to the King's Household.

4. Untraced; not listed among the 'Entries of Musters' remaining in the office in October 1688: BM, Add. 9303, ff. 52–3, 124–5.

my accounts again; and then comes Mrs. Mercer and fair Mrs. Turner, a neighbour of hers that my wife knows by their means – to visit me. I stayed a great while with them, being taken with this pretty woman – though a mighty silly, affected, citizen-woman she is. Then I left them, to come to me to supper anon, and myself out by coach to my old woman in pannyer-alley for my ruled papers, and they are done. And I am much more taken with her black* maid Nan. Thence further to Westminster, thinking to have met Mrs. Martin, but could not find her; so back, and called at Kirton's[1] to borrow 10*s* to pay for my ruled papers – I having not money in my pocket*a* enough to pay for them. But it was a pretty consideration, that on this occasion I was considering where I could with most confidence in a time of need borrow 10*s*; and I protest I could not tell where to do it, and with some trouble and fear did ask*b* it here. So that God keep me from want, for I shall be in a very bad condition to help myself if ever I should come to want or borrow.

Thence called for my papers, and so home, and there comes Mrs. Turner and Mercer and supped*c* with me; and well pleased I was with their company, but especially Mrs. Turner's, she being a very pretty woman of person, and her face pretty good, but colour of her hair very fine and light.

They stayed with me talking till about 11 a-clock, and so home (W. Hewer, who supped with me, leading them home); so I to bed.

17. Up and to the office, where all the morning. At noon dined at home, my brother Balty with me, who is fitting himself to go to sea. So I after dinner to my accounts, and did proceed a good way in settling them; and thence to the office, where all the afternoon late writing my letters and doing business. But Lord, what a conflict I had with myself, my heart tempting me a thousand times to go abroad about some pleasure or other, notwithstanding the weather foul. However, I reproached myself with my weakness in yielding so much my judgment to my sense, and prevailed

---

a repl. 'pockt'   *b* repl. 'asked'   *c* 'and supped' repeated

---

1. Joseph Kirton's bookshop, in Paul's Churchyard.

with difficulty; and did not budge, but stayed within and to my great content did a great deal of business; and so home to supper and to bed.   This day I am told that Mall Davis, the pretty girl that sang and danced so well at the Duke's house, is dead.[1]

18.   And by coach with Sir W. Batten and Sir Tho. Allen to White-hall: and there, after attending the Duke as usual, and there concluding of many things preparative to the Prince and the Generalls going to sea on Monday next – Sir W. Batten and Sir Tho. Allen and I to Mr. Lillys the painter's, and there saw the heads, some finished and all begun, of the Flaggmen in the late great fight with the Duke of Yorke against the Dutch.[2]   The Duke of York hath them done to hang in his chamber, and very finely they are done endeed.[3]   There is the Prince's – Sir G. Askues, Sir Tho. Teddiman's – Sir Chr. Mings, Sir Joseph Jordan, Sir Wm. Barkely, Sir Tho. Allen, and Captain Harman's, as also the Duke of Albemarles – and will be my Lord Sandwiche's, Sir W Pen's, and Sir Jerem. Smiths.   Being very well satisfied with this sight, and other good pictures hanging in the house, we parted; and I left them, and [to] pass away a little time went to the printed picture-seller's in the way thence to the Exchange; and there did see great plenty of fine prints but did not buy any, only a print of

1. This was untrue: see below, 7 March 1667. She eventually became one of Charles II's mistresses and left the stage. (A).

2. The Battle of Lowestoft, June 1665.

3. There were 13 in this set of portraits of flag-officers. Eight were hanging in the Great Chamber at Culford in October 1671 (Bodl., MS. 891, f. 22*r*) and after the Duke's accession they were at St James's Palace. Thereafter they were at Windsor, but in 1824 George IV presented to Greenwich Hospital the portraits of eleven: Harman, Smith, Teddeman, Jordan, the Duke of Albemarle, Myngs, Allin, Sandwich, Penn, Berkeley and Ayscue. These are now in the National Maritime Museum. The portrait of Prince Rupert was retained, however, and is still in the royal collection. That of Sir John Lawson was also kept, probably by accident, and only a copy went with the set to Greenwich. The heads in the series are among Lely's most incisive and sensitive portraits, but in each case the rest of the canvas seems to show extensive participation of assistants in his studio. O. Millar, *Tudor, Stuart and early Georgian pictures in coll. H.M. Queen* (1963), nos 252, 254, with refs. See below, p. 209, n. 2. (OM).

an*a* old pillar in Rome, made for a Navall Triumph, which for the antiquity of the shape of ships I buy and keep.[1]

Thence to the Exchange, that is, the New Exchange, and looked over some play-books, and entend to get all the late new plays. So to Westminster and there at the Swan got a bit of meat and dined alone, and so away toward King's-street; and spying out of my coach Jane that lived heretofore at Jervas my barber's, I went a little further, and stopped and went on foot back and overtook her taking water at Westminster-bridge[2] and spoke to her; and she telling me whither she was going, I over the water and met her at Lambeth, and there drank with her, she telling me how he that was so long her servant* did prove to be a married man, though her maister told me (which she denies) that he had lain with her several times at his house.

There left her, sin hazer alguna cosa con ella; and so away by boat to the Change and took coach and to Mr. Hales, where he would have persuaded me to have had the landskip stand in my picture; but I like it not and will have it otherwise, which I perceive he doth not like so well – however, is so civil as to say it shall be altered. Thence away to Mrs. Pierces, who was not at home, but gone to my house to visit me with Mrs. Knipp. I therefore took up the little girl Betty and my maid Mary that now lives there. And to my house, where they had been but were gone; so in our way back again, met them coming back again to my house in Cornehill, and there stopped, laughing at our pretty misfortunes; and so I carried them to Fish-street and there treated them with prawns and lobsters; and it beginning to grow dark, we away; but the jest is, our horses would not draw us up the Hill, but we were fain to light and stay till the coachman had made them draw down to the bottom of the hill, thereby warming their

a repl. 'a'

---

1. Probably a version of the print (1575) by Antonio Lafreri of the column (now destroyed) raised in celebration of Gaius Duilius's naval victory off Mylae in Sicily over the Carthaginians (260 B.C.). The column was ornamented in bronze with representations of the beaks of the captured vessels which project from the sides. The print (which also contains a drawing of another column) was not retained in the PL. Illust. in Lafreri, *Speculum Romanae magnificentiae* (Rome, n.d.), no. 81.

2. Jetty: the bridge across the river was not completed until 1750.

legs; and then they came up cheerfully enough, and we got up and I carried them home; and coming home, called at my paper ruler's and there found black* Nan, which pleases me mightily; and having saluted her again and again, away home and to bed – apres ayant tocado les mamelles de Mercer, que eran ouverts, con grand plaisir.

So to bed. ⟨In all my riding in the coach, and intervals, my mind hath been full these three weeks of setting to music *It is decreed* &c..⟩[1]

19. Lay long in bed; so to the office, where all the morning. At noon dined with Sir W Warren at the Pope's-head. So back to the office, and there met with the Comissioners of the Ordnance, where Sir W Pen, being almost drunk, vexed me, and the more because Mr. Chichly observed it with me – and it was a disparagement to the office.

They gone, I to my office. Anon comes home my wife from Brampton – not looked for till Saturday; which will hinder me of a little pleasure, but I am glad of her coming. She tells me Palls business with Ensum[2] is like to go on; but I must give, and she consents to it, another 100*l.* She says she doubts my father is in want of money, for rents come in mighty slowly.[3] My mother grows very impatient and troublesome, and my father mighty infirm, through his old distemper[4] – which all together makes me mighty thoughtful. Having heard all this, and bid her welcome, I to the office, where late; and so home, and after a little more talk with my wife, she to bed and I after her.

20. Up, and after an hour or two's talk with my poor wife, who gives me more and more content every day then other, I abroad by coach to Westminster; and there met with Mrs. Martin, and she and I over the water to Stangate; and after a walk in the fields, to the King's-head[5] and there spent an hour or two with pleasure with her, and eat a tansy and so parted. And I to the New Exchange, there to get a list of all the modern plays –

1. See above, p. 91, n. 4. (E).
2. See above, p. 78 & n. 2.
3. There were many complaints of a fall in rents in the 1660s: cf. below, 9 April 1667 & n.

4. Probably the rupture in the groin referred to above, at iv. 118.
5. Probably in the village of Lambeth, nr St Mary's church. (R).

which I entend to collect and to have them bound up together.[1]
Thence to Mr. Hales; and there, though against his perticular
mind, I had my landskip done out, and only a heaven made in the
room of it; which though it doth not please me thoroughly now
it is done, yet it will do better then as it was before.[2]

Thence to Paul's church-yard and there bespoke some new
books. And so to my ruling-woman's and there did see my
work a-doing; and so home and to my office a little, but was
hindered of business I entended by being sent for to Mrs. Turner,[3]
who desired some discourse with me and lay her condition before
me, which is bad and poor. Sir Tho Harvy[4] entends again to
have lodgings in her house, which she prays me to prevent if I can
– which I promised. Thence to talk generally of our neighbours.
I find she tells me the faults of all of them and their bad words of
me and my wife, and endeed doth discover more then I thought.
But I told her, and so will practise, that I will have nothing to do
with any of them. She ended all with a present of shells[5] to my
wife, very fine ones indeed, and seems to have great respect and
honour for my wife. So home and to bed.

21. Up betimes and to the office, there to prepare some things
against the afternoon, for discourse about the business of the
pursers and settling the pursers' matters of the fleet according to
my proposition.[6] By and by the office sat; and they being up, I
continued at the office to finish my matters against the meeting
before the Duke this afternoon; so home about 3 to clap a bit of
meat in my mouth, and so away with Sir W. Batten to White-
hall – and there to the Duke; but he being to go abroad to take
the ayre, he dismissed us presently – without doing anything till
tomorrow morning. So my Lord Brouncker and I down to
walk in the garden, it being a mighty hot and pleasant day; and
there was the King, who, among others, talked to us a little; and
among other pretty things, he swore merrily that he believed the

1. Pepys eventually acquired a
collection, in two volumes, of what
was called in the binder's title 'Loose
Plays': PL 1075, 1604. The first has
14 plays published between 1638 and
1667; the second, 13 published
between 1664 and 1685.

2. See above, pp. 97–8 & n.
(OM).

3. Wife of Thomas Turner of the
Navy Office.

4. Navy Commissioner.

5. Cf. above, i. 148, n. 2.

6. See above, p. 1 & n. 1.

Ketch that Sir W. Batten bought the last year at Colchester was of his own getting, it was so thick to its length.   Another pleasant thing he said of Chr. Pett, commending him that he will not alter his moulds of his ships upon any man's advice ("as", says he, "Comissioner Taylor, I fear, doth of his *New London*, that he makes it differ, in hopes of mending the *Old London*, built by him): for," says he, "he finds that God hath put him into the right, and so will keep in it while he is in.   And," says the King, "I am sure it must be God put him in, for no art of his own ever could have done it" – for it seems he cannot give a good account of what he doth as an Artist.

Thence with my Lord Brouncker in his coach to Hide parke, the first time I have been there this year.   There the King was, but I was sorry to see my Lady Castlemaine; for the mourning[1] forcing all the ladies to go in black, with their hair plain, and without any spots, I find her to be a much more ordinary woman then ever I durst have thought she was; and endeed is not so[a] pretty as Mrs. Stewart – whom I saw there also.   Having done at the park, he set me down at the Exchange, and I by coach home and there to my letters; and they being done, to writing a large letter about the business of the pursers to Sir W. Batten against to-morrow's discourse.[2]   And so home and to bed.

22. *Lords day.*   Up, and put on my new black cloak-Coate: long, down to my knees – and with Sir W. Batten to White-hall, where all in deep mourning for the Queen's mother.   There had great discourse before the Duke and Sir W. Coventry begun the discourse[b] of the day about the pursers business; which I seconded, and with great liking to the Duke – whom, however, afterward my Lord Brouncker and Sir W. Penn did stop by something they said, though not much to the purpose; yet because our proposi-tion had some appearance of certain charge to the King, it was ruled that for this year we should try another way, the same in every respect with ours, leaving out one circumstance, of allowing the pursers the victuals of all men short of the complement.

---

    1. For the Queen's mother: see   Gibson's hand) NMM, LBK/8, pp.
above, p. 84 & n. 2.   377-8; printed in *Further Corr.*, pp.
    2. Dated this day; copy (in   126-30.

I was very well satisfied with it and am contented to try it, wishing it may prove effectual.

Thence away with Sir W. Batten in his coach home – in our way he telling me the certain news, which was afterward confirmed to me this day by several, that the Bishopp of Munster hath made a league [with] the Hollanders, and that our King and Court are displeased much at it – moreover, we are not sure of Sweden.[1] I home to my house and there dined mighty well, my poor wife, and Mercer and I. So back again, walked to White-hall, and there to and again in the park, till, being in the shoemaker's stocks,[2] I was heartily weary. Yet walked however to the Queen's Chappell at St. James's, and there saw a little mayd Baptized – many parts and words whereof are the same with that of our liturgy – and little that is more ceremonious then ours. Thence walked to Westminster and there eat a bit of bread and drank, and so to Worster-house[3] and there stayed and saw the Council up; and then back, walked to the Cockepitt, and there took my leave of the Duke of Albemarle – who is going to-morrow to sea. He seems mightily pleased with me, which I am glad of. But I do find infinitely my concernment in being*a* careful to appear to the King and Duke to continue my care of his business, and to be found diligent as I used to be. Thence walked wearily as far as Fleet*b*-street, and so there met a coach and home – to supper and to bed – having sat a great while with Will Joyce, who came to see me – and it is the first time I have seen him at my house since the plague, and find him the same impertinent prating coxcomb that ever he was.

23. Being mighty weary last night, lay long this morning then up and to the office, where Sir W. Batten, Lord Brouncker,

a repl. 'having'   *b* repl. symbol badly formed

---

1. Münster made peace with the Dutch on 8/18 April at Clèves, largely out of fear of a French attack in the spring. Sweden now repudiated the clumsy overtures England had made for her friendship, and entered into an agreement with the French.

2. Wearing new shoes.

3. On the s. side of the Strand, where Clarendon lodged; council meetings were often held there when he was laid up with gout.

and I met; and toward noon took coach – and to White-hall, where I had the opportunity to take leave of the Prince, and again of the Duke of Albemarle – and saw them kiss the King's hand and the Duke's. And much content endeed there seems to be in all people at their going to sea, and promise themselfs much good from them. This morning the House of parliament have*a* met, only to Adjourne again till winter.[1] The plague I hear encreases in the town much, and exceedingly in the country everywhere.[2]

Thence walked to Westminster-hall; and after a little stay there, there being nothing now left to keep me there, Betty Howlett being gone, I took coach and away home, in my way asking in two or three places the worth of pearl – I being now come to the time that I have long ago promised my wife a necklace.[3]

Dined at home, and took Balty with me to Hales's to show him his sister's picture;[4] and thence to Westminster, and there I to the Swan and drank; and so back again alone to Hales and there met my wife and Mercer – Mrs. Pierce being sitting, and two or three idle people of her acquaintance more standing by. Her picture doth come on well. So stayed till she had done, and then set her down at home; and my wife and I and the girl by*b* coach to Islington, and there eat and drank in the coach; and so home and there find a girl, sent at my desire by Mrs. Michell of Westminster-hall to be my girl under the cook-maid, Susan; but I am a little dissatisfied that the girl, though young, is taller and bigger then Su, and will not I fear be under her command; which will trouble me, and the more because she is recommended by a friend that I would not have any unkindness with. But my wife doth like very well of her.

a MS. 'of' (phonetic spelling)   *b* repl. 'took'

1. Parliament had been prorogued (not adjourned) on 23 February until this day, and was now prorogued again until 18 September: *CJ*, viii. 624.
2. 40 plague victims had been buried in London during 10–17 April; 28 during the previous week (GL, A.1.5, no. 96), and the fear was that the warmer weather would bring still worse news. After May, however, the worst was over in the capital. In the provinces the peak of the epidemic was reached in the summer – a few towns, such as Deal and Colchester, suffering proportionately more heavily than London. See below, pp. 193, 241; Bell, *Plague*, pp. 321+.
3. See above, vi. 201; below, p. 113 & n. 1.
4. See above, p. 93, n. 1. (OM).

So to my accounts and Journall at my chamber – there being bonefires in the street, for being St. George's day and the King's Coronation and the day of the Prince and Duke's going to sea. So having done my business, to bed.

24. Up, and presently am told that the girl that came yesterday hath packed up her things to be gone home again to Enfield, whence she came – which I was glad of, that we might be at first rid of her altogether, rather then be liable to her going away hereafter. The reason was that London doth not agree with her. So I did give her something, and away she went.

By and by comes Mr. Bland to me, the first time since his coming from Tanger, and tells me, in short, how all things are out of order there, and like to be – and the place never likely to come to anything while the soldier governs all and doth not encourage trade.[1] He gone, I to the office, where all the morning. And so to dinner, and there in the afternoon very busy all day till late; and so home to supper and to bed.

25. Up, and to White-hall to the Duke as usual and did our business there. So I away to Westminster (Balty with me, whom I had presented to Sir W. Coventry), and there told Mrs. Michell of her kinswoman's running away, which troubled her. So home, and there find another little girl come from my wife's mother – likely to do well. After dinner I to the office, where Mr Prinn came to meet about the Chest business;[2] and till company came, did discourse with me a good while alone in the garden about the laws of England, telling me the many faults in them; and among others, their obscurity through multitude of long statutes, which he is about to abstract out of all of a sort, and as he lives, and parliaments come, get them put into laws and the other statutes repealed; and then it will be a short work to know

1. Civil government was not established in Tangier until June 1668. John Bland was the principal merchant and first mayor of the town. For the disputes between the garrison and the traders, see Harris, ii. 153–9.

2. William Prynne and Pepys, with the others mentioned later in this entry, were members of the commis-sion appointed in 1662 to inspect the accounts of the Chatham Chest. The commission's minute-book is blank between April 1664 and March 1666: BM, Add. 9317. The orders decided on at this meeting are minuted ib., f. 11*v*. According to the entry there, Penn also attended.

the law – which appears a very noble good thing.[1] By and by Sir W. Batten [and] Sir W Rider met with us, and we did something to purpose about the Chest and hope we shall go on to do so. They up, I to present Balty to Sir W Pen, who at my entreaty did write a most obliging letter to Harman to use him civilly; but the dissembling of that rogue is such, that it doth not oblige me at all.

So abroad to my ruler's of my books, having, God forgive me, a mind to see Nan there, which I did; and so back again, and then out again to see Mrs. Bettons, who were looking out of the window as I came through Fan*a* church-street – so that endeed I am not, as I ought to be,*b* able to command myself in the pleasures of my eye.

So home, and with my wife and Mercer spent our evening upon our new leads by our bedchamber, singing, while Mrs. Mary Batelier[2] looked out of the window to us; and we talked together and at*c* last bade goodnight. However, my wife and I stayed there, talking of several things with great pleasure till 11 a-clock at night; and it is a convenience I would not want for anything in the world, it being methinks better then almost any room in my house. So having supped upon the leads, to bed.

The plague, blessed be God, is decreased [to] 16 this week.[3]

26. To the office, where all the morning. At noon home to dinner; and in the afternoon to my office again, where very busy all the afternoon, and perticulary about fitting of Mr. Yeabsly's accounts for the view of the Lords Commissioners for Tanger.[4] At night home to supper, and to bed.

27. Up (taking Balty with me, who lay at my house last [night] in order to his going away today to sea with the pursers

---

a repl. 'Fanch'-   *b* MS. has full-stop   *c* repl. 'all'

---

1. Possibly the volumes on the royal supremacy which Prynne was now in course of publishing (his *Exact chronologicall . . . demonstration of our . . . King's supreme ecclesiasticall jurisdiction*, 3 vols, 1665, 1666, 1668; usually known as Prynne's *Records*) were a part of this scheme. But the project was never completed.

2. See above, p. 15 & n. 4.
3. From 40 in the previous week: GL, A.1.5, no. 96.
4. Thomas Yeabsley of Plymouth had a victualling contract for Tangier. See below, p. 128 & n. 3.

of the *Henery*, whom I appointed to call him). Abroad to many several places about several businesses: to my Lord Treasurer's, Westminster, and I know not where. At noon to the Change a little, and then bespoke some maps to hang in my new Roome (my boy's room), which will be very pretty. Home to dinner; and after dinner to the hanging up of maps and other things for the fitting of the room, and now it will certainly be one of the handsomest and most useful rooms in my house – so that what with this room and the room on my leads, my house is half as*ª* good again as it was. All this afternoon about this, till I was so *ᵇ* weary, and it was late, I could do no more, but finished the room; so I did not get out to the office all the day long. At night spent a good deal of time with my wife and Mercer, teaching them a song; and so after supper, to bed.

28. Up and to the office. At noon dined at home. After dinner abroad with my wife to Hales's to see only our pictures and Mrs. Pierce's, which I do not think so fine as I might have expected it. My wife to her father's to carry him some ruling work which I have advised her to let him do; it will get him some money. She also is to look out again for another little girl, the last we had being also gone home, the very same day she came. She was also to look after a necklace of pearl, which she is mighty busy about, I being contented to lay out 8*o*l in one for her.

I home to my business. By and by comes my wife, and presently after that, tide serving, Balty took leave of us, going to sea, and upon very good terms, to be muster-maister of a squadron, which will be worth 100*l* this year to him, besides keeping*ᵉ* him the benefit of his pay in*ᵈ* the guard.[1]

He gone, I very busy all the afternoon till night – among other things, writing a letter to my brother John, the first I have done since my being angry with him;[2] and that so sharp a one too, that I was*ᵉ* sorry almost to send it when I had wrote it; but it is pre-

a repl. 'with'   *b* repl. same symbol badly formed
c repl. 'giving'   *d* repl. same symbol badly formed   *e* repl. 'will'

---

1. Pepys this day wrote to Harman (commander of the *Royal Charles* and Rear-Admiral of the Blue), recommending Balty and asking that he be allowed a cabin in which to work: *Further Corr.*, pp. 130–1.

2. For their quarrel, see above, iv. 91.

parative to my being kind to him, and sending for him up hither when he hath passed his degree of Maister in Arts. So home to supper and to bed.

29. *Lords day.* Up and to church, where Mr. Mills; a lazy, simple sermon upon the Devil's having no right to anything in this world. So home to dinner; and after dinner I and my boy down by water to Redriffe; and thence walked to Mr. Evelin's,[1] where I walked in his garden till he came from church, with great pleasure reading Ridlys discourse all my way going and coming, upon the Civill and Ecclesiastical Law.[2] He being come home, he and I walked together in the garden with mighty pleasure, he being a very ingenious man, and the more I know him, the more I love him. His chief business with me was to propose having my Cosen Tho. Pepys in Commission of the Peace; which I do not know what[a] to say to till I speak with him, but should be glad of it – and will put him upon it.[3]

Thence walked back again, reading; and so took water and home, where I find my Uncle and Aunt Wight and supped with them upon my leads with mighty pleasure and mirth. And they being gone, I mighty weary to bed, after having my hair of my head cut shorter, even close to my skull, for coolness, it being mighty hot weather.

30. Up, and being ready to finish my journalls for four days past[b] – to the office, where busy all the morning. At noon dined alone, my wife gone abroad to conclude about her necklace of pearl. I after dinner to even all my accounts of this month; and, bless God, I find myself, notwithstanding great expenses of late – *viz.*, 80*l* now to pay for a necklace – near 40*l* for a set of chairs and couch – near 40*l* for my three pictures[4] – yet I do

a repl. 'not'   *b* repl. same symbol

---

1. John Evelyn lived at Sayes Court, Deptford.

2. Sir Thomas Ridley, *A view of the civile and ecclesiasticall law* (3rd ed. 1662, octavo); PL 899.

3. Evelyn was a neighbour of Thomas Pepys, who lived at Hatcham, Surrey. Presumably he proposed to recommend his name to the

Lord Lieutenant of the county for submission to the Lord Chancellor. See below, p. 114, n. 1. He seems to have escaped the office himself.

4. Presumably the three portraits by Hayls of Pepys himself (£14), his wife (£14) and his father (£10). (OM).

gather, and am now worth 5200*l*. My wife comes home by and by, and hath pitched upon a necklace with three rows, which is a very good one, and 80*l* is the price.[1] In the evening, having finished my accounts to my full content and joyed that I have evened them so plainly, remembering the trouble my last accounts did give me by being let alone a little longer then ordinary,[2] by which to this day I am at a loss for 50*l*. I hope I shall never commit such an error again, for I cannot devise where the 50*l* should be; but it is plain I ought to be worth 50*l* more then I am, and blessed be God the error was no greater.

In the evening with my [wife] and Mercer[a] by coach to take the ayre as far as Bow, and eat and drank in the coach by the way, and with much pleasure and pleased with my company: at night home and up to the leads; but were, contrary to expectation, driven down again with a stink, by Sir W Pen's emptying of a shitten pot in their house of[b] office close by; which doth trouble me, for fear it do hereafter annoy me. So down to sing a little, and then to bed.

So ends this month, with great layings-out – good health and gettings, and advanced well in the whole of my estate; for which God make me thankful.[c]

a l.h. repl. s.h.   *b* 'of' repeated   *c* followed by one blank page

---

1. Pepys had promised on 22 August 1665 to give her a pearl necklace within two years at most, and in less if she pleased him in her painting. According to a family tradition, it survives as an heirloom in the possession of the Pepys Cockerells; at one time there were four such 'Pepys necklaces' (Inf. from J. L. Pepys Cockerell of Aldermaston, Berks.). Cf. illust. in *Country Life*, 4 June 1927, p. 922, fig. 4; *Pepysiana*, p. 23.

2. Cf. above, p. 65.

MAY.

1. Up, and all the morning at the office. At noon my Cosen Tho. Pepys did come to me to consult about the business of his being a Justice of the Peace, which he is much against; and among other reasons, tells me as a confidence*a* that he is not free to exercise punishment according to the act against Quakers and other people, for religion.[1] Nor doth he understand Latin, and so is not capable of the place as formerly, now all warrants do run in Latin.[2] Nor is he in Kent, though he be of Deptford parish, his house standing in Surry. However, I did bring him to encline toward it if he be pressed to take it. I do think it may be some repute to me to have my kinsman in commission there – especially if he behave himself to content in the country.

He gone, and my wife gone abroad, I out also, to and fro to see and be seen; among others, to find out in Thames-street where Betty Howlett is come to live, being married to Mrs. Michells son – which I did about the Old Swan, but did not think fit to go thither or see them. Thence by water to Redriffe, reading a new French book my Lord Brouncker did give me today, *L'histoire amoureuse des Gaules*, being a pretty Libell against the amours of the Court of France.[3] I walked up and down

a MS. 'confident'

---

1. The act was the Conventicle Act (1664); chief of the four acts passed since the Restoration against nonconformity. Thomas Pepys had served as a J.P. in Westminster during the Interregnum. There is no record of his now being put on the commission.

2. In the Interregnum warrants (and most legal proceedings) had been in English, by virtue of two acts of 1650 and 1651.

3. The book was by Roger de Rabutin, Comte de Bussy (d. 1695), and is not in the PL. Composed in 1659–60, it was a *chronique scandaleuse* of the court ladies of the time (thinly disguised under other names) written for the amusement of his mistress. Circulated for a while in MS., it had been published (with a key) early in 1655, against the author's wishes, in Holland. De Bussy was imprisoned in April 1665 by order of Louis XIV, and later banished from court. Several editions appeared in 1665 and 1666, usually without dates; some have intercalations by other hands. See the edition by P. Boiteau (Paris, 1856); esp. vol. i, pp. viii–ix.

Deptford-yard, where I had not been since I came from living at Greenwich – which is some months. There I met with Mr. Castle[1] and was forced against my will to have his company back with me. So we walked and drank at the Halfway-house, and so to his house, where I drank a cup of Syder; and so home – where I find Mr. Norbury, newly come to town, come to see us. After he gone, my wife tells me the ill News that our Su is sick, and gone to bed with great pain in her head and back – which troubles us all. However, we to bed, expecting what tomorrow would produce. She hath, we conceive, wrought a little too much, having neither maid nor girl to help her.

2. Up, and find the girl better, which we are glad of. I with Sir W. Batten to White-hall by coach. There attended the Duke as usual. Thence with Captain Cocke, whom I met there, to London to my office to consult about serving him in getting him some money, he being already tired of his slavery to my Lord Brouncker and the charge it costs him, and gets no manner of courtesy from him for it. He gone, I home to dinner. Find the girl yet better, so no fear of being forced to send her out of doors as we intended. After dinner, by water to White-hall to a Committee for Tanger up[on] Mr. Yeabsly's business,[2] which I got referred to a committee to examine. Thence, among other stops, went to my ruler's house[3] and there stayed a great while with Nan, idling away the afternoon with pleasure. By and by home. So to my office a little, and then home to supper with my wife – the girl being pretty well again; and then to bed.

3. Up, and all the morning at the office. At noon home, and contrary to my expectation find my little*a* girl Su worse then she was, which troubled me; and the more to see my wife minding her painting, and not thinking of her house business (this being the first day of her beginning the second time to paint). This together made me froward, that I was angry with

a repl. 'wife'

---

1. William Castle, shipbuilder, of Redriff Wall; Batten's son-in-law.
2. See above, p. 110 & n. 3.

3. The old woman who ruled his paper: above, p. 98.

I

my wife and would not have Browne[1] to think to dine at my
table with me always, being desirous to have my house to myself,
without a stranger and a Mechanique to be privy[a] to all my
concernments. Upon this my wife and I had a little disagree-
ment, but it ended by and by. And then to send up and down
for a nurse to take the girle home, and would have given anything; I offered to the only one that we could get 20s per week,
and we to find clothes and bedding and physic. And would
have given 30s as demanded, but desired an hour or two's time.
    So I away by water to Westminster and there sent for the
girl's mother to Westminster-hall to me; she came, and undertakes to get her daughter a lodging and nurse at next door to
her, though she dare not, for the parish sake (whose sexton her
husband is), to [take] her into her own house. Thence home,
calling at my bookseller's and other trifling places, three or four,
and so home. And in the evening the mother came, and with a
nurse she hath got, who demanded, and I did agree at, xs per
week to take her. And so she away – and my house mighty[b]
uncouth, having so few in it, and we shall want a servant or two
by it. And the truth is, my heart was a little sad all the afternoon, and jealous of myself. But she went, and we all glad of it.
And so a little to[c] the[d] office; and so to home to supper and
to bed.

    4. Up, and by water to Westminster to Charing-cross (Mr.
Gregory for company with me) to Sir Ph. Warwicke's, who was
not within. So I took Gregory to White-hall, and there spoke
with Joseph Williamson to have leave in the next *Gazette* to
have a general pay for the Chest at Chatham declared upon such
a day in June.[2] Here I left Gregory, and I by coach back again
to Sir Ph. Warwicks and in the park met him walking; so

---

a repl. 'my'   *b* MS. 'my'
c repl. 'and then home'   *d* 'to the office' repeated

---

    1. Alexander Browne, her drawing
master.
    2. The advertisement appeared in
the *London Gazette* of 14 May (not
the next, but the next-but-two) and

announced a general pay at H.M.'s
Pay-house in Chatham on 1 June,
covering the period from Lady Day
past.

discoursed about the business of striking a quarter's tallies for Tanger due this day, which he hath promised to get my Lord Treasurer's warrant for; and so away thence, and to Mr. Hales to see what he had done to Mrs. Pierce's picture; and whatever he pretends, I do not think it will ever be so good a picture as my wife's. Thence home to the office a little, and then to dinner – and had a great fray with my wife again about Brown's coming to teach*[a]* her to paint and sitting with me at table, which I will not yield to. I do thoroughly believe she means no hurt in it, but very angry we were; and I resolved all into my having my will done without disputing, be the reason what it will – and so I will have it. After dinner abroad again, and to the New Exchange about play-books – and to White-hall, thinking to have met Sir G Carteret, but failed. So to the Swan at Westminster, and there spent quarter of an hour with Jane and thence away home. And my wife coming home by and by (having been at her mother's to pray her to look out for a maid for her), by coach into the fields to Bow; and so home back in the evening late home – and after supper to bed – being much out of order for lack of somebody in the room of Su. ⟨This evening, being weary of my late idle courses and the little good I shall do the King or myself in the office, I bound myself to very strict rules till Whitsunday next.⟩*[b]*

5. At the office all the morning. After dinner, upon a letter*[c]* from the fleet from Sir W Coventry, I did do a great deal of work for the sending away of the victuallers that are in the River &c. – too much to remember.[1] Till 10 at night busy about letters and other necessary matters of the office. About 11, I home, it being a fine moonshine;*[d]* and so my wife and Mercer came into the garden, and my business being done, we sang till about 12 at night with mighty pleasure to ourselfs and neighbours, by their Casements opening. And so home to supper and to bed.

a repl.' my'   *b* addition crowded in between entries
     c repl. 'littler'   *d* repl. 'moonship'

---

1. The fleet was now at the Nore. Coventry's letter has not been traced.

6. *Lords day.* To church – home; and after dinner walked to White-hall, thinking to have seen Mr. Coventry, but failed, and therefore walked clear on foot back again. Busy till night in fitting my victualling papers in order, which I fear, through my multitude of*ᵃ* business ⟨and pleasure⟩, have not examined*ᵇ* these several month. Walked*ᶜ* back again home, and so to the Victualling Office, where I met Mr. Gawden and have received some satisfaction, though it be short of what I expected and what might be expected from him.*ᵈ* So this evening I have given.¹ And so to supper and to bed.

7. Up betimes to set my victualling papers in order against Sir W. Coventry comes – which endeed makes me very melancholy, being conscious that I am much to seek in giving a good answer to his queries about the victualling businesses. At the office mighty busy, and brought myself into a pretty plausible condition before Sir W. Coventry came, and did give him a pretty tolerable account of everything; and went with him unto*ᵉ* the Victualling Office, where we sat and examined his businesses and state of the victualling of the fleet; which made me in my heart blush that I could say no more to it then I did or could – but I trust in God I shall never be in that condition again. We parted, and I with pretty good grace; and so home to dinner, where my wife troubled more and more with her swollen cheek. So to dinner ⟨my sister-in-law² with us, who I find more and more a witty woman⟩. And then I to my Lord Treasurer's and the Exchequer about my Tanger businesses. And with mighty*ᶠ* content passed by all things and persons, without so much as desiring any stay or loss of time with them, being by strong vow obliged on no occasion to stay abroad but my public offices. So home again, where I find Mrs. Pierce and Mrs. Ferrers come to see my wife. I stayed a little with them, being full of business; and so to the office, where busy till

---

a repl. symbol rendered illegible   *b* repl. 'passed'   *c* repl. 'or two'
     d MS. 'me'   *e* repl. 'into'   *f* MS. 'my'

---

1. Sentence incomplete.   2. Esther, wife of Balty St Michel.

late at night; and so, weary – and a little conscious of my failures today, yet proud that the day is*a* over without more observation on Sir W. Coventry's part; and so to bed and to sleep soundly.

8. Up and to the office all the morning. At noon dined at home – my wife's cheek bad still. After dinner to the office again; and thither comes Mr. Downing the Anchor-smith, who had given me 50 pieces in gold the last month to speak for him to Sir W. Coventry for his being smith at Deptford. But after I had got it granted him, he finds himself not fit to go on with it, so lets it fall – so hath no benefit of my motion; I therefore in honour and conscience took him home, and though much to my grief, did yet willingly and forcibly force him to take it again, the poor man having no mind to have it. However, I made him take it, and away he went; and I glad I had given him so much cause to speak well of me. So to my office again late; and then home to supper to a good lobster with my wife; and then a little to my office again; and so to bed.

9. Up by 5 a-clock, which I have not a long time done, and down the river by water to Deptford; among other things, to examine the state of Ironworke, in order to the doing something with reference to Downing that may induce him to return me the 50 pieces. Walked back again, reading of my civil law book.[1] And so home and by coach to White-hall, where we did our usual business before the Duke – and heard the Duke commend Deane's ship ⟨the *Rupert*⟩ before the *Defyance*, built lately by Castle, in hearing of Sir W. Batten, which pleased me mightily.[2] Thence by water to Westminster and there looked after my Tanger Order; and so by coach to Mrs. Pierces, thinking to have gone to Hales's; but she was not ready, so away home and to dinner. And after dinner out by coach to Lovett's to have

a MS. 'it'

---

1. See above, p. 112, n. 2.   Castle's ship, above, vi. 7–8. For
2. Cf. the criticisms of William   Castle, see above, p. 115, n. 1.

forwarded*ᵃ* what I have doing there,¹ but find him and his pretty wife gone to my house – to show me something. So away to my Lord Treasurer's; and thence to Pierces, where I find Knipp and I took them to Hales's to see our pictures finished; which are very pretty, but I like not hers half so well as I thought at first, it being not so like, nor so well painted as I expected or as mine and my wife's are. Thence with them to Cornehill to call and choose a chimney-piece² for Pierce's closet; and so home, where my wife in mighty pain, and mightily vexed at my being abroad with these women – and when they were gone, called them "whores" and I know not what; which vexed me, having been so innocent with them. So I with them to Mrs. Turner's and there sat with them a while; anon my wife sends for me; I come, and what was it but to scold at me, and she would go abroad to take the ayre presently, that she would. So I left my company and went with her to Bow, but was vexed and spoke not one word to her all the way, going nor coming – or being come home; but went up*ᵇ* straight to bed. Half an hour after (she in the coach leaning on me, as being desirous to be friends), she comes up, mighty sick with a fit of the Cholique and in mighty pain, and calls for me out of the bed; I rose and held her; she prays me to forgive her, and in mighty pain we put her to bed – where the pain ceased by and by; and so had some sparagus to our beds-side for supper, and very kindly afterward to sleep, and good friends in the morning.

10. So up and to the office, where all the morning. At noon home to dinner, and there busy all the afternoon till past 6 a-clock; and then abroad with my wife by coach – who is now at great ease, her cheek being broke inward. We took with us Mrs. Turner, who was come to visit my wife, just as we were going out. A great deal of tittle-tattle discourse to little purpose;

a   repl. 'bespoke'   *b*   repl. same symbol

1. Lovett was a varnisher, now employed on Pepys's project of varnishing paper on one side to produce a smooth surface for his 'tables'. Pepys appears to have suggested it a year earlier (above, vi.

97), but the invention failed to prosper and was abandoned before being put into use.

2. For the practice of inserting pictures in overmantels, see above, iii. 25, n. 2. (OM).

I finding her (though in other things a very discreet woman) as very a gossip, speaking of her neighbours, as anybody.[1] Going out toward Hackny by coach for the ayre, the silly coachman carries us to Shorditch, which was so pleasant a piece of simplicity in him and us, that made us mighty merry. So back again late, it being wonderous hot all the day [and] night, and it lightening exceedingly all the way we went and came, but without Thunder. Coming home, we called at a little alehouse and had an eele-pie, of which my wife eat part, and brought home the rest. So being come home, we to supper and so to bed. This day came our new cook-maid Mary,[2] commended by Mrs. Batters.

11. Up betimes, and then away with Mr. Yeabsly to my Lord Ashly's; whither by and by comes Sir H. Cholmly and Creed, and then to my Lord and there entered into examination of Mr. Yeabsly's account[3] – wherein, as in all other things, I find him one of the most distinct men that ever I did see in my life. He raised many scruples, which were to be answered another day; and so parted, giving me an alarme how to provide myself against the day of my passing my accounts. Thence I to Westminster to look after the striking of my tallies, but nothing done or to be done therein. So to the Change to speak with Captain Cocke; among other things, about getting of the silver plates[4] of him, which he promises to do. But in discourse, he tells me that I should beware of my fellow-officers; and by name, told me that my Lord Brouncker should say in his hearing, before Sir W. Batten, of me, that he could undo that man if he would – wherein I think he is a foole; but however, it is requisite I be prepared against that man's friendship. Thence home to dinner alone, my wife being abroad. After dinner to the setting some things in order in my dining-room; and by and by comes my wife home, and Mrs. Pierce with her, so I lost most of this afternoon with them; and in the evening abroad with them, our long tour, by coach to Hackney, so to Kingsland, and then to

---

1. But cf. below, 21 May 1667, where Pepys reports her gossip without complaint, perhaps because it was critical of the Penns.

2. She lasted only a few weeks: below, p. 183.

3. See below, p. 128, n. 3.

4. See above, p. 91.

Islington, there entertaining them by candle-light very well; and so home with her, set her down, and so home*ᵃ* and to bed.

12. Up to the office very betimes to draw up a letter for the Duke of Yorke, relating to him the badness of our condition in this office for want of money.¹ That being in good time done, we met at the office and there sat all the morning. At noon home, where I find my wife troubled still at my checking her last night in the coach in her long stories out of *Grand Cyrus*,² which she would tell, though nothing to the purpose nor in any good manner. This she took unkindly, and I think I was to blame endeed – but she doth find, with reason, that in the company of Pierce – Knipp – or other women that I love, I do not value her, or mind her as I ought. However, very good friends by and by, and to dinner, and after dinner up to the putting our dining-room in order, which will be clean again anon, but not as it is to be, because of the pictures, which are not come home.

To the office and did much business; in the evening to Westminster and Whitehall about business, and among other things, met Sir G Downing on Whitehall bridge and there walked half an hour, talking of the success of the late new act; and endeed it is very much that that hath stood really in the room of 800000*l* now since Christmas, being itself but 1250000*l*.³ And so I do really take it to be a very considerable thing done by him, for the beginning, end, and every part of it is to be imputed to him.

So home by water, and there hard, till 12 at night, at work, finishing the great letter to the Duke of York against tomorrow morning; and so home to bed.

This day came home again my girle Susan, her sickness proving an ague, and she had a fit as soon almost as she came home.

a repl. 'to bed'

1. Dated this day: Longleat, Coventry, MSS 97, ff. 19–20. Copy (in Hayter's hand) in NMM, LBK/8, pp. 394–6; printed in *Further Corr.*, pp. 133–6. Another copy in Coventry MSS 96, ff. 110–11 (in Gibson's hand).

2. See above, i. 312, n. 2.

3. The Additional Aid of £1¼ m. levied from December 1665 had by Easter 1666 brought in £798,727 14*s*. 4*d*. according to Dr W. A. Shaw: *CTB*, vol. i, p. xxxi.

The fleet is not yet gone from the Nore. The plague encreases in many places, and is 53 this week with us.[1]

13. Up, and walked to White-hall, where we all met to present a letter to the Duke of York, complaining solemnly of the want of money. And that being done, I to and again up and down Westminster, thinking to have spent a little time with Sarah at the Swan, or Mrs. Martin, but was disappointed in both, so walked the greatest part of the way home – where comes Mr. Symons,[2] my old acquaintance, to dine with me; and I made myself as good company as I could to him, but he was mighty impertinent methought too, yet; and thereby I see the difference between myself now and what it was heretofore, when I reckoned him a very brave fellow.

After dinner he and I walked out together as far as Cheapside, and I quite through to Westminster again, and fell by chance into St. Margett's Church, where I heard a young man play the fool upon the doctrine of purgatory. At this church I spied Betty Howlett, who endeed is mighty pretty, and struck me mightily. I after church time standing in the churchyard, she spied me; so I went to her, her fathers and mothers and husband being with her. They desired, and I agreed, to go home with Mr. Michell; and there had the opportunity to have salute[d] two or three times Betty*a* and make an acquaintance; which they are pleased with, though not so much as I am or they think I am. I stayed here an hour or more, chatting with them in a little sorry garden of theirs by the Bowling Alley;[3] and so left them and I by water home, and there was in great pain in mind lest Sir W. Penn, who is going down to the fleet, should come to me or send for me to be informed in the state of things and perticularly the victualling, that by my pains he might seem wise;[4] so after

a name in s.h.

---

1. This was the London total (for 1–8 May); an increase of 13 over the previous week: GL, A.1.5, no. 96.

2. Will Simons, an underclerk to the Council when Pepys was a clerk in the Exchequer in 1660. In 1669 he was a clerk to the Brooke House Committee.

3. A street running south out of Dean's Yard.

4. On 11 May Penn had been ordered by Albemarle to see to the despatch of victualling ships: HMC, *Portland*, ii. 105.

spending an hour with my wife pleasantly in her closet, I to bed, even by daylight.

14. Comes betimes a letter from Sir W. Coventry that he and Sir G. Carteret are ordered presently down to the fleet. I up, and saw Sir W. Penn gone also after them; and so I, finding it a leisure day, fell to making clean my closet in my office, which[a] I did to my content, and set up my Platts again – being much taken also with Griffin's maid that did clean it – being a pretty maid.

I left her at it and toward Westminster, myself with my wife, by coach; and meeting, took up Mr. Lovett the varnisher with us – who is a pleasant-speaking and humoured man, so my wife much taken with him, and a good deal of work I believe I shall procure him.

I left my wife at the New Exchange, and myself to the Exchequer to look after my Tanger tallies; and there met Sir G. Downing, who showed me his present practice, now begun this day, to paste up upon the Exchequer-door a note of what Orders upon the new Act are paid and now in paying.[1]   And my Lord of Oxford coming by also, took him and showed him his whole method of keeping his books, and everything of it, which endeed is very pretty;[2] and at this day, there is assigned upon the Act 80400*l*.[3]

Thence at the New Exchange took up my wife again, and so home to dinner.   After dinner to my office again to set things in order.   In the evening[b], out with my wife and my aunt Wight to take the ayre, and happened to have a pleasant race between our Hackny-coach and a gentleman's.   At Bow we eat and drank, and so back again, it being very coole in the evening.   Having

a repl. 'when'   *b* repl.? 'men'-

---

1. See above, vi. 292, n. 3. The notices were also inserted in the *London Gazette*.

2. The act required that three books should be kept (for receipts, issues and assignments), and that they should be freely open to public inspection.

3. The bulk of this represented assignments to the Navy. By May c. £500,000 had been reserved for Carteret, and another £200,000 was due for cash loans and goods advanced: PRO, E 403/2800, 3047; E 401/1938.

set home my aunt and come home, I fell to examine my wife's kitchen book, and find 20s mistake, which made me mighty angry, and great difference between us. And so in that difference, to bed.

15. Up, and to the office, where we met and sat all the morning. At noon home to dinner; and after dinner by coach to Sir Ph. Warwickes, he having sent for me, but was not within. So I to my Lord Crew's, who is very lately come to town, and with*a* him talking half an hour of the business of the Warr; wherein he is very doubtful, from our want of money, that we shall fail – and I do concur with him therein. After some little discourse of ordinary matters, I away to Sir Ph. Warwickes again, and was come in and gone out to my Lord Treasurer's, whither I fallowed him, and there my business was to be told that my Lord Treasurer hath got 10000*l* for us in the Navy to answer our great necessities – which I did thank him for, but the sum is not considerable.[1] So home and there busy all the afternoon till night, and then home to supper and to bed.

16. Up very betimes, and so down the River to Deptford to look after some business, being by and by to attend the Duke and Mr. Coventry, and so I was willing to carry something fresh, that I may look as a man minding business, which I have done too much for a great while to forfeit – and is now so great a burden upon my mind night and day, that I do not enjoy myself in the world almost. I walked thither, and came back again by water; and so to White-hall and did our usual business before the Duke; and so I to the Exchequer, where the lazy rogues have not yet done my tallies, which vexes me. Thence to Mr. Hales and paid him for my picture and Mr. Hills: for the first, 14*l* for the picture and 25*s* for the frame; and for the other, 7*l* for the picture, it being a copy of his only, and 5*s* for the frame – in all, 22*l*. 10*s*. I am very well satisfied in my pictures and so took

a repl. 'within'

1. The Board in its letter of 12 May to the Duke of York had put its immediate needs at £167,000 for outstanding bills, and a weekly supply of £20,000: *Further Corr.*, p. 135.

them in another coach home along with me – and there with great pleasure my wife and I hung them up. And that being done, to dinner, where Mrs. Barbara Shelden came to see us and dined with us and we kept her all the day with us, I going down to Deptford; and Lord, to see with what itching desire I did endeavour to see Bagwell's wife, but failed, for which I am glad; only, I observe the folly of my mind, that cannot refrain from pleasure at a season, above all others in my life, requisite for me to show my utmost care in.

I walked both going and coming, spending my time reading of my Civill and Ecclesiastical law-book.[1] Being returned home, I took my wife and Mrs. Barb and Mercer out by coach, and went our Grand Tour[2] and baited at Islington, and so late home about 11 at night – and so, with much pleasure, to bed.

17. Up, lying long, being wearied yesterday with walking. So to the office, where all the morning, with fresh occasions of vexing at myself for my late neglect of business, by which I cannot appear half so useful as I used to do. Home at noon to dinner, and then to my office again, where I could not hold my eyes open for an hour, but I drowsed (so little sensible I apprehend my soul is of my necessity of minding business). But I anon wakened and minded my business, and did a very great deal with very great pleasure; and so home at night to supper and to bed – mightily pleased with myself for the business that I have done, and convinced that if I would but keep constantly to do the same, I might have leisure enough and yet do all my business; and by the grace of God, so I will.   So to bed.

18. Up by 5 a-clock, and so down by water to Deptford and Blackewall to despatch some business. So walked to Dike-shoare,[3] and there took boat again and home. And thence to Westminster and attended all the morning on the Exchequer for a quarter's tallies for Tanger: but Lord,[a] to see what a dull heavy sort of people they are there, would make a man mad. At

a repl. 'now'

---

1. See above, p. 112, n. 2.   3. Duke Shore, Limehouse.
2. See above, pp. 121–2. An
early use of the phrase.

noon had them, and carried them home and there dined with great content with my people, and within and at the office all the afternoon and night; and so home to settle some papers there, and so to bed, being not very well, having eaten too much Lobster at noon at dinner with Mr. Hollyerd, he coming in and commending it so much.

19. Up, and to the office all the morning. At noon took Mr. Deane (lately come to town) home with me to dinner;[a] and there, after giving him some reprimendes and good advice about his deportment in the place where by my interest he is at Harwich,[1] and then declaring my resolution of being his friend still – we did then fall to discourse about his ship *Rupert*, built by him there; which succeeds so well, as he hath got great honour by it, and I some by recommending him – the King, Duke, and everybody saying it is the best ship that was ever built. And then he fell to explain to me his manner of casting the draught of water which a ship will draw beforehand – which is a secret the King and all admire in him; and he is the first that hath come to any certainty beforehand of foretelling the draught of water of a ship before she be launched.[2] I must confess I am much pleased in his success in this business, and do admire * at the confidence of Castle, who did undervalue the draught[b] Deane sent up to me,[3] that I was ashamed to own it or him – Castle asking of me, upon the first sight of it, whether he that laid it

a repl. 'Harwich'   *b* repl. ? 'design'

---

1. Anthony Deane had been Master-Shipwright there since October 1664. Enquiries were being made concerning the conduct of his predecessor, John Browne. Pepys had written to Deane on the subject on 8 March and 5 May (*Further Corr.*, pp. 122–3, 131–2) – letters in which goodwill and frank criticism are admirably mingled. Deane's youthful brashness seems to have brought him into disrepute with Capt. Silas Taylor, Storekeeper at Harwich: ib., pp. 146, 154–5.

2. Such calculations were rare (see G. Naish in C. Singer *et al.*, *Hist. Technol.*, iii. 488+). Deane had now made them not only for his own ship the *Rupert*, but also for the *Royal Katherine*: *Further Corr.*, p. 132. Pepys retained in his library an undated MS. entitled 'Mr Deane's Method of measureing the Body of a Shipp and precalculateing her Draught of Water': PL 2501.

3. For Castle's criticism of the design, see Pepys to Deane, 14 March 1665: *Shorthand Letters*, pp. 36–8.

down had ever built a ship or no – which made me the more doubtful of him.

He being gone, I to the office, where much business and many persons to speak with me. Late home and to bed, glad to be at a little quiet.

20. *Lords day.* With my wife to church in the morning. At noon dined mighty nobly, ourselfs alone. After dinner, my wife and Mercer by coach to Greenwich to be gossip to Mrs. Daniel's child.[1] I out to Westminster, and straight to Mrs. Martin's and there did what I would with her, she staying at home all the day for me. And not being well pleased with her over-free and loose company, I away to Westminster Abbey and there fell in discourse with Mr. Blagrave,[2] whom I find a sober politic man, that gets money*a* and encrease of places; and thence by coach home, and thence by water (after I had discoursed awhile with Mr. Yeabsly, whom I met and took up in my coach with me, and who hath this day presented my Lord Ashly with 100*l* to bespeak his friendship to him in his accounts now before us; and my Lord hath received [it], and so I believe is as bad, as to bribes, as what the world says of him),[3] calling on all the victualling ships to know what they had of their complements; and so to

a MS. 'me'

---

1. John, son of John Daniel. Mrs Daniel was the daughter of Pepys's Greenwich landlady, Mrs Clerke.
2. Thomas or Robert Blagrave; both were court musicians. (E).
3. Yeabsley and his partners, who made an annual payment for the Tangier victualling contract, were claiming demurrage and a rebate for the loss of a ship by capture: PRO, Ao1/310/1220; cf. Rawl. A 193, f. 215r (Pepys to Lanyon, 20 January 1666). The story of the bribe is probably untrue: see K. H. D. Haley, *Shaftesbury*, p. 156. Ashley (Shaftesbury) was not corrupt and in any case was too rich to be corrupted by the gift of £100. Yeabsley had paid Pepys £300 p.a. since getting the contract (above, v. 120), and, according to Professor Haley's guess, may well have invented the story of the bribe in order to encourage Pepys to continue his support. Pepys's relations with the Tangier victuallers had not been frank – in 1665 he had put about a quite untrue story that he had lent money on his own credit to two Tangier contractors: above, vi. 86 & n. 1. Perhaps Yeabsley had discovered the truth.

Deptford to enquire after a little business there; and thence by water back again, all the way coming and going reading my Lord Bacons *Faber Fortunæ*,[1] which I can never read too often. And so back home, and there find my wife come home, much pleased with the reception she had there, and she was godmother and did hold*a* the child at the Font and it is called John.

So back*b* again home, and after setting my papers in order and supping, to bed, desirous to rise betimes in the morning.

21. Up between 4 and 5 a-clock and to set several*c* papers to rights, and so to the office, where we had an extraordinary meeting: but Lord, how it torments me to find myself so unable to give an account of my victualling business, which puts me out of heart in everything else, so that I never had a greater shame upon me in my own mind, nor more trouble as to public business then have now. But I will get out of it as soon as possibly I can.

At noon dined at home. And after dinner comes in my wife's brother Balty and his wife, he being stepped ashore from the fleet for a day or two.

I away in some haste to my Lord Ashly, where it is stupendous to see how favourably, and yet closely, my Lord Ashly carries himself to Mr. Yeabsly in his business, so as I think we shall do his business for him in very good manner. But it is a most extraordinary thing to observe, and that which I would not but have had the observation of for a great deal of money.

Being done there, and much forwarded Yeabsly's business, I with Sir H. Cholmly to my Lord Bellaces (who is lately come from Tanger) to visit him, but is not within; so to Westminster-hall a little about business, and so home by water; and then out with my wife, her brother, sister, and Mercer to Islington, our Grand tour, and there eat and drank. But in discourse I am infinitely please[d] with Balty his deportment in his business of muster-maister, and hope mighty well from him – and am glad with all my heart I put him into this business.

Late home, and to bed – they also lying at my house, he entending to go away tomorrow back again to sea.

a MS. 'holy'   *b* MS. 'to back'   *c* repl. 'my'

1. See above, ii. 102 & n. 1.

22. Up betimes, and to my business of entering some Tanger payments in my books in order; and then to the office, where very busy all the morning. At noon home to dinner – Balty being gone back to sea, and his wife dining with us, whom afterward my wife carried home. I after dinner to the office, and anon out on several occasions; among others, to Lovetts and there stayed by him and her, and saw them (in their poor-conditioned manner) lay on their varnish; which however pleased me mightily to see.

Thence home and to my business, writing letters; and so at night home to supper and to bed.

23. Up by 5 a-clock, and to my chamber, setting several matters in order. So out toward White-hall, calling in my way on my Lord Bellaces – where I came to his bedside and did give me a full and long account of his matters how he left them at Tanger.[1] Declares himself fully satisfied with my care. Seems cunningly to argue for encreasing the number of men there. Told me the whole story of his gains by the Turky prizes, which he owns he hath got about 5000*l* by.[2] Promised me the same profits Povy was to have had. And in fine, I find him a pretty subtle man; and so I left him and to White-hall before the Duke and did our usual business, and eased my mind of two or three things of weight that lay upon me about Lanyon's[3] salary, which I have got to be 150*l* per annum. Thence to Westminster to look after getting some little for some great tallies, but shall find trouble in it. Thence homeward, and met with Sir Ph. Warwicke and spoke about this, in which he is scrupulous. After that, to talk of the wants of the Navy; he lays all the fault now

1. Belasyse (Governor of Tangier, 1665–7) had arrived at Plymouth at the end of April, bringing news of his treaty with the Berbers: *CSPD 1665–6*, p. 363.

2. Belasyse's rapacity was well-known: cf. [?Marvell,] *Third advice to a painter* (1666), ll. 79–80: 'Let Bellasis' autumnal face be seen, /Rich with the spoils of a poor Algerine'. Prizes in Tangier (though technically subject to the jurisdiction of H.M.'s Principal Commissioners for Prizes in Whitehall) were at the disposal of the Governor, acting through powers of admiralty given to him by the Lord High Admiral. In theory, proceeds from their sale went to defray government expenses on the spot. A reorganisation was made in July of this year whereby a commission for prizes was set up in Tangier: Routh, p. 85, n. 3. Cf. Rawl. C 423, ff. 85r, 87r+.

3. Victualler for Tangier.

upon the new act,[1] and owns his own folly in thinking once so well of it as to give way to others' endeavours about it. And is grieved at heart to see what ⟨pass⟩ things are like to come to. Thence to the Excize Office to the Commissioners to get a meeting between them and myself and others about our concernments in the Excise for Tanger. And so to the Change a while, and thence home with Creed and find my wife at dinner with Mr. Cooke, who is going down to Hinchingbrooke; after dinner Creed and I and wife and Mercer out by coach, leaving them at the New Exchange, while I to Whitehall and there stayed at Sir G. Carteret's chamber till the Council rose; and then he and I, by agreement this morning, went forth in his coach by Tiburne to the park – discoursing of the state of the Navy as to money, and the state of the Kingdom too; how ill able to raise more. And of our office, as to the condition of the officers – he giving me caution as to myself, that there are those that are my enemies too, as well as his; and by name, my Lord Bruncker, who hath said some odd speeches against me. So that he advises me to stand on my guard – which I shall do; and unless my too-much addiction to pleasure undo me, will be hard enough for any of them. We rode to and again in the park a good while; and at last home and set me down at Charing-cross; and thence I to Mrs. Pierce's to take up my wife and Mercer – where I find her new picture by Hales doth not please her, nor me endeed, it making no show nor is very like nor no good painting. Home to supper and to bed – having my ⟨right⟩ eye sore and full of humour of late, I think by my late change of my brewer and having of 8*s* beere.[2]

24. Up very betimes, and did much business in my chamber. Then to the office, where busy all the morning. At noon rose, in the pleasantest humour I have seen Sir W. Coventry and the whole board in this twelvemonth – from a pleasant crossing

---

1. For all the effects of the Additional Aid, money was still short, and in June appeals for loans were made to the City. At 27 June Pepys reports Coventry as being pessimistic about the financial situation. See

above, vi. 292, 341–2; below, p. 159 & n. 4, p. 171 & n. 3.

2. I.e. strong beer. It cost in London about 6*s*.–10*s*. a barrel at this time; small beer about 5*s*.–6*s*.: Mdx R.O., Sessions Bk 214, p. 6.

K

humour Sir W. Batten was in, he being hungry and desirous to be gone.

Home; and Mr. Hunt came to dine with me, but I was prevented dining till 4 a-clock by Sir H Cholmly and Sir Jo. Bankes's coming in about some Tanger business. They gone, I to dinner, the others having dined. Mr. Sheply is also newly come out of the country,[1] and came to see us, whom I am glad to see. He left all well there; but I perceive under some discontent in my Lord's behalfe, thinking that he is under disgrace with the King. But he is not so at all, as Sir G. Carteret assures me.

They gone, I to the office and did business; and so in the evening abroad alone with my wife to Kingsland; and so back again and to bed, my right eye continuing very ill of the rheum which hath troubled it four or five days.

25. Up betimes, and to my chamber to do business, where the greatest part of the morning. Then out to the Change to speak with Captain [Cocke], who tells me my silver*a* plates[2] are ready for me, and shall be sent me speedily. And proposes another proposition of serving us with a thousand tons of hemp, and tells me it shall bring me 500*l* if the bargain go forward – which is a good word.[3]   Thence I to Sir G. Carteret, who is at

a repl. 'siver'

---

1. From Hinchingbrooke, where he was Sandwich's steward.

2. See above, pp. 90, 91.

3. Hemp was both expensive and difficult to come by. In the estimate drawn up in November 1666 for the fitting out of the fleet in the next spring it was by far the largest item. This offer of Cocke's met with many objections, chiefly from Coventry, because besides asking a high price (£57 a ton) and offering a late delivery date (November at earliest), Cocke demanded that other goods be taken with it, that the Navy be responsible for fetching it from Hamburg, and

that he be given preferential treatment in payment. It is not surprising that for all his bribes (not only to Pepys but also to Brouncker and his mistress) Cocke should have failed. He found himself in difficulties with the stuff on his hands, and in November, when other hemp had appeared on the market, agreed on a contract which gave him in effect £4 less per ton. Pepys's reward was a piece of plate. See below, esp. pp. 220–1; NMM, LBK/8, pp. 394, 398–9, 461; *Further Corr.*, pp. 138–9, 153; *Shorthand Letters*, p. 88; *CSPD 1666–7*, p. 390.

the pay of the tickets with Sir J. Mennes this day; and here I sat with them a while, the first time I ever was there. And thence to dinner with him – a good dinner. Here came a Gentleman over ⟨from⟩ France, arrived here this day, Mr. Browne of St. Mellos – who, among other things, tells me the meaning of the setting out of dogs every night out of the town walls, which are said to secure the city; but it is not so, but only to secure the Anchors, cables, and ships that lie dry, which might otherwise in the night be liable to be robbed. And these dogs are*a* set out every night and called together in every morning by a man with a horne, and they go in very orderly.[1]

Thence home, and there find Knipp at dinner with my wife, now very big and within a fortnight of lying down. But my head was full of business, and so could have no sport. So I left them, promising to return and take them out at night; and so to*b* the Excise Office, where a meeting was appointed of Sir St. Fox, the Cofferer[2] and myself to settle the business of our tallies; and it was so, pretty well, against another meeting.

Thence away home to the office, and out again to Captain Cocke (Mr. Moore for company walking with me and discoursing and admiring of the learning of Dr Spencer),[3] and there he and I discoursed a little more of our matters; and so home and (Knipp being gone) took out my wife and Mercer to take the ayre a little; and so as far as Hackeny and back again, and then to bed.

26. Up betimes and to the office, where all the morning. At noon dined at home. So to the office again, and a while at

---

a repl. 'go'   *b* repl. 'with'

---

1. Cf. James Howell's letter from St Malo (25 September 1620): 'there is here a perpetual Garrison of *English*, but they are of *English* dogs, which are let out in the Night to guard the Ships, . . . and so they are shut up again in the Morning': *Epist. Ho - Elianae* (ed. Jacobs, i. 54). 'St Malo dogs' were used also to guard the outer defences of Tangier at this time: Routh, p. 41.

2. William Ashburnham.

3. John Spencer, Fellow (later Master) of Corpus Christi College, Cambridge, whose *Discourse concerning prodigies* (1663) Pepys had read on 1 June 1664. He was an eminent Hebraist and a pioneer of the comparative study of religions.

the Victualling Office to understand matters there a little; and thence to the office and despatched much business to my great content; and so home to supper and to bed.

27. *Lords day.* Rose betimes, and to my office till church-time to write two copies of my Will fair, bearing date this day. Wherein I have given my[a] sister Pall 500*l* – my father, for his own and my mother's support, 2000*l* – to my wife, the rest of my estate; but to have 2500*l* secured to her though, by deducting out of what I have given my father and my sister.[1]

I despatched all before church-time, and then home and to church, my wife with me. Thence home to dinner, whither came my uncle Wight and aunt and uncle Norbury – and Mr. Sheply. A good dinner, and very merry. After dinner we broke up, and I by water to Westminster to Mrs. Martin's and there sat with her and her husband and Mrs. Burrows, the pretty, an hour or two; then to the Swan a while; and so home by water, and with my wife by and by, by water as low as Greenwich for ayre only; and so back again home to supper and to bed with great pleasure.

28. Up, and to my chamber to do some business there; and then to the office, where a while; and then by agreement to the Excise Office, where I waited all the morning for the Cofferer and Sir St. Foxe's coming; but they did not, so I and the Commissioners lost their labour and expectation of doing the business we intended. Thence home, where I find Mr. Lovett and his wife come to see us. They are a pretty couple – and she a fine-bred woman; they dined with us and Browne the painter, and she plays finely on the lute. My wife and I were well pleased with her company. After dinner, broke up; I to the office, and they abroad. All the afternoon I busy at the office; and down by water to Deptford – walked back to Redriffe, and so home to the office again, being thoughtful how to answer Sir

a repl. 'Pall'

---

1. Cf. a later note by Pepys (10 June 1681) in Rawl. A 171, f. 91*r*: 'Testamt: Mr. Hayter May 27th. 66'. No will of Pepys's survives except his last (1701, with codicils of 1703). Cf. above, i. 90, n. 1.

W. Coventry against tomorrow in the business of the victualling. But that I do trust to Tom Willson[1] that he will be ready with a book for me tomorrow morning. So to bed – my wife telling me where she hath been today with my aunt Wight; and seen Mrs. Margt Wight, and says she is one of the beautifulest women that ever she saw in her life – the most excellent nose and mouth.[2] They have been also to see pretty Mrs. Batelier; and conclude her to be a prettier woman then Mrs. Pierce, whom my wife led my aunt to see also this day.

29. *King's Birth and Restauracion day.* Waked with the ringing of the bells all over the town. So up before 5 a-clock, and to the office,[a] where we met; and I all the morning with great trouble upon my spirit to think how I should come off in the afternoon when Sir W. Coventry did go to the Victualling Office to see the state of matters there. And methought, by his doing of it without speaking to me, and only with Sir W. Penn, it must be of design to find my negligence. However, at noon I did, upon a small invitation of Sir W Pen's go and dine with Sir W. Coventry at his office, where great good cheer – and many pleasant stories of Sir W. Coventry, but I had no pleasure in them. However, I had last night and this morning made myself a little able to report how matters were – and did readily go with them after dinner to the Victualling Office; and there beyond belief did acquit myself very well, to full content; so that, beyond expectation, I got over this second rub in this business;[3] and if ever I fall on it again, I deserve to be undone.

Being broke up there, I with a merry heart home to my office; and thither my wife comes to me to tell me that if I would see the handsomest woman in England, I shall come home presently; and who should it be but the pretty[b] lady of our parish that did heretofore sit on the other side of our church over against our

---

a 'to the office' repeated   *b* MS. 'prettily'

---

1. Clerk in the Navy Office.
2. On meeting her in February 1665 Pepys had not been able to refrain from kissing her twice, although it cost him 12*d.* in a self-imposed fine: above, vi. 29 & n. 2.
3. The first had been his meeting with Coventry on 7 May.

gallery, that is since married.¹ She, with Mrs. Anne Jones, one of this parish that dances finely, and Mrs.   ª sister did come to see her this afternoon. And so I home, and there found Creed also come to me; so there I spent most of the afternoon with them; and endeed, she is a pretty black woman – her name, Mrs. Horesely. But Lord, to see how my nature could not refrain from the temptation, but I must invite them to go to Fox hall to Spring Garden, though I had freshly received minutes of a great deal of extraordinary business. However, I could not help it; but sent them before with Creed, and I did some of my business, and so after them and find them there in an Arbour; and had met with Mrs. Pierce and some company with her. So here I spent 20s upon them, and were pretty merry. Among other things, had a fellow that imitated all manner of birds and dogs and hogs with his voice, which was mighty pleasant. Stayed here till night; then set Mrs. Pierce in at the New Exchange, and ourselfs took coach and so set Mrs. Horsly home, and then home ᵇ ourselfs, but with great trouble in the streets by bonefires, it being the King's birthday and day of restoration; but Lord, to see the difference, how many there was on the other side, and so few our, the City side of Temple, would make one wonder the difference between the temper of one sort of people and the other – and the difference among all, between what they do now, and what it was the night when Monke came into the City² – such a night as that I never think ᶜ to see again, nor think it can be. ⟨After I came home, I was till one in the morning with Captain Cocke drawing up a contract with him, intended to be offered to the Duke tomorrow – which if it proceeds, he promises me 500l.⟩ ᵈ³

30. Up, and to my office, there to settle some businesses in order to our ᵉ waiting on the Duke today. That done, to Whitehall to Sir W. Coventry's chamber, where I find the Duke gone

---

ª no blank in MS.   ᵇ repl. 'our'   ᶜ repl. 'hope'
ᵈ addition crowded in between entries   ᵉ repl. 'my'

---

1. She appears to have been the 'new Morena' mentioned at 18 December 1664.

2. On 11 February 1660: see above i. 52–3.

3. Cf. above, p. 132 & n. 3.

out with the King today on hunting. So after some discourse with him, I by water to Westminster and there drew a draught of an order for my Lord Treasurer to sign, for my having some little tallies made me in lieu of two great ones of 2000*l* each, to enable me to pay small sums therewith. I showed it to Sir R. Long and had his approbation, and so to Sir Ph. Warwicke's and did give it him to get signed. So home to my office, and there did business. By and by, towards noon, word is brought me that my father and my sister*ᵃ* are come – I expected them today, but not so soon. I to them, and am heartily glad to see them, especially my father, who, poor man, looks very well, and hath rode up this journey on horseback very well – only, his eyesight and hearing*ᵇ* is very bad.[1] I stayed and dined with them, my wife being gone by coach to Barnitt with W. Hewer and Mercer to meet them, and they did come Ware way.[2]

After dinner I left them to dress themselfs, and I abroad by appointment to my Lord Ashly (who, it is strange to see how prettily he dissembles his favour to Yeabsly's business, which none in the world could mistrust, only I that am privy to his being bribed);[3] thence to White-hall, and there stayed till the Council was up with Creed, expecting a meeting of Tanger to end Yeabsly's business, but we could not procure it. So I to my Lord Treasurers and got my warrant; and then to Lovetts, but find nothing done there. So home and did a little business at the office, and so down by water to Deptford, and upon the river and back again home late; and having signed some papers and given order in business, home, where my wife is come home; and so to supper with my father, and mighty pleasant we were and my*ᶜ* wife mighty kind to him and Pall. And so after supper to bed – myself being sleepy, and my right Eye still very sore, as it hath been now about five days or six, which puts me out of tune.

Tonight my wife tells me news hath been brought her that

a repl. 'sist' –   *b* repl. 'h'-   *c* MS. 'mighty'

1. He was now just over 65.
2. From Brampton there were two approaches to London: the easterly route via Ware and Waltham, and the westerly via Stevenage, Hatfield and Barnet. Pepys himself used both.
3. See above, p. 128 & n. 3.

Balty's wife is brought to bed, by some fall or fit, before her time, of a great child, but dead. If the woman do well, we have no reason to be sorry, because his staying a little longer without child will be better for him and her.

31. Waked very betimes in the morning by extraordinary Thunder and rain, which did keep me sleeping and waking till very late; and it being a holiday, and my eye very sore, and myself having had very little sleep for a good while till 9 a-clock – and so up, and so saw all my family up, and my father and sister (who is a pretty good-bodied woman and not over-thicke, as I thought she would have been; but full of Freckles and not handsome in face); and so I out by water among the ships, and to Deptford and Blackewall about business; and so home and to dinner with my father and sister and family, mighty pleasant all of us – and among other things, with a Sparrow that our Mercer hath brought up now for three weeks, which is so tame*a*, that [it] flies up and down and upon the table and eats and pecks, and doth everything so pleasantly, that we are mightily pleased with it.

After dinner I to my papers and accounts of this month, to set all straight – it being a public fast-day, appointed to pray for the good success of the fleet. But it is a pretty thing to consider how little a matter they make of this keeping of a fast, that it was not so much as declared time enough to be read in the churches the last Sunday – but ordered by proclamation since – I suppose upon some sudden news of the Duch being come out.[1]

To my accounts and settled them clear; but to my grief, find myself poorer then I was the last by near 20*l* – by reason of my being forced to return 50*l* to Downing the smith which he had presented me with.[2] However, I am well contented, finding myself yet to be worth 5200*l*.

a   MS. 'time'

---

1. The proclamation was dated 28 May and ordered the use of the same service as was prescribed for the similar occasion in 1665: Steele, no. 3463. Pepys's guess appears to be right: the Dutch battle fleet had come out of the Texel on the 26th, and news of its movements had been sent to Arlington on the 27th (*London Gazette*, 28 May).

2. See above, p. 119.

Having done – to supper with my father – and then to finish the writing fair of my accounts; and so to bed.

《This of Mr. Home-wood ought to come in upon the first of June》 This day came to town Mr. Home-wood, and I took him home ⟨in the evening⟩ to my chamber and discoursed with him about my business of the victual-ling – which I have a mind to imploy him in, and he is desirous of also, but doth very ingenuously declare he understands it not so well as other things and desires to be informed in the nature of it before he attempts it[1] – which I like well, and so I carried him to Mr. Gibson to discourse with him about it,[2] and so home again to my accounts.

Thus ends this month, with my mind oppressed by my defect in my duty of the victualling, which lies upon me as a burden till I get myself into a better posture therein, and hinders me and casts down my courage in everything else that belongs to me – and the jealousy I have of Sir W. Coventry's being displeased with me about it. But I hope in a little time to remedy all.

As to public business: by late tidings of the French Fleete being come to Rochell (how true, though, I know not), our fleet is Divided; Prince Rupert being gone with about 30 ships to the Westward; as is conceived, to meet the French, to hinder their coming to join with the Duch.[3]

My Lord Duke of Albemarle lies in the Downes with the rest, and intends presently to sail to the Gunfleete.

1. Edward Homewood was a clerk in the Navy Office: I have not traced him in the victualling service.
2. Richard Gibson was in charge of the victualling at Yarmouth.
3. This proved a fatal move. In fact Duquesne was still off La Rochelle, and the main French fleet under Beaufort was in the Tagus. The belief that the French were out led to the English defeat in the Four Days Battle which followed. On 1 June, two days after Rupert had gone westward, Albemarle sighted the Dutch battlefleet anchored between Dunkirk and the N. Foreland. Over-confident, he attacked, although heavily outnumbered, and fought a retreating battle. Rupert did not rejoin him until the evening of 3 June.

JUNE.

1. Being prevented yesterday in meeting by reason of the Fast-day, we met today all the morning. At noon I and my father, wife, and sister dined at aunt Wight's here, hard by at Mr. Woollys, upon sudden warning, they being to go out of town tomorrow. Here dined the fair Mrs. Margt. Wight, who is a very fine lady; but the cast of her Eye (got only by an ill habit) doth her much wrong, and her hands are bad – but she hath the face of a noble Roman lady. After dinner, my uncle and Woolly and I out into their yard to talk about what may be done hereafter to all our profits by prize-goods,[1] which did give us reason to lament the loss of the opportunity of the last year; which, if we were as wise as we are now, and [at] the peaceable end of all those troubles that we meet with, all might have been such a height as will*a* never come again in this age – and so I do really believe it. Thence home to my office, and there did much business. And at night home to my father to supper and to bed.

2. Up, and to the office, where certain news is brought us of a letter come to the King this morning from the Duke of Albemarle, dated yesterday at 11 a-clock as they were sailing to the Gunfleet, that they were in sight of the Duch Fleete and were fitting themselfs to fight them[2] – so that they are, ere this, certainly engaged; besides, several do averr they heard the guns all yesterday in the afternoon. This put us at the board into a Tosse.

Presently comes orders for our sending away to the fleet a recruite of 200 soldiers. So I rose from the table, and to the Victualling Office and thence upon the river among several vessels, to consider of the sending them away; and lastly down

a repl. 'would'

---

1. Robert Woolley was a city broker.
2. Cf. Clarke to Williamson, 10 a.m., 1 June (with a postscript, 11 a.m.): *CSPD 1665-6*, p. 424. They had sighted a Dutch fleet of 75 sail.

to Greenwich and there appointed two Yachts to be ready for them – and did order the soldiers to march to Blackewall. Having set all things in order against the next Flood, I went on shore with Captain Erwin[1] at Greenwich and into the parke and there we could hear the guns from the Fleete most plainly. Thence he and I to the King's-head and there bespoke a dish of steaks for our dinner about 4 a-clock. While that was doing, we walked to the water-side, and there seeing the King and Duke come down in their barge to Greenwich-house, I to them and did give them an account what*[a]* I was doing. They went up to the park to hear the guns of the fleet go off. All our hopes now is that Prince Rupert with his fleet is coming back and will be with the fleet this noon – a message being sent to him to that purpose on Wednesday*[b]* last.[2] And a return is come from him this morning, that he did intend to sail from St. Ellens point[3] about 4 in the afternoon on Wednesday,[4] which was yesterday; which gives us great hopes, the wind being very fair, that he is with them this noon; and the fresh going-off*[c]* of the guns makes us believe the same.*[d]*

After dinner, having nothing else to do till flood, I went and saw Mrs. Daniel – to whom I did not tell that the fleets were engaged, because of her husband, who is in the *Royal Charles*.[5] Very pleasant with her half an hour, and so away, and down to Blackewall and there saw the soldiers (who were by this time gotten most of them drunk) shipped off. But Lord, to see how the poor fellows kissed their wifes and sweethearts in that simple manner at their going off, and shouted and let off their guns, was strange sport.

In the evening came up the River the *Katharine* Yacht, Captain

---

a repl. 'what was'   *b* repl. 'Saturday'
c repl. 'of'   *d* several blots hereabouts

---

1. It was Erwin who on 30 May had sent news to Albemarle of the Dutch fleet's approach: BM, Add. 32094, f. 123*r*.

2. For the history of this crucially important message, see below, p. 144, n. 1.

3. On the north-east coast of the Isle of Wight.

4. *Recte* Friday.

5. As it happened, he and a companion brought the news of the action to the King two days later: below, pp. 145–7.

Fazeby, who hath brought over my Lord of Alesbury and Sir Thom. Liddall (with a very pretty daughter, and in a pretty travelling-dress) from Flanders, who saw the Duch fleet on Thursdy and ran from them; but from that hour to this hath not heard one gun, nor any news of any fight.

Having put the soldiers on board, I home and wrote what I had to write by the post; and so home to supper and to bed, it being late.

3. *Lords day* ⟨*Whitsunday*⟩. Up and by water to White-hall; and there met with Mr. Coventry, who tells me the only news from the fleet is brought by Captain Elliott of the *Portland*, which, by being run on board by the *Guernsey*, was disabled from staying abroad – so is come in to Albrough.[1] That he saw one of the ⟨Duch*a*⟩ great ships blown up, and three on fire. That they begun to fight on Friday. And at his coming into port, could make another ship of the King's coming in, which he judged to be the *Rupert*. That he knows of no other hurt to our ships.[2]

With this good news, I home by water again, and to church in the sermon time and with great joy told it my fellows in the pew. So home after church-time to dinner. And after dinner my father, wife, sister, and Mercer by water to Woolwich, while I walked by land and saw the Exchange as full of people, and hath been all this noon, as of any other day, only for news.

I to St. Margaret's Westminster, and there saw at church my pretty Betty Michell. And thence to the Abbey, and so to Mrs. Martin and there did what je voudrais avec her, both devante and backward, which is also muy bon plazer. So by and by he

a repl. 'their'

———

1. Aldeburgh, Suff.
2. Cf. Coventry's fuller account in his letter of this day to Arlington: *CSPD 1665-6*, pp. 426-7. This was the Four Days Battle – the sharpest engagement of the war – fought between the N. Foreland and the

Essex coast during 1-4 June. See below, pp. 146+. It was a victory for the Dutch, though its effects were to some extent offset by the English victory in the Battle of St James's Day (25 July): see below, pp. 225-6.

came in; and after some*ᵃ* discourse with him, I away to White-
hall and there met with this bad news farther: that the Prince
came to Dover but at 10 a-clock last night, and there heard
nothing of a fight – so that we are defeated of all our hopes of his
help to the fleet. It is also reported by some victuallers that the
Duke of Albemarle and Homes their flags were shot down,
and both fain to come to Anchor to renew their Rigging and
sails.

A letter is also come this afternoon from Harman in the
Henery (which is she was taken by Elliott for the *Rupert*), that
being fallen into the body of the Duch fleet, he made his way
through them, was set on by three fireships, one after another –
got two of them off and disabled the third – was set on fire himself; upon which many of his men leaped into the sea and
perished; among others, the Parson first – hath lost above 100
men and a good many wounded*ᵇ* (God knows what is become of
Balty); and at last quenched his own fire and got to Albrough –
being, as all*ᶜ* say, the greatest hazard that ever*ᵈ* any ship scaped,
and as bravely managed by him. The mast of the third fireship
fell into their ship on Fire and hurt Harman's leg, which makes
him lame now, but not dangerous.[1]

I to Sir G. Carteret, who told me there hath been great bad
management in all this; that the King's orders that went on
Friday for calling back the Prince,[2] was sent but by the ordinary
post on Wednesdy, and came to the Prince his hands but on
Friday. And then instead of sailing presently,* he stays till 4 in
the evening; and that which is worst of all – the *Hampshire*,
laden with merchants money come from the Streights, set out
with or but just before the fleet and was in the Downes by
5 of*ᵉ* the clock yesterday morning – and the Prince with his fleet

---

    a repl. 'such'   *b* MS. 'women' repl. 'wound'-
  c repl. 'as also also'   *d* repl. 'every'   *e* MS. 'in'

---

  1. After quick repairs the *Henry*   2. For Rupert's movements, see
under its wounded captain set out   above, p. 139 & n. 3.
the day after (2 June) and rejoined the
fleet.

came to Dover but at 10 of the clock at night.   This is hard to [be] answered, if it be true.[1]

This puts great astonishment into the King and Duke and Court, everybody being out of countenance.   So meeting Creed, he and I by coach to Hide parke alone to talk of these things, and do bless God that my Lord Sandwich was not here at this time – to be concerned in a business like to be so misfortunate.

It was a pleasant thing to consider how fearful I was of being seen with Creed all this afternoon, for fear of people's thinking that by our relation to my Lord Sandwich we should be making ill constructions of the Prince's failure.   But God knows, I am heartily sorry, for the sake of the whole nation; though if it were not for that, it would not be amisse to have these high blades find some check to their presumption – and their[a] disparaging of so good men.

Thence set him down in Common Guarden, and so home by the Change; which is full of people still, and all talk highly of the failure of the Prince in not making more haste after his instructions did come, and of our managements herein, not giving it sooner and with more care and oftener thence.

After supper, to bed.

a   repl. 'to'

---

1. These charges, soon widely repeated, occasioned one of the most hardfought controversies of the war, and after the peace were one of the subjects of the Commons enquiry into naval miscarriages. Coventry drew up the order for Rupert's recall late in the evening of 30 May, and the Duke of York signed it in bed at about midnight. Coventry then took it to Arlington's house to have it despatched by courier, but the minister was asleep and his servants would not disturb him. The orders went therefore by express post sometime before 1 a.m., those directed to Portsmouth arriving there late in the afternoon of 31 May. Rupert, in St Helen's Road off the Isle of Wight, received them at 10 a.m. on 1 June. Rupert's (and Allin's) explanation of why they did not sail until 4 p.m. is that the tides were unfavourable. A later delay occurred through uncertainty as to whether Albemarle was to be found in the Downs or at the Gunfleet. Rupert drew blank at the Downs before sailing on to the Gunfleet. See Coventry's account, below, pp. 178–9, and the narratives of Rupert and Albemarle in CJ, ix. 11+. See also HMC, Eliot Hodgkin, pp. 53–60; Allin, i. 269, ii. pp. xvi+; Rupert and Monck Letter Book, 1666 (ed. J. R. Powell and E. K. Timings), pp. 185+; P. Fraser, Intelligence of Secretaries of State, pp. 83+.

4. Up, and with Sir Jo. Minnes and Sir W Pen to White-hall in the latter's coach – where when we came, we find the Duke at St. James's, whither he is lately gone to lodge.[1] So walking through the park, we saw hundreds of people listening at the Gravell-pits,[2] and to and again in the park to hear the guns. And I saw a letter, dated last night, from Strowd, Governor of Dover Castle, which says that the Prince came thither the night[a] before with his fleet.[3] But that for the guns which we writ that we heard, it is only a mistake for Thunder; and so far as to yesterday, it is a miraculous thing that we all Friday and Saturday and yesterday did hear everywhere most plainly the guns go off, and yet at Deale and Dover, to last night, they did not hear one word of a fight, nor think they heard one gun.[4] This, added to what[b] I have set down before the other day about the *Katharine*,[5] makes room for a great dispute in Philosophy: how we should hear it and not they, the same wind that brought it to us being the same that should bring it to them. But so it is.

Major Halsey,[6] however (he was sent down on purpose to hear news), did bring news this morning that he did see the Prince and his fleet at 9 of the clock yesterday morning, four or five leagues to sea behind the Goodwin. So that by the hearing of the guns this morning, we conclude he is come to the fleet.

After Wayting upon the Duke, Sir W. Penn (who was com-manded to go to rights* by water down to Harwich to despatch away all the ships he can) and I home, drinking two bottles of Cocke ale in the street, in his new fine coach, and so home – where no sooner come, but news is brought me of a couple of men come to speak with me from the fleet. So I down, and who should it be but Mr. Daniel,[7] all muffled up, and his face as

a repl. 'last'   *b* repl. same symbol badly formed

---

1. He usually lived there in summer and at Whitehall in winter.

2. In or just north of St James's Park: Basil H. Johnson, *Berkeley Sq. to Bond St*, pp. 18, 35.

3. Cf. *CSPD 1665–6*, pp. 426, 427.

4. Cf. Evelyn's similar observation (from Deptford) at 1 June. For a possible explanation, see above, vi. 116, n. 1.

5. Above, pp. 141–2.

6. James Halsey (Halsall), Scout-master-General of the army.

7. John Daniel, once a seaman, now a lieutenant on the *Royal Charles*; known to Pepys because he was the son-in-law of Mrs Clerke, Pepys's landlady when he lodged at Green-wich in 1665–6.

black as the chimney and covered with dirt, pitch and tar, and powder, and muffled with dirty clouts and his right eye stopped with Okum. He is come last night at 5 a-clock from the fleet, with a comrade of his that hath endangered another eye. They were set on shore at Harwich this morning at 2 a-clock in a ketch, with about twenty more wounded men from the *Royall Charles*. They being able to ride, took post about 3 this morning and was here between 11 and 12. I went presently into the coach with them, and carried them to Sumersett-house*a* stairs and there took water (all the world gazing upon us and concluding it to be news from the fleet; and everybody's face appeared expecting of news) to the Privy-stairs and left them at Mr. Coventry's lodging (he, though, not being there); and so I into the park to the King, and told him my Lord Generall was well the last night at 5 o'clock, and the Prince come with his fleet and joyned with his about 7. The King was mightily pleased with this news and so took me by the hand and talked a little of it – I giving him the best account I could; and then he bid me to fetch the two seamen to him – he walking into the house. So I went and fetched the seamen into the Vane-room to him, and there he heard the whole account.[1]

The Fight.

How we found the Duch fleet at anchor on Friday, half-seas-over, between Dunkirke and Oastend, and made them let slip their Anchors – they about 90, and we less then 60. We fought them and put them to the run, till they met with about 16 sail of fresh ships and so bore up again. The fight continued till night, and then again the next morning from 5 till 7 at night – and so too, yesterday*b* morning they begun again, and continued till

a l.h. and s.h. repl. s.h. 'White-hall'   *b* repl. 'too'

───────────────

1. A much briefer version of the seamen's story of the Four Days Battle, written by Coventry, is in PRO, SP 29/158, nos 35, 36 (summary in *CSPD 1665–6*, p. 429). An account based on Coventry's version was printed in the *London Gazette*, 7 June, and is reprinted in *Rupert and Monck Letter Book, 1666* (ed. J. R. Powell and E. K. Timings), p. 235. Other contemporary accounts are in PRO, SP 29/158, loc. cit.; *London Gazette*, loc. cit. and *Rupert and Monck Letter Book*, pp. 231+; B. S. Ingram (ed.), *Three sea journals*, pp. 47+. For modern descriptions of the engagement, see Tedder, pp. 153+; Allin, vol. ii, pp. xxiii+ (by R. C. Anderson).

The Four Days Battle, by Abraham Storck

(*National Maritime Museum*)

about 4 a-clock – they chasing us for the most part of Saturday and yesterday; we fleeing from them. The Duke himself, then those people, were put into the ketch, and by and by spied the Prince's fleet coming – upon which, De Ruyter called a little council (being in chase at this time of us); and thereupon their fleet divided into two squadrons, 40 in one and about 30 in the other (the fleet being at first about 90, but by one accident or other supposed to be lessened to about 70); the bigger to fallow the Duke, the less to meet the Prince. But the Prince came up with the Generalls fleet, and the Dutch came together again and bore toward their own coast – and we with them. And now, what the consequence of this day will be, that we [hear] them fighting, we know not. The Duke was forced to come to Anchor on Friday, having lost his sails and rigging. No perticular person spoken of to be hurt but Sir W Clerke, who hath lost his leg, and bore it bravely. The Duke himself had a little hurt in his thigh,[1] but signified little.

The King did pull out of his pocket about twenty pieces in gold, and did give it Daniel for himself and his companion. And so parted, mightily pleased with the account he did give him*a* of the fight and the success it ended with – of the Prince's coming – though it seems the Duke did give way again and again. The King did give order for care to be had of Mr. Daniel*b* and his companion; and so we parted from him, and then met the Duke and gave him the same account; and so broke up, and I left them going to the surgeon's; and I myself by water to the Change, and to several people did give account of the business; and so home about 4 a-clock to dinner and was fallowed by several people home, to be told the news, and good news it is. God send we may hear a good issue of this day's business.

After I had eat something, I walked to Gressham College, where I heard my Lord Bruncker was; and there got a promise

---

a repl. 'it'   *b* l.h. repl. s.h. ? 'Brook'

---

1. The satirists would not allow that it was a thigh-wound. Cf. [?Marvell,] *Third advice to a painter* (1666), ll. 125–6: 'When the rude bullet a large collop tore /Out of that buttock never turn'd before.'

L

of the receipt of the fine Varnish – which I shall be glad to have.[1]
Thence back with Mr. Hooke to my house, and there lent some
of my tables of navall matters, the names of rigging and the
timbers about a ship[2] – in order to Dr. Wilkins's book coming
out about the Universall Language.[3]

Thence (he being gone) to the Crowne behind the Change,
and there supped at the Clubb[4] with my Lord Bruncker, Sir G.
Ent, and others of Gresham College. And all our discourse is of
this fight at sea;[a] and all are doubtful of the success, and conclude all had been lost if the Prince had not come in – they having
chased us the greatest part of Saturdy and Sunday.

Thence with my Lord Brouncker and Creed by coach to
Whitehall – where fresh letters are come from Harwich – where
the *Glocester*, Captain Clerke, is come in. And says that on
Sunday night, upon coming in of the Prince, the Duch did fly.
But all this day they have been fighting; therefore, they did face
again, to be sure. Captain Bacon of the *Bristoll* is killed. They
cry up Jenings of the *Ruby* and Saunders of the *Sweepstakes*.
They condemn mightily Sir Tho. Teddiman for a Coward, but
with what reason, time must show.[5]

Having heard all this, Creed and I walked into the park till 9 or
10 at night, it being fine moonshine – discoursing of the unhappiness* of our fleet. What it would have been if the Prince
had not come in. How much the Duke hath failed of what he
was so presumptuous of.[6] How little we deserve of God
Almighty to give us better fortune. How much this excuse[s]
all that was imputed to my Lord Sandwich; and how much[b]
more he is a man fit to be trusted with all these matters then these

---

a repl. 'say' (? phonetic spelling)   *b* repl. 'he'

---

1. Brouncker was attending a
council meeting of the Royal Society:
Birch, ii. 95. For Pepys's interest in
japanning, see above, iv. 153 & n. 2.
   2. Untraced.
   3. See above, p. 12, n. 6.
   4. Informal suppers were often
held after the weekly meetings of the
society. Later they became formal:
above, vi. 36, n. 4.

5. Pepys controverts this slander
at 8 June, on the Duke of York's
authority: see below, p. 154 & n. 3.
Teddeman (Vice-Admiral of the
Blue) was promoted to the command
of the White on 12 June.
   6. For Albemarle's contempt of
the Dutch, see e.g. *Naval Minutes*,
p. 4; Evelyn, iii. 424–5, 440.

that now command, who act by nor with any advice, but rashly and without any order. How*a* bad we are at intelligence, that should give the Prince no sooner notice of anything, but let him come to Dover without notice of any fight, or where the fleet were, or anything else; nor give the Duke any notice that he might depend upon the Prince's reserve. And lastly, of how good use all may be to check our pride and presumption in adventuring upon hazards upon unequal force, against a people that can fight, it seems now, as well as we, and that will not be discouraged by any losses, but that they will rise again.

Thence by water home, and to supper (my father, wife, and sister having been at Islington today at*b* Pitts's)[1] and to bed.

5. Up, and to the office, where all the morning – expecting every hour more news of the fleet and the issue of yesterday's fight, but nothing came. At noon, though I should have dined with my Lord Mayor and Aldermen at an entertainment of Comissioner Taylors,[2] yet, it being a time of expectation of the success* of the fleet, I did not go – but dined at home; and after dinner by water down to Depford (and Woolwich, where I had not been since I lodged there,[3] and methinks the place is grown natural to me), and thence down to Longreach,[4] calling on all the ships in the way, seeing their condition for sailing and what they want. Home about 11 of the clock; and so eat a bit and to bed – having received no manner of news this day but of the *Raynbows* being put in from the fleet, maimed as the other ships are – and some say that Sir W Clerke is dead of his leg*c* being cut off.[5]

---

a repl. 'Lastly'
b repl. several words rendered illegible except for 'to see . . .'
c repl 'b'-

---

1. Landlord of the King's Head.
2. The dinner was in celebration of the completion of the ship the *Loyal London*, built for the city by John Taylor, who was Navy Commissioner at Harwich. For the launch, see below, p. 160 & n. 3.

3. In the late summer of 1665: above, vi. 140, n. 2.
4. Above Gravesend.
5. Clarke was Secretary at War. He died this day.

6. Up betimes, and vexed with my people for having a key taken out of one of the chamber doors – and nobody knew where it was. As also with my boy for not being ready as soon as I, though I called him, whereupon I boxed him soundly. And then to my business at the office and at the Victualling Office; and thence by water to St. James's*a* ⟨(whither he¹ is now gone)⟩, it being a ⟨monthly⟩ Fast day for the Plague. There we all met and did our business as usual with the Duke; and among other things, had Captain Cockes proposal of East Country goods read,² brought by my Lord Bruncker; which I make use of but as a monkey doth the cat's foot. Sir W. Coventry did much oppose it, and it's ⟨likely it⟩ will not do – so away goes my hopes of 500*l*.

Thence after the Duke into the park, walking through to White-hall; and there everybody listening for guns, but none heard; and every creature is now overjoyed and conclude, upon very good grounds, that the Duch are beaten, because we have heard no guns nor no news of our fleet. By and by, walking a little further, Sir Ph. Frowde did meet the Duke with an express to Sir W. Coventry (who was by) from Captain Taylor, the Storekeeper at Harwich;³ being the narration of Captain Hayward of the *Dunkirke*; who gives a very serious account how upon Monday the two fleets [were] fighting all day till 7*b* at night, and then the whole fleet of Duch did betake themselfs to a very plain flight*c* and never looked back again. That Sir Chr. Mings is wounded in the leg. That the Generall⁴ is well. That it is conceived reasonably that of all the*d* Dutch fleet, which, with what recruits they had, came to 100 sail, there is not above 50 got home – and of them, few, if any, of their flags. And that little Captain Bell in one of the fireships did at the end of the day fire a ship of 70 guns.

We were all so overtaken with this good*e* news that the Duke

a repl. 'White-hall'   *b* repl. '4'   *c* MS. 'fight'
d repl. 'their'   *e* repl. same symbol badly formed

---

1. The Duke of York.
2. See above, p. 132 & n. 3, p. 136.
3. BM, Add. 32094, f. 135r, Harwich, 5 June, 'about 8 at night', endorsed 'Hast, Hast, Hast, post Hast'; summary in HMC, *Rep.*, 5/1/315b. This was an account of the engagement on the last day of the Four Days Battle.
4. Albemarle.

ran with it to the King, who was gone to chapel; and there all the Court was in a hubbub, being rejoiced over head and ears in this good news.

Away go I by coach to the New Exchange and there did spread this good news a little, though I find it had broken out before. And so home to our own church, it being the common fast-day; and it was just before sermon, but Lord, how all the people in the church stared upon me to see me whisper to Sir Jo Minnes and my Lady Pen. Anon I saw*ᵃ* people stirring and whispering below, and by and by comes up the Sexton ⟨from⟩ my Lady Ford to tell me the news (which I had brought), being now sent into the church by Sir W Batten – in writing, and handed from pew to pew. But that which pleased me as much as the news, was to have the fair Mrs. Middleton[1] at our church, who indeed is a very beautiful lady. Here after sermon comes to our office 40 people almost, of all sorts and qualities, to hear the news; which I took great delight to tell them. Then home and found my wife at dinner, not knowing of my being at church. And after dinner my father and she out to Hales's, where my father is to begin to sit today for his picture, which I have a desire to have.[2] I all the afternoon at home doing some business, drawing up of my vows for the *ᵇ* rest of the year to Christmas. But Lord, to see in what a condition of happiness I am, if I could but keep myself so; but my love of pleasure is such, that my very soul is angry with itself for my vanity in so doing. Anon took coach and to Hales's; but he was gone out, and my father and wife gone. So I to Lovetts, and there to my trouble saw plainly that my project of varnish'd books[3] will not take – it not keeping colour, nor being able to take polishing upon a single paper. Thence home, and my father and wife not coming in, I proceeded with my coach to take a little ayre as far as Bow all alone, and there turned back and home. But before I got home,

a   repl. 'hear'   *b*   repl. 'my'

---

1. Either Jane, wife of Charles Myddleton of Ruabon, a famous beauty (see above, vi. 64 & n. 2), or Elizabeth, wife of Richard Myddelton, merchant, of Crutched Friars, whose looks Pepys also admired (above, iv. 200 & n. 3).

2. This portrait (paid for on 27 June) does not survive. (OM).

3. See above, pp. 119–20 & n.

the Boncfircs were lighted all the town over; and I going through Crouched-Friars, seeing Mercer at her mother's gate, stopped and light, and into her mother's (the first time I ever was there) and find all my people, father and all, at a very fine supper at W Hewers's lodging;[1] very neatly, and to my great pleasure. After supper into his chamber, which is mighty fine, with pictures and everything else very curious* – which pleased me exceedingly. Thence to the gate, with the Women all about me; and Mrs. Mercer's son had provided a great many Serpents,[2] and so I made the women all fire some serpents. By and by comes our fair neighbour Mrs. Turner, and two neighbour's daughters, Mrs. Tite; the elder of which, a long red-nosed silly jade; the younger, a pretty black girl, and the merriest sprightly jade that ever I saw. With them idled away the whole night, till 12 at night, at the bonefire in the streets – some of the people thereabouts going about with Musquets, and did give me two or three volleys of their Musquetts, I giving them a crown to drink; and so home – mightily pleased with this happy day's news; and the more because confirmed by Sir Daniel Harvy, who was in the whole fight with the Generall, and tells that there appear but 36 in all of the Duch fleet left at the end of the voyage when they run home.[3] The joy of the City was this night exceeding great.

7. Up betimes, and to my office about business (Sir W. Coventry having sent me word that he is gone down to the fleet to see how matters stand, and to be back again speedily), and with the same expectation of congratulating ourselfs with the victory that I had yesterday. But my Lord Brouncker and Sir T. Harvey, that came from Court, tell me quite contrary news, which astonishes me. That is to say, that we are beaten – lost many ships and good commanders – have not taken one ship of the enemy's, and so can only report ourselfs a victory; nor is it certain that we were left maisters of the field. But above all,

---

1. Will Hewer had ceased to live with the Pepyses in November 1663.
2. Fireworks burning with serpentine motion. Will Mercer was 15.
3. Harvey was a relative of Sandwich by marriage; later Ambas-sador to Turkey. He was wildly wrong. The Dutch losses were much lighter than those of the English – only four out of c. 100 ships: Allin, vol. ii, p. xxvi.

that the *Prince* run on shore upon the Galoper, and there stuck[1] – was endeavoured to be fetched off by the Duch but could not, and so they burned her – and Sir G Ascue is taken prisoner and carried into Holland. This news doth much trouble me, and the thoughts of the ill-consequences of it, and the pride and presumption that brought us to it.

At noon to the Change, and there find the discourse of town, and their countenances, much changed – but yet not very plain. So home to dinner all alone, my father and people being gone all to Woolwich to see the launching of the new ship, the *Greenwich*, built by Chr. Pett – I left alone with little Mrs. Tooker, whom I kept with me in my chamber all the afternoon, and did what I would*ᵃ* with her.

By and by comes Mr. Wayth to me; and discoursing of our ill success, he tells me plainly, from Captain Pages own mouth (who hath lost his*ᵇ* arm in the fight), that the Duch did pursue us two hours before they left us; and then they suffered us to go on homewards, and they retreated toward their coast – which is very sad news.

Then to my office, and anon to White-hall late, to the Duke of York to see what commands he hath and to pray a meeting tomorrow for Tanger in behalf of Mr. Yeabsly – which I did do, and do find the Duke much damped in his discourse touching the late fight, and all the Court talk sadly of it. The Duke did give me several letters he had received from the fleet and Sir W. Coventry and Sir W. Penn, who are gone down thither for me to pick out some works to be done for the setting out the fleet again; and so I took them home with me, and was drawing out an Abstract of them till midnight.[2] And as to news, I do find great reason to think that we are beaten in every respect, and that we are the losers. The *Prince* upon the Galloper, where both the *Royall Charles* and *Royall Katharine*, had come twice aground,

a repl. 'could'   *b* repl. 'is'

---

1. On the evening of the 3rd, six ships struck the Galloper Sand (in the mouth of the Thames *c.* 10 miles north-west of the Foreland); all got off except the *Royal Prince*, a 1st-rate which many considered the best ship in the Navy.

2. A copy of the abstract (8 June; in Hayter's hand) is in Rawl. A 195a, f. 247r.

but got off. The *Essex* carried into Holland. The *Swiftsure* misseing (Sir Wm Barkely) ever since the beginning of the fight. Captains Bacon, Tearne, Wood, Mootham, Whitty, and Coppin Slayne.[1] The Duke of Albemarle writes that he never fought with worse officers in his life, not above 20 of them behaving themselfs like men.[2] Sir Wm. Clerke lost his leg, and in two days died. 〈The *Loyall George, Seven Oakes,* and *Swiftsure* are still missing, having never, as the Generall writes himself, engaged with them.〉[a]

It was as great an [b] alteration to find myself required to write a sad letter, instead of a triumphant one, to my Lady Sandwich this night, as ever on any occasion I had in my life.

So late home, and to bed.

8. Up very betimes, and to attend the Duke of Yorke by order, all of us – to report to him what the works are that are required of us and to divide among us, wherein I have taken a very good share, and more then I can perform I doubt.

Thence to the Exchequer about some Tanger businesses; and then home, where to my very great joy I find Balty come home without any hurt, after the utmost imaginable danger he hath gone through in the *Henery*, being upon the Quarter-deck with Harman all the time; and for which 〈service〉 Harman, I heard this day, commended most seriously, and most eminently by the Duke of Yorke. As also, the Duke did do most utmost right to Sir Tho. Teddiman, of whom a scandal was raised, but without cause, he having behaved himself most eminently brave all the whole fight, and to extraordinary great service and purpose, having given Trump himself such a broadside as was hardly ever given to any ship.[3]

a addition crowded in between paragraphs   *b* repl. 'con'-

---

1. Besides two flag-officers (Myngs and Berkeley), 12 commanders, all told, were lost.

2. Albemarle to Coventry, the *Royal Charles,* 6 June: 'I assure you I never fought with worse officers than now in my life, for not above twenty of them behaved themselves like men' (Smith, i. 110).

3. Cf. the praise given to Teddeman in the account (7 June) of the battle in *CSPD 1665–6,* p. 432. The 'scandal' may have arisen through confusion with his elder brother Henry: see below, p. 163 & n. 3.

Mings is shot through the face and into the shoulder, where*ᵃ* the bullet is lodged. Young Holmes[1] is also ill-wounded, and Utber*ᵇ* in the *Rupert*.

Balty tells me the case of the *Henery*, and it was endeed most extraordinary sad and desperate.

After dinner Balty and I to my office, and there talked a great deal of this fight; and I am mightily pleased in him, and have great content in and hopes of his doing well.

Thence out to White-hall to a Committee for Tanger, but it met not. But Lord, to see how melancholy the Court is under the thoughts of this last overthrow (for so it is), instead of a victory so much and so unreasonably expected.[2]

Thence, the Committee not meeting, Creed and I down the River as low as Sir W Warren's; with whom I did motion a business that may be of profit to me, about buying some lighters to send down to the fleet, wherein he will assist me.[3]

So back again, he and I talking of the last ill-management of this fight, and of the ill-management of fighting at all against so great a force, bigger then ours. And so to the office, where we parted – but with this satisfaction, that we hear the *Swiftsure*, Sir W Barkely, is come in safe to the Nowre after her being absent ever since the beginning of the fight, wherein she did not appear at all from beginning to end. But wherever she hath been, they say she is arrived there well; which I pray God, however, may be true.

At the office late doing business; and so home to supper and to bed.

9. Up, and to St. James's, there to wait on the Duke of York – and had discourse with him about several businesses of the fleet. But Lord, to see how the Court is divided about the *Swiftsure* and the *Essex*'s being safe – and wagers and odds laid on both

a repl. 'his'   *b* repl. ? 'Al'-

---

1. John Holmes, younger brother of Sir Robert. The latter was Rear-Admiral of the Red, and had hoisted his flag on board the *Henry*.

2. The Dutch had won the battle, though at a high cost in men and leaders. Three of their flag-officers were killed. The English, heavily outnumbered, had fought well.

3. For Pepys's reward, see below, p. 244, n. 2. Warren's yard was at Wapping.

sides.[1] I did tell the Duke how Sir W. Batten did tell me this morning that he was sure the *Swiftsure* is safe. This put them all in a great joy and certainty of it, but this I doubt will prove nothing.

Thence to White-hall in expectation of a meeting of Tanger; and we did industriously labour to have it this morning, but we could not get a fifth person there; so after much pains, and thoughts on my side on behalf*a* of Yeabsly, we were fain to break up. But Lord, to see with what patience my Lord Ashly did stay all the morning to get a Committee, little thinking that I knew the rise*b* of his willingness.[2] So I home to dinner, and back again to White-hall; and being come thither a little too soon, went to Westminster-hall and bought a pair of gloves, and to see how people do take this late*c* fight at sea; and I find all give over the thoughts of it as a victory, and do*d* reckon it a great overthrow.

So to White-hall, and there, when we were come all together in certain expectation of doing our business, to Yeabsly's full content and us that were his friends, my Lord Peterborough (whether through some difference between him and my Lord Ashly, or him and me or Povy, or through the falseness of Creed, I know not) doth*e* bring word that the Duke of York (who did expressly bid me wait at the Committee for the despatch of the business) would not have us go forward in this business of allowing the loss of the ships[3] till Sir G. Carteret and Sir W. Coventry were come to town – which was the very thing endeed which we would*f* have avoided. This being told us, we broke up, doing nothing, to my great discontent, though I said nothing. And afterward, I find by my Lord Ashly's discourse to me that he is troubled mightily at it; and endeed it is a great abuse of him – and of the whole Commissioners, that nothing of that nature can be done without Sir G. Carteret or Sir W. Coventry.

No sooner*g* was the Committee up, and I going [from] the

a repl. same symbol badly formed   *b* repl. 'raise'   *c* MS. 'l'
d MS. 'to'   *e* MS. 'I do'   *f* MS. 'could'   *g* MS. 'answer'

1. Neither returned; both had been taken by the Dutch on the 2nd.
2. See above, p. 128 & n. 3.
3. Cf. above, loc. cit.; p. 162 & n. 2.

Court homeward, but I am told Sir W. Coventry is come to town; so I to his chamber, and there did give him an account how matters go in our office. And with some content I parted from him, after we had discoursed several things of the haste requisite to be made in getting the fleet out again and the manner of doing it.[1] But I do not hear that he is at all pleased or satisfied with the late fight. But he tells me more news of our suffering – by the death of one or two captains more then I know before. But he doth give over the thoughts of the safety of the *Swiftsure* or *Essex*.

Thence homewards, landed at the Old Swan, and there find my pretty Betty Michell and her husband at their door in Thamesstreete; which I was glad to find, and went into their shop and they made me drink some of their strong water – the first time I was ever with them there – I do exceedingly love her. After sitting a little, and talking with them about several things at great distance, I parted and home to my business*a* late. But I am to observe how the drinking of some strong water did immediately put my eyes into a fit of sorenesse again, as they were the other day[2] – I mean, my right eye only.

Late at night I have an account brought me by Sir W Warren that he hath gone through four lighters for me[3] – which pleases me very well. So home to bed – much troubled with our disappointment at the Tanger Committee.

10. *Lords day.* Up very betimes, and down the River to Deptford and did a good deal of business in sending away and directing several things to the fleet. That being done, back to London to my office and there at my office till after church-time, fitting some notes to carry to Sir W. Coventry in the afternoon. At noon home to dinner, where my Cosen Joyces, both of them, they and their wifes and little Will, came by invitation to dinner

a   repl. 'of'

---

1. In a letter to Coventry, dated this day (Longleat, Coventry MSS 97, f. 21*r*), Pepys referred to their meeting in the afternoon, and detailed the steps he was taking to victual the

fleet. He kept a note of these preparations: Rawl. A 195a, pp. 247–8.
2. On 23 May strong beer had caused him similar discomfort.
3. See below, p. 161.

to me, and I had a good dinner for them; but Lord, how sick was I of W Joyce's company, both the impertinencies of it and his ill-manners before me at my table to his wife, which I could hardly forbear taking notice of; but being at my table, and for his wife's sake, I did, though I will prevent his giving me the like occasion again at my house, I will warrant him.

After dinner I took leave, and by water to White-hall and there spent all the afternoon in the gallery, till the Council was up, to speak with Sir W. Coventry.

Walking here, I met with Pierce the surgeon – who is lately come from*a* the fleet, and tells me that all the commanders, officers, and even*b* the common seamen, do condemn every part of the late conduct of the Duke of Albemarle.   Both in his fighting at all – in his manner of fighting, running among them – in his retreat, and running the ships on ground – so as nothing can be worse spoken of.   That Holmes, Spragg, and Smith do all the business, and the old and wiser commanders nothing – so as Sir Tho. Teddiman (whom the King and all the world speak well of) is mightily discontented, as being wholly slighted.   He says we lost more after the Prince[1] came then before, too.   The *Prince* was so maimed, as to be forced to be towed home.   He says all the fleet confess their being chased home by the Dutch; and yet the body of the Dutch that did it was not above 40 sail at most – and yet this put us into the fright, as to bring all our ships on ground. He says, however, that the Duke of Albemarle is as high almost as ever, and pleases himself to think that he hath given the Duch their bellies full – without sense of what he hath lost us – and talks how he knows now the way to beat them.   But he says that even Smith himself, one of his creatures, did him himself condemn the late conduct from the beginning to the end.

He tells me further how the Duke of York is wholly given up to his new mistress, my Lady Denham,[2] going at noonday, with all his gentlemen with him, to visit her in Scotland-yard – she declar-

---

a MS. 'to'   *b* repl. 'e'-

---

1. Rupert.
2. For this affair, see Gramont, pp. 169–70, 190. She was the wife of

Sir John Denham, poet and courtier, having married him on 25 May 1665, at the age of 18.

ing she will not be his mistress, as Mrs. Price,[1] to go up and down the privy stairs, but will be owned publicly; and so she is. Mr. Brouncker[2] it seems was the pimp to bring it about, and my Lady Castlemayne, who designs thereby to fortify herself by the Duke – there being a falling-out the other day between the King and her. On this occasion the Queene, in ordinary talk before the ladies in her drawing-room, did say to my Lady Castlemayne that she feared the King did take cold by staying so late abroad at her house. She answered, before them all, that he did not stay so late abroad with her, for he went betimes thence (though[a] he doth not before 1, 2, or 3 in the morning), but must stay somewhere else. The King then coming in, and overhearing, did whisper in the eare aside and told her she was a bold impertinent woman, and bid her be gone out of the Court and not come again till he sent for her – which she did presently;* and went[b] to a lodging in the Pell mell and kept there two or three days, and then sent to the King to know whether she might send for her things away out of her house; the King sent to her, she must first come and view them; and so she came, and the King went to her and all friends again. He tells me she did in her anger say she would be even with the King, and print his letters to her.[3]

So putting all together, we are, and are like to be, in a sad condition.

We are endeavouring to raise money by borrowing it on the City; but I do not think the City will lend a farthing.[4]

By and by the Council broke up, and I spoke with Sir W. Coventry about business; with whom I doubt not in a little time to be mighty well, when I shall appear to mind my business again as I used to do – which, by the grace of God I will do.

Gone from him, I endeavoured to find out Sir G. Carteret;

---

a repl. 'so'   *b* repl. 'took'

---

1. Goditha Price – 'fat Price' (Gramont, p. 243) – a maid of honour to the Duchess, and a daughter of Sir Herbert Price, Master of the King's Household.

2. Henry, brother of Pepys's colleague Lord Brouncker.

3. She was not as good as her word.

4. See below, p. 174 & n. 4. Clarendon wrote to Ormond on 18 June that the government hoped for a loan of £100,000 and that he did not doubt to obtain it: Lister, iii. 434–5.

and at last did at Mr. Ashburnhams in the Old Palace yard: and thence he and I stepped out and walked an hour in the churchyard under Henry the 7th's chapel – he being lately come from the fleet. And tells me, as I hear from everybody else, that the management in the late fight was bad from top to bottom. That several have*a* said this would not have been, if my Lord Sandwich had had the ordering of it. Nay, he tells me that certainly, had my Lord Sandwich had the misfortune to have done as they have done, the King could not have saved him. There is, too, nothing but discontent among the officers; and all the old experienced men are slighted. He tells me, to my question (but as a great secret), that the dividing of the fleet did proceed first from a proposition from the fleet,[1] though agreed to hence. But he confesses it arose from want of due intelligence – which he confesses we do want. He doth, however, call the fight*b* on Sunday a very honourable retreat, and that the Duke of Albemarle did do well in it, and could have been well if he had done it sooner, rather then venture the loss of the fleet and crown, as he must have done if the Prince had not come. He was surprized when I told him I heard that the King did entend to borrow some money of the City, and would know who had spoke of it to me: I told him Sir Ellis Layton,[2] this afternoon. He says it is a dangerous discourse, for that the City certainly will not be invited to do it; and then, for the King to ask it and be denied, will be the beginning of our sorrow. He seems to fear we shall all fall to pieces among ourselfs.

This evening we hear that Sir Chr. Mings is dead of his late wounds – and Sir W. Coventry did commend [him] to me in a most extraordinary manner.

But this day, after three days' trial in vain and the hazard of the spoiling of the ship in lying till next spring, besides the disgrace of it, news is brought that the *Loyall London* is launched – at Deptford.[3]

a MS. 'of' (phonetic spelling)   *b* MS. 'fleet'

1. This seems to have been the case: below, p. 179 & n. 4.

2. Leighton, courtier and lawyer, was a leading member of the Merchant Taylors Company, Secretary to the Royal African Company and one of the secretaries to the Prize Office.

3. Descriptions in *London Gazette*, 14 June.

Having talked thus much with Sir G. Carteret, we parted there; and I home by water, taking in my boat with me Young Michell and my Betty his wife, meeting them accidentally going*a* to look* a boat. I set them down at the Old Swan, and myself went through bridge to the Tower and so home, and after supper, to bed.

11. Up, and down by water to Sir W Warren's (the first time I was in his new house on the other side the water[1] since*b* he enlarged it) to discourse about our lighters that he hath bought for me, and I hope to get 100*l* by this jobb. Having done with him, I took boat again (being mightily struck with a woman in a hat, a seaman's moher that stood on the quay) and home; where at the office all the morning with Sir W. Coventry and some others of our board, hiring of fireships; and Sir W. Coventry begins to see my pains again which I do begin to take, and I am proud of it – and I hope shall continue it. He gone at noon, I home to dinner; and after dinner my father and wife out to the painter's for my father to sit again, and I with*c* my Lady Pen and her daughter to see Harman[2] – who we find lame in bed. His bones*d* of his Anckle is broke, but he hopes to do well soon; and a fine person by his discourse he seems to be, and mighty*e* hearty. And he did plainly tell me that at the council of war before the fight, it was against his reason to begin the fight then, and the reasons of most sober men there[3] – the wind being such, and we to windward, that they could not use their lower tier of guns – which was a very sad thing for us, to have the honour and weal of the nation ventured so foolishly.

I left them there and walked to Deptford, reading in Wallsing-

---

a repl. 'at'   b repl. 'when'   c repl. 'down to'
d repl. 'leg'   e MS. 'my'

---

1. At Rotherhithe, on the Surrey side, opposite his yard at Wapping.
2. Sir John Harman, rear-admiral; a friend of the Penns.
3. This evidence (supported by that of Penn, below, p. 194) contradicts the statement which Albemarle made in defence of his conduct in October 1667 to the Commons. He then alleged that his flag-officers had been unanimous in wanting to engage the enemy, while he had been for a prudent withdrawal into the Thames. *CJ*, ix. 12.

hams *manuall*,[1] a very good book, and there met with Sir W. Batten and my Lady at Uthwayts. Here I did much business, and yet had some little mirth with my Lady; and anon we all came up together to our[a] office, where I was very late, doing much business. Late comes Sir Jo Bankes to see me, and tell me that coming up from Rochester, he overtook above 3 or 400 seamen, and he believes every day they come flocking from the fleet in like numbers; which is a sad neglect there, when it will be impossible to get others and we have little reason to think these will return presently again.

He gone, I to end my letters tonight; and then home to supper and to bed.

12. Up, and to the office, where we sat all the morning. At noon to dinner, and then to White-hall in hopes of a meeting of Tanger about Yeabsly's business, but it could not be obtained – Sir G. Carteret nor Sir W. Coventry being able to be there – which still vexes [me], to see the poor man forced still to attend; as also, being desirous to see what my profit is, and get it.[2]

Walking here in the galleries, I find the Ladies of Honour dressed in their riding garbs, with coats and doublets with deep skirts, just for all the world like men, and buttoned[b] their doublets up the breast, with perriwigs and with hats; so that, only for a long petticoat dragging under their men's coats, nobody could take them for women in any point whatever[3] – which was an odde sight, and a sight did not please me. It was Mrs. Wells[4] and another fine lady that I saw thus.

Thence down by water to Deptford; and there late, seeing some things despatched down to the fleet; and so home (thinking endeed to have met with Bagwell, but I did not) to write my letters, very late; and so to supper and to bed.

---

a s.h. repl. l.h. 'L'-   *b* repl. same symbol badly formed

---

1. See above, v. 10, n. 2.
2. The accounts of Thomas Yeabsley and his partners for the victualling of Tangier were under scrutiny. Pepys received £300 p.a. from them for his good offices: above, v. 210.

3. This was the usual riding-habit: above, vi. 172 & n. 4.
4. Winifred Wells, Maid of Honour to the Queen.

13. Up, and by coach to St. James's, and there did our business before the Duke as usual – having, before the Duke came out of his bed, walked in an antechamber with Sir H. Cholmly, who tells me there is great Jarrs between the Duke of York and the Duke of Albemarle about the latter's turning out one or two of the commanders put in by the Duke of York – among others, Captain Du Tell, a Frenchman,[1] put in by the Duke of York and mightily defended by him; and is therein led by Monsieur Blancford,[2] that it seems hath the same command over the Duke of York as Sir W. Coventry hath – which raises ill-blood between them. And I do in several little things observe that Sir W. Coventry hath of late by the by reflected on the Duke of Albemarle and his Captains, perticularly in that of Old Teddiman, who did deserve to be turned out this fight, and was so; but I heard Sir W. Coventry say that the Duke of Albemarle put in one as bad as he in his room – and one that did as little.[3]

After we had done with the Duke of York, I*a* with others to White-hall, there to attend again a Comittee of Tanger, but there was none, which vexed me to the heart, and makes me mighty doubtful that when we have one, it will be prejudicd against poor Yeabsly, and to my great disadvantage*b* ⟨thereby⟩ – my Lord Peterborough making it his business, I perceive (whether in spite to me, whom he cannot but smell to be a friend to it, or to my Lord Ashly, I know not), to obstruct it, and seems to take delight in disappointing of us; but I shall be revenged of him.

Here I stayed a very great while, almost till noon; and then

     a repl. 'we'   *b* repl. same symbol badly formed

1. Jean-Baptiste du Teil was now removed from the command of the *Jersey* frigate. In a letter to the Duke of 18 June, the Admirals of the fleet, Rupert and Albemarle, remarked on 'some great miscarriages and disorders in the last engagement, which might possibly arise from the difference of language betwixt du Teil and those who ought to have been commanded by him': *Rupert and Monck Letter Book, 1666* (ed. J. R. Powell and E. K. Timings), p. 71. The captain was later knighted, given a post in the Duke's household and

employed on diplomatic missions. James's liking for French servants dated from his service in the French army in the 1650s.

2. The Marquis de Blanquefort (Turenne's nephew, now a naturalised Englishman and after 1677 Earl of Feversham) was a member of the Duke of York's household and a colonel in his troop of guards.

3. Henry Teddeman, sen., of the *Unicorn*, appears to have been replaced by Anthony Langston: *CSPD 1666–7*, p. 439. Cf. above, p. 154, n. 3.

M

(meeting Balty) I took him with me, and to Westminster to the Exchequer, about breaking of two tallies of 2000*l* each into smaller tallies, which I have been endeavouring a good while; but to my trouble, it will not I fear be done, though there be no reason*a* against it, but only a little trouble to the clerks. But it is nothing to me of real profit at all.

Thence with Balty to Hales's by coach (it being the seventh day from my making my last oaths, and by them I am at liberty to dispense with any of my oaths every seventh day, after I had for the six days before-going performed all my vows).*b*

Here I find my father's picture begun;[1] and so much to my content, that it joys my very heart to think that I should have his picture so well done – who, besides that he is my father, and a man that loves me and hath ever done so – is also at this day one of the most careful and innocent men in the world.

Thence with mighty content homeward; and in my way, at the Stockes,[2] did buy a couple of lobsters, and so home to dinner.

Where I find my wife and father had dined, and were going out to Hales's to sit there. So Balty and I alone to dinner; and in the middle of my grace, praying for a blessing upon (these his good creatures), my mind fell upon my Lobsters – upon which I cried, "Cuds zookes!" And Balty looked upon me like a man*c* at a loss what I meant, thinking at first that I meant only that I had said the grace after meat, instead of that before meat; but then I cried, "What is become of my lobsters?", whereupon he run out of doors to overtake the coach, but could not, and so came back again, and mighty merry at dinner to think of my Surprize. After dinner to the Excize office by appointment, and there find my Lord Bellasyse and the Commissioners; and by and by the whole company*d* came to dispute the business of our running so far behind-hand there, and did come to a good issue in it – that is to say, to resolve upon having the debt due to us[3] and the household and the Guards from the Excize stated, and so we shall come to know the worst of our condition and endeavour for some help from my Lord Treasurer.

    a repl. 'reas'-   *b* no bracket in MS.   *c* repl. 'was'
                d repl. 'company'

1. See above, p. 151, n. 2. (OM).   3. The Tangier commissioners.
2. See above, p. 14, n. 1.

Thence home, and put off Balty; and so (being invited) to Sir Chr. Mings's Funerall, but find them gone to church. However, I into the church[1] (which is a fair large church, and a great Chappell), and there heard the service and stayed till they buried him, and then out. And there met with Sir W. Coventry (who was there out of great generosity, and no person of quality there but he) and went with him into his Coach; and being in it with him, there happened this extraordinary case – one of the most Romantique that ever I heard of in my life, and could not have believed but that I did see it*a* – which was this.

About a Dozen able, lusty, proper men came to the coach-side with tears in their eyes, and one of them, that spoke for the rest, begun and says to Sir W. Coventry – "We are here a Dozen of us that have long known and loved and served our dead commander, Sir Chr. Mings, and have now done the last office of laying him in the ground. We would be glad we*b* had any other to offer after him, and in revenge of him – all we have is our lives. If you will please to get his Royal Highness to give us a Fireshipp among us all, here is a Dozen of us, out of all which choose you one to be commander, and the rest of us, whoever he is, will serve him, and, if possible, do that that shall show our memory of our dead commander and our revenge."[2] Sir W. Coventry was herewith much moved (as well as I, who could hardly abstain from weeping) and took their names; and so parted, telling me that he would move his Royal Highness as in a thing very extraordinary (what was done thereon, see the next day in this book)[3], and so we parted.

The truth is, Sir Chr. Mings was a very stout man, and a man of great parts and most excellent tongue* among ordinary men; and as Sir W. Coventry says, could have been the most useful man in the world at such a pinch of time as this. He was come

---

a followed by symbol rendered illegible   *b* repl. 'to'

---

1. St Mary's, Whitechapel; chapel-of-ease to Stepney. The building was reconstructed c. 1675. See Stow, *Survey* (ed. Strype, 1720), bk iv. 44+. (R).
2. Service in fireships was the most dangerous of all naval duties. Their

offer appears to have been accepted: *CSPD 1665–6*, p. 471.
3. There is no mention of the matter either at 14 June or later. But Pepys's work on the diary was at this point 'disturbed': below, p. 167.

into great renowne here at home,*a* and more abroad, in the West
Indys.[1] He had brought his family into a way of being great.
But dying at this time, his memory and name (his father being
always, and at this day, a Shoomaker, and his mother a Hoymans
daughter, of which he was used frequently to boast)[2] will be
quite forgot in a few months, as if he had never been, nor any
of his name be the better by it – he having not had time to
coll[ect] any estate; but is dead poor rather then rich.

So we left the church and crowd, and I*b* home (being set down
on Tower hill) and there did a little business, and then in the
evening went down by water to Deptford, it being very late.
And there I stayed out as much time as I could and then took
boat again homeward. But the officers being gone in, returned
and*c* walked to Mrs. Bagwell's house; and there (it being by this
time pretty dark and past 10 a-clock) went into her house and did
what I would.*d* But I was not a little fearful of what she told
me but now; which is, that her servant was dead of the plague –
that her coming to me yesterday was the first day of her coming
forth, and that she had new-whitened the house all below stairs,
but that above stairs they are not so fit for me to go up to, they
being not so. So I parted thence with a very good will, but very
civil; and away to the waterside and sent for a pint of sack, and
so home, drank what I would and gave the waterman the rest,
and so adieu. Home about 12 at night, and so to bed – finding
most of my people gone to bed.

In my way home I called on a fisherman and bought three
Eeles, which cost me 3*s*.*e*

14. Up, and to the office and there sat all the morning. At
noon dined at home, and thence with my wife and father to
Hales, and there looked only on ⟨my⟩ father's picture (which is
mighty like), and so away to White-hall to a committee for
Tanger – where the Duke of York was and Sir W. Coventry,

---

a MS. 'noon'   *b* repl. 'led'   *c* repl. 'to'
        d repl. 'could'   *e* smudge under '*s*'

---

1. He had served twice in the W.
Indies (in 1655–7 and again shortly
before the second Dutch War) but his
reputation there derived mainly from

his taking Santiago (Cuba) in October
1662.
    2. Cf. above, vi. 278, n. 2.

and a very full committee; and instead of[a] having a very pre-judiced meeting, they did (though endeed inclined against Yeabsly) yield to the greatest part of his account, so as to allow of his demands to the value of 7000*l* and more, and only give time for him to make good his pretence to the rest[1] – which was mighty joy to me; and so we rose up. But I must observe the force of money, which did make my Lord Ashly to argue, and behave himself in the business, with the greatest friendship and yet with all the discretion imaginable – and will be a business of admonition and instruction to me concerning him (and other men too, for aught I know) as long as I live. Thence took Creed, with some kind of violence and some hard words between us, to St. James's, to have found out Sir W. Coventry to have signed the order for his payment, among others that did stay on purpose to do it. (And which is strange, among the rest, my Lord Ashly; who did cause Creed to write it presently, and kept two or three of them with him by cunning to stay and sign it); but Creed's ill-nature (though never so well bribed, as it hath lately in this case, by 20 pieces) will not be overcome from his usual delays.

Thence, failing of meeting Sir W. Coventry, I took leave of Creed (very good friends) – and away home; and there took out my father, wife, sister, and Mercer our grand Tour[2] in the evening, and made it 10 at night before we got home. Only, drink at the door at Islington, at the Katherin wheele, and so home and to the office a little, and then to bed.

15. Up betimes, and to my Journall entries – but disturbed by many businesses. Among others, by Mr. Houblons coming to me about evening their freight for Tanger, which I did. And then Mr. Bland, who presented me yesterday with a very fine Affrican Matt (to lay upon the ground under a bed of state), being the first fruits of our peace with Guyland.[3]

a repl. 'a'

---

1. Cf. above, p. 128 & n. 3. Yeabsley and his partners were allowed £7519 for victualling a transport for 22 weeks: PRO, AO1/310/1220.

2. See above, pp. 121-2.

3. A treaty of peace and alliance concluded on 2 April with the Berber leader: Routh, p. 90.

So to the office, and thither came my pretty widow Mrs. Burrows, poor woman, to get*a* her ticket paid for her husband's service – which I did pay her myself, and did bezar her muchas vezes – and I do hope may hereafter have mas de su company.

Thence to Westminster to the Exchequer, but could not persuade the blockheaded fellows to do what I desire, of breaking my great tallies into less, notwithstanding my Lord Treasurer's order – which vexed so much, that I would not bestow more time and trouble among a company of dunces; and so back again home and to dinner, whither Creed came and dined with me.

And after dinner Mr Moore and he and I abroad, thinking to go down the River together; but the tide being against me, could*b* not, but returned and walked an hour in the garden; but Lord, to hear how he pleases himself in behalf of my Lord Sandwich in the miscarriage of the Duke of Albemarle – and doth inveigh against Sir W. Coventry as a cunning knave; but I think that without any manner of reason at all, but only his passion.

He being gone, I to my chamber at home to set my Journall right, and so to settle my Tanger accounts – which I did in very good order: and then in the evening comes Mr. Yeabsly to reckon with me, which I did also, and have above*c* 200*l* profit therein to myself; which is a great blessing, the God of Heaven make me*d* thankful for it. That being done, and my eyes beginning to be sore with overmuch*e* writing, I to supper and to bed.

16. Up betimes, and to my office – and then we sat all the morning – and despatched much business – the King – Duke of York – and Sir W. Coventry being gone down to the fleet. At noon home to dinner, and then down to Woolwich and Deptford to look after things, my head akeing from the multitude of businesses I had in my head yesterday in settling my accounts.

a 'to get' repeated   *b* MS. 'would'   *c* repl. 'near'

d repl. 'is'   *e* repl. 'con'-

All the way down and up, reading of *The Mayor of Quinborough*, a simple play.¹

At Deptford while I am there, comes Mr. Williamson, Sir Arth. Ingram, and Jacke Fen to see the new ships,² which they had done; and then I with them home in their boat, and a very fine gentleman Mr. Williamson is.

It seems the Dutch do mightily insult of their victory, and they have great reason. Sir Wm. Barkely was killed before his ship taken – and there he lies dead in a Sugar Chest for everybody to see, with his Flagg standing up by him³ – and Sir George Ascue is carried up and down The Hague for people to see.

Home to my office, where late; and then to bed.

17. *Lords day.* Being invited to Anthon. Joyces to dinner, my wife and sister and Mercer and I walked out in the morning, it being fine weather, to Christ Church; and there heard a silly sermon, but sat where we saw one of the prettiest little boys, with the prettiest mouth, that ever I saw in life.⁴

Thence to Joyces, where Wm. Joyce and his wife were – and had a good dinner; but Lord, how sick was I of the company, only hope I shall have no more of it a good while. But am invited to Will's this week; and his wife, poor unhappy woman, cried to hear me say that I could not be there, she thinking that I slight her – so they got me to promise to come.

Thence my father and I walked to Grayse Inn-fields and there spent an hour or two, walking and talking of several businesses. First, as to his estate, he told me it produced about 80*l* per annum. But then there goes 30*l* per annum taxes and other things, certain charge – which I do promise to make good,ᵃ as far as this 30*l* – at which the poor manᵇ was overjoyed and wept.

a repl. 'go'   *b* repl. 'was'

---

1. A history play by Thomas Middleton (written c. 1618, but not published until 1661: PL 1075). (A).
2. Two ships had just been built at Woolwich and Deptford: above, p. 153; *CSPD 1665–6*, p. 343.
3. His body had been embalmed by the anatomist Ruysch, and lay in the Grote Kerk in The Hague. It was brought home and buried in Westminster Abbey in August. *London Gazette*, 15 July; *Gent. Mag.*, 57 (1787)/214.
4. Christ Church, Newgate St, served as the chapel of Christ's Hospital school.

As to Pall, he tells me he is mightily satisfied with Ensum; and so I promised to give her 500*l* presently, and to oblige myself to 100*l* more on the birth of her first child, he insuring her in 10*l* per annum for every 100*l*.[1] And in the meantime, till she doth marry, I promise to allow her 10*l* per annum.

Then as to John, I tell him I will promise him nothing, but will supply him as so much lent him – I declaring that I am not pleased with him yet.[2] And that when his degree is over, I will send for him up hither, and if he be good for anything, doubt not to get him preferment.[3]

This discourse ended to the joy of my father, and no less to me, to see that I am able to do this; we return[a] to Joyces and there, wanting a coach to carry us home, I walked out as far as the New Exchange to find one, but could not. So down to the Milke-house[4] and drank three glasses of whey, and then up into the Strand[b] again, and there met with a coach. And so to Joyces and took up my father, wife, sister, and Mercer, and to Islington, where we drank, and then our Tour by Hackny home – where, after a little business at my office and then talk with my Lady and Pegg Pen in the garden, I home and to bed – being very weary.

18. Up betimes, and in my chamber most of the morning, setting things to right there, my Journall and accounts with my father and brother. Then to the office a little, and so to Lumberd-street to borrow a little money upon a tally, but cannot. Thence to Exchequer, and there after much wrangling got consent that I should have a great tally broken into little ones. Thence to Hales's to see how my father's picture goes on, which pleases me

---

a repl. 'up'   *b* MS. 'Strang' (s.h.)

---

1. Sc. Ensum was to settle on Pall 10% of her portion. This was a high rate: cf. above, vi. 138 & n. 1.
2. For their quarrel, see above, v. 91.
3. See above, p. 50, n. 2.

4. Possibly the whey-house mentioned at 10 June 1663. Both references suggest a location near to the New Exchange and between the Thames and the Strand. (R.)

mighty well, though I find again, as I did[a] in Mrs. Pierces, that a picture may have more of likeness in the first or second working then it shall have when finished; though this is very well, and to my full content; but so it is. And contrarily, mine was not so like at the first, second, or third sitting as it was afterward.

Thence to my Lord Bellasyse by invitation, and there dined with him and his lady and daughter; and at dinner there played to us a young boy lately come from France, where he had been learning a year or two on the viallin, and plays finely. But impartially, I do not find any goodness in their ayres (though very good) beyond ours, when played by the same hand; I observed in several of Baptiste's (the present great composer) and our Bannisters.[1] But it was pretty to see how passionately my Lord's daughter loves music, the most that ever I saw creature in my life. Thence, after dinner, home and to the office; and anon to Lombard-street again – where much talk at Colvill's, he censuring the times and how matters are ordered – and with reason enough. But above all, the thinking to borrow money of the City, which will not be done but will be denied (they being little pleased with the King's affairs), and that must breed differences between the King and the City.[2] Thence down the water to Deptford to order things away to the fleet; and back again, and after some business at my office late, home to supper and to bed.

Sir W. Coventry is returned this night from the fleet – he being the activest man in the world, and we all (myself perticularly) more afeared of him then of the King or his service, for aught I see; God forgive us. ⟨This day the great news is come of the French their taking the Island of St. Christophers from us – and it is to be feared they have done the like of all those Islands there-abouts.[3] This makes the City mad.⟩[b]

---

    a   repl. 'ever'   *b*   addition crowded in between entries

---

1. John Banister directed the King's string band of 24 performers. 'Baptiste' was Jean-Baptiste Lully.

2. See above, p. 159 & n. 4.

3. St Kitt's (one of the Leeward Is.) was shared between the English and the French. The latter took control of the whole island after a short campaign in April; but no other island was now taken. The peace of 1667 restored the *status quo* in St Kitt's.

19. Up and to my office, there to fit business against the rest meet; which they did by and by, and sat late. After the office rose (with Creed with me), to Wm. Joyce's to dinner, being invited; and there find my father and sister, my wife and Mercer, with them, almost dined. I made myself as complaisant as I could till I had dined, but yet much against my will; and so away after dinner with Creed to Pennys my tailor – where I bespoke a thin stuff suit – and did spend a little time evening some little accounts with Creed. And so parted, and I to Sir G Carterets by appointment – where I perceive by him the King is going to borrow some money of the City; but I fear it will do no good, but hurt. He tells me how the Generall is displeased, and there have been some high words between the Generall and Sir W Coventry. And it may be so, for I do not find Sir W. Coventry so highly commending the Duke as he used to be, but letting fall now and then some little jerkes. As this day, speaking of news from Holland, says, "I find their victory begins to shrinke there, as well as ours here."[1]

Here I met with Captain Cocke, and he tells me that the first thing the Prince said to the King upon his coming, was complaining of the Commissioners of the Navy – that they could have been abroad in three or four days but for us; that we do not take care of them – which I am troubled at, and do fear may in violence break out upon this office some time or other; for we shall not be able to carry on the business.

Thence home, and at my business till late at night; then with my wife into the garden, and there sang with Mercer – whom I feel myself beginning to love too much, by handling of her breasts in a morning when she dresses me, they being the finest that ever I saw in my life; that is the truth of it.

So home, and to supper with beans and bacon, and to bed.

20. Up, but in some pain of the Collique – hav[ing] of late taken too much cold by washing my feet and going in a thin silk waistcoat, without any other coat over it, and open-breasted. But I hope it will go*a* over.

a MS. 'be go'

---

1. Cf. the similar news reported   *Gazette*, 14 and 18 June.
from The Hague in the *London*

I did this morning (my father being to go away tomorrow) give my father some money to buy him a horse, and for other things, to himself and my mother and sister, among them, 20*l* – besides undertaking to pay for other things for them to about 3*l* – which the poor man takes with infinite kindness, and I do not think I can bestow it better. Thence by coach to St. James's as usual, to wait on the Duke of York (after having discoursed with Collonell Fitzgerald,[1] whom I met in my way and he returned with me to Westminster, about paying him a sum of 700 and odd pounds, and he bids me defalk 25*l* for myself, which is a very good thing). Having done with the Duke, I to Exchequer and there after much ado do get my business quite over, of the difficulty of breaking a great tally into little ones; and so shall have it done tomorrow.

Thence to the Hall, and with Mrs. Martin home and stayed with her a while; and then away to the Swan and sent for a bit of meat and dined there. And thence to Faythorne the picture-seller's, and there chose two or three good Cutts to try to Vernish. And so to Hales's to see my father's picture, which is now near finished and is very good. And here I stayed and took a nap of an hour, thinking my father and wife would have come; but they did not, so I away home as fast as I could, fearing lest my father, this day going abroad to see Mr. Honiwood at Major Russells, might meet with any trouble; and so in great pain home. But to spite me, in Cheapside I met Mrs. Williams in a coach, and she called me, so I must needs light and go along with her and poor Knipp (who is as big as she can tumble, and looks every day to lie down) as far as PaterNoster row; which I did do, and there stayed in Bennet's shop with them, and was fearful lest the people of the shop, knowing me, should ask after my father and give Mrs. Williams any knowledge of me to my disgrace.

Having seen them done there, and accompanied them to Ludgate, I light, and into my owne coach and home, where I find my father and wife had had no intent of coming at all to Hales's. So I at home all the evening doing business, and at night in the garden (it having been these three or four days mighty hot weather) singing in the evening; and then home to supper and to bed.

1. Lieutenant-Governor of Tangier.

21. Up, and at the office all the morning – where, by several circumstances, I find Sir W. Coventry and the Duke of Albemarle do not agree as they used to do – Sir W. Coventry commending Aylett (in some reproach to the Duke), whom the Duke hath put out for want of courage[1] – and found fault with Steward, whom the Duke keeps in, though as much in fault as any commander in the fleet.[2]

At noon home to dinner – my father, sister, and wife dining at Sarah Giles's, poor woman – where I should have been, but my pride would not suffer me.[3]

After dinner, to Mr. Debusty's to speak with Sir Robt. Viner – a fine house and a great many fine ladies. He used me mighty civilly. My business was to set the matter right about the letter of Credit he did give my Lord Bellaces, that I may take up the tallies lodged with Viner for his security in the answering of my Lord's bills – which we did set right very well; and Sir R Viner went home with me and did give me the 5000*l* tallies presently. Here at Mr. Debusty's, I saw in a gold frame a picture of a Fluter playing on his Flute – which for a good while I took for painting, but at last observed it a piece of Tapstry and is the finest that ever I saw in my life – for figures and good natural Colours, and a very fine thing it is indeed.[4]

So home, and met Sir George Smith by the way, who tells me that this day my Lord Chancellor and some of the Court have been with the City, and the City have voted to lend the King 100000*l* – which, if soon paid (as he says he believes it will), will be a greater service then I did ever expect at this time from the City.[5]

So home to my letters, and then with my wife in the garden, and then upon our leads singing in the evening, and so to supper

1. Capt. John Aylett, of the *Port-land*, had another but inferior command (that of the *Forester*) in 1668.

2. Capt. Francis Steward, of the *Golden Phoenix*, seems to have held no further command.

3. She was a connection of Pepys's mother – a poor relation, like the Joyces. She and her husband Thomas lived in St Giles's, Cripplegate. She was illiterate, and attested her will

(1670) with a mark.

4. Unidentified. (OM).

5. A loan was voted, *nem. con.*, to be raised on the credit of the Additional Aid: LRO, Letter Bk WW, f. 78*v*. The last instalment was paid in early September: Sharpe, ii. 414. Clarendon was accompanied by Southampton, the Lord Treasurer, among others: Lister, iii. 434–5.

(and while at supper comes young Michell, whose wife I love, little Betty Howlet, to get my favour about*a* a ticket;[1] and I am glad of this occasion of obliging him and give occasion of his coming to me, for I must be better acquainted with him and her); and after supper, to bed.

22. Up, and before I went out, Mr. Peter Barr[2] sent me a Terce of Clarret, which is very welcome. And so abroad, down the River to Deptford and there did some business; and then to*b* Westminster and there did with much ado get my tallies (my small ones instead of one great one of 2000*l*); and so away home*c* – and there all day upon my Tanger accounts with Creed; and he being gone, with myself in settling other accounts till past 12 at night; and then everybody being in bed, I to bed –
My father, wife, and sister having been late abroad upon the water. And Mercer being gone to her mother's and stayed so late, she could not get into the office, which vexed me.

23. My father and sister very betimes took their leave; and my wife, with all possible kindness, went with them to the Coach – I being mightily pleased with their company thus long, and my father with his being here; and it rejoices my heart that I am in condition to do anything to comfort him, and could, were it not for my mother, have been contented he should have stayed alway here with me – he is such innocent company. They being gone, I to my papers, but vexed at what I heard but a little of this morning before my wife went out: that Mercer and she fell out last night, and that the girl is gone home to her mother's for altogether. This troubles me, though perhaps it may be an ease to me of so much charge.*d* But I love the girle, and another we must be forced to keep, I do foresee; and then*e* shall be sorry to part with her.
At the office all the morning, much disquiet[ed] in my mind in the middle*f* of my business about this girl. Home at noon to

a repl. 'a'   *b* repl. 'home'   *c* repl. 'to'   *d* repl. 'hab'-
     e repl. 'I'   *f* repl. same symbol

---

1. Tavern keepers such as Mitchell were often used by sailors to cash their pay-tickets.
2. A London merchant trading principally with France. In April he had supplied provisions to the Navy at Portsmouth: *CSPD 1665–6*, p. 335.

dinner; and what with the going away of my father today and
the loss of Mercer, I after dinner went up to my chamber and
there could have cried to myself, had not people come to me
about business.   In the evening down to Tower wharfe, thinking
to go by water; but could not get watermen, they being now so
scarce by reason of the great press.^a¹   So to the Custome-house;
and there with great threats got a couple to carry me down to
Deptford, all the way reading *Pompey the Great* (a play translated
from French by several noble persons; among other, my
Lord Buckehurst);² but to me is but a mean play, and the words
and sense not very extraordinary.   From Deptford I walked to
Redriffe, and was in my way overtaken by Bagwell, lately
come from sea in the *Providence*; who did give me an account of
several perticulars in the late fight, and how his ship was deserted
basely by the *Yorke*, Captain Swanly, commander.³   So I home;
and there, after writing my letters, home to supper and to bed –
fully resolved to rise betimes and go down the River tomorrow
morning, being vexed this night to find none of the officers in
the yard at 7 at night, nor anybody concerned, as if it were a
Dutch warr.   ⟨It seems Mercer's mother was here in the morning
to speak with my wife, but my wife would not.   In the afternoon I and my wife, in writing, did instruct W. Hewers in some
discourse to her; and she in the evening did come and satisfy
my wife; and by and by Mercer did come – which I was mighty
glad of, and eased of much pain about her.⟩^b

---

a MS. 'price'   *b* addition crowded into bottom of page

---

1. Either they had been pressed, or
were in hiding for fear of it.   Regulations governing watermen's liability
to the press are in Duke of York,
Mem. (naval), pp. 149–50, 274, 276;
cf. H. Humpherus, *Hist. Watermen*, i.
296, 297.   Masters of barges and
watermen to privileged persons were
usually exempt.

2. A translation of Corneille's
*Pompée: Pompey the Great, a tragedy.
As it was acted by the servants of His*
*Royal Highness the Duke of York.
Translated out of French by certain
Persons of Honour* (1664; quarto):
PL 1604 (2).   The translators, apart
from Buckhurst (Dorset), were Ed-
mund Waller, Sir Charles Sedley,
Edward Filmer and Sidney Godol-
phin (A).

3. Capt. John Swanley, appointed
to command of the *York* in 1664,
appears to have received no further
command.

24. *Sunday.* *Midsummer Day.*

Up, but, being weary the last night, not so soon as I intended. Then being dressed, I down by water to Deptford and there did a great deal of business, being in a mighty hurry – Sir W. Coventry writing to me that there was some thoughts that the Duch fleet were out or coming out.[1] Business being done, in providing for the carrying down of some provisions to the fleet, I away back home. And after dinner, by water to White-hall and there waited, till the Council rose, in the boarden gallery.

And there, among other things, I hear that Sir Francis Prugean is dead – after being married to a widow about a year or thereabouts. ⟨He died⟩ very rich*a* and had for the last year lived very handsomely – his lady bringing him to it.[2] He was no great painstaker in person, yet died very rich. And as Dr. Clerke says, was of a very great judgment, but hath writ nothing to leave his name to posterity by.

In the gallery, among others, met with Major Halsey[3] – a great creature of the Duke of Albemarle's; who tells me that the Duke, by name, hath said that he expected to have the work here up in the river done, having left Sir W. Batten and Mr. Phipps there.

He says that the Duke of Albemarle doth say that this is a victory we have had, having, as he was sure, killed them 8000 men, and sunk about 14 of their ships; but nothing like this appears true.[4] He lays much of*b* the little success we had, however, upon the fleet's being divided by order from above and the want of spirit in the commanders. And that he was com-

---

a sentence revised from 'Very rich he is left'   *b* repl. 'up'

---

1. They were out by the 26th: G. Brandt, *Michel de Ruiter* (trans., 1698), p. 368. The letter has not been traced.

2. Prujean, a 'skillfull & learned' physician (Evelyn, iii. 294), was five times President of the Royal College of Physicians. He had died on the previous day. His marriage to Margaret, daughter of Lord Gorges and widow of Sir Thomas Fleming, had taken place on 13 February 1664.

His will suggests that he was well-to-do before his second marriage, and in 1664 he was living in a largish house (12 hearths) in St Martin's Ludgate. (R).

3. See above, p. 145, n. 6.

4. Modern estimates are 2000 killed and 4 ships sunk: Clowes, ii. 276; Allin, vol. ii, p. xxvi. For Albemarle's boastfulness, see above, p. 148 & n. 6.

manded by order to go out of the Downes to the Gunfleete; and in the way meeting the Dutch fleet, what should he do? Should he not fight them? – especially having beat them heretofore at as great disadvantage. He tells me further, that having been down with*a* the Duke of Albemarle, he finds that Holmes and Spragg do govern most business of the Navy – and by others I understand that Sir Tho. Allen is offended thereat; that he is not so much advised with as he ought to be. He tells me also, as he says of his own knowledge, that several people, before the Duke went out, did offer to supply the King with 100000*l*, provided he *b*I would be Treasurer of it, to see it laid out for the Navy; which he refused, and so it died. But I believe none of this.

This day I saw my Lady Falmouth, with whom I remember now I have dined at my Lord Berkely's heretofore: a pretty pretty woman. She was now in her second or third mourning, and pretty pleasant in her looks.²

By and by the Council rises, and Sir W. Coventry comes out and he and I went aside and discoursed of much business of the Navy; and afterwards took his coach and to Hide parke, he and I alone. There we had much talk. First, he started a discourse of a talk he hears about the town, which, says he, is a very bad one, and fit to be suppressed if we knew how: which is the comparing of the success* of the last year³ with that of this, saying that that was good and that bad. I was as sparing in speaking as I could, being jealous* of him, and myself also, but wished it could be stopped; but said I doubted it could not, otherwise then by the fleet's*c* being abroad again, and so finding other work for men's minds and discourse. Then to discourse of himself, saying that he heard that he was under the lash of people's discourse about the Princes not having notice of the Dutch being out and

a repl. 'by'   *b* repl. 'the King would'   *c* repl. 'fleeting'

1. Albemarle.
2. Her husband (Charles Berkeley, Earl of Falmouth, an intimate of the King) had been killed in battle on 3 June 1665. She was a maid of honour to the Duchess of York, and, according to Gramont (p. 223) the only one among them who 'really had some semblance of virtue and beauty'. The reference here to mourning is to the second and third periods of its observance. Each lasted for several months.
3. At the Battle of Lowestoft: see above, vi. 122–3.

for him to come back again, nor the Duke of Albemarle notice that the Prince was sent for back again. To which, he told me very perticularly how careful he was, the very same night that it was to resolve to send for the Prince back, to cause orders to be writ;[1] and waked the Duke,[2] who was then in bed, to sign them; and that they went by express that very night, being the Wednesdy night before the Fight, which begun on the Friday; and that, for sending them by the post express and not by gentlemen on purpose, he made a sport of it, and said, "I knew none to send it with but would at least have lost more time in fitting themselfs out then any diligence of theirs beyond that that the ordinary post would have recovered."

I told him that this was not so much the towne-talk as the reason of dividing the Fleete. To this, he told me he ought not to say much; but did assure me in general, that the proposition did first come from the Fleete; and the resolution not being prosecuted[a] with orders so soon as the Generall[3] thought fit, the Generall did send Sir Edwd Spragge up on purpose for them; and that there was nothing in the whole business which was not done with the full consent and advice of the Duke of Albemarle.[4] But he

a repl. 'taken'

---

1. See above, pp. 143–4 & n.
2. The Duke of York.
3. Albemarle.
4. Coventry repeated this version of the events to the Commons in the debates of 20 October 1667 and 17 February 1668: Milward, pp. 90, 187–8; Grey, i. 80. His notes (probably written for the debates) are in Longleat, Coventry MSS 95, pp. 214, 393, 395 (partially printed in *Rupert and Monck Letter Book, 1666*, ed. J. R. Powell and E. K. Timings, pp. 201–3, 207). Pepys's account here is fuller than those of the parliamentary diarists who reported the debates. For discussion of the evidence, see authorities cited above, p. 144, n. 1. The fleet had divided on receiving the (false) news that a French force was approaching from

the west: see above, p. 139 & n. 3. This information had been sent from the government to Albemarle and Rupert at the Nore on 13 May, and they had agreed on the 14th to detach a squadron under Rupert to meet the French. Spragge was sent back to Whitehall for the official orders, but it was not until the 24th that Coventry was able to give them to him. (The choice of the ships which were to sail under Rupert was not made until the 22nd, and for reasons of secrecy Coventry had written out all the documents in his own hand.) Albemarle had agreed not only to the division of the fleet but also to the size of Rupert's squadron. He had however received none of the extra ships he had asked for as soon as the division was decided on.

did adde (though as the Catholiques call*ª le Secret de la Messe*) that Sir Edwd. Spragge, who had even in Sir Chr. Mings's time put in to be the great favourite of the Prince, but much more now had a mind to be the great man with him, and to that end had a mind to have the Prince at a distance from the Duke of Albemarle, that they might be doing something alone, did, as he believed, put on this business of dividing the fleet, and that thence it came.[1]

He tells me, as to the business of Intelligence, the want whereof the world did complain much of, that for that it was not his business,[2] and as he was therefore to have no share in the blame, so he would not meddle to lay it anywhere else.

That De Ruyter was ordered by the States not to make it his business to come into much danger, but to preserve himself, as much as was fit, out of harm's way, to be able to direct the fleet.

He doth, I perceive, with some violence forbear saying anything to the reproach of the Duke of Albemarle, but, contrarily, speaks much of his courage; but I do as plainly see that he doth not like the Duke of Albemarle's proceedings, but, contrarily, is displeased therewith. And he doth plainly diminish the commanders put in by the Duke, and doth lessen the miscarriages of any that have been removed by him.

He concurs with me that the next bout will be a Fatall one to one side or other; because if we be beaten, we shall not be able to set out our fleet again.

He doth confess, with me, that the hearts of our Seamen are much saddened – and for that reason, among others, wishes Sir Chr. Mings alive, who might inspire courage and spirit into them.

Speaking of Holmes, how great a man he is, and that he doth for the present, and hath done all this voyage, kept himself in good order and within bounds – "But," says he, "a Catt will be a Catt still; and some time or other, out his humour must break again."

a repl. 'say'

---

1. The news that the Dutch had come out was known to Albemarle two days before Rupert and his squadron left him on 29 May.

2. The responsibility rested primarily on Arlington as Secretary of State.

He doth not dis=owne but that the dividing of the fleet, upon the presumptions that was then had (which I suppose was the French fleet being come this*ᵃ* way), was a good resolution. Having had all this discourse, he and I back to White-hall; and there I left him (being [in] a little doubt whether I had behaved myself in my discourse with the policy and circumspection which ought to be used to so great a courtier as he is and so wise and factious¹ a man) and by water home; and so after supper, to bed.

25. Up, and all the morning at my Tanger accounts, which the chopping and changing of my tallies makes mighty*ᵇ* troublesome; but however, I did end them with great satisfaction to myself. At noon, without staying to eat my dinner, I down by water to Deptford; and there coming, find Sir W. Batten and Sir Jeremy Smith (on whom the despatch of the *Loyall London* depends) at dinner at Greenwich at the Beare tavern; and thither I to them, and there dined with them. Very good company of strangers there*ᶜ* was, but I took no great pleasure among them, being desirous to be back again. So got them to rise as soon as I could – having told them the news Sir W. Coventry just now writ me to tell them; which is, that the Duch are certainly come out. I did much business at Deptford, and so home by an old poor man, a Sculler, having no oares to be got; and all this day on the water entertained myself with the play of Commenius;² and being come home, did go out to Allgate, there to be overtaken by Mrs. Marget Pen in her father's coach, and my wife and Mercer with her; and ⟨Mrs. Pen⟩*ᵈ* carried us to two gardens at Hackeny (which I every day grow more and more in love with) – Mr. Drakes one, where the garden is good, and house and the prospect admirable³ – the other, my Lord

a repl. 'to' *b* MS. 'my'
c repl. same symbol written too high *d* repl. 'she'

---

1. The reference here is to the anti-Sandwich faction.
2. John Wilson, *Andronicus Comnenius, a tragedy* (1664); PL 1604 (1). (A).

3. Nothing appears to be known with certainty of either the house or its owner.

Brookes's, where the gardens are much better, but the house not so good, nor the prospect good at all[1] – but the gardens are excellent; and here I first saw Oranges grow,[2] some green, some half, some a quarter, and some full ripe on the same tree, and one fruit of the same tree doth come a year or two after the other. I pulled off a little one by stealth (the man being mighty curious* of them) and eat it; and it was just as other little green small oranges are; as big as half the end of my little finger. Here were also great variety of other exoticque plants, and several Labarinths and a pretty Aviary. Having done there with very great pleasure, we away back again, and called at the Taverne in Hackny by the church[3] and there drank and eate; and so in the cool of the evening, home – this being the first day of my putting on my black stuff Bombazin suit, and I hope to feel no inconvenience by it, the weather being extremely hot. So home and to bed – and this night the first night of my lying without a waistcoat, which I hope I shall very well indure. So to bed.

This morning I did with great pleasure hear Mr. Cæsar play some good things on his lute, while he came to teach my boy Tom, and I did give him 40*s* for his encouragement.

26. Up, and to the office betimes, and there all the morning – very busy to get out the fleet, the Dutch being now for certain out, and we shall not, we think, be much behindhand with them. At noon to the Change about business, and so home to dinner, and after dinner to the setting my Journall to rights; and so to the office again – where all the afternoon full of business, and there till night, that my eyes were sore, that I could not write no longer.

1. According to Evelyn (8 May 1654) the garden of Brooke House was 'one of the neatest, & most celebrated in England', but the house in itself was 'a despicable building'. See E. A. Mann, *Brooke House, Hackney* (LCC, *Survey*, Monograph 5), esp. pl. 1 (Hollar's engraving, 1642); LCC, *Survey*, vol. 60; William Robinson, *Hist. Hackney* (1842), i. 109+. Mulberry trees survived in

the garden as late as 1954. The house (on the west side of Upper Clapton Rd between Brooke and Kenninghall Rds) has been demolished. (R).

2. Pepys had first seen orange-trees in St James's Park on 19 April 1664.

3. Probably the tavern on the east side of Church St (now Mare St) known in the 19th century as The Old Mermaid. (R).

Then into the garden; then my wife and Mercer, and my Lady Pen and her daughter with us. And here we sang in the dark very finely half an hour, and so home to supper and to bed. This afternoon, after a long drowth, we had a good shoure of rain, but it will not signify much if no more come. This day, in the morning came Mr. Chichly to Sir W. Coventry to tell him the ill-successe of the guns made for the *Loyall London*; which is, that in the trial, every one of the great guns, the whole Cannon of seven (as I take it), broke in pieces[1] – which is a strange mishap, and that which will give more occasion to people's discourse of the King's business being done ill. This night Mary my cook-maid, that hath been with us about three months,[2] but finds herself not able to do my work so, is gone with great kindness away, and another (Luce) come, very ugly and plain, but may be a good servant for all that.

27. Up, and to my office awhile. Then down the River a little way to see vessels ready for the carrying down of 400 land-soldiers to the fleet. Then back to the office for my papers, and so to St. James's, where we did our usual attendance on the Duke. Having done with him, we all of us down to Sir W. Coventry's chamber (where I saw his father my Lord Coventry's picture hung up, done by Stone, who then brought it home. It is a good picture, drawn in his judge's robes, and the Great Seal by him.[3] And while it was hanging up, "This," says Sir W. Coventry, merrily, "is the use we make of our fathers") to discourse about the proposition of serving us with Hemp, delivered*a*

a repl. 'sent'

---

1. The newly-built *Loyal London* did not reach the fleet at the Nore until 13 July, and then without guns: *CSPD 1665–6*, p. 528. Thomas Chicheley was a Commissioner of the Ordnance.
2. In fact only since 10 May.
3. The 1st Baron Coventry had been Lord Keeper from 1625 until his death in 1640. This copy of his portrait was probably made by Symon Stone, a professional copyist: O. Millar in *Burl. Mag.*, 97/256.

The original portrait was almost certainly by Cornelius Johnson, to whom Lord Coventry seems to have sat on a number of occasions. The portrait (1631) in the possession of the Earl of Clarendon shows the Lord Keeper in legal robes with the Great Seal: A. J. Finberg in *Pub. Walpole Soc.*, vol. x, pl. xxxvi. Copies and derivations of this are common: one of them, signed and dated 1634, is at Longleat and may have belonged to Sir William Coventry. (OM).

in by my Lord Brouncker as from an unknown person, though I know it to be Captain Cocke's.[1]   My Lord and Sir W. Coventry had some earnest words about it; the one promoting it for his private ends (being, as Cocke tells me himself,[a] to have 500*l* if the bargain goes on; and I am to have as much); and the other opposing it for the unreasonableness of it, not[b] knowing at all whose the proposition is, which seems the more ingenious of the two.   I sat by and said nothing, being no great friend to the proposition, though Cocke intends me a convenience by it.   But what I observed most from the discourse was this of Sir W. Coventry, that he doth look upon ourselfs in a desperate condition – the issue of all standing[c] upon this one point, that by the next fight, if we beat, the Dutch will certainly be content to take eggs for their money[2] (that was his expression); or if we be beaten, we must be contented to make peace, and glad if we can have it without paying too dear for it.   And withal, we do rely wholly upon the Parliament's giving us more money the next sitting, or else we are undone.

Being gone thence, I by coach to the Old Exchange, but did not go into it – but to Mr. Cade's the Stacioner; stood till the shower was over, it being a great and welcome one after so much dry weather.   Here I understand that Ogleby is putting out some new fables of his own, which will be very fine and very Satyricall.[3]   Thence home to dinner; and after dinner carried my wife to her sister's, and I to Mr. Hales's to pay for my father's picture – which cost me 10*l* the head and 25*s* the frame.   Thence to Lovett's, who hath now done something towards the varnishing of single paper for the making of books which will do, I think, very well.[4]   He did also carry me to a Knight's chamber in Grayes Inne, where there is a frame of his making, of counterfeit

a repl. closing bracket   *b* repl. 'though'   *c* repl. 'being'

---

1. See above, p. 132 & n. 3.
2. Sc. will be happy to cut their losses and make peace.
3. John Ogilby had already published a verse translation of Aesop (above, ii. 6, n. 4); these fables of his own were never published.   At this time he also had ready for publication a long epic poem on Charles I, but it was, in the words of the *DNB*, 'fortunately burnt'.   He had no original talent.
4. See above, pp. 119–20 & n.

Tortoy'shell, which endeed is most excellently done. Then I took him with me to a picture-shop to choose a print for him to varnish, but did not agree on one then.

Thence to my wife to take her up; and so carried her home, and I at the office till late, and so to supper with my wife and to bed.

I did this afternoon visit my Lord Bellasses – who professes all imaginable satisfaction in me. He spoke dissatisfiedly with Creed, which I was pleased well enough with. My Lord is going down to his Guarrison to Hull, by the King's command to put it in order, for fear of an invasion[1] – which course I perceive is taken upon the sea-coasts round; for we have a real apprehension of the King of France's invading us.

28. Up, and at the office all the morning. At noon home to dinner; and after dinner abroad to Lumbardstreete, there to reckon with Sir Rob. Viner for some money, and did set all straight to my great content; and so home, and all the afternoon and evening*a* at the office, my mind full at this time of getting my accounts over, and as much money in my hands as I can, for a great turn is to be feared in the times – the French having some great design (whatever it is, in hand), and our necessities on every side very great. The Dutch are now known to be out, and we may expect them every hour upon our coast. But our fleet is in pretty good readiness for them.

29. Up, and within doors most of the morning, sending a porter (Sanders) up and down to several people to pay them money to clear my month's debts everywhere, being mighty desirous to have all clear – as soon as I can – and to that end, did do much in settling my Tanger accounts clear. At noon dined,

a repl. 'night'

---

1. Belasyse (Governor of Tangier) was also Governor of Hull, 1661–73. Fears of an invasion by the French and Dutch (particularly of the north country) were now common: see the 'Advice from the Hague', 30 June/9 July, which Pepys preserved (Rawl. A 195a, f. 169r), and cf. HMC, *Le Fleming*, p. 40. For the government's preparations, see *CSPD 1665–6*, pp. 475–6. Alarms of this sort were frequent throughout the war: P. Fraser, *Intelligence of Secretaries of State, 1660–88*, pp. 11–12.

having first been down at Deptford; and did a little business there and back again. After dinner to White-hall to a Committee of Tanger, but I came a little too late, they were up; so I to several places about business. Among others, to Westminster-hall, and there did meet with Betty Michell at her own mother's shop.*ᵃ* I would fain have carried her home by water, but she was to sup at that end of the town.

So I away to White-hall; and thence, the Council being up, walked to St. James's and there had much discourse with Sir W. Coventry at his chamber – who I find quite weary of the war. Decries our having any war at all, or himself to have been any occasion of it.¹ That he hopes this will make us shy of any war hereafter, or to prepare better for it. Believes that one overthrow on the Duch side would make them desire peace, and that one on ours will make us willing to accept of one. Tells me that Comissioner Pett is fallen infinitely under the displeasure of the Prince and Duke of Albemarle, not giving them satisfaction in the getting out of the fleet;² and that that complaint, he believes, is come to the King. And by Sir W. Coventry's discourse I find he doth concur in it, and speaks of his having of no authority in that place where he is;³ and I do believe at least it will end in his being removed to some other yard – and I am not sorry for it; but do fear that though he deserves as bad, yet at this time the blame may not be so well deserved.

Thence home, and to the office – where I met with a letter from Dover which tells me (and it did come by express) that news is brought over by a gentleman from Callice that the Duch fleet, 130 sail, are come upon the French coast – and that the country is bringing in Pickeaxes and Shovells and wheel-barrows into Callice.⁴ That there are 6000 men, armed with head, back, and breast (Frenchmen), ready to go on board the Duch fleet, and will be fallowed by 12000 more. That they pretend they

a repl. 'ship'

---

1. Cf. above, v. 159 & n. 3.
2. Cf. Rupert and Albemarle to Arlington, 24 June: *CSPD 1665–6*, p. 455.
3. Peter Pett was resident Navy Commissioner at Chatham.

4. Francis Hosier to Pepys, Dover, 29 June: Rawl. A 195a, f. 227r. The 'gentleman from Callice' had been on his way to Whitehall with the news.

are to come to Dover. And that thereupon the Governor of Dover Castle is getting the victuallers' provision out of the town into the castle, to secure it – but I do think this is a ridiculous conceit. But a little time will show.[1] At night, home to supper and to bed.

30. Up and to the office; and mightily troubled all this morning with going to my Lord Mayor (Sir Tho. Bludworth, a silly man I think)[2] and other places about getting shipped some men that they have these two last nights pressed in the City out of houses – the persons wholly unfit for sea,[3] and many of them people of very good fashion – which is a shame to think of; and carried to Bridewell they are, yet without being impressed with money legally, as they ought to be.

But to see how the King's business is done, my Lord Mayor himself did scruple, at this time of extremity, to do this thing, because he had not money to pay the prest-money to the men – he told me so[a] himself; nor to take up boats to carry them down through bridge to the ships I have prepared to carry them down in. Insomuch that I was forced to promise to be his pay-maister; and he did send his City Remembrancer[4] afterward to the office, and at the table, in the face of the officers, I did there out of my own purse disburse 15*l.* to pay for their pressing and diet last night and this morning – which is a thing worth record of my Lord Mayor.[5]

a   MS. 'sold'

---

1. The alarm proved needless. De Ruyter had been out since the 27th with 75 sail. He was at the moment playing with the idea of a landing in Kent, for which he had equipped himself with 7000 soldiers: G. Brandt, *Michel de Ruiter* (trans. 1698), p. 368. The Governor of Dover Castle was Capt. John Strode. Guards were set and beacons laid on the 30th, and a French ship did in fact fire into the town on 2 July: *London Gazette*, 2, 5 July.

2. Cf. below, p. 393, n. 2.
3. A common feature of the press system: cf. J. Hollond, *Discourses* (ed. Tanner), p. 50 & n.
4. Edward Manning.
5. In a note written a few days later Pepys states that this £15 was 'W. Hewer's mony': Rawl. A 195a, f. 289r. Bludworth's bills were sent in on 6 July, and an imprest for £100 more given him on the 7th: ib., ff. 287–9. For the press system, see above, v. 168, n. 2.

Busy about this all the morning. At noon dined, and then to the office again, and all the afternoon, till 12 at night, full of this business and others. And among those others, about the getting of men*ᵃ* pressed by our officers of the fleet into the service, even our own men that [are] at the office*ᵇ* and the boats that carries us – so that it is now become impossible to have so much as a letter carried from place to place, or any message done for us. Nay, out of victualling-ships full loaden to go down to the fleet, and out of the vessels of the Officers of the Ordinance, they press men; so that for want of discipline in this respect, I do fear all will be undone. Vexed with these things, but eased in mind by my ridding of a great deal of business from the office, I late home to supper and to bed. But before I was in bed, while I was undressing myself, our new ugly maid Luce had like to have broke her neck in the dark, going down our upper stairs; but (which I was glad of) the poor girl did only bruise her head. But at first did lie on the ground groaning, and drawing her breath like one a-dying.

This month I end in much hurry of business, but in much more trouble in mind to think what will become of public businesses, having so many enemies abroad, and neither force – nor money at all – and but little Courage for ourselfs. It being really true that the spirits of our seamen, and commanders too, are really broke by the last defeat with the Duch; and this is not my conjecture*ᶜ* only, but the real and serious thoughts of Sir G. Carteret and Sir W. Coventry, whom I have at distinct times hear[d] the same thing come from, with a great deal of grief and trouble.

But lastly, I am providing against a foul day, to get as much money into my hands as I can, at least out of the public hands, that so, if a turn (which I fear) do come, I may have a little to trust to. I pray God give me good success in my choice how*ᵈ* to dispose*ᵉ* of what little I have, that I may not take it out of public hands and put it into worse.

JULY.

1. *Sunday.* Up betimes and to the office, receiving letters, two or three one after another, from Sir W. Coventry, and sent as many to him – being full of variety of business and hurry; but among the chiefest, is the getting of these pressed men out of the City down the River to the fleet.[1]
While I was hard at it, comes Sir W Pen to town, which I little expected, having invited my Lady and her daughter Pegg to dine with me today – which at noon they did, and Sir W. Penn with them, and pretty merry we were. And though I do not love him, yet I find it necessary to keep in with him – his good service at Sherenesse in getting out the fleet being much taken notice of, and reported to the King and Duke even from the Prince and Duke of Albemarle themselfs, and made the most of to me and them by Sir W. Coventry.[2] Therefore, I think it discretion, great and necessary discretion, to keep in with him.[a]
After dinner to the office again, where busy; and then down to Deptford to the yard, thinking to have seen Bagwell's wife, whose husband is gone yesterday back to the fleet; but I did not see her, so missed what I went for; and so back and to the Tower several times about the business of the pressed men, and late at it, till 12 at night, shipping of them. But Lord, how some poor women did cry, and in my life I never did see such natural expression of passion as I did here – in some women's bewailing themselfs, and running to every parcel of men that were brought, one after another, to look for their husbands, and wept over every vessel that went off, thinking they might be there, and looking after the ship as far as ever they could by moone-light – that it grieved me to the heart to hear them. Besides, to see poor

a   repl. 'them'

---

1. See Duke of York to Navy Board, 30 June: PRO, Adm. 106/13, ff. 165-7. In reply, Pepys complained to Coventry that he was unable to despatch half the work he used to, 'so backwardly everything moves': NMM, LBK/8, p. 388 (copy in Hewer's hand; printed incompletely in *Further Corr.*, p. 137).
2. Clarendon mentions it, with some exaggeration of the speed of the achievement: *Life*, iii. 77.

patient labouring men and housekeepers, leaving poor wifes and families, taken up on a sudden by strangers, was very hard; and that without press-money, but forced against all law to be gone. It is a great tyranny.[1]   Having done this, I to the Lieutenant of the Tower and bade him good-night, and so away home and to bed.

2.   Up betimes, and forced to go to my Lord Mayors[2] about the business of the pressed men; and endeed, I find him a mean man of understanding and despatch of any public business. Thence, out of curiosity, to Bridewell to see the pressed men, where there is about 300; but so unruly that I durst not go among them, and they have reason to be so, having been kept these three days prisoners, with little or no victuals, and pressed out, and contrary to all course of law, without press-money, and men that are not liable to it.[3]

Here I met with prating Collonell Cox, one of the City Collonells, heretofore a great presbyterian.[4]   But to hear how the fellow did commend himself and the service he doth the King, and like an asse at Paul's did take me out of my way on purpose to show me the gate (the little North gate) where he had two men*a* shot close by him on each hand, and his own hair burnt by a bullet*b*-shot in the insurrection of Venner, and himself escaped.[5]   Thence home, and to the Tower to see the men from Bridewell Shipped.

Being rid of him, I home to dinner; and thence to the Excise office by appointment to meet my Lord Bellasses and the Commissioners, which we did and soon despatched; and so I home, and there was called by Pegg Pen to her house, where her father and mother and Mrs. Norton, the Second Roxalana,[6] a fine woman,

---

a repl. 'me'   *b* repl. 'bult'

---

1. Pepys's later views (1692) are in *Naval Minutes*, pp. 267–8. He regarded the system as an evil which would have to be accepted as long as the navy was starved of funds.
2. Sir Thomas Bludworth's.
3. Only able-bodied seamen aged between 18 and 60 were in theory liable, with certain exemptions; see e.g. above, p. 176, n. 1.
4. Thomas Cox, now Lieutenant-

Colonel of the Blue regiment of the city militia; formerly a commissioner of the London militia under the Commonwealth.
5. For Venner's rising (January 1661), see above, ii. 7, n. 2.
6. Mrs Norton of the Duke of York's Company had succeeded Mrs Davenport as Roxalana in Davenant's opera *The siege of Rhodes*; see above, iii. 273, n.1.   (A).

indifferent handsome, good body and hand – and good mine;* and pretends to sing, but doth*a* it not excellently; however, I took pleasure there; and my wife was sent for and Creed came in to us, and so there we spent the most of the afternoon. Thence, weary of losing so much time, and to the office, and thence presently down to Deptford; but to see what a consternation there is upon the water by reason of this great press, that nothing is able to get a waterman to appear almost. Here I meant to have spoke with Bagwell's moher; but her face was sore, and so I did not; but returned, and upon the water found one of the vessels loaden with the Bridewell-birds in*b* a great mutiny, and they would not sail, not they; but with good words, and cajolling the ringleader into the Tower (where when he was come, he was clapped up in the Hole), they were got very quietly; but I think it is much if they do not run the vessel on ground. But away they went, and I to the Lieutenant of the Tower; and having talked with him a little, then home to supper very late, and to bed weary.

3. Being very weary, lay long in bed. Then to the office and there sat all the day. At noon dined at home, Balty's wife with us – and in very good humour I was, and merry at dinner, and after dinner a song or two; and so I abroad to my Lord Treasurer's (sending my sister home by the coach), while I stayed there by appointment to have met my Lord Bellasses and Commissioners of Excise, but they did not meet, my Lord being abroad. However, Mr. Finch,[1] one of the Commissioners, I met there, and he and I walked two hours together in the garden talking of many things; sometimes of Mr. Povy, whose vanity, prodigality, neglect of his business, and committing it to unfit hands hath undone him and outed him of all his public imployments, and the thing set on foot by an accidental revivall of a business wherein he had three or four years ago, by surprise, got the Duke of Yorke to sign to the having a sum of money paid out of the Excise before some that was due to him, and now the

1. Francis Finch, M.P. for Winchelsea, Sussex.

money is fallen short and the Duke never likely to be paid. This, being revived, hath undone Povy.[1]

Then we fell to discourse of the Parliament and the great men there; and among others, Mr. Vaughan, whom he reports as a man of excellent judgment and learning, but most passionate and opiniastre.[2] He had done himself the most wrong (though he values it not), that is, the displeasure of the King, in his standing so long against the breaking of the act for a Trienniall parliament.[a][3] But yet doth believe him to be a most loyall gentleman.

He told me Mr. Prin's Character; that he is a man of mighty labour and reading and memory, but the worst judge of matters, or layer-together of what he hath read, in the world – (which I do not however believe him in);[4] that he believes him very true to the King in his heart,[b] but can never be reconciled to Episcopacy. That the House doth not lay much weight upon him or anything he says.[5]

He told me many fine things; and so we parted, and I home and hard to work a while at the office; and then home, and till midnight about settling my last month's accounts, wherein I have been interrupted by public business, that I did not state them two or three days ago; but I do now,[c] to my great joy,

---

a repl. 'par'-   b repl. 'times'   c repl. 'not'

---

1. In March 1665 he had resigned to Pepys his place as Treasurer for Tangier; in September 1666 he was replaced as Treasurer to the Duke of York by Sir Allen Apsley.
2. John Vaughan was M.P. for Cardiganshire and a leading member of the country party. To Clarendon (whose impeachment Vaughan was to support in 1667) he was 'proud and insolent . . . magisterial and supercilious': *Life*, i. 37. He was made Chief Justice of Common Pleas and knighted in 1668.
3. See above, v. 102–3 & n.
4. The consensus of opinion is with Finch not Pepys: William Prynne's method of writing a book was to discharge his materials pell-mell on to the page and into the margins.
5. Prynne had always supported monarchy, but opposed *jure divino* episcopacy. In the Commons he had been reprimanded in 1661 for a pamphlet addressed to the Lords against the Corporation Bill (*CJ*, viii. 301–2), and in 1664 for altering a bill after its committal (above, v. 148 & n. 3). He was too bookish and long-winded – too fond of perambulating among his precedents – to be a good parliamentarian: cf. *The Moderate*, 12 December 1648; John Price, *Mystery of . . . Restauration . . .* (1680), p. 131; Milward, p. 130.

find myself worth above 5600*l*, for which the Lord's name be praised. So with my heart full of content, to bed.

News came yesterday from Harwich that the Dutch had appeared upon our coast with their fleet, and we believe did go to the Gunfleete;[1] and they are supposed to be there now, but I have heard nothing of them today.

Yesterday Dr. Whistler, at Sir W Pen's, told me that Alexander Broome, the great Songmaker, is lately dead.[2]

4. Up, and visited very betimes by Mr. Sheply, who is come to town upon business from Hinchingbrooke, where he left all well. I out, and walked along with him as far as Fleetestreete, it being a fast-day, the usual fast for the plague, and few coaches to be had. Thanks be to God, the plague is as I hear encreased but two this week.[3] But in the country in several places it rages mightily, and perticularly in Colchester, where it hath long been, and is believed will quite depopulate the place.[4]

To St. James's, and there did our usual business with the Duke, all of us. Among other things, discoursing about the places where to build ten great ships, the King and Council have resolved on none to be under third-rates;[5] but it is impossible to do it – unless we have more money towards the doing it then yet we have in any view. But however, the show must be made to the world.

Thence to my Lord Bellaces to take my leave of him, he being going down to the North – to look after the Militia there, for fear of an invasion.[6]

Thence home and dined; and then to the office, where busy

1. Cf. *CSPD 1665-6*, p. 487.
2. Brome (lawyer, versifier and dramatist) had died on 29 June.
3. In the week of 26 June-3 July plague burials were 35 as against 33 in the previous week: GL, A.1.5, no. 96.
4. The outbreak raged from August 1665 to December 1666, reaching its height in late June, and accounting for over 4800 deaths – a higher proportion of deaths to total population than in London. It was probably the worst provincial plague since the Black Death, and is said to have led to the economic decline of the town in the 18th century. PRO, PC2/59, f. 8; R. Josselin, *Diary* (ed. Hockcliffe), pp. 148+; C. Creighton, *Hist. Epidemics*, i. 688-91; J. F. D. Shrewsbury, *Hist. bubonic plague in Brit. Isles*, pp. 499+.
5. For the order (30 June), see PRO, PC 2/59, f. 42r. Estimates were prepared on 19 July for two 2nd-rates and four 3rd-rates: *CSPD 1665-6*, p. 554. Cf. *Further Corr.*, p. 153. For rates of ships, see above, iii. 128, n. 1.
6. See above, p. 185 & n. 1.

all day. And in the evening Sir W Pen came to me, and we walked together and talked of the late fight. I find him very plain that the whole conduct of the late fight was ill, and that that of truth's all, and he tells me that it is not he, but two-thirds of the commanders of the whole fleet have told him so – they all saying that they durst not oppose it at the council of war, for fear of being called Cowards,[1] though it was wholly against their judgment to fight that day with that disproportion of force; and then we not being able to use one gun of our lower tire, which was a greater disproportion then the other.[2] Besides, we might very well have*a* stayed in the Downs without fighting, or anywhere else, till the Prince could have come up to them – or at least till the weather was fair, that we might have the benefit of our whole force in the ships that we had.

He says three things must [be] remedied, or else we shall be undone, by this fleet.

1. That we must fight in a line, whereas we fight promis-cuously, to our utter and demonstrable ruine – the Duch fighting otherwise – and we, whenever we beat them.[3]

2. We must not desert ships of our own in distress as we did, for that makes a captain desperate, and will fling away his ship when there is no hopes left him of succour.

3. That ships, when they are a little shattered, must not take the liberty to come in of themselfs; but refit themselfs the best they can, and stay out – many of our ships coming in with very small disablings.

a MS. 'of' (phonetic spelling)

1. For Albemarle's accusations against his commanders, see above, p. 154; below, p. 222. For his over-confidence, see above, p. 148 & n. 6.

2. Sc. the Dutch were able to open the gun-ports of their lower tiers of guns, whereas the English ships were too low in the water to follow suit.

3. The fighting instructions of April 1665 (of which Penn was probably the author) insisted on the line-ahead formation; those of 1666 had reminded commanders that they must not obey this general rule to the extent of neglecting chances of des-troying the enemy. Pepys himself (through his attachment to Sandwich) had a prejudice in favour of the tactics of 1665. Hence his warm (and quite unusual) agreement with Penn. But Penn, if correctly reported, was wrong. The fleet did fight in line in the Four Days Battle, and the Dutch (who won) did not. See *Fighting Instructions, 1530–1816* (ed. J. S. Corbett), pp. 110+. Cf. Ehrman, pp. 21–2.

He told me that our very commanders, nay, our very flag-officers, do stand in need of exercizing among themselfs and discoursing the business of commanding a fleet – he telling me that even one of our flag-men in the fleet did not know which Tacke[a] lost the wind or which kept it in the last engagement.

He says it was pure dismaying and fear that made them all run upon the Galloper, not having their wits about them; and that it was[b] a miracle they were not all lost. He much inveighs upon my discoursing of Sir John Lawson's saying heretofore, that 60 sail would do as much as 100. And says that he was a man of no counsel at all, but had got the confidence to say as the gallants did, and did propose to himself to make himself great by them, and saying as they did; but was no man of judgment in his business, but had been out in the greatest points that have come before them. And then in the business of Forecastles, which he did oppose, all the world sees now the use of them for shelter of men.[1]

He did talk very rationally to me, insomuch that I took more pleasure this night in hearing him discourse then I ever did in my life in anything that he said.

He gone, I to the office again; and so after some business, home to supper and to bed.

5. Up, and to the office, where we sat all the morning busy. Then at noon dined, and Mr. Sheply with me – who came to town the other day. I lent him 30*l* in silver upon 30 pieces in gold; but to see how apt everybody is to neglect old kindnesses, I must charge myself with the ingratitude of being unwilling to lend him so much money without some pawne, if he should have asked it; but he did not ask it, poor man, and so no harm done. After dinner, he gone, I to my office and Lumbardstreet about money; and then to my office again, very busy, and so till late; and then a song with my wife and Mercer in the garden, and so with great content to bed.

---

a l.h. repl. s.h.   *b* repl. 'is'

1. This was one aspect of the perennial controversy of armour *versus* manœuvrability. Penn and Lawson may well have taken opposing views on it in the Jamaican expedition, 1655–6. Cf. Oppenheim, p. 338.

o

6. Up, and after doing some business at my office, abroad to Lumbardstreete about the getting of a good sum of money; thence home, in preparation for my having some good sum in my hands, for fear of a trouble in the State, that I may not have all I have in the world out of my hands and so be left a beggar. Having put that in a way, I home to the office; and so to the Tower about shipping of some more pressed-men – and that done, away to Broadstreete to Sir G. Carteret, who is at a pay of Tickets all alone. And I believe not less then 1000 people in the streets. But it is a pretty thing to observe, that both there and everywhere else a man shall see many women nowadays of mean sort in the streets, but no men; men being so afeared of the press.[1]

I dined with Sir G. Carteret; and after dinner had much discourse about our public business, and he doth seem to fear every day more and more what I do, which is a general confusion in the State. Plainly answering me to the question, Who is it that the weight of the Warr depends? that it is only Sir W Coventry.

He tells me too, that the Duke of Albemarle is dissatisfied, and that the Duchesse doth curse Coventry as the man that betrayed her husband to the sea – though I believe that it is not so.

Thence to Lumberdstreete, and received 2000*l* and carried it home – whereof, 1000*l* in gold, the greatest quantity, not only that I ever had*a* of gold, but that ever I saw together; and is not much above half a 100lb bag full – but is much weightier. This I do for security sake, and convenience of carriage – though it costs me above 70*l* the change of it, at*b* 18½*d* per peece.

That being at home, I there met with a letter from Bab Allen to invite me to be godfather to her boy with Mrs. Williams; which I consented to, but know not the time when it is to be.[2]

Thence down to the Old Swan, calling at Michells, he not being

a repl. 'saw'   *b* repl. 'it coming'

---

1. On 19 July it was calculated that 2751 had been shipped to the fleet from the Tower since 30 June: *CSPD 1665–6*, p. 555. Pepys's phrase 'of mean sort' is revealing about who was subject to the press.

2. 'Bab Allen' was Pepys's nickname for Mrs Knepp. On 6 August her child was named Samuel after Pepys: *Harl. Soc. Reg.*, 36/40.

within; and there I did steal a kiss or two of her, and staying a little longer, he came in, and her father, whom I carried to Westminster, my business being thither; and so back again home, and very busy all the evening; at night, a song in the garden and to bed.

7. At the office all the morning. At noon dined at home, and Creed with me; and after dinner he and I two or three hours in my chamber, discoursing of the fittest way for a man to do that hath money. And find all he offers, of turning some into gold and leaving some in a friend's hand, is nothing more then what I thought of myself; but is doubtful, as well as I, what is best to be done of all those, or other ways to be thought on.

He tells me he finds all things mighty dull at Court, and that they now begin to lie long in bed – it being, as we suppose, not seemly for them to be found playing and gaming as they used to be; nor that their minds are at ease enough to fallow their*a* sports; and yet not knowing how to imploy themselfs (though there be work enough for their thoughts and counsels and pains), they keep long in bed. But he thinks with me, that there is nothing in the world can help us but the King's personal looking after his business and his officers, and that with that we may yet do well; but otherwise must be undone, nobody at this day taking care of anything, nor hath anybody to call him to account for it.

Thence left him and to my office, all the afternoon busy, and in some pain in my back by some bruise or other I have given myself in my right Testicle this morning. And the pain lies there, and hath done, and in my back thereupon all this day.[1]

At night into the garden to my wife and Lady Pen and Pegg and Creed, who stayed with them, till 10 at night. My Lady Pen did give us a Tart and other things; and so broke up late, and I to bed.

It proved the hottest night that ever I was in in my life, and thundered and lightened all night long, and rained hard. But Lord, to see in what [fear] I lay a good while, hearing of a little

a MS. 'them'

---

1. Dr C. E. Newman writes: 'This was probably the result of an inflammation. The epididymis (princi- pally the first part of the duct leading away from the testis) is always liable to infection.'

noise of somebody walking in the house. So rung the bell, and it was my maids going to bed about one a-clock in the morning. But the fear of being robbed, having so much money in the house, was very great; and is still so, and doth much disquiet me.

8. *Lordsday.* Up, and pretty well of my pain, so that it did not trouble me at all; and I do clearly find that my pain in my back was nothing, but only accompanied my bruise*ᵃ* in my stone.

To church, wife and Mercer and I, in expectation of hearing some mighty preacher today, Mrs. Mary Batelier sending us word so; but it proved our ordinary silly Lecturer,¹ which made me merry, and she laughed upon us to see her mistake.

At noon W. Hewer dined with us – and a good dinner. And I expected to have had news sent me of Knepp's christening today; but hearing nothing of it, I did not go, though I fear it is but their forgetfulness – and so I may disappoint them.

To church after dinner again; a thing I have not done a good while before, go twice in one day.²

After church, with my wife and Mercer and Tom by water through bridge to the Spring guarden at Fox hall; and thence down to Depford and there did a little business; and so back home and to bed.

9. Up betimes, and with Sir W. Penn in his coach to Westminster to Sir G Downing's, but missed of him; and so we parted, and I by water home, where busy all the morning. At noon dined at home; and after dinner to my office, where busy till come to by Lovett and his wife, who have brought me some sheets of paper varnished on one side, which lies very white and smooth – and I think will do our business most exactly and will come up to the use that I entended them for, and I am apt to believe will be an invention that will take in the world.³ I have

a repl. 'broke'

---

1. The unidentified (and insufferable) Scotsman: see above, iv. 12, n. 1.

2. The last occasion appears to have been on 9 April 1665.

3. See above, pp. 119–20 & n.

made up a little book of it to give Sir W. Coventry tomorrow – and am very well pleased with it.

Home with them; and there find my aunt Wight with my wife, come to take her leave of her, being going for the summer into the country.[1] And there was also Mrs. Mary Batelier and her sister, newly come out of France, a black, very black, woman; but mighty good-natured people both,*a* as ever I saw. Here I made the black one sing a French song, which she did mighty innocently – and then Mrs. Lovett play on the lute, which she doth very well, and then Mercer and I sang; and so with great pleasure – I left them, having showed them my chamber and 1000*l* in gold, which they wondered at – and given them sweet-meats, and shown my aunt Wight my father's picture, which she admires.

So I left them, and to the office, where Mr. Moore came to me; and talking of my Lord's family business, tells me that Mr. Sheply is ignorantly, we all believe, mistaken in his accounts, above 700*l* more then he can discharge himself of; which is a mighty misfortune, poor man, and may undo him, and yet everybody believes that he doth it most honestly. I am troubled for him very much.[2]

He gone, I hard at the office till night; then home to supper – and to bed.

10. Up, and to the office, where busy all the morning sitting. And there presented Sir W. Coventry with my little book made up of Lovetts varnished paper, which he and the whole board liked very well. At noon home to dinner, and then to the office, the yard being very full of women (I believe above 300) coming to get money for their husbands and friends that are prisoners in Holland; and they lay clamouring and swearing, and cursing us, that my wife and I were afeared to send a venison-pasty that we have for supper tonight to the cook's to be baked, for fear of their offering violence to it – but it went, and no hurt done. Then I took an opportunity, when they were all gone

a repl. same symbol

---

1. The Wights had a house at Artington, near Guildford, Surrey.
2. Edward Shipley (steward at Hinchingbrooke) was in 1669 dismissed from Sandwich's service for incompetence.

into the fore*ᵃ*=yard, and slipped into the office and there busy all the afternoon. But by and by the women got into the garden, and came all to my closet window and there tormented me; and I confess, their cries were so sad for money, and laying down the condition of their families and their husbands, and what they have done and suffered for the King, and how ill they are used by us, and how well the Duch are used here by the allowance of their masters, and what their husbands are offered to serve the Duch abroad,[1] that I do most heartily pity them, and was ready to cry to hear them – but cannot help them;[2] however, when the rest was gone, I did call one to me, that I heard complain only and pity her husband, and did give her some money; and she blessed me and went away.

Anon, my business at the office*ᵇ* being done, I to the Tower to speak with Sir Jo Robinson about business – principally, the bad condition of the pressed men for want of clothes, as it is represented from the fleet; and so to provide them shirts and stockings and drawers. Having done with him about that, I home, and there find my wife and the two Mrs. Bateliers walking in the garden; I with them till almost 9 at night, and then they and we, and Mrs. Mercer the mother and her daughter Anne, and our Mercer to supper, to a good venison-pasty and other good things, and had a good supper and very merry – Mrs. Bateliers being both very good-humoured. We sang and talked, and then led them home; and there they made us drink, and among other things, did show us in Cages some Birds*ᶜ* brought from about Bourdeaux, that are all fat; and examining one of them, they are so, almost all fat. Their name is   ,[3] which are brought over to the King for him to eat, and endeed are excellent things.

We parted from them, and so home to bed, it being very late; and to bed.

---

a l.h. repl. l.h. 'forey'-   b repl. same symbol badly formed
c l.h. repl. s.h.

---

1. There were Englishmen serving in the Dutch fleet which invaded the Medway in the following year: below, 14 June 1667.

2. The Board ordered this day that 'speedy relief' for prisoners should be made (out of pay) 'without any trouble to be given to any of there relations in attendance here for the same': PRO, Adm. 106/3520, f. 31r.

3. ? ortolans.

11. Up, and by water to Sir G Downings, there to discourse with him about the relief of the prisoners in Holland – which I did, and we do resolve of the manner of sending them some.[1] So I away by coach to St. James's, and there hear that the Duchesse is lately brought to bed of a Boy.[2] By and by called to wait on the Duke, the King being present – and there agreed, among other things, of the places to build the ten new great ships ordered to be built[3] – and as to the relief of prisoners in Holland. And then about several stories of the basenesse of the Kings of Spain's being served[a] with officers – they in Flanders having as good common-men as any prince in the world; but the veriest Cowards for the officers, nay, for the general officers, as the Generall and Lieutenant Generall,[4] in the whole world. But above all things, the King did speak most in contempt of the ceremoniousnesse of the King of Spain, that he doth nothing but under some ridiculous form or other; and will not piss but another must hold the chamber-pot.[5]

Thence to Westminster-hall and there stayed a while, and then to the Swan and kissed Sarah, and so home to dinner; and after dinner, out again to Sir Rob. Viner and there did agree with him to accomodate some business of tallies, so as I shall get in near 2000*l* into my own hands, which is in the King's, upon tallies – which will be a pleasure to me, and satisfaction to have a good

a repl. 'several'

---

1. See *CSPD 1665–6*, p. 533 for a reference (14 July) to a report about conditions in Flushing gaol: food and medical attention were badly needed.

2. Charles Stuart, born to the Duchess of York on the 4th; cr. Duke of Kendal; d. 22 May 1667.

3. See above, p. 193 & n. 5.

4. The Spanish forces were outnumbered by the French invaders and were rapidly defeated in the following spring. Their commander was the Marquis de Castelrodrigo (Governor of the Spanish Netherlands, 1664–8). His lieutenant was a French-born soldier of fortune, Jean-Gaspar-Ferdinand de Marsin, companion in arms of the great Condé,

They did not greatly trust each other but neither was a coward.

5. Charles had paid only one very brief visit to Spain, to Saragossa and Fuenterrabia, at the end of 1659, but knew the Spanish court at Brussels well in his exile. Cf. the comment of John Sheffield, Duke of Buckingham on Charles (*Works*, 1740, ii. 81): 'He had so natural an aversion to formality . . . he could not on premeditation act the part of a King for a moment, either at Parliament or Council . . . which carried him into the other extreme . . . of letting all distinction and ceremony fall to the ground as useless and foppish.'

sum in my own hands whenever evil disturbances should be in the state – though it troubles me to lose so great a profit as the King's interest of 10 per cent for that*ᵃ* money.¹

Thence to Westminster, doing several things by the way, and there failed of meeting Mrs. Lane; and so by coach took up my wife at her sister's, and so away to Islington, she and I alone, and so through Hackny, and home late – our discourse being about laying up of some money safe, in prevention to the troubles I am afeared we may have in the state. And so, sleepy (for want of sleep the last night, going to bed late and rising betimes in the morning), home; but when I came to the office, I there met with a command from my Lord Arlington to go down to a Galliott at Greenwich (by the King's perticular command) that is going to carry the Savoy Envoyé² over. And we fear there may be many Frenchmen there on board – and so I have a power and command to search for and seize all that have not passes from one of the Secretary's of State, and to bring them and their papers and everything else in custody some-whither. So I to the Tower, and got a Couple of Musquetiers with me and Griffen and my boy Tom, and so down, and being come, found none on board but two or three servants, looking to horses and doggs, there on board. And seeing no more, I stayed not long there; but away, and on shore at Greenwich, the night*ᵇ* being late and the tide against us. So (having sent before) to Mrs. Clerkes, and there I had a good bed, and well received, the whole people rising to see me;³ and among the rest, young Mrs. Daniel, whom I kissed again and again alone; and so by and by to bed, and slept

《12.》 pretty well; but was up again by 5 a-clock, and was forced to rise, having much business; and so up and dressed myself (enquiring, was told that Mrs. Tooker was gone thence to live at London), and away with Poundy to the Tower; and thence, having shifted myself, but being mighty drowzy for

---

a repl. 'it'   *b* repl. 'weather'

---

1. The legal maximum was 6%, but in times of difficulty the government paid more, the extra being disguised as 'gratuities'.

2. Conte di Piossasco, envoy from Savoy until July 1667.

3. Pepys had lodged there during the Plague.

want of sleep, I by coach to St. James's to Goring-house[1] – there to wait on my Lord Arlington to give him an account of my night's work, but he was not up – being not long since married;[2] so after walking up and down the house below (being the house I was once at Hartlibbs sister['s] wedding,[3] and is a very fine house and finely furnished); and then, thinking it too much for me to lose time to wait my Lord's rising, I away to St. James's, and there to Sir W. Coventry and wrote a letter to my Lord Arlington, giving him an account of what I have done; and so with Sir W. Coventry[a] into London to the office. And all the way I observed him mightily to make mirth of the Duke of Albemarle and his people about him; saying that he was the happiest man in the world for doing of great things by sorry instruments – and so, perticularized in Sir W Clerke and Riggs and Halsey and others. And then again said that the only quality eminent in him was that he did persevere. And endeed, he is a very drudge and stands by the King's business. And this he said: that one thing he was good at, that he never would receive an excuse if the thing was not done; listening to no reason for it, be it good or bad. But then I told him, which he confessed, that he would however give the man that he imploys orders for the removing of any obstruction that he thinks he shall meet with in the world – and instanced in several warrants that he issued, for breaking open of houses and other outrages about the business of prizes;[4] which people bore with, either for affection or fear, which he believes would not have been borne with from the King nor Duke nor any man else in England; and I think he is in the right, but it is not from their love[b] of him, but from something else I cannot presently say.

Sir W. Coventry did further say, concerning Warcupp his kinsman,[5] that had the simplicity to tell Sir W. Coventry that the

a repl. 'GC' *b* repl. 'live'

1. In St James's Park on the site of the present Buckingham Palace. (R).
2. He had married a Dutchwoman, Isabella van Beverweerd, on 16 May 1666.
3. See above, i. 196.
4. For the prize goods affair, see above, vi. 231, n. 1.

5. Edmond Warcupp, Albemarle's kinsman, had acted as his agent in much river business (e.g. over prize goods), being a magistrate and Bailiff of Southwark. For his disgrace at this time, see below, p. 219 & n. 4.

Duke did intend to go to sea and to leave him his Agent on shore for all things that related to the sea – "But," says Sir W. Coventry, "I did believe, but the Duke of York would expect to be his Agent on shore for all sea-matters." And then he begin to say what a great man Warcupp was, and something else, and what was that but a great Lyer; and told me a story how at table he did (they speaking about Antipathys) say that a rose touching his skin anywhere would make it rise and pimple.[1] And by and by, the Dessert coming with roses upon it, the Duchess bid him try, and they did; but they rubbed and rubbed, but nothing would do in the world – by which his lie was found out*a* then.

He spoke contemptibly of Holmes and his Mermidons that came to take down the ships from hence, and have carried them without any necessaries or anything almost, that they will certainly be longer getting ready then if they had stayed here.

In Fine, I do observe he hath no esteem nor kindness for the Duke's matters, but, contrarily, doth slight him and them; and I pray God the Kingdom do not pay too dear by this jarring, though this Blocke-headed Duke I did never expect better from.

At the office all the morning. At noon home, and thought to have slept, my head all day being full of business, and yet sleepy and out of order; and so I lay down on my bed in my gowne to sleep, but I could not. Therefore, about 3 a-clock up and to dinner, and thence to the office, where Mrs. Burroughs my pretty widow was; and so I did her business and sent her away by agreement; and presently *b* I by coach after her and took her up in Fanchurch-street – and away through the City, hiding my face as much as I could. But she being mighty pretty and well enough clad, I was not afeared; but only lest somebody shall see me and think me idle. I quite through with her, and so into the fields Uxbridge way, a mile or two beyond Tyburne, and then back, and then to Paddington, and then back to Lyssen-

---

a MS. 'at'   b repl. 'by and by'

---

1. Evelyn (18 June 1670) has a story of a lady who had her cheek blistered by a rose laid upon it when she was asleep. The story derived from Kenelm Digby (cf. his *Two Treatises*, 1644, p. 336), but Digby was, as Evelyn said, 'a teller of strange things'. See Evelyn, iii. 550 & n.

green, a place the coachman led me to (I never knew in my life), and there we eat and drank; and so back to Charing Crosse and there I set her down – all the way most excellent pretty company. I had her lips as much as I would; and a mighty pretty woman she is and very modest, and yet kind in all fair ways.

All this time I passed with mighty pleasure, it being what I have for a long time wished for; and did pay this day 5s^a forfeit for her company.

She being gone, I to White-hall, and there to Lord Arlingtons and met Mr. Williamson and find there is no more need of my trouble about the Galliott last night; so with content departed and went straight home – where at the office did the most at the office in that wearied and sleepy state I could; and so home and to supper; and after supper, falling to singing with Mercer, did however sit up with her (she pleasing me with her singing of *Help, Helpe*)[1] till past midnight, and I not a whit Drowzy. And so to bed.

13. Lay sleepy in bed till 8 in the morning. Then up and to the office, where till about noon; then out to the Change and several places; and so home to dinner. Then out again to Sir R Viner, and there to my content settled the business of two tallies, so as I shall have 2000l almost more of my own money in my hand – which pleases me mightily. And so home and there to the office, where mighty busy;^b and then home to supper, and to even my Journall, and to bed –

Our fleet being now in all points ready to sail, but for the carrying of the two or three new ships with them, which will keep them a day or two or three more.

It is said the Duch is gone off our coast; but I have no good reason to believe it, Sir W. Coventry not thinking any such thing.

14. Up betimes to the office, to write fair a laborious letter I wrote, as from the Board,^c to the Duke of York, laying out our

a repl. '4s'   *b* repl. 'business'
c l.h. repl. same l.h. word badly written

1. See above, i. 169, n. 3. (E).

want of money again.[1] And perticularly the business of Captain Cockes tender[a] of hemp,[2] which my Lord Bruncker brought in under an unknown hand, without name – wherein his Lordshipp will have no great success I doubt.

That being done, I down to Thames Streete and there agreed for four or five Tons of Corke to send this day to the fleet, being a new device to make Barrecados with, instead of Junke.[3] By this means I came to see and kiss Mr. Hill's young wife; and a blithe young woman she is. So to the office, and at noon home to dinner; and then sent for young Michell and imployed him all the afternoon about weighing and shipping off of the Corke – having by this means an opportunity of getting him 30 or 40*s*. Having set him a-doing, I home and to the office very late, very busy, and did endeed despatch much business; and so to supper and to bed – after a song in the garden – which, and after dinner, is now the greatest pleasure I take, and endeed doth please me mightily. ⟨To bed, after washing my legs and feet with warm water in my Kitchin. This evening I had Davila brought home to me, and I find it a most excellent history as ever I read.⟩[b4]

15. ⟨*Lords day*.⟩ Up, and to church, where our lecturer made a sorry silly sermon upon the great point of proving the truth of the Christian religion. Home, and had a good dinner, expecting Mr. Hunt, but there comes only young Michell[c] and his wife – whom my wife concurs with me to be a pretty woman, and with her husband, is a pretty innocent couple. Mighty pleasant we were, and I mightily pleased in her company and to find my wife

---

a repl. 'contract'   *b* addition crowded in between entries
c MS. 'Miichell'

---

1. Copies in NMM, LBK/8, pp. 398–400 (printed in *Further Corr.*, pp. 137–40); Longleat, Coventry MSS 96, ff. 112–13. The Board reminded the Duke that since 12 May (when their last full statement of needs was made to him) they had received only £124,000 of the £327,000 they had required as a minimum.

2. See above, p. 132 & n. 3.

3. Coventry had written to Pepys

on the 13th asking him to look out a 'considerable quantity' of cork for fenders (for the defence of quarter-decks): Rawl. A 195a, f. 170r.

4. Probably the translation by William Aylesbury (1647) of E. C. Davila's *Storia delle guerre civili di Francia*. Pepys retained the translation by Sir Charles Cotterell published in 1678: PL 2430.

so well pleased with them also. After dinner he and I walked to White-hall, not being able to get a coach – he to the Abbey and I to White-hall; but met with nobody to discourse with, having no great mind to be found idling there and be asked questions of the fleet; so walked only through to the park, and there, it being mighty hot, and I weary, lay down by the Canaille[1] upon the grasse and slept awhile, and was thinking of a Lampoone which hath run in my head this week, to make upon the late fight at sea and the miscarriages there – but other businesses put it out of my head.[2]

Having lain there a while, I then to the Abbey and there called Michell; and so walked in great pain, having new shoos on, as far as Fleet-street; and there got a coach, and so in some little ease home – and there drank a great deal of small beer. And so took up my wife and Betty Michell and her husband, and away into the fields to take the ayre – as far as beyond Hackny, and so back again. In our way drinking a great deale of Milke,[3] which I drank to take away my Heartburne, wherewith I have been of late mightily troubled. But all the way home I did break abundance of wind behind – which did presage no good, but a great deal of cold gotten. So home and supped; and away went Michell and his wife – of whom I stole two or three salutes. And so to bed, in some pain and in fear of more – which accordingly I met with, for I was in mighty pain all night long, of the Winde griping of my belly*a* and making of me shit often, and vomit too – which is a thing not usual with me. But this I impute to the milk that I drank, after so much beer. But the cold, to my washing my feet the night before.

16. Lay in great pain in bed all the morning and most of the afternoon – being in much pain, making little or no water, and endeed having little within to make any with. And had great Twinges with the wind all the day, in my belly with wind – and a looseness with it; which, however, made it not so great as I have heretofore had it. ⟨A wonderful dark sky and shower of rain

a repl. same symbol

1. For waterworks in the park, see above, i. 246 & n. 2.

2. He does not appear to have written it. For a well-known anony-mous lampoon on this subject, see below, p. 407, n. 4.

3. For the perils of milk-drinking, see above, iv. 164, n. 2.

this morning – which at Harwich proved so too, with a shower of hail as big as walnuts.⟩*a*1

I had some broth made me to drink, which I love*b* – only to fill up room.

Up in the afternoon, and passed the day with Balty, who is come from sea for a day or two before the fight; and I perceive could be willing fairly to be out of the next fight, and I cannot much blame him, he having no reason by his place to be there. However, would not have him to be absent manifestly to avoid being there.

At night grew a little better and took a glister of Sacke; but taking it but by*c* halfes, it did me not much good, I taking but a little of it.   However, to bed, and had a pretty good night of it –

⟪17.⟫ so as to be able to rise to go to the office; and there sat, but now and then in pain, and without making much water, or freely.   However, it grew better and better, so as after dinner, believing the jogging in a coach would do me good, I did take my wife out to the New*d* Exchange to buy things. She there, while I with Balty went and bought a common riding-cloak for myself, to save my best.   It cost me but 30s, and will do my turn mighty well.

Thence home, and walked in the garden with Sir W. Penn a while; and saying how the riding in the coach doth me good (though I do not yet much find it), he ordered his to be got ready while I did some little business at the office; and so abroad, he and I, after 8 a-clock at night, as far almost as Bow, and so back again, and so home to supper and to bed.   This day I did bid Balty to agree with   ,2 the Duch painter which he once led me to (to see landskips), for a winter-piece of Snow, which endeed is a good piece, and costs me but 40s – which I

---

a   addition crowded into bottom of page   *b*   repl. 'loved'
         c   repl. 'by'   *d*   repl. 'Ch'-

---

1. Dr D. J. Schove writes: 'There were storms, with heavy rain and sometimes hail, in many parts of England and Scotland on or about this date. See e.g. *CSPD 1665–6*, p. 543; *Philos. Trans.*, ii (for 1667), no. 26, p. 481.'

2. Unidentified; conceivably either Hendrick Danckerts or Jan Lo(o)ten, both of whom were in London at this date. (OM).

would not take the money again for, it being I think mighty good. After a little supper, to bed – being in less pain still, and had very good rest.

18. Up in good ease, and so by coach to St. James's after my fellows, and there did our business, which is mostly every day to complain of want of money – and that only will undo us in a little time.

Here, among other things, before us all, the Duke of York did say that now at length he*ᵃ* is come to a sure knowledge that the Duch did lose in the late engagements 29 captains and 13 ships[1] – upon which, Sir W. Coventry did publicly move that if his Royal Highness had this of a certainty, it would be of use to send this down to the fleet, and to cause it to be spread about the fleet for the recovering of the spirits of the officers and seamen – who are under great dejectedness for want of knowing that they did do anything against the enemy, notwithstanding all that they did to us – which though it be true, yet methought was one of the most dishonourable motions to our countrymen that ever was made – and is worth remembering.

Thence with Sir W Pen home, calling at Lillys to have a time appointed when to be drawn among the other Commanders of Flags the last year's fight.[2] And so full of work Lilly is, that he was fain to take his table-book out to see how his time is appointed; and appointed six days hence for him to come, between 7 and 8 in the morning.

Thence with him home; and there by appointment I find Dr. Fuller, now Bishop of Limbricke in Ireland – whom I knew in his low condition at Twittenham.[3] I had also, by his desire, Sir W. Penn, and with him his lady and daughter. And had a good dinner, and find the Bishopp the same good man as*ᵇ* ever; and in a word, kind to us, and methinks one of the comeliest and

a repl. 'is'   *b* MS. 'that'

1. The Dutch lost nine captains: G. Brandt, *Michel de Ruiter* (trans., 1698), p. 363. For their losses of ships, see above, p. 177, n. 4.
2. Sir William Penn's portrait is among the set now at Greenwich: above, p. 102 & n. 3. (OM).
3. Fuller had been a schoolmaster at Twickenham: cf. above, i. 20, n. 2.

most becoming Pr[e]lates in all respects that ever I saw in my life. During dinner comes an acquaintance of his, Sir Thomas Little-ton[1] – whom I knew not while he was in my house, but liked his discourse. And afterward by Sir W. Penn do come to know that he is one of the greatest speakers in the House of Commons, and the usual Second to the great Vaughan.[2] So was sorry I did observe him no more and gain more of his acquaintance.

After dinner, they being gone, and I mightily pleased with my guests – I down the River to Greenwich about business; and thence walked to Woolwich, reading *The Rivall Ladys*[3] all the way, and find it a most pleasant and fine-writ play. At Wool-wige saw Mr. Shelden, it being late, and there eat and drank, being kindly used by him and Bab; and so by water to Depford, it being 10 a-clock before I got to Depford, and dark – and there to Bagwell's. And having stayed there a while, away home; and after supper to bed.

The Duke of York said this day, that by letters from the Generalls, they would sail with the fleet this day or tomorrow.

19. Up, in very good health in every respect; only, my late Feavor got by my pain doth break out about my mouth.

So to the office, where all the morning sitting – full of wants of money; and much stores to buy for to replenish the stores, and no money to do it with, nor[a] anybody to trust us without it.

So at noon home to dinner, Balty and his wife with us. By and by Balty takes his leave of us, he going away just now toward the fleet; where he will pass through one great engagement more before he be two days older I believe.

I to the office, where busy all the afternoon, late; and then home, and after some pleasant discourse with my wife, to bed. After I was in bed, I had a letter from Sir W. Coventry that tells

a repl. 'And so'

---

1. M.P. for Much Wenlock, Salop; a leader of the country interest: 'the ablest and vehementest arguer of them all' (Burnet, ii. 92); 'great *Littleton*' (Marvell, *Last Instructions*, l. 298).

2. For Vaughan, see above, p. 192, n. 2.

3. A tragicomedy by Dryden: see above, v. 232 & n. 3; PL 1604 (1664 ed.). (A).

me that the fleet is sailed this morning. God send us good news of them.

20. Up, and finding by a letter late last night that the fleet is gone[1] and that Sir W. Penn is ordered to go down to Sherenesse, and finding him ready to go to St. James's this morning, I was willing to go with him to see how things go; and so with him thither (but no discourse with the Duke) but to White-hall, and there the Duke of York did bid Sir W. Penn to stay to discourse with him and the King about business of the fleet; which troubled me a little, but it was only out of envy, for which I blame myself – having no reason to expect to be called to advise in a matter I understand not.

So I away to Lovetts, there to see[a] how my picture goes on to be varnished (a fine crucifix),[2] which will be very fine. And here I saw some fine prints, brought from France by Sir Tho. Crew, who is lately returned. So home, calling at the stationer's for some paper fit to varnish; and in my way home met with Lovett, to whom I gave it. And he did present me with a varnished staff, very fine, and light[b] to walk with.

So home and to dinner, there coming young Mrs. Daniel and her sister Sarah and dined with us – and old Mr. Hawly, whose condition pities me, he being forced[c] to turn under-parish-clerk at St. Gyles's I think, at the other end of the town.[3]

Thence I to the office, where busy all the afternoon; and in the

---

a repl. same symbol   *b* MS. 'late'   *c* repl. same symbol

---

1. They fell down the river in the early morning of the 19th, but did not get beyond the Shoe on the 20th (*CSPD 1665–6*, p. 558), and did not engage the Dutch, who waited for them in the mouth of the river, until the 25th.

2. An unidentified print of the Passion: below, p. 353. Possibly this was the picture which in 1674 gave grounds to Pepys's political enemies to accuse him of being (like his master, the Duke of York) a papist. Cf. *CJ*, ix. 306 (10 February

1674): 'Mr Pepis, standing up in his Place, did heartily and flatly deny, that he ever had any Altar, or Crucifix, or the Image or Picture of any Saint whatsoever in his House, from the Top to the Bottom of it.' Cf. also Longleat, Coventry MSS 2, ff. 38+.

3. Presumably at St Giles-in-the-Fields. His name does not occur in the records of the Parish Clerks' Company. For the other guests, see above, vi. 261, n. 3.

P

evening with Sir W. Penn, walking with whom in the garden, with whom I am of late mighty great; and it is wisdom to continue myself so, for he is, of all the men of the office at present, most manifestly useful,*a* and best thought of. He and I supped together upon the seat in the garden; and thence, he gone, my wife and Mercer came and walked, and sang late, and then home to bed.

21. Up, and to the office, where all the morning sitting. At noon walked in the garden with Comissioner Pett (newly come to town), who tells me how infinite the disorders are among the commanders and all officers of the fleet – no discipline – nothing but swearing and cursing, and everybody doing what they please; and the Generalls, understanding no better, suffer it, to the reproaching of this Board*b* or whoever it will be. He himself hath been challenged twice to the field, or something*c* as good, by Sir Edwd Spragg and Captain Seamour; he tells me the captains carry, for all the late orders, what men*d* they please.[1] Demand and consume what provisions they please. So that he fears, and I do no less, that God Almighty can[not] bless us while we keep in this disorder that we are in. He observing to me too, that there is no man of counsel or advice in the fleet; and the truth is, the gentlemen Captains will undo us,[2] for they are not to be kept in order, their friends about the King and Duke and their own houses* is so free, that it is not for any person but the Duke himself to have any command over them. He gone, I to dinner, and then to the office, where busy all the afternoon. At night walked in the garden with my wife, and so home to supper and to bed.

Sir W Pen is gone down to Sherenesse today, to see things made ready against the fleet shall come in again – which makes

a repl. 'usual'   *b* repl. ? 'mor'-   *c* repl. 'things'   *d* repl. 'orders'

---

1. Supernumeraries (men carried aboard extra to the ships' complements) were to cause a great deal of trouble to Pepys as Surveyor-General of Victualling. Sometimes they were authorised by the flag-officers and the Lord Admiral. On 20 February the Admiral had ordered the Navy Board to remedy abuses in the system. BM, Add. 36782, f. 33*v*.

2. Cf. above, p. 11, n. 1.

Pett mad; and calls him dissembling knave, and that himself takes all the pains and is blamed, while he doth nothing but hinder business, and takes all the honour of it to himself. And tells me plainly, he will fling up his commission rather then bear*ᵃ* it.

22. *Lords day.* Up, and to my chamber and there till noon, mighty busy setting money-matters and other things of mighty moment to rights, to the great content of my mind, I finding that accounts but a little let go can never be put in order by strangers, for I cannot without much difficulty do it myself. After dinner to them again till about 4 a-clock, and then walked to White-hall, where saw nobody*ᵇ* almost, but walked up and down with Hugh May,[1] who is a very ingenious man – among other things, discoursing of the present fashion of gardens, to make them plain[2] – that we have the best walks of Gravell in the world – France having none, nor Italy; and our green of our bowling-alleys is better then any they have. So our business here being ayre, this is the best way, only with a little mixture of Statues or pots,*ᶜ* which may be handsome, and so filled with another pot of such or such, a flower or greene, as the season of the year will bear. And then for Flowers, they are best seen in a little plat by themselfs; besides, their borders spoil ⟨the walks of⟩ any other garden. And then for fruit, the best way is to have Walls built Circularly, one within another, to the South, on purpose for fruit, and leave the walking-garden only for that use.

Thence walked through the house, where most people mighty*ᵈ* hush, and methinks melancholy, I saw not a smiling face through the whole Court; and in my conscience, they are doubtful of the

---

a repl. 'do so'   *b* repl. 'few'   *c* repl. 'pts'   *d* MS. 'my'

---

1. Deputy-Surveyor of the King's Works.
2. This was the French fashion of composing large formal effects by means of sweeps of grass, water and gravelled paths; exemplified by Le Nôtre, and copied by John Rose, the royal gardener, in the reconstruction (now proceeding) of Greenwich and St James. May was closely connected with these changes. The abandonment of the native Elizabethan tradition (flowers in profusion, and small walled and 'knotted' gardens) was regretted by some experts (e.g. John Rea, *Flora*, 1665, p. 1). But the high quality of English grass and gravel was usually remarked on in the gardening books of the time.

conduct again of the Generalls – and I pray God they may not make their fears reasonable. Sir Rd Fanshaw is lately dead at Madrid.¹

Guyland is lately over-throwne wholly in Barbary, by the King of Taffiletta.² The Fleete cannot yet*ᵃ* get clear of the River; but expect the first wind to be out, and then to be sure they fight.

The Queene and Maids of Honour are at Tunbridge.³

23. Up and to my chamber, doing several things there of moment. And then comes Simpson the Joyner, and he and I with great pains contriving presses to put my books up in;⁴ they now growing numerous, and lying one upon another on my chairs, I lose the use, to avoid the trouble of removing them when I would open a book.

Thence out to the Excise Office about business, and then homewards; met Colvill, who tells me he hath 1000*l* ready for me upon a tally – which pleases me, and yet I know not now what to do with it, having already as much money as is fit for me to have in the house.⁵ But I will have it. I did also meet Alderman Backewell, who tells me of the hard usage he now finds from Mr. Fen, in not getting him a bill or two paid – now that he can be no more useful to him.⁶ Telling me that what by his being

a repl. 'again'

---

1. He was Ambassador to Spain and had died on 16/26 June.

2. 'Guyland' was the local chieftain who had menaced Tangier, and 'the King of Tafiletta' his overlord, El Rashid II, Emperor of Morocco since 1664. In June Guyland's forces had been overthrown near Alcazar. He held out in Azila for two years more, but was no longer able to challenge Tafiletta's control of the country. Guyland fled to the protection of the English on the fall of Azila in 1668, and was killed in battle five years later. Routh, pp. 90–1.

3. They stayed from 9 July to 5 August: *London Gazette* (12 July; 9 August). It was the Queen's patronage which made the wells there fashionable at this period.

4. The two cases now made survive, with ten similar ones, in the Pepys Library at Magdalene College. Description by R. W. Symonds in *Connoisseur*, 85/275+, 353+; see illust. opp. Thomas Simpson was Master-Joiner at the Deptford and Woolwich dockyards.

5. Over £2,000; above, p. 196.

6. See above, vi. 292, n. 3.

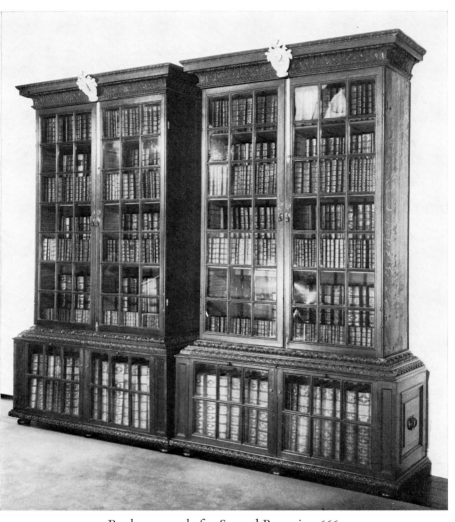

Bookcases made for Samuel Pepys in 1666
(*Pepys Library, Magdalene College, Cambridge*)

abroad and Shaws death,[1] he hath lost the Ball; but that he
doubts not to come to give a Kicke at it still, and then he shall be
wiser and keep it while he hath it.   But he says he hath a good
maister, the King, who[a] will not suffer him to be undone, as
other[wise] he must have been; and I believe him.[2]

So home and to dinner, where I confess, reflecting upon the
ease and plenty that I live in, of money, goods, servants, honour,
everything, I could not but with hearty[b] thanks to Almighty God
ejaculate my thanks to Him while I was at dinner, to myself.

After dinner to the office, and there till 5 or 6 a-clock, and then
by coach to St. James and there with Sir W. Coventry and Sir
G Downing to take the ayre in the park – all full of expectation
of the fleet's engagement, but it is not yet.   Sir W. Coventry says
they are 89 men-of-war, and but one fifth-rate, and that the *Sweepstakes*, which carries 40 guns.[3]   They are most infinitely manned
he tells me; the *Loyall London*, Sir J. Smith (which by the way
he commends to be the best ship in the world, large and by),
hath above 800 men.[4]   And more, takes notice, which is
worth notice, that the fleet hath lain now near fourteen days
without any demand for a fardingworth of anything of any
kind, but only to get[c] men.   But also observes that with this
excess of men, nevertheless they have thought fit to leave behind
them 16 ships, which they have robbed of their men; which
certainly might have been manned, and they been serviceable
in the fight, and yet the fleet well-manned, according to the
excess of supernumeraries which we hear they have.   At least,

---

a repl. 'he'   *b* MS. 'heartily'   *c* repl. 'carry'

---

1. Robin Shaw, his principal assis-
tant (an old friend of Pepys) had died
in July 1665. For several months in
that year Backwell had been in
Antwerp raising money for subsidies
which were to be paid to the allied
forces of Münster: above, vi. 150 &
n. 1; Sir W. Temple, *Select Letters*
(1701), i. 212.

2. The Exchequer had helped to

save him from bankruptcy a year
earlier: see above, loc. cit. Cf. *CTB*,
i. 677.

3. Her normal war-time complement was 36 guns.   She was made a
4th-rate in 1669: *Cat.*, i. 279.

4. This was the new 2nd-rate
launched in June: above, p. 160.
Her normal war-time complement
was officially 730 men: *Cat.*, i. 267.

two or three of them might have been[a] left manned, and sent away with the Gottenburgh ships.[1]

They conclude this to be much the best fleet, for force of guns, greatness, and number of ships and men, that ever England did see – being, as Sir W. Coventry reckons,[2] besides those left behind, 89 men of war, and 20 fire-ships, though we cannot hear that they have with them above 18.

The French are not yet joyned with the Duch, which doth dissatisfy the Hollanders,[3] and if they should have a defeat, will undo De Witt; the people generally of Holland do hate this league with France.

We cannot think of any business but lie big with expectation of the issue of this fight; but do conclude that this fight being over, we shall be able to see the whole issue of the war, good or bad.

So homeward, and walked over the park (St. James's) with Sir G. Downing; and at White-hall took a coach, and there to supper with much pleasure, and to bed.

24. Up, and to the office – where little business done, our heads being full of expectation of the fleet's being engaged, but no certain notice of it; only, Shepheard in the Duke's Yacht left them yesterday morning, within[b] a league of the Dutch fleet and making after them, they standing into the sea. At noon to dinner; and after dinner, with Mercer (as of late my practice is) a song. And so to the office, there to set up again my frames about my Platts,[c] which I have got to be all gilded, and look very fine. And then to my business, and busy very late, till midnight, drawing up a representation of the state of my victualling business

---

a 'been' repeated   *b* repl. 'in'   *c* repl. 'draughts'

---

1. The Hamburg and Gothenburg fleets had been lying for some weeks at Harwich, awaiting escort. After the battle on St James's Day (25 July), two ships were sent from the fleet to convoy them. *CSPD 1666–7*, p. 6.

2. Pepys made a briefer note of Coventry's report in Rawl. A 195a, f. 31*r*.

3. Cf. the similar report in *London Gazette*, 23 July.

to the Duke,¹ I having never appeared to him doing anything too yet; and therefore I now do it in writing, I having now the advantage of having had two fleets*ᵃ* dispatched in better condition then ever any fleets were yet I believe; at least, with least complaint – and by this means I shall with the better confidence get my bills out for my salary.²

So home to bed.

25. Up betimes to write fair my last night's paper*ᵇ* for the Duke; and so along with Sir W. Batten by hackney-coach to St. James – where the Duke is go[ne] abroad with the King to the park, but anon came back to White-hall; and so we, after an hour's waiting, walked thither (I having desired Sir W. Coventry in his chamber to read over my paper about the victualling, which he approves of, and I am glad I showed it him first;*ᶜ* it makes it the less necessary to show it the Duke at all, if I find it best to let it alone); at White-hall we find [the Court] gone to chapel, it being St. James's day. And by and by, while they are at chapel and we waiting chapel being done, comes people out of the parke, telling us that the guns are heard plain.³ And so everybody to the park, and by and by, the chapel done, and the King and Duke into the bowling-green and upon the leads (whither I went) and there the guns were plain to be heard (though it was pretty to hear how confident some would be in the lowdnesse of the guns, when it was as much as ever I could do to hear them);

---

a MS. 'fls'   *b* repl. symbol rendered illegible   *c* repl. 'him'

---

1. Copy (in Pepys's hand) in NMM, LBK/8, pp. 400–1; dated this day; partially printed in *Further Corr.*, pp. 141–2. 'Two fleets have been provided for . . . the latter (though conceived the greatest ever yet set forth) dispatched without one day's loss of time, or the least complaint . . . and . . . with a sufficiency to complete the whole fleet with four months provisions to determine the 3rd of October next . . .'.

2. His salary as Surveyor-General of the Victualling was £300 p.a.

3. Arlington wrote to Sandwich on the 26th that he and the King heard them plainly from the morning of the 25th onwards, and that on the 26th they grew fainter: Sandwich MSS, Letters from Ministers, i, f. 140*v*.

by and by the King to dinner, and I waited there his dining; but Lord, how little I should be pleased, I think, to have so many people crowding about me.[1] And among other things, it astonished me to see my Lord Barkeshire,[2] waiting at table and serving the King drink, in that dirty pickle as I never saw man in my life. Here I met Mr. Williams,[3] who in serious discourse told me he did hope well of this fight, because of the equality of force, or rather our having the advantage in number, and also because we did not go about it with that presumption that we did heretofore – when, he told me, he did before the last fight look upon us by our pride fated[a] to be overcome.

He would have me to dine where he was invited to dine, at the backe stayres. So after the King's meat was taken away, we thither, but he could not stay; but left me there among two or three of the King's servants, where we dined with the meat that came from his table; which was most excellent, with most brave drink, cooled in Ice (which at this hot time was welcome); and I, drinking no wine, had Metheglin for the King's own drinking, which did please me mightily.

Thence, having dined mighty nobly, I away to Mrs. Martin's new lodgings, where I find her, and was with her alone; but Lord, how big she is already. She is, at least seems, in mighty trouble for her husband at sea, when I am sure she cares not for him, and I would not undeceive her, though I know his ship is one of those that is not gone, but left behind without men.

Thence to White-hall again to hear news, but found none; so back toward Westminster, and there met Mrs. Burroughs, whom I had a mind to meet, but being undressed did appear a mighty ordinary woman. Thence by water home, and out again by coach to Lovetts to see my Crucifix, which is not done. So to White-hall again to have met Sir G. Carteret, but he is gone abroad; so back homewards, and seeing Mr. Spong, took

a MS. 'fitted'

---

1. The royal practice of dining in public on certain days of each week was discontinued during the war: Evelyn, 7 August 1667. The crowding was by courtiers and servants.

2. Gentleman of the Bedchamber; aged c. 76.

3. Probably Vincent Williams, Groom of the Chamber in ordinary.

him up; and he and I to Reeves the glass-maker's and did see several glasses, and had pretty discourse with him; and so away and set down Mr. Spong in*ᵃ* London, and so home, and with my wife late, twatling at my Lady Penns; and so home to supper and to bed.

I did this afternoon call at my woman*ᵇ* that ruled my paper to bespeak a Musique Card,[1] and there did kiss Nan.

No news tonight from the fleet how matters go yet.

26. Up and to the office, where all the morning. At noon dined at home, Mr. Hunt and his wife (who is very gallant, and newly come from Cambrige because of the sickness)[2] with us – very merry at table, and the people I do love mightily. But being in haste to go to White-hall, I rose, and Mr. Hunt with me, and by coach thither; where I left him in the boarded gallery, and I by appointment to attend the Duke of York at his closet. But being not come, Sir G. Carteret and I did talk together, and advises me that if I could, I would get the papers of examination touching the business of the last year's prizes[3] which concern my Lord Sandwich out of Warcupps hand; who being now under disgrace and poor, he believes may be brought easily to part with them.[4] My Lord Crew it seems is fearful yet that matters may be enquired into. This I will endeavour to do – though I do not think it signifies much.

By and by the Duke of York comes and we had a meeting; and among other things, I did read my declaration of the proceedings of the Victualling action this year,[5] and desired his Royal Highness to give me the*ᶜ* satisfaction of knowing whether his

---

a repl. 'at'   *b* repl. 'w'-   *c* repl. 'an'

1. Perhaps a card used for composing or for recording rules of composition. (E).
2. John Hunt was a subcommissioner of the excise for Cambridgeshire. The plague, which first struck Cambridge in the summer of 1665, reached its height in July–August 1666: J. F. D. Shrewsbury, *Hist. bubonic plague in Brit. Isles*, pp. 514–16.
3. See above, vi. 231, n. 1.

4. Edmond Warcupp (above, p. 203, n. 5), employed in the examination of prizes, had been imprisoned on 20 July on a charge of making improper use of Arlington's name to cover some financial transactions: PRO, PC2/59, f. 56*v*. In a petition of August 1666 he pleaded 'nine small lamenting children': *CSPD 1666–7*, p. 14.
5. See above, p. 217, n. 1.

Royal Highness were pleased therewith. He told me he was, and that it was a good account, and that the business of the victualling was much in a better condition then it was the last year – which did much joy me, being said in the company of my fellows, by which I shall be able with confidence to demand my salary, and the rest of the Sub-Surveyors.[1]

Thence away, mightily satisfied, to Mrs. Pierces, there to find my wife. Mrs. Pierce hath lain*a* in of a boy about a month – the boy is dead this day.[2] She lies in in good state, and very pretty she is. But methinks doth every day grow more and more great, and a little too much – unless they got more money then I fear they do.

Thence with my wife and Mercer to my Lord Chancellors new house,[3] and there carried them up to the Leads – where I find my Lord Chamberlaine, Lauderdale, Sir Rob. Murray, and others. And do find it the most delightful place for prospect that ever was in the world, it even ravishing me; and that is all, in short, I can say of it.

Thence to Islington to our old house[4] and eat and drank, and so round by Kingsland home; and there to the office a little and Sir W. Batten's (but no news at all from the fleet), and so home to bed.

27. Up and to the office, where all the morning busy. At noon dined at home, and then to the office again, and there walking in the garden with Captain Cocke till 5 a-clock. No news yet of the fleet. His great bargain of Hemp with us, by*b* his

---

a repl. 'lie'   *b* repl. 'by'

---

1. From Pepys's shorthand memorandum of this meeting it appears that he persuaded the Duke, who had already expressed his satisfaction, to repeat his words of praise for the benefit of Batten, who had arrived late: NMM, LBK/8, p. 401 (printed *Shorthand Letters*, p. 84). There was a reduction in the number of complaints about victualling in 1666

compared with those of 1665: see *Cat.*, i. 154.

2. One month was the usual period of lying-in. The boy was Vincent, son of James and Elizabeth Pearse, baptised on 9 July.

3. In Piccadilly: see above, p. 32 & n. 2.

4. The King's Head.

unknown proposition,[1] is disliked by the King, and so is quite off – of which he is glad, by this means being rid of his obligation to my Lord Bruncker, which he was tired with, and especially his mistress Mrs. Williams; and so will fall into another way about it, wherein he will advise only with myself – which doth not displease me, and will be better for him, and the King too. Much common talk of public businesses. The want of money. The uneasiness that Parliament will find in raising any – and the ill condition we shall be in if they do not. And his confidence that the Swede is true to us, but poor[2] – but would be glad to do us all manner of service in the world. He gone, I away by water from the Old Swan to White-hall. The waterman tells me that news is come that our ship *Resolution* is burnt, and that we had sunk four or five of the enemy's ships. When I came to White-hall, I met with Creed, and he tells me the same news. And walking with him into the park, I to Sir W. Coventry's lodging, and there he showed me Captain Talbots letter, wherein he says that the fight begun on the 25th.[3] That our White squadron begun with one of the Duch squadrons, and then the Red with another, so hot, that we put them both to giving way, and so they continued in pursuit all the day, and as long as he stayed with them. That the Blew fell to the Zealand squadron; and after a long dispute, he against two or three great ships, he received eight or nine dangerous[a] shots, and so came away; and says he saw the *Resolucion* burned by one of their Fireshipps, and four or five of the enemy's – but says that two or three of our great ships were in danger of being fired by our own fireships, which Sir W. Coventry nor I cannot understand. But upon the whole, he and I walked two or three turns in the park under the great trees – and do doubt that this gallant is come away

a repl. 'great'

---

1. See above, p. 132 & n. 3. Brouncker had proposed it but had concealed Cocke's interest.

2. Cocke, as an Eastland merchant, was knowledgeable about Scandinavia.

3. This was the engagement which became known as the Battle of St James's Day: see below, p. 225 & n.

1. Charles Talbot commanded the *Elizabeth*; his letter was used in the account of the battle published in the *London Gazette* of 2 August.

a little too soon, having lost never a mast nor sail[1] – and then we did begin to discourse of the young gentlemen-captains, which he was very free with me in speaking his mind of the unruliness of them. And what a loss the King hath of his old men, and now of this Hannum of the *Resolucion*, if he be dead.[2] And that there is but few old sober men in the fleet,[a] and if those few of the Flags that are so should die, he fears some other gentlemen-captains will get in; and then what a council we shall have, God knows. He told me how he is disturbed to hear the commanders at sea called Cowards here on shore. And that he was yesterday concerned publicly, at a dinner, to defend them against somebody that said that not above 20 of them fought as they should do (and endeed it is derived from the Duke of Albemarle himself, who wrote so to the King and Duke),[3] and that he told them how they fought four days – two of them with great disadvantage. That Count de Guiche, who was on board De Ruyter, writing his narrative home in French of the fight, doth lay all the honour that may be upon the English courage, above the Duch.[4] And that himself was sent down from the King and Duke of York after the fight to pray them to spare none that they thought had not done their parts, and that they have removed but four, whereof Du Tell is one, of whom he would say nothing (but it seems the Duke of York hath been much displeased at his removal, and hath now taken him into his service, which is a plain affront to the Duke of Albemarle),[5] and two of the others Sir W. Coventry did speak very slenderly of their faults; only the last, which was old Teddiman,[6] he says is in

a repl. 'world'

---

1. Talbot (a gentleman-captain) was said to have come into Aldeburgh 'with his vessel in good condition, walking the deck in his silk morning gown and powdered hair': *CSPD 1665–6*, p. 591.

2. Willoughby Hannam, in fact, was saved, together with most of his men, by boats sent from neighbouring ships.

3. See above, p. 154 & n. 2; cf. above, p. 194 & n. 1.

4. Armand de Gramont, Comte de Guiche, eldest son of the Duc de Gramont, had served as a volunteer in the Four Days Battle (1–4 June) along with the Prince of Monaco, who fell in the water. The *Relation* which he (and Monaco) wrote of the battle was incorporated in de Guiche's *Memoires* (1744), pp. 234+.

5. See above, p. 163 & n. 1.

6. See above, p. 163 & n. 3.

fault and hath little to excuse himself with; and that therefore we should not be forward in condemning men of want of courage, when the Generals, who are both men of mettle and hate Cowards, and had the sense of our ill-success upon them (and by the way, must either let the world think it was the miscarriage of the captains, or their own conduct), have thought fit to remove no more of them, when desired by the King and Duke of York to do it, without respect to any favour any of them can pretend to in either of them.

At last we concluded that we never can hope to meet the Duch with such advantages as now, in number and force, and a fleet in want of nothing; and he hath often repeated, now and at other times, industriously, that many of the Captains have declared that they want nothing. And again, that they did lie ten days together at the Nore without demanding of anything in the world but men; and of them, they afterward, when they went away, the Generals themselfs acknowledge that they have permitted several ships to carry Supernumerarys.[1]

But that if we do not speed well, we must then play small games, and spoil their trade in small parties.

And so we parted; and I meeting Creed in the park again, did take him by coach and to Islington, thinking to have met my Lady Pen and wife, but they were gone; so we eat and drank, and away back – setting him down in Cheapside; and I home, and there, after a little while mending of my tune to *It is decreed*,[2] to bed.

28. Up and to the office, where no more news of the fleet then was yesterday. Here we sat. And at noon to dinner to[a] the Popes head, where my Lord Brouncker (and his mistress dined) and Comissioner Pett, Dr. Charleton, and myself entertained with a venison pasty by Sir W Warren. Here, very pretty discourse of Dr. Charleton concerning Nature's fashioning[b]

a repl. 'with' *b* repl. 'fashion'-

---

1. Pepys later attributed the short-age of supplies to the number of un-authorised supernumeraries: see his evidence (1669) to the Brooke House Committee: PL 2874, p. 480. Cf. above, p. 212, n. 1.

2. See above, p. 91 & n. 4. (E).

every creature's teeth according to the food she intends them. And that man's, it is plain, was not for flesh, but for fruit.[1] And that he can at any time tell the food of a beast unknown, by the teeth. My Lord Brouncker made one or two objections to it; that creatures find their food proper for their teeth, rather then that the teeth was fitted for the food. But the Doctor, I think, did well observe that creatures do naturally, and from the first, before they have had experience to try, do love such a food rather then another. And that all children love fruit, and none brought to flesh but against their wills at first.

Thence with my Lord Brouncker to White-hall, where no news; so to St. James's to Sir W. Coventry, and there hear only of the *Bredah's* being come in, and gives the same small account that the other did yesterday, so that we know not what is done by the body of the fleet at all – but conceive great reason to hope well.

Thence with my Lord to his Coach-house, and there put in six horses into his coach and he and I alone to Highgate – all the way, going and coming, I learning of him the principles of Optickes, and what it is that makes an object seem less or bigger. And how much distance doth lessen an object. And that it is not the eye at all, or any rule in optiques, that can tell distance; but it is only an act of reason, comparing of one mark with another. Which did both please and inform me mightily. Being come thither, we went to my Lord Lauderdale's house[2] to speak with him about getting a man at Lieth to join with one we imploy to buy some prize-goods for the King. We find [him] and his lady and some Scotch people at supper – pretty odd company; though my Lord Brouncker tells me my Lord Lauderdale is a man of mighty good reason and judgment.[3] But at supper there played one of their servants upon the viallin, some Scotch tunes only – several – and the best of their country, as they seemed to esteem them by their praising and admiring them; but Lord, the strangest ayre that ever I heard in my life, and all of

1. Dr Walter Charlton was a physician to the King; a prolific author on anatomy and antiquities, and much given to hypotheses. This theory, however, does not appear in his *Nat. hist. of nutrition* (1659).

2. Lauderdale House on Highgate Hill; now Waterlow Park. (R).

3. Lauderdale, Secretary for Scottish affairs, 1660–80, had generally a reputation not only for ability but also for lack of scruple.

one cast. But strange to hear my Lord Lauderdale say himself, that he had rather hear a Catt mew then the best Musique in the world – and the better the music, the more sick it makes him. And that of all instruments, he hates*a* the Lute most; and next to that, the Baggpipe.

Thence back with my Lord to his house; all the way good discourse, informing of myself about optiques still; and there left him, and by a hackney home; and after writing three or four letters, home to supper and to bed.

29. *Lords day.* Up and all the morning in my chamber, making up my accounts in my book with my father and brother, and stating them. Towards noon, before sermon was done at church, comes news by a letter to Sir W. Batten (to my hand) of the late fight – which I sent to his house, he at church: but Lord, with what impatience I stayed till sermon was done, to know the issue of the fight, with a thousand hopes and fears and thoughts about the consequences of either. At last sermon is done and he came home, and the bells immediately rung as soon as the church was done;[1] but coming to Sir W. Batten to know the news, his letter said nothing of it – but all the town is full of a victory. By and by, a letter from Sir W. Coventry tells me that we have the victory. Beat them into the Weelings.[2] Had taken two of their great ships, but by the orders of the Generals they are burned[3] – this being methought but a poor result after the fighting of two so great fleets; and four days having no tidings of them, I was still impatient – but could know no more; so away

a s.h. repl. l.h. 'h'-

---

1. Pepys kept a copy of the announcement of the St James's Day victory made from the pulpit at Bow church this day and given to him by William Batelier: Rawl. A 195a, f. 201r; printed in Braybrooke (1825), ii. 297–8. He also kept a copy of the account and plan of the battle by his friend James Pearse, Surgeon-General of the fleet: Rawl., loc. cit., ff. 202–5. Other contemporary accounts are in *Rupert and Monck Letter Book, 1666* (ed. J. R. Powell and E. K. Timings), pp. 270+; Allin, i. 277+; *Naval Misc.* (Navy Rec. Soc.), pp. 8+; B. S. Ingram (ed.), *Three sea journals*, pp. 53+. For modern accounts, see Tedder, pp. 171+; Allin, vol. ii, pp. xxvii+ (by R. C. Anderson).

2. The Weilings: the channels south-west of Flushing.

3. Allin ordered their destruction, so as 'not to unman his ships': *CSPD 1665–6*, p. 579.

home to dinner, where Mr. Spong and Reeves dined with me by invitation. After dinner to our business of my Microscope, to be shown some of the observables of that; and then down to my office to look in a dark room with my glasses and Tube,*a* and most excellently things appeared indeed, beyond imagination. This was our work all the afternoon, trying the several glasses and several objects; among others, one of my plats, where the lines appeared so very plain, that it is not possible to think how plain it was done.

Thence, satisfied exceedingly with all this, we home, and to discourse many pretty things; and so stayed out the afternoon till it begun to be dark and then they away, and I to Sir W. Batten, where the Lieutenant of the Tower was, and Sir J. Mennes; and the news, I fear, is nor more [nor] less then what I had heard before. Only, that our Blue Squadron, it seems, was pursued the most of the time, having more ships, a great many, then its number allotted to her share.[1]   Young Seamour is killed, the only captain slain.[2]   The *Resolution* burned; but, as they say, most of her [men] and commander saved.*b*[3]   This is all; only, we keep the sea; which*c* denotes a victory, or at least that we are not beaten. But no great matters to brag*d* on, God knows.[4]   So home to supper and to bed.

30.   Up and did some business in my chamber; then by and by comes my boy's lute-maister,[5] and I did direct him hereafter

a   l.h. repl. l.h. 'Tubee'   b   repl. symbol rendered illegible
c   repl. 'what'   d   repl. 'God'

---

1. The Blue, under Sir Jeremy Smith, had to take on more than its fair share of opposition. Its fight against Tromp, commanding the Dutch rear, developed into a separate battle.

2. Hugh Seymour was captain of the *Foresight*. Sir Thomas Clifford's letter to Arlington of 27 July contains Pepys's news, and reports that Seymour, a 'brave commander', was the only captain lost: *CSPD 1665–6*, p. 579. Four others were in fact killed: Clowes, ii. 283.

3. See above, p. 222 & n. 2.

4. The Dutch fleet had been beaten back into harbour with heavy losses, but Smith, in charge of the pursuit on the 26th, had missed an opportunity of cutting off and destroying Tromp's squadron.

5. Smegergill (alias Caesar): see above, v. 344, n. 1. (E).

to begin to teach him to play his part on the Theorbo, which he will do, and that in a little time I believe. So to the office, and there with Sir W Warren, with whom I have spent no time a good while. We set right our business of the Lighters, wherein I think I shall get 100*l.*[1] At noon home to dinner, and there did practise with Mercer one of my new tunes that I have got Dr Childe to set me a bass to, and it goes prettily. Thence abroad to pay several debts at the end of the month. And so to Sir W. Coventry at St. James's, where I find him in his new closet, which is very fine and well supplied with handsome books. I find him speak very slightly of the late victory. Dislikes their staying with the fleet up their coast, believing that the Duch will come out in fourteen days; and then we, with our unready fleet, by reason of some of the ships being maymed, shall be in bad condition to fight them upon their own coast. Is much dissatisfied with the great number of men, and their fresh demands of 24 victualling ships, they going out but the other day as full as they could stow. I asked him whether he did never desire an[a] account of the number of Supernumerarys, as I have done several ways, without which we shall be in great errour about the victuals; he says he hath done it again and again, and if any mistake should happen, they must thank themselfs. He spoke slightly of the Duke of Albemarle, saying, when De Ruyter came to give him a broadside – "Now," says he (chawing of Tobacco the while), "will this fellow come and give me two broadsides, and then he will run;" but it seems he held him to it two hours, till the Duke himself was forced to retreat to refit ⟨and was towed off⟩, and De Ruyter stayed for him till he came back again to fight. One in the ship saying to the Duke, "Sir, methinks De Ruyter hath given us more then two broadsides." "Well," says the Duke, "but you shall find him run by and by." "And so he did," says Sir W. Coventry; "but after the Duke himself had been first made to fall off."

The *Resolucion* had all brass guns, being the same that Sir J Lawson had in her in the Straights.[2]

a   repl. 'a'

---

1. See above, pp. 157, 161.
2. The *Resolution* had been burnt in the battle. 'Brass' (i.e. bronze) guns were more accurate and more expensive than those of cast iron.

It is observe[d] that the two fleets were even in number, to one ship.¹

Thence home, and to sing with my wife and Mercer in the garden; and coming in, I find my wife plainly dissatisfied with me, that I can spend so much time with Mercer, teaching her to sing, and could never take that pains with her – which I acknowledge; but it is because that the girl doth take music mighty readily, and she doth not; and music is the thing of the world that I love most, and all the pleasure almost that I can now take. So to bed in some little discontent, but no words from me.

31. Good friends in the morning; and up to the office – where sitting all the morning. And while at table, we were mightily joyed with news, brought by Sir J. Mennes and Sir W. Batten, of the death of De Ruter; but when Sir W. Coventry came, he told us there was no such thing, which quite dashed me again; though, God forgive me, I was a little sorry in my heart before, lest it might give occasion of too much glory to the Duke of Albemarle.

Great bandying this day between Sir W. Coventry and my Lord Brouncker about Captain Cocke – which I am well pleased with – while I keep from any open violence on either side, but rather on Sir W. Coventry.

At noon had a haunch of venison boiled, and a very good dinner beside, there dining with me, on a sudden invitation, the two maiden-sisters Batelier's and their elder brother, a pretty man, understand[ing] and well-discoursed.² Much pleased with his company.

Having dined myself, I rose to go to a Committee of Tanger, and did come thither time enough to meet Povy and Creed, and none else – the Court being empty, the King gone to Tunbrige, and the Duke of York a-hunting. I had some discourse with Povy, who is mightily discontented, I find, about his disappointments at Court;³ and says of all places, if there be hell, it is here –

---

1. Cf. Clifford's letter to Arlington, 27 July, in which the two fleets were estimated at 90 men-of-war each: *CSPD 1665–6*, pp. 579–80. Dr Anderson puts the figures at 89 ships of the line (English) and 88 (Dutch):

Allin, vol. ii, p. xxviii.

2. William Batelier, was a wine merchant living in Crutched Friars. He and his sisters became close friends of the Pepyses.

3. Cf. above, pp. 191–2 & n.

no faith, no truth, no love, nor any agreement between man and wife, nor friends. He would have spoke broader, but I put it off to another time, and so parted.

Then with Creed, and read over with him the Narrative of the late [fight],[1] which he makes a very poor thing of, as endeed it is, and speaks most slightingly of that whole matter.

Povy discoursed with me about my Lord Peterborough's 5o*l* which his man did give me from him, the last year's salary I paid him, which he would have Povy pay him again; but I have not taken[a] it to myself yet, and therefore will most heartily return him, and mark him out for a coxcomb.

Povy went down to Mr. Williamsons, and brought me up this extract out of the Flanders letters today come.[2] That Admirall Everson and the Admirall and Vice-admirall of Freezeland,[3] with many Captains and men, are slain. That De Ruyter is safe, but lost 250 men out of his own ship. But that he is in great disgrace – and Trump in better Favour.[4] That Bankert's ship is burned, himself hardly scaping with a few men on board De Haes.[5] That 15 captains are to be tried the 7th of August. And that the hangman was sent from Flushing to assist the Council of Warr. How much of this is true, time will show.

Thence to Westminster-hall and walked an hour with Creed, talking of the last fight and observing the ridiculous management thereof and success* of the Duke of Albemarle.

a repl. symbol rendered illegible

---

1. This was the official account: *The victory over the fleet of the States General . . . in the late engagement begun the 25 of July inst., as it came from His Highness Prince Rupert and His Grace the Duke of Albemarle*; reprinted in *Rupert and Monck Letter Book, 1666* (ed. J. R. Powell and E. K. Timings), pp. 266–8.

2. This news (sent by one of Williamson's intelligencers) was reported in the *London Gazette* of 2 August.

3. I.e. Jan Evertsen, Tjerk Hiddes de Vries, and Rudolph Koenders.

4. On the contrary: de Ruyter received the thanks of the States-General, but made a critical report on Tromp's action in breaking off from the main engagement to pursue Smith's squadron. Tromp was dismissed on 14/24 August: G. Brandt, *Michel de Ruiter* (trans., 1698), pp. 380, 383–4.

5. Bankert's ship the *Tholen* was burnt by Allin. He went on board Adriaen de Haes of the Zeeland squadron, and covered the retreat: Allin, i. 278.

Thence parted, and to Mrs. Martin's lodgings and sat with her a while; and then by water home, all the way reading the Narrative of the last fight, in order, it may be, to the making some marginal notes upon it.

At the Old Swan found my Betty Michell at the door, where I stayed talking to her a pretty while, it being dusky, and kissed her; and so away home and writ my letters, and then home to supper, where the brother and Mary Batelier are still, and Mercer's two sisters. They have spent the time dancing this afternoon, and we were very merry; and then after supper into the garden and there walked, and then home with them; and then back again, my wife and I and the girl, and sang in the garden, and then to bed.

Colvill[1] was with me this morning; and to my great joy, I could now have all my money in that I have in the world. But the times being open again, I think it is best to keep some*a* of it abroad.

Mighty well, and end this month in content of mind and body – the public matters looking more safe for the present then they did. And we having a victory over the Duch, just such as I could have wished, and as the Kingdom was fit to bear – enough to give us the name of conquerors and leave us masters of the sea. But without any such great matters done as should give the Duke of Albemarle any honour at all, or give him cause to rise to his former insolence.

a repl. 'it'

---

1. John Colvill, goldsmith-banker.

AUGUST.

1. Up betimes to the settling of my last month's accounts, and I bless God I find them very clear, and that I am worth 5700*l*, the most that ever*a* my book did yet make out. So prepared to attend the Duke of York as usual. But Sir W Pen, just as I was going out, comes home from Sheerenesse, and held me in discourse about public business, till I came by coach too late to St. James, and there find that everything stood still, and nothing done for want of me. Thence walked over the Park with Sir W. Coventry, who I clearly see is not thoroughly pleased with the late management of the fight,[1] nor with anything that the Generals do. Only, is glad to hear that De Ruyter is out of favour, and that this fight hath cost them 5000 men, as they themselfs do report.[2] And it is a strange thing, as he observes, how now and then the slaughter runs on one hand; there being 5000 killed on theirs, and not above 400 or 500 killed and wounded on ours,[3] and as many flag-officers on theirs as ordinary captains in ours; there being Everson and the Admiral and Vice-admiral of Freezeland on theirs, and Seamour, Martin, and [4] on ours. I left him going to chapel, it being the common fast-day, and the Duke of York at chapel; and I to Mrs. Martins, but she abroad; so I sauntered to or again to the Abbey, and then to the parish church,[5] fearful of being seen to do so; and so after the parish church was ended, I to the Swan and

a repl. 'every'

---

1. The St James's Day Battle.
2. Losses on both sides were abnormally high. Those of the Dutch were put at 4000–5000 men in the Dutch news printed in the *London Gazette*, 6, 13 August. They were probably about 2000: J. C. de Jonge, *Geschiedenis van het nederlandsche zeewesen*, ii. 84.
3. A modern estimate is c. 300: Clowes, ii. 282–3.
4. Supply 'John Parker of the

Yarmouth, Joseph Saunders of the *Breda* and Arthur Ashby of the *Guinea*': Clowes, ii. 283. The English lost no flag-officers and the Dutch five. The Dutch admirals mentioned here were Jan Evertsen (Lt-Admiral of the Zeeland squadron), Lt-Adm. de Vries and Vice-Adm. Coenders of the Vriesland squadron. De Jonge, loc. cit.; *Mar. Mirr.*, 24/45.
5. St Margaret's, Westminster.

there dined upon*ᵃ* a rabbit; and after dinner to Mrs. Martins and there find Mrs. Burroughs, and by and by comes a pretty widow, one Mrs. Estwood, and one Mrs. Fenton, a maid. And here merry, kissing and looking on their breasts and all the innocent pleasure in the world. But Lord, to see the dissembling of this widow; how upon the singing of a certain Jigg by Doll, Mrs. Martin's sister, she seemed* to be sick, and fainted and God knows what, because the Jigg which her husband (who died this last sickness) loved. But by and by I made her as merry as is possible, and tossed and tumbled her as I pleased, and then carried her and her sober pretty kinswoman, Mrs. Fenton, home to their lodging in the new market of my Lord Treasurers,¹ and there left them. Mightily pleased with this afternoon's mirth – but in great pain to ride in a coach with them, for fear of being seen.

So home, and there much pleased with my wife's drawing today in her pictures; and so to supper and to bed, very pleasant.

2. [Up] and to the office, where we sat; and in discourse at the table with Sir W. Batten, I was urged to tell him it was an untruth, which did displease him mightily, and parted at noon very angry with me. At home find Lovett, who brought me some papers varnished, and showed me my crucifix,² which will be very fine when done. He dined with me and Baltys wife, who is in great pain for her husband, not hearing of him since the fight; but I understand he was not in it, going hence too late – and I am glad of it. Thence to the office, and thither Creed comes to me, and he and I walked a good while, and then to the Victualling ⟨Office⟩ together, and there with Mr. Gawden I did much business; and so away with Creed again, and by coach to see my Lord Brouncker, who it seems was not well yesterday; but being come thither, I find his coach ready to carry him abroad, but Tom his footman, whatever the matter was, was loath to desire me to come in, but I walked a great while in the Piatza³ till I was going away. But by and by my

a repl. 'with'

---

1. Southampton Market. For Southampton's development of Bloomsbury, see above, v. 286, n. 2. (R).

2. See above, p. 211 & n. 2.
3. In Covent Garden. (R).

Lord himself comes down, and coldly received me – so I soon parted, having enough for my over-officious folly in troubling myself to visit him, and I am apt to think that he was fearful that my coming was out of design to see how he spent his time then to enquire after his health: so parted, and I with Creed down to the New Exchange stairs, and there I took water and he parted. So home, and then down to Woolwich, reading and making an end of *The Rivall Ladys*,[1] and find it a very pretty play. At Woolwich, it being now night, I find my*a* wife and Mercer and Mr. Batelier and Mary there, and a supper getting ready. So I stayed in some pain, it being late and post-night. So supped and merrily home, but it was 12 at night first. However, sent away some letters, and home to bed.

3. Up and to the office, where Sir W. Batten and I sat to contract for some fire ships – I there close all the morning. At noon home to dinner, and then abroad to Sir Philip Warwick*b* at White-hall about Tanger quarter tallies.[2] And there had some serious discourse touching money and the case of the Navy, wherein all I could get of him was that we had the full understanding of the treasure, as much as my Lord Treasurer himself, and know*c* what he can do. And that whatever our case is, more money cannot be got till the Parliament. So talked of getting an account ready as soon as we could to give the Parliament, and so, very, melancholy parted. So I back again, calling my wife at her sister's, from whose husband we do now hear that he was safe this week, and going in a ship to the fleet – from the buoy of the Nore, where he hath been all this while – the fleet being gone before he got down. So home, and busy till night; and then to Sir W. Penn with my wife to sit and chat; and a small supper, and home to bed.

The death of Everson, and the report of our success, beyond expectation, in the killing of so great a number of men, hath

---

a repl. 'them get'   *b* MS. 'Sir W Ph'   *c* blot under symbol

---

1. See above, p. 210, n. 3. (A).   Warwick was secretary to the Lord
2. Tallies for the payment of the   Treasurer.
Tangier garrison for one quarter.

raised the estimation of the late victory considerably; but it is only among fools, for all that was but accidental. But this morning, getting Sir W. Penn to read over the Narrative[1] with me – he did sparingly, yet plainly, say that we might have intercepted their Zealand squadron coming home, if we had done our parts. And more, that we might have spooned before the wind as well as they, and have overtaken their ships in the pursuite in all that while.[2]

4. Up and to the office, where all the morning; and at noon to dinner, and Mr. Cooke dined with us, who is lately come from Hinchingbrooke, who[3] is also come to town. The family all well. Then I to the office, where very busy, to state to Mr. Coventry the account of the victuals of the fleet;[4] and late at it, and then home to supper and to bed.

This evening Sir W. Penn came into the garden and walked with me, and told me that he had certain notice that at Flushing they are in great distraction. De Ruyter dares not come on shore for fear of the people. Nor anybody open their houses or shops for fear of the tumult – which is a very good hearing.[5]

5. *Lords day.* Up, and down to the old Swan; and there called Betty Michell and her husband and had two or three long salutes from her out of sight of su marido, which pleased me mightily. And so carried them ⟨by water⟩ to Westminster; and I to St. James's and there had a meeting before the Duke of

1. See above, p. 229, n. 1.
2. The main English fleet had had a chance of intercepting Tromp who returned to the Dutch coast, pursued by Smith's squadron, on the evening of the 26th. But the ships had lost touch in the night, and the Dutch had slipped in behind the shoals. (To 'spoon' is to run before wind without any sail.)
3. I.e. Lord Hinchingbrooke: see below, p. 236.
4. Letter dated this day; copy (in clerk's hand) in NMM, LBK/8, pp. 432–3. Rupert and Albemarle, the

commanders of the fleet, on being sent an extract from this letter, complained that Pepys had omitted to account for many defective provisions, particularly the beer: *Rupert and Monck Letter Book, 1666* (ed. J. R. Powell and E. K. Timings), pp. 137–8.
5. A canard. There was a strong rumour in Holland itself that de Ruyter did not come ashore for fear of being tried for the fleet's failure in the St James's Day Battle: cf. *London Gazette*, 6 August. But in fact it was Tromp who was blamed: cf. above, p. 229, n. 4.

York, complaining of want of money; but nothing done to any purpose, for want we shall; so that now our advices to him signify nothing. Here Sir W. Coventry did acquaint the Duke of York how the world doth discourse of the ill method of our books, and that we would consider how to answer any enquiry which shall be made after our practice therein – which will, I think, concern the Controller most. But I shall make it a memento to myself.

Thence walked to the parish church[1] to have one look upon Betty Michell; and so away homeward by water, and landed to go to the church, where I believe Mrs. Horsly goes,*a* by Merchant-Taylor hall.[2] And there I find in the pulpit Elborough,[3] my old schoolfellow and a simple rogue; and yet I find preaching a very good sermon, and in as right a parson-like manner, and in good manner too, as I have heard anybody; and the church very full – which is a surprizing consideration. But I did not see her.

So home, and had a good dinner; and after dinner, with my wife and Mercer and Jane by water all the afternoon up as high as Moreclacke, with great pleasure, and a fine day – reading over the second part of *The Siege of Rhodes*[4] with great delight. We landed and walked at Barne elmes; and then at the neat-houses[5] I landed and bought a Millon (and we did also land and eat and drink at Wandsworth); and so to the Old Swan, and there walked home – it being a mighty fine evening, cool evening; and there being come, my wife and I spent an hour in the garden, talking of our living in the country when I shall be turned out of the office, as I fear the Parliament may find faults enough with the office to remove us all. And I am joyed to think in how good a condition I am to retire thither, and have wherewith very well to subsist. ⟨Nan at Sir W. Penn's, lately married to one Markeham, a kinsman of Sir W. Penn's – a pretty wench she is.⟩*b* Thence home and to bed.

6. Up and to the office a while. And then by water to my Lady Mountagu's at Westminster and there visited my Lord

---

a repl. 'went'   *b* addition crowded in between entries

1. Probably St Margaret's, Westminster. (R).

2. ? St Martin Outwich. (R).

3. Curate of St Lawrence Poultney.

4. See above, ii. 130 & n. 2. (A).

5. In Chelsea; see above, ii. 198, n. 2. (R).

Hinchingbrooke, newly come from Hinchingbrooke; and find him a mighty sober gentleman – to my great content. Thence to Sir Ph. Warwickes and my Lord Treasurer's, but failed in my business. So home, and in Fanchurch-street met with Mr. Battersby; says he, "Do you see Dan Rawlinson's door shut up?"[1] (which I did, and wondered); "Why," says he, "after all the sickness, and himself spending all the last year in the country[2] – one of his men is now dead of the plague, and his wife and one of his maids sick, and himself shut up;" which troubles me mightily. So home, and there do hear also from Mrs. Sarah Daniel that Greenwich is at this time much worse then ever it was, and Deptford too;[3] and she told us that they believed all the town would leave the town and come to London; which is now the receptacle of all the people from all infected places. God preserve us. So by and by to dinner; and after dinner in comes Mrs. Knepp; and I being at the office, went home to her, and there I sat and talked with her, it being the first time of her being here since her being brought to bed. I very pleasant with her, but perceive my wife hath no great pleasure in her being here, she not being pleased with my kindness here to her. However, we talked and sang, and were very pleasant.[a] By and by comes Mr. Pierce and his wife, the first time she also hath been here since her lying-in (both having been brought to bed of boys, and both of them dead). And here we talked and were pleasant; only, my wife in a chagrin humour, she not being pleased with my kindness to either of them. And by and by she fell into some silly discourse, wherein I checked[b] her, which made her mighty pettish, and discoursed very offensively to Mrs. Pierce, which did displease me; but I would make no words, but put the discourse

a   preceding part of entry crowded into bottom of page
b   repl. 'opposed'

1. Rawlinson kept the Mitre Tavern, Fenchurch St.
2. At his death in 1680 he had lands in Lancashire (where his family had come from), Warwickshire and Essex.
3. At Deptford 406 deaths by plague were said to have occurred in 1665 and 522 in 1666: N. Dews, *Hist. Deptford*, p. 310; D. Lysons, *Environs of London* (1792–1811), iv. 373. Evelyn several times refrained from going to church for fear of infection at this time: Evelyn, 22, 29 July, 12, 19, 26 August. See also ib., 30 December 1665.

by as much as I could (it being about a report that my wife said was made of herself, and meant by Mrs. Pierce, that she was grown a gallante, when she had but so few suits of clothes these two or three years, and a great deal of that silly discourse); and by and by Mrs. Pierce did tell her that such discourses should not trouble her, for there went as bad on other people, and perticularly of herself, at this end of the town (meaning my wife) that she was crooked, which was quite false; which my wife had the wit not to acknowledge herself to be the speaker of, though she hath said it twenty times. But by this means we had little*a* pleasure in their visit; however, Knipp and I sang, and then I offered them to carry them home and to take my wife with me, but she would not go: so I with them, leaving my wife in a very ill humour, and very slighting to them, which vexed me. However, I would not be removed from my civility to them, but sent for a coach and went with them; and in our way, Knipp saying that she came out of doors without a dinner to us, I took them to old Fishstreete,[1] to the very house and room where I kept my wedding-dinner, where I never was since; and there I did give them a jole of Salmon and what else was to be had. And here we talked of the ill-humour of*b* my wife, which I did excuse as much as I could, and they seemed to admit of it but did both confess they wondered at it; but from thence to other discourse, and among others, to that of my Lord Bruncker and Mrs. Williams, who it seems doth speak mighty hardly of me for my not treating them and not giving her something to her closet, and doth speak worse of my wife, and dishonourably; but it is what she doth of all the world, though she be a whore herself, so I value it not. But they told me how poorly my Lord carried himself the other day to his kinswoman, Mrs. Howard, and was displeased because she called him uncle to a little gentlewoman that is there with him, which he will not admit of – for no relation is to be challenged from others to a lord – and did treat her thereupon very rudely and ungenteely. Knipp tells me also that my Lord keeps another woman besides Mrs. Williams; and that when I was there the other day, there was a great hubbub

a repl. 'much'   *b* repl. 'which'

---

1. Now Knightrider St. (R).

in the house, Mrs. Williams being fallen sick because my Lord was gone to his other mistress, making her wait for him till his return from the other mistress. And a great deal of do there was about it, and Mrs. Williams swounded at it – at that very time when I was there, and wondered at the reason of my being received so negligently.

I set them both at home – Knipp at her house, her husband being at the Doore; and glad she was to be found to have stayed out so long with me and Mrs. Pierce, and none else – and Mrs.*a* Pierce at her house; and am mightily pleased with the discretion of her during the simplicity and offensiveness of my wife's discourse this afternoon. ⟨I perceive by the new face at Mrs. Pierces door that our Mary is gone from her⟩.*b*

So I home, calling on W. Joyce in my coach, and stayed and talked a little with him, who is the same silly prating*c* fellow that ever he was; and so home, and there find my wife mightily out of order and reproaching of Mrs. Pierce and Knipp as wenches, and I know not what. But I did give her no words to offend her, quietly let all pass; and so to bed, without any good look or words to or from my wife.

7. Up and to the office, where we sat all the morning; and home to dinner, and then to the office again, being pretty good friends with my wife again, no angry words passing; but she finding fault with Mercer, suspecting that it was she that must have told Mary, that must have told her mistress*d* of my wife's saying that she was crooked. But the truth is, she is jealous of my kindness to her. After dinner to the office and did a great deal of business. In the evening comes Mr. Reeves with a 12-foote glasse; and so I left the office and home, where I met Mr. Batelier[1] with my wife, in order to their going tomorrow by agreement to Bow to see a dancing meeting. But Lord, to see how soon I could conceive evil fears and thought concerning them. So Reeves and I and they up to the top of the house, and there we endeavoured to see the moon and Saturne and Jupiter; but the heaven proved cloudy, and so we lost our labour, having taken pains to get things together in order to the manag-

---

a repl. 'with'   *b* addition crowded in between paragraphs
c repl. 'fellow'   *d* 'mistress' in s.h. repeated in l.h.

1. See above, p. 228 & n. 2.

ing of our long glass. So down to supper and then to bed, Reeves lying at my house; but good discourse I had from him in his own trade concerning glasses. And so all of us late to bed.

I receive fresh intelligence that Deptford and Greenwich are now afresh exceedingly afflicted with the sickness, more then ever.

8. Up, and with Reeves walk as far as the Temple, doing some business in my way, at my bookseller's and elsewhere; and there parted, and I took coach (having first discoursed with Mr. Hooke a little, whom we met in the street, about the nature of Sounds, and he did make me understand the nature of Musicall sounds made by Strings, mighty prettily; and told me that having come*a* to a certain Number of Vibracions proper to make any tone, he is able to tell how many strokes a fly makes with her wings (those flies that hum in their flying) by the note that it answers to in Musique during their flying.[1]   That, I suppose, is a little too much raffined; but his discourse in general of sound was mighty fine).

There I left them, and myself by coach to St. James's, where we attended with the rest of my fellows on the Duke, whom I found with two*b* or three patches upon his nose and about his right eye, which came from his being struck with the bow of a tree the other day in his hunting; and it is a wonder it did not strike out his eye. After we had done our business with him, which is now but little, the want of money being such as leaves us little to do but to answer complaints of the want thereof, and nothing to offer to the Duke – the representing of our wants

a repl. 'coming'   *b* repl. 'his'

---

1. Robert Hooke was the curator of the Royal Society and probably its most active member. He refers to these experiments with insects in his pioneer work on microscopy, *Micrographia* (1665), pp. 172–4. He had observed and recorded the structure of insects' wings under the microscope. He had also determined the pitch of their wing-sound by tuning a 'musical string' in unison with it, thence deducing the wing-stroke frequency. His results seem to have been only approximate. Flies made 'many hundreds if not some thousands' of vibrations per second. Bees' motions were quicker, and might be, he thought, 'the quickest vibrating *spontaneous* motions of any in the world'. Cf. also Gunther, vi. 186. Some modern research is summarised in *Nature*, 20 December 1952, pp. 1057+.

of money being now become uselesse – I into the park, and there
I met with Mrs. Burroughs by appointment, and did agree (after
discoursing upon some business of hers) for her to meet me at the
New Exchange; while I by coach to my Lord Treasurer's, and
then called at the New Exchange, and thence carried her by water
to parliament stayres, and I to the Exchequer about my Tanger
Quarters tallies; and that done, I took coach and to the west
door of the abby, where she came to me; and I with her by coach
to Lissen greene, where we were last, and stayed an hour or two
before dinner could be got for us, I in the meantime having much
pleasure with her, but all honest.   And by and by dinner came
up, and then to my sport again, but still honest; and then took
coach, and up and down in the country*a* toward Acton, and then
toward Chelsy, and so to Westminster, and there set her down
where I took her up, with mighty pleasure in her company;
and so I by coach home, and thence to Bow with all the haste
I could, to my Lady Pooly's, where my wife was with Mr.
Batelier and his sisters;[1] and there I found a noble Supper, and
everything exceeding pleasant; and their mother, Mrs. Batelier,
a ⟨fine⟩ woman (but mighty passionate upon sudden news
brought her of the loss of a dog, borrowed of the Duke of
Albemarle's son to lime a bitch of hers that is very pretty; but
the dog was by and by found, and so all well again); their
company mighty innocent and pleasant, we having never been
here before.*b*   About 10 a-clock we rose from table, and sang a
song, and so home in two coaches (W. Batelier and his sister
Mary and my wife and I in one, and Mercer alone in the other);
and after being examined at Allgate whether we were husbands
and wifes, home.   And being there come and sent away W.
Batelier and his sister, I find Reeves there, it being a mighty fine
bright night; and so upon my leads, though very sleepy, till one
in the morning, looking on the moon and Jupiter with this 12-foot
glass,*c* and another of 6-foot that he hath brought with him
tonight, and the sights mighty pleasant.*d*   And one of the glasses
I will buy, it being very usefull.

a   repl. same symbol badly formed
b repl. same word badly written in both l.h. and s.h.   *c* repl. 'cl'-
d repl. same symbol badly formed

1. See above, p. 228 & n. 2.

So to bed, mighty sleepy, but with much pleasure – Reevs lying at my house again; and mighty proud I am (and ought to be thankful to God Almighty) that I am able to have a spare bed for my friends.

9. Up, and to the office to prepare business for the Board – Reeves being gone, and I having lent him 5*l* upon one of the glasses.[1] Here we sat, but to little purpose, nobody coming at us but to ask for money – not to offer us any goods. At noon home to dinner, and then to the office again, being mightily pleased with a Virgins head that my wife is now doing of.

In the evening to Lumbardstreet about money – to enable me to pay Sir G. Carteret's 3000*l*, which he hath lodged in my hand in behalf of his son and my Lady Jemimah toward their portion – which, I thank God, I am able to do at a minute's warning.

In my way enquired and find Mrs. Rawlinson is dead of the sickness, and her maid continues mighty ill – he himself[2] is got out of the house. I met also with Mr. Eveling in the street, who tells me the sad condition at this very day at Deptford for the plague, and more at Deale (within his precinct, as one of the Commissioners for sick and wounded seamen), that the towne is almost quite depopulated.[3]

Thence back home again; and after some business at my office, late home to supper and to bed – I being sleepy by my late want of rest, notwithstanding my endeavouring to get a nap of an hour this noon after dinner.

So home and to bed.

10. Up, and to my chamber; there did some business, and then to my office; and towards noon by water to the Exchequer

1. Apparently it was the 12 ft telescope which Pepys bought: below, p. 254. Monconys (ii. 17) speaks of Reeves in 1663 as charging £6 for his telescopes. (He does not specify the size.)

2. Her husband Daniel Rawlinson. His servant, William Chombley, had been buried on the 6th; his wife and her maid were buried on the day of this entry: *Harl. Soc. Reg.*, iii. 237.

3. For Deptford, see above, p. 236 & n. 3. For Deal, see the account sent to the government on 10 August; *CSPD 1666–7*, p. 26. On 26 August, 20 victims in one week were reported. Ships still avoided the port in December: C. Creighton, *Hist. epidemics in Britain*, i. 688. See also J. F. D. Shrewsbury, *Hist. bubonic plague in Brit. Isles*, pp. 490–1.

about my Tanger order. And thence back again and to the*ᵃ* Exchange, where little news but what is in the book. And among ⟨other⟩ things, of a man sent up for by the King and Council for saying that Sir W Coventry did give intelligence to the Duch of all our matters here.¹ I met with Colvill, and he and I did agree about his lending me 1000*l* upon a tally of 1000*l* for Tanger. Thence to Sympson the Joyner, and I am mightily pleased with what I see of my presses*ᵇ* for my books which he is making for me.² So homeward, and hear in Fanchurch-street that now the mayde also is dead at Mr. Rawlinsons; so that there is three dead in all, the wife, a manservant, and maidservant. Home to dinner, where sister Balty dined with us, and met a letter come to me from him. He is well at Harwich, going to the fleet. After dinner to the office, and anon with my wife and sister abroad; left them in Paternoster row, while Creed (who was with me at the office) to Westminster; and leaving him in the Strand, I to my Lord Chancellors and did very little business; and so away home by water, with more and more pleasure every time, I reading over my Lord Bacons *Faber Fortunæ*.³ So home and there did little business; and then walked an hour, talking of sundry things in the garden, and find him a cunning knave, as I always observed him to be; and so home to supper and to bed – pleased that this day I find, if I please, that I can have all my money in that I have out my hands; but am at a loss whether to take it in or no. And pleased also to hear of Mrs. Barb. Sheldons good fortune, who is like to have Mr. Woods son, the Mastmaker, a very rich man; and to be married speedily, she being already mighty fine upon it.⁴

11. Up and to the office, where we sat all the morning. At noon home to dinner, where mightily pleased with my wife's beginnings of a little Virgin's head. To the office and did much

---

a s.h. repl. l.h. 'Col'-   *b* badly-written l.h. (?'præsses')

---

1. Three men had in fact been summoned for the aspersion on Coventry; another was accused of a similar offence against Arlington: PRO, PC 2/59, ff. 63r, 64r. It was this last who was here referred to. Misunderstanding was possibly caused

be the brevity of the newspaper's account: *London Gazette*, 9 August.
2. See above, p. 214, & n. 4.
3. See above, ii. 102, n. 1.
4. She was the niece of William Sheldon, Clerk of the Cheque at Woolwich.

business; and then to Mr. Colvills, and with him did come to an agreement about my 2600*l* assignment on the Exchequer which I had of Sir W Warren; and to my great joy, I think shall get above 100*l* by it, but I must leave it to be finished on Monday. Thence to the office, and there did the remainder of my business, and so home to supper and to bed. This afternoon I hear as if we had landed some men upon the Dutch coasts, but I believe it is but a foolery, either in the report or the attempt.[1]

12. *Lords day.* Up and to my chamber, where busy all the morning; and my thoughts very much upon the manner of my removal of my closet things the next week into my present Musique-room,[2] if I find I*ᵃ* can spare or get money to furnish it. By and by comes Reeves by appointment, but did not bring the glasses and things I expected for our discourse and my information today, but we have agreed on it for next Sunday. By and by in comes Betty Michell and her husband; and so to dinner, I mightily pleased with their company. We passed the whole day talking with them, but without any pleasure but only her being there. In the evening all parted, and I and my wife up to her closet to consider how to order that the next summer, if we live to it. And then down to my chamber at night to examine her kitchen accounts; and there I took occasion to fall out with her, for her buying of a laced handkercher and pinner without my leave; though the thing is not much, yet I would not permit her begin to do so, lest worse should fallow; from this we begin both to be angry very much, and so continued till bed, and did not sleep friends.

13. Up, without being friends with my wife, nor great enemies, being both quiet and silent. So out to Colvills; but he not being come to town yet, I to Paul's churchyard to treat with a bookbinder to come and gild*ᵇ* the backs of all my books to make them handsome, to stand in my new presses when they come.[3] So back again to Colvills, and there did end*ᶜ* our treaty

a repl. 'it'   *b* repl. 'bind'   *c* repl. 'make'

1. See below, p. 247 & n. 1.
2. Cf. above, p. 95. (E).
3. For Pepys's care of his books,

see above, vi. 31–2. The bookbinder was possibly Edmond Richardson.

R

to my full content, about my Chequer assignment of 2600*l* of Sir W. Warren's, for which I gave him[1] 170*l* to stand to the hazard of receiving it.   So I shall get clear by it, 230*l*, which is a very good jobb.[2]   God be praised for it.   Having done with him, then he and I took*a* coach, and I carried him to Westminster and there set him down – in our way speaking of several things. I find him a bold man to say anything of anybody, and finds faults with our great Ministers of State, that nobody looks after anything.   And I thought it dangerous to be free with him, for I do not think he can keep counsel – because he blabs to me what hath passed between other people and him.   Thence I to St. James's, and there missed Sir W. Coventry; but taking up Mr. Robinson[3] in my coach, I towards London, and there in the way met Sir W. Coventry and fallowed him to White-hall, where a little discourse, very kind; and so I away with Robinson, and set him down at the Change, and thence I to Stokes's the goldsmith and sent him to and again to get me 1000*l* in gold.   And so home to dinner, my wife and I friends, without any words almost of last night.   After dinner, I abroad to Stokes, and there did receive 1000*l*-worth in gold, paying 18¾*d* and 19*d* for others exchange.[4]   Home with them, and there to my office to business; and anon home in the evening, there to settle some of my accounts; and then to supper and to bed.

a 'took' repeated

1. Colvill.
2. For this transaction, see above, pp. 89–90 & n. Pepys kept a memorandum on it among his loose papers: 'Aug. 13. 1666.   I delivered up to Mr Colvill Sir W. Warrens Order, allowing him 170*l*. for the forbearance till (when ever it shall bee) hee shall bee payd.   Soe hee gave me 2432*l*. 02*s*. 07*d*., presently, with a written promise to give mee 5*l* if the Order bee payd him before Lady Day next' (Rawl. A 174, f. 436*v*).   Pepys

went on to observe that Colvill got 10% p.a. for six months. The £230 which Pepys now gained was in addition to the gift of £300 from Warren.
3. Thomas Robson, Coventry's clerk.
4. This was the charge per piece. For the varying rate at which gold coins were exchanged for silver and other coins, see e.g. below, pp. 346, 348, 366–7; 13 June 1667.

14. *Thanksgiving day.*[1] Up, and comes Mr. Foly[2] and his man with a box of great variety of Carpenters and Joyners tooles which I had bespoke, to me, which please me mightily, but I will have more. Then I abroad down to the Old Swan, and there I called and kissed Betty Michell and would have got her to go with me to Westminster, but I find her a little colder then she used to be methought, which did a little molest me. So I away, not pleased, and to White-hall, where I find them at Chappell; and met with Povy, and he and I together, who tells me how mad my letter makes my Lord Peterbrough, and what a furious letter he hath writ to me in answer, though it is not come yet.[3] This did trouble me; for though there be no reason, yet to have a nobleman's mouth open against a man may do a man hurt; so I endeavoured to have found him out and spoke with him, but could not. So to the chapel, and heard a piece of the Dean of Westminsters sermon[4] and a special good Anthemne before the king after sermon. And then home by coach with Captain Cocke – who is in pain about his Hemp, of which he says he hath bought great quantities, and would gladly be upon good terms with us for it – wherein I promise to assist him.[5] So we light*a* at the Change, where after a small turn or two, taking no pleasure nowadays to be there, because of answering questions that would be asked there which I cannot answer. So home and dined. And after dinner with my wife and Mercer to the Beare=garden, where I have not been I think of many years, and saw some good sport of the bull's tossing of the dogs –

a repl. 'set'

---

1. Proclaimed on 6 August for the victory of 25 July (Steele, no. 3467); in the provinces the celebration was held on 23 August.

2. Robert Foley, ironmonger to the Navy.

3. The letters are untraced. Peterborough (for whose Tangier pension see above, iv. 94, n. 1) now successfully claimed a refund: below, p. 335.

4. Dr John Dolben (later Bishop of Rochester and Archbishop of York) was Clerk of the Closet and Dean of Westminster, 1662–6. The sermon (on Ps. xviii. 1–3) was printed soon afterwards by the King's command: *A sermon preached before the King, Aug. 14, 1666; being the day of thanksgiving for the late victory at sea* (1666).

5. See below, p. 359, p. 385 & n. 2.

one into the very boxes. But it is a very rude and nasty pleasure.[1]
We had a great many hectors in the same box with us ⟨(and
one, very fine, went into the pit and played his dog for a wager,
which was a strange sport for a gentleman)⟩, where they drank
wine, and drank Mercer's health first, which I pledged with my
hat off. And who should be in the house but Mr. Pierce the
surgeon, who saw us and spoke to us. Thence home, well[a]
enough satisfied however with the variety of this afternoon's
exercise; and so I to my chamber, till in the evening our company
came to supper we had invited to a venison pasty – Mr. Batelier
and his sister Mary, Mrs. Mercer – her daughter Anne, Mr. Le
Brun, and W Hewers. And so we supped, and very merry.
And then about 9 a-clock to Mrs. Mercers gate, where the fire
and boys expected us and her son had provided abundance of
Serpents[b] and rockets; and there mighty merry (my Lady Pen
and Pegg going thither with us ⟨and Nan Wright⟩) till about
12 at night, flinging our fireworks and burning one another and
the people over the way. And at last, our businesses being most
spent – we into Mrs. Mercers, and there mighty merry, smutting
one another with Candlegresse and soot, till most of us were like
devils; and that being done, then we broke up and to my house,
and there I made them drink; and upstairs we went, and then
fell into dancing (W Batelier dancing well) and dressing, him
and I and one Mr. Banister (who with his wife came over also
with us) like women; and Mercer put on a suit of Toms, like a
boy, and mighty mirth we had, and Mercer danced a Jigg, and
Nan Wright and my wife and Pegg Pen put on periwigs. Thus
we spent till 3 or 4 in the morning, mighty merry; and then
parted and to bed.

a repl. same symbol   *b* repl. 'Crackers'

---

1. When Evelyn went to the same
place (in Southwark) on 16 June 1670
'one of the Bulls tossd a Dog full
into a Ladys lap, as she sate in one of
the boxes at a Considerable height
from the *Arena*'. Evelyn (iii. 549 &
n. 4) also thought the business 'rude
and dirty'. So too, at an earlier
period, did Philip Sidney and Francis
Bacon: C. E. Raven, *English Natural-
ists*, p. 232. Cf. Z. C. von Uffenbach,
London in 1710 (ed. Quarrell and
Mare), pp. 59–60. For Pepys's dislike
of bloodthirsty sports, see above, iv.
427–8 & n.

15. Mighty sleepy; slept till past 8 of the clock, and was called up by a letter from Sir W. Coventry; which, among other things, tells me how we have burned 160 ships of the enemy within the Fly.[1] I up, and with all possible haste,[a] and in pain for fear of coming late, it being our day of attending the Duke of York, to St. James's, where they are full of the perticulars – how they are generally good merchant-ships, some of them laden, and supposed rich ships. We spent five fireships upon them. We landed on the Schelling (Sir Ph. Howard with some men, and Holmes I think with others, about 1000 in all), and burned a town – and so came away. By and by the Duke of York with his books showed us the very place and manner – and that it was not our design or expectation to have done this, but only to have landed on the Fly and burned some of their stores; but being come in, we spied these ships, and with our longboats one by one fired them, our ships running all aground, it being so shoal water. We were led to this by, it seems, a Renegado Captain of the Hollanders,[2] who found himself ill-used by De Ruyter for his good service, and so came over to us; and hath done us good service, so that now we trust him, and he himself did go on this expedition. The service is very great – and our joys as

a repl. same symbol

---

1. Coventry to Pepys, 15 August, '7 in morn.': Rawl. A 195a, f. 195*r*. This action ('Sir Robert Holmes's Bonfire') took place on 9–10 August. The English fleet had unchallenged command of the Dutch seas at this moment, and (with the help of information from a Dutch deserter, Heemskerck, later knighted) it was decided to venture a bold stroke – a landing on the island of Vlieland where naval stores, both of the E. India Company and of the government, could be destroyed. Holmes was detached for the purpose with a small squadron of low-rate ships, some fireships and a force of soldiers and mariners under Sir Philip Howard. As they sailed into the Fly (the channel between Vlieland and Ter-

schelling) they saw the masts of a great concentration of merchantmen lying at anchor beyond the islands. Holmes decided to attack them first, with his fireships. Having no protection beyond a couple of men-of-war, they were burnt and destroyed right and left. This was on the 9th. On the 10th, the weather prevented a landing on Vlieland, but a force was sent ashore on Terschelling to plunder the little town of Westterschelling (Westeinde). Allin, i. 281+; *Naval Misc.* (Navy Records Soc.), iii. 18+; *CSPD 1666–7*, pp. 21, 27; R. Ollard, *Man of War*, ch. xiii. Pepys preserved Hollar's print of the action: PL 2985, pt ii, f. 312*r*.

2. Capt. Louis Heemskerck.

great for it. All is, it will make the Duke of Albemarle in repute again I doubt – though there be nothing of his in this. But Lord, to see what success doth, whether with or without reason, and making a man seem wise, notwithstanding never so late demonstration of the profoundest folly in the world.

Thence walked over the park with Sir W. Coventry, in our way talking of the unhappy state of our office. And I took an opportunity to let him know that, though the backwardnesses of all our matters of the office may be well imputed to the known want of money, yet perhaps there might be personal and perticular failings; and that I did therefore depend still upon his promise of telling*a* me whenever he finds any ground to believe any defect or neglect on my part; which he promised me still to do, and that there was none he saw– "Nor endeed," says he, "is there room nowadays to find fault with any perticular man, while we are in this condition for money." This methought did not so well please me; but however, I am glad I have said this, thereby giving myself good grounds to believe that at this time he did not want an occasion to have said what he pleased to me, if he had had anything in his mind; which by his late distance and silence, I have feared. But then again, I am to consider he is grown a very great man, much greater then he was, and so must keep more distance; and next, that the condition*b* of our office will not afford me occasion of showing myself so active and deserving as heretofore; and lastly, the muchness of his business cannot suffer him to mind it, or give him leisure to reflect on anything or show the freedom and kindness that he used to do. But I think I have done something considerable to my satisfaction in doing this (and that if I do but my duty remarkably from this time forward, and not neglected it, as I have of late done, and minded my pleasures, I may be as well as ever I was).

Thence to the Exchequer, but did nothing, they being all gone from their offices; and so to the Old Exchange, where the town full of this good news; but I did not stay to tell or hear any, but home, my head akeing and drowzy, and to dinner; and then lay down upon the couch, thinking to get a little rest, but could not. So down the River, reading *The Adventures of*

---

a repl. same symbol   *b* repl. 'cons'–

five houres,[1] which the more I read the more I admire. So down below Greenwich; but the wind and tide being against us, I back again to Deptford and did a little business there, and thence walked to Redriffe, and so home – and to the office a while; in the evening comes W. Batelier and his sister and my wife and fair Mrs. Turner into the garden, and there we walked; and then with my Lady Pen and Pegg in a-doors, and eat and were merry; and so pretty late broke up and to bed – the guns of the Tower going off, and there being bonefires also in the street for this late good Successe.

16. Up, having slept well; and after entering my journall, to the office – where all the morning; but of late Sir W. Coventry hath not come to us, he being discouraged from the little we have to do but to answer the clamours of people for money. At noon home, and there dined with me my Lady Pen only, and W. Hewer, at a haunch of venison boiled – where pretty merry. Only, my wife vexed me a little about demanding money to go with my Lady Pen to the Exchange to lay out. I to the office, where all the afternoon very busy and doing much business. But here I had a most eminent experience of the evil of being behind-hand in business; I was the most backward to begin anything, and would fain have framed to myself an occasion of going abroad, and should I doubt have done it – but some business coming in, one after another, kept me there, and I fell to the ridding away of a great deal of business; and when my hand was in it, was so pleasing a sight to [see] my papers disposed of, and letters answered which troubled my book[2] and table, that I could have continued there with delight all night long; and did, till called away by my Lady Pen and Pegg and my wife to their house to eat with them; and there I went, and exceeding merry, there being Nan Wright, now Mrs. Markeham, and sits at table with my Lady. So mighty merry, home and to bed.

This day, Sir W. Batten did show us at the table a letter from Sir T. Allen, which says that we have taken ten or twelve ships (since the late great expedition of burning their ships and town), laden with hemp, flax, tar, deals, &c; this was good news, but

---

1. A comedy by Sir Samuel Tuke; see above, iv. 8 & n. 2. (A).

2. Possibly a memorandum book, or the office day-book.

by and by comes in Sir G. Carteret, and he asked us with full mouth* what we would give for good news. Says Sir W. Batten, "I have better then you, for a wager." They laid sixpences, and we that were by were to give sixpence to him that told the best news. So Sir W. Batten told his, of the ten or twelve ships. Sir G. Carteret did then tell us that upon the news of the burning of the ships and town, the common people of Amsterdam did besiege De Witts house, and he was forced to fly to the Prince of Orange, who is gone to Cleve to the marriage of his sister.[1] This we concluded all the best news, and my Lord Brouncker and myself did give Sir G. Carteret our sixpence apiece, which he did give Mr. Smith to give the poor. Thus we made ourselfs mighty merry.

17. Up, and betimes with Captain Erwin down by water to Woolwich, I walking alone from Greenwich thither – making an end of *The Adventures of five houres*, – which when all is done, is the best play that ever I read in my life.[2] Being come thither, I did some business there and at the Ropeyard, and had a piece of Bridecake sent me by Mrs. Barbary into the boate after me – she being here at her uncles with her husband (Mr. Woods son, the mast-maker), and mighty nobly married: they say she was very fine, and he very rich[3] – a strange fortune for so odd a looked maid, though her hands and body be good, and nature very good I think.

Back with Captain Erwin, discoursing about the East Indys, where he hath often been. And among other things, he tells me how the King of Syam seldom goes out without 30 or 40000 people with him, and not a word spoke nor a hum or cough in the whole company to be heard.[4] He tells me the punishment

1. There was no truth in this rumour about de Witt. William of Orange (his political enemy) had gone to the wedding of Mary, Princess of Orange (William's aunt, not his sister) to Ludwig Heinrich, Count Palatine of Simmern (d. 1674).
2. Pepys was probably impressed by its close-knit plot. (A).
3. See above, p. 242 & n. 4.
4. Cf. the descriptions in F. Caron

and J. Schouten, *A true description of the mighty kingdoms of Japan and Siam* (trans. 1663; ed. Boxer), esp. pp. 98–9; [F. T. de Choisy,] *Journal du voyage de Siam* (1687). The usual royal train consisted of 1200 or 1400; only once a year when the King visited the Temple of the Gods would he be accompanied by an entourage of 20,000 or 30,000.

frequently there for malefactors is cutting off the Crowne of their head, which they do very dexterously, leaving their brains bare, which kills them presently.[1] He told me, what I remember he hath once done heretofore – that everybody is to lie flat down at the coming by of the King, and nobody to look upon him, upon pain of death.[2] And that he and his fellows, being strangers, were invited to see the sport of taking of a wild Eliphant. And they did only kneel and look toward the King. Their Druggerman did desire them to fall down, for otherwise he should suffer for their contempt of the King. The sport being ended, a messenger comes from the King, which the Druggerman thought had been to have taken[a] away his life. But it was to enquire how the strangers liked the sport. The Druggerman answered that they did cry it up to be the best that ever they saw, and that they never heard of any prince so great in everything as this King. The messenger being gone back, Erwin and his company asked their Druggerman what he had said, which he told them. "But why," say they, "would you say that without our leave, it being not true?" "It is no matter for that," says he, "I must have said it, or have been hanged, for our King doth not live by meat nor drink, but by having great lyes told him."

In our way back we came by a little vessel that came into the river this morning, who says he left the fleet in Sole Bay – and that he hath not heard (he belonging to Sir W. Jenings in the fleet) of any such prizes taken as the ten or twelve I enquired about, and said by Sir W. Batten yesterday to be taken; so I fear it is not true.[3]

So to Westminster, and there to my great content did receive my 2000*l* of Mr. Spicer's telling which I was to receive of Colvill; and brought it home with me [to] my house by water, and there I find one of my new presses for my books brought home, which pleases me mightily – as also doth my wife's progress upon her head that she is making.

a repl. 'm'-

---

1. Cf. de Choisy, op. cit., pp. 33–40.

2. He was held to be divine. For the same reason his subjects were forbidden to pronounce his name: de Choisy, p. 339.

3. Allin had anchored off Lowestoft on the 15th. His journal mentions the prizes only vaguely; one ship laden with hemp and flax was taken on the 9th: Allin, i. 282, 284.

So to dinner, and thence abroad with my wife. Leaving her at Unthankes, I to White-hall, waiting at the Council door till it rose; and there spoke with Sir W. Coventry, who, and I, doth much fear our victuallers, they having missed the fleet in their going.[1] But Sir W. Coventry says it is not our fault, but theirs, if they have not left ships to secure them. This he spoke in a chagrin sort of way methought. After a little more discourse of several businesses, I away homeward, having in the gallery the good fortune to see Mrs. Steward, who is grown a little too tall, but is a woman of most excellent features.

The Narrative of the late expedition in burning the ships is in print,[2] and makes it a great thing; and I hope it is so.

So took up my wife, and home; and I to the office, and thence with Symson the Joyner home to put together the press he hath brought me for my books this day, which pleases me exceedingly. Then to Sir W. Batten's, where Sir Rd Ford[3] did, very understandingly methought, give us an account of the Originall of the Hollands Bank and the nature of it, and how they do never give any Interest at all to any person that brings in their money – though what is brought in upon the public faith, interest is given by the state for[4] –

The unsafe condition of a bank under a monarch, and the little safety to a Monarch to have any City or Corporacion alone (as London in answer to Amsterdam) to have so great a wealth or credit, is it that makes it hard to have a bank here.[5] And as to the former, he did tell us how it sticks in the memory of most mer-

1. Cf. Coventry to Pepys, 15 August: Rawl. A 195a, f. 195r. The *Marmaduke*, for example, had six weeks' dry provisions but only two days' beer.

2. *A true and perfect narrative of the great and signal success of a part of His Majesty's fleet*; published by command; not in the PL.

3. A prominent merchant and an M.P.

4. The Bank of Amsterdam, founded in 1609, confined its activities until 1683 to exchange and deposit banking, and was at this time the most important in Europe. Deposi-

tors normally got no interest, but full security (the bank survived a run on it during the French invasion of 1672), full value for clipped coins, and above all, transferability. It was managed by the city of Amsterdam. Government loans in 1666 were usually at 4%. See Adam Smith, *Wealth of Nations* (ed. Cannan), i. 443–52; V. Barbour, *Capitalism in Amsterdam in 17th cent.*, pp. 43+, 82.

5. Cf. the memorandum on the Bank of Amsterdam, possibly by Ford but not in his hand, in Bodl., Clar. 83, ff. 419–20; summarised in *CSP Clar.*, v. 745–6.

chants, how the late King (when by the war between Holland and France and Spayne all the Bullen of Spain was brought hither, one-third of it to be coyned; and endeed it was found advantageous to the merchant to coyne most of it) was persuaded in a strait by my Lord Cottington, to seize[a] upon the money in the Towre – which, though in a few days the merchants concerned did prevail to get it released, yet the thing will never be forgot.[1]

So home to supper and to bed – understanding this evening, since I came home, that our victuallers are all come in to the fleet; which is good news.

Sir J. Mennes came home tonight, not well, from Chatham, where he hath been at a pay – holding it at Upner castle, because of the plague so much in the towne of Chatham.[2] He hath they say got an ague, being so much on the water.

18. All the morning at the office. Then to the Exchange (with Lord Brouncker in his coach) at noon, but it was only to avoid Mr. Chr. Petts being invited by me to dinner. So home, calling at my little Mercer's in Lumbardstreet who hath the pretty wife like the old Queene – and there cheapened some

a repl. 'cease'

---

1. This occurred in July 1640 when Charles I was hard pressed for money for the Scottish war. For some time during the Thirty Years War, Spanish bullion had been coined in the English mint and shipped to Dunkirk for the use of the troops. Charles suddenly seized £130,000-worth of it late one Saturday afternoon, promising to pay it back in six months. The Merchant Adventurers and others trading to Spain, whose credit and trade abroad would have been ruined, successfully protested. (Ford, Pepys's informant, was a Spanish merchant.) S. R. Gardiner, on what appears to be slender evidence, attributed the inspiration to Hamilton (*Hist. Engl.*, 1884, x. 170), and does not seem to have noticed this entry. Cottington was Chancellor of the Exchequer and Constable of the Tower. The bankers' distrust of the powers of the monarch was reinforced by the Stop of the Exchequer (1672), and it was not until after his powers had been somewhat limited, in the Glorious Revolution, that the Bank of England was founded in 1694.

2. Mennes had also asked for the money to be sent by river, to avoid infection; see his letter of 11 August to the Navy Board: *CSPD 1666–7*, p. 31. He had then reported that 30 had died in Chatham in the previous week. The plague reached its height there at about this time: see J. F. D. Shrewsbury, *Hist. bubonic plague in Brit. Isles*, pp. 488–9.

stuffs to hang my room that I entend to turn into a closet. So home to dinner; and after dinner comes Creed to discourse with me about several things of Tanger concernment, and accounts; among others, starts the doubt (which I was formerly aware^a of, but did wink at it) whether or no Lanyon and his partners[1] be not paid for more then they should be – which he presses, so that it did a little discompose me; but however, I do think no harm will arise thereby.   He gone, I to the office, and there very late, very busy; and so home to supper and to bed.

19. *Lords day.*   Up, and to my chamber, and there begun to draw out fair and methodically my accounts of Tanger in order to show them to the Lords.[2]   But by and by comes by agreement Mr. Reeves, and after him Mr. Spong; and all day with them, both before and after dinner till 10 a-clock at night, upon Opticke enquiries – he bringing me a frame with closes on, to see how the Rays of light do cut one another, and in a dark room with smoake, which is very pretty.   He did also bring a lantern, with pictures in glass to make strange things appear on a wall, very pretty.[3]   We did also at night see Jupiter and his girdle and Satellites very fine with my 12-foot glass, but could not Saturne, he being very dark.   Spong and I also had several fine discourses upon the globes this afternoon, perticularly why the fixed stars do not rise and set at the same hour all the year long, which he could not demonstrate, nor I neither, the reason of.   So it being late, after supper they away home.

But it vexed me to understand no more from Reeves and his glasses touching the nature and reason of the several refractions of the several figured glasses, he understanding the acting part but not one bit the theory, nor can make anybody understand it – which is a strange dullness methinks.

a   repl. 'aw'-

---

1. Victuallers.
2. The Tangier commissioners.
3. There were several types of 'picture-box' at this time.   Reeves's is described (1663) by Monconys (ii. 17–18) as 'une lanterne sourde qui a un demi-globe tout entier de cristal, d'environ 3 poulces de diametre, & qui porte bien loin la representation des objets qu'il met entre la lumiere, & ce cristal, par le moyen d'une feuille de verre sur laquelle ces objects sonts peints . . .'.

I did not hear anything yesterday, or at all, to confirm either Sir Tho. Allin's news of the ten or twelve ships taken, nor of the disorder at Amsterdam upon the news of the burning of the ships – that he[1] should be fled to the Prince of Orange, it being generally believed that he was gone to France before.[a]

20. Wakened this morning about 6 a-clock with a violent knocking at Sir J Minnes's door to call up Mrs. Hammon[2] – crying[b] out that Sir J Minnes is a-dying (he came home ill of an ague on Friday night – I saw him on Saturday after his fit of the Ague, and then was pretty lusty); which troubles me mightily, for he is a very good, harmless, honest gentleman, though not fit for the business. But I much fear a worse may come, that may be more uneasy to me.

Up and to Deptford by water, reading *Othello, Moore of Venice*, which I ever heretofore esteemed a mighty good play; but having so lately read *The Adventures of five hours*,[3] it seems a mean thing.

Walked back, and so home and then down to the old Swan and drank at B. Michells; and so to Westminster to the Exchequer about my quarter's tallies;[4] and so to Lumberdstreete to choose stuff to hang my new intended closet, and have chosen purple. So home to dinner, and all the afternoon, till almost midnight, upon my Tanger accounts, getting Tom Willson to help me in writing as I read, and at night, W Hewers; and find myself most happy in the keeping of all my accounts, for that after all the changings and turnings necessary in such an account, I find myself right to a farding, in an account of 127000*l*. This afternoon I visited Sir J. Mennes, who, poor man, is much impaired by these few days sickness; and I fear endeed it will kill him.

21. Up and to the office, where much business – and Sir W. Coventry there, who of late hath wholly left us, most of our business being about money, to which we can give no answer;

a followed by 'Upon the score' struck through   *b* repl. 'say'-

---

1. de Witt: see above, p. 250, n. 1.   4. Payments for a quarter's expen-
2. Mary Hammon(d), Mennes's   diture for Tangier.
widowed sister.
3. See above, p. 249 & n. 1, p. 250
& n. 2. (A).

which makes him weary of coming to us. He made an experiment today, by taking up a heap of petitions that lay upon the table. They proved seventeen in number. And found them thus – One for money for reparation for clothes – four desired to have tickets made out to them; and the other twelve were for money.[1] Dined at home, and sister Balty with us – my wife snappish because I denied her money to lay out this afternoon. How[ever], good friends again; and by coach set them down at the New Exchange, and I to Exchequer and there find my business of my tallies in good forwardness. I passed down into the hall,[a] and there hear that Mr. Bowles the grocer, after four or five days' sickness, is dead, and this day buried. So away, and taking up my wife, went homewards. I light, and with Harman to my Mercers in Lumberdstreet and there agreed for our purple Serge for my closet; and so I away home. So home and late at the office; and then home and there find Mr. Batelier[2] and his sister Mary, and we sat chatting a great while, talking of Wiches and Spirits; and he told me of his own knowledge, being with some others at Bourdeaux, making a bargain with another man at a taverne for some Claretts, they did hire a fellow to thunder (which he had the art of doing upon a deale board) and to rain and hail; that is, make the noise of – so as did give them a pretence of undervaluing their Merchants wines, by saying this thunder would spoil and turn them – which was so reasonable to the Merchant that he did abate two *pistolls* per Ton for the wine, in belief of that – whereas, going out, there was no such thing. This Batelier did see and was the cause of, to his profit, as is above said.

By and by broke up, and to bed.

22. Up and by coach with 100*l* to the Exchequer to pay fees there. There left it, and I to St. James's and there with the Duke of York. I had opportunity of much talk with Sir W.

a MS. 'hill'

---

1. Most of these petitions are listed in *CSPD 1665–6*, p. 668. The petitioners included a purser making his fourth application for money, an anchor-smith who had attended the office for three weeks to get payment, and a hoyman wanting 23 months' wages.

2. See above, p. 228, n. 2.

Penn today (he being newly come from the fleet); and he doth much undervalue the honour that is given to the conduct of the late business of Holmes in burning the ships and town, saying it was a great thing endeed, and of great profit to us, in being of great loss to the enemy; but that it was wholly a business of chance, and no conduct imployed in it. I find Sir W. Penn doth hold up his head at this time higher then ever he did in his life. I perceive he doth look after Sir J. Mennes's place if he dies; and though I love him not, nor do desire to have him in, yet I do think him the ablest man in England for it.

To the Chequer, and there received my tallies and paid my fees in good order. And so home, and there find Mrs. Knipp and my wife going to dinner. She tells me my song of *Beauty Retire* is mightily*ᵃ* cried up – which I am not a little*ᵇ* proud of; and do think I have done *It is Decreed* better, but*ᶜ* I have not finished it.[1] My Closet is doing by Upholsters, which I am pleased with, but fear my purple will be too sad for that melancholy room.

After dinner and doing something at the office, I with my wife, Knepp, and Mercer by coach to Moore fields and there saw *Polichinelle*,[2] which pleases me mightily; and here I saw our Mary, our last chamber-maid, who is gone from Mrs. Pierce's it seems. Then carried Knipp home, calling at the Cocke ale-house at the door and drank. And so home and there find Reeves; and so up to look upon the Starrs, and do like*ᵈ* my glass very well and did even with him for it, and a little perspective and the*ᵉ* Lanthorne that shows tricks – all together costing me 9*l* 5*s*. So to bed, he lying at our house.

23. At the office all the morning, whither Sir W. Coventry sent me word that the Duch fleet is certainly*ᶠ* abroad, and so we

---

a repl. 'the'   *b* repl. 'able'   *c* repl. symbol rendered illegible
    d repl. 'kil'   *e* repl. 'my'   *f* repl. 'cert'-

---

1. For these songs, see above, vi. 320 & n. 4; above, p. 91 & n. 4. (E).
2. The most popular of the puppet-plays of Italian origin. The hook-nosed, hump-backed Polichinello of this play is one of the ancestors of the English 'Punch'. (A).

are to hasten all we have to send to our fleet with all speed.[1] But Lord, to see how my Lord Bruncker undertakes the despatch of the fireships, when he is no more fit for it then a porter. And all the while, Sir W. Penn,[a] who is the most fit, is unwilling to displease him, and doth not look after it – and so the King's work is [not] like to be well done.

At noon[b] dined at home, Lovett with us; but he doth not please me in his business, for he keeps things long in hand, and his paper doth not hold so good as I expected – the varnish wiping off in a little time, a very spunge.[2]   And I doubt by his discourse, he is an odde kind of fellow, and in plain terms, a very rogue.

He gone, I to the office (having seen and liked the Upholsters work in my room, which they have almost done) and there late, and in the evening find Mr. Batelier and his sister there; and there we talked and eat and were merry; and so parted late, and to bed.

24. Up, and despatched several businesses at home in the morning; and then comes Sympson to set up my other new Presse for my books; and so he and I fell in to the Furnishing of my new closet, and taking out the things out of my old.   I kept him with me all day, and he dined with me; and so all the afternoon, till it was quite dark – hanging things; that is, my maps and picture[s] – and Draughts – and setting up my books, and as much as we could do – to my most extraordinary satisfaction; so that I think it will be as[c] noble a closet as any man hath, and light enough; though endeed, it would be better to have had a little more light.

He gone, my wife and I to talk – and sup; and then to setting right my Tanger accounts and enter my Journall; and then to bed, with great content in my day's work.

This afternoon came Mrs. Barbary Shelden, now Mrs. Wood,

---

a repl. 'WC'   *b* repl. 'd'-   *c* repl. 'as'

---

1. Coventry to Pepys, St James's, 23 August: Rawl. A 195a, f. 197r. Fifty-six Dutch ships were already at sea and the rest about to come out. Coventry urged that the fireships should be immediately sent out of the river to the fleet; their combustible materials could be roughly stowed aboard and stacked properly later.

2. See above, pp. 119-20 & n.

to see my wife. I was so busy, I*ᵃ* would not see her. But she came, it seems, mighty rich in rings and fine clothes, and like a lady; and says she is matched mighty well – at which I am very glad, but wonder at her good fortune and the folly of her husband – and vexed at myself for not paying her the respect of seeing her. But I will come out of her debt another time.

25. All the morning at the office. At noon dined at home; and after dinner, up to my new closet, which pleases me mightily, and there I proceeded to put many things in order, as far as I had time; and then set it in washing, and stood by myself a great while to see it washed; and then to the office and there wrote my letters and other things; and then, in mighty good humour, home to supper and to bed.

26. *Lords day.* Up betimes, and to the finishing the setting things in order in my new closet out of my old; which I did thoroughly by the time sermon was done at church – to my exceeding joy; only, I was a little disturbed with news my Lord Bruncker brought me, that we are to attend the King at White-hall this afternoon, and that it is about a complaint from the Generals[1] against us.

Sir W. Penn dined by invitation with me,*ᵇ* his Lady and daughter being gone into the country. We very merry. After dinner we parted, and I to my office, whither I sent for Mr. Lewes[2] and instructed myself fully in the business of the victualling, to enable me to answer in that matter; and then Sir W.

---

a repl. symbol rendered illegible   *b* repl. 'us'

---

1. Rupert and Albemarle, in command of the fleet. Men had been on short allowance since 2 August, and now that the Dutch fleet was known to be out the matter was more than ever urgent. The English fleet did not get away until the 30th, mainly through shortage of beer and water. Pepys's victualling organisation had suffered in the past three weeks from lack of cash, bad weather,

desertion, and above all from the failure of some victualling ships to rendezvous with the fleet. He had been forced to use colliers to carry victuals to the fleet. Gauden blamed the press-gangs who took sailors from the victualling ships; NWB, p. 103. *CSPD 1666–7*, pp. 52, 56, 57, 71, 78; NMM, MSS Wyn, 14/9.

2. Thomas Lewis, Clerk of the Issues in the Victualling Office.

S

Penn and I by coach to White-hall and there stayed till the King and Cabinet was met in the green Chamber, and then were called in; and there the King begun with me, to hear how the victualls of the fleet stood; I did in a long discourse tell him and the rest (the Duke of York, Lord Chancellor, Lord Treasurer, both the Secretarys,[1] Sir G. Carteret, and Sir W. Coventry) how it stood; wherein they seemed satisfied, but press mightily for more supplies; and the letter of the Generals, which was*a* read, did lay their not going, or too soon returning from the Duch coast, this next bout, to the want of victuals. Then they proceeded to the enquiry after the fireships; and did all very superficially – and without any severity at all. But however, I was in pain, after we came out, to know how I had done – and hear, well enough. But however, it shall be a caution to me to prepare myself against a day of inquisition.

Being come out, I met with Mr Moore; and he and I an hour together in the gallery – telling me how far they*b* are gone in getting my Lord's pardon, so as the Chancellor is prepared in it. And Sir H. Bennet doth promote it, and the warrant for the King's signing is drawn.[2] The business between my Lord Hinchingbrooke and Mrs. Mallet is quite broke off, he attending her at Tunbridge, and she declaring her affections to be settled – and he not being fully pleased with the vanity and liberty of her carriage.[3] He told me how*c* my Lord hath drawn a bill of exchange from Spain of 1200*l*, and would have me supplied him with 500*l* of it; but I avoided it – being not willing to imbark myself in money there where I see things going to ruine. Thence to discourse of the times, and he tells me he believes both my Lord Arlington and Sir W. Coventry, as well as my Lord Sandwich and Sir G. Carteret, have reason to fear, and are

a repl. 'were'   *b* repl. 'he'   *c* 'how' repeated

---

1. Arlington and Morice.
2. This was the pardon to Sandwich for the prize-goods affair: see above, vi. 231, n. 1. The King signed the warrant on 29 August and the patent was issued on 17 September. PRO, SP 29/169, no. 76;

C 66/3086, no. 6. Henry Moore was a lawyer and Sandwich's man of business.
3. Sandwich has a note of the news in Sandwich MSS, Journal, iii. 36. Elizabeth Malet married the Earl of Rochester in the following year.

afeared, of this parliament now coming on.[1] He tells me that Bristoll's faction is getting ground apace against my Lord Chancellor. He told me that my old Lord Coventry[2] was a cunning, crafty man, and did make as many bad Decrees in Chancery as any man;[3] and that in one case, that occasioned many years' dispute, at last when the[a] King came in, it was hoped by the party greived to get my Lord Chancellor to reverse a Decree of his. Sir W. Coventry took the opportunity of the business between the Duke of York and the Duchess[4] and came to my Lord Chancellor, that he had rather be drawn up Holborne to be hanged then live to see his father pissed upon (in these very terms), and any decree of his reversed. And so the Chancellor did not think fit to do it; but it still stands, to the undoing of one Norton, a printer, about his right to the printing of the Bible and Grammer, &c.[5]

Thence Sir W. Penn and I to[b] Islington, and there drank at the Katherine Wheele; and so down the nearest way home, where there was no kind of pleasure at all. Being come home, hear that Sir J. Mennes hath had a very bad fit all this day. And a Hickup do[c] take him, which is a very bad sign – which troubled me truly. So home to supper a little, and then to bed.

27. Up and to my new closet, which pleases me mightily, and there did a little business; then to break open a window to the leads-side in my old closet, which will enlighten the room mightily and make it mighty pleasant. So to the office, and

a repl. 'my'   *b* repl. 'by'   *c* MS. 'to'

---

1. The sixth session of the Cavalier Parliament began on 18 September.
2. Sir William's father, Thomas Coventry, 1st Baron Coventry, Lord Keeper 1625–40.
3. His reputation as a judge in fact stood high: Clarendon, *Hist.*, i. 57, 172; cf. Lord Campbell, *Lives of Lord Chancellors* (1845 ed.), ii. 507–8.
4. Their secret marriage.
5. Bonham Norton (d. 1635) had in 1618–29 engaged in a series of Chancery suits against his partner Robert Barker, with whom he had shared the lucrative business of King's Printer. Being defeated, he had accused Lord Keeper Coventry of having received a bribe, and was in consequence fined and imprisoned. His son Roger (d. 1662) had at the Restoration filed a suit, challenging Coventry's decree, and had petitioned the King, but to no avail. Roger's son Roger had now succeeded to the family business. See H. R. Plomer in *The Library*, n.s. 2/353+.

then home about one thing or other about my new closet, for my mind is full of nothing but that. So at noon to dinner, mightily pleased with my wife's picture that she is upon.[1] Then to the office, and thither came and walked an hour with me Sir G*a* Carteret – who tells me what is done about my Lord's pardon; and is not for letting the Duke of York know anything of it beforehand, but to carry it as speedily and quietly as we can. He seems to be very apprehensive that the Parliament will be troublesome, and inquisitive into faults – but seems not to value them as to himself.

He gone, I to the Victualling Office, there with Lewes and Willson setting the business of the state of the fleet's victualling even and plain; and that being done, and other good discourse about it over, Mr. Willson and I by water down the River for discourse only – about business of the office; and then back, and I home; and after a little at my office, home to my new closet and there did much business on my Tanger account and my Journall for three days. So to supper and to bed.

We are not sure that the Duch fleet is out.[2] I have another Memento from Sir W. Coventry of the want of provisions in the fleet[3] – which troubles me, though there is no reason for it. But will have the good effect of making me more wary. So, full of thoughts, to bed.

28. Up, and in my new closet a good while, doing business. Then called on by Mrs. Martin and Burroughs of Westminster, about business of the former's husband – which done, I to the office, where we sat all the morning. At noon I with my wife and Mercer to Philpott lane, a great cook's shop, to the wedding of Mr. Longracke our Purveyor,[4] a good sober civil man, and hath married a sober serious mayde. Here I met much ordinary company, going thither at his great request – but there was Mr.

a repl. 'W'

---

1. See above, p. 241. (OM).
2. It did not leave the Dutch coast until 1/11 September: G. Brandt, *Michel de Ruiter* (trans., 1698), p. 389.
3. On 25 August the Duke of York had written to the Navy Board com-

plaining that the slopsellers would not provide clothes until paid something of what was already owed them: PRO, Adm. 2/1745, f. 144*v*.
4. John Longrack, purveyor of timber to the navy.

Madden[1] and his lady, a fine noble pretty lady – and he[a] a fine gentleman seems to be. We four were most together; but the whole company was very simple and innocent. A good dinner, and what was best, good Musique. After dinner the young women went to dance – among others, Mr. Chr. Pett his daughter, who is a very pretty modest girl – I am mightily taken with her. And that being done, about 5 a-clock home, very well pleased with the afternoon's work. And so we broke up mighty civilly, the bride and bridegroom going to Greenwich (they keeping their dinner here only for my sake) to lie; and we home – where I to the office. And anon am on a sudden called to meet Sir W. Coventry and Sir W. Penn at the Victualling Office, which did put me out of order to be so surprized. But I went, and there Sir W. Coventry did read me a letter from the Generalls to the King, a most scurvy letter, reflecting most upon Sir W. Coventry, and then upon me for my accounts (not that they are not true, but that we do not consider the expense of the fleet), and then of the whole office in neglecting them and the King's service; and this in very plain and sharp and menacing terms.[2] I did give a good account of matters, according to our computation of the expense of the fleet. I find Sir W. Coventry willing enough to accept of anything to confront the Generals. But a great supply must be made, and shall be, in grace of God; but however, our accounts here will be found the true ones. Having done here, and much work set me, I with greater content home then I thought I should have done; and so to the office awhile, and then home and a while in my new closet, which delights me every day more and more. And so late to bed.

a MS. 'he and'

---

1. Probably John Madden, Surveyor of the Woods on this side Trent.

2. Rupert and Albemarle to the King, 27 August (PRO, SP 29/169, no. 34; summary in *CSPD 1666–7*, p. 71; copy in *Rupert and Monck Letter Book, 1666*, ed. J. R. Powell and E. K. Timings, pp. 142–3). It was a long letter complaining that 'we are not supplied with provisions according to the necessity of our affairs . . . and that when we send up our demands, instead of having them answered, we have accounts sent to us, which are prepared by Mr. Pepys of what hath been supplied . . .'. They asked for provisions, wet and dry, to last the fleet until October; otherwise they would have to return to port ahead of time.

29. Up betimes, and there to fit some Tanger accounts, and then by appointment to my Lord Bellasses;[1] but about Pauls thought of the chief paper I should carry with me, and so fain to come back again, and did; and then met with Sir W. Penn, and with him to my Lord Bellasses (he sitting in the coach the while), while I up to my Lord and there offered him my account of the bills of exchange I have received and paid for him – wherein we agree, all but one 200*l* bill of Vernattys drawing, wherein I doubt he hath endeavoured to cheat my Lord – but that will soon appear.[2] Thence took leave, and found Sir W. Penn talking to Orange Mall of the King's House – who, to our great comfort, told us that they begin to act on the 18th of this month.[3] So on to St. Jam[e]s's, in the way Sir W. Penn telling me that Mr. Norton, that married Sir J Lawson's daughter, is dead. She left 800*l* a year Joynter, a son to inherit the whole estate. She freed from her father-in-law's tyranny, and is in condition to help her mother – who needs it – of which I am glad, the young lady being very pretty.[4]

To St. James's, and there Sir W. Coventry took Sir W. Penn and me apart and read to us his answer to the Generalls letter to the King that he read last night; wherein he is very plain, and states the matter in full defence of himself, and of me with him, which he could not avoid – which is a good comfort to me, that I happen to be involved with him in the same cause.[5] And then speaking of the supplies which have been made to this fleet,

1. Governor of Tangier.
2. Philibert Vernatti was Muster-Master and Treasurer of the Tangier garrison. In Tangier, he had lived 'like a prince', allegedly from profits in the slave trade (John Luke to Nathaniel Luke, 16 May 1664: BM, Sloane 3509, f. 56*v*), though according to the not disinterested Charles Harbord (1662) he was 'a very careful honest Gent': Carte 75, f. 28*r*. His accounts remained mysterious and he took flight in October 1666.
3. 'Orange Mall' was Mary Meggs, who had a monopoly of the sale of oranges in the pit, boxes and middle gallery of the Theatre Royal in Bridges St, Drury Lane. She was an assiduous gossip and scandalmonger. Though the London theatres did not resume regular activities after the plague until the latter part of November 1666, some performances were attempted a few weeks earlier and were suppressed. Moll was probably referring to one of these. (A).
4. Cf. above, vi. 150 & n. 3.
5. Coventry to Rupert and Albemarle, 29 August; copy in Rawl. A 174, ff. 211–12, endorsed (in Hayter's hand): 'In answer among other things to their complaints of want of victualls'.

more then ever in all kinds to any, even that wherein the Duke of York himself was – "Well," says he, "if this will not do, I will say, as Sir J Falstaffe did to the Prince – 'Tell your father, that if he do not like this, let him kill the next Piercy himself.'"[1] And so we broke up, and to the Duke and there did our usual business.

So I into the parke, and there met Creed and he and I walked to Westminster to the Chequer – and thence to White-hall, talking of Tanger matters and Vernattys knaveries; and so parted, and then I homeward and met Mr. Povy in Cheapside. And stopped and talked a good while – upon the profits of that place which my Lord Bellasses hath made this last year, and what share we are to have of it – but of this, all imperfect; and so parted, and I home and there find Mrs. Mary Batelier[2] and she dined with us; and thence I took them to Islington and there eat a Custard, and so back to Moore-fields and showed Batelier, with my wife, *Polichienelli*[3] – which I like the more I see it. And so home with great content, she being a mighty good-natured pretty woman. And thence I to the victualling Office, and there with Mr. Lewes and Willson upon our victualling matters till 10 at night; and so home and there late, writing a letter to Sir W. Coventry;[4] and so home to supper and to bed.

No news where the Duch are. We begin to think they will steal through the Channel to meet Beaufort.[5] We think our fleet sailed yesterday, but we have no news of it.

30. Up and all the morning at the office. Dined at home; and in the afternoon, and at night till 2 in the morning, framing my great letter to Mr. Hayes about*a* the victualling of the fleet, about which there hath been so much ado and exceptions taken by the Generals.[6]

a repl. 'at'

1. '... if your Father will do me any honor, so: if not, let him kill the next Percie himselfe': *King Henry IV, Pt I*, V, 4. (A).

2. See above, p. 15 & n. 4.

3. See above, p. 257 & n. 2. (A).

4. Pepys to Coventry, 29 August: Longleat, Coventry MSS 97, f. 27r; about the victualling.

5. The Duc de Beaufort, commander of the French fleet.

6. Cf. above, p. 259 & n. 1. James Hayes was Rupert's secretary. His letter to Pepys (Southwold Bay, 19 August; endorsed 'arrived 23 Aug.') is in Rawl. A 176, ff. 207-8.

31. To bed at 2 or 3 in the morning, and up again at 6 to go by appointment to my Lord Bellasses; but he out of town, which vexed me. So back, and got Mr. Poynter to enter into my book[1] while I read from my last night's notes the letter; and that being done, to writing it fair. At noon home to dinner, and then the boy and I to the office, and there he read while I writ it fair – which done, I sent it to Sir W. Coventry to peruse and send to the fleet by the first opportunity; and so pretty betimes to bed – much pleased today with thoughts of gilding the backs of all my books alike in my new presses.[a]

a followed by two blank pages

---

1. His letter-book: NMM, LBK/8, pp. 434, 425–7 (pages in wrong order).

The Fire of London, by an anonymous artist
(*The London Museum*)

SEPTEMBER

1. Up and at the office all the morning, and then dined at home. Got my new closet made mighty clean against tomorrow. Sir W. Penn and my wife and Mercer and I to *Polichenelly*, but were there horribly frighted to see young Killigrew come in with a great many more young sparks; but we hid ourselfs, so as we think they did not see us.[1] By and by they went away, and then we were at rest again; and so the play being done, we to Islington and there eat and drank and mighty merry – and so home, singing; and after a letter or two at the office, to bed.

2. *Lords day.* Some of our maids sitting up late last night to get things ready against our feast today, Jane called us up, about 3 in the morning, to tell us of a great fire they saw in the City.[2]

1. Henry Killigrew (son of Thomas, the dramatist) was a Groom of the Bedchamber to the Duke of York; hence perhaps the Principal Officers' fear of being seen at a play: cf. below, p. 399 & n. 3. For the play, see above, p. 257, n. 2.

2. This was the Fire of London, which had begun about an hour before in Pudding Lane, near Fish Street Hill, not far from London Bridge (see map below, p. 430). It was to rage for four days and nights. Caused by an accidental fire in a bakery which spread quickly because of the dry season, it was widely believed to have been started deliberately by foreign enemies or Papists, or both. The worst was over after the east wind abated during the night of the 4th–5th. By then it is said to have destroyed c. 13,200 houses and levelled an area of c. 436 acres, leaving only about one-fifth of the city standing. Some 100,000 people were made homeless, but few lives were lost. Among the famous buildings which suffered were St Paul's (which was gutted, along with 84 parish churches, three others being badly damaged), Guildhall, and the Royal Exchange. Four stone bridges (including London Bridge) suffered damage, and 52 Company Halls were destroyed. Pepys's house and the Navy Office were not touched, but his birthplace in Salisbury Court off Fleet St was burnt down. In the absence of fire insurance (which in England began only after this disaster) municipal enterprise played a great part in the rebuilding of the city. The process was necessarily slow and piecemeal: meantime some trade moved away to the West End. But the bulk of private building was completed or well under way by 1670; Guildhall and the Royal Exchange were rebuilt by 1671, 25 of the parish churches by 1683, the Company Halls by 1685, and St Paul's by 1710. See Bell, *Fire*; T. F. Reddaway, *Rebuilding of London after the Great Fire*, pp. 281+ ; *Comp.*: 'Fire'.

So I rose, and slipped on my nightgown and went to her window, and thought it to be on the back side of Markelane at the furthest;[a] but being unused to such fires as fallowed, I thought it far enough off, and so went to bed again and to sleep.   About 7 rose again to dress myself, and there looked out at the window and saw the fire not so much as it was, and further off.   So to my closet to set things to rights after yesterday's cleaning.   By and by Jane[b] comes and tells me that she hears that above 300 houses have been burned down tonight by the fire we saw, and that it was now burning down all Fishstreet by London Bridge.   So I made myself ready presently, and walked to the Tower and there got up upon one of the high places, Sir J Robinsons little son going up with me;   and there I did see the houses at that end of the bridge all on fire, and an infinite great fire on this and the other side the end of the bridge – which, among other people, did trouble me for poor little Michell and our Sarah on the Bridge.   So down, with my heart full of trouble, to the Lieutenant of the Tower, who tells me that it begun this morning in the King's bakers[1] house in Pudding-lane, and that it hath burned down St. Magnes Church and most part of Fishstreete already.   So I down to the water-side and there got a boat and through bridge, and there saw a lamentable fire.   Poor Michells house,[2] as far as the Old Swan, already burned that way and the fire running further, that in a very little time it got as far as the Stillyard while I was there.   Everybody endeavouring to remove their goods, and flinging into the River or bringing them into lighters that lay off.   Poor people staying in their houses as long as till the very fire touched them, and then running into boats or clambering from one pair of stair by the water-side to another. And among other things, the poor pigeons I perceive were loath to leave their houses, but hovered about the windows and balconies till they were some of them burned, their wings, and fell down.

a repl. 'further'   *b* repl. 'a'

---

1. Thomas Farriner, sen. The question of whether the fire was due to his carelessness is discussed in Bell, *Fire*, p. 22.

2. Probably in or near Old Swan Lane: for its rebuilding, see below, 19 March 1668. (R).

Having stayed, and in an hour's time seen the fire rage every way, and nobody to my sight endeavouring to quench it, but to remove their goods and leave all to the fire; and having seen it get as far as the Steeleyard, and the wind mighty high and driving it into the city, and everything, after so long a drougth, proving combustible, even the very stones of churches, and among other things, the poor steeple by which pretty Mrs.   [1] lives,[a] and whereof my old school-fellow Elborough is parson, taken fire in the very top and there burned till it fall down – I to White-hall with a gentleman with me who desired to go off from the Tower to see the fire in my boat – to White-hall, and there up to the King's closet in the chapel, where people came about me and I did give them an account dismayed them all; and word was carried in to the King, so I was called for and did tell the King and Duke of York what I saw, and that unless his Majesty did command houses to be pulled down, nothing could stop the fire. They[b] seemed much troubled, and the King commanded me to go to my Lord Mayor from him and command him to spare no houses but to pull[c] down before the fire every way. The Duke of York bid me tell him that if he would have any more soldiers, he shall; and so did my Lord Arlington afterward, as a great secret. Here meeting with Captain Cocke, I in his coach, which he lent me, and Creed with me, to Pauls; and there walked along Watling-street as well as I could, every creature coming away loaden with goods to save – and here and there sick people carried away in beds. Extraordinary good goods carried in carts and on backs. At last met my Lord Mayor[2] in Canning Streete, like a man spent, with a hankercher about his neck. To the King's message, he cried like a fainting woman, "Lord, what can I do? I am spent. People will not obey me. I have been pull[ing] down houses. But the fire overtakes us faster then we can do it." That he needed no more soldiers; and that for himself, he must go and refresh himself, having been up all night. So he left me, and I him, and walked home – seeing people all almost distracted

a 'lives' repeated   *b* MS. 'the'   *c* MS. 'pulled'

---

1. Supply 'Horsley': above, p. 235. The church was St Lawrence Pountney.

2. Sir Thomas Bludworth.

and no manner of means used to quench the fire. The houses too, so very thick thereabouts, and full of matter for burning, as pitch and tar, in Thames-street – and warehouses of oyle and wines and Brandy and other things. Here I saw Mr. Isaccke Houblon, that handsome man – prettily dressed and dirty at his door at*ᵃ* Dowgate, receiving some of his brothers things whose houses were on fire; and as he says, have been removed twice already, and he doubts (as it soon proved) that they must be in a little time removed from his house also – which was a sad consideration.¹ And to see the churches all filling with goods, by people who themselfs should have been quietly there at this time.

By this time it was about 12 a-clock, and so home and there find my guests, which was Mr. Wood and his wife, Barbary Shelden, and also Mr. Moone² – she mighty fine, and her husband, for aught I see, a likely man.³ But Mr. Moones design and mine, which was to look over my closet and please him with the sight thereof, which he hath long desired, was wholly disappointed, for we were in great trouble and disturbance at this fire, not knowing what to think of it. However, we had an extraordinary good dinner, and as merry as at this time we could be.

While at dinner, Mrs. Batelier came to enquire after Mr. Woolfe and Stanes (who it seems are related*ᵇ* to them), whose houses in Fishstreet*ᶜ* are all burned, and they in a sad condition. She would not stay in the fright.

As soon as dined, I and Moone away and walked through the City, the streets full of nothing but people and horses and carts loaden with goods, ready to run over one another, and removing goods from one burned house to another – they now removing out of Canning-street (which received goods in the morning) into Lumbard Streete and further; and among others, I now saw my little goldsmith Stokes receiving some friend's goods, whose house itself was burned the day after. We parted at Pauls, he

---

a repl. 'receiving'   *b* repl. 'acq'-   *c* l.h. repl. s.h. 'Fish'

---

1. James Houblon sen., and all his sons, except James, lost their houses as a result of the fire. They probably moved temporarily to James's house in Winchester St. Lady A. A. Houblon, *Houblon Family*, i. 145, 149.
2. Lord Belasyse's secretary.
3. See above, p. 242 & n. 4.

home and I to Pauls-Wharf, where I had appointed a boat to attend me; and took in Mr. Carcasse and his brother, whom I met in the street, and carried them below and above bridge, to and again, to see the fire, which was now got further, both below and above, and no likelihood of stopping it. Met with the King and Duke of York in their Barge, and with them to Queen-Hith and there called Sir Rd. Browne[1] to them. Their order was only to pull down houses apace, and so below bridge at the water-side; but little was or could be done, the fire coming upon them so fast. Good hopes there was of stopping it at the Three Cranes above, and at Buttolphs-Wharf below bridge, if care be used; but the wind carries it into the City, so as we know not by the water-side what it doth there. River full of lighter[s] and boats taking in goods, and good goods swimming in the water; and only, I observed that hardly one lighter or boat in three that had the goods of a house in, but there was a pair* of virginalls in it. Having seen as much as I could now, I away to White-hall by appointment, and there walked to St. James's Park, and there met my wife and Creed and Wood and his wife and walked to my boat, and there upon the water again, and to the fire up and down, it still increasing and the wind great. So near the fire as we could for smoke; and all over the Thames, with one's face in the wind you were almost burned with a[a] shower of Firedrops – this is very true – so as houses were burned by these[b] drops and flakes of fire, three or four, nay five or six houses, one from another. When we could endure no more upon the water, we to a little alehouse on the Bankside over against the Three Cranes, and there stayed till it was dark almost and saw the fire grow; and as it grow darker, appeared more[c] and more, and in Corners and upon steeples and between churches and houses, as far as we could see up the hill of the City, in a most horrid malicious bloody flame, not like the fine flame of an ordinary fire. Barbary[2] and her husband away before us. We stayed till, it being darkish, we saw the fire as only one entire arch of fire from this to the other side the bridge, and in a bow

a repl. 'little'   *b* repl. 'this'   *c* repl. 'till'

---

1. Alderman of the nearby Lang-bourn ward, and a colonel in the city militia.

2. Mrs Knepp: see above, p. 4. (E).

up the hill, for an arch of above a mile long. It made me weep to see it. The churches, houses, and all on fire and flaming at once, and a horrid noise the flames made, and the cracking of houses at their ruine. So home with a sad heart, and there find everybody discoursing and lamenting the fire; and poor Tom Hater came with some few of his goods saved out of his house, which is burned upon Fish-street hill.[1] I invited him to lie at my house, and did receive his goods: but was deceived in his lying there, the noise coming every moment of the growth of the Fire, so as we were forced to begin to pack*a* up our own goods and prepare for their removal. And did by Moone-shine (it being brave, dry, and moonshine and warm weather) carry much of my goods into the garden, and Mr. Hater and I did remove my money and Iron-chests into my cellar – as thinking that the safest place. And got my bags of gold into my office ready to carry away, and my chief papers of accounts also there, and my tallies into a box by themselfs. So great was our fear, as Sir W. Batten had carts come out of the country to fetch away his goods this night. We did put Mr. Hater, poor man, to bed a little; but he got but very little rest, so much noise being in my house, taking down of goods.

3.   About 4 a-clock in the morning, my Lady Batten sent me a cart to carry away all my money and plate and best things to Sir W Riders at Bednall greene;[2] which I did, riding myself in my nightgown in the Cart; and Lord, to see how the streets and the highways are crowded with people, running and riding and getting of carts at any rate to fetch away thing[s]. I find Sir W Rider tired with being called up all night and receiving things from several friends. His house full of goods – and much of Sir W. Batten and Sir W. Penn's. I am eased at my heart to have my treasure so well secured. Then home with much ado to find a way. Nor any sleep all this night to me nor my poor

a repl. 'remove'

---

1. The street of that name immediately north of London Bridge.
2. Rider lived in a large Elizabethan mansion: see above, iv. 200 & n. 5.

He was a prosperous merchant and an associate of several officers of the Navy Board, including Pepys, on the Tangier and other committees.

wife. But then, and all this day, she and I and all my people labouring to get away the rest of our things, and did get Mr. Tooker[1] to get me a lighter to take them in, and we did carry them (myself some) over Tower-hill, which was by this time full of people's goods, bringing their goods thither. And down to the lighter, which lay at the next quay above the Tower-dock. And here was my neighbour's wife, Mrs. ,[2] with her pretty child and some few of her things, which I did willingly give way to be saved with mine. But there was no passing with anything through the postern, the crowd was so great.

The Duke of York came this day by the office and spoke to us, and did ride with his guard up and down the City to keep all quiet (he being now General, and having the care of all).[3]

This day, Mercer being not at home, but against her mistress order gone to her mother's, and my wife going thither to speak with W. Hewer, met her there and was angry; and her mother saying that she was not a prentice girl, to ask leave every time she goes abroad, my wife with good reason was angry, and when she came home, bid her be gone again. And so she went away, which troubled me; but yet less then it would, because of the condition we are in fear of coming into in a little time, of being less able to keep one in her quality. At night, lay down a little upon a quilt of W. Hewer in the office (all my own things being packed up or gone); and after me, my poor wife did the like – we having fed upon the remains of yesterday's dinner, having no fire nor dishes, nor any opportunity of dressing anything.

4. Up by break of day to get away the remainder of my things, which I did by a lighter at the Iron-gate; and my hands so few, that it was the afternoon before we could get them all away.

Sir W. Penn and I to Tower-street, and there met the fire

---

1. River agent to the Navy Board.
2. Supply 'Buckworth'. She had a little boy of four: see below, pp. 419–20.
3. He had this day been put in charge of the fire-fighting, and gave tireless and distinguished service.

For the organisation he commanded, see *CSPD 1666–7*, pp. 94–5; T. F. Reddaway, *Rebuilding of London*, p. 24. He acted in the absence of Albemarle, Captain-General of the kingdom, who was away with the fleet until the 7th.

Burning three or four doors beyond Mr. Howells;[1] whose goods, poor man (his trayes and dishes, Shovells &c., were flung all along Tower-street in the kennels, and people working therewith from one end to the other), the fire coming on in that narrow street, on both sides, with infinite fury. Sir W. Batten, not knowing how to remove his wind,* did dig a pit in the garden and laid it in there; and I took the opportunity of laying all the papers of my office that I could not otherwise dispose of. And in the evening Sir W. Penn and I did dig another and put our wine in it, and I my parmazan cheese as well as my wine and some other things.

The Duke of York was at the office this day at Sir W. Penn's, but I happened not to be within. This afternoon, sitting melancholy with Sir W. Penn in our garden and thinking of the certain burning of this office without extraordinary means, I did propose for the sending up of all our workmen from Woolwich and Deptford yards (none whereof yet appeared), and to write to Sir W. Coventry to have the Duke of York's permission to pull*a* down houses rather then lose this office, which would much hinder the King's business. So Sir W. Penn he went down this night, in order to the sending them up tomorrow morning; and I wrote to Sir W. Coventry about the business,[2] but received no answer.

This night Mrs. Turner (who, poor woman, was removing her goods all this day – good goods, into the garden, and knew not how to dispose of them) – and her husband supped with my wife and I at night in the office, upon a shoulder of mutton from the cook's, without any napkin or anything, in a sad manner but were merry. Only, now and then walking into the garden and saw how horridly the sky looks, all on a fire in the night, was enough to put us out of our wits; and endeed it was extremely dreadfull – for it looks just as if it was at us, and the whole heaven*b* on fire. I after supper walked in the dark down to Tower-street, and there saw it all on fire at the Trinity house on that side and the Dolphin tavern on this side, which was very near

a repl. 'pulled'　　　*b* repl. 'sky'

---

1. Turner to the Navy Board.　　　2. NMM, LBK/8, p. 456 (copy in Pepys's hand).

The Fire of London, by Thomas Wyck

(His Grace the Duke of Beaufort)

us – and the fire with extraordinary vehemence. Now begins the practice of blowing up of houses in Tower-street, those next the Tower, which at first did frighten people more then any-thing; but it stop[ped] the fire where it was done – it bringing down the houses to the ground in the same places they stood, and then it was easy to quench what little fire was in it, though it kindled nothing almost. W. Hewer this day *a* went to see how his mother did, and comes late home, but telling us how he hath been forced to remove her to Islington, her house in pye=Corner being burned. So that it is got so far that way and all the Old Bayly, and was running down to Fleetestreete. And Pauls is burned, and all Cheapside. I wrote to my father this night; but the post-house being burned, the letter could not go.

5. I lay down in the office again upon W. Hewer's quilt, being mighty weary and sore in my feet with going till I was hardly able to stand. About 2 in the morning my wife calls me up and tells of new Cryes of "Fyre!" – it being come to Barkeing Church,[1] which is the bottom of our lane. I up; and finding it so, resolved presently to take her away; and did, and took my gold (which was about 2350*l*), W. Hewer, and Jane down by Poundy's boat to Woolwich. But Lord, what a sad sight it was by moonlight to see the whole City almost on fire – that you might see it plain at Woolwich, as if you were by it. There when *b* I came, I find the gates[2] shut, but no guard kept at all; which troubled me, because of discourses now begun that there is plot in it and that the French had done it.[3] I got the gates open, and to Mr. Shelden's,[4] where I locked up my gold and charged my wife and W. Hewer never to leave the room without one of them in it night nor day. So back again, by the way

---

1. All Hallows, Barking, which, until the making of Byward St curtailed Seething Lane, stood at its south-east end. (R).
2. Of the dockyard.
3. It was said that 50,000 French and Dutch had landed, and were

entering the city: Evelyn, 7 September; W. Sandys to Viscount Scudamore, n.d., qu. Bell, *Fire*, p. 317.
4. Clerk of the Cheque, Woolwich; Mrs Pepys's host during the Plague. She now appears to have stayed there until 13 September.

T

seeing my[a] goods well in the lighters at Deptford and watched well by people. Home, and whereas I expected to have seen our house on fire, it being now about 7[b] a-clock, it was not. But to the Fyre, and there find greater hopes then I expected; for my confidence of finding our office on fire was such, that I durst not ask anybody how it was with us, till I came and saw it not burned. But going to the fire, I find, by the blowing up of houses and the great help given by the workmen out of the King's yards, sent up by Sir W. Penn, there is a good stop given to it, as well at Marke-lane end as ours – it having only burned the Dyall of Barkeing Church, and part of the porch, and was there quenched.[1] I up to the top of Barkeing steeple, and there saw the saddest sight of desolation that I ever saw. Everywhere great fires. Oyle-cellars and brimstone and other things burning. I became afeared to stay there long; and therefore down again as fast as I could, the fire being spread as far as I could see it, and to Sir W. Penn's and there eat a piece of cold meat, having eaten nothing since Sunday but the remains of Sunday's dinner.

Here I met with Mr. Young and Whistler; and having re-moved all my things, and received good hopes that the fire at our end is stopped, they and I walked into the town and find Fan-church-street, Gracious-street, and Lumbard-street all in dust.[2] The Exchange a sad sight, nothing standing there of all the statues or pillars but Sir Tho. Gresham's picture in the corner.[3] Walked into Moore-fields (our feet ready to burn, walking through the town among the hot coles) and find that full of people, and poor wretches carrying their goods there, and every-body keeping his goods together by themselfs (and a great blessing it is to them that it is fair weather for them to keep

a repl. 'on'   *b* repl. '6 a'-

---

1. Bell (*Fire*, pp. 160–1) gives reasons for doubting the statement about the porch.
2. Cf. Evelyn's account of his walk in the city on the 7th.
3. Along the sides of the quad-rangle, above the arcades, had stood statues of the sovereigns from Edward the Confessor to Charles II. All were destroyed – only that of Gresh-am, the founder, remained: a fact which provoked comment. Evelyn saw it on the 7th.

abroad night and day); drank there, and paid twopence for a plain penny loaf.¹

Thence homeward, having passed through Cheapside and Newgate-market, all burned – and seen Anthony Joyces house in fire. And took up (which I keep by me) a piece of glass of Mercer's chapel in the street, where much more was, so melted and buckled with the heat of the fire, like parchment. I also did see a poor Catt taken out of a hole in the chimney joyning to the wall of the Exchange, with the hair all burned off the body and yet alive. So home at night, and find there good hopes of saving our office – but great endeavours of watching all night and having men ready; and so we lodged them in the office, and had drink and bread and cheese for them. And I lay down and slept a good night about midnight – though when I rose, I hear that there had been a great alarme of French and Duch being risen – which proved nothing. But it is a strange thing to see how long this time did look since Sunday, having been alway full of variety of actions, and little sleep, that it looked like a week or more. And I had forgot almost the day of the week.

6. Up about 5 a-clock, and there met Mr Gawden at the gate of the office (I entending to go out, as I used every now and then to do, to see how the fire is) to call our men to Bishopps-gate, where no fire had yet been near, and there is now one broke out – which did give great grounds to people, and to me too, to think that there is some kind of plott in this (on which many by this time have been taken, and it hath been dangerous for any stranger to walk in the streets);² but I went with the

---

1. The King made a reassuring speech to the crowds in Moorfields on the following morning: Evelyn, 7 September.

2. Suspicion fell on foreigners and dissenters of all sorts, but principally on the Catholics and the French. The latter were insulted in the streets and many were arrested and examined by the government. One demented Frenchman, Hubert, made a false confession of guilt. In January 1667 parliament concluded, after en-

quiry, that the papists were responsible (a view which Pepys shared: see below, 23 September 1667). The government however decided to see no more in it than the hand of Providence. Cf. *Verney Mem.*, ii. 254–5 (letter of 3 September about the attacks on foreigners); Evelyn, 7 September; W. Taswell, *Autobiography* (*Camden Soc. Misc.*, vol. ii, p. 11); HMC, *Portland*, iii. 298; Bell, *Fire*, ch. xi.

men and we did put it out in a little time, so that that was well again.   It was pretty to see how hard the women did work in the cannells sweeping of water;   but then they would scold for drink and be as drunk as devils.   I saw good Butts of sugar broke open in the street, and people go and take handfuls out and put into beer and drink it.   And now all being pretty well, I took boat and over to Southwarke, and took boat on the other side the bridge and so to Westminster, thinking to Shift myself, being all in dirt from top to bottom.   But could not there find any place to buy a Shirt or pair of gloves, Westminster-hall being full of people's goods – those in Westminster having removed all their goods, and the Exchequer money put into vessels to carry*ᵃ* to Nonsuch.¹   But to the Swan, and there was trimmed. And then to White-hall, but saw nobody, and so home.   A sad sight to see how the River looks – no houses nor church near it to the Temple – where it stopped.   At home did go with Sir W. Batten and our neighbour Knightly (who, with one more, was the only man of any fashion left in all the neighbourhood hereabouts, they all removing their goods and leaving their houses to the mercy of the fire) to Sir R. Ford's, and there dined, in an earthen platter a fried breast of mutton, a great many of us. But very merry;   and endeed as good a meal, though as ugly a one, as ever I had in my life.   Thence down to Deptford, and there with great satisfaction landed all my goods at Sir G Car-teret's,² safe, and nothing missed I could see, or hurt.   This being done to my great content, I home;   and to Sir W. Batten's, and there with Sir R. Ford, Mr Knightly, and one Withers,³ a professed lying rogue, supped well;   and mighty merry and our fears over.   From them to the office and there slept, with the office full of labourers, who talked and slept and walked all night long there.   But strange it was to see Cloathworkers-hall

a 'to carry' repeated

---

1. On 4 September the Exchequer of the Receipt and the Tally Office had been ordered to remove to Nonsuch House, near Epsom, their temporary home during the Plague: *CSPD 1666–7*, p. 99.

2. He had an official residence there, as Navy Treasurer.

3. Probably Robert Withers, ship-builder, of Bolton-le-Sands, Lancs.

on fire these three days and nights in one body of Flame – it being the cellar, full of Oyle.

7. Up by 5 a-clock and, blessed be God, find all well, and by water to Paul's wharfe. Walked thence and saw all the town burned, and a miserable sight of Pauls church, with all the roofs fallen and the body of the Quire fallen into St Fayths[1] – Paul's school also – Ludgate – Fleet street – my father's house, and the church, and a good part of the Temple the like. So to Creeds lodging near the New Exchange, and there find him laid down upon a bed – the house all unfurnished, there being fears of the fire's coming to them. There borrowed a shirt of him – and washed. To Sir W. Coventry at St. James's, who lay without Curtains, having removed all his goods – as the King at White-hall and everybody had done and was doing. He hopes we shall have no public distractions upon this fire, which is what everybody fears – because of the talk of the French having a hand in it. And it is a proper time for discontents – but all men's minds are full of care to protect themselfs and save their goods. The Militia is in armes everywhere. Our Fleetes, he tells me, have been in sight one of another, and most unhappily by Fowle weather were parted, to our great loss, as in reason they do conclude – the Duch being come out only to make a show and please their people; but in*a* very bad condition as to stores, victuals, and men. They are at Bullen, and our fleet come to St. Ellens.[2] We have got nothing, but have lost one ship, but he knows not what.[3]

Thence to the Swan and there drank; and so home and find all well. My Lord Brouncker at Sir W. Batten's, and tells us the Generall is sent for up to come to advise with the King about business at this juncture, and to keep all quiet – which is great

a repl. 'against'

---

1. Cf. Evelyn, 7 September. 'St Faith's-under-St Paul's' was the popular name for the crypt under the choir of the cathedral. (R).

2. St Helen's Road, off the north-east coast of the Isle of Wight.

3. This encounter took place on 1 September off Calais. Rupert's slowness in giving the order to attack, as well as the storm, seems to have caused the failure to make contact. The English lost several ships, not one. Allin, i. 286+; *Naval Misc.* (Navy Rec. Soc.), iii. 32–3.

honour to him, but I am sure is but a piece of dissimulation.[1] So home and did give order for my house to be made clean; and then down to Woolwich and there find all well. Dined, and Mrs. Markeham came to see my wife. So I up again, and calling at Deptford for some things of W. Hewer, he being with me; and then home and spent the evening with Sir R. Ford, Mr. Knightly, and Sir W. Penn at Sir W. Batten's. This day our Merchants first met at Gresham College, which by proclamation[2] is to be their Exchange. Strange to hear what is bid for houses all up and down here – a friend of Sir W Riders having 150*l* for what he used to let for 40*l* per annum. Much dispute where the Custome-house shall be; thereby the growth of the City again to be foreseen. My Lord Treasurer, they say, and others, would have it at the other end of the town. I home late to Sir W. Penn, who did give me a bed – but without curtains or hangings, all being down. So here I went the first time[3] into a naked bed,*a* only my drawers on – and did sleep pretty well; but still, both sleeping and waking, had a fear of fire in my heart, that I took little rest. People do all*b* the world over cry out of the simplicity of my Lord Mayor in general, and more perticularly in this business of the fire, laying it all upon him.[4] A proclamation is come out for markets to be kept at Leaden hall and Mile=end greene and several other places about the town,

a repl. 'bod'   *b* 'do all' repeated

---

1. Albemarle, whose prestige with the London public was great, was sent for on the 4th from Portsmouth (where the fleet was fitting out), and arrived in London on the 7th: *CSPD 1666–7*, pp. 99, 102, 105. It was not true that this was 'a piece of dissimulation': see Arlington to Clifford, 4 September (*CSPD 1666–7*, p. 99).
2. Steele, no. 3473 (6 September).
3. I.e. since the Fire.
4. A MS. newsletter reported that on the first night of the disaster Bludworth refused to order the destruction of houses, saying that the

fire was slight and 'a woman might piss it out': qu. J. P. Malcolm, *Londinium Redivivum* (1802–7), iv. 74. For his attempts to save his reputation, see his letter to Williamson, 29 September: *CSPD 1666–7*, pp. 167–8. He had been guilty of a certain indecision perhaps, and after the second day of the Fire had been displaced from control of affairs by the Duke of York. But no Lord Mayor could act as autocratically as the Privy Council. For a defence of him, and a criticism of Pepys's report, see Bell, *Fire*, pp. 344–7.

and Tower hill, and all churches to be set open to receive poor people.[1]

8. Up, and with Sir W. Batten and Sir W. Penn by water to White-hall, and they to St. James's. I stopped with Sir G[a] Carteret, to desire him to go with us and to enquire after money. But the first he cannot do, and the other as little, or says, "When can we[b] get any, or what shall we do for it?" He, it seems[c], is imployed in the correspondence between the City and the King every day, in settling of things. I find him full of trouble to think how things will go. I left him, and to St. James's, where we met first at Sir W. Coventry's chamber and there did what business we can without any books. Our discourse, as everything else, was confused. The fleet is at Portsmouth, there staying a wind to carry them to the Downes or toward Bullen, where they say the Dutch fleete is gone and stays. We concluded upon private meetings for a while, not having any money to satisfy any people that may come to us. I bought two eeles upon the Thames, cost me 6s.[2] Thence with Sir W. Batten to the Cockpit, whither the Duke of Albemarle is come. It seems the King holds him so necessary at this time, that he hath sent for him and will keep ⟨him⟩ here. Endeed, his interest in the City, being acquainted, and his care in keeping things quiet, is reckoned that wherein he will be very serviceable. We to him. He is courted in appearance by everybody. He very kind to us. I perceive he lays by all business of the fleet at present and minds the City, and is now hastening to Gresham-College[3] to discourse with the Aldermen. Sir W. Batten and I home (where met by my Brother John, come to town to see how things are with us). And then presently he with me to Gresham-College – where infinite of people; partly through novelty to see the new place, and partly to find out and hear what is become one man of

---

a repl. 'W' *b* MS. 'we can' *c* 'He, it seems' repeated

---

1. There were two proclamations, of 5 and 6 September: Steele, nos 3470, 3473.
2. Three times the price he paid on 13 June.

3. Used as both Guildhall and Royal Exchange as a result of the Fire.

another. I met with many people undone, and more that have extraordinary great losses. People speaking their thoughts variously about the beginning of the fire and the rebuilding of the City. Then to Sir W. Batten and took my brother with me, and there dined with a great company of neighbours, and much good discourse; among others, of the low spirits of some rich men in the City, in sparing any encouragement to the poor people that wrought for the saving their houses. Among others, Alderman Starling, a very rich man, without children, the fire at next door to him in our Lane – after our men had saved his house, did give 2s 6d among 30 of them, and did quarrel with some that would remove the rubbish out of the way of the fire, saying that they came to steal.¹ Sir W. Coventry told me of another this morning in Holborne, which he showed the King – that when it was offered ᵃ to stop the fire near ᵇ his house for such ᶜ a reward, that came but to 2s 6d a man among the neighbours, he would give but 18d.² Thence to Bednall-green by coach, my brother with me, and saw all well there and fetched away my Journall-book to enter for five days past; and then back to the office, where I find Bagwells wife and her husband come home. Agreed to come [to] their house tomorrow,³ I sending him away back to his ship today. To the office, and late writing letters; and then to Sir W. Penn, my brother lying with me, and Sir W. Penn gone down to rest himself at Woolwich. But I was much frighted, and kept awake in my bed, by some noise I heard a great while below-stairs and the boys not coming up to me when I knocked.ᵈ It was by their discovery of people stealing of some neighbours' wine that lay ᵉ in vessels in the street. So to sleep. And all well all night.

a repl. 'ordered'   b repl. 'a'   c repl. '2s'
d repl. 'hear'   e MS. 'lain'

---

1. His house (small for an alderman, having only nine hearths) was on the west side of Seething Lane. His will showed that he could be prudently generous. Pepys gave a tip of 5s. for the recovery of some books on 21 September. (R).

2. Sir Richard Browne is said to have given £4 to the men who risked their lives to rescue a chest containing £10,000: *N. & Q.*, 15 April 1876, p. 306.

3. Apparently a mistake for Monday the 10th.

9. *Sunday.* Up, and was trimmed, and sent my brother to Woolwich to my wife to dine with her. I to church, where our parson made a melancholy but good sermon – and many, and most, in the church cried, especially the women. The church mighty full, but few of fashion, and most strangers. I walked to Bednall-green; and there dined well, but a bad venison pasty, at Sir W Rider's. Good people they are, and good discourse. And his daughter*ᵃ* Middleton, a fine woman and discreet. Thence home, and to church again, and there preached Deane Harding;[1] but methinks a bad poor sermon, though proper for the time – nor eloquent, in saying at this time that the City is reduced from a large Folio to a Decimo tertio. So to my office, there to write down my journall and take leave of my brother, whom I sent back this afternoon, though rainy – which it hath not done a good while before.[2] But I had no room nor convenience for him here till my house is fitted; but I was very kind to him, and do take very well of him his journey. I did give him 40s for his pocket; and so he being gone, and it presently rayning, I was troubled for him, though it is good for the Fyre. Anon to Sir W. Penn to bed, and made my boy Tom to read me asleep.

10. All the morning clearing our cellars and breaking in pieces all my old Lumber, to make room and to prevent fire. And then*ᵇ* to Sir W. Batten and dined, and there hear that Sir W Rider says that the town is full of the report of the wealth that is in his house, and would be glad that his friends would provide for the safety of their goods there. This made me get a cart; and thither, and there brought my money all away – took a hackney-coach myself (the hackney-coaches now standing at Allgate); much wealth endeed there is at his house. Blessed be God, I got all mine well thence and lodged it in my office;*ᶜ* but vexed to have all the world see it – and with Sir W. Batten,

a 'And his daughter' repeated
b repl. 'there hear that Sir'   *c* repl. 'house'

1. Nathaniel Hardy, Dean of Rochester.

2. Dr D. J. Schove writes: 'In south-east England there had been little rain, except for a few thunderstorms, since October of the previous year, and August had been particularly hot. The drought contributed to the destructiveness of the fire. Cf. Evelyn, iii. 451–2; Bell, *Fire*, pp. 17–18; D. J. Schove in *Weather*, 21/271+'.

who would have taken away my hands before they were stowed. But by and by comes Brother Balty from sea, which I was glad of; and so got him and Mr. Tooker and the boy to watch with them all in the office all night, while I, upon Janes coming, went down to my wife; calling at Deptford, intending to Bagwell, but did not ouvrir la porta como yo did expect. So down late to Woolwich, and there find my wife out of humour and indifferent, as she uses upon her having much liberty abroad.

11. Lay there; and up betimes, and by water with my gold and laid it with the rest in my office, where I find all well and safe. So with Sir W. Batten to the New Exchange by water, and to my Lord Brouncker's house, where Sir W. Coventry and G. Carteret met. Little business before us but want of money. Broke up, and I home by coach round the town. Dined at home, Balty and myself putting up my papers in my closet in the office. He away. I down to Deptford, and there spoke with Bagwell and agreed upon tomorrow, and came home in the rain by water. In the evening, at Sir W. Penn with my wife at supper: he in*a* a mad, ridiculous, drunken humour – and it seems there have been some late distastes between his lady and him, as my [wife] tells me. After supper I home, and with Mr. Hater, Gibson, and Tom alone, got all my chests and money into the further cellar, with much pains but great content to me when done. So, very late and weary, to bed.

12. Up, and with Sir W. Batten [and] Sir W. Penn to St. James's by water, and there did our usual business with the Duke of York. Thence I to Westminster, and there speak with Michell and Howlett, who tell me how their poor young ones are going to Shadwell.[1] The latter told me of the unkindness of that young man to his wife; which is now over, and I have promised to appear a counsellor to him. I am glad she is like to be so near us again. Thence to Martin, and there did tout ce que je voudrais avec her, and drank, and away by water home and to dinner, Balty and his wife there. After dinner I took

a MS. 'is'

---

1. Young Mitchell (newly married to Betty Howlett) had kept a strong-water house in Thames St, now destroyed in the Fire.

him down with me to Deptford; and there, by the *Bezan*, loaded above half my goods and sent them away.   So we back home, and then I found occasion to return in the dark, and to Bagwell*a* and there nudo in lecto con ella did do all that I desired; but though I did intend para aver demorado con ella toda la night, yet when I had done ce que je voudrais, I did hate both ella and la cosa; and taking occasion from the uncertainty of su marido's return esta*b* noche, did me levar; and so away home late to Sir W. Penn (Balty and his wife lying at my house); and there, in the same simple humour, I found Sir W. Penn, and so late to bed.

13.   Up, and down to Tower wharfe; and there with Balty and labourers from Deptford did get my goods housed well at home.   So down to Deptford again to fetch the rest, and there eat a bit of dinner at the Globe, with the maister of the *Bezan* with me, while the labourers went to dinner.   Here I hear that this poor town doth bury still of the plague seven or eight in a day.[1]   So to Sir G. Carteret's to work; and there did, to my great content, ship off into the *Bezan* all the rest of my goods, saving my pictures and fine things, that I will bring home in wherrys when my house is fit to receive them.   And so home and unloaden them by carts and hands before night, to my exceeding satisfaction; and so after supper to bed in my house, the first time I have lain there; and lay with my wife in my old closet upon the ground, and Balty and his wife in the best chamber, upon the ground also.

14.   Up, and to work, having Carpenters come to help in setting up bedsteads and hangings; and at that trade my people and I all the morning, till pressed by public business to leave them, against my will, in the afternoon; and yet I was troubled in being at home, to see all my goods lie up and down the house in a bad condition, and strange workmen going to and fro might take what they would almost.   All the afternoon busy; and Sir W. Coventry came to me, and found me, as God would have it, in my office, and people about me setting my papers to rights; and there discoursed about getting an account ready against the Parliament, and thereby did create me infinite of

a   name in s.h.   *b*   preceded by blot

1.   Cf. above, p. 236 & n. 3; Evelyn, 7 September.

business, and to be done on a sudden, which troubled me; but however, he being gone, I about it late and to good purpose; and so home, having this day also got my wine*a* out of the ground again and set it in my cellar; but with great pain to keep the port[er]s that carried it in from observing the money-chests there. So to bed as last night; only, my wife and I upon a bedstead with curtains in that which was Mercer's chamber, and Balty and his wife (who are here and do us good service) where we lay last night. This day poor Tom Pepys the turner was with me, and Kate Joyce, to bespeak places; one for himself, the other for her husband. She tells me he hath lost 140*l* per annum, but hath seven houses left.

15. All the morning at the office, Harman being come, to my great satisfaction, to put up my beds and hangings; so I am at rest, and fallowed my business all day. Dined with Sir W. Batten. Mighty busy about this account,[1] and while my people were busy, myself wrote near 30 letters and orders with my own hand. At it till 11 at night; and it is strange to see how clear my head was, being eased of all the matter of all those letters; whereas one would think that I should have been dozed – I never did observe so much of myself in my life. In the evening there comes to me Captain Cocke, and walked a good while in the garden; he says he hath computed that the rents of houses lost this fire in the City comes to 600000*l* per annum.[2] That this will make the Parliament more quiet then otherwise they would have been, and give the King a more ready supply. That the supply must be by excise, as it is in holland.[3] That the Parliament will see it necessary to carry on the war. That the late storm hindered our beating the Duch fleet, who were gone out only to satisfy the people, having no business to do but to avoid

a repl. 'wife'

---

1. See below, p. 288 & n. 1.
2. This is far in excess of the estimate which may be calculated from the statistics drawn up shortly after the Fire and given in Stow, *Survey* (ed. Strype, 1720), bk i. 227. 13,200 houses are there stated to have been destroyed, and their average

rental value (at 12 years' purchase) is put at £25 p.a. The total loss of rent in that case would be £340,000.
3. For the attempt to extend the excise, see below, p. 356 & n. 3. For the Dutch excise, see above, v. 69 & n. 1.

us. That the French, as late in the year as it is, are coming. That the Duch are really in bad condition, but that this unhappiness of ours doth give them heart. That there was a late difference between my Lord Arlington and Sir W. Coventry, about neglect in that Lord to send away an express of the other's in time.[1] That it came before the King, and the Duke of York concerned himself in it – but this fire hath stopped it. The Duch fleet is not gone home, but rather to the North; and so dangerous to our Gottenburgh fleet. That the Parliament is likely to fall foul upon some persons; and among others, on the Vicechamberlaine, though we both believe with little ground. That, certainly, never so great a loss as this was borne so well by citizens in the world as this; he believing that not one merchant upon the Change will break upon it.[2] That he doth not apprehend there will be any disturbances in estate upon it, for that all men are busy[a] in looking after their own business, to save themselfs. He gone, I to finish my letters; and home to bed and find, to my infinite joy, many rooms clean, and myself and wife lie in our own chamber again. But much terrified in the nights nowadays, with dreams of fire and falling down of houses.

16.[b] *Lords day.* Lay with much pleasure in bed, talking with my wife about Mr. Haters lying here, and W. Hewer also, if Mrs. Mercer leaves her house.[3] To the office, whither also all my people about this account, and there busy all the morning. At noon with my wife (against her will, all undressed and dirty) dined at Sir W. Penn, where was all the company of our families in town. But Lord, so sorry a dinner – venison baked in pans, that the dinner I have had for his lady alone hath been worth four of it. Thence after dinner, displeased with our entertainment, to my office again, and there till almost midnight, and my

a repl. 'business'
b from here to end of 11 October entries written in very small hand with lines close together; for explanation, see Pepys's memorandum below, p. 318

---

1. See above, p. 179 & n. 4.
2. Cf. Evelyn's similar comment (in a letter, 27 September: *Diary and corr.*, ed. Wheatley, iii. 344); and Pepys's reports, below, p. 323; 25 September 1667. But see below, 3 December 1667; Bell, *Fire*, ch. xii, esp. p. 218. There was no fire insurance at this time.
3. Hewer lodged with the Mercers.

people with me. And then home, my head mightily akeing about our accounts.

17. Up betimes, and shaved myself after a week's growth; but Lord, how ugly I was yesterday and how fine today. By water, seeing the City all the way, a sad sight endeed, much fire being still in – to Sir W. Coventry, and there read*a* over my yesterday's work; being a collection of the perticulars of the excess of charge created by a war[1] – with good content. Sir W. Coventry was in great pain lest the French fleet should be passed by our fleet – who had notice of them on Saturday, and were preparing to go meet them; but their minds altered, and judged them merchant-men, when the same day, the *Success*, Captain Ball, made their whole fleet, and came to Brighthemson and thence at 5 a-clock afternoon, Saturday, wrote Sir W. Coventry news thereof. So that we do much fear our missing*b* them.[2] Here came in and talked with him, Sir Tho Clifford, who appears a very fine gentleman, and much set by at Court for his activity in going to sea, and stoutness everywhere and stirring up and down.[3]   Thence by coach over the ruines, down Fleete-

a repl. same symbol   *b* repl. same symbol badly formed

1. Longleat, Coventry MSS 97, ff. 29-33 (16 September); copy (in Hayter's hand) in PL 2589, pp. 56+ .
2. News from the Duke of York of the approach of the French reached the fleet off Dungeness on the 15th. They found a small force of eight sail which were chased by frigates, two being driven ashore and burnt. Below, pp. 327-8 & n.; Allin, i. 289-90; *Naval Misc.* (Navy Rec. Soc.), iii. 36. Ball's letter from Brighton ('Brighthemson') is referred to in *CSPD 1666-7*, p. 133.
3. Clifford (later Lord Treasurer, 1672-3) was sub-commissioner for the Sick and Wounded and a Commissioner for Prizes, and had served in the fleet in all the major engagements of 1665-6, sailing on board a flagship usually, and taking part in the councils of war. His work in pre-

venting the embezzlement of prizes, in sending detailed reports of naval actions to Secretary Arlington and in organising the relief of the wounded in the west country had already been recognised in 1665 by the grant of a prize-ship and a lease of royal lands. He was now (28 November and 5 December) made Comptroller to the King's Household and a Privy Councillor 'for his singular Zeal . . . in the honourable dangers of this war . . . where he has been all along a constant Actor . . . taking his share in the warmest parts of those services': C. H. Hartmann, *Clifford*, p. 123; see also ib., pp. 38, 43, 45; Sandwich, pp. 241, 267. Evelyn (iii. 470) wrote of him as 'a valiant & daring person' 'advanc'd by my Lord Arlington . . . to the greate astonishment of all the Courte'.

streete and Cheapside to Broad-street to Sir G. Carteret, where Sir W. Batten (and Sir J. Mennes, whom I had not seen a long time before, being his first coming abroad) and Lord Brouncker passing his accounts. Thence home a little to look after my people at work, and back to Sir G. Carteret to dinner; and thence, after some discourse with him upon our public accounts, I back home, and all the day with Harman and his people finishing the hangings and beds in my house; and the hangings will be as good as ever, and perticularly in my new closet. They gone, and I weary, my wife and I, and Balty and his wife, who came hither today to help us, to a barrel of oysters I sent from the River today, and so to bed.

18. Strange, with what freedom and quantity I pissed this night, which I know not what to impute to but my oysters – unless the coldness of the night should cause it, for it was a sad rainy and tempestuous night.[1] As soon as up, I begun to have some pain in my blather and belly as usual, which made me go to dinner betimes to fill my belly; and that did ease me, so as I did my business in the afternoon, in forwarding the settling of my house, very well. Betimes to bed, my wife also being all this day ill in the same manner. Troubled at my wife's hair coming off so much. This day the Parliament met, and adjourned till Friday, when the King will be with them.

19. Up, and with Sir W. Penn by coach to St. James's, and there did our usual business before the Duke of York; which signified little, our business*a* being only complaints of lack of money. Here I saw a bastard of the late King of Sweden's, come to kiss his hands – a mighty modish French-like gentleman.[2] Thence to White-hall with Sir W. Batten and Sir W. Pen to

a repl. 'complaints'

---

1. Dr D. J. Schove writes: 'Wood (*L. &. T.*, ii. 88) has a description of what was presumably the same wind (? tornado) on the previous day. "All the morning a grievous and blustery wind: the devill appeared at Westminster at [? and] Whitehall and

frighted the gards out of their wits." '
2. Gustaf, later Count Carlsson (d. 1708), bastard son of Charles X (d. 1660). He spent the period 1659–68 travelling with a tutor in W. Europe, and later became a soldier in the service of William of Orange.

Wilkes's; and there did hear the many profane stories of Sir Henr. Wood[1] – damning the parsons for spending so much wine at the sacrament, cursing that ever they took the cup to themselfs; and then another story, that he valued not all the world's curses, for, for twopence he shall get at any time the prayers of some poor body, that is worth a thousand of all their curses. Lord Norwich drawing a Tooth at a health. Another time, he and pinchbacke and Dr. Goffe,[2] now a religious* man, Pinchbacke did begin a frolic of drink[ing] out of a glass, with a toad in it that he had taken up going out to shit – he did it without harm. Goffe, who knew Sacke would kill the toad, called for sack. And when he saw it dead, says he, "I will have a quick toad; I will not drink from a dead toad;" by that means, no other being to be found, he escaped the health. Thence home and dined, and to Deptford and got all my pictures put into wherries, and my other fine things, and landed them all very well, and brought them home and got Symson to set them up all tonight; and he gone, I and the boy to finish and set up my books and everything else in my house, till 2 in the morning, and then to bed. But mightily troubled, and even in my sleep, at my missing four or five of my biggest books – Speed's Chronicle – and maps, and the two parts of Waggoner, and a book of Cards; which I suppose I have put up with too much care, that I have forgot where they are, for sure they are not stole.[3] Two little pictures of sea and ships, and a little gilt frame belonging to my platt of the River I want; but my books do heartily trouble me. Most of my gilt frames are hurt, which also troubles me; but

---

1. Clerk of the Board of Green Cloth: Evelyn (17 November 1651) thought him 'odd'. His brother Thomas (Dean of Lichfield) was even odder: see below, 31 January 1668 & n.

2. John Pinchbeck served in the army under both Charles I and Charles II. Stephen Goffe (once a royal chaplain) had been a Roman convert since 1641 and Superior of the Paris Oratory since 1655.

3. They were found later: below, p. 292. John Speed's *History of Great Britaine* (1650) and *Prospect of the most famous parts of the world* (1631), and Wagenaer's *Mariner's Mirrour* (1588; q.v. above, iv. 240, n. 1) – all large folios – are still in the PL: nos 2906, 2901, 3000. See also below, 2 March 1667. The 'book of Cards' was presumably a collection of sea-cards (charts): cf. below, p. 292.

most my books. This day I put on two shirts,[1] the first time this year, and do grow well upon it; so that my disease is nothing but wind.

20. Up, much troubled about my books; but cannot imagine where they should be. Up to the setting my closet to rights, and Sir W. Coventry takes me at it – which did not displease me. He and I to discourse about our accounts and the bringing them to the Parliament, and with much content to see him rely so well on my part.[a] He and I together to Broad-street to the Vice-chamberlain; and there discoursed a while, and parted. My Lady Carteret came to town, but I did not see her. He tells me how the fleet is come into the Downes; nothing done, nor French fleet seen. We drove all from our anchors.[2] But he says news is come that De Ruter is dead, or very near it, of a hurt in his mouth, upon the discharge of one of his own guns; which put him into a fever, and he likely to die, if not already dead.[3] We parted, and I home and to dinner; and after dinner to the setting things in order, and all my people busy about the same work. In the afternoon out by coach, my wife with me (which we have not done several weeks now), through all the ruines to show her them, which frets her much – and is a sad sight endeed. Set her down at her brother's; and thence I to Westminster-hall, and there stayed a little while and called her home. She did give me an account of great differences between her mother and Balty's wife. The old woman charges her with going abroad, and staying out late, and painting in the absence of her husband, and I know not what; and they grow proud, both he and she, and do not help their father and mother out of what I help them to; which I do not like, nor my wife. So home, and to the office to even my Journall, and then home and very

a repl. 'paper'

---

1. A second shirt was a common form of underwear.

2. Rupert to Coventry, 19 September: Sir Henry Ellis (ed.), *Orig. Corr.* (ser. 3), iv. 294–6. A storm had disturbed the ships: see letters in *CSPD 1666–7*, p. 143 and C. Batters

to Pepys, n.d. (? 20 September), *CSPD Add. 1660–85*, p. 164.

3. The news of his wound was correct, but not that of his death: G. Brandt, *Michel de Ruiter* (trans. 1698), p. 392.

U

late up with Jane, setting my books in perfect order in my closet; but am mightily troubled for my great books that I miss. And I am troubled the more, for fear there should be more missing then what I find, though by the room they take on the shelves, I don't find any reason to think it. So to bed.

21. Up, and mightily pleased with the setting of my books the last night in order; and that which did please me most of all, is that W. Hewer tells me that upon enquiry, he doth find that Sir W. Penn hath a hamper more then his own, which he took for a hamper of bottles of wine, and are books in it. I was impatient to see it, but they were carried into a wine-cellar, and the boy is abroad with him at the House, where the Parliament meet today, and the King to be with them. At noon, after dinner, I sent for Harry, and he tells me it is so, and brought me by and by my hamper of books, to my great joy, with the same books I missed, and three more great ones and no more – I did give him 5s for his pains; and so home with great joy, and to the setting some of them right; but could not finish it, but away by coach to the other end of the town, leaving my wife at the Change. But neither came time enough to the Council to speak with the Duke of York nor with Sir G. Carteret; and so called my wife and paid for some things she bought, and so home, and there, after a little doing at the office about our accounts, which now draw near the time they should be ready, the House having order[ed] Sir G. Carteret, upon his offering them to bring them in on Saturday next – I home; and there with great pleasure very late, new setting all my books; and now I am in as good condition as I desire to be in all worldly respects, the Lord of heaven make me thankful and continue me therein. So to bed. This day I had new stairs of main timber put to my cellar going into the yard.

22. To my closet and had it new washed, and now my house is so clean as I never saw it, or any other house in my life, and everything in as good condition as ever before the fire; but with I believe about 20*l* cost one way or other, besides about 20*l* charge in removing my goods; and do not find that I have lost anything but two little pictures of shipping and sea, and a little gold frame for one of my sea-cards. My glazier, endeed, is so

full of work that I cannot get him to come to perfect my house. To the office, and there busy now for good and all about my accounts. My Lord Brouncker came thither, thinking to find an office, but we have not yet met. He doth now give me a watch, a plain one, in the room of my former watch with many motions[1] which I did give him. If it goes well, I care not for the difference in worth – though I believe there is above 5*l*. He and I to Sir G. Carteret to discourse about his account; but Mr. Waith[2] not being there, nothing could be done; and therefore I home again, and busy all day. In the afternoon comes Ant. Joyce to see me, and with tears told me his loss, but yet that he hath something left that he can live well upon, and I doubt it not. But he would buy some place that he could have, and yet keep his trade where he is settled in St. Jones's.[3] He gone, I to the office again, and then to Sir G. Carteret and there find Mr. Wayth; but Lord, how fretfully Sir G. Carteret doth discourse with Mr. Wayth about his accounts, like a man that understands them not one word. I held my tongue, and let him go on like a passionate fool. In the afternoon I paid for the two lighters that carried my goods to Deptford, and they cost me 8*l*. Till past midnight at our accounts, and have brought them to a good issue, so as to be ready to meet Sir G. Carteret and Sir W. Coventry tomorrow – but must work tomorrow; which Mr. T. Hater had no mind to, it being the Lord's day;[4] but being told the necessity, submitted, poor man. This night, writ for Brother John to come to town. Among other reasons, my estate lying in money, I am afeared of any sudden miscarriage. So to bed, mightily contented in despatch[ing] so much business and find[ing] my house in the best condition that ever I knew it. Home to bed.

23. 《*Sunday*》 Up, and after being trimmed, all the morning at the office, with my people about me, till about one a-clock; and then home, and my people with me, and Mr. Wayth; and eat a bit of victuals in my old closet, now my little dining-room, which makes a pretty room; and my house being so clean makes

1. Cf. above, vi. 221, n. 3. Possibly it had astronomical dials.

2. Paymaster to the Navy Treasurer.

3. St John's, Clerkenwell. Whether he remained there is uncertain. His will (1668) shows him in St Giles without Cripplegate. (R).

4. He was a nonconformist – a Baptist or a Quaker.

me mightily pleased, but only I do lack Mercer or somebody in the house to sing with. As soon as eat a bit, Mr. Wayth and I by water to White-hall, and there at Sir G. Carteret's lodgings Sir W. Coventry met, and we did debate the whole business of our account to the Parliament – where it appears to us that the charge of the war, from September 1 1664 to this Michaelmas, will have been but 3200000*l*, and we have paid in that time somewhat about 2200000*l*; so that we owe above 900000*l*: but our method of accounting, though it cannot I believe be far wide from the mark, yet will not abide a strict examination if the Parliament should be troublesome.[1] Here happened a pretty question of Sir W. Coventry, whether this account of ours will not put my Lord Treasurer to a difficulty to tell what is become of all the money the Parliament hath given in this time for the war, which hath amounted to about 4000000*l*[2] – which nobody there could answer; but I perceive they did doubt what his answer could be. Having done, and taken from Sir W. Coventry the minutes of a letter to my Lord Treasurer, Wayth and I back again to the office. And thence back down to the water with my wife, and landed him in Southworke, and my wife and I for pleasure to Fox hall, and there eat and drank, and so back home; and I to my office till midnight, drawing the letter we are to send with our account to my Lord Treasurer; and that being done to my mind, I home to bed.

24. Up, and with Sir W. Batten and W. Penn to St. James's, and there with Sir W. Coventry – read, and all approved of my letter; and then home, and after dinner, Mr. Hater and Gibson dining with me, to the office and there very late, new moulding my accounts and writing fair my letter – which I did against the evening; and then by coach, left my wife at her brother's, and I

1. These accounts were presented (with a covering letter) to the Lord Treasurer on 24 September: BM, Add. 28084, ff. 24*r*, 30*r*; copies are ib., 9311, ff. 115*v*–116*v* and PL 2589, pp. 13+ (summary of accounts in *Cat.*, i. 102). Abstracts and other papers are in PL 2589 ('Collections towards the Stateing the Expence of his Majesty's Navy from the begin-

ning of the present warr . . .'). Cf. below, p. 317 & n. 3; 3 August 1667. Cf. also Coventry to Pepys, 12 October: Rawl. A 195a, f. 233*r* (wrongly dated 12 October 1667).

2. This was roughly the total voted by the Royal and Additional Aids of 1665 and the Poll tax of 1666. The actual revenue was less.

to St. James's and up and down to look Sir W. Coventry; and at last found him and Sir G. Carteret with Lord Treasurer at White-hall – consulting how to make up my Lord Treasurer's general account, as well as that of the Navy perticularly. Here I brought the letter, but found that Sir G. Carteret hath altered his account since he did give me the abstract of it; so all my letter must be writ over again, to put in his last abstract. So to Sir G. Carteret's lodgings to speak a little about the alteration, and there looking over the book that Sir G. Carteret entends to deliver to the Parliament of his payments since September 1 1664; and there I find my name the very second, for flags which I had bought for the Navy, of calico once, about 500*l* and odd pounds[1] – which vexed me mightily. At last I concluded of scraping out my name and putting in Mr. Tookers[2] – which eased me, though the price was such as I should have had glory by. Here I saw my Lady Carteret, lately come to town, who, good lady, is mighty kind, and I must make much of her – for she is a most excellent woman. So took up my wife, and away home, and there to bed. And up betimes with all my people, to get the letter writ over and other things done; which I did, and by coach to Lord Brouncker and got his hand to it. And then to Parliament-house and got it signed by the rest, and then delivered it at the House door to Sir Ph. Warwicke – Sir G. Carteret being gone into the House with his book of accounts under his arme, to present to the House. I had brought my wife to Westminster-hall; and leaving her with Mrs. Michell, where she sat in her shop and had burned wine sent for her – I walked in the hall, and among others, with N. Pickering, who continues still a lying, bragging coxcomb, telling me that my Lord Sandwich may thank himself for all his misfortune, for not suffering him and two or three good honest fellows more to take them by the throats that spoke ill of him. And told me how basely Lionell Walden[3] hath carried himself towards my Lord, by speaking slightly of him – which I shall remember.

Thence took my wife home to dinner; and then to the office,

《25.》

---

1. See above, v. 289 & n. 3. The Principal Officers were forbidden to trade in naval stores.

2. Shipping agent in the river to the Board.

3. M.P. for Huntingdon borough; Deputy-Lieutenant (under Sandwich and Manchester) for the county.

where Mr. Hater all the day putting in order and entering in a book[1] all the measures that this account of the Navy hath been made up by. And late at night to Mrs. Turner's, where she had got my wife and Lady Pen and Peg, and supped; and after supper, and the rest of the company by design gone, Mrs. Turner and her husband did lay their case to me about their lodgings,[2] Sir J. Mennes being now gone wholly to his own; and now, they being empty, they doubt Sir T. Harvy or Lord Brouncker may look after the lodgings. I did give them the best advice, poor people, that I could, and would do them any kindness, though it is strange that now they should have ne'er a friend of Sir W. Batten or W. Penn to trust to but me, that they have disobliged. So home to bed – and all night still mightily troubled in my sleep with fire and houses pulling down.

26. Up, and with Sir J. Mennes to St. James's; where, everybody going to the House, I away by coach to Westminster hall; and after a few turns, and hearing that our accounts came into the House but today, being hindered yesterday by other business, I away by coach home, taking up my wife and calling at Bennet's, our late mercer, who is come into Covent-garden to a fine house looking down upon the Exchange;[3] and I perceive many Londoners every day come, and Mr. Pierce hath let his wife's closet, and the little blind bed-chamber, and a garret to a silkman for 50*l* fine and 30*l* per annum, and 40*l* per annum more for dieting the master and two prentices. So home, not agreeing for silk for a petticoat for her which she desired; but home to dinner, and then back to White-hall, leaving my wife by the way to buy her petticoat of Bennet; and I to White-hall, waiting all the day on the Duke of York to move the King for getting Lanyon some money at Plymouth, out of some oyle-prizes

1. Probably PL 2589.
2. Thomas Turner, Mennes's clerk, had lodgings next to Pepys's, and Mennes had apparently occupied part of them. It seems that the Turners now feared that the whole of their lodgings would be taken over by either Harvey or Brouncker. The latter did in fact displace them in

February 1667 and they were given accommodation elsewhere at the Board's expense.
3. The New Exchange. The house was probably in or near Half Moon St (now Bedford St), which would loosely be called Covent Garden though actually in St Martin's-in-the-Fields. (R).

brought in thither – but could get nothing done.[1] But here by Mr. Dugdale[2] I hear the great loss of books in St. Pauls churchyard, and at their hall also – which they value at about 150000*l*;[3] some booksellers being wholly undone; and among others, they say, my poor Kirton.[4] And Mr. Crumlum,[5] all his books and household stuff burned; they trusting to St. Fayths, and the roof of the church falling, broke the Arch down into the lower church, and so all the goods burned[6] – a very great loss. His father hath lost above 1000*l* in books – one book newly-printed, a discourse it seems of Courts.[7] Here I had the hap to see my Lady Denham;[8] and at night went into the drawing-room and saw several fine ladies; among others, Castlemayne, but chiefly Denham again, and the Duke of York taking her aside and talking to her in the sight of all the world, all alone; which was strange – and what also I did not like. Here I met with good Mr. Eveling, who cries out against it and calls it bichering,[9] for the Duke of York talks a little to her, and then she goes away and then he fallows her again, like a dog.

1. On 9 September Lanyon (Navy agent at Plymouth) had written to Pepys that a good supply of train oil could be had from two Greenland ships brought in as prizes: *CSPD 1666–7*, pp. 111, 136. Pepys hoped (in vain) to use this windfall as a means of paying some of the debts owing at Plymouth: *Further Corr.*, p. 151.

2. John, son of the herald and antiquarian, William Dugdale; chief gentleman-usher to the Lord Chancellor, Clarendon.

3. Stationers' Hall, along with St Faith's and Christ Church, had been used for storage by the booksellers. Evelyn, in a letter of 27 September, put the estimated loss at £200,000 (*Diary and corr.*, ed. Wheatley, iii. 344); Dr de Beer (Evelyn, iii. 459, n. 3) believes that 'the stationers probably suffered greater losses through the Fire than any other traders'. Evelyn (7 September)

stated that the books in St Faith's burnt for a whole week. Cf. below, pp. 309–10 & n.

4. Joseph Kirton had been Pepys's bookseller until the Fire.

5. Samuel Cromleholme, High Master of St Paul's. His library was reputedly the best private collection in London at that time, and its loss is said to have hastened his death: Sir M. McDonnell, *Hist. St Paul's School*, p. 225.

6. For a different version of the origin of this outbreak, see below, p. 309; 14 January 1668.

7. William Dugdale's losses are described in his letters of 15 October and 28 May 1667 (*Life, diary and corr.*, ed. W. Hamper, 1827, p. 364; HMC, *Le Fleming*, p. 48), and included all but a few copies of his *Originales Juridiciales*, just published.

8. The Duke of York's mistress.

9. A word Evelyn never uses in his diary.

He observes that none of the nobility came out of the country at all to help the King or comfort him or prevent commotions at this fire, but do as if the King were nobody;[1] nor ne'er a priest comes to give the King and Court good counsel or to comfort the poor people that suffer; but all is dead – nothing of good in any of their minds. He bemoans it, and says he fears more ruin hangs over our heads. Thence away by coach and called away my wife at Unthankes, where she tells me she hath bought a gown of 15*s* per yard; the same, before her face, my Lady Castlemaine this day bought also – which I seemed vexed for; though I do not grudge it her, but to encline her to have Mercer again – which I believe I shall do, but the girl, I heare, hath no mind to come to us again – which vexes me. Being come home, I to Sir W. Batten, and there hear our business was tendered to the House today and a Committee of the whole House chosen to examine our accounts,[2] and a great many hotspurs enquiring into it – and likely to give us much trouble and blame, and perhaps (which I am afeared of) will find faults enow to demand better officers. This I truly fear. Thence*a* away with Sir W. Penn, who was there; and he and I walked in the garden by moonlight, and he proposes his and my looking out into Scotland about timber, and to use Pett there; for timber will be a good commodity this time of building the City. And I like the motion, and doubt not that we may do good in it.[3]

a repl. 'this'

---

1. Evelyn himself had been active in organising fire prevention in Fetter Lane: Evelyn, 4 September.

2. *Recte* a select committee of 45, appointed to examine the accounts of the Ordnance Office and Treasury as well as the Navy. A subcommittee was appointed to deal with the naval accounts: *CJ*, viii. 628.

3. Nothing came of this proposal, though Scottish timber was used for houses about a year later: *Bulstrode Papers*, i. 10. The navy itself normally used little wood from Scotland since it was reckoned inferior to English and foreign varieties, but

Phineas Pett was there on the Board's service during the war years and afterwards, 1665–70. Not much rebuilding of the city had yet been done; the act of 1667 which controlled it defined the dimensions of the timber in the new brick houses, and (in a 'scheme' annexed to the act) stated that the 'sawed timber' had usually come from the West country. Building timber fetched £5 a ton in November 1666: HMC, *Hastings*, ii. 372. Evelyn was now busy with a similar project for making bricks; see below, 23 September 1668 & n.

We did also discourse about our Privateer,[1] and hope well of that also, without much hazard, as, if God blesses us, I hope we shall do pretty well toward getting a penny. I was mightily pleased with our discourse; and so parted, and to the office to finish my Journall for three or four days; and so home to supper and to bed. Our fleet abroad, and the Duch too, for all we know. The weather very bad; and under the command of an unlucky man[2] I fear. God bless him and the fleet under him.

27. A very furious blowing night all the night, and my mind still mightily perplexed with dreams and burning the rest of the town – and waking in much pain for the fleet. Up, and with my wife by coach as far as the Temple;[a] and there she to the mercer's again, and I to look out Penny, my tailor, to speak for a cloak and cassock for my brother, who is coming to town and I will have him in a canonical dress – that he may be the fitter to go abroad with me. I then to the Exchequer; and there, among other things, spoke to Mr. Falconbrige about his girl I heard sing at Nonsuch;[3] and took him and some other Chequer-men to the Sun tavern, and there spent 2s 6d upon them; and he sent for the girl, and she hath a pretty way of singing, but hath almost forgot, for want of practice. She is poor in clothes, and not bred to any carriage, but will be soon taught all. And if Mercer do not come again, I think we may have her upon better terms, and breed her to what we please. Thence to Sir W. Coventry, and there dined with him and Sir W. Batten, the Lieutenant of the Tower, and Mr. Thin, a pretty gentleman, going to Gottenburgh:[4] having dined, Sir[b] W. Coventry, W. Batten, and I walked into his closet to consider of some things more to be done in a list to be given to the Parliament of all our ships,

a repl. 'Parliament'   b l.h. repl. s.h. 'with'

---

1. See below, p. 301, n. 1.
2. Rupert had been in sole command of the fleet, since the 6th, Albemarle having been recalled to help to direct the measures taken against the Fire.
3. See above, vi. 235 & n. 4.

4. Thomas Thynne (Coventry's nephew, later Viscount Weymouth) was now appointed envoy-extraordinary to Sweden. He did not set out until November: *CSPD 1666–7*, p. 268.

and time of entry and discharge.[1] Sir W. Coventry seems to think they will soon be weary of the business and fall quietly into the giving the King what is fit. This he hopes. Thence I by coach home to the office, and there intending a meeting; but nobody being there but[a] myself and Sir J. Mennes, who is worse then nothing, I did not answer anybody, but kept to my business in the office till night; and then Sir W. Batten and W. Penn to me, and thence to Sir W. Batten and eat a barrel of oysters I did give them; and so home and to bed – I having this evening discoursed with W. Hewer about Mercer, I having a mind to have her again; and I am vexed to hear him say that he thinks she hath no mind to come again; though her mother hath. No news of the fleet yet, but that they went by Dover on 25th toward the Gunfleet, but whether the Duch be yet abroad or no, we hear not. De Ruyter is not dead, but like to do well. Most think that the gross of the French fleet are gone home again.[2]

28. Lay long in bed, and am come to agreement with my wife to have Mercer again, on condition she may learn this winter two months to dance, and she promises me she will endeavour to learn[b] to sing; and all this I am willing enough to. So up, and by and by the glazier comes to finish the windows of my house, which pleases me, and the bookbinder to gild the backs of my books. I got the glass of my book-presses to be done presently,* which did mightily content me. And to setting my study in a little better order; and so to my office to my people, busy about our Parliament accounts; and so to dinner – and then at them again close. At night comes Sir W. Penn,[c] and he and I a turn in the garden, and he broke to me a proposition of his and my joining in a design of fetching timber and deals from Scotland by the help of Mr. Pett upon the place; ⟨which⟩ while London is building, will yield good money.[3] I approve it. We judged a third man, that is knowing, is necessary; and concluded on Sir W. Warren, and sent for him to come to us tomorrow morning. I full of this all night, and the project of

a MS. 'by'   *b* repl. same symbol badly formed   *c* repl. 'WB'

---

1. Copy (in Hewer's hand) in PL 2589, pp. 70+.

2. See below, pp. 327–8 & n.

3. See above, p. 298 & n. 3.

our man-of-war;[1] but he and I both dissatisfied with Sir W. Batten's proposing his son[2] to be Lieutenant, which we neither of us like.   He gone, I discoursed with W. Hewer about Mercer, having a great mind she should come to us again; and instructed him what to say to her mother about it.   And so home to supper and to bed.

29. A little meeting at the office by Sir W. Batten, W. Penn, and myself – being the first since the fire.   We rose soon; and comes Sir W. Warren by our desire, and he, W. Penn, and I talked of our Scotch motion, which W. Warren did seem to be stumbled at; and did give no ready answer, but proposed some thing previous to it which he knows would find us work, or writing to Mr. Pett to be informed how matters go there as to cost – and ways of providing Sawyers or sawmills.   We were parted without coming to any good resolution in it – I discerning plainly that Sir W. Warren had no mind to it, but that he was surprized at our motion.   He gone, I to some office business, and then home to dinner, and then to office again, and then got done by night the lists that are to be presented to the Parliament committee, of the ships, number of men, and time imployed since the war.   And then I with it (leaving my wife at Unthankes) to St. James's, where Sir W. Coventry stayed for me; and he and I perused our *a* lists, and find, to our great joy, that the wages, victuals, wear, and tear, cast by the Medium of the men, will come

a repl. 'it'

---

1. A Dutch prize, the *Flying Grey-hound* of Amsterdam, captured by the *Pembroke*, was now lent to Pepys, Batten and Penn as a privateer, on condition that it would be restored to the King's service, as a fireship, in the following spring.   The partners paid nothing for the loan, but themselves met all other expenses, Batten being in charge of the accounts.   Pepys soon sold one-third of his share to Sir Richard Ford: below, p. 338.   The ship, commanded by Edward Hogg, was now at Harwich.   It was com-missioned on 25 October and in December put out to sea.   For its exploits, see below, pp. 418, 424 etc. See also BM, Harl. 1510, f. 90*v* (order of Prize Commissioners, 30 July 1666); PL 2871, p. 665 (copy of Admiral's warrant, 22 September); ib., p. 667 (copy of letters of marque, 4 October); PRO, HCA 25/228, f. 68*v* (commission, 25 October); Rawl. A 174, ff. 291+ (accounts); *Shorthand Letters*, pp. 85–6; *CSPD 1666–7*, pp. 48–9, 67, 308.

2. His younger son, Benjamin.

to above three Millions; and that the extraordinaries, which all the world will allow us, will arise to more then will justify the expense we have declared to have been at since the war – *viz.*, 320000*l*[1] – he and I being both mightily satisfied; he saying to me that if God send us over this rubb, we must take another course for a better Controller.   So we parted, and I to my wife, who stayed for the[a] finishing her new best gown (the best that ever he[b][2] made her), colourd tabby Flowred.   And so took her and it home; and then I to my people, and having cut them out a little more work then they expected, *viz.*, the writing over the lists in a new[c] method, I home to bed, I being in good humour and glad of the end we have brought this matter to.

30. *Lords day.* Up and to church, where I have not been a good while;[3] and there the church infinitely thronged with strangers since the fire came into our parish; but not one handsome face in all of them, as if endeed there was a curse, as Bishopp Fuller heretofore said, upon our parish. Here I saw Mercer come into the church; which I had a mind to, but she avoided looking up – which vexed me. A pretty good sermon; and then home, and comes Balty and dined with us – a good dinner; and then to have my hair cut against winter close to my head, and then to church again. A sorry sermon, and away home. W. Penn and I to walk, to talk about several businesses; and then home, and my wife and I to read in Fullers *Church History*,[4] and so to supper and to bed.

This month ends with my mind full of business and concernment how this office will[d] speed with the Parliament, which begins to be mighty severe in the examining our accounts and the expense of the Navy this war.

a repl. 'me'   *b* MS. ? 'I'   *c* repl. 'm'-   *d* repl. 'sp'-

---

1. *Recte* £3,200,000. These accounts (in Pepys's hand) are in Longleat, Coventry MSS 98, f. 214r: 'Expense of the Navy from Sept. 1 1664 to Sept. 29 1666 and the Debt then'; copy (in Gibson's hand) in PL 2589, p. 91. The expense was £3,200,516 (£2,195,560 being paid by the Navy Treasury and £74,460 by the Exchequer). Debts at 29 September stood at £930,496.

2. Her tailor, Unthanke.

3. The last occasion was on 9 September.

4. See above, i. 56, n. 6.

OCTOBER.[a]

1. Up, and all the morning at the office getting the list of all the ships and vessels imployed since the war for the committee of Parliament.[1] At noon with it to Sir W. Coventry's chamber, and there dined with him and W. Batten [and] W. Penn; and after dinner examined it, and find it will do us much right in the number of men, rising to near the expense we delivered to the Parliament. W. Coventry and I (the others going before to the committee) to Lord Brouncker for his hand, and find him simply mighty busy in a council of the Queen's.[2] He came out, and took in the papers to sign, and sent them mighty wisely out again. So W. Coventry away to the committee, and I to the Mercer's and there took a bill of what I owe of late, which comes to above 17*l*. Thence to White-hall, and there did hear Betty Michell was at this end of the town; and so, without breach of vow, did stay to endeavour to meet with her and carry her home; but she did not come, so I lost my whole afternoon. But pretty, how I took another pretty woman for her, taking her a clap on the breech, thinking verily it had been her. Stayed till W. Batten and W. Penn came out; and so away home by water with them, and to the office to do some business; and then home, and my wife doth tell me that W. Hewer tells her that Mercer hath no mind to come. So I was angry at it, and resolve with her to have Falconbrige's girl; and I think it will be better for us, and will please me better with singing. With this resolution, to supper and to bed.

2. Up, and am sent for to Sir G. Carteret; and to him, and there he tells me how our lists are referred to a sub-committee to consider and examine, and that I am ordered to be there this afternoon. So I away thence to my new bookbinder[3] to see my books

a repl. 'September.'

1. See above, p. 298 & n. 2.
2. Since 1662 he had been Chancellor to the Queen.

3. See above, p. 243, n. 3.

gilding in the backs, and then to Westminster-hall to the House and spoke with Sir W. Coventry, where he told me I must attend the committee in the afternoon, and received some hints of more work to do. So I away to the Chequer, and thence to an alehouse and found Mr. Falconbrige, and agreed for his kinswoman to come to me. He says she can dress my wife and will do anything we would have her to do, and is of a good spirit*a* – and mighty*b* cheerful. He is much pleased therewith, and so we*c* shall be. So agreed for her coming the next week. So away home, and eat a short dinner, and then with Sir W. Penn to Westminster-hall, and do give his boy my book of papers to hold, while he went into the committee-chamber in the inner Court of Wardes and I walked without with Mr. Slingsby of the tower[1] (who was there, and did in walking inform me mightily in several things; among others, that the heightening*d* or lowering of money is only a cheat, and doth good to some perticular men; which, if I can but remember how, I am now by him fully convinced of); anon Sir W. Penn went away, telling me that W. Coventry, that was within, had told him that the fleet is all come in to the buoy of the Nore, and that he must hasten down to them, and so went away. And I into the committee-chamber before the committee sat, and there heard Birch discourse highly and understandingly about the Navy business and a proposal made heretofore to farm the Navy.[2] But W. Coventry did abundantly answer him – and is a most excellent person. By and by the committee met, and*e* I walked out; and anon they rose and called me in, and appointed me to attend a committee of them tomorrow at the office to examine our lists. This put me into a mighty fear and trouble, they doing it in a very ill humour methought. So I away, and called on my Lord Brouncker to desire him to be there tomorrow. And so home, having taken

a followed by 'but will do anything we would have her do'   *b* MS. 'my'
c repl. 'am I'   *d* repl. 'highering'   *e* repl. 'and there heard Birch discourse'

---

1. Henry Slingsby was Master of the Mint, which was housed in the Tower.

2. Col. John Birch was an acknowledged expert on naval administration. Some navy business had been farmed during 1577–96 when Hawkins was Navy Treasurer: Oppenheim, pp. 162–3. No more recent farms or proposals to farm have been traced.

up my wife at Unthankes – full of trouble in mind to think what I shall be obliged to answer, that am neither fully fit, nor in any measure concerned to take the shame and trouble of this office upon me; but only from the inability and folly of the Controller occasions it. When come home, I to Sir W. Penn to his boy for my book, and there find he hath it not, but delivered it to the doorkeeper of the committee for me. This, added to my former disquiet, made me stark mad, considering all the naked-ness of the office lay open in papers within those Covers. I could not tell in the world what to do, but was mad on all sides; and that which made me worse, Captain Cocke was there, and he did so swear and curse at the boy that told me. So Cocke, Griffin, and the boy with me – they to find out the housekeeper*ᵃ* of the Parliament, Hughes, while I to Sir W. Coventry, but could hear nothing of it there; but coming to our Rendezvous at the Swan tavern in Kings-street, I find they have found the house-keeper, and the book simply locked up in the Court. So I stayed and drank, and rewarded the doorkeeper and away home, my heart lighter by all this; but to bed very sad notwithstanding, in fear of what will happen tomorrow upon their coming.

3. Waked betimes, mightily troubled in mind, and in the most true trouble that I ever was in my life, saving in that business last year of the East India prizes.[1] So up, and with Mr. Hayter and W. Hewer and Gibson to consider of our business and books and papers necessary for this examination; and by and by, by 8 a-clock, comes Birch the first, with the list and books of accounts delivered in. He calls me to work, and there he and I begin; when by and by comes Garraway, the first time I ever saw him, and Sir W Thomson and Mr. Boscawen.[2] They to it, and I did make shift to answer them better then I expected. Sir W. Batten, Lord Brouncker, W. Penn came in, but presently went out; and J. Mennes came in, and said two

a repl. 'housekeeper doorkeeper'

---

1. See above, vi. 231, n. 1.
2. The M.P.'s were Col. John Birch (Penryn; see above, p. 304, n. 2); William Garroway (Chichester; a leading critic of the Court); Sir

William Thompson (London) and Edward Boscawen (Truro). Pepys's memorandum on this meeting (in Gibson's hand) is in PL 2589, pp. 94–5.

or three words from the purpose but to do hurt; and so away he went also – and left me all the morning with them alone, to stand or fall. At noon W. Batten comes to them to invite them*a* (though fast-day)[1] to dinner – which they did, and good company they were, but especially Garraway. Here I have news brought me of my father's com[ing] to town, and I presently to him. Glad to see him, poor man, he being come unexpected to see us and the City. I could*b* not stay with him, but after dinner to work again, only the committee and I, till dark night; and by that time they cast up all the lists and found out what the medium of men was borne all the war, of all sorts – and ended with good peace and much seeming satisfaction; but I find them wise and reserved, and instructed to hit all our blots – as, among others, that we reckon*c* the ships full manned from the beginning. They gone, and my heart eased of a great deal of fear and pain, and reckoning myself to come off with victory, because not overcome in anything or much foiled, I away to Sir W. Coventry's chamber, but he not within; then to White-hall and there among the ladies, and saw my Lady Castlemaine never looked so ill, nor Mrs. Stewart neither, as in this plain natural dress; I was not pleased with either of them. Away, not finding W. Coventry; and so home, and there find my father and my brother come to town – my father without my expectation; but glad I am to see him. And so to supper with him, and to work again at the office; then home to set up all my Folio books, which are come home gilt on the backs, very handsome to the eye; and then at midnight to bed. This night W. Penn told me W. Batten swears he will have nothing to do with the privateer if his son do not go Lieutenant; which angers me and him, but we will be even with him one way or other.

4. Up, and mighty betimes to W. Coventry to give him an account of yesterday's work, which doth give him good content. He did then tell me his speech lately to the House in his own vindication, about the report of his selling of places – he having a

---

a MS. 'them to'　　　*b* MS. 'would'　　　*c* 'that we reckon' repeated

---

1. For the Plague.

small occasion offered him by chance, which he did desire, and took and did it to his content; and he says to the House's seeming to approve of it, by their hum.[1] He confessed how long he had done it, and how he desired to have something else;[2] and since then he had taken nothing, and challenged all the world. I was glad of this also. Thence up to the Duke of York by appointment, with fellow-officers, to complain, but to no purpose, of want of money; and so away – I to Sir G. Carteret to his lodging, and there discoursed much of the want of money and our being designed for destruction. How the King hath lost his power by submitting himself to this way of examining his accounts - and is become but as a private man. He says the King is troubled at it, but they talk an entry shall be made[3] that it is not to be brought into example. That the King must, if they do not agree presently, make them a courageous speech; which he says he may do (the City of London being now burned, and himself master of an army)[4] better then any prince before him – and so I believe. Thence home about noon and to dinner. After dinner the bookbinder came, and I sent by him some more books to gild. I to the office all day, and spent most of it with W. Warren, whom I have had no discourse with a great while. And when all is done, I do find him a mighty wise man as any I know, and his counsel as much to be fallowed. Late with Mr. Hayter, upon comparing the charge and husbandry of the last Duch war with ours now; and do find good room to think we have done little worse then they – whereof good use may and will be made.[5] So home to supper and to bed.

1. This was possibly during the debate on the navy's finances on 26 September. Cf. above, iv. 331 & n. 4.

2. I.e. a salary in lieu of the right to sell places. He had been given a salary since September 1664: Longleat, Coventry MSS 98, ff. 119r, 127r; ib., 102, f. 2v. He made a similar defence against these charges in 1668: cf. below, 23 February 1668 & n.

3. In the Commons' journals.

4. The forces recently raised against the French: cf. above, p. 185 & n. 1.

5. A copy of this calculation, and of Coventry's letter of 3 October asking for it (in Pepys's hand) is in PL 2589, pp. 117-18. According to these figures, the Commonwealth government paid, in the opening year of the First Dutch War, £171,785 more than was paid by the Restoration government for similar goods and services during the opening year of the Second War.

x

5. Up, and with my father talking awhile; then to the office, and there troubled with a message from Lord Peterborough about money;[1] but I did give as kind answer as I could, though I hate him. Then to Sir G. Carteret to discourse about paying off part of the great ships come in; and so home again to prepare the comparison of the two Duch wars' charges for W. Coventry; and then by water (and saw old Mr. Michell digging like a painful father for his son) to him, and find him at Dinner. After dinner, to look over my papers; and comparing them with some notes of his [he] brought me the sight of some good Navy notes of his, which I shall get. Then examined and liked well my notes; and away together to White-hall, in the way discoursing the inconvenience of the King's being thus subject to an account; but it will be remedied for the time to come he thinks, if we can get over this. And I find he will have the Controller's business better done, swearing he will never be for a Witt to be imployed on business again. Thence I home, and back again to White-hall; and, meeting Sir H Cholmly, to Westminster-hall and there walked till night that the Committee came down, and there W. Coventry tells me that the sub-committee have made their report to the grand-committee, and in pretty kind terms, and have agreed upon allowing us 4*l* per head, which I am sure will do the business.[2] But he had endeavoured to have got more, but this doth well; and he and I are both mighty glad it*a* is come to this, and the heat of this present business seems almost over. But I have more work cut out for me, to prepare a list of the extraordinaries not to be included within the 4*l*, against Monday.[3] So I away from him and met with the Vicechamberlaine, and I told him that*b* I had this evening in coming thither

a repl. 'of'   *b* MS. 'what'

---

1. For his pension as late Governor of Tangier: see above, iv. 94, n. 1; below, p. 335 & n. 3.

2. This became the normal monthly allowance per man on which naval estimates were based throughout the rest of the century, and comprised 30*s*. for wages, 30*s*. for wear and tear (material, including ships), and 20*s*. for victuals. Ehrman, pp. 159–60.

3. Copies of the list (in Gibson's hand), with accompanying papers, are in PL 2589, pp. 98+ ; BM, Add. 28084, f. 30*r*. The 'extraordinary charge' of the war from 1 September 1664 to 30 September 1666 amounted to £269,186.

met with Captain Cocke, and he told me of a wild motion made
in the House of Lords by the Duke of Buckingham, for all men
that had cheated the King to be declared traitors and felons –
and that my Lord Sandwich was named.[1] This put me into a
great pain; so the Vice-Chamberlain, who had heard nothing of it,
having been all day in the City, away with me to White-hall, and
there ᵃ came to me and told me that upon my Lord Ashly's
asking their direction whether being a peere he should bring
in his accounts to the Commons, which they did give way to,
the Duke of Buckingham did move that for the time to come
what I have written above might be declared, by some fuller law
then heretofore. Lord Ashly answered it was not the fault of the
present laws, but want of proof – and so said the Lord Chancellor; he[2] answered that a better law, he thought, might be
made; so the House, laughing, did refer it to him to bring in a
bill to that purpose, and this was all. So I away with joyful
heart home, calling on Cocke and telling him the same. So I
away home to the office to clear my Journall for five days, and so
home to supper and to bed, my father, who had stayed out late
and troubled me thereat, being come home well and gone to
bed, which pleases me also. This day, coming home, Mr.
Kirton's kinsman my bookseller came in my way; and so I am
told by him that Mr. Kirton is utterly undone, and made 2 or
3000*l* worse then nothing, from being worth 7 or 8000*l*. That
the goods laid in the churchyard fired, through the window,
those in St. Fayths church – and those coming to the warehouses doors fired them, and burned all the books and the
pillars of the church, so as the roof falling down, broke quite
down, which it did not do in the other places of the church,
which is alike pillared (which I knew not before); but being not
burned, they stand still. He doth believe there is above 150000*l*
of books burned; all the great booksellers almost undone – not
only these, but their warehouses at their hall, and under Christ-
church and elsewhere, being all burned. A great want thereof
there will be of books, especially Latin books and foreign books;

a no blank in MS.

1. The motion is not noticed in the
Lord's Journals. Buckingham seems
to have been persuaded by Coventry
to abandon this move: see below, p.
325; 27 February, 4 March 1667.
2. Buckingham.

and among others, the polyglottes and new Bible, which he believes will be presently worth 40*l* apiece.[1]

6. Up, and having seen my brother in his Cassocke, which I am not the most satisfied in, being doubtful at this time what course to have him profess too soon – to the office, and there busy about a list of the extraordinaries of the charge of the fleet this war; and was led to go to the Office of the Ordinance to be satisfied in something, and find their accounts and books kept in mighty good order – but that they can give no light, nor will the[a] nature of their affairs permit it, to tell what the charge of the ordinance comes to, a man a month. So home again and to dinner, there coming Creed to me; but what with business and my hatred to the man, I did not spend any time with him; but after dinner, wife and he and I took coach and to Westminster, but he light about Paul's, and I set her at her tailor's, and myself to St. James's; but there missing W. Coventry, returned and took up my wife and, calling at the Exchange, home – whither Sir H. Cholmly came to visit me, but my business suffered me not to stay with him: so he gone, I by water to Westminster-hall, and thence to St. James and there found W. Coventry waiting for me; and I did give him a good account, to his mind, of the business he expected about extraordinaries, and then fell to other talk; among others, our sad condition contracted by want of a Controller; and it was his words, that he believes, besides all the shame and trouble he hath brought on the office, the King had better have given 100000*l* then ever have had him there. He did discourse about some of these discontented parliament-men, and says that Birch is a false rogue, but that Garraway is a man that hath not been well used by the Court, though very stout to death and hath suffered all that is possible for the King from the beginning. But discontented as he is, yet he never knew a session of Parliament but he hath done some good deed

a repl. 'into'

1. Original subscribers to the *Biblia Polyglotta* (ed. Brian Walton, 6 vols, 1657) had had their copies for £10 each: *DNB*. Pepys retained a copy in his library; PL 2948–53. For the new Bible, see A. S. Herbert, *Hist. cat. Engl. Bible, 1525–1961*, p. 210, no. 694. For the burning of the books, see above, p. 297 & n. 3.

for the King before it rose.[1] I told him the passage Cocke told me of – his having begged a brace of bucks of the Lord Arlington for him, and when it came to him, he sent it back again. Sir W. Coventry told me it is much to be pitied that the King should lose the service of a man so able and faithful – and that he ought to be brought over, but that it is always observed, that by bringing over one discontented man you raise up three in his room – which is a State lesson I never knew before – but when others discover[a] your fear, and the discontent procures favour, they will be discontented too, and impose on you. Thence to White-hall, and got a coach and home, and there did business late; and so home and set up my little books[2] of one of my presses, come home gilt, which pleases me mightily; and then to bed. This morning my wife told me of a fine gentlewoman my Lady Pen tells her of, for 20*l* per annum, that sings, dances, plays on four or five instruments, and many other fine things, which pleases me mightily, and she sent to have her see her; which she did this afternoon, but sings basely, and is a tawdry wench, that would take 8*l*, but my wife nor I think her fit to come.

7. *Lords day.* Up, and after visiting my father in his chamber, to church, and then home to dinner. Little Michell and his wife came to dine with us – which they did; and then presently after dinner, I with Sir J. Mennes to White-hall, where met by W. Batten and Lord Brouncker, to attend the King and Duke of York at the Cabinet; but nobody had determined what to speak of, but only in general to ask for money – so I was forced immediately to prepare in my mind a method of discoursing.[3]

a   repl. same symbol badly formed

1. On 24 September Garroway had carried to the King the thanks of the House for his speech, and the offer of a subsidy: Milward, p. 6. For his help in securing a grant of £1,220,000 in 1673, see Burnet, ii. 16–17. (Marvell and others regarded him as corruptible.) Although now usually a critic of the court, he had been a royalist in the Civil War period.

2. In Pepys's library, in its finished state, the books were arranged by size. This entry (and that of 3 October about the folios) suggest that he may have adopted this plan from the beginning.

3. Naval accounts were at this period presented to the Council or Cabinet; after the fall of Clarendon in 1667, to the Treasury. See e.g. below, 3, 4 June 1667.

And anon we were called in to the green-room, where the King, Duke of York, Prince Rupert, Lord Chancellor, Lord Treasurer, Duke of Albemarle, G. Carteret, W. Coventry, Morrice. Nobody beginning, I did, and made a current and, I thought, a good speech, laying open the ill state of the Navy – by the greatness of the debt – greatness of work to do against next year – the time and materials it would take – and our incapacity, through a total want of money. I had no sooner done, but Prince Rupert rose up and told the King in a heat that whatever the gentleman had said, he had brought home his fleet in as good a condition as ever any fleet was brought home – that twenty boats would be as many as the fleet would want – and all the anchors and cables left in the storm might be taken up again.[1] This arose from my saying, among other things we had to do, that the fleet was come in, the greatest fleet that ever his Majesty had yet together, and that in as bad condition as the enemy or weather could put it. And to use Sir W. Penn's words, who is upon the place taking a Survey, he dreads the reports he is to receive from the Surveyors of its defects.[2] I therefore did only answer that I was sorry for his Highness's offence,[a] but that what I said was but the report we received from those entrusted in the fleet to inform us. He muttered, and repeated what he had said; and so after a long silence on all hands, nobody, not so much as the Duke of Albemarle, seconding the Prince, nor taking notice of what he said, we withdrew. I was not a little troubled at this passage; and the more, when speaking with Jacke Fenn about it, he told me that the Prince will now be asking[b] who this Pepys[3] is, and find him to be a creature of my Lord Sandwiches, and therefore this was done only to disparage him. Anon they broke up and Sir W. Coventry came out, so I asked his advice: he told me he had said something to salve it, which was that his Highnesse had, he believed, rightly informed the King that the fleet is in

a repl. 'what'   *b* preceded by 'will be asking now'

---

1. For their recovery (off Dungeness), see *CSPD 1666–7*, p. 204; Allin, i. 297.

2. Penn (writing from the *Katherine* yacht, at the Nore buoy) had sent a pessimistic report to the Board on the 5th: *CSPD 1666–7*, p. 185.

3. The name is here written in shorthand. Cf. above, vi. 173 & n. 1.

good condition to have stayed out yet longer, and hath fought the enemy; but yet that Mr. Pepys his meaning might be that though in so good condition, if they should come in and lie all the winter, we shall be very loath to send them to sea for another year's service with[out] great repairs. He said it would be no hurt if I went to him and showed him the report himself brought up from the fleet, where every ship, by the commander's report, doth need more or less – and not to mention more of Sir W. Penn for doing him a mischief; so I said I would – but do not think that all this will redound to my hurt, because the truth of what I said will soon appear. Thence, having been informed that after all this pains the King hath found out how to supply us with 5 or 6000*l*, when 100000*l* were at this time but absolutely necessary, and we mentioned 50000*l* – this*ᵃ* is every day a greater and greater omen of Ruine – God fit us for it – Sir J. Mennes and I home (it raining) by coach (calling only on Sir G. Carteret at his lodging, who is, I find, troubled at my Lord Treasurer and Sir Ph. Warwick bungling in his accounts);[1] and being come home to supper, with my father, and then all to bed. I made my brother in his Cassocke to say grace this day, but I like his voice so ill, that I begin to be sorry he hath taken this order upon him.

8. Up, and to my office, called up by Comissioner Middleton, newly come to town, but stayed not with me. So I to my office, busy all the morning. Towards noon by water to Westminster-hall, and there by several hear that the Parliament doth resolve to do something to retrench Sir G. Carteret's great salary[2] – but cannot hear of anything bad they can lay to his charge. The House did this day order to be ingrossed the bill against importing Irish cattle – a thing, it seems, carried on by

a   repl. 'which'

---

1. For Southampton's inefficiency, see above, vi. 218 & n. 1.
2. This was possibly a resolution of the Commons' committee on war expenses which reported on the 11th; it is not recorded in the *Journals*. The Treasurer (much the best paid of the

Principal Officers of the Navy) had received a fixed stipend of £2000 p.a. in 1660–2, but since then had been paid by the traditional and more lucrative method of fees, allowances and poundage. After 1668 a salary was paid; details in *Cat.*, i. 8, n. 3,

the Westerne parliament-men, wholly against the sense[a] of most of the rest of the House; who think if you do this, you give the Irish again cause to rebel.[1] Thus, plenty on both sides makes us mad. The Committee of the Canary Company, several of both factions, came to me for my Cosen Roger that is of the Committee.[2] Thence with W. Coventry when the House rose, and W. Batten, to St. James's, and there agreed of and signed our paper of extraordinaries;[3] and there left them, and I to Unthankes, where Mr. Falconbriges girl is; and by and by comes my wife – who likes her well, though I confess I cannot (though she be of my finding out and sings pretty well), because she will be raised from so mean a condition to so high, all of a sudden. But she will be much to our profit, more then Mercer, less expense. Here we bespoke a new gown for her, and to come to us on Friday. She being gone, my wife and I home by coach; and then I presently by water with Mr. Pierce[4] to Westminster-hall – he in the way telling me how the Duke of York and Duke of

a repl. 'since'

---

1. *CJ*, viii. 632. The bill to prohibit the import of Irish fat cattle had been introduced in 1663 and was promoted by the enemies of Clarendon and Ormond, led by Buckingham. For its passage, see below, 18 January 1667. The division of opinion was now close, the government being against it, and recommittal had been voted on 5 October by a majority of four: ib., p. 631. Welsh members and those from the west and north of England were strongly for it, in the belief that the prohibition would raise the value of English cattle, and increase rents, which had been falling. They represented the 'breeding' interest. The counties which thrived on fattening Irish cattle (the 'feeding' land) – especially Norfolk and Suffolk – opposed the bill, together with the Londoners, who represented the biggest con-

sumers' market. BM, Add. 4706, ff. 39–40; *CSP Ireland, 1666–9*, pp. 533–42; Milward, pp. 3–4, 9, 47; Clarendon, *Life*, iii. 155+.

2. The agitation against the Canary Company (incorporated 17 March 1665) ended in the revocation of its charter in 1667. On 1 October 1666 a petition had been presented by a group of merchants aggrieved by the monopoly, and the Commons had appointed a committee of 35 which included 'both factions' – both opponents and supporters of the company. Its report (29 October) was hostile, and a conference with the Lords was held in December to gain their concurrence. On 18 September 1667 the King cancelled the patent. See *EHR*, 31/529+. For Clarendon's part in the affair, see below, p. 342.

3. See above, p. 308, n. 3.

4. Surgeon to the Duke of York.

Albemarle do not agree. The Duke of York is wholly given up to this bitch of Denham. The Duke of Albemarle and Prince Rupert do less agree. So that we are all in pieces, and nobody knows what will be done the next year. The King hath yesterday in council declared his resolution of setting a fashion for clothes, which he will never alter.[1] It will be a vest, I know not well how. But it is to teach the nobility thrift, and will do good. By and by comes down from the Comittee W. Coventry, and I find him troubled at several things happened this afternoon – which vexes me also; our business looking worse and worse, and our work growing on our hands – time spending, and no money to set anything in hand with; the end whereof must be speedy ruine. The Duch insult,* and have taken off Bruants head, which they have not dared to do (though found guilty of the fault he did die for, of something of the Prince of Oranges faction) till just now[2] – which speaks more confidence in our being worse then before. Alderman Maynell, I hear, is dead.[3] Thence returned in the dark by coach all alone, full of thoughts of the consequences of this ill complexion of affairs, and how to save myself and the little I have; which if I can do, I have cause to bless God that I am so well, and shall be well contented to retreat to Brampton and spend the rest of my days there. So to my office, and did some business and finished my Journall, with resolutions, if God bless me, to apply myself soberly to settle all matters for myself and expect the event of all with comfort. So home to supper and to bed.

---

1. See below, p. 324 & n. 3. There is no entry about this in the Privy Council Register; presumably the announcement was made at a meeting of the Committee for Foreign Affairs.

2. Henri Fleury de Culan, Heer van Buat, once a member of the household of William II of Orange, was in Arlington's pay, and had been engaged in an attempt to start negotiations for peace with England. He had been arrested on a charge of treason on 8 August but his trial had been delayed by the discovery that several members of the States-General had been involved in the conspiracy with him. Buat was sentenced on 30 September and executed on 1 October. (The execution was reported in the *London Gazette* published on the day of this entry.) His death meant a defeat for the Orangists and a closer alliance between the republican government and the French. *London Gazette*, 27 August, 13, 24 September, 8 October; Feiling, pp. 197+.

3. Francis Meynell, goldsmith, died on the 6th.

9. Up and to the office, where we sat, the first day since the fire I think.[1] At noon home, and my uncle Tho was there, dined with my brother and I (my father and wife was gone abroad); and then to the office again in the afternoon, and there close all day long – and did much business. At night to W. Batten, where Sir R Ford did occasion some discourse of sending a convoy to the Maderas; and this did put us upon some new thoughts of sending our privateer thither on merchants accounts, which I have more mind to – the profit being certain, and occasion honest withal.[a] [2] So home, and to supper with my father; and then to set my remainder of my books gilt in order, with much pleasure; and so late to bed.

10. *Fast day for the Fire.* Up, with Sir W. Batten by water to White-hall, and anon had a meeting before Duke of York; where pretty to see how Sir W. Batten, that carried the Surveys of all the fleet with him to show their ill condition to Duke of York, when he found the Prince there, did not speak one word, though the meeting was of his asking, for nothing else. And when I asked him, he told me he knew the Prince too well to anger him – so that he was afeared to do it. Thence with him to Westminster to the parish church, where the parliament-men, and Stellingfleete in the pulpit[3] – so full, no standing there; so he and I to eat herrings at the Dog tavern. And then to church again, and then was Mr. Frampton in the pulpit they cry up so much – a young man, and of mighty[b] ready tongue.[4] I heard a little of his sermon, and liked it, but the crowd so great, I could

a MS. 'with trouble'   *b* MS. 'my'

1. There had been 'a little meeting' on 29 September: above, p. 301.
2. The *Flying Greyhound*, however, went privateering. See above, p. 301, n. 1; below, p. 360, n. 3.
3. His sermon (at St Margaret's) was on Amos, iv. 11; printed as *A sermon preached before the House of Commons Octob. 10; being the fast-day appointed for the late dreadfull fire* (1666); reprinted in his *Sermons preached on several occasions* (1673), pp.

1–22. The fast had been appointed by a proclamation of 13 September: Steele, no. 3474. Service in *A form of common prayer . . .* [for] *a day of fasting and humiliation in consideration of the late dreadful fire.*

4. Robert Frampton was now 44. On 20 January 1667 he delivered the best sermon Pepys had ever heard. In 1680 he became Bishop of Gloucester. None of his sermons appears to have been published.

not stay; so to the Swan, and baisai la fille[1] and drank, and then home by coach and took father, wife, brother, and W. Hewer to Islington, where I find mine Host dead.[2] Here eat and drank, and merry; and so home and to the office a while. And then to Sir W. Batten to talk a while, and with Captain Cocke into the office to hear his news, who is mighty conversant with Garraway and those people; who tells me what they object as to the Mal=administracion of things as to money – but that they mean well, and will do well; but their reckonings are very good, and show great faults, as I will here insert here. They say the King hath had towards this war expressly, thus much:[3]

Royall Ayde	2450000*l*
more	1250000.
Three months' tax given the King by a power of raising a month's tax of 70000*l* every year for three years	0210000.
Customes, out of which the King did promise to pay 240000*l*, which for two years comes to	0480000.
Prizes, which they moderately reckon at	0300000.
A debt declared by the Navy, by us	0900000.
	5590000.
The whole charge of the Navy, as we state it for two years and a month, hath been but	3200000.
So what then is become of all this sum?	2390000.

He and I did bemoan our public condition. He tells me the Duke of Albemarle is under a cloud, and they have a mind at

---

1. Sarah Udall, of the Swan, New Palace Yard.
2. Pitt, of the King's Head.
3. The accounts covered 1 September 1664–30 September 1666: see above, p. 294 & n. 1. Further figures are in Milward, pp. 26–7; *CJ*, viii. 634. The committee's report was accepted 'with favour' by the House on the 11th: Milward, p. 20. Pepys kept a copy of it given to him (on 8 February 1678) by Sir William Lowther, chairman of the committee: PL 2266, no. 151. Another copy is in BM, Harl. 6277, pp. 3–6.

Court to lay him aside. This I know not, but all things I believe are not right with him – and I am glad of it, but sorry for the time. So home to supper and to bed – it being my wedding night; but how many years I cannot tell, but my wife says ten.[1]

11. Up, and discoursed with my father of my sending some money for safety into the country, for I am in pain what to do with what*a* I have. I did give him money, poor man, and he overjoyed. So left him, and to the office, where nothing but sad evidences of ruine coming on us for want of money. So home to dinner,*b* which was a very good dinner, my father, brother, wife and I; and then to the office again, where I was all the afternoon till very late, busy; and then home to supper and to bed.

《*Memorandum.*》*c* I had taken my Journall during the fire and the disorders fallowing in loose papers until this very day, and could not get time to enter them in my book till January 18 in the morning, having made my eyes sore by frequent attempts this winter to do it. But now it is done, for which I thank God, and pray never the like occasion may happen.

12. Up, and after taking leave of my poor father, who is setting out this day for Brampton by the Cambrige coach, he having taken a journey to see the city burned and to bring my brother to town – I out by water; and so [by] coach to St. James's, the weather being foul – and there from Sir W. Coventry do hear how the House hath cut us off 150000*l* of our wear and tear – for that which was saved by the King while the fleet lay in harbour in winter. However, he seems pleased, and so am I, that they have abated no more – and do intend to allow of 28000 men for the next*d* year; and this day have*e* appointed to declare the sum they will give the King, and to propose the way of raising it – so that this is likely to be the great day.[2] After

a repl. 'it'   *b* repl. 'supper'
c crowded into bottom of the page; written on or after 18 January 1667
d repl. 'one'   *e* repl. 'to'

---

1. Presumably a mistake for eleven: see above, ii. 194 & n. 3.
2. A committee of the whole this day voted a supply of £1,800,000, but postponed the vote on ways and means: *CJ*, viii. 635.

done*ᵃ* in his chamber, I with him to Westminster-hall and there took a few turns, the Hall mighty full of people and the House likely to be very full today about the money business. Here I met with several people, and do find that people have a mighty mind to have a fling at the vice chamberlain, if they could lay hold of anything, his place being endeed too much for such, they think, or any single subject of no greater parts and quality then he to enjoy. But I hope he may weather all – though it will not be by any dexterity of his, I dare say, if he do stand, but by his fate only, and people's being taken off by other things. Thence home by coach, mighty dirty weather, and then to the Treasurer's office and got a ticket paid for my little Michell;[1] and so again by coach to Westminster, and came presently after the House rose; so to the Swan, and there sent for a piece of meat, and dined alone and played with Sarah; and so to the Hall a while, and thence to Mrs. Martin's lodging and did what I would with her. She is very big, and resolves I must be godfather. Thence away by water with Cropp[2] to Deptford. It was almost night before I got thither, so I only did give direction concerning a press that I have making there, to hold my turning and Joyners tooles that were lately given me, which will be very handsome;[3] and so away back again, it being now dark; and so home, and there find my wife come home and hath brought her new Girle I have helped her to of Mr. Falconbrige's. She is wretched poor and but ordinary favoured, and we fain to lay out seven or eight pound-worth of clothes*ᵇ* upon her back, which methinks doth go against my heart, and do not think I can ever esteem her as I could have done another that had come fine and handsome; and*ᶜ* which is more, her voice, for want of use, is so Furr'd, that it doth not at present please me;[4] but her manner of singing is such, that I shall, I think, take great pleasure in it. Well, she is come, and I wish us good fortune in her.

        a repl. 'part'   *b* repl. 'cloth'   *c* repl. 'but'

---

1. Cf. above, pp. 174–5 & n.
2. A waterman.
3. For the gift, see above, p. 245. The press would probably be made by Simpson, the master-joiner at Deptford yard who had just made two

bookcases for Pepys (see above, p. 214 & n. 4).
4. Her name (by a happy chance) was Barker. She stayed until 13 May 1667.

Here I met with notice of a meeting of the Commissioners for Tanger tomorrow, and so I must have my accounts ready for them; which caused me to confine myself to my chamber presently and set to the making up my accounts, which I find very clear, but with much difficulty, by reason of my not doing them sooner, things being out of my mind. It cost me ⟪13.⟫ till 4 a-clock in the morning; and which was pretty, to think I was above an hour, after*a* I had made all right, in casting up of about twenty sums, being dozed with much work, and had for 40 times together forgot to carry the 60 which I had in my mind in one denomination*b* which exceeded 60 – and this did confound me for above an hour together. At last all even and done, and so*c* to bed.

Up at 7, and so to the office, after looking over my last night's work. We sat all the morning. At noon by coach with my Lord Brouncker and light at the Temple, and so alone I to dinner at a Cookes, and thence to my Lord Bellasses,[1] whom I find kind; but he had drawn some new proposal to deliver to the Lords Commissioners today, wherein one was that the garrison would not be well paid without some goldsmith's undertaking the paying of the bills of exchange for tallies. He professing so much kindness to me, and saying that he would not be concerned in the garrison without me, and that if he continued in that imployment, no man should have to do with the money but myself, I did ask his Lordships meaning of that proposition in his paper: he told me he had not much considered it, but that he meant no harm to me; I told him I thought it would render me useless; whereupon he did very frankly (after my seeming denials for a good while) cause it to be writ over again, and that clause left out – which did satisfy me abundantly. It being done, he and I together to White-hall, and there the Duke of York (who is gone over to all his pleasures again, and leaves off care of business, what with his woman, my Lady Denham, and his hunting three times a week) was just come in from hunting. So I stood and saw him dress himself and try on his Vest, which is the King's new fashion,[2] and will be in it for good and all on Monday

---

a repl. 'in'   *b* repl. 'demom'-   *c* repl. 'wrote fair all'

---

1. Governor of Tangier.   2. See below, p. 324 & n. 3.

next, the whole Court: it is a fashion the King says he will never change. He being ready, he and my Lord Chancellor and Duke of Albemarle and Prince Rupert, Lord Bellasses, Sir H. Cholmly, Povy, and myself met at a committee for Tanger. My Lord Bellasses propositions were read and discoursed of, about reducing the garrison to less charge. And endeed, I am mad in love with my Lord Chancellor, for he doth comprehend and speak as well, and with the greatest easiness and authority, that ever I saw man in my life. I did never observe how much easier a man doth speak, when he knows all the company to be below him, then in him; for though he spoke endeed excellent well, yet his manner and freedom of doing it, as if he played with it and was informing only all the rest of the company, was mighty pretty.[1] He did call again and again upon Mr. Povy for his accounts. I did think fit to make the solemn tender of my accounts that I entended. I said somethink*a* that was liked, touching *b* the want of money and the bad Creditt of our tallies. My Lord Chancellor moved that without any trouble to any of the rest of the Lords, I might alone attend the King when he was with his private council, and open the state of the garrison's want of credit; and all that could be done, should. Most things moved were referred to committees, and so we broke up; and at the end Sir W. Coventry came, so I away with him and he discoursed with me something of the Parliament's business. They have voted giving the King*c* for the next year, 1800000*l*; which, were it not for his debts, were a great sum. He says he thinks the House may say no more to us for the present, but that we must mend our manners against the next trial – and mend them we will. But he thinks it is not a fit time to be found making of trouble among ourselfs,*d* meaning about Sir J. Mennes, who most certainly must be removed, or made a Commissioner and some-body else Controller. But he tells me that the House hath a great envy at Sir G. Carteret – and that had he ever thought fit in all his discourse to have touched upon the point of our want

a phonetic spelling   *b* repl. 'one of my'   *c* MS. 'giving'   *d* repl. 'other'

---

1. Cf. Burnet: 'He spake well, his style had no flaw in it, but had a just mixture of wit and sense, only he spoke too copiously' (*Hist.*, *Supp.*, ed. Foxcroft, p. 53).

of money and badness of payments, it would have been laid
hold on to Sir G. Carteret's hurt; but he hath avoided it, though
without much reason for it, most studiously; and in short, did
end thus: that he hath never shown so much of the pigeon in
all his life as in his innocence to Sir G. Carteret at this time –
which I believe, and will desire Sir G. Carteret to thank him for it.
So we broke up, and I by coach home, calling for a new pair of
shoes; and so, little being to do at the office, did go home;
and after spending a little at righting some of my books which
stood out of order, I to bed.

14. *Lords day.* Lay long in bed, among other things, talking
of my wife's renewing her acquaintance with Mrs. Pierce, which,
by my wife's ill using her when she was here last, hath been
interrupted.[1] Herein we were a little angry together, but
presently friends again; and so up, and I to church – which was
mighty full, and my beauties, Mrs. Lethulier and fair Batelier,
both there. A very foul morning – rained, and sent for my
cloak to go out of the church with. So dined, and after dinner
and good discourse thereat, to my brother; he and I by water to
White-hall, and he to Westminster Abbey. Here I met with
Sir Steph. Fox, who told me how much right I had done myself
and how well it was represented by the committee to the House,
my readiness to give them satisfaction in everything when they
were at the office. I was glad of this. He did further discourse
of Sir W. Coventry's great abilities, and how necessary it were
that I were of the House to assist him.[2] I did not own it, but
do myself think it were not unnecessary, if either he should die
or be removed to the Lords,[3] or anything to hinder his doing
the like service the next trial – which makes me think that it
were not a thing*a* very unfit – but I will not move in it. He and
I parted, I to Mrs. Martins, thinking to have met Mrs. Burrows,

a   repl. same symbol badly formed

---

1. See above, pp. 236–7.
2. Coventry already had the assistance in the House of Batten, Carteret
and Penn. Pepys did not try to enter
Parliament until late in 1669 (when he
unsuccessfully contested Aldeburgh,

Suff.) and did not become a member
until 1673, when he was elected for
Castle Rising, Norf.
3. There had been a rumour in May
1666 that Coventry would be made a
peer: *CSPD 1665–6*, p. 398.

but she was not there; so away, and took my brother out of the Abbey and home, and there to set some accounts right, and to the office to even my Journall, and so home to supper and to bed.

15. Called up, though a very rainy morning, by Sir H. Cholmly, and he and I most of the morning together, evening of accounts, which I was very glad of. Then he and I out to Sir Robt. Viner's at the Affrican-house[1] (where I had not been since he came thither) but he was not there; but I did some business with his people, and then to Colvill's, who I find lives now in Lymestreete – and with the same credit as ever – this fire having not done them any wrong that I hear of at all.[2] Thence he and I together to Westminster-hall – in our way talking of matters and passages of state. The viciousness of the Court. The contempt the King brings himself into thereby. His minding nothing, but doing all things just as his people about him will have it. The Duke of York becoming a slave to this whore Denham – and wholly minds her. That there really was amours between the Duchesse and Sidny.[3] That there is reason to fear that as soon as the Parliament have raised this money,[4] the King will see that he hath got all that he can get, and then make up a peace. He tells me, which I wonder at but that I find it confirmed by Mr. Pierce, whom I met by and by in the Hall, that Sir W. Coventry is of the Caball with the Duke of York and Brouncker, with this Lady Denham, which is a shame and I am sorry for it; and that Sir W. Coventry doth make her visits. But yet I hope it is not so. Pierce tells me that, as little agreement as there is between the Prince and Duke of Albemarle, yet they are likely to go to sea again – for the first will not be trusted alone, and nobody will go with him but this Duke of Albemarle. He tells me much, how all the commanders of the fleet and officers that are sober men do cry out upon their bad discipline, and the ruine that must fallow it if it continue. But that which I wonder most at, it seems their secretaries have been the most exorbitant in their fees to all sorts of people, that it is not to be believed that they durst do it, so as it is believed they

1. Vyner's city house in Lombard St had been destroyed by the Fire. (R).

2. Cf. above, p. 287 & n. 2.

3. See above, p. 8 & n. 1.

4. The vote of £1,800,000: see above, p. 318, n. 2.

Y

have got 800*l* apiece by the very vacancies in the fleet.[1] He tells me that Lady Castlemayne is concluded to be with child again.[2] And that all the people about the King do make no scruple of saying that the King doth lie with Mrs. Stuart, whom he says is a most excellent-natured lady. This day the King begins to put on his Vest, and I did see several persons of the House of Lords, and Commons too, great courtiers, who are in it – being a long Cassocke close to the body, of black cloth and pinked with white silk under it, and a coat over it, and the legs ruffled with black riband like a pigeon's leg – and upon the whole, I wish the King may keep it, for it is a very fine and handsome garment.[3] Walking with Pierce in the Court of Wards, out comes Sir W. Coventry and he and I talked of business. Among others, I proposed the making Sir J. Mennes a Commissioner, and make somebody else Controller. He tells me it is the thing he hath been thinking of, and hath spoke to the Duke of York of it, and he believes it will be done. But that which I

1. James Hayes was secretary to Rupert, and Matthew Locke to Albemarle. On a much smaller scale, Pepys had himself made money by this means: above, i. 90.

2. She had given birth to a son in 1665 (later the Duke of Northumberland), but her sixth child by Charles (a daughter, Barbara, later a nun) was not born until 1672.

3. Cf. above, p. 315. The costume was in two senses a war measure, being both economical and anti-French. Evelyn describes the King as first appearing in it on 18 October, 'changing doublet, stiff collar, bands and Cloake etc: into a comely Vest, after the *Persian* mode with girdle or shash, & Shoe strings & Garters, into bouckles, of which some were set with precious stones . . .'. According to Rugge (ii, f. 179r) it was 'a close coat of Cloath pinkt with a taffety under the cutts this in length reachd the calf of the legg and upon that a sercoat cutt att the brest which hung loose and shorter then the vest six inches the breeches the Spanish cutt and buskins some of Cloath and som of leather but of the same colour as the vest or Garment, of never inn like fashion since William the Conqueror . . .'. Both Rugge and Anthony Wood (*L. & T.*, ii. 90) state that the King first wore the costume on the 14th, but Pepys's statement is probably to be preferred. Several courtiers had wagered that the King would soon abandon it and the King was said to have accepted the bet at 100 to 1: Evelyn, 18 October; A. Browning, *Danby*, ii. 17. Description (by E. S. de Beer, with illustrations) in *Journ. Warburg Inst.*, 2/105–15; Cunnington, pp. 133–4, fig. 62. Cf. Marvell, *The Kings vowes*, ll. 49–51. Pepys very soon bought an outfit for himself: see below, p. 353. It became the prototype of the later coat and waistcoat, displacing jerkin and doublet, and was worn until c. 1670–2. For the story of Louis XIV's countermeasure, see below, p. 379 & n. 4.

fear is that Pen will be Controller, which I shall grudge a little – the Duke of Buckingham called him aside and spoke a good while with him, I did presently fear it might be to discourse something of his design to blemish my Lord of Sandwich, in pursuance of the wild motion he made the other day in the House.[1] Sir W. Coventry, when he came to me again, told me that he had wrought a miracle, which was the convincing the Duke of Buckingham that something (he did not name what) that he had entended to do was not fit to be done, and that the Duke is gone away of that opinion. This makes me verily believe it was something like what I feared.

By and by the House rose, and then we parted; and I with Sir G. Carteret and walked in the Exchequer Court, discoursing of businesses. Among others, I observing to him how friendly Sir W. Coventry[a] had carried himself to him in these late enquiries, when, if he had borne him any spleen, he could have had what occasion he pleased offered him – he did confess he found the same thing, and would thank him for it.

I did give him some other[b] advices, and so away with him to his lodgings at White-hall to dinner, where my Lady is – and mighty kind, both of them, to me. Their son and my Lady Jemimah will be here very speedily. She tells me the ladies are to go into a new fashion shortly; and that is to wear short coats above their anckles[2] – which she nor I do not like, but conclude this long Trayne to be mighty graceful. But she cries out of the vices of the Court, and how they're going to set up playes already.[3] And how the next day after the late great fast, the Duchesse of York did give the King and Queen a play. Nay, she told me that they have heretofore had plays at Court the very nights before the fast for the death of the late King.

---

a repl. 'WC'   *b* repl. 'thing'

---

1. See above, p. 309. For the replacement of Mennes, see below, 20 January 1667 & n.

2. The Queen favoured this fashion: below, p. 335.

3. On 18 October Evelyn saw a performance of *Mustapha* at the Cockpit, the royal private theatre adjoining Whitehall Palace. For the reopening of the theatres after the Fire, see below p. 341, n. 3. (A).

She doth much cry out upon these things, and that which she believes will undo the whole nation – and I fear so too.

After dinner away home, Mr. Brisband along with me as far as the Temple; and there looked upon a new book, set out by one Rycault, secretary to my Lord Winchelsea, of the policy and customs of the Turkes, which is it seems much cried up[1] – but I could not stay; but home, where I find Balty come back, and with him some ⟨muster⟩ books, which I am glad of, and hope he will do me credit in his imployment. By and by took coach again, and carried him home and my wife to her tailor's, while I to White-hall to have found out Povy; but miss him, and so call my wife and home again – where at Sir W. Batten I met Sir W. Penn, lately come from the fleet at the Nore; and here was many goodfellows, among others, Sir R. Holmes, who is exceeding kind to me, more then usual; which makes me afeared of him,[a] though I do much wish his friendship. Thereupon, after a little stay, I withdrew, and to the office[b] awhile; and then home to supper, and to my chamber to settle a few papers, and then to bed.

This day the great debate was in Parliament the manner of raising the 1800000*l* they voted him on Friday.[2] And at last, after many proposals, one moved that the Chimny-money might be taken from the King and an equal revenue of something else might be found for the King – and people be enjoined to buy off this Tax of Chimny-money for ever, at eight years' purchase, which will raise present money, as they think, 1600000*l* – and the State eased of an ill burthen, and the King be supplied of something as good or better for his use.[3] The House seems to like this, and put off the debate to tomorrow.

a repl. 'it'   *b* MS. 'office and'

---

1. *The present state of the Ottoman Empire By Paul Rycaut, Esq. secretary to his Excellency the Earl of Winchilsea, Embassadour Extraordinary for His Majesty Charles the Second etc. to Sultan Mahomet Han the Fourth, Emperour of the Turks.* Pepys bought it on 8 April 1667.

2. Reported in Milward, pp. 23–4.

3. The unpopular hearth-tax dated from 1662 and was part of the revenue granted to the Crown in perpetuity. Hence the need for compensation. But the project failed and the tax was not abolished until 1689. Other debates on the method of raising supply are noted below, pp. 330, 331, 332, 356, 387–8, 408–9.

16. Up, and to the office, where sat to do little business but hear clamours for money. At noon home to dinner, and to the office again, after hearing my brother play a little upon the Lyra viall, which he doth so as to show that he hath a love to Musique and a spirit for it – which I am well pleased with. I all the afternoon at the office, and at night with Sir W. Batten, W. Penn, J. Mennes at W. Penn's lodgings, advising about business and orders fit presently to make about*a* discharging of ships come into the river, and which to pay first, and many things in order thereto. But it vexed me, that it being now past 7 a-clock, and the businesses of great weight and I had done them by 8 a-clock and sending them to be signed, they were all gone to bed, and Sir W. Penn, though awake, would not, being in bed, have them brought him to sign. This made me quite angry.

Late at work at the office, and then home to supper and to bed.

Not come to any resolution at the Parliament today about the manner of raising this 1800000*l*.[1]

17. Up, and busy about public and private business all the morning at the office. At noon home to dinner, alone with my brother, with whom I had now the first private talk I have had, and find he hath preached but twice in his life. I did give him some advice to study pronunciation; but I do fear he will never make a good speaker – nor, I fear, any general good scholar – for I do not see that he minds Optickes or Mathematics of any sort, nor anything else that I can find – I know not what he may be at divinity and ordinary school-learning. However, he seems sober, and that pleases me. After dinner took him and my wife and Barker (for so is our new woman called, and is yet but a sorry girl) and set them down at Unthankes; and so to Whitehall and there find some of my brethren with the Duke of York; but so few, I put*b* off the meeting. We stood and heard the Duke discourse, which he did mighty scurrilously, of the French, and with reason; that they should give Beaufort orders, when he was to bring, and did bring, his fleet hither, that his Rendevous of his

a repl. 'above'   *b* repl. same symbol badly formed

---

1. The Commons debated whether to choose a land-tax or a general excise: Milward, p. 25.

fleet and for all sluggs to come to should be between Calais and Dover – which did prove the taking of La Roche, who, among other slugs behind, did by their instructions make for that place to Rendevous with the fleet.[1]   And Beaufort, seeing them as he was returning, took them for the English fleet, and wrote word to the King of France that he had passed by the English fleet and the English fleet durst[a] not meddle with him.

The Court is all full of Vests; only, my Lord St. Albans not pinked, but plain black – and they say the King says the pinking upon white makes them look too much like magpyes, and therefore hath bespoke one of plain velvet.   Thence to St. James by coach, and spoke, at 4 a-clock or 5, with Sir W. Coventry, newly come from the House, where they have sat all this day and not come to an end of the debate how the money shall be raised. He tells me that what I proposed to him the other day was what he had himself thought on and determined, and that he believes it will speedily be done: the making Sir J. Mennes a Commissioner and bringing somebody else to be Controller, and that (which doth not please me I confess, for my own perticular, so well as Sir J. Mennes) will I fear be Sir W. Penn, for he is the only fit man for it.

Away from him, and took up my wife and left her at Templebar[b] to buy some lace for a petticoat, and I took coach and away to Sir R Viner's about a little business; and then home, and by and by to my chamber and there late alone, making up an account for the Board to pass tomorrow, if I can get them, for the clearing all my imprest bills; which, if I can do, will be to my very good satisfaction.   Having done this, then to supper and to bed.

18.   Up and to the office, where we sat all the morning.   The waters so high in the road by the late rains, that our letters came

---

a   repl. 'would not m' –   *b*   repl. 'the'

---

1. For Beaufort's movements, see above, pp. 288, 300 & nn. He sailed out from La Rochelle to join de Ruyter in the Channel, but when off Dieppe was ordered back into port, the French authorities fearing that the Dutch fleet was going to leave him unsupported: Allin, vol. ii, pp. xxxiii-iv. La Roche, captain of the *Rubis*, was one of the 'slugs' (stragglers) captured by Allin on 18 September: see below, p. 350 & n. 1.

not in till today; and now I understand that my father is got well home, but had a painful journy of it.

At noon with Lord Brouncker to St. Ellens, where the master of the late Pope's-head tavern[1] is now set up again, and there dined at Sir W. Warren's cost, a very good dinner. Here my Lord Brouncker proffered to carry me and my wife in to a play at Court tonight, and to lend me his coach home; which tempted me much, but I shall not do it. Thence rose from table before dinner ended, and homewards, met my wife, and so away by coach toward Lovetts (in the way wondering at what a good pretty wench our Barker makes, being now put into good clothes and fashionable[2] at my charge, but it becomes her so, that I do not now think much of it, and is an example of the power of good clothes and dress), where I stood godfather. But it was pretty that being a Protestant, a man stood by and was my proxy to answer for me. A priest christened it, and the boy's name is Samuel. The ceremonies many, and some foolish. The priest in a gentleman's dress, more then my own; but is a Capuchin, one of the Queen-mother's priests.[3] He did give my proxy and the woman-proxy (my Lady Bills, absent, had a proxy also) good advice to bring up the child, and at the end, that he ought never to marry the child nor the godmother, nor the godmother the child, or the godfather. But which is strange, they say that the mother of the child and the godfather may marry. This is strange.[4] By and by the Lady[a] Bills came in, a well-bred but crooked woman. The poor people of the house had good wine and a good cake; and she a pretty woman in her[b] lying-in dress. It cost me ⟨near⟩ 40s the whole christening: to midwife, 20s –

---

a repl. 'g'-   *b* repl. 'this'

---

1. The parish of St Helen's Bishopsgate had escaped the Fire. The Pope's Head Tavern, in Pope's Head Alley, off Lombard St, had been destroyed. Its landlord, John Sawyer, returned there after it was rebuilt on the same site. PRO, E 179/252/23, no f.; ib. 32(3), p. 1. (R).

2. For maids' dress, see above, vi. 238, n. 3.

3. It was usual for Roman Catholic priests to wear lay clothes to save themselves from prosecution.

4. The spiritual affinity between godparents was an impediment to valid marriage, but the mother and the godfather might marry if not connected by blood or marriage relationship.

nurse, 10*s* – maid, 2*s* 6*d*, and the coach, 5*s* – I was very well satisfied with what I have done; and so home and to the office, and thence to Sir W. Batten's and there hear how the business of buying off the chimney-money is passed in the House, and so the King to be satisfied some other way, and the King supplied with the money raised by this purchasing off of the chimneys.[1] So home, mightily pleased in mind that I have got my bills of imprest cleared by bills signed this day, to my good satisfaction. To supper and to bed.

19. Up, and by coach to my Lord Ashlys, and thence (he being gone out) to the Exchequer chamber, and there find him and my Lord Bellasses about my Lord Bellasses' accounts – which was the business I went upon. This was soon ended, and then I with Creed back home to my house, and there he and I did even accounts for salary.[2] And by that time dinner was ready, and merry at dinner and then abroad to Povy's, who continues as much confounded in all his businesses as ever he was; and would have had me paid money as*a* like a fool as himself, which I troubled him in refusing, but I did persist in it. After a little more discourse, I left them and to White-hall, where I met with Sir Rob. Viner, who told me a little of what in going home I had seen; also, a little of the disorder and mutiny among the seamen at the Treasurer's office[3] – which did trouble me then and all this day since, considering how many more seamen will come to town every day, and no money for them – a Parliament sitting – and the Exchange close by, and an enemy to hear of and laugh at it.

Viner too, and Backewell, were sent for this afternoon and

a repl. 'to'

---

1. A committee was appointed: *CJ*, viii. 627. Debate in Milward, pp. 27–8.

2. For Pepys's salary as Treasurer for Tangier, and Creed's as Secretary.

3. As a result of the disorders this day at the Navy Treasurer's, in Broad St, 24 soldiers were detailed to keep guard on pay-days, and a supply of

12 firelocks, with powder and bullets, was ordered for the Navy Office: *CSPD 1666–7*, p. 218; HMC, *Eliot Hodgkin*, pp. 167–8. In addition no seamen were to be sent up to London until their pay was ready for them: *Further Corr.*, p. 144. More riots occurred on 19 December.

was before*ᵃ* the King and his Cabinet about money; they declaring they would advance no more – it being discourse in the House of Parliament for the King to issue out his privy-seals to them to command them to trust him,[1] which gives them reason to decline trusting. But more money they are persuaded to lend, but so little, that (with horrour I speak it) coming after the Council was up, with Sir G. Carteret, Sir W. Coventry, Lord Brouncker, and myself, I did lay the state of our condition before the Duke of York. That the fleet could not go out without several*ᵇ* things it wanted and we could not have without money – perticularly broom and reed, which we had promised the man Swan[2] to help him to 200*l* of his debt, and a few other small sum[s] of 200*l* a-piece to some others.*ᶜ* And that I do foresee the Duke of York would call us to an account why the fleet is not abroad, and we cannot answer otherwise then our want of money. And that endeed we do not do the King any service now, but do rather abuse and betray his service, by being there and seeming to do something while we do not. Sir G. Carteret asked me (just in these words, for in this and all the rest I set down the very words for memory sake, if there should be occasion) whether 50 or 60*l* would do us any good; and when I told him the very broom-man must have 200*l*, he held up his eyes as if we had asked a million. Sir W. Coventry told the Duke of York plainly, he did rather desire to have his commission called in then serve in so ill a place, where he cannot do the King service; and I did concur in saying the same. This was all very plain, and the Duke of York did confess that he did not see how we could do anything without a present supply of 20000*l*, and that he would speak to the King next council-day, and I promised to wait on him to put him in mind of it. This I

---

a repl. ? 'mighty'   *b* repl. 'some'   *c* repl. same symbol

---

1. I.e. writs for a forced loan: a device used by Charles I, and condemned in parliament by the Petition of Right (1628). It was never used by Charles II.
2. Humphrey Swan; there are several payments of smaller sums to him, March–July, in PRO, Adm. 20/7, pt i. 93, 199. Broom and reed were used in fireships, as combustible material, and for cleaning ships' bottoms by singeing off the tar ('breaming').

set down for my future justification, if need be. And so we broke up, and all parted – Sir W. Coventry being not very well, but I believe made much worse by this night's sad discourse.[1]

So I home by coach, considering what the consequence of all this must be in a little time – nothing but distraction and confusion – which makes me wish with all my heart that I were well and quietly settled with what little I have got, at Brampton, where I might live peaceably and study and pray for the good of the King and my country.

Home, and to Sir W. Batten, where I saw my Lady, who is now come downstairs after a great sickness. Sir W. Batten was at the pay today, and tells me how rude the men were; but did go away quietly, being promised pay on Wednesday next. God send us money for it.

So to the office, and then to supper and to bed.

Among other things proposed in the House today to give the King in lieu of Chimnys, there was the bringing up of Sealed= paper, such as Sir J. Mennes showed me tonight at Sir W. Batten's is used in Spayne, and brings the King a great revenue.[2] But it shows what shifts we are put to, too much.

20. Up, and all the morning at the office, where none met but myself. So I walked a good while with Mr. Gauden in the garden, who is lately come from the fleet at the Buoy of the Nore. And he doth tell me how all the sober commanders, and even Sir Tho. Allen himself, do complain of the ill government of the fleet. How Holmes and Jenings have commanded all the fleet this year. That nothing is done upon deliberation, but if a sober man give his opinion otherwise then the Prince would have it, the Prince would cry, "Damn him, do you Fallow your orders, and that is enough for you!" He tells me he hears of nothing

1. Pepys told the 'melancholy story' of this interview with the Duke in a letter of the same day to Penn: *Further Corr.*, p. 144.

2. See *CJ*, viii. 639; for the abortive schemes to abolish the hearth-tax, see above, p. 326 & n. 3. The stamp-duty here referred to (proposed also in 1661–2 as an alternative to the hearth-tax) was not imposed until 1671: see below, pp. 408–9; E. Hughes in *EHR*, 56/234+. For the Spanish stamp-duty (introduced into Castile in 1636 and afterwards into the rest of the kingdom), see G. Desdevises du Dézert, *L'Espagne de l'ancien régime*, ii. 391.

but of swearing and drinking and whoring, and all manner of profaneness quite through the whole fleet.

He being gone, there comes to me Comissioner Middleton, whom I took on purpose to walk in the garden with me and to learn what he observed when the fleet was at Portsmouth. He says that the fleet was in such a condition as to discipline, as if the Devil hath commanded it – so much wickedness of all sorts.

Enquiring how it came to pass that so many ships miscarried this year, he tells me that he enquired, and the pilots do say that they dare not do nor go but as the captains will have them; and if they offer to do otherwise, the captains swear they will run them through.

He says that he heard Captain Digby (my Lord of Bristoll's son, a young fellow that never was but one year, if that, in the fleet) say that he did hope he should not see a tarpaulin have the command of a ship within this twelve months.[1]

He observed while he was on board the Admirall when the fleet was at Portsmouth, that there was a faction there. Holmes commanded all on the Prince's side, and Sir Jerem. Smith on the Dukes – and everybody that came did apply themselfs to one side or other. And when the Duke of Albemarle was gone away to come hither – then Sir Jer. Smith did hang his head and walked in the General's ship but like a private commander.

He says he was on board the Prince when the news came of the burning of London; and all the Prince said was that now Shipton's prophecy was out.[2] And he heard a young Commander presently swear that now a citizen's wife, that would not take under half-a-piece before, would now[a] be occupied for half-a-Crowne – and made mighty sport of it.

He says that Hubberd, that commanded this year the Admiral's ship, is a proud conceited fellow (though I thought otherwise of

a MS. 'not'

---

1. For the controversy about tarpaulins *versus* gentlemen-captains, see above, p. 11, n. 1.

2. 'Mother Shipton' was allegedly a prophetess of the early 16th century, but there is no trace of her before 1641 when a book of her prophecies was published. It is not true that she had

foretold the Fire of London, as many thought she had: cf. W. Sandys to Viscount Scudamore, 6 September 1666, qu. Bell, *Fire*, p. 361. But she had vaguely forecast the destruction of London from some unknown cause: *Mother Shiptons prophecies* (1663 ed.), p. 4.

him), and fit to command a single ship, but not a fleet; and he doth wonder that there hath not been more mischief this year then there hath. He says the fleet came to anchor between the Horse and the Island,[1] so that when they came to weigh, many of the ships could not turn, but run foul of the Horse and there stuck but that the weather was good.

He says that nothing can do the King more disservice, nor please the standing-officers[2] of the ship better, then these silly commanders that now we have, for they sign to anything that their*a* officers desire of them, nor have judgment to contradict them if they would.

He told me many good*b* things, which made me bless God that we have received no greater disasters this year then we have, though they have been the greatest that ever was known in England before, put all their losses of the King's ships by want of skill and seamanship together from the beginning.

He being gone, comes Sir G. Carteret, and he and I walked together awhile – discoursing upon the sad condition of the time, what need we have, and how impossible it is to get money.

He told me my Lord Chancellor the other day did ask him how*c* it came to pass that his friend Pepys doth so much magnify all things to worst, as I did on Sunday last, in the bad condition of the fleet. Sir G. Carteret tells me that he answered him that I was but the mouth of the rest, and spoke what they have dictated to me – which did, as he says, presently take off his displeasure. So that I am well at present with him, but I must have a care not to be over-busy in that office again – and burn my fingers.

He tells me he wishes he had sold his place at some good rate to somebody or other at the beginning of the war. And that he would*d* do it now, but nobody will deal with him for it.

He tells me the Duke of Albemarle is very much discontented – and the Duke of York doth not, it seems, please him.

He tells me that our case as to money is not to be made good

a repl. 'the com'- *b* repl. 'made'
c repl. 'why' *d* MS. 'could'

---

1. The Horse Sand (in Spithead) and the Isle of Wight. 2. See below, p. 410, n. 2.

at present, and therefore wishes a good and speedy peace before it be too late. And from his discourse methinks^a I find that there is something moving towards it.[1]

Many people at the office; but having no more of the office, I did put it off till the next meeting.^b

Thence with Sir G. Carteret home to dinner, with him, my Lady and Mr. Ashburnham the cofferer. Here they talk that the Queene hath a great mind to alter her fashion and to have the feet seen, which she loves mightily – and they do believe that it [will] come into it in a little time.

Here I met with the King's Declaracion about his proceedings with the King of Denmarke – and perticularly the business of Bergen.[2] But it is so well writ, that if it be true – the King of Denmarke is one of the most absolute wickedness in the world for a person of his quality.

After dinner home, and there met Mr. Povy by appointment. And^c there he and I all the afternoon, till late at night, evening of all accounts between us – which we did to both our satisfaction. But that which troubles me most, is that I am to refund to the ignoble Lord Peterborough what he had given us six months ago – because we did not supply him with money.[3] But it is no great matter.

He gone, I to the office and there did some business; and so home, my mind in good ease by having done with Povy, in order^d to the adjusting of all my accounts in a few days.

So home to supper and to bed.

21. *Lords day.* Up, and with my wife to church, and her new woman Barker with her the first time. The girl will I think do very well.

a repl. 'methought'   *b* repl. 'day'
c repl. 'But did it to find what was the first'   *d* repl. same symbol

---

1. Attempts were now being made to separate the Dutch and the French, and to drive a bargain with the former: Feiling, pp. 209–10. No treaty was concluded until the following August.

2. *A true deduction of all transactions between his Majesty of Great Britain and the King of Denmark*; published on the occasion of the declaration of war on Denmark on 19 September 1666: *CSPD 1666–7*, p. 140. For the Bergen affair, see above, vi. 196, n. 1.

3. His Tangier pension: see above, iv. 94 & n. 1.

Here*ᵃ* a lazy sermon, and so home to dinner and took in my Lady Pen and Peg (Sir Wm being below[1] with the fleet), and mighty merry we were. And then after dinner, presently (it being a mighty foul day) I by coach to White-hall and there attended the Cabinet, and was called in before the King and them to give an account of our want of money for Tanger; which troubles me that it should be my place so often, and so soon after one another, to come to speak there of their wants, the thing of the world that they love least to hear of – and that which is no welcome thing to be the solicitor for. And to see how like an image the King sat, and could not speak one word when I had delivered myself, was very strange. Only, my Lord Chancellor did ask me whether I thought it was in nature at this time to help us to anything. So I was referred to another meeting of the Lords Commissioners for Tanger and my Lord Treasurer – and so went away. And by coach home, where I spent the evening in reading Stillingfleetes defence of the Archbishop, that part about Purgatory,[2] a*ᵇ* point I had never considered before what was said for it or against it. And though I do believe we are in the right, yet I do not see any great matter in this book.

So to supper; and my*ᶜ* people being gone most of them to bed – my boy and Jane and I did get two of my Iron chests out of the cellar into my closet, and the money, to my great satisfaction to see it there again, and the rather because the damp cellar spoils all my chests. This being done, and I weary, to bed.

This afternoon, walking with Sir H. Cholmly long in the gallery, he told me, among many other things, how young Harry Killigrew is banished the Court lately for saying that my Lady Castlemayne was a little lecherous girl when she was young,

---

a or 'Hear'   *b* repl. 'that'   *c* repl. 'to'

---

1. Down river at the Nore.
2. Edward Stillingfleet's *A rational account of the grounds of Protestant religion* (1665; PL 2325); a commentary on Archbishop Laud's book (1639) enlarging on his controversy in 1622 with the Jesuit John Fisher. In ch. vi of pt iii (pp. 636–54) Stilling-

fleet considers 'the advantage which comes to the Church of Rome by the doctrine of Purgatory'; the lack of patristic basis for it; 'the churches infallibility made at last the Foundation of the belief . . . , The Falsity of that Principle: and the whole concluded'.

and used to rub her thing with her fingers or against the end of forms, and that she must be rubbed with something else. This she complained to the King of – and he sent to the Duke of York, whose servant he is, to turn him away.[1] The Duke of York hath done it, but takes it ill of my Lady that he was not complained to first. She attended him to excuse it, but ill blood is made by it.

He told me how Mr. Williamson stood in a little place to have come into the House of Commons,[a] and they would not choose him; they said, "No Courtier!" And which is worse, Bab May went down in great state to Winchelsea with the Duke of York's letters, not doubting to be chosen, and there the people chose a private gentleman in spite of him, and cried out they would have no Court pimp to be their Burgesse – which are things that boade very ill.[b][2] This afternoon, I went to see, and sat a good while with[c] Mrs. Martin; and there was her sister Doll, with whom, contrary to all expectation, I did what I would, and might have done anything else.

22. Up, and by coach to Westminster-hall, there thinking to have met Betty Michell, who I heard yesterday stayed all night at her father's, but she was gone. So I stayed a little, and then

---

a repl. 'Parliament'   *b* '22' in margin struck through   *c* repl. 'what'

---

1. He was the son of Thomas Killigrew, sen., the dramatist, and a Groom of the Bedchamber to the Duke of York. Cf. the newsletter report (25 October) in HMC, *Rep.*, 7/1/485 in which he is said to have used 'raw words' against 'a lady of pleasure'. The King, writing to his sister Minette a year later, said of Killigrew, 'Have one caution of him, that you believe not one word he says of us here, for he a most notorious liar . . .' (C. H. Hartmann, *The King my brother*, p. 202).

2. In September Joseph Williamson (head of Arlington's secretariat) had been defeated at Morpeth, Northumberland, by, Lord Morpeth.

Cf. the account by his brother, who acted as his agent, in *CSPD Add. 1660–85*, p. 163: 'They say openly that after Sir George Downing no courtier nor stranger shall be chosen by them'. Baptist May (Groom of the Bedchamber to the Duke of York) was defeated at Winchelsea in early October by Robert Austin of Tenterden despite (or because of) the Duke's letter of recommendation. Williamson failed on two further occasions before being elected in 1669. These defeats were remarkable but not untypical: bye-elections (numerous at this time) were going heavily against the government.

down to the bridge by water and there overtook her and her father; so saluted her, and walked over London Bridge with them and there parted, the weather being very foul; and so to the Tower by water, and so home – where I find Mr. Cæsar playing the treble to my boy upon the Theorbo, the first time I heard him, which pleases me mightily. After dinner I carried him and my wife toward Westminster by coach, myself lighting at the Temple; and there, being a little too soon, walked in the Temple church, looking with pleasure on the monuments and epitaphs. And then to my Lord Bellasses, where Creed and Povy by appointment met to discourse of some of their Tanger accounts between my Lord and Vernatty, who will prove a very knave. That being done, I away with Povy to White-hall, and thence I to Unthankes and there take up my wife; and so home, it being very foul and dark. Being there come, I to the settling of some of my money matters in my chests, and evening some accounts; which I was at late and to my extraordinary content, and especially to see all things hit so even and right, and with an apparent profit and advantage since my last accounting, but how much I cannot perticularly yet come to adjudge.

Late to supper and to bed.

23. Up, and at the office all the morning. At noon Sir W. Batten told me Sir Rd. Ford would accept*a* of one-third of my profit in our private man-of-war and bear one-third of the charge, and be bound in the Admiralty – so I shall be excused being bound; which I like mightily of, and did draw up a writing as well as I could to that purpose, and signed and sealed it, and so he and Sir R. Ford are to go to enter into bond this afternoon.[1]

Home to dinner; and after dinner, it being late, I down by water to Shadwell to see Betty Michell, the first time I ever was at their new dwelling since the fire – and there find her in the house all alone. I find her mighty modest – but had her lips as much as I would. And endeed, she is mighty pretty, that I love her exceedingly. I paid her 10*l*. 1*s*. that I received upon a ticket

a repl. 'acc'-

---

1. See above, p. 301 & n. 1. The captains, masters and owners of privateers had to enter into bonds to render to the Admiral his share (one tenth) of their profits.

for her husband, which is a great kindness I have done them.[1]
And having kissed her as much as I would, I away, poor wretch,
and down to Deptford to see Sir J. Mennes's ordering of the pay
of some ships there, which he doth most miserably, and so home.
Bagwell's wife, seeing me come the fields way, did get over her
pales to come after and talk with me – which she did for a good
way, and so parted; and I home and to the office, very busy,
and so to supper and to bed.

24. Up, and down to the Old Swan, and there find little
Michell come to his new shop[2] that he hath built there in the
room of his house that was burned – I hope he will do good
here. I drank and bade him joy, for I love him and his wife
well – him for his care, and her for her person. And so to
White-hall, where we attended the Duke. And to all our complaints for want of money, which now we are tired out with
making, the Duke only tells us that he is sorry for it, and hath
spoke to the King of it, and money we shall have as soon as it
can be found; and though all the issue of the war lies upon it,
yet that is all the answer we can get, and that is as bad or worse
then nothing. Thence to Westminster-hall, where the term is
begun; and I did take a turn or two, and so away by coach to
Sir R Viners and there received some money, and then home
and to dinner. After dinner, to little business, and then abroad
with my wife – she to see her brother who is sick, and she believes
is from some discontent his wife hath given him by her loose
carriage, which he is told, and he hath found hath been very
suspicious in his absence,[3] which I am sorry for. I to the Hall,
and there walked long; among others, talking with Mr. Hayes,
Prince Rupert's Secretary, a very ingenious man, and one I think
fit to contract some friendship with. Here I stayed late, walking
to and again, hearing how the Parliament proceeds, which is
mighty slowly, in the settling of the money business, and great
factions growing every day among them.
I am told also how Holmes did last Sunday deliver in his articles
to the King and Cabinet against Smith, and that Smith hath

1. Cf. above, pp. 174–5 & n. 3. Cf. above, p. 291.
2. Probably a strong-water house:
above, p. 81 & n. 1.

z

given in his answer, and lays his not accompanying the fleet to his pilott, who would not undertake to carry the ship further – which the pilot acknowledges. The thing is not accommodated, but only taken up; and both sides commanded to be quiet, but no peace like to be. The Duke of Albemarle is Smiths friend, and hath publicly swore that he would never go to sea again unless Holmes's commission were taken from him.[1]

I find by Hayes that they did expect great glory in coming home in so good condition as they did with the fleet; and there-fore, I the less wonder that the Prince was distasted with my dis-course the other day about the bad state of the fleet.[2] But it pleases me to hear that he did expect great thanks, and lays the fault of the want of it upon the Fire, which deadened everything, and glory of his services.

About 7 at night home, and called my wife, and it being moonshine, took her into the garden and there laid open our condition as to our estate, and the danger of my having it all in the house at once, in case of any disorder or troubles in the State; and therefore resolved to remove part of it to Brampton, and part somewhither else, and part in my own house – which is very necessary, and will tend to our safety, though I shall not think it safe out of my own sight.

So to the office, and then to supper and to bed.

1. For these charges (preferred in August), see BM, Add. 29597, f. 23. They relate to the pursuit of the Dutch after the Battle of St James's Day (25 July). Sir Jeremy Smith, in command of the Blue, was said to have failed to press home his attack, and to have allowed Tromp's ships, separated from the main force, to make harbour. He lost touch with them on the night of the 26th–27th, and called off the chase on the 27th when he found himself in shallow water. Cf. above, p. 234 & n. 2. According to a report made at the time: 'Holmes fired several guns to induce . . . Smith to bear up to them, and soon after the Zealand squadron ran and got home, but had they been chased as they ought, every ship had been lost' (*CSPD 1665–6*, p. 596). A court-martial, demanded by Rupert, referred the matter to the King and the Admiral, who after examining Smith allowed the charges to drop. Albemarle's defence of Smith was perhaps inspired by his jealousy of Rupert (cf. his warm commendation of Smith to the King in August: ib., *1666–7*, p. 40). Holmes and Smith dealt with the matter by a duel: below, p. 348. The House of Commons held an enquiry in March 1668 and decided in Smith's favour: below, 6 March 1668; *CSPD 1666–7*, pp. 14, 40, 222, 231. But Holmes was never deprived of his commis-sion.

2. See above, pp. 331–2.

25. Up betimes and by water to White-hall, and there with Sir G. Carteret to Sir W. Coventry, who is come to his winter lodgings at White-hall, and there agreed upon a method of paying of tickets. And so I back again home, and to the office, where we sat all the morning, but to little purpose but to receive clamours for money. At noon home to dinner, where the two Mrs. Daniels came to see us – and dined with us. After dinner, I out with my wife to Mrs. Pierces, where she hath not been a great while, from some little unkindness of my wife's to her when she was last here.[1] But she received us with mighty respect and discretion – and was making herself mighty fine, to go to a great Ball tonight at Court, being the Queenes birthday. So the ladies for this one day do wear Laces, but to put them off again tomorrow.[2] Thence I to my Lord Bruncker, and with him to Mrs. Williams's, where we meet Knipp. I was glad to see the Jade – made her sing – and she told us they begin at both houses to act on Monday next.[3] But I fear, after all this sorrow, their gains will be but little. Mrs. Williams says the Dukes house will now be much the better of the two, because of their women – which I am glad to hear.[4]

Thence with Lord Brouncker to White-hall, and there spoke with Sir W. Coventry about some office business, and then I away to Mrs. Pierces and there saw her new closet, which is mighty rich and fine. Her daughter Betty grows mighty pretty.

Thence with my wife home, and to do business at the office. Then to Sir W. Batten, who tells me that the House of Parliament makes mighty little haste in settling the money, and that

1. See above, pp. 236–7.

2. The court was still in mourning for the death of the Queen's mother: above, p. 106 & n. 1.

3. The public theatres in Lincoln's Inn Fields and Bridges St, Drury Lane, did not, in fact, re-open for regular performances after the Fire until very late in November 1666, possibly on the 29th. See *London Stage 1600–1800, pt 1, 1660–1700* (ed. W. van Lennep), p. 98. (A).

4. Mrs Williams (who may have been the actress of that name in the Duke's Company) was probably right in claiming at this time that the actresses there were superior to those in the King's Company. Their principal, Mrs Betterton, the finest actress of her day, was now at the height of her powers, and the leading actress of the King's Company, Anne Marshall, appears to have gone into temporary retirement between June 1665 and February 1667. See J. H. Wilson, *All the King's ladies*, pp. 169, 191. (A).

he knows not when it will be done. But they fall into faction, and Libells have been found in the House. Among others, one yesterday, wherein they reckon up divers great sums to be given away by the King – among others, 10000*l* to Sir W. Coventry for Weare and Teare (the point he stood upon to advance that sum by, for them to give the King); Sir G. Carteret, 50000*l* for something else, I think Supernumerarys. And so, to Matt Wren, 5000*l* for passing the Canary Company's patent. And so, a great many other sums to other persons.[1]

So home to supper and to bed.

26. Up, and all the morning and most of the afternoon within doors, beginning to set my accounts in order from before this Fire, I being behindhand with them ever since. And this day I got most of my tradesmen to bring in their bills, and paid them. Dined at home, and busy again after dinner; and then abroad by water to Westminster-hall, where I walked till the evening; and then out, the first time I ever was abroad with Doll Lane, to the Dog tavern, and there drank with her – a bad face, but good-bodied girl. Did nothing but salute and play with her, and talk; and thence away by coach home, and so to do a little more in my accounts, and then to supper and to bed.

Nothing done in the House yet as to the finishing of the Bill for money – which is a mighty sad thing, all lying at stake for it.

27. Up, and there comes to see me my Lord Bellasses, which was a great honour. He tells me great news, yet but what I suspected: that Vernatty is fled, and so hath cheated him and twenty more; but most of all, I doubt, Mr. Povy.[2]

Thence to talk about public business; he tells me how the two Houses begin to be troublesome, the Lords to have quarrels one with another, my Lord Duke of Buckingham having said to the Lord Chancellor (who is against the passing of the Bill

1. In the recent debates on naval expenses (Milward, pp. 9, 14, 20, 26–7), Coventry and Carteret had urged the Commons to provide more money for the wear and tear of ships etc., and for the extra cost of victualling ships which carried men addi-tional to their complements. Wren, Clarendon's secretary, had been accused of corruption by the enemies of the Canary Company: see above, p. 314 & n. 2.

2. See above, p. 264 & n. 2.

for prohibiting the bring[ing] over of Irish Cattle),¹ that whoever was against the Bill was there led to it by an Irish Interest
or an Irish understanding, which is as much as to say he is a fool.
This bred heat from my Lord Chancellor, and something he²
said did offend my Lord of Ossory (my Lord Duke of Ormond's
son), and they two had hard words; upon which the latter sends
a challenge to the former – of which the former complains to the
House, and so the business is to be heard on Monday next.³

Then as to the Commons; some ugly Knifes, like poignards
to stob people with, about 2 or 300 of them were brought in
yesterday to the House, found in one of the houses rubbish that
was burnt, and said to be the house of a Catholique.⁴ This, and
several letters out of the country, saying how high the Catholiques
are everywhere and bold in the owning their religion, have made
the Commons mad; and they presently voted that the King be
desired to put all Catholiques out of imployment, and other high
things⁵ – while the business of money hangs in the hedge. So
that upon the whole, God knows we are in a sad condition like
to be – these being the very beginnings of the late troubles.
He gone, I at the office all the morning. At noon home to
dinner, where Mrs. Pierce and her boy and Knipp – who sings as

1. See above, pp. 313–14 & n.
2. Buckingham.
3. The quarrel followed the debate on the 25th: Ossory's challenge was made outside the House, but in consequence of remarks made in debate by Buckingham. Both were imprisoned by the Lords for three days, and released on the 31st after apologising to the House: *LJ*, xii. 18–22. Full accounts of the quarrel are in Clarendon, *Life*, iii. 135+; Thomas Brown, *Misc. Aulica* (1702), pp. 423–6 (where Arlington's letter to Ormond of '20 October' should be dated 30 October).
4. The report of the committee appointed 'to receive information of the Insolency of the Popish priests and Jesuits, and of the Increase of Popery' (*CJ*, viii. 641–2) does not mention the poignards. According to Milward (p. 32), only two daggers were brought into the house as samples. They were knives used in whale fishing, belonging to two French Papists – 'as desperate instruments . . . as ever I saw'. Cf. HMC, *Portland*, iii. 302.
5. The Commons' resolutions of the 26th asked the King to banish Catholic priests and Jesuits, to put the recusancy laws into force by proclamation, to disarm all Papists and to require all officers, military and civil, to take the oaths of allegiance and supremacy on pain of dismissal: *CJ*, viii. 641–2. The Lords concurred (ib., p. 645), and the King issued a proclamation banishing priests and Jesuits (apart from those in the Queen's service) and enforcing the recusancy laws: Steele, no. 3478 (10 November).

well, and is the best company in the world – dined with us, and infinite mirth. The playhouses begin to play next week.

Toward evening I took them out to the New Exchange, and there my wife bought things, and I did give each of them a pair of Jesimy plain gloves and another of white. Here Knipp and I walked up and down to see handsome faces, and did see several. Then carried each of them home, and with great pleasure and content home myself; where, having writ several letters, I home; and there, upon some serious discourse between my wife and I about that business, I called to us my brother, and there broke to him our design to send him into the country with some part of our money; and so did seriously discourse the whole thing, and then away to supper and to bed. I pray God give a blessing to our resolution, for I do much fear we shall meet with speedy distractions for want of money.

28. ⟨*Lords day*⟩ Up, and to church with my wife; and then home, and there is come ⟨little⟩ Michell and his wife; I sent for them – and also comes Captain Guy[1] to dine with me, and he and I much talk together: he cries out of the discipline of the fleet, and confesses really that the true English valour we talk of is almost spent and worn out – few of the commanders doing what they should do, and he much fears we shall therefore be beaten the next year. He assures me we were beaten home the last June fight, and that the whole fleet was ashamed to hear of our Bone=fires.[2] He commends Smith, and cries out of Holmes for an idle, proud, conceited, though stout fellow. He tells me we are to owe the loss of so many ships on the sands, not to any fault of the pilots, but to the weather; but in this I have good authority to fear there was something more. He[a] says the Dutch do fight in very good order, and we in none at all. He says that in the July fight,[3] both the Prince and Holmes had their belly-

a repl. 'But'

---

1. Thomas Guy, who commanded the *Assurance* during the recent campaign. He was himself a 'stout and able seaman' according to Coventry: Longleat, Coventry MSS 99, f. 91*v*.

2. For the Four Days Battle, see above, pp. 146+. Pepys reported bonfires at 6 June.

3. The Battle of St James's Day: see above, p. 221 & n. 3.

fulls, and were fain to go aside – though, if the wind had continued, we had utterly beaten them. He doth confess the whole to be governed by a company of fools, and fears our ruine.

After dinner, he gone, I with my brother to White-hall, and he to Westminster Abby. I presently to Mrs. Martin's, and there met widow Burroughs and Doll and did tumble them all the afternoon as I pleased; and having given them a bottle of wine, I parted, and home by boat (my brother going by land) and thence with my wife to sit and supped with my Uncle and Aunt Wight, and see Woolly's wife, who is a pretty woman. And after supper, being very merry in abusing my Aunt with Dr. Venner,[1] we home, and I to do something in my accounts, and so to bed.

The *Revenge* having her Forecastle blown up with powder, to the killing of some men in the River, and the *Dyamonds* being overset in the careening at Sheerenesse, are further marks of the method all the King's work is now done in. The *Foresight* also, and another, came to disasters in the same place this week in the careening – which is strange.[2]

29. Up, and to the office to do business, and thither comes to me Sir Tho. Teddiman, and he and I walked a good while in the garden together, discoursing of the disorder and discipline of the fleet, wherein he told me how bad everything is but was very wary in speaking anything to the dishonour of the Prince or Duke of Albemarle; but doth magnify my Lord Sandwich much before them both for ability to serve the King, and doth heartily wish for him here – for he fears that we shall be undone the next year, but that he will, however, see an end of it.

To prevent the necessity of his dining with me, I was forced to pretend occasion of going to Westminster; so away I went, and Mr. Barber the clerk, having a request to make to me to get him into imployment, did walk along with me and by water to Westminster with me – he professing great love to me, and an

---

1. On 8 December 1664 Pepys had teased his Aunt Wight about her 'doating on Dr. Venner'.

2. An enquiry into these accidents (except that to the *Revenge*) was immediately made by Penn: see *CSPD 1666–7*, p. 216; cf. Allin, i. 297. The unnamed ship was the *Greenwich*.

able clerk he is.[1] When I come thither, I find the new Lord Mayor Bolton a-swearing at the Exchequer with some of the Aldermen and Livery; but Lord, to see how meanly they now look, who upon this day used to be all little lords, is a sad sight and worthy consideration. And everybody did reflect with pity upon the poor City, to which they are now coming to choose and swear their Lord Mayor, compared with what it heretofore was.[2]

Thence by coach (having in the Hall bought me a velvet riding*a* cap, cost me 20s) to my Taylors, and there bespoke a plain vest. And so to my goldsmith to bid him look out for some gold for me; and he tells me that Ginnys, which I bought 2000 of not long ago, and cost me but 18½d change, will now cost me 22d, and but very few to be had at any price.[3] However, some more I will have, for they are very convenient – and of easy disposal.

So home to dinner, and to discourse with my brother upon his translation of my Lord Bacon's *Faber Fortunæ*[4] which I gave him to do; and he hath done it but meanly, I am not pleased with it at all – having done it only literally, but without any life at all.

About 5 a-clock I took my wife (who is mighty fine, and with a new fair pair of locks, which vex me,[5] though like a

a MS. 'reading'

---

1. William Barbour, clerk in the Navy Office, had in March 1666 been employed by Evelyn in the Commission for the Sick and Wounded. In 1667 he became one of the four clerks of the Ticket Office.

2. The scene is described in a newsletter of 1 November: 'The new Lord Mayor was sworn in at the Exchequer bar, where they seemed as hearty though not as numerous as before the fire; all the companies were excused attendance, except those of the two lord mayors and two sheriffs, who went to and from Westminster in coaches' (H. Muddiman to G. Powell, *CSPD 1666–7*, p. 231). There was no Lord Mayor's show, no

banquet, no procession of barges from London to Westminster. The mayor's own company (Merchant Taylors') having itself suffered from the Fire, asked him to forego the 100 marks customarily paid for the beautifying of his house. But he refused. R. T. D. Sayle, *Lord Mayors' pageants of the Merchant Taylors' Co.*, pp. 130–1.

3. Guineas had been first minted in 1663. The 'change' mentioned by Pepys was the goldsmith's fee for supplying gold in return for silver; the previous occasion referred to was on 13 August.

4. Bacon's essay: see above, ii. 102, n. 1.

5. Cf. below, 11 May 1667.

fool I helped her the other night to buy them), and to Mrs. Pierce's; and there staying a little, I away before to White-hall and into the new playhouse there, the first time I ever was there, and the first play I have seen since before the great plague.[1] By and by Mr. Pierce comes, bringing my wife and his, and Knipp. By and by the King and Queen, Duke and Duchesse, and all the great ladies of the Court; which endeed was a fine sight – but the play, being *Love in a Tubb*,[2] a silly play; and though done by the Duke's people, yet having neither Baterton nor his wife[3] – and the whole thing done ill, and being ill also, I had no manner of pleasure in the play. Besides, the House, though very fine, yet bad for the voice – for hearing.[4] The sight of the ladies, endeed, was exceeding noble; and above all my Lady Castlemayne.

The play done by 10 a-clock, I carried them all home; and then home myself and, well satisfied with the sight but not the play, we with great content to bed.

30. Up and to the office, where sat all the morning; and at noon home to dinner, and then to the office again, where late, very busy and despatching much business. Mr. Hater staying most of the afternoon abroad, he came to me, poor man, to make excuse; and it was that he had been looking out for a little house for his family, his wife being much frightened in the country with the discourses about the country of troubles and disorders like to be,*a* and therefore durst not be from him; and therefore

a MS. 'me'

1. This was in the Great Hall, Whitehall, which John Webb had converted into a permanent theatre in 1665. See above, vi. 85 & n. 3. The last play Pepys had seen was *Love's Mistress* at the TR, Drury Lane, on 15 May 1665. (A).

2. A comedy by Sir George Etherege; see above, vi. 4 & n. 2. (A).

3. According to Downes (pp. 24–5), Betterton usually played Lord Beaufort; Mrs Betterton, Graciana. (A).

4. The Great Hall Theatre measured $87 \times c. 39\frac{1}{2}$ ft and had a proscenium arch 23 ft high and 25 ft wide. Pepys's criticism of its acoustics was thoroughly justified, however. It was a very high building; in February 1671 it was equipped with a cloth ceiling, and in 1675 with a permanent ceiling 'that the Voices may the better be heard'. See E. Boswell, *Restoration court stage*, pp. 28, 38, 46, 50. (A).

he is forced to bring her to town, that they may be together. This is now the general apprehension of all people. Perticulars I do not know, but my own fears are also great, and I do think it time to look out to save something if a storm should come. At night home to supper and singing with my wife, who hath lately begun to learn,[1] and I think will come to do something, though her ear is not good; nor I, I confess, have patience enough*a* to teach her or hear her sing now and then a note out of tune, and am to blame that I cannot bear*b* with that in her which is fit I should do with her as a learner, and one that I desire much could sing, and so should encourage her. This I was troubled at, for I find that I do put her out of heart and make her fearful to sing before me.

So after supper to bed.

31. Out with Sir W. Batten toward White-hall, being in pain in my cods by being squeezed the other night in a little coach when I carried Pierce and his wife and my people.[2] But I hope I shall be soon well again. This day is a great day at the House; so little to do with the Duke of York, but soon parted. Coming out of the Court, I met Collonell Atkins, who tells me the whole City ring today of Sir Jer Smiths killing of Holmes in a Duell; at which I was not much displeased, for I fear every day more and more mischief from that man, if he lives. But the thing is not true, for in my coach I did by and by meet Sir Jer Smith going to Court.

So I by coach to my goldsmith, there to see what gold I can get – which is but little, and not under 22*d*. So away home to dinner. And after dinner to my closet, where I spent the whole afternoon till late at evening of all my accounts, public and private; and to my great satisfaction I do find that I do bring my accounts to a very near balance, notwithstanding all the hurries and troubles I have been put to by the late Fire, that I have not been able to even my accounts since July last before. And I bless God, I do find that I am worth more then ever I yet

a repl. 'have'   *b* MS. 'can tear'

1. Goodgroome taught her: see below, p. 397 and n. 3. (E).   2. Cf. above, ii. 194 & n. 4.

was, which is 6200*l* – for which the holy name of God be praised. And my other accounts, of Tanger, in a very plain and clear condition, that I am not liable to any trouble*ᵃ* from them. But in fear great I am, and I perceive the whole City is, of some distractions and disorders among us, which God of his goodness prevent.

Late to supper with my wife and brother, and then to bed.

And thus ends the month – with an ill aspect. The business of the Navy standing wholly still. No credit. No goods sold us. Nobody will trust. All we have to do at the office is to hear complaints for want of money. The Duke of York himself, for now three weeks, seems to rest satisfied that we can do nothing without money, and that all must stand still till the King gets money – which the Parliament have been a great while about, but are so dissatisfied with the King's management, and his giving himself up to pleasures, and not minding the calling to account any of his officers – and they observe so much the expense of the war, and yet that after we have made it the most we can, it doth not amount to what they have given the King for the Warr, that they are backward of giving any more. However, 1800000*l* they have voted, but the way of gathering it hath taken up more time then is fit to be now lost. The seamen grow very rude, and everything out of order – commanders having no power over their seamen, but the seamen do what they please. Few stay on board, but all coming running up hither to town; and nobody can with justice blame them, we owing them so much money, and their families must starve if we do not give them money or they procure upon their tickets from some people that will trust them. A great folly is observed by all people, in the King's giving leave to so many merchantmen to go abroad this winter, and some upon voyages where it is impossible they should be back again by the spring; and the rest will be doubtful, but yet we let them go.[1] What the reason of state is, nobody can tell, but all condemn it. The Prince and

a   repl. 'default'

1. Passes for this purpose were issued by a secretary of state: *CSPD 1665-6*, pp. 219, 229. For the embargo, see above, p. 20, n. 3. It was thought that possibly the ships, and certainly the men, ought to be available for the State's service.

Duke of Albemarle have got no great credit by this year's service, our losses, both of reputation and ships, having been greater then is thought have ever been suffered in all ages put together before – being beat home and fleeing home the first fight, and then losing so many ships then and since upon the sands, and some falling into the enemy's hands, and not one taken this year but the *Ruby*, French prize, now at the end of the year, by*ᵃ* the*ᵇ* Frenchmen's mistake in running upon us.[1]

Great folly in both Houses of Parliament, several persons falling together by the eares; among others, in the House of Lords, the Duke of Buckingham and my Lord Ossory. Such is our case, that everybody fears an invasion the next year; and for my part, I do methinks foresee some great unhappiness coming upon us, and do provide for it by laying by something against a rainy day – dividing what I have and laying it in several places – but with all faithfulness to the King in all respects – my grief only being that the King doth not look after his business himself, and thereby will be undone, both himself and his nations – it being not yet, I believe, too late, if he would apply himself to it, to save all and conquer the Duch; but while he and the Duke of York mind their pleasure as they do, and nothing else, we must be beaten.

So late, with my mind in good condition of quiet after the settling all my accounts, and to bed.*ᶜ*

---

a MS. 'but'   *b* repl. 'their'   *c* followed by one blank page

---

1. The *Rubis*, a flagship in Beaufort's fleet, sailing on 18 September near the Isle of Wight, mistook the white flag of Allin's squadron for the French: Allin to Williamson, 20 September, *CSPD 1666–7*, p. 143; Allin, i. 291. Cf. above, pp. 327–8 & n.

NOVEMBER.

1. Up, and was presented by Burton one of our smiths wifes, with a very noble cake – which I presently resolved to have my wife go with today, and some wine, and house-warme my Betty Michell; which she readily resolved to do. So I to the office and sat all the morning, where little to do but answer people about want of money. So that there is little service done the King by us, and great disquiet to ourselfs; I am sure there is to me very much, for I do not enjoy myself as I would and should do in my imployment if my pains could do the King better service, and with the peace that we used to do it.

At noon to dinner; and from dinner my wife and my brother and W. Hewer and Barker away to Betty Michells to Shadwell, and I to my office, where I took in Mrs. Bagwell[a] and did what I would with her; and so she went away, and I all the afternoon till[b] almost night there; and then my wife being come back, I took her and set her at her brother's, who is very sick, and I to White-hall and there all alone a pretty while with Sir W. Coventry at his chamber; I find him very melancholy under the same considerations of the King's service that I am. He confesses with me, he expects all will be undone and all ruined. He complains, and sees perfectly what I with grief do, and said it first himself to me: that all discipline is lost in the fleet, no order nor no command. And concurs with me that it is necessary we do again and again represent all things more and more plainly to the Duke of York, as a guard to ourselfs hereafter when things shall come to be worse. He says the House goes on slowly in finding of money, and that the discontented party do say they have not done with us, for they will have a further bout with us as to our accounts – and they are exceedingly well instructed where to hit us. I left him with a thousand sad reflections upon the times and the state of the King's matters, and so away and took up my wife, and home, where a little at the office and then home to supper and talk with my wife (with whom I have much comfort) and my brother, and so to bed.

a name in s.h.   *b* repl. 'all'

2. Up betimes, and with Sir W. Batten to Woolwich, where first we went on board the *Ruby*, French prize, the only ship of war we have taken from any of our enemies this year. It seems a very good ship, but with galleries quite round the Sterne to walk in, as a Balcone, which will be taken down. She had also about 40 good brass guns, but will make little amends to our loss in the *Prince*.[1]

Thence to the Ropeyard and the other yards to do several businesses. He, and I also, did buy some apples and pork; by the same token, the Bucher commended it as the best in England for Cloath and Colour – and for his beef, says he, "Look how fat it is; the lean appears only here and there a speck, like Beauty= spots."

Having done at Woolwich, we to Depford (it being very cold upon the water) and there did also a little more business; and so home, I reading all the way to make end of *The Bondman*[2] (which the oftener I read, the more I like), and begin *The Duchesse of Malfy*,[3] which seems a good play.

At home to dinner, and there came Mr. Pierce, Chyrurgeon, to see me; and after I had eat something, he and I and my wife by coach to Westminster; she[a] set us down at White-hall and she to her brother's – I up into the House, and among other things walked a good while with the Serjeant Trumpet, who tells me, as I wished, that the[b] King's Italian here is about setting three parts for Trumpets and shall teach some to sound them, and believes they will [be] admirable·Musique.[4] I also walked with Sir St. Fox[5] an hour, and good discourse of public business

a repl. 'and s'–   *b* repl. 'they'

---

1. For the *Rubis*, see above, p. 350 & n. 1. According to Hosier's letter to Pepys (20 September), she had '50 Brass Guns' (PRO, SP 29/172, no. 65); Allin reported 40 out of a total armament of 54: ib., no. 71. For the loss of the *Prince* on the Galloper sands, see above, pp. 152–3 & n.

2. Massinger's tragicomedy: see above, ii. 47, n. 2; ib., p. 106, n. 4. Pepys had bought a copy on 25 May 1661. (A).

3. Webster's tragedy; see above, iii. 209, n. 1; PL 1075. (A).

4. The Serjeant-Trumpeter to the King was Gervase Price. The Italian was possibly Giovanni Battista Draghi: G. D. Weiss, *Samuel Pepys curioso*, p. 94. (E).

5. Comptroller of the King's Household.

with him – who seems very much satisfied with my discourse, and desired more of my acquaintance.

Then comes out the King and Duke of York from the Council, and so I spoke a while to Sir W. Coventry about some office business; and so called my wife (her brother being now a little better then he was) and so home; and I to my chamber to do some business, and then to supper and to bed.

3. This morning comes Mr. Lovett and brings me my print of the Passion,[1] varnished by him, and the frame black; which endeed is very fine, though not so fine as I expected – however, pleases me exceedingly. This, and the sheets of paper he prepared for me, come to 3*l*, which I did give him; and though it be more then is fit to lay out*a* on pleasure, yet it being ingenious I did not think much of it.

He gone, I to the office, where all the morning to little purpose, nothing being before us but clamours*b* for money. So at noon home to dinner; and after dinner to hang up my new varnished pictures and set my chamber in order to be made clean; and then to the office again and there all the afternoon till late at night. and so to supper and to bed.

4. *Lords day.* Comes my Taylors man in the morning and brings my vest home, and coat to wear with it[2], and belt and silver-hilted sword. So I rose and dressed myself, and I like myself mightily in it, and so doth my wife. Then being dressed, to church; and after church pulled my Lady Pen and Mrs. Markeham into my house to dinner; and Sir J. Mennes, he got Mrs. Pegg along with him. I had a good dinner for them, and very merry. And after dinner to the waterside, and so, it being very cold, to White-hall, and was mighty fearful of an ague (my vest being new and thin, and the*c* Coate cut not to meet before upon my breast). Here I waited in the gallery till the Council was up; and among others, did speak with Mr. Cooling, my Lord Chamberlain's secretary – who tells me my Lord-

---

a MS. 'in on'   *b* repl. 'clim'-   *c* repl. 'open'

---

1. See above, p. 211 & n. 2.   2. This was the new fashion: see above, p. 324, n. 3.

Generall is become mighty low in all people's opinion, and that he hath received several slurs from the King and Duke of York. That people at Court do see the difference between his and the Prince's management and my Lord Sandwiches. That this business which he is put upon, of crying out against*ᵃ* the Catholiques and turning them out of all imployment, will undo him when he comes to turn out the officers out of the army – and this is a thing of his own seeking.¹ That he is grown a drunken sot, and drinks with nobody but Troutbecke,² whom nobody else will keep company with – of whom he told me this story: That once, the Duke of Albemarle in his drink taking notice as of a wonder that Nan Hide should ever come to be Duchess of Yorke – "Nay," says Troutbecke, "ne'er wonder at that; for if you will give me another bottle of wine, I will tell you as great, if not greater, a miracle." And what was that but that "Our Dirty Besse" (meaning his*ᵇ* Duchesse) should come to be Duchesse of Albemarle.³ Here we parted, and so by and by the Council rose, and out comes Sir G. Carteret and Sir W. Coventry and they and my Lord Brouncker and I went to Sir G. Carteret's lodgings, there to discourse about some money demanded by Sir W Warren; and having done that, broke up – and Sir G. Carteret and I alone together a while, where he shows me a long*ᶜ* letter, all in cipher, from my Lord Sandwich to him. The contents he hath not yet found out – but he tells me that my Lord is not sent for home, as several people have enquired after of me. He spoke something reflecting upon me in the business of pursers: that their present bad behaviour is but what he did foresee and had convinced me of; and yet when it came last year to be argued before the Duke of York, I turned and said as the*ᵈ* rest said.⁴ I answered nothing to it, but let it go. And so to other discourse of the ill state of things, of which all people are full

---

a repl. 'on'   b repl. 'the'
c repl. 'letter'   d repl. 'they'

---

1. He was supporting the parliamentary campaign against catholics in office: see above, p. 343 & n. 5. Cf. also above, p. 163.

2. John Troutbeck, surgeon to the King and to Albemarle's troop of the Life Guards; an associate of Albemarle since at least 1659.

3. See above, p. 56, n. 2.

4. This is possibly the meeting recorded above, p. 106.

of sorrow and observation; and so parted, and then by water (landing in Southwarke) home to the Tower; and so home, and there begun to read Potters discourse upon 666,[1] which pleases me mightily; and then broke off, and to supper and to bed.

5. A holiday – lay long; then up and to the office, where vexed to meet with people come from the fleet at the Nore, where so many ships are laid up and few going abroad; and yet Sir[a] Tho. Allen hath sent up some Lieutenants with warrants to press men for a few ships to go out this winter, while every day thousands appear here, to our great trouble and affright, here every day before our office and the ticket office, and no Captain able to command one man aboard.

Thence by water to Westminster, and there at the Swan find Sarah is married to a shoemaker yesterday,[2] so I could not see her, but believe I shall hereafter at good leisure. Thence by coach to my Lord Peterborough's and there spoke with my Lady[b], who had sent to speak with me. She makes mighty moan of the badness of the times, and her family as to money – my Lord's passionateness for want thereof, and his want of coming in of rents, and no wages from the Duke of York; no money to be had there for wages nor disbursements, and therefore prays my assistance about his pension.[3] I was moved with her story, which she largely and handsomely told me, and promised[c] I would try what I could do – in a few days. And so took leave, being willing to keep her Lord fair with me, both for his respect to my Lord Sandwich and for my own sake hereafter when I come to pass my accounts.

Thence to my Lord Crews, and there dined and mightily made

---

a repl. 'he hath sent up'   *b* MS. 'Lord'   *c* MS. 'presented'

---

1. The prophetic book about the number of the Beast: see above, p. 47 & n. 1.

2. Sarah Huedell (Udall) was married to John Harmond on 4 November at St Margaret's, Westminster.

3. Peterborough had relinquished

AA

the governorship of Tangier in 1662 in return for a life pension of £1000 p.a., but had great difficulty in obtaining its payment. He also served in the household of the Duke of York. The fall of rents was a common complaint of landowners at this time.

of, having not, to my shame, been there in eight months[a][1] before. Here my Lord and Sir Tho. Crew, Mr. John, and Dr Crew – and two strangers.[2] ⟨The⟩ best family in the world for goodness and sobriety. Here, beyond my expectation, I met my Lord Hinchingbrooke, who is come to town two days since from Hinchingbrooke, and brought his sister and brother Carteret with him – who are at Sir G. Carteret's. After dinner I and Sir Tho Crew went aside to discourse of public matters, and do find by him that all the country gentlemen are publicly jealous of the Courtiers in the Parliament, and that they do doubt everything that they propose. And that the true reason why the country-gentleman is for a land Tax and against a general Excize, is because they are fearful that if the latter be granted, they shall never get it down again; whereas the land-tax will be but for so much, and when the war ceases there will be no ground got by the Court to keep it up.[3] He doth much cry out upon our accounts, and that all that they have had from the King hath[b] been but Estimates, both from my Lord[c] Treasurer and us, and from all people else – so that the Parliament is weary of it. He says the House would be very glad to get something against Sir G. Carteret, and will not let their enquiries die till they have got something.

He doth, from what he hath heard at the Committee for examining the burning of the City, conclude it as a thing certain, that it was done by plot – it being proved by many witnesses that endeavours were made in several places to encrease the fire, and that both in city and country it was bragged by several

---

a repl. 'or ten'   *b* repl. 'will be but'   *c* l.h. repl. s.h. 'Lord'

---

1. In fact, five-and-a-half: see above, p. 125.

2. On this day Dr Nathaniel Crew, son of Lord Crew, and brother of Sir Thomas and John, was appointed chaplain-in-ordinary to the King.

3. Crew was M.P. for Brackley, Northants. The government was pressing for an extension of the limited excise imposed in 1660 into a general one, on the ground that it would not reduce cash reserves so quickly as other methods, with the result that the public, as well as paying taxes, would be able to lend money: cf. Warwick's views above, v. 68. But the country party preferred a temporary land-tax to another excise, which they distrusted as leading too easily to the establishment of a horde of officials and above all of a standing army, like Cromwell's redcoats. See Milward, pp. 25, 309. The critics won and a land-tax was voted: below, p. 408 & n. 4.

papists that upon such a day or in such a time we should find the hottest weather that ever was in England, and words of plainer sense.[1] But my Lord Crew was discoursing at table how the Judges have determined in that case whether the Landlords or the Tenants (who are in their leases all of them generally tied to maintain and uphold their houses) shall bear the loss of the fire. And they say that ⟨Tenants*a*⟩ should, against all Casualtys of fire beginning either in their own or in their neighbour's; but where it is done by an Enemy, they are not to do it. And this was by an enemy, there having been one Convict and hanged upon this very score – which is an excellent Salvo for the Tenants, and for which I am glad – because of my father's house.[2]

After dinner and this discourse, I took coach, and at the same time find my Lord Hinchingbrooke and Mr. Jo. Crew and the Doctor going out to see the ruins of the City; so I took the Doctor into my Hackny-coach (and he is a very fine sober gentleman), and so through the City; but Lord, what pretty and sober observations he made of the City and its desolation – till anon we come to my house, and there I took them upon Tower hill to show them what houses were pulled down there since the fire; and then to my house, where I treated them with good wine of several sorts, and they took it mighty respectfully, and a fine

a repl. 'they'

---

1. A committee of enquiry had been appointed by the Commons on 25 September, and reported on 22 January 1667: below, 16 September 1667. Crew was not a member of it. Cf. Sir T. Osborne (2 October): 'I have bin this afternoon imployed in the committee of examining persons suspected for fireing the Citty, but all the allegations are very frivolous, and people are generally satisfied that the fire was accidentall' (A. Browning, *Danby*, ii. 15).

2. Lord Crew was referring to the bill drafted by the judges to deal with the situation affecting landlords and tenants which followed the Fire. Houses were not insured, and strict application of the terms of the leases would have been impossible to enforce in most cases, and would indeed have been unjust if enforceable. But in October Hubert, a Frenchman, was convicted of starting the fire, and hanged on the 29th. Tenants were thereby exempt from responsibility. On 6 November the city sent a deputation to parliament thanking them for this decision. The bill became law in February 1667 and set up a Fire Court, staffed by common law judges but employing an equitable jurisdiction, to settle disputes. See below, 24 February 1667 & n.; T. F. Reddaway, *Rebuilding of London*, pp. 76–7.

company*a* of gentlemen they are; but above all, I was glad to see my Lord Hinchingbrooke drink no wine at all. Here I got them to appoint Wednesday come sennit to dine here at my house; and so we broke up, and all took coach again, and I carried the Doctor to Chancery-Lane and thence I to White-hall, where I stayed walking up and down till night, and then got almost into the Playhouse, having much mind to go and see the play at Court this night; but fearing how I should get home, because of the bonefires[1] and the lateness of the night to get a coach, I did not stay; but having this evening seen my Lady Jemimah, who is come to town and looks very well*b* and fat, and heard how Mr. John Pickering[2] is to be married this week and to a fortune with 5000*l*, and seen a rich necklace of pearl and two pendants of Dyamonds, which Sir G. Carteret hath presented her with since her coming to town – I home by coach, but met not one bonefire through the whole town in going round by the Wall; which is strange, and speaks the melancholy disposition of the City at present, while never more was said of and feared of and done against the Papists then just at this time. Home, and there find my wife and her people at Cards; and I to my chamber and there late, and so to supper and to bed.

6. Up and to the office, where all the morning sitting. At noon home to dinner; and after dinner down alone by water to Depford, reading *Duchess of Malfy*, the play,[3] which is pretty good – and there did some business; and so up again, and all the evening at the office. At night home to supper, and there find Mr. Batelier,[4] who supped with us and good company he is; and so after supper to bed.

7. Up, and with Sir W. Batten to White-hall, where we attended as usual the Duke of York; and there was, by the folly

a repl. 'compl'-   *b* MS. 'fell'

---

1. For Gunpowder Plot Day.
2. Presumably a mistake for Gilbert, son of Sir Gilbert Pickering (a brother-in-law of Sandwich), who on 16 November obtained a licence for his marriage to Elizabeth, daughter of Thomas Pinchon, a London draper.

John, the eldest son, did not marry until 1669. *Visit. Northants., 1681*, Harl. Soc., 87/171.
3. Webster's tragedy: see above, iii. 209, n. 1. (A).
4. See above, p. 228 & n. 2.

of Sir W. Batten, prevented in obtaining a bargain for Captain Cocke which would, I think, have [been] at this time (during our great want of hemp) both profitable to the King and of good convenience to me.[1]   But I matter it not – it being done only by the folly, not any design, of Sir W. Batten.   Thence to Westminster-hall; and it being fast-day,[2] there was no shops open; but meeting with Doll Lane, did go with her to the Rose tavern and there drank and played with her a good while.   She went away, and I stayed a good while after, and was seen going out by one of our neighbours near the office and two of the Hall people that I had no mind to have been seen by; but there was no hurt in it, nor can be alleged from it – therefore I am not solicitous in it; but took coach and called[a] at Faythornes to buy some prints for my wife to draw by this winter; and here did see my Lady Castlemaynes picture, done by him from Lillys, in red chalke and other colours, by which he hath cut it in copper to be printed.[3]   The picture in chalke[b] is the finest thing I ever saw in my life I think, and did desire to buy it; but he says he must keep it awhile to correct his Copper plate by, and when that is done, he will sell it me.

Thence home, and found my wife gone out with my brother to see her brother.   I to dinner, and thence to my chamber to read, and so to the office (it being a fast-day and so a holiday), and then to Mrs. Turner's, at her request, to speak and advise about Sir Tho. Harvys coming to lodge there,[4] which I think must be submitted to, and better now then hereafter when he gets more ground, for I perceive he intends to stay by it and begins to crow mightily upon his late being at the payment of

a repl. 'stayed at'   *b* l.h. repl. l.h. 'Calk'

---

1. Cf. below, p. 385, n. 2.
2. For the Plague.
3. Faithorne's drawing, and the engraving for which it was made, were based on the portrait by Lely of which a version had been given to Lord Sandwich: above, v. 200, n. 3; L. Fagan, *Descriptive cat. of engraved works of William Faithorne*, p. 27.

Pepys later bought three impressions of the engraving and appears to have had one of them varnished and framed: below, p. 393; 21 January, 8 May 1667. (OM).

4. Harvey's plan to live there dated back over a year: above, vi. 37 & n. 2. But in the event Brouncker took the lodgings: below, 10 February 1667.

tickets. But a coxcomb he is, and will never be better in the business of the Navy. Thence home, and there find Mr. Batelier come to bring my wife a very fine puppy of his mother's spaniel, a very fine one endeed – which my wife is mighty proud of.[1] He stayed and supped with us, and they to Cards – I to my chamber to do some business, and then out to them to play, and were a little merry, and then to bed.

By the Duke of York his discourse today in his chamber, they have it at Court, as well as we here, that a fatal day is to be expected shortly, of some great mischiefe in[a] the remainder of this week;[b] whether by the papists, or what, they are not certain.[2] But the day is disputed; some say next Friday, others a day sooner, others later; and I hope all will prove a foolery. But it is observable how everybody's fears are busy at this time.

8. Up, and before I went to the office, I spoke with Mr. Martin for his advice about my proceeding in the business of the Private man-of-Warr, he having heretofore served in one of them – and now I have it in my thoughts to send him purser in ours.[3] After this discourse, I to the office, where I sat all the morning – Sir W. Coventry with us, where he hath not been a great while; Sir W. Penn also, newly come from the Nore, where he hath been some time fitting of the ships out. At noon home to dinner, and then to the office a while, and so home for my sword, and there find Mercer come to see her mistress. I was glad to see her there, and my wife mighty kind also; and for my part, much vexed that the jade is not with us still. Left them together, designing to go abroad tomorrow night to Mrs. Pierces to dance; and so I to Westminster-hall and there met Mr. Grey,[4] who tells me the House is sitting still (and now it was 6 a-clock) and likely to sit till midnight; and have proceeded[c]

a MS. 'to'   b MS. 'day'   c repl. 'voted'

---

1. For the puppy's quasi-ducal lineage, see above, p. 240.

2. See below, pp. 364–5 & n.

3. The *Flying Greyhound*: above, p. 301, n. 1. Martin is referred to as 'my purser' at 5 March 1667. Cf.

above, p. 75.

4. Probably Thomas Grey, M.P. for Ludgershall, Wilts., a colleague of Pepys on the committee of the Royal Fishery.

far to give the King his supply presently – and herein have done more today then was hoped for.[1] So to White-hall to Sir W. Coventry, and there would fain have carried Captain Cocke's business for his bargain of hemp, but am defeated and disappointed and knew hardly how to carry myself in it between my interest and desire not to offend Sir W. Coventry. Sir W. Coventry did this night tell me how the business is done about Sir J. Mennes; that he is to be a Commissioner, and my Lord Brouncker and Sir W. Penn are to be Controller joyntly;[2] which I am very glad of, and better then if they were either of them alone, and do hope truly that the King's business will be better done thereby, and infinitely better then now it is.

Thence by coach home, full of thoughts of the consequence of this alteration in our office, and I think no evil to me. So at my office late, and then home to supper and to bed.

Mr. Grey did assure me this night that he was told this day by one of the greater Ministers of State in England and one of the King's Cabinet, that we had little left to agree on between the Duch and us towards a peace, but only the place of Treaty[3] – which doth astonish me to hear, but am glad of it, for I fear the consequence of the war. But he says that the King having all the money he is like to have, we shall be sure of a peace in a little time.

9. Up and to the office, where did a good deal of business. And then at noon to the Exchange and to my little goldsmith's,[4]

---

1. See *CJ*, viii. 647: the means agreed on were a post-charge of eleven months' assessment, a poll tax, a stamp duty and an increase of duties on foreign imports. The vote 'that candles be brought in' was carried by 136 to 109.

2. The reorganisation of the comptrollership in the following January turned out slightly differently: see below, 20 January 1667. The attempt to shunt Mennes into a commissionership failed both now and in 1668.

3. In fact much manoeuvring

about terms followed: cf. Clarendon, *Life*, iii. 210+; Feiling, pp. 209–10. The question of venue was really part of the issue of whether the peace was to be a separate treaty with the Dutch or a joint treaty with the Dutch and the French. The Dutch government favoured a joint treaty negotiated on neutral soil; the English were pressing for a separate treaty negotiated on Dutch or English territory.

4. Humphrey Stokes's.

whose wife is very pretty and modest, that ever I saw any.
Upon the Change, where I have seldom of late been, I find all
people mightily at a loss what to expect, but confusion and
fears in every man's head and heart. Whether war or peace,
all fear the event will be bad. Thence home and with my
brother to dinner, my wife being dressing herself against night.
After dinner I to my closet all the afternoon, till the porter
brought my vest back from the Taylors, and then to dress myself
very fine, about 4 or 5 a-clock; and by that time comes Mr.
Batelier and Mercer, and away by coach to Mrs. Pierces by
appointment, where we find good company – a fair lady, my
Lady Prettyman – Mrs. Corbet – Knipp. And for men, Captain
Downing – Mr. Lloyd, Sir W. Coventry's clerk – and one Mr.
Tripp, who dances well. After some trifling discourse, we to
dancing and very good sport, and mightily pleased I was with
the company. After our first bout of dancing, Knipp and I to
sing,*a* and Mercer and Captain Downing (who loves and understands music) would by all means have my song of *Beauty Retire*[1] –
which Knipp hath spread abroad, and he extols it above anything
he ever heard. And without flattery, I think it is good in its
kind. This being done, and going to dance again, comes news
that White-hall was on fire[2] – and presently more*b* perticulars,
that the Horse guard was on fire. And so we run up to the
garret and find it so, a horrid great fire – and by and by we saw
and heard part of it blown up with powder. The ladies begun
presently*c* to be afeared – one fell*d* into fits. The whole town in
an Alarme. Drums beat and trumpets, and the guards everywhere
spread – running up and down in the street. And I begun to
have mighty apprehensions how things might be at home, and

a   MS. 'sins' or 'since'   b   repl. 'better'
c   repl. 'present'- badly written   d   repl. same symbol

1. See above, vi. 320, n. 4. (E).
2. A fire broke out between 7 and
8 p.m. in the Horse Guard House in
the Tilt Yard but was put out by
10 p.m., 'with the loss only of that
part of the Building it had at first
seized': *London Gazette*, 10 November. The *Gazette* did not suggest
that it was caused by anything other
than a pure accident, and Sir E.
Harley wrote to his wife that it was
'occasioned by a drunken groom in
the hayloft': HMC, *Portland*, iii. 303.
Milward (p. 39) reports that it began
at about 4 or 5 p.m. The palace was
destroyed by fire in 1698.

so was in mighty pain to get home; and that that encreased all is that we are in expectation (from common fame) this night or tomorrow to have a Massacre – by the having so many fires one after another – as that in the City. And at the same time begun*ª* in Westminster by the Palace, but put out – and since in Southworke, to the burning down some houses; and now this, doth make all people conclude there is something extraordinary in it, but nobody knows what. By and by comes news that the fire is slackened; so then we were a little cheered*ᵇ* up again, and to supper and pretty merry. But above all, there comes in that Dumb boy that I knew in Olivers time, who is mightily acquainted here and with Downing; and he made strange signs of the fire, and how the King was abroad, and many things they understood but I could not – which I wondering at, and discoursing with Downing about it, "Why," says [he], "it is only a little use, and you will understand him and make him understand you, with as much ease as may be." So I prayed him to tell*ᶜ* him that I was afeared that my coach would be gone, and that he should go down and steal one of the seats out of the coach and keep it, and that would make the coachman to stay. He did this, so that the Dumb boy did go down, and like a cunning rogue went into the coach, pretending to sleep; and by and by fell to his work, but finds the seats nailed to the coach; so he did all he could, but could not do it; however, stayed there and stayed the coach, till the coachman's patience was quite spent, and beat the dumb boy by force, and so went away. So the Dumb boy came up and told him all the story, which they below did see all that passed and knew it to be true. After supper another dance or two, and then news that the fire is as great as ever, which put us all to our wit's end, and I mightily [eager] to go home; but the coach being gone, and it being about 10 at night and rainy dirty weather, I knew not what to do but to walk out with Mr. Batelier, myself resolving to go home on foot and leave the women there. And so did; but at the Savoy got a coach and came back and took up the women; and so (having by people come from the fire understood that the fire was overcome, and all well) we merrily parted, and home. Stopped by several

a repl. symbol rendered illegible *b* repl. 'merry'
c repl. 'bid him by signs go down'

guards and Constables quite through the town (round the wall as we went), all being in armes.   We got well home; and in the way I did con mi mano tocar la jambe de Mercer*ᵃ* sa chair.   Elle retirait sa jambe modestement, but I did tocar sa peau with my naked hand.   And the truth is, la fille hath something that is assez jolie.   Being come home, we to Cards till 2 in the morning; and drinking lamb's-wool, to bed.

10.   Up, and to the office, where Sir W. Coventry came to tell us that the Parliament did fall foul of our accounts again*ᵇ* yesterday,[1] and we must arme to have them examined – which I am sorry for; it will bring great trouble to me and shame upon the office.   My head full this morning how to carry on Captain Cockes bargain of hemp, which I think I shall by my dexterity do, and to the King's advantage as well as my own.   At noon with my Lord Brouncker and Sir Tho. Harvy to Cockes house, and there Mrs. Williams and other company, and an excellent dinner.   Mr. Temples wife after dinner fell to play on the Harpsicon, till she tired everybody, that I left the house without taking leave, and no creature left standing by her to hear her. Thence I home and to the office, where late doing of business; and then home and read an hour, to make an end of Potters discourse of the Number 666, which I like all along, but his close is most excellent; and whether it be right or wrong, is mighty ingenious.[2]   Then to supper and so to bed.

This is the fatal day that everybody hath discoursed for a long time to be the day that the papists, or I know not who, had

---

a   name in s.h.   *b*   repl. same symbol

---

1. See Milward, p. 39.
2. For the book, see above, p. 47, n. 1. In the concluding chapter the author answered objections and conducted an elaborate enquiry into the area and cubic space of Jerusalem on the one hand, and of Rome (seat of Antichrist) on the other. He argued throughout that 666 represents Antichrist, the Beast of Revelations, and that its root (which he calculated, ignoring fractions, to be 25) is an evil number: the number of the original body of Cardinals and parish priests of Rome. 144 signifies Christ, and its square root (12) is the number of the disciples, and of the angels, and of the tribes of Israel. For Pepys's scepticism about the Pope as Antichrist, see above, v. 256.

designed to commit a Massacre upon;[1] but however, I trust in God we shall rise tomorrow morning as well as ever.

This afternoon[a] Creed comes to me, and by him, as also my Lady Pen, I hear that my Lady Denham is exceeding sick,[b] even to death; and that she says, and everybody else discourses, that she is poysoned;[2] and Creed tells me that it is said that there hath been a design to poison the King. What the meaning of all these sad signs are, the Lord knows; but every day things look worse and worse. God fit us for the worst.

11. *Lords day.* Up, and to church, myself and wife – where that old dunce Meriton, brother to the known Meriton of St. Martins Westminster, did make a very good sermon, beyond my expectation.[3] Home to dinner, and we carried in Pegg Pen and there also came to us little Michell and his wife, and dined very pleasantly. Anon to church, my wife and I and Betty Michell, her husband being gone to Westminster. Here at church (God forgive me), my mind did courir upon Betty Michell, so that I do hazer[c] con mi cosa in la eglisa même.

---

a repl. 'day'   *b* repl. 's'-   *c* MS. 'hozer'

---

1. Cf. above, p. 360. Fear of a Catholic rising had been widespread ever since the Fire, which was interpreted (especially by puritan fanatics) as the first step towards the overthrow of Protestantism. Preachers at court and in many churches on Gunpowder Plot Day had warned their hearers that the political principles of the papists were still those of Guy Fawkes; Parliament had asked for measures against them, and a proclamation banishing priests had been issued on this day. But I have found no other references than Pepys's to 10 November as the fatal day. One report (21 November, from Lyme) had it that 23 November was the day appointed: *CSPD 1666–7,* p. 276.

2. Lady Denham was the Duke of York's mistress: the poison was variously alleged to have been administered by the Duchess, by her husband, and by the Countess of Rochester. Cf. *CSPD 1666–7,* pp. 262–3; Marvell, i. 273. She recovered now, but the rumours of poisoning were revived when she died in earnest in January 1667.

3. Thomas Meriton, Rector of St Nicholas Cole Abbey, London, had graduated from Magdalene in 1652, two years before Pepys. He appears to have been the uncle, not brother, of John Meriton, a well-known preacher, once lecturer at St Martin's, now Rector of St Michael's Cornhill and of St Mary Bothaw.

After church, home, and I to my chamber and there did finish the putting time to my song of *It is decreed*.[1]   And do please myself at last, and think it will be thought a good song.   By and by little Michell comes and takes away his wife home, and my wife and brother and I to my Uncle Wights, where my aunt is grown so ugly, and their entertainment so bad, that I am in pain to be there, nor will go thither again a good while if sent for – for we were sent for tonight; we had not gone else.   Woolly's wife a silly woman and not very handsome, but no spirit in her at all – and their discourse mean.   And the fear of the troubles of the times hath made them not to bring their plate to town since it was carried out upon the business of the Fire, so that they drink in earth and a wooden can, which I do not like.   So home, and my people to bed.   I late to finish my song, and then to bed also.   And the business of the firing of the City, and the fears we have of new troubles and violences, and the fear of fire among ourselfs, did keep me awake a good while, considering the sad condition I and my family should be in.   So at last to sleep.

12.   Lay long in bed.   And then up, and Mr. Carcasse brought me near 500 tickets to sign; which I did, and by discourse find him a cunning, confident, shrowd man – but one that I do doubt hath, by his discourse of the ill-will he hath got with my Lord Marquis of Dorchester (with whom he lived), he hath had cunning practices in his time, and would not now spare to use the same to his profit.[2]   That done, I to the office, whither by and by comes Creed to me and he and I walked in the garden a little, talking of the present ill condition of things, which is the common subject of all men's discourse and fears nowadays, and perticularly of my Lady Denham, whom everybody says is poisoned, and he tells me she hath said it to the Duke of York; but is upon the mending hand, though the town says she is dead this morning.   He and I to the Change, where I had several little errands;   and going to Sir R. Viners, I did get such a splash and spots of dirt upon my new Vest, that I was out of countenance to be seen in the street.   This day I received 450 pieces of gold

1. See above, p. 91 & n. 4. (E).
2. James Carkesse (clerk in the Ticket Office) was in 1667 dismissed for issuing double-tickets, but later reinstated.

more of Mr. Stokes, but cost me 22½d change.[1] But I am well contented with it, I having now near 2800l in gold, and will not rest till I get full 3000l – and then will venture my fortune for the saving that and the rest.

Home to dinner, though Sir R Viner would have stayed us to dine with him, he being Sheriffe (but, poor man, was so out of countenance that he had no wine ready to drink to us, his butler being out of the way; though we know him to be a very liberal man); and after dinner I took my wife out, entending to have gone and have seen my Lady Jemimah at White-hall; but so great a stop there was at the New Exchange, that we could not pass in half an hour,[2] and therefore light and bought a little matter at the Exchange; and then home and there at the office awhile, and then home to my chamber; and after my wife and all the maids abed but Jane (whom I put confidence in), she and I and my brother, and Tom and W. Hewer, did bring up all the remainder of my money and my plate-chest out of the cellar, and placed the money in my study with the rest, and the plate in my dressing-room. But endeed, I am in great pain to think how to dispose of my money, it being wholly unsafe to keep it all in coin*a* in one place. But now I have it all at my hand, I shall remember it better to think of disposing of it. This done by one in the morning, to bed.

This afternoon, going toward Westminster, Creed and I did step [in]*b* (the Duke of York being just going away from seeing of it) at Pauls, and in the Convocation-house yard did there see the body of Robt. Braybrooke, Bishop of London, that died 1404.[3] He fell down in his tomb out of the great church into St. Fayths this late Fire, and is here seen his Skeleton with the flesh on; but all tough and dry*c* like a spongy dry leather or

---

a MS. 'kind' (a closely similar symbol) *b* 'in' struck through
c 'and dry . . . ' to end of entry crowded into bottom of page

---

1. For rates of exchange for silver into gold, see above, p. 244 & n. 4.
2. For traffic-blocks, see above, i. 303, n. 1.

3. The brass inscription, recording the name, title and date, had survived.

Touchwood all upon his bones.   His head turned aside.[1]   A great man in his time, and Lord Chancellor – and now exposed to be handled and derided by some, though admired for its duration by others.   Many flocking to see it.

13.   At the[a] office all the morning.   At noon home to dinner, and then out to Bishops-gate-street and there bought some drinking-glasses – a case of knifes, and other things against tomorrow, in expectation of my Lord Hinchingbrooke coming to dine with me.   So home; and having set some things in the way of doing, also against tomorrow, I to my office, there to despatch business, and do here receive notice from my Lord Hinchingbrooke that he is not well, and so not in condition to come to dine with me tomorrow – which I am not in much trouble for, because of the disorder my house is[b] in by the Bricklayers coming to mend the chimney in my dining-room for smoking, which they were upon almost till midnight, and have now made it very pretty, and doth carry smoke exceeding well.

This evening came all the Houblons to me, to invite me to sup with them tomorrow night.   I did take them home, and there we sat and talked a good while, and a glass of wine, and then parted till tomorrow night.

So at night, well satisfied in the alteration of my chimney, to bed.

14.   Up, and by water to White-hall; and thence to West-minster, where I bought several things – as, a hone – ribband –

a   repl. 'my'   *b*   repl. 'in'

---

1.   William Dugdale saw three such bodies.   Braybrooke's was 'so dried up, the flesh, sinews, and skin cleaving fast to the bones, that, being set upon the feet, it stood stiff as a plank, the skin being tough like leather, and not at all inclined to putrefaction, which some attributed to the sanctity of the person . . . but herein was nothing supernatural': *Hist. St. Paul's* (ed. Ellis, 1818), p. 124.   Aubrey (i. 181) has a ghoulish story of the discovery under similar circumstances of the body of Dean Colet, preserved in embalming fluid within a lead coffin.   'Mr.   Wyld and Ralph Greatorex tested [the fluid], and 'twas of a kind of insipid tast, something of an ironish tast.   The body felt, to the probe of a stick which they thrust into a chinke, like brawne.'

gloves – books. And then took coach and to Knipp's lodging, whom I find not ready to go home with me, so I away to do a little business; among others, to call upon Mr. Osborne[1] for my Tanger warrant for the last Quarter, and so to the New Exchange for some things for my wife, and then to Knipp again and there stayed, reading of Wallers verses[2] while she finished her dressing – her husband being by, I had no other pastime. Her lodging very mean, and the condition she lives in; yet makes a show without doors, God bless us. I carried him along with us into the City, and set him down in Bishopsgate-street and then home with her. She tells me how Smith of the Duke's house hath killed a man upon a quarrel in play – which makes everybody sorry, he being a good actor, and they say a good man, however this happens.[3] The ladies of the Court do much bemoan him, she says. Here she and we alone at dinner, to some good victuals that we could not put off, that was intended for the great dinner of my Lord Hinchingbrooke, if he had come. After dinner, I to teach her my new Recitative of *It is decreed* – of which she learnt a good part; and I do well like it, and believe shall be well pleased when she hath it all, and that it will be found an agreeable thing. Then carried her home, and my wife and I intended to have seen my Lady Jemimah at White-hall; but the Exchange street[4] was so full of coaches, everybody as they say going thither to make themselfs fine against tomorrow night, that after half an hour's stay we could not do any; but only, my wife to see her brother, and I to go speak one word with Sir G. Carteret about office business. And talk of the general complexion of matters; which he looks upon, as I do, with horror, and gives us all for an undone people – that there is no such thing as a peace in hand, nor a possibility of any without our begging it, they being as high, or higher, in their terms[a] then

a repl. 'times'

---

1. Clerk to Gauden, Navy victualler.

2. *Poems etc. written upon several occasions*; first published in 1645. Pepys kept the fourth edition (1682): PL 1155.

3. William Smith was a leading performer in Davenant's company. He soon returned to the stage. (A).

4. Presumably the street by the New Exchange – i.e. the Strand.

ever.[1]   And tells me that just now my Lord Hollis[2] had been
with him, and wept to think in what a condition [we] are fallen.
He showed me my Lord Sandwiches letter to ⟨him⟩, complaining of the lack of money; which Sir G. Carteret is at a loss how in
the world to get the King to supply him with – and wishes him
for that reason here, for that he fears he will be brought to
disgrace there, for want of supplies.[3]   He says the House is yet
in a bad humour; and desiring to know whence[a] it is that the
King[b] stirs not, he says he minds it not, nor will be brought
to it – and that his servants of the House do, instead of making the
Parliament better, rather play the rogue one with another, and
will put all in Fire.[4]   So that upon the whole, we are in a wretched
condition, and I went from him in full apprehensions of it.   So
took up my wife, her brother being yet very bad, and doubtful
whether he will recover or no; and so to St. Ellens[5] and there sent
my wife home, and myself to the Popeshead, where all the
Houblons were, and Dr. Croone;[6] and by and by to an exceeding
pretty supper – excellent discourse of all sorts; and endeed, are[c] a
set of the finest gentlemen that ever I met withal in my life.   Here
Dr. Croone told me that at the meeting at Gresham College
tonight (which it seems they now have every Wednesday again)[7]
there was a pretty experiment, of the blood of one Dogg let out
(till he died) into the body of another on one side, while all his
own run out on the other side.   The first died upon the place,

    a repl. 'when'   *b* MS. 'Kings'   *c* MS. 'or'

---

1. Since accepting the Swedish
mediators in July 1666, Britain had
abated her terms, abandoning, e.g.
her attempt to foist the Prince of
Orange on to the Dutch. The latter
still refused to make a separate treaty
without French agreement. See
Feiling, pp. 209–11.
    2. The 1st Baron Holles, ambassa-
dor to France from July 1663 until
May 1666.
    3. For Sandwich's accounts for the
embassy to Spain, see below, 4
October 1667; 8 February 1669, n.
His pay (now in arrears) had been
fixed at the high rate of £8,000 p.a.

4. For the inefficiency of the
Court's spokesmen in the Commons
at this time, see esp. below, pp.
380–1, 388, 408, 416.
    5. St Helen's, Bishopsgate.
    6. William Croone, anatomist and
a leading F.R.S.
    7. Since the Fire the Royal Society
had met regularly on its usual day –
Wednesday – with only two exceptions: 5 September because of the
Fire itself, and 10 October because of
the fast. Birch, ii, *passim*. Pepys
had not attended any meeting since
11 April.

and the other very well, and likely to do well.[1] This did give occasion to many pretty wishes, as of the blood of a Quaker to be let into an Archbishop, and such like. But, as Dr Croone says, may if it takes be of mighty use to man's health, for the amending of bad blood by borrowing from a better body.

After supper James Houblon and another brother took me aside, and to talk of some businesses of their own, where I am to serve them, and will. And then to talk of public matters; and I do find that they, and all merchants else, do give over trade and the nation for lost – nothing being done with care or foresight – no convoys granted, nor anything done to satisfaction. But do think that the Duch and French will master us the next year, do what we can; and so do I, unless God Almighty makes the King to mind his business; which might yet save all.[a]

Here we sat talking till past one in the morning, and then home – where my people sat up for me, my wife and all; and so to bed.

15. This [morning] came Mr. Sheply (newly out[b] of the country) to see me; after a little discourse with him, I to the office, where we sat all the morning. And at noon home, and there dined, Sheply with me, and after dinner I did pay him 70l, which he had paid my father for my use in the country. He being gone, I took coach and to Mr. Pierce's, where I find her as fine as possible, and himself going to the Ball at night at Court, it being the Queenes Birthday. And so I carried them in my coach; and having set them into the house, and gotten Mr. Pierce to undertake the carrying in my wife, I to Unthankes, where she appointed to be, and there told her; and back again about business to White-hall while Pierce went and fetched her and carried her in. I, after I had met with Sir W. Coventry and given him some account of matters, I also to the Ball, and with much ado got up to the Loft, where with much trouble I could see very well. Anon the house grew full, and the candles

a repl. 'us'   *b* repl. ? 'forth'

---

1. The experiment was conducted on a mastiff and a spaniel: Birch, ii. 123; *Philos. Trans.*, i (for 1665-6), 353-8. For transfusion of blood, see below, 30 November 1667 & n.

BB

light, and the King and Queen and all the ladies set. And it was endeed a glorious sight to see Mrs. Steward in black, and white[a] lace – and her head and shoulders dressed with Dyamonds. And the like a[b] great many great ladies more (only, the Queene none); and the King in his rich vest of some rich silk and silver trimming, as[c] the Duke of York and all the dancers were, some of cloth of silver, and others of other sorts, exceeding rich.[1] Presently after the King was come in, he took the Queene, and about fourteen more couple there was, and begun the Bransles. As many of the men as I can remember presently, were: the King – Duke of York – Prince Rupert – Duke of Monmouth – Duke of Buckingham – Lord Douglas – Mr. Hamilton – Collonell Russell – Mr. Griffith – Lord Ossory – Lord Rochester. And of the ladies – the Queene – Duchess of York – Mrs. Steward – Duchess of Monmouth – Lady Essex Howard – Mrs. Temple – Swedes Embassadresse[2] – Lady Arlington – Lord George Barkely's daughter. And many others I remember not. But all most excellently dressed, in rich petticoats and gowns and Dyamonds – and pearl.

After the Bransles, then to a Corant, and now and then a French[d] Dance; but that so rare that the Corants grew tiresome, that I wished it done. Only, Mrs. Steward danced mighty finely, and many French dances, especially one the King called the New Dance,[3] which was very pretty. But upon the whole matter, the business of the dancing of itself was not extraordinary pleasing. But the clothes and sight of the persons was indeed very pleasing, and worth my coming, being never likely to see more gallantry while I live – if I should come twenty times.[e]

About 12 at night it broke up, and I to hire a coach with much difficulty; but Pierce had hired a chair for my wife, and so she

---

a MS. 'while'   *b* repl. 'too'   *c* 'as' repeated
d l.h. repl. l.h. 'Figure'   *e* followed by blot

---

1. Cf. Lord Herbert to Lady Herbert, London, 17 November: 'Never saw greater bravery . . . a hundred vests that at the least cost a hundred pounds. Some were adorned with jewels above a thousand. . . . The ladies much richer than the men . . . the gloriousest assembly everybody said that has been in England since the King's return, except the Coronation' (HMC, *Beaufort*, p. 55).

2. Baroness Leiyonbergh.

3. Unidentified. (E).

being gone to his house – he and I (taking up Barker at Un-thankes) to his house – whither his wife was come home a good while ago, and gone to bed. So away home with my wife – between displeased at the dull dancing, and satisfied at the clothes and persons (my Lady Castlemayne (without whom all is no-thing) being there, very rich, though not dancing*a*); and so after supper, it being very cold, to bed.

16. Up again betimes to attend the examination of Mr. Gawden's accounts[1] – where we all met, but I did little but fit myself for*b* the drawing my great letter to the Duke of York of the state of the Navy for want of money.[2] At noon to the Change, and thence back to the new tavern come by us, the Three Tuns, where D. Gawden did feast us all with a chine of beef and good other things, and an infinite dish of fowl; but all spoiled in the dressing.

This noon I met with Mr. Hooke, and he tells me the Dogg which was filled with another*c* dog's blood at the College the other day, is very well, and like to be so as ever. And doubts not its being found of great use to men; and so doth Dr Whistler, who dined with us at the tavern. Thence home in the evening;*d* and I to my preparing my letter, and did go a pretty way in it, staying late upon it. And then home to supper and to bed, the weather being on a sudden set in to be very cold.

17. Up, and to the office, where all the morning. At noon home to dinner, and in the afternoon shut myself in my chamber,

a MS. 'danced'   *b* repl. 'against and'
    c repl. 'anothers'   *d* repl. 'after'

1. For Pepys's notes on these accounts (November 1666), see NWB, pp. 115–16: Rawl. A 174, ff. 450–1.

2. Navy Board to Duke of York, 17 November; copies in Longleat, Coventry MSS 97, ff. 38–42 (in Pepys's hand) and in NMM, LBK/8, pp. 413–20 (in Hayter's hand, printed in *Further Corr.*, pp. 146–54). The letter includes a brief summary of the reports made on this subject earlier in the year, and concludes with an estimate of the money required to set out the fleet the next spring, and to fit out the new ships then building. To that charge (amounting to c. £180,000) had to be added the debts (£934,000) recently reported to Parliament: cf. above, p. 294.

and there till 12 at night finishing my great letter to the Duke of York; which doth lay the ill condition of the Navy so open to him, that it is impossible, if the King and he minds anything of their business, but it will operate*a* upon them to set all matters right, and get money to carry on the war before it be too late, or else lay out for a peace upon any Tearmes.   It was a great convenience tonight, that what I had writ fowle in shorthand, I could read to W. Hewer and he take it fair in shorthand[1] so as I can read it tomorrow to Sir W. Coventry, and then come home and he read to me, while I take it in longhand to present – which saves me much time.   So to bed.

18.   *Lords day*.   Up by Candle-light and on Foote to White-hall, where by appointment I met Lord Brouncker at Sir W. Coventry's chamber, and there I read over my great letter and they approved it; and as I do do our business in defence of the Board, so I think it is as good a letter in the manner, and believe it is the worst in the matter of it, as ever came from any office to a prince.

Back home in my Lord Brouncker's coach, and there W. Hewer and I to write it over fair.   Dined at noon, and Mercer with us, and mighty merry.   And then to finish my letter, and it being 3 a-clock ere I had done, when I came to Sir W. Batten he was in a huffe, which I made light of.   But he signed the letter, though he would not go, and liked the letter well.   Sir W. Penn, it seems, he would not stay for it; so making slight of Sir W. Penn's putting so much weight upon his hand to Sir W. Batten, I down to the Tower-wharf and there got a Sculler, and to White-hall and there met Lord Brouncker and he signed it; and so I delivered it to Mr. Chevins,[2] and he to Sir W. Coventry in the Cabinet, the King and Council being sitting – where I leave it to its fortune, and I by water home again, and to my

a repl. 'be'

---

1. Hewer used a variety of Shelton's system – not exactly the same as that used by Pepys. A small notebook of Hewer's, consisting mostly of sermon notes in shorthand, is now in the Houghton Library at Harvard.

The last entry is for 4 February 1666. See above, p. 35, n. 3.

2. Will Chiffinch, Page of the Bedchamber and Keeper of the Privy Closet to the King.

chamber to even my Journall. And then comes Captain Cocke to me, and he and I a great deal of melancholy discourse of the times, giving all over for gone, though now the Parliament will soon finish the Bill for money. But we fear if we had it, as matters are now managed, we shall never make the best of it, but consume it all to no purpose – or a bad one. He being gone, I again to my Journall and finished it; and so to supper – and to bed.

19. Lay pretty long in bed, talking with pleasure with my wife; and then up, and all the morning at my own chamber, fitting some Tanger matters against the afternoon for a meeting. This morning also came Mr. Cæsar, and I heard him on the Lute very finely, and my boy begins to play well. After dinner I carried and set my wife down at her brother's, and then to Barkeshire-house, where my Lord Chancellor hath been ever since the fire[1] – but he is not come home yet. So I to West-minster-hall, where the Lords newly up and the Commons still sitting. Here I met withal Mr. Robinson, who did give me a printed paper wherein he states his pretence to the post office, and entends to petition the parliament in it.[2] Thence I to the Bull head tavern (where I have not been since Mr. Chetwin and the time of our club)[3] – and here had six bottles of claret filled, and I sent [them] to Mrs. Martin, whom I had promised some of my own, and having none of my own, sent her this. Thence to my Lord Chancellors, and there met Mr. Creed and Gawden, Cholmly and Sir G. Carteret walking in the park over against the House. I walked with Sir G. Carteret, who I find displeased*a* with the letter I have drawn and sent in yesterday, finding fault

a repl. 'discourse'

1. Berkshire House was near St James's Palace. Clarendon had pre-viously lodged at Worcester House in the Strand.
2. A copy of Robinson's printed petition (4 pp.) is in PRO, SP 29/142, no. 199 (1): *The case and title of Henry Robinson of London unto a deputation and management of both the Letter-* offices. He, and his father Henry before him, claimed the office by virtue of a grant of deputation made by Lord Stanhope who had been appointed to the post in 1577.
3. A weekly meeting, mostly of young government clerks, held in the 1650s: above, i. 208 & n. 4.

with the account we give of the ill state of the Navy; but I said little, only will justify the truth of it. Here we walked to and again till one dropped away after another; and so I took coach and to White-hall and there visited my Lady Jemimah at Sir G. Carteret's lodgings. Here was Sir Tho. Crew, and he told me how hot words grew again today in the House of Lords between my Lord Ossory and Ashly, the former saying that something said by the other was said like one of Olivers council. Ashly said that he must give him reparation, or he would take it his own way. The House therefore did bring my Lord Ossory to confess his fault and ask pardon for it – as he was also to my Lord Buckingham, for saying that something was not truth that my Lord Buckingham had said.¹ This will render my Lord Ossory very little in a little time. By and by away, and calling my wife, went home; and there a little at Sir W. Batten's to hear news, but nothing. And then home to supper, whither Captain Cocke, half-foxed, came and sat with us, and so away and then we to bed.

20. Called up by Mr. Sheply, who is going into the country today to Hinchingbrooke; I sent my service to my Lady and, in general, for news – that the world doth think well of my Lord and doth*ᵃ* wish he were here again. But that the public matters of the State as to the war are in the worst condition that is possible. By and by Sir W Warren, and with him half an hour discoursing of several businesses, and some I hope will bring me a little profit. He gone, and Sheply, I to the office a little, and then to church, it being Thanksgiving day for the cessation of the plague.² But Lord, how the town doth say that it is hastened

a   repl. 'of'

---

1. In the debate on the bill prohibiting the import of Irish cattle this day, Ossory was twice reprehended by the House on these two counts, and twice apologised. He had used 'indecent Expression to the Duke of Bucks' (*LJ*, xiii. 31–2) in the course of defending Irish interests (his father, Ormond, was Lord Lieutenant) against Buck-

ingham's attacks. Cf. above, pp. 342–3 & nn.

2. Appointed by a Council order of 9 November: PRO PC 2/59, f. 108*v*. Service in *A form of common prayer with prayer for thanksgiving . . . for asswaging the late contagion and pestilence* (1666).

before the plague is quite over, there dying some people still,[1] but only to get ground of Plays to be publicly acted, which the Bishops would not suffer till the plague was over. And one would think so, by the suddenness of the notice given of the day, which was last Sunday, and the little ceremony: the sermon being dull, of Mr Milles,[a] and people with great indifferency came to hear him.

After church, home, where I met Mr. Gregory[2] who I did then agree with to come to teach my wife to play on the Viall; and he being an able and sober man, I am mighty glad of it. He had dined, therefore went away, and I to dinner; and after dinner by coach to Barkeshire-house, and there did get a very great meeting, the Duke of York being there, and much business done, though not in proportion to the greatness of the business, and my Lord Chancellor sleeping and snoring the greater part of the time. Among other things, I declared the state of our Credit as to tallies to raise money by. And there was an order for payment of 5000*l*[3] to Mr. Gauden, out of which I hope to get something against Christmas. Here we sat late, and here I did hear that there are some troubles like to be in Scotland, there being a discontented party already risen, that hath seized on the Governor of Dumfreeze and imprisoned him. But the story is yet very uncertain, and therefore I set no great weight on it.[4]

I home, by Mr. Gauden in his coach; and so with great pleasure to spend the evening at home upon my Lyra Viall, and then to supper and to bed – with mighty peace of mind,

a MS. 'Minnes'

---

1. Eight died of plague during 13–20 November; seven in the following week: GL, A.1.5, no. 96.

2. About this time there were two William and two Henry Gregorys, all court musicians. (E).

3. *Recte* £5858: Rawl. A 174, ff. 450–1.

4. This was the beginning of the Pentland Rising: a rebellion of the Covenanters in the South-West. On 15 November, Sir James Turner, Governor of Dumfries and a prominent enemy of the Covenanters, had

been seized by the rebels, and imprisoned in Maxwell Town, Galloway. For the letters from Scotland carrying the news to which Pepys refers, see *CSPD 1666–7*, pp. 262, 268; the *Gazette* had nothing until its issue of 22 November. In the notices Pepys gives later of the rising, his information is usually slightly different (in e.g. estimates of numbers) from that reaching the office of the Secretary of State: see *CSPD 1666–7*, passim.

and a hearty desire that I had but what I have quietly in the country – but I fear I do at this day see the best that either I, or the rest of our nation, will ever see.

21. Up; with Sir W. Batten to Charing-cross, and thence I to wait on Sir Ph. Howard,[1] whom I find dressing himself in his night-gown and Turban like a Turke; but one of the finest persons that ever I saw in my life. He had several gentlemen of his own waiting on him, and one playing finely on the gittarr. He discourses as well as ever I heard man, in few words and hand-some. He expressed all kindness to Balty, whom I told how sick he is. He says that before he comes to be mustered again, he must bring certificate of his swearing the oaths of Allegiance and Supremacy and having taken the sacrament according to the rites of the Church of England.[2] This I perceive is imposed on all – and he will be ready to do. I pray God he may have his health again to be able to do it. Being mightily satisfied with his civility, I away to Westminster-hall; and there walked with several people, and all the discourse is about some trouble in Scotland I heard of yesterday, but nobody can tell the truth of it.

Here was Betty Michell with her mother; I would have carried her home, but her father entends to go with her, so I lost my hopes. And thence I to the Excize-Office about some tallies,[3] and then to the Exchange, where I did much business; and so home to dinner, and then to the office, where busy all the after-noon till night; and then home to supper, and after supper an hour reading to my wife and brother something in Chaucer[4] with great pleasure, and so to bed.

22. Up, and to the office, where we sat all the morning. And my Lord Brouncker did show me Holler's new print of the City, with a pretty representation of that part which is burnt,

---

1. Captain of Albemarle's troop of the Life Guard; younger brother of the 1st Earl of Carlisle.

2. This last requirement was made by an order in council of 9 Novem-ber, following resolutions passed by both houses of Parliament. This and similar measures taken at the time were inspired by the anti-Catholic feeling provoked by the Fire. PRO, PC 2/59, f. 108r.

3. See above, p. 92 & n. 2.

4. Probably from Thomas Speght's 1602 edition of the *Workes*: PL 2365.

very fine endeed. And tells me that he was yesterday sworn the King's servant, and that the King hath commanded him to go on with his great map of the City which he was upon before the City was burned,[1] like Gombout of Paris;[2] which I am glad of. At noon home to dinner, where my wife and I fell out, I being displeased with her cutting away a*ᵃ* lace hankercher so wide about the neck, down to her breasts almost, out of a belief, but without reason, that it is the fashion. Here we did give one another the lie too much, but were presently friends; and then I to my office, where very late and did much business; and then home, and there find Mr. Batelier[3] – and did sup and play at Cards awhile. But he tells me the news how the King of France hath, in defiance to the King of England, caused all his footmen to be put into Vests, and that the noblemen of France will do the like;[4] which, if true, is the greatest indignity ever done by one prince to another, and would incite a stone to be revenged; and I hope our King will, if it be so as he tells me it is – being told by one that came over from Paris with my Lady Fanshaw

a repl. 'her'

---

1. Wenceslaus Hollar and Francis Sandford had been appointed shortly after the Fire to produce maps and surveys showing the damage done to the city, and on 12 November a warrant had been issued for Hollar to be sworn in as 'scenographer and designer of prospects': *CSPD 1666–7*, pp. 111, 256. His map had already been shown, partially finished, to the King (ib., p. 228), and was now published as *A Map or groundplott of the citty of London the blanke space signifying the burnt part....* He also published in this year two 'prospects' of the city, taken before and after the Fire from Southwark, copies of which are in PL 2972, pp. 32–3. His 'great map of the City' was either *A new map of the citties of London, West-minster* (1675), or, more probably, his *A large and accurate map of the city of London*, based on a survey by John

Ogilby and William Morgan published in 1677. See A. M. Hind, *Wenceslaus Hollar and his views of London*, pp. 40–3. Pepys's collection of London maps and prospects is in PL 2972; see esp. pp. 31, 34–5.

2. Jacques Gomboust had published a large map of Paris in 1652. Pepys kept a copy of the issue of 1665: PL 2974, pp. 4–13. Cf. *Further Corr.*, p. 280.

3. Will Batelier, wine merchant.

4. The story is unconfirmed; it was allegedly Louis' revenge on Charles's new anti-French costume: see above, p. 324, n. 3. Halifax, in his *Character of a Trimmer* (1684–5; *Complete Works*, ed. Raleigh, pp. 90–1), wrote that Louis instructed Henriette d'Orléans, on her visit to England in 1670, to 'laugh us out of these vests'.

(who is come over with the dead body of her husband)[1] and that saw it before he came away. This makes me mighty merry, it being an ingenious kind of affront; but yet makes me angry to see that the King of England is become so little as to have that affront offered him.

So I left my people at Cards, and to my chamber to read, and then to bed. Batelier did bring us some oysters tonight, and some bottles of new French wine of this year, mighty good – but I drank but little.

This noon Bagwell's[a] wife was with me at the office, and I did what I would; and at night came Mrs. Burroughs, and appointed to meet upon the next holiday and go abroad together.

23. Up, and with Sir J Minnes to White-hall, where we and the rest attended the Duke of York – where, among other things, we had a complaint of Sir Wm. Jennings against his Lieutenant, Le Neve, one that had been long the Dukes page, and for whom the Duke of York hath great kindness.[2] It was a drunken quarrel, where one was as blameable as the other. It was referred to further examination, but the Duke of York declared that as he would not favour disobedience, so neither drunkenness – and thereon he said very well.

Thence with Sir W. Coventry to Westminster-hall, and there parted – he having told me how Sir J. Mennes doth disagree from the proposition of resigning his place, and that so the whole matter is again at a stand – at which I am sorry for the King's sake, but glad that Sir W. Penn is again defeated, for I would not have him come to be Controller if I could help it, he will be so cruel proud. Here I spoke with Sir G Downing about our prisoners in Holland and their being released; which he is con-cerned in, and most of them are.[3] Then discoursing of matters of the House of Parliament, he tells me that it is not the fault of the House, but the King's own party that hath hindered the

a name in s.h.

---

1. See above, p. 214 & n. 1.
2. Jennings commanded the *Ruby*. Richard Le Neve (now 20) was made a captain in 1671.
3. Downing, lately envoy-extra-ordinary to the United Provinces, supervised the exchange of prisoners of war in the winters of 1665-6 and 1666-7. Cf. *CSPD 1665-6*, p. 432.

passing of the Bill for money, by their popping in of new projects for raising it[1] – which is a strange thing. And mighty confident he is that what money is raised will be raised and put into the same form that the last was, to come into the Exchequer.[2] And for aught I see, I must confess I think it is the best way.

Thence down to the Hall and there walked awhile, and all the talk is about Scotland, what news thence; but there is nothing come since the first report, and so all is given over for nothing.

Thence home; and after dinner to my chamber with Creed, who came and dined with me, and he and I to reckon for his salary; and by and by comes in Collonell Atkins[3] and I did the like with him; and it was Creeds design to bring him only for his own ends, to seem to do him a courtesy. And it is no great matter – the fellow I hate, and so I think all the world else do. Then to talk of my report I am to make of the state of our wants of money to the Lord Treasurer; but our discourse came to little. However, in the evening, to be rid of him, I took coach and saw him to the Temple, and there light; and he being gone, with all the haste back again and to my chamber late, to enter all this day's matter of accounts in my book ⟨and*a* draw up my report to my Lord Treasurer, and so⟩ to bed. At the Temple I called at Playfords and there find that his new impression of his Ketches are not yet out, the fire having hindered it; but his man tells me that it will be a very fine piece – many things new being added to it.[4]

24. Up, and to the office, where we sat all the morning. At noon rose, and to my closet and finished my report to my Lord Treasurer of our Tanger wants; and then with Sir J. Mennes by coach to Stepny to the Trinity-house – where it is kept again now, since the burning of their other house[5] in London. And

a   repl. 'so'

---

1. See below, p. 408 & n. 4.
2. The Eleven Months Tax of 1666 was in this respect like the Additional Aid of 1665: see above, vi. 292 & n. 3.
3. Samuel Atkins had supplied the Tangier garrison with oats, coals, etc.: PRO, AO1/310/1220.

4. John Playford, *Catch that catch can, or The Musical companion* (1667); Pepys bought it on 15 April 1667. Earlier books in the series had appeared in 1652, 1658 and 1663. (E).
5. In Water Lane, near the Tower. (R).

here a great many met at Sir Tho. Allen's feast of his being made an Elder Brother – but he is sick, and so could not be there. Here was much good company, and very merry. But the discourse of Scotland, it seems, is confirmed; and that they are 4000 of them in armes and do declare for King and Covenant – which is very ill news.[1] I pray God deliver us from the ill consequences we may justly fear from it. Here was a good venison pasty or two, and other good victuals. But towards the latter end of the dinner I rose, and without taking leave, went away from table, and got Sir J. Mennes' coach and away home; and thence with my report to my Lord Treasurer's, where I did deliver to Sir Ph. Warwicke for my Lord (who was busy) my report, for[a] him to consider against tomorrow's council. Sir Ph. Warwick, I find, is full of trouble in his mind to see how things go and what our wants are; and so I have no delight to trouble him with discourse, though I honour the man with all my heart, and I think him to be a very able and right honest man. So away home again, and there to my office[b] to write my letters very late; and then home to supper, and then to read the late printed discourse of Witches by a member of Gresham College, and then to bed – the discourse being well writ in good style, but methinks not very convincing.[2] ⟨This day Mr. Martin came to tell me his wife is brought to bed of a girl, and I promised to christen it next Sunday.⟩[c]

25. *Lords day.* Up, and with Sir J. Mennes by coach to White-hall; and there coming late, I to rights* to the chapel – where in my usual place I heard one of the King's chaplains,

---

a repl. 'to'　　b repl. 'cl'-
c addition crowded in between entries

---

1. The rebels (whose numbers are here greatly exaggerated) renewed the Covenant of 1638 at Lanerick, in Clydesdale, declaring their loyalty to the King and their enmity to nothing but episcopacy: Burnet, i. 420. Cf. *London Gazette*, nos 106, 108, 109.

2. Joseph Glanvill, *Some philosophical considerations touching the being of witches*; in which the author tried to find scientific ground for the existence of witchcraft. His book was twice re-issued in 1667; the fourth edition appeared in 1668 under a new title (*A blow at modern Sadducism, in some philosophical considerations about witchcraft*). Pepys retained Glanvill's *Saducismus Triumphatus, or Full and plain evidence concerning witches and apparitions* (1681): PL 1211.

one Mr. Floyd,[1] preach. He was out two or three times in his prayer, and as many in his sermon; but yet he made a most excellent good sermon, of our duty to imitate the lives and practice of Christ and the saints departed. And did it very handsomely, and excellent style – but was a little over-large in magnifying the graces of the nobility and prelates that we have seen in our memories in the world, whom God hath taken from us.

At the end of the sermon, an excellent Anthemne. But it was a pleasant thing, an idle companion in our pew (a prating, bold counsellor, that hath been heretofore at the Navy Office, and noted for a great[a] eater and drinker, not for quantity but of the best – his name Tom Bales) said, "I know a fitter Anthem for this sermon, speaking only of our duty of fallowing the saints, and I know not what – Cooke should have sung *Come[b] Fallow Fallow mee*."[2]

After sermon, up into the gallery, and then to Sir G. Carteret's to dinner, where much company. Among others, Mr. Carteret and my Lady Jem. And here was also Mr. Ashburnham, the great man[3] – who is a pleasant man, and that hath seen much of the world and more of the Court.

After dinner Sir G. Carteret and I to another room, and he tells me more and more of our want of money and in how ill condition we are likely to be soon in. And that he believes we shall not have a fleet at sea the next year; and so do I believe, but he seems to speak it as a thing expected[c] by the King – and as if their matters were laid accordingly.

Thence into the Court, and there delivered copies of my report to my Lord Treasurer, to the Duke of York, Sir W. Coventry, and others. And attended there till the Council met, and then was called in and I read my letter. My Lord Treasurer declared that the King had nothing to give till the Parliament did give

a repl. 'greater'   *b* l.h. repl. s.h.   *c* repl. 'intended'

---

1. William Lloyd, Prebendary of Ripon, appointed chaplain to the King in July 1666; later (1680) Bishop of St Asaph.

2. Possibly the popular catch composed by John Hilton (d. 1657): see

Catch that catch can (1652), p. 22, and later editions. But the first line is common to several songs and ballads. (E).

3. William Ashburnham, Cofferer of the King's Household.

him some money.   So the King did of himself bid me to declare
to all that would take our tallies for payment, that he should,
as soon as the Parliament's money doth come in, take back their
tallies and give them money – which I giving him occasion to
repeat to me (it*ᵃ* coming from him against the *gré*, I perceive, of
my Lord Treasurer), I was content therewith and went home –
and glad that I have got so much.   Here stayed till the Council
rise, walking in the galleries; all the talk*ᵇ* being of Scotland, where
the highest report, I perceive, runs but upon 3 or 400¹ in armes.
But they believe that it will grow more, and do seem to apprehend
it much, as if the King of France had a hand in it.²   My Lord
Lauderdale³ doth make nothing of it, it seems; and people do
censure him for it – he from the beginning saying that there was
nothing in it, whereas it doth appear to be a pure rebellion.   But
no persons of quality being in it, all do hope that it cannot amount
to much.⁴

Here I saw Mrs. Steward this afternoon, methought the
beautifullest creature that ever I saw in my life, more then ever
I thought her, as often as I have seen her – and I begin to think
doth exceed my Lady Castlemayne, at least now.

This being St. Katherines day, the Queene was at masse by
7 a-clock this morning.   And Mr. Ashburnham doth say that
he never saw anything have so much zeale in his life as she hath –
and (the Question being asked by my Lady Carteret) much
beyond the bigotery that ever the old Queen-mother had.

I spoke with Mr. May, who tells me that the*ᶜ* design of building
the City doth go on apace; and by his description, it will be

a repl. 'though'   *b* repl. 'talking'   *c* MS. 'I'

---

1. This is presumably a mistake for
'3 or 4000'.   The rebels were at first
rumoured to be 4000 strong; estimates were now a little lower:
CSPD 1666–7, p. 295.   That given
at about this time to the Scottish
Privy Council was c. 3000: *Reg. P.
C. Scot. 1665–9*, p. 226.
2. The Scottish government feared
Dutch rather than French influence:

ib., p. xi; *CSPD 1666–7*, p. 284.   In
fact it was a purely local rising.
3. Secretary for Scottish affairs.
4. Only two lairds, both of them
said to be 'mad fellows', joined the
rebellion, and ministers of the kirk
were serving as officers. *CSPD 1666–
7*, p. 268; *Reg. P. C. Scot., 1665–9*,
p. 226; Burnet, i. 418.

mighty handsome, and to the satisfaction of people. But I pray God it come not out too late.[1]

The Council up, after speaking with Sir W. Coventry a little, away home with Captain Cocke in his coach; discourse about the forming of his contract he made with us lately for hemp.[2] And so home, where we parted, and I find my Uncle Wight and Mr. Wight and Woolly, who stayed and supped, and mighty merry together. And then I to my chamber to even my journall, and then to bed. ⟨I will remember that Mr. Ashburnham today at dinner told how the rich fortune Mrs. Mallett reports of her servants: that my Lord Herbert would have had her – my Lord Hinchingbrooke was indifferent to have her – my Lord Jo. Butler might not have her – my Lord of Rochester would have forced her; and Sir   Popham (who nevertheless is likely to have her) would kiss her breech to have her.⟩ [a3]

26. Up and to my chamber to do some business. Then to speak with several people; among others, with Mrs. Burroughs, whom I appointed to meet me at the New Exchange in the afternoon. I by water to Westminster, and there to enquire after my tallies, which I shall get this week. Thence to the Swan,

a addition crowded in between entries

---

1. The government and city were anxious to lose no time; committees were hard at work, and on 19 November the work of clearing the rubble had been started. Hugh May (Controller of the King's Works) had been appointed early in October to the commission set up jointly by the Privy Council and the city to prepare a survey of the ground (there was no map or street-plan in existence) and to devise regulations for the new streets and buildings. It is to these plans, and not to the famous schemes of Wren and others, that Pepys refers as 'handsome'. When he speaks of the satisfaction of 'people', he means the property-owners and tenants.

His fear of the rebuilding being too late was a generally felt fear that inhabitants would migrate or establish themselves in the suburbs rather than wait for the new buildings. See T. F. Reddaway, *Rebuilding of London*, pp. 40+, esp. 60–1.

2. Under a contract of 30 October Cocke had obtained £56 per ton, less £3 per ton for convoy charges: *CSPD 1666–7*, p. 390. Cf. above, p. 245 & n. 5.

3. Elizabeth Malet married Rochester in 1667. Popham was probably Sir Francis (of the Wiltshire family). For the proposal to marry her to Hinchingbrooke, see above, p. 56 & n. 1.

having sent for some burnt claret, and there by and by comes Doll Lane, and she and I sat and drank and talked a great while; among other things, about her sister being brought to bed – and I too to be the godfather to the girl. I did tumble Doll, and do almost what I would with her; and so parted, and I took coach and to the New Exchange, buying a neat-tongue by the way, thinking to eat it out of town. But there I find Burroughs in company of an old woman, an aunt of hers, which she could not leave – for half an hour. So after buying a few baubles to while away time, I down to Wesminster, and there into the House of Parliament, where at a great committee[1] I did hear, as long as I would, the great case against my Lord Mordaunt for some arbitrary proceedings of his against one Taylor, whom he imprisoned and did all the violence to imaginable, only to get him to give way to his abusing his daughter.[2] Here was Mr. Sawyer, my old Chamberfellow, a counsel against my Lord, and I am glad to see him in so good play.[3] Here I met, before the committee sat, with my Cosen Roger Pepys, the first time I have spoke with him this parliament; he hath promised to come and bring Madam Turner with him (who is come to town to see the City but hath lost all her goods of all kinds in Salsbury-Court, Sir Wm. Turner having not endeavoured in her absence to save

---

1. A Grand Committee of Grievances of the Commons, which Pepys, as a member of the public, had no right to attend. Its proceedings are not noticed in the official *Journals* of either House or in Milward.

2. This was a *cause célèbre*. Mordaunt, appointed Governor of Windsor Castle and High Steward of the town for his royalist services, was now accused by William Tayleur (Paymaster and Surveyor of the castle) of ejecting him from his chambers and imprisoning him because he had presumed to stand as parliamentary candidate for Windsor in 1661. He was also said to have 'made sundry uncivil addresses' to Tayleur's daughter in 1664. The examination which

Pepys attended led to Mordaunt's impeachment in the following January. Saved by the prorogation of parliament in February 1667, he resigned his Windsor office, and received a royal pardon in the following July. *LJ*, xii. 60–2, 77–9; *State Trials* (ed. Howell), vi. 785+; *CSPD 1667*, p. 277; ib., *1667–8*, p. 608; R. R. Tighe and J. E. Davis, *Annals of Windsor*, ii. 283+.

3. Robert Sawyer had been an undergraduate at Magdalene from 1648 to 1652 (Pepys from 1651 to 1654). He had became a fellow of the college (1654) and was now a barrister of the Inner Temple. He was knighted in 1677 and made Attorney-General in 1681.

one penny)[1] to dine with me on Friday next – of which I am glad. Roger bids me to help him to some good rich widow, for he is resolved to go and retire wholly into the country; for he says he is confident we shall be all ruined very speedily by what he sees in the State – and I am much of his mind. Having stayed as long as I thought fit for meeting of Burroughs, I away and to the Change again, but there do not find her now, I having stayed too long at the House – and therefore very hungry, having eat nothing today; home, and there to eat presently. And then to the office a little, and so to Sir W. Batten, where Sir J. Mennes and Captain Cocke was; but no news from the North at all today. And the news-book makes that business nothing,[2] but that they are all dispersed. I pray God it may prove so. So home; and after a little at my chamber, to bed.

27. Up, and to the office, where we sat all the morning. And here I had a letter from Mr. Brisband on another occasion, which by the by intimates my Lord Hinchingbrooke's intention to come and dine with me tomorrow. This put me into a great surprize, and therefore endeavoured all I could to hasten over our business at the office; and so home at noon and to dinner, and then away by coach, it being a very foul day, to White-hall; and there at Sir G. Carteret find my Lord Hinchingbrooke, who promises to dine with me tomorrow and bring Mr Carteret along with him. Here I stayed a little while, talking with him and the ladies; and then away to my Lord Crews, and there did by the by make a visit to my Lord Crew and had some good discourse with him – he doubting that all will break in pieces in the Kingdom. And that the taxes now coming out, which will tax the same man in three or four several capacities; as, for lands – office – profession – and money at interest – will be the hardest that ever came out.[3] And doth think that we owe it, and the

<hr>

1. Jane Turner had been living at Kirkleatham, Yorks.: below, p. 403. Sir William was her brother-in-law.

2. The report (19 November) from Carlisle in the *London Gazette* of this day said that the rebels were few, and engaged only in a family quarrel with the Governor of Dumfries. The large forces of horse and foot sent by

the Scottish Privy Council would 'no doubt suddenly give a good account of the mutineers.' Cf. also the report from Edinburgh of 21 November in *CSPD 1666–7*, p. 276.

3. The Land Tax and Poll Tax bills, passed on 8 February 1667. For Pepys's poll tax, see below, 25 January, 5 April 1667.

lateness of its being given, wholly to the unpreparedness of the King's own party to make their demand[a] and choice; for they have obstructed the giving it by land-tax, which had been done long since. Having ended my visit with him, I spoke to Sir Tho. Crew to invite him and his brother John to dinner tomorrow at my house to meet Lord Hinchingbrooke; and so homeward, calling at the cook's who is to dress it to bespeak him; and then home, and there set things in order for a very fine dinner; and then to the office, where late, very busy and to good purpose as to despatch of business; and then home – to bed – my people sitting up to get things in order against tomorrow. This evening was brought me, which Griffin had, as he says, taken this afternoon off of the table in the office, a letter sealed and directed to the Principal Officers and Comissioners of the Navy.[1] It is a serious and just Libell against our disorder in paying of our money, making ten times more people wait then we have money for, and complaining by name of Sir W. Batten for paying away great sums to perticular people – which is true. I was sorry to see this way of reproach taken against us, but more sorry that there is true ground for it.

28. Up, and with Sir W. Penn to White-hall (setting his Lady and daughter down by the way at a mercer's in the Strand, where they are going to lay out some money); and to White-hall, where, though it blows hard and rains hard, yet the Duke of York is gone a-hunting. We therefore lost our labour, and so back again – and I by hackney-coach to several places to get things ready against dinner,[b] and then home and did the like there, to my great satisfaction; and at noon comes my Lord Hinchingbrooke, Sir Tho. Crew, Mr. John Crew, Mr. Carteret,[c] and Brisband. I had six noble dishes for them, dressed by a man-cook, and commended, as endeed they deserved, for exceedingly well done. We eat with great pleasure, and I enjoyed myself in it with reflections upon the pleasures which I at best can expect, yet not to exceed this – eating in silver plates, and all things mighty rich and handsome about me. A great deal of fine

---

a repl. 'dement'   *b* repl. 'tomorrow'   *c* repl. 'Herb'-

---

1. Untraced.

discourse, sitting almost till dark at dinner; and then broke up with great pleasure, especially to myself, and they away; only, Mr. Carteret and I to Gresham College, where they meet now weekly again. And here they had good discourse how this late experiment of the dog (which is in perfect good health) may be improved to good uses to men – and other pretty things, and then broke up.¹ Here was Mr. Henery Howard, that will here-after be Duke of Norfolke, who is admitted this day into the Society; and being a very proud man, and that values himself upon his family, writes his name, as he doth everywhere: *Henery Howard of Norfolke.*²

Thence home, and there comes my Lady Pen, Pegg, and Mrs. Turner, and played at cards and supped with us, and were pretty merry – and Pegg with me in my closet a good while, and did suffer me a la besar mucho et tocar ses cosas upon her breast – wherein I had great pleasure, and so spent the evening; and then broke up, and I to bed, my mind mightily pleased with this day's entertainment.

29. Up, and to the office, where busy all the morning. At noon home to dinner, where I find Balty come out to see us, but looks like death, and I do fear he is in a consumption. He hath not been abroad many weeks before – and hath now a well day, and a fit day of the head-ake, in extraordinary torture. After dinner, left him and his wife, they having their mother hard by; and my wife and I, a wet afternoon, to White-hall to have seen my Lady Carteret and Jemimah; but as God would have it, they were abroad, and I was well contented at it. So my wife and I to Westminster-hall, where I left her a little, and to the Exchequer and then presently home again, calling at our Man=cooke's for his help tomorrow, but he could not come. So I home to the office, my people all busy to get a good dinner

---

1. Birch, ii. 128.
2. He was the second son of the Earl of Arundel, and became 6th Duke of Norfolk in 1677. For his benefac-tions to the Royal Society he had received a message of thanks, and was now elected a fellow and shortly afterwards a member of Council:

Birch, ii. 128, 131. He is referred to in the society's minutes as 'Mr. Henry Howard of Norfolk'. Later at the prompting of the Duke of York he was to provide Pepys with a parlia-mentary seat at Castle Rising, Norf., in 1673.

tomorrow again. I late at the office, and all the news I hear I put into a letter[1] this night to my Lord Brouncker at Chatham. Thus – "I doubt not of your Lordshipp's hearing of Sir Tho. Clifford's succeeding Sir H. Pollard in the Controllership of the King's house.[2] But perhaps our ill (but confirmed) tidings[a] from the Berbados may not yet, it coming but yesterday; *viz.* that about eleven ships (whereof two of the King's, the *Hope* and *Coventry*) going thence with men to attack St. Christophers, were seized by a violent Herricana and all sunk – two only of thirteen escaping, and those with loss of masts, &c; my Lord Willoughby himself is involved in the disaster, and I think two ships thrown upon an island of the French, and so all the men (to 500) become their prisoners.[3] Tis said, too, that eighteen Dutch men-of-war are passed the Channell, in order to meet with our Smyrna ships;[4] and some, I hear, do fright us with the King of Sweden's seizing our mast-ships at Gottenburgh.[5] But we have too much ill news true, to afflict ourselfs with what[b] is uncertain. That which I hear from Scotland is the Duke of York's saying yesterday that he is confident the Lieutenant Generall there hath driven them into a pound, somewhere towards the mountains."[6]

Having writ my letters, I home to supper and to bed – the

---

a repl. 'news'   *b* repl. same symbol badly formed

---

1. Original untraced.

2. For Clifford's rise, see above, p. 288, n. 3. The order for his swearing-in was issued on 28 November: *CSPD 1666–7*, p. 298. His predecessor had died on the 27th.

3. This disaster had occurred on 16 August. Willoughby of Parham, Governor of Barbados and the Leeward Islands since 1663, had led an expedition to retake St Christopher's, captured by the French in the spring of 1666. He himself was drowned. Details of the disaster were given in letters from Plymouth to the Navy Board and to Williamson, 27 November: *CSPD 1666–7*, pp. 292–4. The *Hope* was lost – it was the ship in

which Willoughby was drowned – and the *Coventry* captured. Pepys appears to be uncertain about the total number of the ships. There were in fact eight merchant ships as well as the two frigates: A. P. Thornton, *W. India policy under Restoration*, p. 128, n. 7.

4. See below, p. 404 & n. 3.

5. See below, p. 424.

6. The rebels had attempted to march from the south-west on to Edinburgh, but on the 28th the government forces under Thomas Dalziel overwhelmed them at Rullion Green in the Pentland Hills. See below, pp. 396–7.

world being mightily troubled at the ill news from Berbados and the consequence of the Scotch business, as little as we do make of it.

And to show how mad we are at home*a* here, and unfit for any troubles – my Lord St. John's did a day or two since openly pull a gentleman in Westminster-hall by the nose (one Sir Andr. Henly) while the Judges were upon their benches, and the other gentleman did give him a rap over the pate with his cane – of which fray, the Judges they say will make a great matter; men are only sorry the gentleman did proceed to return a blow, for otherwise my Lord would have been soundly fined for the affront – and may be yet for his affront to the judges.[1]

30. Up and with Sir W. Batten to White-hall, and there we did attend the Duke of York and had much business with him. And pretty to see (it being St. Andrew's day) how some few did wear St. Andrew's Crosse; but most did make a mockery at it, and the House of Parliament, contrary to practice, did sit also – people having no mind to observe that Scotch saint's day till they hear better news from Scotland.

Thence to Westminster-hall and the abby, thinking, as I had*b* appointed, to have met Mrs. Burroughs there; but not meeting*c* her, I home and just overtook my Cosen Rogr. Pepys, Mrs. Turner, Dike, and Joyce Norton, coming by invitation to dine with me – these ladies I have not seen since before the plague. Mrs. Turner is come to town to look after her things in her house; but all is lost. She is quite weary of the country, but

---

a repl. same symbol badly formed   *b* repl. 'entend'   *c* repl. 'coming'

---

1. The affray happened on the 28th, when the Court of Common Pleas was sitting, and was thus committed *coram rege*. The offenders were Charles Lord St John of Basing, son and heir of the Marquess of Winchester, and M.P. for Hampshire, and Sir Andrew Henley, Bt, of Henley, Som. Henley was arrested immediately; St John escaped but later admitted his offence (which he said was committed in passion), and by intercession of the Commons received a royal pardon in June 1667. *CSPD 1666–7*, p. 299; ib., *1667*, p. 67; *CJ*, viii. 656–7. St John was an eccentric. Later, as Marquess of Winchester, he lived a queer life, turning night into day – his dinner parties commonly going on till 7 or 8 a.m.: Reresby, *Memoirs* (ed. A. Browning), p. 467.

cannot get her husband to let her live here any more, which troubles her mightily. She was mighty angry with me, that in all this time I never writ to her; which I do think and take to myself as a fault, and which I have promised to mend. Here I had a noble and costly dinner for them, dressed by a man=cooke, as that the other day was. And pretty merry we were, as I could be with this company and so great charge. We sat long; and after much talk of the plenty of her country[1] in Fish, but in nothing also that is pleasing, we broke up with great kindness; and when it begun to be dark, we parted, they in one coach home, and I in another to Westminster hall – where by appointment Mrs. Burroughs and I were to meet, but did not, after I had spent the whole evening there. Only, I did go drink at the Swan, and there did meet with Sarah,[2] who is now newly married; and there I did lay the beginnings of a future amor con ella, which in time may come para laisser me hazer alguna cosa con elle. Thence, it being late, away; called at Mrs. Burroughs mother's door, and she came out to me and I did hazer whatever I would con su mano tocando mi cosa; and then parted and home; and after some playing at cards with my wife, we to supper and to bed.

1. North Riding, Yorkshire.   2. Sarah Harmond, *née* Udall.

DECEMBER.

1. Up and to the office, where we sat all the morning. At home to dinner, and then abroad, walking to the Old Swan, and in my way*a* did see a cellar in Tower streete in a very fresh Fire, the late great winds having blown it up; it seemed to be only of Loggwood, that hath kept the fire all this while in it.[1] Going further, I met my late Lord Mayor ⟨Bludworth⟩, under whom the City was burned, and went with him by water to White-hall. But Lord, the silly talk that this fellow had – only, how ready he would be to part with all his estate in these difficult times to advance the King's service, and complaining that now (as everybody did lately in the Fire) everybody endeavours to save himself and let the whole perish – but a very weak man he seems to be.[2] I left him at White-hall, he giving 6*d* towards the boat, and I to Westminster-hall, where I was again defeated in my expectation of Burroughs – however, I was not much sorry for it; but by coach home in the evening, calling at Faythornes and buying three of my Lady Castlemaynes heads, printed this day; which endeed is, as to the head, I think a very fine picture, and like her.[3] I did this afternoon get Mrs. Michell to let me*b* only have a sight of a pamphlett lately printed, but suppressed and much called after, called *The Catholiques Apology*,[4] lamenting the severity of the Parliament against them – and comparing it

a MS. 'wife' *b* MS. 'him'

---

1. Fires had continued to smoulder in cellars despite the wet weather of October. Rugge (ii. 187*v*) noticed one on the following 28 January; Pepys saw a smoking cellar on 16 March.

2. Cf. above, p. 280 & n. 4. An anonymous comment on him in 1672 was that he was 'willing, though it may be not very able, to doe great things': qu. A. B. Beaven, *Aldermen of London*, ii. 186.

3. See above, p. 359 & n. 3. (OM).

4. *The Catholique apology* (1666); usually attributed to Roger Palmer, Earl of Castlemaine (husband of Barbara, the King's mistress); not in the PL. An order for its suppression had been issued on 28 November: *CSPD 1666–7*, p. 296.

with the lenity of other princes to protestants. Giving old and late instances of their Loyalty to their princes, whatever is objected against them. And excusing their disquiets in Queen Elizabeths time, for that it was impossible for them to think her a lawful queen, if Queene Mary, who had been owned as such, were so; one being the*a* daughter of the true, and the other of a false wife – and that of the Gunpowder Treason, by saying that it was only the practice of some of us, if not the King, to trapan some of their religion into it, it never being defended by the generality of their Church, nor endeed known by them. And ends with a large Catalogue in red Letters, of the Catholiques which have lost their lives in the quarrel of the late King and this. The thing is very well writ endeed. So home to my letters, and then to my supper and to bed.

2. *Lords day.* Up and to church; and after church home to dinner, where I met B. Michell and her husband. Very merry at dinner; and after dinner, having borrowed Sir W Pen's coach, we to Westminster, they two and my wife and I, to Mr. Martins, where find the company almost all come to the christening of Mrs. Martin's child,*b* a girl. A great deal of good plain company. After sitting long, till the church was done, the parson comes, and then we to christen the child;*c*[1] I was godfather, and Mrs. Holder (⟨her⟩ husband, a good man, I know well)[2] and a pretty lady that waits it seems on my Lady Bath at White-hall – her name Mrs. Noble, were godmothers. After the christening comes in the wine and the sweetmeats, and then to prate and tattle, and then very good company they were, and I among them. Here was old Mrs. Michell, and Howlett, and several married women of the Hall whom I knew mayds. Here was also Mrs. Burroughs – and Mrs. Boles the young widow, whom I led home; and having stayed till the moon was up, I took my pretty gossip to White-hall with us and I saw her in her lodging, and then my own company again took coach; and no sooner

a repl. 'a'   *b* MS. 'church'   *c* MS. 'church'

1. She was christened Catherine, the name made fashionable by the Queen. She only lived to be two.

2. Possibly Joseph Holden, a haberdasher of St Bride's Lane.

in the coach but something broke, that we were fain there to stay till a smith could be fetched, which was above an hour, and then it costing me 6*s* to mend. Away round by the wall and Cow-lane,[1] for fear it should break again, and in pain about the coach all the way. But to ease myself therein, Betty Michell did sit at the same end with me, and there con su mano under my manteau, I did pull off her cheirotheca and did tocar mi cosa con su mano through my chemise,*a* but yet so as to hazer me hazer la grande cosa – and she did let me hazerle sin mucho trabaho. Being very much pleased with this, we at last came home; and so to supper, and then sent them by boat home, and we to bed.

When I came home, I went to Sir W. Batten's, and there I hear more ill news still; that all our New England fleet which went out lately are put back a third time by foul weather, and dispersed, some to one port and some to another, and their convoys also to Plymouth; and whether any of them be lost or no, we do not know.[2] This, added to all the rest, doth lay us flat in our hopes and courages, everybody prophesying destruction to the nation.

3. Up, and among a great many people that came to speak with me, one was my Lord Peterborough's gentleman, who comes to me to dun me to get some money advanced for his Lord.[3] And I demanding what news, he tells me that at Court they begin to fear the business of Scotland more and more, and that the Duke of York entends to go to the North to raise an army, and that the King would have some of the nobility and others to go and assist; but they were so served the last year (among others, his Lord) in raising forces at their own charge for fear of the French invading us, that they will not be got out now, without money advanced to them by*b* the King. And this is like to be the King's case for certain, if ever he comes to have need of any army.

a repl. ? same symbol badly formed   *b* repl. 'to'

---

1. Famous for its coachmakers. (R).
2. Lanyon to Navy Board, 30 November, Plymouth: *CSPD 1666–7*, p. 301. They set out again on 4 and 7 December: ib., p. 326.
3. See above, p. 355 & n. 3.

He and others gone, I by water to Westminster, and there to the Exchequer and put my tallies in a way of doing for the last Quarter.   But my not fallowing it the last week hath occasioned the clerks some trouble, which I am sorry for and they are mad*a* at. Thence at noon home, and there find Kate Joyce, who dined with me. Her husband and she are weary of their new life of being an Inn Keeper, and will leave it, and would fain get some office; but I know none the fool is fit for.[1]   But would be glad to help them if I could, though they have enough to live on, God be thanked; though their loss hath been to the value of 3000*l*. W Joyce now hath all the trade, she says, the trade being come to that end of the town.[2]   She dined with me, my wife being ill of her months in bed.   I left her with my wife, and away myself to Westminster-hall by appointment, and there found out Burroughs; and I took her by coach as far as my Lord Treasurers, and called at the Cake-house by Hales's, and there in the coach eat and drank, and then carried her home – with much ado making her to tocar mi cosa, she being endeed very averse a alguna cosa of that kind. However, time can hazer-la, the same as it hath hecho others. So having set her down in the palace, I to the Swan and there did the first time bezar the little sister of Sarah, that is come into her place;[3] and so away by coach home, where to my Vyall and supper, and then to bed, being weary of the fallowing of my pleasure and sorry for my omitting (though with a true salvo to my vows) the stating my last month's accounts in time, as I should.   But resolve to settle and clear all my business before me this month, that I may begin afresh the next year and enjoy some little pleasure freely at Christmasse. So to bed – and with more cheerfulness then I have done a good while, to hear that for certain the Scott rebells are all routed – they having been so bold as to come within three

a repl. 'made'

---

1. Anthony Joyce was now an inn-keeper in Clerkenwell. He had suffered in the Fire from the loss of several of the houses he owned. He committed suicide in January 1668.

2. William Joyce, her brother-in-law, was a tallow-chandler in Covent Garden. The Fire had driven trade westwards.

3. Sarah (Udall) had left to be married to a shoemaker: above, p. 355 & n. 2. Her sister appears to have been Frances: below, 24 April 1667.

mile of Edingburgh, and there given two or three repulses to the King's forces, but at last were mastered – 3 or 400 killed or taken; among which, their leader, one Wallis, and seven ministers (they having all taken the Covenant a few days before, and sworn to live and die in it, as they did); and so all is likely to be there quiet again.[1] There is also the very good news come, of 7[a] New-England ships come home safe to Falmouth with masts for the King;[2] which is a blessing mighty unexpected, and without which (if for nothing else) we must have failed the next year. But God be praised for thus much good fortune, and send us the continuance of his favour in other things. So to bed.

4. Up and to the office, where we sat all the morning. At noon dined at home. After dinner presently to my office and there late, and then home to even my Journall and accounts; and then to supper, much eased in mind and last night's good news, which is more and more confirmed, with perticulars to very good purpose; and so to bed.

5. Up and by water to White-hall, where we did much business before the Duke of York; which being done, I away home by water again, and there to my office till noon, busy. At noon home, and Goodgroome[3] dined with us – who teaches my wife to sing.[b] After dinner I did give him my song, *Beauty retire*,[4] which he hath often desired of me; and without flattery, I think is a very good song. He gone, I to the office and there late very busy, doing much business; and then home to supper and talk; and then scold with my wife for not reckoning well the times that her music masters have been with her, but setting down more then I am sure, and did convince her, they had been with her; and in a ill humour of anger with her, to bed.

a repl. '4'   *b* MS. 'since'

---

1. This was the battle of Rullion Green, fought seven miles south-south-west of Edinburgh: see above, p. 390 & n. 6.
2. John Lanyon to Navy Board; Plymouth, 30 November: *CSPD 1666–7*, p. 301.

3. Probably the Goodgroome who was Pepys's singing-master in 1661. (E).
4. See above, vi. 320, n. 4. (E).

6. Up, but*a* very good friends with her before I rose; and
so to the office, where we sat all the forenoon; and then home to
dinner, where Harman dined with us, and great sport to hear
him tell how Will Joyce grows rich by the custom of the City
coming to his end of the town, and how he rants over his brother
and sister for their keeping an Inn, and goes thither and tears like
a prince, calling him "hosteller," and his sister "hostess." Then
after dinner my wife and brother (in another habit)[1] go out to
see a play; but I am not to take notice that I know of my brother's
going. So I to the office, where very busy till late at night, and
then home. My wife not pleased with the play, but thinks that
it is because she is grown more Criticall then she used to be. But
my brother, she says, is mightily taken with it. So to supper and
to bed.

This day in the gazette was the whole story of defeating the
Scotch Rebells, and of the creation of the Duke of Cambrige
Knight of the Guarter.[2]

7. Up and by water to the Exchequer, where I got my
tallies finished for the last Quarter for Tanger; and having paid
all my fees, I to the Swan, whither I sent for some oysters; and
thither comes Mr. Falconbrige and Spicer and many more clerks,
and there we eat and drank, and a great deal of their sorry discourse; and so parted, and I by coach home, meeting Balty in
the street about Charing-cross, walking; which I was glad to
see,[3] and spoke to him about his mustering business, I being now
to give an account how the several muster-maisters have behaved
themselfs; and so home to dinner, where finding the cloth laid,
and much crumpled but clean, I grew angry and flung the
trenchers about the room, and in a mighty heat I was; so a clean
cloth was laid, and my poor wife very patient; and so to dinner,
and in comes Mrs. Barbara Shelden, now Mrs. Wood,[4] and dined

a repl. 'and 5'-

---

1. I.e. in layman's dress, being
about to go to the theatre.
2. *London Gazette,* 6 December.
The Duke of Cambridge (second son
of the Duke of York) had been
installed as a knight of the Garter at

Whitehall on 3 December, in the
place of the 2nd Earl of Lindsey, who
had died on 29 July.
3. He had been ill: see above, p.
389.
4. See above, p. 242 & n. 4.

with us. She mighty fine – and lives, I perceive, mighty happily; which I am glad for her sake, but hate her husband for a blockhead in his choice.[1] So away after dinner, leaving my wife and her,[a] and by water to the Strand and so to the King's playhouse, where two acts were almost done when I came in; and there I sat with my cloak about my face and saw the remainder of *The Mayds Tragedy* – a good play, and well acted, especially by the younger Marshall, which is become a pretty good actor.[2] And is the first play I have seen in either of the houses since before the great plague – they having acted now about fourteen days publicly. But I was in mighty pain lest I should be seen by anybody to be at a play.[3] As soon as done, I home and there to my office awhile; and then home and spent the night evening my Tanger accounts,[b] much to my satisfaction; and then to supper, and mighty good friends with my poor wife, and so to bed.

8. Up and to the office, where we sat all the morning; and at noon home to dinner, and there find Mr. Pierce and his wife and Betty, a pretty girl – who in discourse at table told me of the great Proviso passed the House of Parliament yesterday, which makes the King and Court mad – the King having given order to my Lord Chamberlain to send to the playhouses (and bawdy houses) to bid all the Parliament-men that were there to go to the Parliament presently – this is true, it seems – but it was carried against the Court by 30 or 40 voices. It is a Proviso to the Poll Bill, that there shall be a committee of nine persons that shall have the inspection, upon oath and ⟨power of⟩ giving oaths, of

a repl. 'them'   *b* repl. 'business'

---

1. Sc. in her choice of him.
2. The play was by Beaumont and Fletcher; see above, ii. 100 & n. 4. Rebecca Marshall (younger sister of Anne Marshall, another actress at this theatre) played Evadne. (A).
3. Pepys had not visited a public theatre since 15 May 1665, though he

had seen a play at the royal private theatre in the Great Hall at Whitehall on 29 October 1666. He presumably felt that playgoing was a dangerous and unbecoming pastime in the midst of the war and so soon after the Plague and the Fire. Cf. above, p. 347. (A).

all the accounts of the money given*ᵃ* and spent for this warr.¹
This hath a most sad face, and will breed very ill blood – he tells
me brought in by Sir Robt. Howard, who is one of the King's
servants, at least hath a great office and hath got, they say,
20000*l* since the King came in.²

Mr. Pierce did also tell me as a great truth, as being told it by
Mr. Cowly,³ who was by and heard it – that Tom Killigrew⁴
should publicly tell the King that his matters were coming into a
very ill state, but that yet there was a way to help all – which is,
says he, "There is a good honest able*ᵇ* man that I could name,
that if your Majesty would imploy and command to see all things
well executed, all things would soon be mended; and this is one
Charles Stuart – who now spends his time in imploying his lips
and his prick about the Court, and hath no other imployment.
But if you would give him this imployment, he were the fittest
man in the world to perform it." This he says is most true.

But the King doth not profit by any of this, but lays all aside
and remembers nothing, but to his pleasures again – which is a
sorrowful consideration.

Very good company we were at dinner, and merry; and after
dinner, he being gone about business, my wife and I, and Mrs.
Pierce and Betty and Balty, who came to see us today, very sick,
and went home not well, together out. And our coach broke

---

a repl. 'sp'-   *b* repl. 'man'

---

1. The voting was 119–83. There
was doubt whether parliament could
properly authorise the administration
of oaths to the servants of the King.
According to Milward (pp. 48, 56), it
was Garroway who introduced the
proposal to tack the provision on to
the poll bill: cf. *CJ*, viii. 659. In the
event a separate bill was introduced
but never passed. The King appointed his own commission of
enquiry. See below, p. 404; *CTB*,
vol. ii, pp. xlii–xlvi. Pepys's informant was Pearse, the Duke of York's
surgeon, and Groom of the Bedchamber to the Queen.

2. Howard (the dramatist; M.P.
for Stockbridge, Hants.), as well as
enjoying other court emoluments, had
been Serjeant-Painter to the King
(1660–3) and Clerk of the Patents in
Chancery (1660–4), surrendering each
office to a purchaser. See H. J.
Oliver, *Sir R. Howard*, pp. 38–9, 40.
With two others, he had lent £20,000
to the King in 1665: ib., p. 124. But
he was a constant critic of the government in parliament.

3. Abraham Cowley, the poet.

4. Groom of the Bedchamber to
the King.

the wheel off upon Ludgate-hill – so we were fain to part ourselfs and get room in other people's coaches. And Mrs. Pierce and I in one, and I carried her home and set her down, and myself to the King's playhouse (which troubles me since, and hath cost me a forfeit of xs, which I have paid)¹ and there did see a good part of *The English Monsieur*,² which is a mighty pretty play, very witty and pleasant – and the women do very well; but above all, little Nelly³ – that I am mightily pleased with the play and much with the House, more then ever I expected, the*ᵃ* women doing better then ever I expected, and very fine women.

Here I was in pain to be seen, and hid myself; but as God would have it, Sir John Chichly⁴ came and sat just by me.

Thence to Mrs. Pierces, and there took up my wife, and away home and to the office and Sir W. Batten's, of whom I hear that this Proviso in Parliament is mightily ill taken by all the Court-party, as a mortal blow and that that strikes deep into the King's prerogative – which troubles me mightily.

Home, and set some papers right in my chamber; and then to supper and to bed – we being in much fear of ill news of our Colliers – a fleet of 200 sail – and fourteen Duch men-of-war between them and us. And they coming home with small con-voy – and the City in great want, [coals] being at 3*l* 3*s* per Chaldron as I am told.⁵ I saw smoke in the ruines this very day.⁶

a MS. 'but'

---

1. In accordance with his vow not to visit playhouses more than once a month; see above, v. 33. (A).
2. A comedy by James Howard, first acted in 1663, and published in 1674. (A).
3. Nell Gwynn, who played Lady Wealthy. She had made her début in 1664, but this is the first time that Pepys mentions having seen her on the stage. (A).
4. Naval captain; son of Thomas Chicheley, Ordnance Commissioner.
5. The colliers were dispersed by the Dutch, but none were taken. Bad weather drove some back to Newcastle. *CSPD 1666–7*, pp. 285, 335, 343, 364. Pepys reports that at the end of the winter the price of coal had gone up to £4 a chaldron (c. £3 a ton): below, 6 March 1667. In the following summer, when the Dutch invaded the Thames, it was still dearer: £5 10s. a chaldron (over £4 a ton): below, 26 June 1667 & n. Prices of fuel, light, and textiles were higher in 1666–7 than at any time in the late 17th century: J. K. Horse-field, *Brit. monetary experiments 1650–1710*, p. 4.
6. Cf. above, p. 393 & n. 1.

9. *Lords day.* Up, not to church but to my chamber, and there begun to enter into this book my Jou[r]nall of September, which in the Fire time I could not enter here, but in loose papers.[1] At noon dined, and then to my chamber all the afternoon and night, looking over and tearing and burning all the unnecessary letters which I have had upon my File for four or five years backward – which I entend to do quite through all my papers, that I may have nothing by me but what is worth keeping, and fit to be seen if I should miscarry. At this work till midnight, and then to supper and to bed.

10. Up, and at my office all the morning, and several people with me; Sir W. Warren, who I do every day more and more admire for a miracle of cunning and Forecast in his business – and then Captain Cocke, with whom I walked in the garden. And he tells me how angry the Court is at the late proviso brought in by the House. How still my Lord Chancellor is, not daring to do or say anything to displease the Parliament. That the Parliament is in a very ill humour, and grows every day more and more so. And that the unskilfulness of the Court and their difference among one another is the occasion of all, not agreeing in what they would have, and so give leisure and occasion to the other part to run away with what the Court would not have.

Then comes Mr. Gawden, and he and I in my chamber discoursing about his business[2] and to pay him some Tanger orders, which he delayed to receive till I have money instead of tallies. But doth promise me consideration for my Victualling business for this year, and also as Treasurer for Tanger, which I am glad of, but would have been gladder to have just now received it. He gone, I alone to dinner at home, my wife and her people being gone down the River today for pleasure, though a cold day, and dark night to come up.

In the afternoon, I to the Excize Office to enter my tallies; which I did, and came presently back again. And then to the office and did much business; and then home to supper, my

---

1. Cf. above, vol. i, p. xcix & n. 6.
2. Cf. Gauden to Pepys, 3 December (summary in NWB, p. 103),

complaining of the impressment of seamen from his victualling ships.

wife and people being come well and hungry home from Erith. Then I to begin the setting of a Base to *It is Decreed*,[1] and so to bed.

11. Up, and to the office, where we sat; and at noon home to dinner, a small dinner because of a good supper. After dinner my wife and I by coach to St. Clements church, to Mrs. Turner's lodgings hard by to take our leaves of her. She is returning into the North to her child, where I perceive her husband hath clearly got the mastery of her, and she is likely to spend her days [there]; which for her sake I am a little sorry for, though for his, it is but fit she should live where he hath a mind.[2] Here were several people come to see and take leave of her, she going tomorrow. Among others, my Lady Mordant, which was Betty Turner, a most homely widow, but young and pretty rich and good-natured.[3] Thence, having promised to write every month to her – we home; and I to my office, while my wife to get things together for supper. Despatched my business at the office. Anon comes our guests: old Mr. Batelier[4] and his son and daughter – Mercer – which was all our company. We had a good venison pasty and other good cheer, and as merry as in so good, innocent, and understand[ing] company I could be. He is much troubled that wines laden by him in France before the late proclamation was out, cannot now be brought into England, which is much to his and other merchants' loss.[5]

We sat long at supper, and then to talk, and so late parted – and so to bed. This day the Pole bill was to be passed, and great endeavours used to take away the Proviso.

12. Up, and to the office, where some accounts of Mr. Gawdens were examined. But I home most of the morning to even some accounts with Sir H. Cholmly – Mr. Moone – and others, one after another. Sir H. Cholmly did with grief tell

1. See below, p. 414, n. 2. (E).
2. See above, p. 387 & n. 1. The Turners, who had lost their house in Salisbury Court in the Fire, returned to live in London in the following spring. John Turner, the husband, became a serjeant-at-law in 1669.
3. With her sister Mrs Steward, she became a close friend of Pepys in the 1670s. Pepys is mistaken in calling her Betty Turner; she was the daughter of Nicholas Johnson, of London, who had married Sir William Turner's sister. Her first husband (Sir George Mordaunt, Bt) had died in 1665.
4. Joseph Batelier, sen.
5. A proclamation of 10 November had prohibited the import from France of all goods or manufactures of French origin: Steele, no. 3481.

DD

me how the Parliament*a* hath been told plainly that the King hath been heard to say that he would dissolve*b* them rather then pass this Bill with the Proviso. But tells me that the Proviso is removed, and now carried that it shall be done by a Bill by itself.[1] He tells me how the King hath lately paid above 30000*l* to clear debts of my Lady Castlemaynes – and that she and her husband are parted for ever, upon good terms, never to trouble one another more.[2] He says that he hears that above 400000*l* hath gone into the Privy-purse since this Warr, and that that hath consumed so much of our money and makes the King and Court so mad to be brought to discover it.

He gone, and after him the rest – I to the office; and at noon to the Change, where the very good newes is just come of our*c* four ships from Smyrna come safe without convoy even into the Downes, without seeing any enemy[3] – which is the best, and endeed only considerable good news to our Exchange since the burning of the City; and it is strange to see how it doth cheer up men's hearts. Here I saw shops now come to be in this Exchange. And met little Batelier – who sits here, but at 3*l* per annum, whereas he sat at the other at 100*l* – which he says he believes will prove of as good account to him now, as the other did at that rent. From the Change to Captain Cockes, and there by agreement dined. And there was Charles Porter – Temple – Fenn – De Busty[4] (whose bad English and pleasant discourses was exceeding good entertainment), Matt Wren – Major Cooper, and myself. Mighty merry, and pretty discourse.

They talked for certain that now the King doth fallow Mrs. Steward wholly – and my Lady Castlemayne not above once a week. That the Duke of York doth not haunt my Lady Denham so much. That she troubles him with matters of state, being of

---

a repl. 'the'   *b* repl. 'deserve'   *c* repl. 'our four (rich) Smyrna ships'

---

1. By a vote of 11 December: *CJ*, viii. 661. For this attempt to appoint a committee of enquiry, see above, p. 400 & n. 1.

2. Cf. above, iii. 147 & n. 1. Gifts to Lady Castlemaine (and with them her extravagance) are said to have increased after she had arranged for the appointment of her friend Baptist May as Keeper of the Privy Purse. Cf. Clarendon, *Life*, iii. 61–2.

3. They carried a cargo valued at £700,000 and had been in danger of capture by a Dutch squadron: above, p. 390; *CSPD 1666–7*, pp. 340, 341, 343–4.

4. Lawrence Debussy, merchant.

my Lord Bristoll's faction, and that he avoids.   That she is ill still.[1]

After dinner I away to the office, where we sat late upon Mr. Gaudens accounts – Sir J. Mennes being gone home sick.   I late at the office, and then home to supper and to bed, being mightily troubled with a pain in the small of my back, through cold, or (which I think most true) by straining last night to get open my plate=chest.   In such pain all night, I could not turn myself in my bed.   ⟨News this day from Brampton of Mr. Ensum, my sister's sweetheart, being dead – a clowne.*⟩[a]

13.   Up, and to the office, where we sat.   At noon to[b] the Change, and there met Captain Cocke and had a second time[2] his direction to bespeak 100*l* of plate, which I did at Sir R Viner's – being twelve plates more – and something else I have to choose. Thence home to dinner;   and there W. Hewer dined with me, and showed me a Gazett in Aprill last (which I wonder should never be remembered by anybody) which tells how several persons were then tried for their lives, and were found guilty of a design of killing the King and destroying the government;   and as a means to it, to burn the City;   and that the day entended for the plot was the 3rd of last September.   And that fire did endeed break out on the 2nd of September – which is very strange me-thinks – and I shall remember it.[3]

At the office all the afternoon – late;   and then home to even my accounts in my Tanger book, which I did to great content in all respects, and joy to my heart;   and so to bed.

---

a   addition crowded in between entries   *b*   repl. 'home'

---

1. For her illness, see above, p. 365 & n. 2.   The Bristol faction was anti-Clarendonian and therefore in bad odour with the Duke.

2. Cf. above, pp. 90, 91.

3. The *London Gazette*, 29 April 1666, reported that eight Common-wealthsmen had been convicted at the Old Bailey of high treason.   They had plotted the capture of the Tower, the death of the King and the over-throw of the government, and meant to declare 'for an equal division of Lands etc.'   'The better to effect this Hellish Design, the City was to have been fired . . . the third of *September* was pitched on for the Attempt, as being found by *Lillies* Almanack, and a Scheme erected for that purpose, to be a lucky day, a Planet then ruling which prognosticated the Downfal of Monarchy.'   Cf. Burnet, i. 411.   In fact 3 September was always a date of preternatural importance to the fana-tics, since it was the anniversary of Dunbar and of Cromwell's death.

This afternoon Sir W. Warren and Mr Moore, one after another, walked with me in the garden; and they both tell me that my Lord Sandwich is called home.[1] And that he doth grow more and more in esteem everywhere, and is better spoken of – which I am mighty glad – though I know well enough his deserving the same before, and did foresee that it will come to it.

In mighty great pain in my back still. But I perceive it changes its place – and doth not trouble me at all in making of water; and that is my joy, so that I believe it is nothing but a strain. And for these three or four days I perceive my[a] overworking of my eyes by Candle light doth hurt them, as it did the last winter. That by day I am well and do[b] get them right – but then after candle-light they begin to be sore and run – so that I entend to get some green spectacles.

14. Up, and very well again of my pain in my back, it having been nothing but cold. By coach to White-hall, seeing many smokes of the Fire by the way yet. And took up into the coach with me a country gentleman, who asked me room to go with me, it being dirty – one come out of the North to see his son after the burning his house – a merchant. Here endeavoured to wait on the Duke of York, but he would not stay from the Parliament. So I to Westminster-hall – and there met my good friend Mr. Eveling and walked with him a good while – lamenting our condition, for want of good counsel and the King's minding of his business and servants. I out to the Bell Taverne, and thither comes Doll to me and yo did tocar la cosa of her as I pleased; and after an hour's stay away, and stayed in Westminster-hall till the rising of the House, having told Mr. Eveling, and he several others, of my Gazette which I had about me, that mentioned in April last a plot for which several were condemned of treason at the Old bayly for many things; and among others, for a design of burning the City on the 3rd of September. The House sat till 3 a-clock; and then up, and I home with Sir St. Fox to his house to dinner, and the Cofferer with us. There I find his lady, a fine[c] woman, and seven the prettiest children of theirs that ever I knew almost. A very gent dinner, and in

a repl. 'the'   *b* repl. 'did'   *c* repl. 'b'–

1. A canard: Sandwich did not   in Madrid until September 1668.
return to England from his embassy

great state and fashion, and excellent discourse – and nothing like an old experienced man and a Courtier, and such is the Cofferer Ashburnham. The House hath been mighty hot today against the Paper bill – showing all manner of averseness*[a]* to give the King money; which these Courtiers do take mighty notice of, and look upon the others as bad rebells as ever the last were. But ⟨the Courtiers⟩ did carry it against those men, upon a division of the House, a great many, that it should be committed; and so it was – which they reckon good news.[1] After dinner we three to the Excise Office, and there had long discourse about our monies, but nothing to satisfaction; that is, to show any way of shortening the time which our tallies take up before they become payable – which is now full two years – which is 20 per cent of all the King's money for interest[2] – and the great disservice of his Majesty otherwise.

Thence in the evening round by coach home, where*[b]* I find Founds's his present of a fair pair of Cand[l]estickes and half a dozen of plates come; which costs him full 50*l* and is a very good present.[3]

And here I met with, sealed up, from Sir H. Cholmly, the*[c]* Lampoone or the Mocke=advice to a Paynter, abusing the Duke of York and my Lord Sandwich, Pen, and everybody, and the King himself, in*[d]* all the matters of the Navy and Warr.[4]

a repl. 'ill'   *b* MS. 'which'   *c* repl. 'his'   *d* repl. 'for'

1. The vote to commit the stamp-duty bill passed by 89 to 52: *CJ*, viii. 662. Cf. above, p. 332, n. 2.

2. I.e. the King had to borrow from the bankers for two years at 10%.

3. William Fownes, clerk to the Storekeeper at Deptford yard, had been appointed Clerk of the Cheque there at Michaelmas. On 1 February 1667 Pepys found him to be a 'very child' in his business and had to give him a lesson in it.

4. In parody of Waller's *Instructions to a painter* (1665, celebrating the Battle of Lowestoft), there had just been published *The second advice to a painter, being the last work of Sir John Denham* (dated 1667), a satirical description of the same battle. Neither this nor any of its sequels (below, 20 January, 1 July, 16 September 1667) is in the PL. This and *The third advice* have been attributed (uncertainly) to Marvell: see M. T. Osborne, *Advice-to-a-painter poems*, pp. 28–9; G. deF. Lord, (ed.) *Poems of State*, vol. i (*1660–78*), p. 21, n. The copy Pepys here refers to appears to have been in MS. Pepys had himself once thought of writing something similar: above, p. 207.

I am sorry for my Lord Sandwich having so great a part in it.[1]
Then to supper and Musique, and to bed.

15. Up, and to the office, where my Lord Brouncker (newly
come to town from his being at Chatham and Harwich to spy
enormities); and at noon I with him and his Lady Williams to
Captain Cocke's, where a good dinner and very merry. Good
news today upon the Exchange: that our Hamburgh fleet is got
home[a] – and good hopes that we may soon have the like of our
Gottenburgh, and then we shall be well for this winter.[2] Very
merry at dinner. And by and by comes in Matt Wrenn from
the Parliament-house, and tells us that he and all his party of the
House, which is the Court-party, are fools, and have been made
so this day by the wise men of the other side[3] – for after the
Court-party had carried it yesterday so powerfully for the Paper
Bill, yet now it is laid aside wholly, and to be supplied by a land-
Tax – which, it is true, will do well and will be the sooner finished,
which was the great argument for the doing of it – but then it
shows them fools, that they would not permit this to have been
done six weeks ago, which they might have had.[4] And next,
they have parted with the Paper Bill;[5] which, when once begun,
might have proved a very good flower in the Crowne as any
there. So doth really say that they are truly outwitted by the
other side.

a MS. 'him'

---

1. It attacked his part in the Bergen
and prize-ships affairs, and sneered at
his appointment to Spain: 'There let
him languish a long quarantine,/And
ne'er to England come till he be
clean' (ll. 315–16).
2. See below, p. 424 & n. 3.
3. Cf. the similar report in the
letter from Sir John to Sir Edward
Nicholas, 19 December: BM, Eger-
ton 2539, f. 76r. For the court
party's mismanagement of parliament
(in 1667–8), see C. Roberts in *Hunt.*

Lib. Quart., 20/137+. Matthew
Wren (M.P. for St Michael, Corn-
wall) was secretary to Clarendon.
4. Cf. above, p. 356 & n. 3. It
was now ordered that the House
should go into Committee of the
Whole on the following Monday to
proceed on the bill for a monthly
assessment: *CJ*, viii. 663. The bill
passed the House on 25 January.
5. I.e. the proposal to levy a stamp-
duty: see above, p. 332 & n. 2.

Thence away to Sir Robt. Viners and there chose some plate, besides twelve plates, which I purpose to have with Captain Cocke's gift of 100*l*. And so home and there busy late, and then home and to bed.

16. *Lords day.* Lay long, talking with my wife in bed. Then up with great content, and to my chamber to set right a picture*a* or two – Lovett having sent me yesterday Santa Clara's head varnished, which is very fine.[1] And now my closet is so full stored and so fine, as I would never desire to have it better.

Dined without any strangers with me – which I do not like on Sundays. Then after dinner by water to Westminster to see Mrs. Martin, whom I found up in her chamber and ready to go abroad. I sat there with her and her husband and others a pretty while; and then away to White-hall and there walked up and down to the Queen's side, and there saw my dear Lady Castle-mayne, who continues admirable methinks – and I do not hear but that the King is the same to her still as ever. Anon to chapel, by the King's closet, and heard a very good Anthemne. Then with Lord Brouncker to Sir W. Coventry's chamber, and there we sat with him and talked. He is weary of anything to do, he says, in the Navy. He tells us this Committee of Accounts will enquire sharply into our office;[2] and (speaking of Sir J. Mennes) he says he will not bear anybody's faults but his own. He discoursed as bad of Sir W. Batten almost. And cries out upon the discipline of the fleet, which*b* is lost. And that there is not, in any of the fourth-rates and under, scarce left one Sea=Comander, but all young gentlemen. And which troubles him, he hears that the gentlemen do give out that in two or three years a Tarpawlin shall not dare to look after being better then a Boatswain[3] – which he is troubled at, and with good reason. And at this day Sir Robt. Holmes is mightily troubled that his brother doth not command in chief, but is commanded

a repl. 'a'   *b* repl. 'with'

---

1. Unidentified. (OM).
2. See below, 2 January 1667 & n,
3. Cf. above, p. 11 & n. 1,

by Captain Hannum – who, Sir W. Coventry says he believes to be at least of as good blood – is a longer bred seaman – an elder officer, and an elder commander.[1] But such is Sir R. Holmes's pride, as never to be stopped – he being greatly troubled at my Lord Brouncker's late discharging all his men and officers but the standing-officers at Chatham;[2] and so are all other Commanders, and a very great cry hath been to the King from them all in my Lord's absence. But Sir W. Coventry doth undertake to defend it, and my Lord Brouncker got ground by it I believe – who is angry at Sir W. Batten and W. Penn's bad words concerning it. And I have made it worse by telling him that they refuse to sign to a paper which he and I signed on Saturday to declare the reason of his actions – which Sir W. Coventry likes, and would have it sent him and he will sign it – which pleases me well.

So we parted, and I with Lord Brouncker to Sir P. Neale's chamber, and there sat and talked awhile – Sir Edwd. Walker being there, and telling us how he hath lost many fine Rowles of antiquity in Heraldry by the late fire, but hath saved the most of his papers.[3] Here was also Dr. Wallis, the famous scholar and mathematician; but he promises little.[4]

1. A squadron under Kempthorne was about to sail for the Mediterranean. John Holmes (later a distinguished admiral) was now only 26, and had held his first commands in the summer engagements of this year. Pepys thought him idle and proud: below, 8 April 1668. Willoughby Hanham had commanded four ships since 1660.

2. The principle of continuous employment for naval officers was gradually introduced (largely through Pepys's own efforts) in 1668–75. Even so, they were mostly unemployed during the winter months when the ships were refitting. Rigging wages (half-pay) were later in the century paid to junior officers in winter. See below, 6 July 1668, n.;

Cat., i. 145+ ; Ehrman, esp. pp. 139–40. The standing officers were warrant officers and were normally not removable from their ships.

3. Walker was Garter King-of-Arms. The heralds had had about one day in which to move their records (to Whitehall), and they appear to have saved almost all of them. See *CSPD 1670*, p. 566; A. R. Wagner, *Records Coll. of Arms*, p. 20.

4. Pepys's acquaintance with John Wallis later prospered; in the 1690s they corresponded on mathematical subjects: see *Priv. Corr.*, esp. vol. i, p. xiii. In 1701 Pepys commissioned Kneller to paint Wallis's portrait for Oxford University.

Left them, and in the dark and cold home by water; and so to supper and to*a* read, and so to bed – my eyes being better today – and I cannot impute it to anything but by my being much in the dark tonight, for I plainly find that it is only excess of light that makes my eyes sore.

This afternoon I walked with Lord Brouncker into the park, and there talked of the times. And he doth think that the King sees that he cannot never have much more money or good from this Parliament, and that therefore he may hereafter dissolve them. That as soon as he hath the money settled, he believes a peace will be clapped up; and that there are overtures of a peace[1] – which, if such as the Lord Chancellor can excuse, he will take. For it is the Chancellors interest, he says, to bring peace again, for in peace he can do all and command all; but in war he cannot, because he understands not the nature of the war – as to the management thereof. He tells me he doth not believe that the Duke of York will go to sea again, though there are a great many about the King that would be glad of any occasion to take him out of the world – he standing in their ways; and seemed to mean the Duke of Monmouth – who spends his time the most viciously and idly of any man, nor will be fit for anything – yet he speaks as if it were not impossible but the King would own him for his son, and that there was a marriage between his mother and him[2] – which God forbid should be, if it be not true; nor will the Duke of York easily be gulled in it. But this, put to our other distractions, makes things appear very sad, and likely to be the occasion of much confusion in a little time. And my Lord Brouncker seems to say that nothing can help us but the King's making a peace as soon as he hath this money; and thereby*b* putting himself out of debt, and so becoming a good husband;* and then he will neither need this, nor any other Parliament till he can have one to his mind. For no Parliament can, as he says, be kept long good – but they will spoil one another. And that therefore it hath been the practice of kings

a repl. 'there'   *b* repl. 'then'

---

1. Negotiations with both the Dutch and the French were now under way: Feiling, p. 210.

2. See above, iii. 238 & n. 4.

to tell Parliaments what he hath for them to do, and give them so long time to do it in, and no longer.

Harry Kembe, one of our messengers, is lately dead.

17. Up, and several people to speak with me. Then comes Mr. Cæsar, and then Goodgroome, and what with one and the other, nothing but Musique with me this morning, to my great content; and the more to see that God Almighty hath put me into condition to bear the charge of all this. So out to the Change I, and did a little business; and then home, where they two musicians and Mr. Cooke came to see me – and Mercer, to go along with my wife this afternoon to a play. To dinner, and then our*a* company all broke up, and I to my chamber to do several things – among other things, to write a letter to my Lord Sandwich,[1] it being one of the burdens upon my mind that I have not writ to him since*b* he went into Spain. But now I do intend to give him a brief account of our whole year's action since he went, which will make amends. My wife well home in the evening from the play; which I was glad of, it being cold and dark, and she having her necklace of pearl on, and none but Mercer with her. Spent the evening in fitting my books, to have the number set upon each in order to my having an Alphabet of my whole, which will be of great ease to me.[2] This day Captain Batters came from sea in his Fireshipp, and came to see me, poor man, as his patron[3] – and a poor painful wretch he is as can be. After supper, to bed.

a repl. 'my'   *b* repl. 'when'

---

1. Untraced.
2. This was the first of his catalogues. His books were now contained in two presses. For their numbering and listing, see succeeding entries. Neither this list nor the revisions mentioned below at 15–16 February 1668 and 24 May 1669 are known to survive. In October 1681 Pepys records having 'put up in the Greate Chest 2 old Cathalogues of my Books': Rawl. A 183, f. 239r.

Paper 'tickets' were now pasted on the spines: below, pp. 416, 417. (The volumes at the ends of the shelves still retain their small diamond shaped slips; but these represent the final 'adjustment' of the library by John Jackson.) The shelfmarks (in arabic numerals) were pencilled by Pepys on the fly-leaves, but possibly not before 1672. (Inf. from H. M. Nixon).
3. Cf. above, vi. 37 & n. 4.

18. Up and to the office, where I hear the ill news that poor Batters, that hath been born and bred a seaman, and brought up his ship from sea but yesterday, was, going down from me to his ship, drownded in the Thames – which is a sad fortune, and doth make me afeared, and will do, more then ever I was.[1]

At noon dined at home; and then by coach to my Lord Bellasses, but not at home; so to Westminster hall, where the Lords are sitting still. I to see Mrs. Martin, who is very well, and intends to go abroad tomorrow after her childbed. She doth tell me that this child did come la même jour that it ought to hazer after my avoir été con elle before her marido did venir home. And she would now have done anything cum ego; and did endeavour, but su cosa stava mala, which did empescar. Thence to the Swan, and there I sent for Sarah[a] and mighty merry we were, but contra my will were very far[b] from hazer algo. So to Sir Rob. Viner's about my plate, and carried home another dozen of plates, which makes my stock of plates up $2\frac{1}{2}$ dozen. And at home find Mr. Tho. Andrews,[2] with whom I stayed and talked a little, and invited him to dine with me at Christmas; and then I to the office, and there late doing business, and so home and to bed – sorry for poor Batters.

19. Up and by water to White-hall, and there with the Duke of York did our usual business. But nothing but complaints of want of money, with[out] success, and Sir W. Coventry's complaint of the defects of our office (endeed Sir J. Mennes's), without any amendment. And he tells us so plainly of the committee of Parliament's resolution to enquire home into all our managements, that it makes me resolve to be wary and to do all things betimes to be ready for them. Thence, going away,

a name in s.h.   *b* MS. 'free'

---

1. Christopher Batters was in command of the *Joseph* fireship. He had just sold £10-worth of fish to a fishmonger and appears to have been drinking in celebration: *CSPD 1666-7*, pp. 505-6. The body was not found until the end of the following March.

2. Merchant, of Crutched Friars. Possibly a slip for John Andrews, of Bow: below, p. 422.

met Mr. Hingston the Organist (my old acquaintance)[1] in the Court, and I took him to the Dogg tavern and got him to set me a bass to my *It is decreed*,[2] which I think will go well; but he commends the song, not knowing the words, but says the ayre is good, and believes the words are plainly expressed. He is of my mind, against having of eighths unnecessarily[a] in composition.[3] This did all please me mightily. Then to talk of the King's family:* he says many of the Musique are ready to starve, they being five[b] years behindhand for their wages. Nay, Evens, the famous man upon the Harp, having not his equal in the world, did the other day die for mere want, and was fain to be buried at the almes of the parish – and carried to his grave in the dark at night, without one Linke,[c] but that Mr Hingston met it by chance and did give 12*d* to buy two or three links. He says all must come to ruin at this rate, and I believe him.

Thence I up to the Lords' House to enquire for Lord Bellasses; and there hear[d] how at a conference this morning between the two Houses, about the business of the Canary Company[4] – my Lord Buckingham leaning rudely over my Lord Marquis of Dorchester, my Lord Dorchester removed his elbow. Duke of Buckingham asked whether he was uneasy. Dorchester replied, "Yes", and that he durst [not] do this, were he anywhere else. Buckingham replied, yes he would, and that he was a better man then himself. Dorchester[e] answered that he lyed. With this, Buckingham struck off his hat, and took him by his periwigg and pulled it a-t'o[ther]-side, and held him. My Lord Chamberlain and others interposed. And upon coming into the House,

a repl. 'in'   *b* repl. 'some'
c l.h. repl. l.h. 'Torch'
d repl. symbol rendered illegible   *e* repl. 'And that he Lyed'

---

1. John Hingston, teacher of keyboard instruments, had been Cromwell's organist and was now a court musician. (E).

2. Pepys's attempt (above, p. 403) had apparently failed. For the song, see above, p. 91, n. 4. (E).

3. Octave leaps for the voice, or octave intervals between voice-line and bass. (E).

4. See above, p. 314 & n. 2.

the Lords did order them both to the Tower, whither they are to go this afternoon.[1]

I down into the Hall, and there the Lieutenant of the Tower took me with him and would have me to the Tower to dinner; where I dined – at the head of his table next his lady – who is comely, and seeming sober and stately, but very proud and very cunning, or I am mistaken – and wanton too.[2] This day's work will bring the Lieutenant of the Tower 350*l*.[3] But a strange conceited, vain man he is, that ever I met withal, in his own praise – as I have heretofore observed of him. Thence home, and upon Tower hill saw about 3 or 400 seamen get together; and one, standing upon a pile of bricks, made his sign with his hand-kercher upon his stick, and called all the rest to him, and several shouts they gave. This made me afeared, so I got home as fast as I could – and hearing of no present hurt, did go to Sir Robt. Viners about my plate again; and coming home, do hear of 1000 seamen said in the streets to be in armes. So in great fear home, expecting to find a tumult about our house, and was doubtful of my riches there – but I thank God, I found all well. But by and by Sir W. Batten and Sir R Ford do tell me that the seamen have been at some prisons to release some seamen,

1. Cf. Clarendon (*Life*, iii. 153–4): 'As they were sitting down in the painted chamber, which is seldom done in good order, it chanced that the marquis of Dorchester sat next the duke of Buckingham, between whom there was no good correspond-ence. The one changing his posture for his own ease, which made the station of the other the more uneasy, they first endeavoured by justling to recover what they had dispossessed each other of, and afterwards fell to direct blows; in which the marquis, who was the lower of the two in stature, and was less active in his limbs, lost his periwig, and received some rudeness, which nobody im-puted to his want of courage, which was ever less questioned than that of the other. The marquis had much of the duke's hair in his hands to recompense for his pulling off his periwig, which he could not reach high enough to do to the other.' (Clarendon is mistaken in stating that the conference was about the Irish Cattle bill.) Both were sent to the Tower and not released until the 22nd: *LJ*, xii. 52–3, 55. Dorchester was a man of violent temper. In 1638 he had obtained a pardon for an assault committed within the precincts of Westminster Abbey in service-time; in 1641 he had been imprisoned by the House of Lords for words spoken in debate; and in 1660 he had challenged his son-in-law Lord Roos to a duel.
2. Anne, wife of Sir John Robin-son: for her reputation, see Pepys's story above, vi. 290.
3. From prisoners' fees.

and that the Duke of Albemarle is in armes, and all the Guards at the other end of the town; and the Duke of Albemarle is gone with some forces to Wapping to quell the seamen – which is a thing of infinite disgrace to us.[1]

I sat long, talking with them. And among other things, Sir R. Ford[2] did make me understand how the House of Commons is a beast not to be understood – it being impossible to know beforehand the success almost of any small plain thing – there being so many to think and speak to any business, and they of so uncertain minds and interests and passions.

He did tell me, and so did Sir W. Batten, how Sir Allen Brodericke and Sir Allen Apsly did come drunk the other day into the House, and did both speak for half an hour together, and could not be either laughed or pulled or bid to sit down and hold their peace – to the great contempt of the King's servants and cause – which I am aggrieved at with all my heart.[3]

We were full in discourse of the sad state of our times. And the horrid shame brought on the King's service by the just clamours of the poor seamen. And that we must be undone in a little time.

Home, full of trouble on these considerations. And among other things, I to my chamber and there to ticket a good part of my books, in order to the Numbring of them – for my easy finding them to read, as I have occasion.

So to supper and to bed – with my heart full of trouble.

20. Up and to the office, where we sat all the morning. And here, among other things, came Captain Cocke, and I did get him to sign me a note for the 100*l*, to pay for the plate he

---

1. 'Some seamen being sent to Newgate for discontented words, about 600 other seamen went to rescue them and broke open the prison gates . . . some were apprehended, but forgiven by the Duke of York' (D. de Repas to Sir R. Harley, London, 22 December): HMC, *Portland*, iii. 303.

2. M.P. for Southampton; a prominent merchant and a member of the Council for Trade.

3. Marvell describes them as 'late and disorder'd' leaders of the drinking crew in the Commons (*Last Instructions*, ll. 209-12), and as 'the two *Allens*' who ply Clarendon 'with gallons' (*Clarendon's House-warming*, l. 50). But I have not traced this incident elsewhere.

doth present me with,[1] which[a] I am very glad of. At noon home to dinner, where was Balty come; who is well again, and the most recovered in his countenance that ever I did see. Here dined with me also Mrs. Batters, poor woman, now left a sad widow by the drowning of her husband the other day. I pity her, and will do her what kindness I can; yet I observe something of ill-nature in myself, more then should be: that I am colder towards her in my charity then I should be to one so painful as he and she have been, and full of kindness to their power to my wife and I. After dinner out with Balty, setting him down at the Maypole in the Strand; and then I to my Lord Bellasses, and there spoke with Mr. Moone about some business; and so away home to my business at the office, and then home to supper and to bed, after having finished the putting of little papers upon my books, to be numbered hereafter.

21. Lay long; and when up, find Mrs. Clerke of Greenwich and her daughter Daniel. Their business, among other things, was a request her daughter was to make; so I took her into my chamber, and there it was to help her husband to the command of a little new pleasure-boat building – which I promised to assist in.[2] And here I had opportunity para besar elle and tocar sus mamelles, so as to make mi mismo espender with great pleasure. Then to the office and there did a little business; and then to the Change and did the like; so home to dinner, and spent all the afternoon in putting some things, pictures especially, in order, and pasting my Lady Castlemaynes print[3] on a frame, which I have made handsome and is a fine piece. So to the office in the evening to marshall my papers[b] of accounts presented to the Parliament, against any future occasion to recur to them – which I did do to my great content. So home and did some Tanger work, and so to bed.

<hr>

a repl. 'my' *b* repl. 'account of'

<hr>

1. A gift for Pepys's help with the recent hemp contract: above, p. 385 & n. 2.

2. For the Daniel family, see above, vi. 261, n. 3. I have not traced any such appointment for Daniel.

3. See above, p. 359 & n. 3. (OM).

22.   At the office all the morning, and there came news from Hogg that our Shipp hath brought in a Lubecker to Portsmouth, likely to prove prize – of deals – which joys us.[1]   At noon home to dinner, and then Sir W. Penn, Sir R. Ford, and I met at Sir W. Batten to examine our papers, and have great hopes to prove her prize.   And Sir R. Ford I find a mighty yare man in this business, making exceeding good observations from the papers on our behalf.   Hereupon concluded what to write to Hogg and Middleton, which I did.   And also with Mr. Oviatt (Sir R. Ford's son, who[a] is to be our solicitor) to fee some counsel in the Admiralty, but none in town; so home again, and after writing letters by the post – I with all my clerks, and Carcasse and Whitfield,[2] to the ticket-office, there to be informed in the method and disorder of that office, which I find infinite great – of infinite concernment to be mended; and did spend till 12 at night, to my great satisfaction, it being a point of our office I was wholly unacquainted in.   So with great content ⟨home and⟩ to bed.

23.   *Lords day.*   Up, and alone to church; and meeting Nan Wright at the gate, had opportunity to take two or three besados,[b] and so to church – where a vain fellow with a periwig preached, Chaplain (as by his prayer appeared) to the Earl of Carlisle. Home, and there dined with us Betty Michell and her husband. After dinner, I to White-hall by coach, and took them with me; and in the way I would have taken su mano as I did the last time, but she did in a manner withhold it.   So set them down at White-hall, and I to the Chapel to find Dr. Gibbons;[3] and from him to the Harp and Ball to transcribe the Treble which I would have him to set a bass to.   But this took me so much time, and it growing night, I was fearful of missing a coach; and therefore took a coach, and to rights to call Michell and his wife at their father Howletts; and so home, it being cold and the ground

a   repl. ') to'   b   repl. 'mer'-

1. This capture by Pepys's privateer was also reported to him in a letter from Commissioner Middleton (Portsmouth, 25 November): *CSPD 1666–7*, p. 288.

2. The two latter were clerks of the Ticket Office.

3. Christopher Gibbons, organist of Westminster Abbey. (E).

all snow, but the moon shining. In the way, I did prender su mano with some little violence; and so in every motion she seemed para hazer contra su will, but yet did hazer whatever I would. I did by degrees poner mi cosa en su mano nudo, and did hazerla tenerle et fregarle et tocar mi thigh; and so all the way home, and then did doner ella su gans para put on encore – she making many little endeavours para ôter su mano, but yielded still. We came home, and there she did seem a little*a* ill, but I did take several opportunities afterward para*b* besar la, and so goodnight. They gone, I to my chamber, and with my brother and wife did Number all my books in my closet and took a list of their names; which pleases me mightily, and is a jobb I wanted much to have done. Then to supper and to bed.

24. Up and to the office, where Lord Brouncker, J. Mennes, W. Penn, and myself met; and there I did use my notes I took on Saturday night about tickets, and did come to a good settle-ment in that business of that office, if it be kept to[1] – this morning being a meeting on purpose. At noon, to prevent my Lord Brouncker's dining here, I walked as if upon business with*c* him (it being frost and dry)as far as Paul's, and so back again through the City by Yildhall,[2] observing the ruines thereabouts, till I did truly lose myself; and so home to dinner. I do truly find that I have overwrought my eyes, so that now they are become weak and apt to be tired, and all excess of light makes them sore, so that now, to the candlelight I am forced to sit by, adding the Snow upon the ground all day, my eyes are very bad, and will be worse if not helped; so my Lord Brouncker doth advise me, as a certain cure, to use Greene Spectacles, which I will do. So to dinner, where Mercer with us, and very merry. After dinner, she goes and fetches a little son of Mr. Buckeworths, the whitest-haired and of the most spirit that ever I saw in my life – for dis-

a repl. same symbol badly formed
b repl.? same symbol badly formed
c repl. 'to'

---

1. New regulations for the issue of pay tickets were concluded by the Board on 17 January 1667, but proved difficult to enforce in war conditions: PL 2874, p. 479.

2. Guildhall (common pronuncia-tion-spelling). (WM).

EE

course of all kind, and so ready and to the purpose, not above four year old. Thence to Sir Robt. Viners and there paid for the plate I have bought, to the value of 94*l*, with the 100*l* Captain Cocke did give me to that purpose, and received the rest in money. I this evening did buy me a pair of green spectacles, to see whether they will help my eyes or no. So to the Change, and went to the Upper Change, which is almost as good as the old one; only, shops are but on one side. Then home to the office and did business till my eyes begun to be bad; and so home to supper (my people busy making mince-pies) and so to bed. No news yet of our Gottenburgh fleet;[1] which makes [me] have some fears, it being of mighty concernment to have our supply of masts safe. I met with Mr. Cade tonight, my stationer, and he tells me that he hears for certain that the Queene-Mother is about and hath near finished a peace with France; which, as a Presbyterian, he doth not like, but seems to fear it will be a means to introduce Popery.[2]

25. *Christmas day.* Lay pretty long in bed. And then rise, leaving my wife desirous to sleep, having sat up till 4 this morning seeing her maids make mince-pies.*a* I to church, where our parson Mills made a good sermon. Then home, and dined well on some good ribbs of beef roasted and mince pies; only my wife, brother, and Barker, and plenty of good wine of my own; and my heart full of true joy and thanks to God Almighty for the goodness of my condition at this day. After dinner I begun to teach my wife and Barker my song, *It is decreed* – which pleases me mightily,*b* as now I have Mr. Hinxton's bass.[3] Then out, and walked alone on foot to Temple, it being a fine frost, thinking to*c* have seen a play all alone; but there missing of any

a MS. 'pays'   *b* repl. 'highly'   *c* repl. 'it'

1. See below, p. 424, n. 3.

2. St Albans, the Queen-Mother's confidant, and a leader of the pro-French faction at court, was now engaged in negotiations with France which had begun in profound secrecy in the autumn and were confided at first only to the King himself. In January 1667 he was sent to Paris where he made an agreement by which Charles promised to enter no alliance contrary to France's interests. He was later (in 1669–70) prominent in the negotiations which led to the treaty of Dover which was (by some) meant to be the 'means to introduce Popery'.

3. See above, p. 414 & n. 2. (E).

Bills,[1] concluded there was none; and so back home, and there with my brother, reducing the names of all my books to an Alphabet, which kept us till 7 or 8 at night; and then to supper, W. Hewer with us, and pretty merry; and then to my chamber to enter this day's journal only, and then to bed – my head a little thoughtful how [to] behave myself in the business of the victualling, which I think will be prudence to offer my service[a] in doing something in passing the pursers' accounts – thereby to serve the King – get honour to myself, and confirm me in my place in the victualling, which at present hath not work enough to deserve my wages.[2]

26. Up, and walked all the way (it being a most fine frost) to White-hall to Sir W. Coventry's chamber; and thence with him up to the Duke of York; where, among other things at our meeting, I did offer my assistance to Sir J. Mennes to do the business of his office relating to the pursers' accounts – which was well accepted by the Duke of York, and I think I have and shall do myself good in it – if it be taken; for it will confirm me in the business of my victualling office – which I do now very little for. Thence home, carrying home a barrel of oysters with me. Anon comes Mr. John Andrews and his wife by invitation from Bow to dine with me, and young Batelier[3] and his wife, with her great belly, which hath spoiled her looks mightily already. Here was also ⟨Mercer (and)⟩ Creed, whom I met coming home – who tells me of a most bitter Lampoone now out against the Court and the management of State from head to foot, mighty witty and mighty[b] severe).[4] By and by to dinner – a very good one – and merry. After dinner I put the women into coach, and they to the Duke's house to a play which was acted, *The*   .[5] It was indifferently done, but was

---

a MS. 'to offer my offer my service'   *b* MS. 'my'

---

1. Playbills advertising perform-ances. They were exhibited on posts, etc., in the streets. (A).
2. Pepys had been Surveyor-General of Victualling since Novem-ber 1665. The work on pursers' accounts was ordered by the Duke of York on 23 November and 17

December 1666: Tanner 45, f. 123r; Duke of York, *Mem. (naval)*, p. 56.
3. Joseph Batelier, jun.
4. Possibly *The third advice to a painter*, which Pepys copied out on 20 January 1667.
5. Untraced. (A).

not pleased with the song, Gosnell[1] not singing it, but[a] a new wench that sings naughtily.* Thence home, all by coach. And there Mr. Andrews to the vyall, who plays[b] most excellently on it – which I did not know before. Then to dance, here being Pendleton[2] sent (by my wife's direction), and a fiddler; and we got also the elder Batelier tonight, and Nan Wright – and mighty merry we were, and I danced; and so till 12 at night, and to supper, and then to cross-purposes,[3] mighty merry; and then to bed – my eyes being sore. Creed lay here in Barker's bed.

27. Up, and called up by the King's Trumpets, which cost me 10s.[4] So to the office, where we sat all the morning. At noon, by invitation, my wife (who had not been there these ten months I think) and I to meet, all our families, at Sir W. Batten's at dinner; where neither a great dinner for so much company, nor anything good or handsome. In middle of dinner I rose, and my wife, and by coach to the King's playhouse; and meeting Creed, took him up, and there[c] saw *The Scornfull Lady*[5] well acted, Doll Common[6] doing Abigail most excellently, and Knipp the Widow very well (and will be an excellent actor I think); in other parts, the play not so well done as used to be by the old actors.[7] Anon to White-hall by coach, thinking to have seen a play there tonight – but found it a mistake; so back again, and missed our coach, who was gone, thinking to come time enough three hours hence; and we could not blame him. So forced to get another coach, and all three home to my house; and there to Sir W. Batten's and eat a bit of cold chine of beef, and then stayed and

---

a repl. 'as'　　*b* MS. 'pleases'　　*c* repl. 'to the'

---

1. Winifred Gosnell, formerly maid to Pepys's wife, now one of the leading actresses at the Duke's theatre. (A).

2. Pembleton, the dancing-master who had given lessons to both Pepys and his wife in 1663.

3. A question-and-answer game, with forfeits.

4. A Christmas box.

5. A comedy by Beaumont and Fletcher (see above, i. 303 & n. 3) now at the TR, Vere St. (A).

6. Mrs Corey ('Doll Common' after the part she played in Jonson's *The Alchemist*) was a leading actress in the King's Company. Other roles are listed by Downes (p. 6) as follows: Elder Loveless, Burt; Younger Loveless, Kynaston; Welford, Hart; Sir Roger, Lacy; The Lady, Mrs Marshall. (A).

7. As in the performances seen by Pepys on 27 November 1660 and 4 January 1661. (A).

talked; and then home, and sat and talked a little by the fire's side with wife and Creed; and so to bed, my left*ª* eye being very sore. No business, public nor private, minded all these two days. ⟨This day a house or two was blown up with powder in the Minorys, and several people spoiled, and many dug out from under the rubbish.⟩*ᵇ*

28. Up, and Creed and I walked (a very fine walk in the frost) to my Lord Bellasses; but missing him, did find him at White-hall, and there spoke with him about some Tanger business. That done, we to Creeds lodgings, which are very pretty, but he is going from them.¹ So we to Lincolnes Inne-fields, he to Ned Pickerings (who it seems lives there, keeping a good house) and I to my Lord Crews, where I dined and hear the news how my Lord's brother, Mr. Nath. Crew, hath an estate of 6 or 700*l* per annum left him by the death of an old acquaintance of his, but not akinned to him at all. And this man is dead without will, but had, above ten years since, made over his estate to this Mr. Crew, to him and his heirs for ever, and given Mr. Crew the keeping of the deeds in his own hand all this time – by which, if he would, he might have taken present possession of the estate – for he knew what they were. This is as great an act of confident friendship as this latter age, I believe, can*ᶜ* show.² From hence to the Duke's house, and there saw *Mackbeth* most excellently acted, and a most excellent play for variety.³ I had sent for my wife to meet me there, who did come. And after the play done, I out so soon to meet her at the other door, that I left my cloak in the playhouse; and while I returned to get it, she was gone out and missed me, and with W. Hewer away home. I, not sorry for it much, did go to White-hall and got my Lord Bellasses to get me into the playhouse; and there, after all

---

a repl. symbol rendered illegible
b addition crowded in between entries   *c* followed by blot

---

1. When last mentioned (above, p. 279), they were near the New Exchange. He was often changing them.

2. When Crew died, he was possessed of land in four counties, but

his will (1693) does not reveal anything of this transaction.

3. This was probably the first of Davenant's spectacular adaptations of the play (see above, v. 314 & n. 3); now at the LIF. (A).

staying above an hour*ª* **for** the players (the King and all waiting, which was absurd), saw *Henry the 5th*[1] – well done by the Dukes people, and in most excellent habit, all new vests, being put on but this night. But I sat so high and far off, that I missed most of the words; and sat*ᵇ* with a wind coming into my back and neck, which did much*ᶜ* trouble me.

The play continued till 12 at night; and then up, and a most horrid cold night it was, and frosty – and moonshine. But the worst is, I had left my cloak at Sir G. Carteret's; and they being abed, I was forced to go home without it. So by chance got a coach, and to the Golden Lion tavern in the Strand*ᵈ* and there drank some mulled sack; and so home – where find my poor wife staying for me. And then to bed – mighty cold.

29. Up, called up with news from Sir W. Batten that Hogg hath brought in two prizes more; and so I thither and hear the perticulars, which are good – one of them, if prize, being worth 4000*l* – for which God be thanked.[2]   Then to the office, and have the news brought us of Captain Robinsons coming with his fleet from Gottenburgh – dispersed, though, by foul weather. But he hath light of five Dutch men-of-war and taken three, whereof one is sunk[3] – which is very good news to close up the year with, and most of our merchantmen already heard of to be safely come home – though after long lookings-for; and now to several ports, as they could make them. At noon home to dinner, where Balty is, and now well recovered. Then to the office to do business; and at night, it being very cold, home to my chamber and there late, writing. But my left eye still very sore – I write by

a repl. same symbol badly formed   *b* repl. same symbol badly formed
            c repl. 'l'-   *d* MS. 'Strang' (s.h.)

---

1. Probably the history play by Roger Boyle, Earl of Orrery; see above, v. 240 & n. 2. (A).

2. See Hogg to Penn (27 December): *CSPD 1666–7*, p. 373. He had sailed from Cowes on the 23rd. Marvell (ii. 49) mentions the captures – by 'a Privateer of Sir William Battens' – in a letter of 29 December. But for some of the prize, protection was claimed under the Swedish flag: see below, 21 January 1667.

3. Capt. Robert Robinson, with a squadron of six ships, had escorted the Gothenburg fleet there and back. His action against the Dutch men-of-war took place on Christmas Day. The fleet came home in ragged order; it seems that two ships foundered: *CSPD 1666–7*, pp. 317, 374–81, 438.

spectacles all this night. Then to supper and to bed – this day's good news making me very lively; only, the arrears of much business upon my hands, and my accounts to be settled for the whole year past, do lie as a weight*a* on my mind.

30. *Lords day.* Lay long; however, up and to church, where Mills made a good sermon. Here was a collection for the Sexton.[1] But it came into my head, why we should be more bold in making the collection while the psalm is singing then in the sermon or prayer. Home, and without any strangers to dinner; and then all the afternoon and evening in my chamber preparing all my accounts in good condition against tomorrow, to state them for the whole year past – to which God give me a good issue when I come to close them.
So to supper and to bed.

31. Rising this day with a full design to mind nothing else but to make up my accounts for the year past, I did take money and walk forth to several places in the town, as far as the New Exchange, to pay all my debts, it being still a very great frost and good walking. I stayed at the Fleece tavern in Coventgarden, while my*b* boy Tom went to W. Joyces to pay what I owed for candles there. Thence to the New Exchange to clear my wife's score; and so going back again, I met Doll Lane (Mrs. Martin's sister) with another young woman of the Hall, one Scott, and took them to the Half-Moon tavern and there drank some burned wine with them, without more pleasure; and so away home by coach, and there to dinner and then to my accounts, wherein at last I find them clear and right; but to my great discontent, do find that my gettings this year have been 573*l* less then my last – it being this year in all, but 2986*l*; whereas the last I got 3560*l*. And then again, my spendings this year have exceeded my spendings the last, by 644 – my whole spendings last year being but 509*l*; whereas this year it appears I have spent 1154*l* – which is a sum not fit to be said that ever I should spend in one year, before I am maister of a better estate

a repl. 'mind'   *b* repl. 'the'

---

1. For these collections, see above, ii. 6 & n. 5.

then I am. Yet, blessed be God, and I pray God make me thankful for it, I do find myself worth in money, all good, above 6200*l*; which is above 1800*l* more then I was the last year. This, I trust in God, will make me thankful for what I have, and careful to make up by care next year what by my negligence and prodigality I have lost and spent this*a* year.

The doing of this and entering it fair, with the sorting of all my expenses to see how and in what points I have exceeded, did make it late work, till my eyes became very sore and ill; and then did give over, and supper and to bed.

Thus ends this year of public wonder and mischief to this nation – and therefore generally wished by all people to have an end. Myself and family well, having four maids and one clerk, Tom, in my house; and my brother now with me, to spend time in order to his preferment. Our healths all well; only, my eyes, with overworking them, are sore as soon as candle-light comes to them, and not else. Public matters in a most sad condition. Seamen discouraged for want of pay, and are become not to be governed. Nor, as matters are now, can any fleet go out next year. Our enemies, French and Duch, great, and grow more, by our poverty. The Parliament backward in raising, because jealous of the spending of the money. The City less and less likely to be built again,[1] everybody settling elsewhere, and nobody encouraged to trade. A sad, vicious, negligent Court, and all sober men there fearful of the ruin of the whole Kingdom this next year – from which, good God deliver us. One thing I reckon remarkable in my own condition is that I am come to abound in good plate, so as at all entertainments to be served wholly with silver plates, having two dozen and a half.*b*

a MS. 'next'   *b* followed by one blank page

---

1. The bills governing the rebuilding and the settling of claims were still before parliament. The two main ones were shortly to receive royal assent on 8 February 1667.

LONDON
IN THE SIXTEEN-SIXTIES

Western half (omitting most minor streets & alleys)

Scale of yards

0	220	440	660	880

⋯⋯ Area of Great Fire

To Harr...

Tyburn
Gibbet⋯⋯ To Oxford ⋯⋯

Burlington
House
Clarendon
House
Piccadilly

Berkeley
House

St Jam...
Fields
(being
develo...

To Knightsbridge & Kensington

Berkshire
House

St James
Palace

Goring
House

To Chelsea

Ca...

PettyFr...

1 St Martin-in-the-Fields
2 Wallingford House
3 The Cockpit, Whitehall
4 Axe Yard
5 St Margaret's Ch, Westminster
6 The Gate House, Westminster
7 Westminster Hall
8 The King's House, Drury Lane
9 Maypole in the Strand
10 St Clement Danes Ch, Strand
11 The Duke's Ho., Lincoln's Inn Fields
12 Gaming House in Bell Yard
13 Temple Bar
14 St Dunstan-in-the-West
15 St Andrew's Ch, Holborn

Map prepared by the late Professor T. F. Reddaway

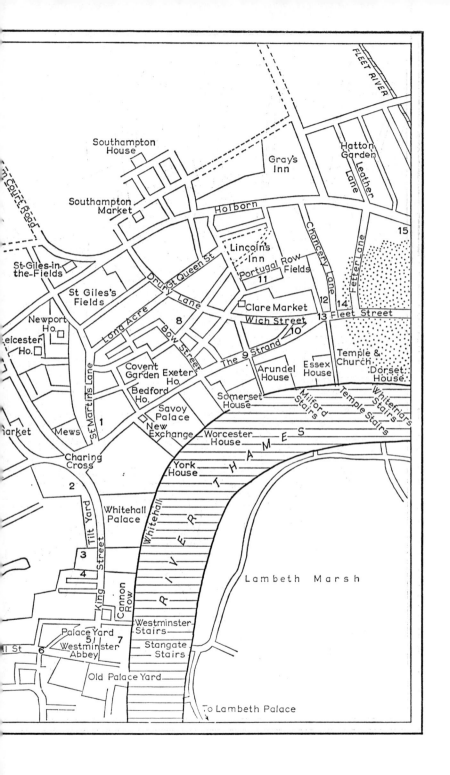

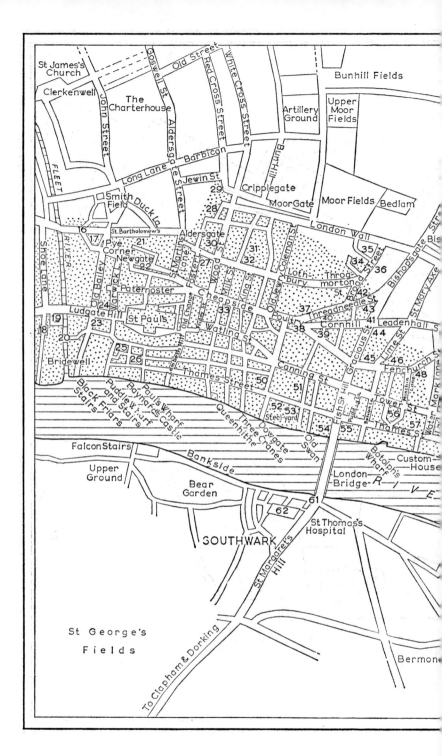

LONDON
IN THE SIXTEEN-SIXTIES

Eastern half (omitting most minor streets & alleys)

Scale of yards

0	220	440	660	880

Area of Great Fire

Petticoat Lane

tillery ard

To Colchester

Whitechapel

sditch

Aldgate

Minories

Goodman's
Fields

er ll

The
Tower

Victualling
Office

East Smithfield

To Ratcliff

16 Holborn Conduit
17 St Sepulchre's Ch.
18 Salisbury Court
19 St Bride's Church
20 Bridge in Bridewell
21 Christ Ch. Newgate
22 Newgate Market
23 Ludgate
24 St Martin's Ch.
25 The Wardrobe
26 Doctors' Commons
27 Goldsmiths' Hall
28 Barber Surgeons' Hall
29 St Giles, Cripplegate
30 Haberdashers' Hall
31 Guildhall
32 St Lawrence Jewry
33 St Mary le Bow
34 Dutch Ch. Austin Friars
35 Treasury Office, Navy
36 Gresham College
37 The Post Office, 1666
38 Stocks Market

39 The Great Coffee House
40 Royal Exchange
41 Cornhill Conduit
42 French Church
43 Merchant Taylors' Hall
44 Leadenhall Market
45 St Dionis Backchurch
46 The Mitre, Fenchurch St
47 St Katherine Cree
48 Clothworkers' Hall
49 St Olave's Ch. Hart St
50 Skinners' Hall, Dowgate Hill
51 St Lawrence Poultney
52 All Hallows the Great
53 All Hallows the Less
54 Fishmongers' Hall
55 St Magnus's Church
56 St Dunstan in the East
57 Trinity House
58 All Hallows, Barking
59 Navy Office
60 St Katherine's by the Tower
61 The Bear at the Bridge Foot
62 St Mary Overie (now
Southwark Cath.)

f

Iron Gate Stairs

60

T H A M E S

Pasture
Grounds

Wapping
Church

To Ratcliff & Limehouse

Sir William
Warren's shipyard

To
Deptford,
Woolwich
& Chatham

Rotherhithe
Church

Map prepared by the late Professor T. F. Reddaway

SELECT LIST OF PERSONS

ADMIRAL, the: James, Duke of York, Lord High Admiral of England

ALBEMARLE, 1st Duke of (Lord Monke): Captain-General of the Kingdom

ARLINGTON, 1st Earl of (Sir Henry Bennet): Secretary of State

ASHLEY, 1st Baron (Sir Anthony Ashley Cooper, later 1st Earl of Shaftesbury): Chancellor of the Exchequer

ATTORNEY-GENERAL: Sir Geoffrey Palmer

BACKWELL, Edward: goldsmith–banker

BAGWELL, Mrs: Pepys's mistress; wife of ship's carpenter

BALTY: Balthasar St Michel; brother-in-law; minor naval official

BATTEN, Sir William: Surveyor of the Navy

BETTERTON (Baterton), Thomas: actor in the Duke's Company

BIRCH, Jane: maidservant

BOOKSELLER, my: Joseph Kirton (until the Fire)

BOWYER, my father: Robert Bowyer, senior Exchequer colleague

BRISTOL, 2nd Earl of: politician

BROUNCKER (Bruncker, Brunkard, Brunkerd), 2nd Viscount: Commissioner of the Navy

BUCKINGHAM, 2nd Duke of: politician

CARKESSE (Carcasse), James: clerk in the Ticket Office

CARTERET, Sir George: Treasurer of the Navy and Vice-Chamberlain of the King's Household

CASTLEMAINE, Barbara, Countess of: the King's mistress

CHANCELLOR, the: see 'Lord Chancellor'

CHILD, the: usually Edward, eldest son and heir of Sandwich

CHOLMLEY, Sir Hugh: courtier, engineer

COCKE, George: hemp merchant

COFFERER, the: William Ashburnham

COMPTROLLER (Controller), the: the Comptroller of the Navy (Sir Robert Slingsby, 1660–1; Sir John Mennes, 1661–71)

COVENTRY, Sir William: Secretary to the Lord High Admiral, 1660–7; Commissioner of the Navy (occasionally called 'Mr.' after knighted, 1665)

CREED, John: household and naval servant of Sandwich

CREW, 1st Baron: Sandwich's father-in-law; Presbyterian politician

CUTTANCE, Sir Roger: naval captain

DEANE, Anthony: shipwright

DEB: *see* 'Willet, Deborah'

DOWNING, Sir George: Exchequer official, Envoy-Extraordinary to the United Provinces, and secretary to the Treasury Commission

DUKE, the: usually James, Duke of York, the King's brother; occasionally George (Monck), Duke of Albemarle

DUKE OF YORK: *see* 'James, Duke of York'

EDWARD, Mr: Edward, eldest son and heir of Sandwich

EDWARDS, Tom: servant

EVELYN, John: friend, *savant*; Commissioner of Sick and Wounded

FENNER, Thomas (m. Katherine Kite, sister of Pepys's mother): uncle; ironmonger

FERRER(S), Capt. Robert: army captain; Sandwich's Master of Horse

FORD, Sir Richard: Spanish merchant

FOX, Sir Stephen: Paymaster of the Army

GAUDEN, Sir Denis: Navy victualler

GENERAL(S), the: Albemarle, Captain-General of the Kingdom, 1660–70; Prince Rupert and Albemarle, Generals-at-Sea in command of the Fleet, 1666

GIBSON, Richard: clerk to Pepys in the Navy Office

GWYN, Nell: actress (in the King's Company) and King's mistress

HARRIS, Henry: actor in the Duke's Company

HAYTER, Tom: clerk to Pepys in the Navy Office

HEWER, Will: clerk to Pepys in the Navy Office

HILL, Thomas: friend, musician, Portuguese merchant

HINCHINGBROOKE, Viscount (also 'Mr Edward', 'the child'): eldest son of Sandwich

HOLLIER (Holliard), Thomas: surgeon

HOLMES, Sir Robert: naval commander

HOWE, Will: household and naval servant of Sandwich

JAMES, DUKE OF YORK: the King's brother and heir presumptive (later James II); Lord High Admiral

JANE: usually Jane Birch, maidservant

JOYCE, Anthony (m. Kate Fenner, 1st cousin): innkeeper

JOYCE, William (m. Mary Fenner, 1st cousin): tallow-chandler

JUDGE-ADVOCATE, the: John Fowler, Judge-Advocate of the Fleet

KNIPP (Knepp), Mrs: actress in the King's Company

LADIES, the young/ the two/ the: often Sandwich's daughters

LAWSON, Sir John: naval commander

LIEUTENANT OF THE TOWER: Sir John Robinson

L'IMPERTINENT, Mons.:   [?Daniel] Butler, friend, ? clergyman

LORD CHAMBERLAIN: Edward Mountagu, 2nd Earl of Manchester; Sandwich's cousin

LORD CHANCELLOR: Edward Hyde, 1st Earl of Clarendon (often called Chancellor after his dismissal, 1667)

LORD KEEPER: Sir Orlando Bridgeman

LORD PRIVY SEAL: John Robartes, 2nd Baron Robartes (later 1st Earl of Radnor)

LORD TREASURER: Thomas Wriothesley, 4th Earl of Southampton

MARTIN, Betty (*née* Lane):   Pepys's mistress; shopgirl

MENNES (Minnes), Sir John: Comptroller of the Navy

MERCER, Mary: maid to Mrs Pepys

MILL(E)S, Rev. Dr John: Rector of St Olave's, Hart St; Pepys's parish priest

MONCK (Monke), George (Lord):   soldier. *See* 'Albemarle, 1st Duke of'

MONMOUTH, Duke of: illegitimate son of Charles II

MOORE, Henry: lawyer; officer of Sandwich's household

MY LADY: usually Jemima, wife of Sandwich

MY LORD: usually Sandwich

NELL, NELLY: usually Nell Gwyn

PALL: Paulina Pepys; sister (sometimes spelt 'pall')

PEARSE (Pierce), James: courtier, surgeon to Duke of York, and naval surgeon

PENN, Sir William: Commissioner of the Navy and naval commander (father of the Quaker leader)

PEPYS, Elizabeth (*née* St Michel):   wife

PEPYS, John and Margaret: parents

PEPYS, John (unm.):   brother; unbeneficed clergyman

PEPYS, Tom (unm.):   brother; tailor

PEPYS, Paulina (m. John Jackson):   sister

PEPYS, Capt. Robert: uncle, of Brampton, Hunts.

PEPYS, Roger: 1st cousin once removed; barrister and M.P.

PEPYS, Thomas: uncle, of St Alphege's, London

PETT, Peter: Commissioner of the Navy and shipwright

PICKERING, Mr (Ned):   courtier, 1662-3; Sandwich's brother-in-law and servant

POVEY, Thomas: Treasurer of the Tangier Committee

PRINCE, the: usually Prince Rupert

QUEEN, the: (until May 1662) the Queen Mother, Henrietta-Maria, widow of Charles I;   Catherine of Braganza, wife of Charles II (m. 21 May 1662)

RIDER, Sir William: merchant

ROBERT, Prince: Prince Rupert

RUPERT, Prince: 1st cousin of Charles II;   naval commander

St MICHEL, Alexandre and Mary: parents-in-law

St MICHEL, Balthasar ('Balty';   m. Esther Watts):   brother-in-law; minor naval official

SANDWICH, 1st Earl of: 1st cousin once removed, and patron; politician, naval commander and diplomat

SHIPLEY, Edward: steward of Sandwich's household

SIDNY, Mr: Sidney Mountagu, second son of Sandwich

SOLICITOR, the: the Solicitor-General, Sir Heneage Finch

SOUTHAMPTON, 4th Earl of: Lord Treasurer

SURVEYOR, the: the Surveyor of the Navy (Sir William Batten, 1660–7;   Col. Thomas Middleton, 1667–72)

TEDDIMAN, Sir Thomas: naval commander

THE: Theophila Turner

TREASURER, the: usually the Treasurer of the Navy (Sir George Carteret, 1660–7;   1st Earl of Anglesey, 1667–8);   sometimes the Lord Treasurer of the Kingdom, the Earl of Southampton, 1660–7

TRICE, Tom: relative by marriage;   civil lawyer

TURNER, John (m. Jane Pepys, distant cousin):   barrister

TURNER, Betty and Theophila: daughters of John and Jane Turner

TURNER, Thomas: senior clerk in the Navy Office

VICE-CHAMBERLAIN, the: Sir George Carteret, Vice-Chamberlain of the King's Household and Treasurer of the Navy

VYNER, Sir Robert: goldsmith–banker

WARREN, Sir William: timber merchant

WARWICK, Sir Philip: Secretary to the Lord Treasurer

WIGHT, William: uncle (half-brother of Pepys's father);   fishmonger

WILL: usually Will Hewer

WILLET, Deborah: maid to Mrs Pepys

WILLIAMS ('Sir Wms. both'):   Sir William Batten and Sir William Penn, colleagues on the Navy Board

WREN, Matthew: Secretary to the Lord High Admiral, 1667–72

SELECT GLOSSARY

A Large Glossary (of words, phrases and proverbs in all languages) will be found in the *Companion*. This Select Glossary is restricted to usages, many of them recurrent, which might puzzle the reader. It includes words and constructions which are now obsolete, archaic, slang or dialect; words which are used with meanings now obsolete or otherwise unfamiliar; and place names frequently recurrent or used in colloquial styles or in non-standard forms. The definitions given here are minimal: meanings now familiar and contemporary meanings not implied in the text are not noted, and many items are explained more fully in *Companion* articles ('Language', 'Food', 'Drink', 'Music', 'Theatre' etc.), and in the Large Glossary. A few foreign words are included. The spellings are taken from those used in the text: they do not, for brevity's sake, include all variants.

ABLE: wealthy
ABROAD: away, out of doors
ACHIEVEMENT: hatchment, representation of heraldic arms
ACTION: acting, performance
ACTOR: male or female theatrical performer
ADDES: adze
ADMIRAL SHIP: flagship carrying admiral
ADMIRATION, ADMIRE: wonder, alarm; to wonder at
ADVENTURER: investor, speculator
ADVICE: consideration
AFFECT: to be fond of, to be concerned
AFFECTION: attention
AIR: generic term for all gases
ALL MY CAKE WILL BE DOE: all my plans will miscarry
ALPHABET: index
AMBAGE: deceit, deviousness
AMUSED, AMUZED: bemused, astonished
ANCIENT: elderly, senior
ANGEL: gold coin worth c. 10s.
ANGELIQUE: small archlute
ANNOY: molest, hurt

ANOTHER GATE'S BUSINESS: different altogether
ANSWERABLE: similar, conformably
ANTIC, ANTIQUE: fantastic
APERN: apron
APPREHENSION: apprehension
APPROVE OF: criticise
AQUA FORTIS (FARTIS): nitric acid
ARTICLE: to indict
ARTIST: workman, craftsman, technician, practitioner
ASPECT (astrol.): position of stars as seen from earth
ASTED: Ashtead, Surrey
AYERY: airy, sprightly, stylish

BAGNARD: bagnio, prison, lock-up
BAILEY, BAYLY: bailiff
BAIT, BAYTE: refreshment on journey (for horses or travellers). Also v.
BALDWICK: Baldock, Herts.
BALK: roughly-squared beam of Baltic timber
BALLET: ballad, broadside
BAND: neckband
BANDORE: musical instrument resembling guitar

BANQUET, BANQUETTING HOUSE: summer-house

BANQUET: course of fruits, sweets and wine

BARBE (s.): Arab (Barbary) horse

BARBE (v.): to shave

BARN ELMS: riverside area near Barnes, Surrey

BARRICADOES (naval): tenders

BASE, BASS: bass viol

BASTE HIS COAT: to beat, chastise

BAVINS: kindling wood, brushwood

BAYLY: see 'Bailey'

BAYT(E): see 'Bait'

BEARD: facial hair, moustache

BEFOREHAND, to get: to have money in hand

BEHALF: to behave

BEHINDHAND: insolvent

BELL: to throb

BELOW: downstream from London Bridge

BELOW STAIRS: part of the Royal Household governed by Lord Steward

BEST HAND, at the: the best bargain

BEVER: beaver, fur hat

BEWPERS: bunting, fabric used for flags

BEZAN, BIZAN (Du. bezaan): small yacht

BIGGLESWORTH: Biggleswade, Beds.

BILL: (legal) warrant, writ; bill of exchange; Bill of Mortality (weekly list of burials; see iii. 225, n. 2)

BILLANDER (Du. bijlander): bilander, small two-masted merchantman

BIRD'S EYE: spotted fabric

BIZAN: see 'Bezan'

BLACK (adj.): brunette, dark in hair or complexion

BLACK(E)WALL: dock on n. shore of Thames below Greenwich used by E. Indiamen

BLANCH (of coins): to silver

BLIND: out of the way, private, obscure

BLOAT HERRING: bloater

BLUR: innuendo, charge

BOATE: boot or luggage compartment on side of coach

BODYS: foundations, basic rules; structure; (of ship) sectional drawings

BOLTHEAD: globular glass vessel with long straight neck

BOMBAIM: Bombay

BORDER: toupée

BOTARGO: dried fish-roe

BOTTOMARYNE, BOTTUMARY, BUMMARY: mortgage on ship

BOWPOTT: flower pot

BRAINFORD: Brentford, Mdx

BRAMPTON: village near Huntingdon in which Pepys inherited property

BRANSLE: branle, group dance in duple or triple measure

BRAVE (adj.): fine, enjoyable

BRAVE (v.): to threaten, challenge

BREAK BULK: to remove part of cargo

BREDHEMSON, BRIGHTHEMSON: Brighton, Sussex

BRIDEWELL-BIRD: jailbird

BRIDGE: usually London Bridge; also jetty; landing stairs

BRIEF: collection authorised by Lord Chancellor for charity

BRIG, BRIGANTINE: small vessel equipped both for sailing and rowing

BRIGHTHEMSON: see 'Bredhemson'

BRISTOL MILK: rum-and-milk punch

BROTHER: brother-in-law; colleague

BRUMLY: Bromley, Kent

BRUSH (s.): graze

BUBO: tumour

BULLEN: Boulogne

BUMMARY: see 'Bottomaryne'

BURNTWOOD: Brentwood, Essex

BURY (of money): pour in, salt away, invest

BUSSE: two- or three-masted fishing boat

CABARETT (Fr. cabaret): tavern

CALES: Cadiz

CALICE, CALLIS: Calais

CALL: to call on/for; to drive

CAMELOTT, CAMLET, CAMLOTT: light cloth usually made from goat hair

CANAILLE, CHANNEL, KENNEL: drainage gutter (in street); canal (in St James's Park)

CANCRE: canker, cold-sore

CANNING ST: Cannon St

CANONS: boot-hose tops

CANTON (heraldic): small division of shield

CAPER (ship): privateer

CARBONADO: to grill, broil

CARESSE: to make much of

CAST OF OFFICE: taste of quality

CATAPLASM: poultice

CATCH: round song; (ship) ketch

CATT-CALL: whistle

CAUDLE: thin gruel

CELLAR: box for bottles

CERE CLOTH: cloth impregnated with wax and medicaments

CESTORNE: cistern

CHAFE: heat, anger

CHALDRON: 1½ tons (London measure)

CHAMBER: small piece of ordnance for firing salutes

CHANGE, the: the Royal (Old) Exchange

CHANGELING: idiot

CHANNELL: see 'Canaille'

CHANNELL ROW: Cannon Row, Westminster

CHAPEL, the: usually the Chapel Royal, Whitehall Place

CHAPTER: usually of Bible

CHARACTER: code, cipher; verbal portrait

CHEAP (s.): bargain

CHEAPEN: to ask the price of, bargain

CHEQUER, the: usually the Exchequer

CHEST, the: the Chatham Chest, the pension fund for seamen

CHILD, with: eager, anxious

CHIMNEY-PIECE: picture, etc., over a fireplace; the structure over and around fireplace

CHINA-ALE: ale flavoured with china root

CHINE: rib (of beef), saddle (of mutton)

CHOQUE: attack

CHOUSE: to swindle, trick

CHURCH: after July 1660, usually St Olave's, Hart St

CLAP: gonorrhoea

CLERK OF THE CHEQUE: principal clerical officer of a dockyard

CLOATH (of meat): skin

CLOSE: shutter; (of music) cadence

CLOUTERLY: clumsily

CLOWNE: countryman, clodhopper

CLUB (s.): share of expenses, meeting at which expenses are shared. Also v.

CLYSTER, GLISTER, GLYSTER: enema

COACH: captain's state-room in a large ship

COCK ALE: ale mixed with minced chicken

COCKPIT(T), the: usually the theatre in the Cockpit buildings, Whitehall Palace; the buildings themselves

COD: small bag; testicle

CODLIN TART: apple (codling) tart

COFFEE: coffee-house

COG: to cheat, banter, wheedle

COLEWORTS: cabbage

COLLAR DAY: day on which knights of chivalric orders wore insignia at court

COLLECT: to deduce

COLLIER: coal merchant; coal ship

COLLOPS: fried bacon

COLLY-FEAST: feast of collies (cullies, good companions) at which each pays his share

COMEDIAN: actor

COMEDY: play

COMFITURE (Fr.): jam, marmalade

COMMEN, COMMON GUARDEN: Covent Garden

COMMEND: to comment

COMMONLY: together

COMPASS TIMBER: curved timber

COMPLEXION: character, humour

COMPOSE: to put music to words

CONCEIT (s.): idea, notion
CONCLUDE: to include
CONDITION (s.): disposition; social position, state of wealth
CONDITION (v.): to make conditions
CONDITIONED: having a (specified) disposition or social position
CONGEE: bow at parting
CONJURE: to plead with
CONSIDERABLE: worthy of consideration
CONSTER: to construe, translate
CONSUMPTIVE: suffering from (any) wasting disease
CONTENT, by, in: by agreement, without examination, at a rough guess
CONVENIENCE: advantage
CONVERSATION: demeanour, behaviour; acquaintance, society
COOLE: cowl
CORANT(O): dance involving a running or gliding step
COSEN, COUSIN: almost any relative
COUNT: to recount
COUNTENANCE: recognition, acknowledgement
COUNTRY: county, district
COURSE, in: in sequence
COURSE, of: as usual
COURT BARON: manorial court (civil)
COURT-DISH: dish with a cut from every meat
COURT LEET: local criminal court
COUSIN: *see* 'Cosen'
COY: disdainful; quiet
COYING: stroking, caressing
CRADLE: fire-basket
CRAMBO: rhyming game
CREATURE (of persons): puppet, instrument
CRUSADO: Portuguese coin worth 3s.
CUDDY: room in a large ship in which the officers took their meals
CULLY: dupe; friend
CUNNING: knowledgeable; knowledge
CURIOUS: careful, painstaking, discriminating; fine, delicate
CURRANT: out and about

CUSTOMER: customs officer
CUT (v.): to carve meat
CUTT (s.): an engraving

DAUGHTER-IN-LAW: stepdaughter
DEAD COLOUR: preparatory layer of colour in a painting
DEAD PAYS: sailors or soldiers kept on pay roll after death
DEALS: sawn timber used for decks, etc.
DEDIMUS: writ empowering J.P.
DEFALK: to subtract
DEFENCE: supplies
DEFEND: to prevent
DEFY, DEFYANCE (Fr.): to mistrust; mistrust
DELICATE: pleasant
DELINQUENT: active royalist in Civil War and Interregnum
DEMORAGE: demurrage, compensation from the freighter due to a shipowner for delaying vessel beyond time specified in charter-party
DEPEND: to wait, hang
DEVISE: to decide; discern
DIALECT: jargon
DIALL, double horizontal: instrument telling hour of day
DIRECTION: supervision of making; arrangement
DISCOVER: to disclose, reveal
DISCREET: discerning, judicious
DISPENSE: provisions
DISTASTE (s.): difference, quarrel, offence
DISTASTE (v.): to offend
DISTINCT: discerning, discriminating
DISTRINGAS: writ of distraint
DOATE: to nod off to sleep
DOCTOR: clergyman, don
DOE: dough. *See* 'All my cake ...'
DOGGED: awkward
DOLLER: *see* Rix Doller
DORTOIRE: dorter, monastic dormitory
DOTY: darling
DOWNS, the: roadstead off Deal, Kent
DOXY: whore, mistress

DRAM: timber from Drammen, Norway

DRAWER: tapster, barman

DRESS: to cook, prepare food

DROLLING, DROLLY: comical, comically

DRUDGER: dredger, container for sweetmeats

DRUGGERMAN: dragoman

DRY BEATEN: soundly beaten, without drawing blood

DRY MONEY: hard cash

DUANA: divan, council

DUCCATON: ducatoon, large silver coin of the Netherlands worth 5s. 9d.

DUCKET(T): ducat, foreign gold coin (here probably Dutch) worth 9s.

DUKE'S [PLAY] HOUSE, the: playhouse in Lincoln's Inn Fields used by the Duke of York's Company from June 1660 until 9 November 1671; often called 'the Opera'. Also known as the Lincoln's Inn Fields Theatre (LIF)

DULL: limp, spiritless

EARTH: earthenware

EASILY: slower

EAST INDIES: the territory covered by the E. India Company, including the modern sub-continent of India

EAST COUNTRY, EASTLAND: the territory (in Europe) covered by the Eastland Company

EFFEMINACY: love of women

ELABORATORY: laboratory

ELECTUARY: medicinal salve with a honey base

EMERODS: haemorrhoids

ENTENDIMIENTO (Sp.): understanding

ENTERTAIN: to retain, employ

EPICURE: glutton

ERIFFE: Erith, Kent

ESPINETTE(s): spinet, small harpsichord

ESSAY: to assay

EUPHROES: uphroes, large Norwegian spars

EVEN (of accounts): to balance

EVEN (of the diary): to bring up to date

EVEN (adv.): surely

EXCEPT: to accept

FACTION: the government's parliamentary critics

FACTIOUS: able to command a following

FACTORY: trading station

FAIRING: small present (as from a fair)

FAIRLY: gently, quietly

FAMILY: household (including servants)

FANCY (music): fantasia

FANFARROON: fanfaron, braggart

FARANDINE, FARRINDIN: *see* 'Ferrandin'

FASHION (of metal, furniture): design, fashioning

FAT: vat

FATHER: father-in-law (similarly with 'mother' etc.)

FELLET (of trees): a cutting, felling

FELLOW COMMONER: undergraduate paying high fees and enjoying privileges

FENCE: defence

FERRANDIN, FARRINDIN, FARANDINE: cloth of silk mixed with wool or hair

FIDDLE: viol; violin

FINE (s.): payment for lease

FINE FOR OFFICE (v.): to avoid office by payment of fine

FIRESHIP: ship filled with combustibles used to ram and set fire to enemy

FITS OF THE MOTHER: hysterics

FLAG, FLAGGMAN: flag officer

FLAGEOLET: end-blown, six-holed instrument

FLESHED: relentless, proud

FLUXED (of the pox): salivated

FLYING ARMY, FLEET: small mobile force

FOND, FONDNESS: foolish; folly

FOND: fund

FORCE OUT: to escape

FORSOOTH: to speak ceremoniously

FORTY: many, scores of

FOXED: intoxicated

FOX HALL: Vauxhall (pleasure gardens)

FOY: departure feast or gift

FREQUENT: to busy oneself

FRIENDS: parents, relatives

FROST-BITE: to invigorate by exposure to cold

FULL: anxious

FULL MOUTH, with: eagerly; openly, loudly

GALL: harass

GALLIOTT: small swift galley

GALLOPER, the: shoal off Essex coast

GAMBO: Gambia, W. Africa

GAMMER: old woman

GENERAL-AT-SEA: naval commander (a post, not a rank)

GENIUS: inborn character, natural ability; mood

GENT: graceful, polite

GENTILELY: obligingly

GEORGE: jewel, forming part of insignia of Order of Garter

GERMANY: territory of the Holy Roman Empire

GET UP ONE'S CRUMB: to improve one's status

GET WITHOUT BOOK: to memorise

GIBB-CAT: tom-cat

GILDER, GUILDER: Dutch money of account worth 2s.

GIMP: twisted thread of material with wire or cord running through it

GITTERNE: musical instrument of the guitar family

GIVE: to answer

GLASS: telescope

GLEEKE: three-handed card game

GLISTER, GLYSTER: see 'Clyster'

GLOSSE, by a fine: by a plausible pretext

GO TO ONE'S NAKED BED: to go to bed without night-clothes

GO(O)D BWYE: God be with ye, goodbye

GODLYMAN: Godalming, Surrey

GOODFELLOW: boon companion

GOOD-SPEAKER: one who speaks well of others

GORGET: neckerchief for women

GOSSIP (v.): to act as godparent, to attend a new mother; to chatter. Also s.

GRACIOUS-STREET(E): Gracechurch St

GRAIN (? of gold): sum of money

GRAVE: to engrave

GREEN (of meat): uncured

GRESHAM COLLEGE: meeting-place of Royal Society; the Society itself

GRIEF: bodily pain

GRUDGEING, GRUTCHING: trifling complaint, grumble

GUEST: nominee; friend; stranger

GUILDER: see 'Gilder'

GUN: flagon of ale; cannon, salute

GUNDALO, GUNDILOW: gondola

GUNFLEET, the: anchorage in mouth of Thames off Essex coast

HACKNEY: hack, workhorse, drudge

HALF-A-PIECE: gold coin worth c. 10s.

HALF-SHIRT: sham shirt front

HALFE-WAY-HOUSE: Rotherhithe tavern halfway between London Bridge and Deptford

HALL, the: usually Westminster Hall

HANDSEL: to try out, use for first time

HAND-TO-FIST: hastily

HANDYCAPP: handicap, a card game

HANG IN THE HEDGE: to be delayed

HANGER: loop holding a sword; small sword

HANGING JACK: turnspit for roasting meat

HANK: hold, grip

HARE: to harry, rebuke

HARPSICHON: see 'Harpsichord'

HARPSICHORD, HARPSICHON: keyboard instrument of one or two manuals, with strings plucked by quills or leather jacks, and with stops which vary the tone

HARSLET: haslet, pigmeat (esp. offal)

HAVE A GOOD COAT OF [HIS] FLEECE: to have a good share

HAVE A HAND: to have leisure, freedom

HAVE A MONTH'S MIND: to have a great desire

HEAD-PIECE: container; helmet

HEAVE AT: to oppose

HERBALL: botanical encyclopaedia; *hortus siccus* (book of dried and pressed plants)

HERE (Du. *heer*): Lord

HIGH: arrogant, proud, high-handed

HINCHINGBROOKE: Sandwich's house near Huntingdon

HOMAGE: jury of presentment at a manorial court

HONEST (of a woman): virtuous

HOOKS, off the: angry, mad

HOOKS, to put off the: to anger

HOPE, the: reach of Thames downstream from Tilbury

HOPEFUL: promising

HOUSE: playhouse; parliament; (royal) household or palace building

HOUSE OF OFFICE: latrine

HOY: small passenger and cargo ship, sloop-rigged

HOYSE: to hoist

HUMOUR: mood; character, characteristic; good or ill temper

HUSBAND: one who gets good/bad value for money, supervisor, steward

HYPOCRAS: hippocras, spiced white wine

ILL-TEMPERED: out of sorts, ill adjusted (to weather etc.; cf. 'Temper')

IMPERTINENCE: irrelevance, garrulity, folly. Also 'Impertinent'

IMPOSTUME: abscess

IMPREST: money paid in advance by government to public servant

INDIAN GOWN: loose gown of glazed cotton

INGENIOUS, INGENUOUS: clever, intelligent

INGENUITY: wit, intelligence; freedom

INGENUOUS: see 'Ingenious'

INSTITUCIONS: instructions

INSTRUMENT: agent, clerk

INSULT: to exult over

INTELLIGENCE: information

INTRATUR: warrant authorising payment by Exchequer

IRISIPULUS: erysipelas

IRONMONGER: often a large-scale merchant, not necessarily a retailer

JACK(E): flag used as signal or mark of distinction; rogue, knave. *See also* 'Hanging jack'

JACKANAPES COAT: monkey coat, sailor's short close-fitting jacket

JACOB(US): gold sovereign coined by James I

JAPAN: lacquer

JARR, JARRING: quarrel

JEALOUS: fearful, suspicious, mistrustful. Also 'Jealousy'

JERK(E): captious remark

JES(S)IMY: jasmine

JEW'S TRUMP: Jew's harp

JOCKY: horse-dealer

JOLE (of fish): jowl, a cut consisting of the head and shoulders. *See also* 'Pole'

JOYNT-STOOL: stout stool held together by joints

JULIPP: julep, a sweet drink made from syrup

JUMBLE: to take for an airing

JUMP WITH: to agree, harmonise

JUNK (naval): old rope

JURATE (of Cinque Ports): jurat, alderman

JUSTE-AU-CORPS: close-fitting long coat

KATCH (ship): ketch

KEEP A QUARTER: to make a disturbance

KENNEL: see 'Canaille'

KERCHER: kerchief, head-covering

KETCH (s.): catch, song in canon

KETCH (v.): to catch

KING'S [PLAY] HOUSE, the: playhouse in Vere St, Clare Market, Lincoln's Inn Fields, used by the King's Company from 8 November 1660 until 7 May 1663; the playhouse in Bridges St, Drury Lane, used by the same company from 7 May 1663 until the fire of 25 January 1672. Also known as the Theatre Royal (TR)

KITLIN: kitling, kitten, cub

KNEES: timbers of naturally angular shape used in ship-building

KNOT (s.): flower bed; difficulty; clique, band

KNOT (v.): to join, band together

KNOWN: famous

LACE: usually braid made with gold- or silver-thread

LAMB'S-WOOL: hot ale with apples and spice

LAMP-GLASS: magnifying lens used to concentrate lamp-light

LAST: load, measure of tar

LASTOFFE: Lowestoft, Suff.

LATITUDINARIAN: liberal Anglican

LAVER: fountain

LEADS: flat space on roof top, sometimes boarded over

LEAN: to lie down

LEARN: to teach

LEAVE: to end

LECTURE: weekday religious service consisting mostly of a sermon

LESSON: piece of music

LETTERS OF MART: letters of marque

LEVETT: reveille, reveille music

LIBEL(L): leaflet, broadside; (in legal proceedings) written charge

LIE UPON: to press, insist

LIFE: life interest

LIFE, for my: on my life

LIGHT: window

LIGNUM VITAE: hard W. Indian wood with medicinal qualities, often used for drinking vessels

LIMB: to limn, paint

LIME (of dogs): to mate

LINK(E): torch

LINNING: linen

LIPPOCK: Liphook, Hants.

LIST: pleasure, desire

LOCK: waterway between arches of bridge

LOMBRE: *see* 'Ombre'

LONDON: the city of London (to be distinguished from Westminster)

LOOK: to look at, for

LOOK AFTER: to have eyes on

LUMBERSTREETE: Lombard St

LUTE: pear-shaped instrument with six courses of gut strings and a turned-back peg-box; made in various sizes, the larger instruments having additional bass strings

LUTESTRING: lustring, a glossy silk

LYRA-VIALL: small bass viol tuned for playing chords

MADAM(E): prefix used mainly of widows, elderly ladies, foreign ladies

MAIN (adj.): strong, bulky

MAIN (s.): chief purpose or object

MA(I)STER: expert; professional; sailing master

MAKE (s.): (of fighting cocks) match, pair of opponents

MAKE (v.): to copulate

MAKE LEGS: to bow, curtsey

MAKE SURE TO: to plight troth

MALLOWS: St Malo

MAN OF BUSINESS: executive agent, administrator

MANAGED-HORSE (cf. Fr. *manège*): horse trained in riding school

MANDAMUS: royal mandate under seal

MARGARET, MARGETTS: Margate, Kent

MARGENTING: putting margin-lines on paper

MARK: 13s. 4d.

MARMOTTE (Fr., affectionate): young girl

MARROWBONE: Marylebone, Mdx.

MASTY: burly

MATCH: tinderbox and wick

MATHEMATICIAN: mathematical instrument-maker

MEAT: food

MEDIUM: mean, average

METHEGLIN: strong mead flavoured with herbs

MINCHEN-LANE: Mincing Lane

MINE: mien

MINIKIN: fishing line of varnished gut; treble string of stringed instrument

MISTRESS: prefix used of unmarried girls and women as well as of young married women

MISTRESS: sweetheart

MITHRYDATE: drug used as an antidote

MOHER (Sp. *mujer*): woman, wife

MOIS, MOYS: menstrual periods

MOLD, MOLDE, MOLLE (archit.): mole

MOLEST: to annoy

MOND: orb (royal jewel in form of globe)

MONTEERE, MOUNTEERE: huntsman's cap; close-fitting hood

MOPED: bemused

MORECLACK(E): Mortlake, Surrey

MORENA (Sp.): brunette

MORNING DRAUGHT: drink (sometimes with snack) taken instead of breakfast

MOTHER-IN-LAW: stepmother (similarly with 'father-in-law' etc.)

MOTT: sighting line in an optical tube

MOUNTEERE: *see* 'Monteere'

MOYRE: moire, watered silk

MUM: strong spiced ale

MURLACE: Morlaix, Brittany

MUSCADINE, MUSCATT: muscatel wine

MUSIC: band, choir, performer

MUSTY: peevish

NAKED BED: *see* 'Go to one's n.b.'

NARROWLY: anxiously, carefully

NAUGHT, NOUGHT: worthless, bad in condition or quality, sexually wicked

NAVY: Navy Office

NAVY OFFICERS: Principal Officers of the Navy – i.e. the Comptroller, Treasurer, Surveyor, Clerk of the Acts, together with a variable number of Commissioners; members of the Navy Board. Cf. 'Sea-Officers'

NEARLY: deeply

NEAT: ox, cattle

NEITHER MEDDLE NOR MAKE: to have nothing to do with

NEWSBOOK: newspaper (weekly, octavo)

NIBBLE AT: to carp at

NICOTIQUES: narcotics, medicines

NIGHTGOWN(E): dressing gown

NOISE: group of musical instruments playing together

NORE, the: anchorage in mouth of Thames

NORTHDOWNE ALE: Margate Ale

NOSE: to insult, affront

NOTE: business

NOTORIOUS: famous, well-known

NOUGHT: *see* 'Naught'

OBNOXIOUS: liable to

OBSERVABLE (adj.): noteworthy, notorious

OBSERVABLE (s.): thing or matter worthy of observation

OF: to have

OFFICE DAY: day on which a meeting of the Navy Board was held

OFFICERS OF THE NAVY: *see* 'Navy Officers'

OLEO (Sp. *olla*): stew

OMBRE (Sp. *hombre*): card game

OPEN: unsettled

OPERA: spectacular entertainment (involving use of painted scenery and stage machinery), often with music

OPERA, the: the theatre in Lincoln's Inn Fields. *See* 'Duke's House, the'

OPINIASTRE, OPINIASTREMENT (Fr.): stubborn, stubbornly

OPPONE: to oppose, hinder

ORDER: to put in order

ORDINARY (adj.): established

ORDINARY (s.): eating place serving fixed-price meals; peace-time establishment (of navy, dockyard, etc.)

OVERSEEN: omitted, neglected; guilty of oversight

OWE: to own

PADRON (?Sp., ?It. *patrone*): master

PAGEANT: decorated symbolic float used in procession

PAINFUL: painstaking

PAIR OF OARS: large river-boat rowed by two watermen, each using a pair of oars. Cf. 'Sculler'

PAIR OF ORGANS/VIRGINALS: a single instrument

PANNYARD: pannier, basket

PARAGON: heavy rich cloth, partly of mohair

PARALLELOGRAM: pantograph

PARCEL: share, part; isolated group

PARK, the: normally St James's Park (Hyde Park is usually named)

PARTY: charter-party

PASQUIL: a lampoon

PASSION: feeling, mood

PASSIONATE: touching, affecting

PATTEN: overshoe

PAY: to berate, beat

PAY A COAT: to beat, chastise

PAYSAN (Fr.): country style

PAY SICE: to pay dearly (sixfold)

PENDANCES, PENDENTS: lockets; earrings

PERPLEX: to vex

PERSPECTIVE, PERSPECTIVE GLASSES: binoculars

PESLEMESLE: pell-mell, early form of croquet

PETTY BAG: petty cash

PHILOSOPHY: natural science

PHYSIC: laxative, purge

PHYSICALLY: without sheets, uncovered

PICK: pique

PICK A HOLE IN A COAT: to pick a quarrel, complain

PICKAROON (Sp. *picarón*): pirate, privateer

PIECE: gold coin worth c. 20s.

PIECE (PEECE) OF EIGHT: Spanish silver coin worth 4s. 6d.

PIGEON: coward

PINK(E): small broad-beamed ship; poniard, pointed weapon

PINNER: coif with two long flaps; fill-in above low *décolletage*

PIPE: measure of wine (c. 120 galls)

PIPE (musical): before 14 August 1668 usually a flageolet; afterwards usually a recorder

PISTOLE: French gold coin worth 16s.

PLACKET: petticoat

PLAIN: unaffected

PLAT(T): plate, engraving, chart, map; arrangement; level; [flower] plot

PLATERER: one who works silver plate

PLAY (v.): to play for stakes

POINT, POYNT: piece of lace

POINT DE GESNE: Genoa lace

POLE: head; head-and-shoulder (of fish); poll tax

POLICY: government: cunning; self-interest

POLLARD: cut-back, stunted tree

POMPOUS: ceremonious, dignified

POOR JACK: dried salt fish

POOR WRETCH (affectionate): poor soul

POSSET: drink made of hot milk, spices, wine (or beer)

POST (v.): to expose, pillory

POST WARRANT: authority to employ posthorses

POSY: verse or phrase engraved on inside of ring

POWDERED (of meat): salted

PRACTICE: trick

PRAGMATIC, PRAGMATICAL: interfering, conceited, dogmatic

PRATIQUE: ship's licence for port facilities given on its presenting clean bill of health

PRESBYTER JOHN: puritan parson

PRESENT (s.): shot, volley

PRESENT, PRESENTLY: immediate, immediately

PRESS BED: bed folding into or built inside a cupboard

PREST MONEY (milit., naval): press money

PRETTY (of men): fine, elegant, foppish

PRICK: to write out music; to list

PRICK OUT: to strike out, delete

PRINCE: ruler

PRINCIPLES (of music): natural ability, rudimentary knowledge

PRISE, PRIZE: worth, value, price

PRIVATE: small, secret

PRIZE FIGHT: fencing match fought for money

PROPRIETY: property, ownership

PROTEST (a bill of exchange): to record non-payment

PROUD (of animals): on heat

PROVOKE: to urge

PULL A CROW: to quarrel

PURCHASE: advantage; profit; booty

PURL(E): hot spiced beer

PUSS: ill-favoured woman

PUT OFF: to sell, dispose of

PYONEER: pioneer (ditch digger, labourer)

QU: cue

QUARREFOUR: crossroads

QUARTRE: position in dancing or fencing

QUARTERAGE: charge for lodgings or quarters; quarterly allowance

QUEST HOUSE: house used for inquests, parish meetings

QUINBROUGH: Queenborough, Kent

QUINSBOROUGH: Königsberg, E. Prussia

RACE: to rase, destroy

RAKE-SHAMED: disreputable, disgraceful

RARE: fine, splendid

RATE: to berate, scold

RATTLE: to scold

RATTOON: rattan cane

READY: dressed

REAKE: trick

RECEPI: writ of receipt issued by Chancery

RECONCILE: to settle a dispute, to determine the truth

RECORDER: family of end-blown, eight-holed instruments (descant, treble, tenor, bass)

RECOVER: to reconcile

RECOVERY (legal): process for re-establishment of ownership

REDRIFFE: Rotherhithe, Surrey

REFERRING: indebted, beholden to

REFORM: to disband

REFORMADO: naval (or military) officer serving without commission

REFRESH (of a sword): to sharpen

RELIGIOUS: monk, nun

REPLICACION (legal): replication, plaintiff's answer to defendant's plea

RESEMBLE: to represent, figure

RESENT: to receive

RESPECT: to mean, refer to

RESPECTFUL: respectable

REST: wrest, tuning key

RETAIN (a writ): to maintain a court action (from term to term)

REVOLUTION: sudden change (not necessarily violent)

RHODOMONTADO: boast, brag

RIDE POST: to travel by posthorse, to ride fast

RIGHT-HAND MAN: soldier on whom drill manoeuvres turn

RIGHTS, to: immediately, directly

RISE: origin

RIS (v.): rose

RIX DOLLER: Dutch or N. German silver coin (*Rijksdaalder, Reichsthaler*) worth c. 4s. 9d.

ROCKE: distaff

ROMANTIQUE: having the characteristics of a tale (romance)

ROUNDHOUSE: uppermost cabin in stern of ship

ROYALL THEATRE, the: *see* 'Theatre, the'
RUB(B): check, stop, obstacle
RUFFIAN: pimp
RUMP: remnant of the Long Parliament
RUMPER: member or supporter of the Rump
RUNLETT: cask
RUNNING: temporary

SACK: white wine from Spain or Canaries
SALT: salt-cellar
SALT-EELE: rope's end used for punishment
SALVE UP: to smooth over
SALVO: excuse, explanation
SARCENET: thin taffeta, fine silk cloth
SASSE (Du. *sas*): sluice, lock
SAVE: to be in time for
SAY: fine woollen cloth
SCALE (of music): key; gamut
SCALLOP: scalloped lace collar
SCALLOP-WHISK: *see* 'Whisk'
SCAPE (s.): adventure
SCAPE (v.): to escape
SCARE-FIRE: sudden conflagration
SCHOOL: to scold, rebuke
SCHUIT (Du.): Dutch canal boat barge
SCONCE: bracket, candlestick
SCOTOSCOPE: portable *camera obscura*
SCOWRE: to beat, punish
SCREW: key, screw-bolt
SCRUPLE: to dispute
SCULL, SCULLER: small river-boat rowed by a single waterman using one pair of oars. Cf. 'Pair of oars'
SEA-CARD: chart
SEA-COAL: coal carried by sea
SEA-OFFICERS: commissioned officers of the navy. Cf. 'Navy Officers'
SECOND MOURNING: half mourning
SEEL (of a ship): to lurch
SEEM: to pretend
SENNIT: sevennight, a week
SENSIBLY: perceptibly, painfully
SERPENT: firework

SERVANT: suitor, lover
SET: sit
SET UP/OFF ONE'S REST: to be certain, to be content, to make an end, to make one's whole aim
SEWER: stream, ditch
SHAG(G): worsted or silk cloth with a velvet nap on one side
SHEATH (of a ship): to encase the hull as a protection against worm
SHIFT (s.): trial, attempt, arrangement
SHIFT (v.): to change clothes; to dodge a round in paying for drinks (or to get rid of the effects of drink)
SHOEMAKER'S STOCKS: new shoes
SHOVE AT: to apply one's energies to
SHROUD: shrewish, peevish
SHUFFLEBOARD: shovelboard, shove-ha'penny
SHUTS: shutters
SILLABUB, SULLYBUB, SYLLABUB: milk mixed with wine
SIMPLE: foolish
SIT: to hold a meeting
SIT CLOSE: to hold a meeting from which clerks are excluded
SITHE: sigh
SKELLUM: rascal, thief
SLENDERLY: slightingly
SLICE: flat plate
SLIGHT, SLIGHTLY: contemptuous; slightingly, without ceremony
SLIP A CALF/FILLY: to abort
SLOP(P)S: seamen's ready-made clothes
SLUG(G): slow heavy boat: rough metal projectile
SLUT: drudge, wench (sometimes used playfully)
SMALL (of drink): light
SNAP(P) (s.): bite, snack, small meal; attack
SNAP (v.): to ambush, cut down, out, off
SNUFF: to speak scornfully
SNUFFE, take/go in: to take offence
SOKER: old hand; pal; toper
SOLD(E)BAY: Solebay, off Southwold, Suff.

SOL(L)ICITOR: agent
SON: son-in-law (similarly with 'daughter' etc.)
SON-IN-LAW: stepson
SOUND: fish-bladder
SOUND, the: strictly the navigable passage between Denmark and Sweden where tolls were levied (Oversund), but more generally (and usually in Pepys) the Baltic
SPARROWGRASS: asparagus
SPEAK BROAD: to speak fully, frankly
SPECIALITY: bond under seal
SPECIES (optical): image
SPEED: to succeed
SPIKET: spigot, tap, faucet
SPILT, SPOILT: ruined
SPINET: single-manual wing-shaped keyboard instrument with harpsichord action
SPOIL (of people): to deflower; (of animals) to injure seriously
SPOTS: patches (cosmetic)
SPRANKLE: sparkling remark, *bon mot*
SPUDD: trenching tool
STAIRS: landing stage
STAND IN: to cost
STANDING WATER: between tides
STANDISH: stand for ink, pens etc.
STATE-DISH: richly decorated dish; dish with a round lid or canopy
STATESMAN: Commonwealth's-man
STATIONER: bookseller (often also publisher)
STEMPEECE: timber of ship's bow
STICK: blockhead
STILLYARD, the: the Steelyard
STIR(R): rumour
STOMACH: courage, pride; appetite
STOMACHFULLY: proudly
STONE-HORSE: stallion
STOUND: astonishment
STOUT: brave, courageous
STOWAGE: storage, payment for storage
STRAIGHTS, STREIGHTS, the: strictly the Straits of Gibraltar: more usually the Mediterranean
STRANGERS: foreigners

STRIKE (nautical): to lower the topsail in salute; (of Exchequer tallies) to make, cut
STRONG WATER: distilled spirits
SUBSIDY MAN: man of substance (liable to pay subsidy-tax)
SUCCESS(E): occurrence, eventuality (good or bad), outcome
SUDDENLY: in a short while
SULLYBUB: *see* 'Sillabub'
SUPERNUMERARY: seamen extra to ship's complement
SURLY: imperious, lordly
SWINE-POX: chicken-pox
SWOUND: to swoon, faint
SYLLABUB: *see* 'Sillabub'
SYMPHONY: instrumental introduction, interlude etc., in a vocal composition

TAB(B)Y: watered silk
TABLE: legend attached to a picture
TABLE BOOK: memorandum book
TABLES: backgammon and similar games
TAILLE, TALLE (Fr. *taille*): figure, shape (of person)
TAKE EGGS FOR MONEY: to cut one's losses, to accept something worthless
TAKE OUT: to learn; perform
TAKE UP: to agree on
TAKING (s.): condition
TALE: reckoning, number
TALL: fine, elegant
TALLE: *see* 'Taille'
TALLY: wooden stick used by the Exchequer in accounting
TAMKIN: tampion, wooden gun plug
TANSY, TANZY: egg pudding flavoured with tansy
TARPAULIN: 'tar', a sea-bred captain as opposed to a gentleman-captain
TAXOR: financial official of university
TEAR: to rant
TELL: to count
TEMPER (s.): moderation; temperament, mood; physical condition

TEMPER (v.): to moderate, control
TENT: roll of absorbent material used for wounds; (Sp. *tinto*) red wine
TERCE, TIERCE: measure of wine (42 galls; one-third of a pipe)
TERELLA: terrella, spherical magnet, terrestrial globe containing magnet
TERM(E)S: menstrual periods
THEATRE, the: before May 1663 usually Theatre Royal, Vere St; afterwards usually Theatre Royal, Drury Lane (TR)
THEM: *see* 'Those'
THEORBO: large double-necked tenor lute
THOSE: menstrual periods
THRUSH: inflammation of throat and mouth
TICKELED: annoyed, irritated
TICKET(T): seaman's pay-ticket
TIERCE: *see* 'Terce'
TILT: awning over river-boat
TIMBER: wood for the skeleton of a ship (as distinct from plank or deals used for the decks, cabins, gun-platforms etc.)
TIRE: tier
TOKEN, by the same: so, then, and
TONGUE: reputation, fame
TOPS: turnovers of the protective stockings worn with boots
TOUCHED: annoyed
TOUR, the: coach parade of *beau monde* in Hyde Park
TOUSE: to tousle, tumble a woman
TOWN(E): manor
TOY: small gift
TOYLE: foil, net into which game is driven
TRADE: manufacture, industry
TRANSIRE: warrant allowing goods through customs
TRAPAN, TREPAN: to perform brain surgery; cheat, trick, trap, inveigle
TREASURY, the: the Navy Treasury or the national Treasury
TREAT: to handle (literally)
TREAT, TREATY: negotiate, negotiation

TREBLE: treble viol
TREPAN: *see* 'Trapan'
TRIANGLE, TRYANGLE: triangular virginals
TRILL(O): vocal vibrato
TRIM: to shave
TRUCKLE/TRUNDLE-BED: low bed on castors which could be put under main bed
TRYANGLE: *see* 'Triangle'
TRY A PULL: to have a go
TUITION: guardianship
TURK, the: used of all denizens of the Turkish Empire, but usually of the Berber pirates of the African coast, especially Algiers
TURKEY WORK: red tapestry in Turkish style
TURKY-STONE: turquoise
TUTTLE FIELDS: Tothill Fields
TWIST: strong thread

UGLY: awkward
UMBLES (of deer): edible entrails, giblets
UNBESPEAK: countermand
UNCOUTH: out of sorts or order, uneasy, at a loss
UNDERSTAND: to conduct oneself properly; (s.) understanding
UNDERTAKER: contractor; parliamentary manager
UNHAPPY, UNHAPPILY: unlucky; unluckily
UNREADY: undressed
UNTRUSS: to undo one's breeches: defecate
UPPER BENCH: name given in Interregnum to King's Bench
USE: usury, interest
USE UPON USE: compound interest

VAPOURISH: pretentious, foolish
VAUNT: to vend, sell
VENETIAN CAP: peaked cap as worn by Venetian Doge
VESTS: robes, vestments
VIALL, VIOL: family of fretted, bowed instruments with six gut strings; the

bowing hand is held beneath the bow and the instrument held on or between the knees; now mostly superseded by violin family

VIRGINALS: rectangular English keyboard instrument resembling spinet; usually in case without legs

VIRTUOSO: widely learned man, scholar of the Royal Society kind

WASTCOATE, WAISTCOAT: warm undergarment

WAIT, WAYT (at court etc.): to serve a turn of duty (usually a month) as an official

WARDROBE, the: the office of the King's Great Wardrobe, of which Lord Sandwich was Keeper; the building at Puddle Wharf containing the office; a cloak room

WARM: comfortable, well-off

WASSAIL, WASSELL: entertainment (e.g. a play)

WASTECLOATH: cloth hung on ship as decoration between quarter-deck and forecastle

WATCH: clock

WAY, in/out of the: accessible/inaccessible; in a suitable/unsuitable condition

WAYTES: waits; municipal musicians

WEATHER-GLASS(E): thermometer (or, less likely, barometer)

WEIGH (of ships): to raise

WELLING: Welwyn, Herts.

WESTERN BARGEMAN (BARGEE): bargee serving western reaches of Thames

WESTMINSTER: the area around Whitehall and the Abbey; not the modern city of Westminster

WHISKE: woman's neckerchief

WHITE-HALL: royal palace, largely burnt down in 1698

WHITSTER: bleacher, launderer

WIGG: wig, cake, bun

WILDE: wile

WIND (s.): wine

WIND LIKE A CHICKEN: to wind round one's little finger

WIPE: sarcasm, insult

WISTELY: with close attention

WIT, WITTY: cleverness, clever

WONDER: to marvel at

WOODMONGER: fuel merchant

WORD: utterance, phrase

WOREMOODE: wormwood

WRETCH: *see* 'Poor wretch'

YARD: penis

YARE: ready, skilful

YILDHALL: Guildhall

YOWELL: Ewell, Surrey